Frontier and Overseas Expeditions from India

Frontier and Overseas Expeditions from India

(in 7 Volumes)

Compiled in the Intelligence Branch, Army Headquarters, India

Vol. 1 (Part 1)
Tribes-North of the Kabul River

Low Price Publications
Delhi-110052

Distributed by
D.K. Publishers Distributors (P) Ltd.
4834/24, Ansari Road, Darya Ganj,
New Delhi-110002
Phones: 23278584, 23278368, 23261465
e-mail: dkpd@del3.vsnl.net.in
url: www.dkpd.com

First Published 1907-11

Reprinted in **LPP** 2004

ISBN 81-7536-323-1 (Set)
ISBN 81-7536-324-X (Vol.1)

Published by
Low Price Publications
A-6, Nimri Commercial Centre,
Near Ashok Vihar Phase-IV,
Delhi-110052
Phones: 27401672, 27452453
e-mail: lpp@nde.vsnl.net.in
url: www.lppindia.com

Printed at
D K Fine Art Press P Ltd.
Delhi-110052

PRINTED IN INDIA

Frontier and Overseas Expeditions from India

Frontier and Overseas Expeditions from India

(in 7 Volumes)

Compiled in the
Intelligence Branch,
Army Headquarters, India

Vol. 1 (Part 1)
Tribes-North of the Kabul River

Low Price Publications
Delhi-110052

Distributed by
D.K. Publishers Distributors (P) Ltd.
4834/24, Ansari Road, Darya Ganj,
New Delhi-110002
Phones: 23278584, 23278368, 23261465
e-mail: dkpd@del3.vsnl.net.in
url: www.dkpd.com

First Published 1907-11

Reprinted in **LPP** 2004

ISBN 81-7536-323-1 (Set)
ISBN 81-7536-324-X (Vol.1)

Published by
Low Price Publications
A-6, Nimri Commercial Centre,
Near Ashok Vihar Phase-IV,
Delhi-110052
Phones: 27401672, 27452453
e-mail: lpp@nde.vsnl.net.in
url: www.lppindia.com

Printed at
D K Fine Art Press P Ltd.
Delhi-110052

PRINTED IN INDIA

CHAPTER IV.

BLACK MOUNTAIN TRIBES—(continued).

CHAPTER V.

YUSAFZAI AND GADUN TRIBES BETWEEN THE BLACK MOUNTAIN AND SWAT.

CHAPTER VI.

YUSAFZAI AND GADUN TRIBES BETWEEN THE BLACK MOUNTAIN AND SWAT—(continued).

The Ambela Expedition, 1863.

CHAPTER VII.

YUSAFZAI AND GADUN TRIBES BETWEEN THE BLACK MOUNTAIN AND SWAT—(continued).

CONTENTS.

INTRODUCTION.

CHAPTER I.

THE GILGIT AGENCY.

CHAPTER II.

CHITRAL.

CHAPTER III.

CIS-INDUS, SWATI, AND BLACK MOUNTAIN TRIBES.

CHAPTER VIII.

SWAT TRIBES.

CHAPTER IX.

SWAT TRIBES—(*continued*).

CHAPTER X.

THE UTMAN KHEL TRIBE.

CHAPTER XI.

THE MOHMAND TRIBE.

CHAPTER XII.

AKOZAI-YUSAFZAI AND TARKANRI TRIBES OF DIR AND BAJAUR.

CHAPTER XIII.

AKOZAI-YUSAFZAI AND TARKANRI TRIBES—contd.

LIST OF MAPS AND ILLUSTRATIONS.

PREFACE.

IN 1866 the Punjab Government considered it desirable that a "Record should be composed of the expeditions made from time to time against the North-West Frontier Tribes, with such further information as might render the work a valuable guide to those who might have future dealings with these turbulent neighbours." The first edition of the work was compiled in 1873 by Colonel W. H. Paget, 5th Punjab Cavalry, under the title of "A Record of Expeditions against the North-West Frontier Tribes," and was revised and brought up to date in 1884 by Lieutenant A. H. Mason, R.E.

Similar considerations have now prompted the compilation of a record of expeditions against frontier tribes on all the frontiers of India, and of operations embarked in by the Indian Government overseas; and as the latest edition of Paget and Mason had become out of print, it was decided to incorporate that work, revised and brought up to date, in the present volumes, instead of again issuing it as a separate compilation.

The arrangement adopted in the former work, namely, each tribe being dealt with separately, has been followed in the present instance, but for the sake of convenience the present record has been divided into six volumes, each volume dealing with a distinct geographical division. This division is as follows:—

Vol. I.—North-West Frontier Tribes north of the Kabul river.

Vol. II.—North-West Frontier Tribes between the Kabul and Gumal rivers.

Vol. III.—Baluchistan, and the First Afghan War.

Vol. IV.—North and North-Eastern Frontier Tribes.

Vol. V.—Burma.

Vol. VI.—Overseas Expeditions, including Part I, Africa; Part II, Ceylon and the islands of the Indian Ocean; Part III, Arabia and Persia; Part IV, Malay Peninsula and Archipelago; Part V, China.

Of the first three volumes, the accounts of dealings with the North-West Frontier and Baluchistan Tribes previous to 1884 have been extracted from Paget and Mason's book, while the history of subsequent operations has been compiled for these volumes by Major O. K. Tancock, R. G. A., Major E. J. M. Molyneux, D. S. O., 12th Cavalry, Captain W. L. Maxwell, 127th Baluch Light Infantry, and Lieutenant C. F. Aspinall, Royal Munster Fusiliers. The remaining three volumes are new, and of these Volume IV has been compiled by Lieutenant J. L. Mowbray, R. H. A., and Volume V by Lieutenant C. F. Aspinall. The latter officer has also been responsible for the editing of Volumes I, II, IV, and V. Volume VI has been compiled by Major R. G. Burton, 94th Russell's Infantry, Major W. H. Brown, 103rd Mahratta Light Infantry, Captain R. S. Phillips, 52nd Sikhs, and Lieutenant G. P. Morris, 30th Lancers. The general editorship of Volumes III and VI has been undertaken by Major R. G. Burton.

It is especially requested that any errors in these volumes may be brought to the notice of this Division as speedily as possible.

W. MALLESON, *Lieut.-Colonel,*
Assistant Quarter Master General for Intelligence,
Division of the Chief of the Staff.

SIMLA:

17*th September* 1907.

INTRODUCTION TO VOLS. I, II, AND III.

SINCE 1884, the year in which Paget and Mason's "Records of Expeditions against the North-West Frontier Tribes" was published, the Frontier of British Influence has, by the Durand Agreement, extended far beyond the limits therein described, and now, including as it does nearly all the frontier tribes, is coterminous with Afghanistan from the Kilik pass in the north to the borders of Persia in the west.

The boundary line of 1884 was what is now, roughly, the administrative border of the North-West Frontier Province. In the present work, in order to differentiate between these two boundary lines, that of British Influence and that of British Administration, the former will be called the Frontier and the latter the Administrative Border Line.

The border line skirts the six districts of Hazara, Kohat, Peshawar, Bannu, Dera Ismail Khan, and Dera Ghazi Khan, the first five of which belong to the North-West Frontier Province, and the last to the province of the Punjab. Of these six districts, two, Hazara and Kohat, are hilly and in parts mountainous. The other four are almost level plains, only broken by deep ravines and torrent beds, which make even the Peshawar valley difficult for the movements of cavalry and guns. The characteristics of the people inhabiting them differ very greatly, and it is necessary, in as few words as possible, to describe each district before giving an account of the tribes beyond their border.

The Hazara district is the most northern. The upper portion of it, especially that known as Kaghan, is entirely composed of mountain ranges covered with magnificent forests; the lower portion of the district is, although elevated, more level, and, possessing an abundant supply of water, produces excellent crops. The population is generally peaceable and unwarlike. Its largest element consists of immigrants expelled, some centuries ago, from the neighbouring Swat valley, a physically weak and contemptible race. These form nearly a third of the inhabitants of the Hazara district ; nearly half the remainder is composed of descendants from Rajput and other Hindu tribes, Gujars,[1] Ghakkars, Dunds, and Karals, who have for the most part adopted the Muhammadan creed. They are industrious and good cultivators, and form the best part of the Hazara population. Descendants of Afghan immigrants, related to the Yusafzai and other tribes in the neighbourhood, constitute a fifth of the whole.

The Peshawar district contrasts remarkably with that just described. Consisting of a wide level plain, it is abundantly watered by the large rivers of Swat and Kabul, and is broken only by deep ravines which intersect it in all directions. The length from north to south is 54 miles, but the western border is 170 miles long, and adjoins the lands of the Gaduns, Bunerwals, Baizais, Ranizais, Utman Khels, Mohmands, and Afridis. From Sikh and Afghan days Peshawar has had an infamous reputation for the character of its inhabitants, who required for their control the sternest administrators of the Sikh Government, and for its climate, which, owing to excessive irrigation, and also from the valley being enclosed by lofty hills, is, at certain seasons of the year, extremely unhealthy. The inhabitants are strangely mixed. About ninety-two per cent. are Muhammadans, the few Hindus being found as merchants and shopkeepers in Peshawar and the larger villages. The total population of the district is about three-quarters of a million, of which about one-sixth are Yusafzais, an Afghan clan inhabiting the high plain to the north. After the Yusafzais the most important tribes are the Mohmands and the Khattaks. The remainder of the population is made up of numerous Afghan tribes, and of Punjabi Muhammadans from cis-Indus districts.

The district of Kohat is almost entirely composed of a system of low, barren hills, from which it derives its name, intermingled with small but fertile valleys. The importance of the district is

1 The Gujars are found amongst many of the independent tribes between the Kunar river and the Hazara district. Their occupation is chiefly cattle rearing, as their name implies, and the cultivation of land which they hold in lease from the owners, whom they are bound to serve in time of war. They are a fine, stalwart race, and, though as a rule quiet and industrious, are apt to break out into lawlessness like the people amongst whom they dwell. They are supposed to be the descendants of the possessors of the country previous to the arrival of the Pathans.

due to the existence of extensive salt mines, the produce of which is used throughout trans-Indus territory and Afghanistan, and which, chiefly from political considerations, is taxed much more lightly than the produce of the Jhelum mines, which supply the greater part of Northern India to the east of the Indus. About 1883 the price of salt at the Kohat mines was raised, and this subject will again be referred to further on, when we come to speak of our relations with the Afridis, who are the principal carriers of the Kohat salt. The city of Peshawar is the central depôt of the salt trade, whence it is taken by traders to Jalalabad, Kashmir, and Kashgar, and exchanged for the produce of these countries. About two-thirds of the population of the Kohat district are Afghans, and of these one-third are Khattaks, who, inhabiting the north of the district, are one of the finest tribes on the whole frontier, and supply our regiments with many of their best soldiers. The Bangash tribe is almost as numerous, and is generally quiet and well disposed.

The Bannu district consists of a flat open plain like Peshawar, and, like it, is abundantly watered by the Kurram and Gumbela rivers. The rainfall being very scanty, cultivation is almost entirely dependent upon irrigation from the streams. In the trans-Indus portion of the district are the Bannuchis, a mongrel Afghan tribe, who are about the worst specimens of the race on the frontier. Their physique, owing to the malarious climate, is as degraded as their morals. They are cowardly and unwarlike, and on this account give less trouble than the next most important section of the population, the Wazirs, who are in appearance and in character immeasurably their superiors. The south of the Bannu district is inhabited by the Marwatis, a high-caste Pathan race, brave, simple, and honest, who form as great a contrast as can be conceived to their northern neighbours, the Bannuchis.

In the Dera Ismail Khan district, owing to the rainfall being very small and irrigation wanting, the country for the most part is little better than a desert, and can only be cultivated in those exceptional years when abundant rain may happen to fall. That portion of the district, however, which has a sufficiency of irrigation, and especially the Tank valley, is fertile. The country on the west of the Indus falls with an almost imperceptible slope from the hills to the Indus. The original population of the district seems to have been Jats. Then came an immigration of Balochis from the south, forming the bulk of the present population of the Kulachi sub-division, below the Ustarana country, few being found north of the town of Dera Ismail Khan. In the south they are the dominant class ; in the country cis-Indus they are mixed with, and practically on an equality with, the Jats. The only Baloch tribe found together in any numbers are the Kasranis, inhabiting the country about Daulatwala. The Pathans occupy the north of the district up to Isa Khel, together with Marwatis, all recent settlers, and rapidly increasing in numbers.

The characteristics of the Dera Ghazi Khan district resemble closely those of the trans-Indus portion of Dera Ismail Khan. It consists of a strip of country lying between the Indus and the hills, here entirely occupied by Baloch tribes. The character of its trans-border neighbours has exercised as great an influence upon the interior of Dera Ghazi Khan as it has in the districts to the north. One-third of the population is Baloch, one-half are Jats, and the remainder is composed of Pathan immigrants, and a larger proportion of pure Hindus than are found elsewhere on the border. The character of the population of Dera Ghazi Khan may generally be described as being as well disposed and law-abiding as that of any district in Northern India.

Until 1903 the military defence of the frontier was, with the exception of the Peshawar district, entrusted to the Punjab Frontier Force, consisting of—

- 4 Regiments of Punjab Cavalry,
- 1 Regiment, Corps of Guides, Cavalry and Infantry,
- 4 Mountain Batteries of Artillery,
- 1 Garrison Battery of Artillery,
- 4 Regiments of Sikh Infantry,
- 5 „ „ Punjab Infantry,
- 1 Regiment of Gurkhas,

and was commanded by a Brigadier-General. Peshawar itself was the head-quarters of a brigade of the Bengal Army, and, with Nowshera and five outlying fortresses in the valley, absorbed nearly a fourth of the whole Bengal force in the Punjab.

In 1903, however, the Punjab Frontier Force was abolished, and the frontier is now defended by the Peshawar and Quetta Divisions and the Kohat, Derajat, and Bannu Brigades, assisted by the Frontier Militias.

We now come to the consideration of the tribes beyond the administrative border. The two great nations, the Baloch and Pathan, hold the whole country to the west of the Punjab, the former lying roughly to the south and the latter to the north of a line drawn from the western face of the Suleimans, opposite Dera Ghazi Khan, almost due west to Quetta.

The Balochis and Pathans[1] are both foreigners in the Punjab proper, and have entered its political boundaries within the last few hundred years, though it is not impossible that in doing so the Pathans only re-entered a country which their ancestors had left more than a thousand years before. Yet their freedom from the irksome and artificial restrictions of caste, and the comparative licence which their tribal customs permit them in the matter of inter-marriage, have caused their example to produce a marked effect upon the neighbouring Indian races; and it is the proximity of these races, and the force of that example daily set before them by nations living next door, to which, far more than to the mere political supremacy of a Muhammadan dynasty, or adoption of the Muhammadan creed, may be attributed the laxity of caste rules and observances which characterizes the people of our western plains.

The Baloch presents in many respects a very strong contrast to his neighbour the Pathan. Both have most of the virtues and many of the vices peculiar to a wild and semi-civilized life. To both, hospitality is a sacred duty and the safety of the guest inviolable; both look upon the exaction of "blood for blood" as the first duty of man; both follow strictly a code of honour of their own, though one very different from that of modern Europe; both believe in one God, whose name is *Allah* and whose prophet is Muhammad. But the one attacks his enemy from the front, the other from behind; the one is bound by his promises,[2] the

1 This account of the Baloch and Pathan races is taken from Ibbetson's Report of the Census, 1881.

2 There is in the hills above Harrand a "stone, or cairn of cursings," erected as a perpetual memorial of one who betrayed his fellow.

other by his interests ; in short, the Baloch is less turbulent, less treacherous, less bloodthirsty, and less fanatical than the Pathan ; he has less of God in his creed and less of the devil in his nature. His frame is shorter and more spare and wiry than that of his neighbour to the north, though generations have given to him, too, a bold and manly bearing. Frank and open in his manners, and without severity, fairly truthful when not corrupted by our courts, faithful to his word, temperate and enduring, and looking upon courage as the highest virtue, the true Baloch of the Derajat is a pleasant man to have dealings with. As a revenue payer he is not so satisfactory; his want of industry, and the pride which looks upon manual labour as degrading, making him but a poor husbandman. He is an expert rider ; horse racing is his national amusement, and the Baloch breed of horses is celebrated throughout northern India. He is a thief by tradition and descent, for he says, "God will not favour a Baloch who does not steal and rob," and "The Baloch who steals secures heaven to seven generations of his ancestors." But he has become much more honest under the civilizing influences of our rule. His face is long and oval, his features finely cut, and his nose aquiline ; he wears his hair long, and usually in oily curls, and lets his beard and whiskers grow, and he is very filthy in person, considering cleanliness as a mark of effeminacy. He usually carries a sword, knife, and shield ; he wears a smock-frock reaching to his heels and pleated across the waist, loose drawers, and a long cotton scarf, and all these must be white, or as near it as dirt will allow of, insomuch that he will not enter our army because he there would be obliged to wear a coloured uniform. His wife wears a sheet over her head, a long sort of night-gown reaching to her ankles, and wide drawers ; her clothes may be red or white ; and she plaits her hair in a long *queue.*

As the true Baloch is nomad in his habits, he does not seclude his women ; but he is extremely jealous of female honour. In cases of detected adultery, the man is killed and the woman hangs herself by order. Even when on the war trail, the women and children of his enemy are safe from him. The Baloch of the hills lives in huts or temporary camps, and wanders with his herds from place to place. In the plains he has settled in small villages ;

but the houses are of the poorest possible description. A tally of lives due is kept between the various tribes or families. and when the accounts grow complicated, it can be settled by betrothals, or even by payment of cattle.

The Balochis are nominally Musalmans, but singulary ignorant of their religion and neglectful of its rites and observances; and though, if their ejection from Arabia be true, they must have originally been Shia, they now belong almost without exception to the Sunni sect. The Balochis themselves claim to be Arabs by origin, while some hold them to be of Turkoman stock; their customs are said to support the latter theory; their features certainly favour the former. Their language is a branch of the old Persian, but it is being gradually superseded on the Punjab frontier by Multani or Jatki. They have no written character and no literature; but they are passionately fond of poetry, chiefly consisting of ballads describing the events of national or tribal history, and of love songs; and local poets are still common among them.

When the Balochis moved northwards towards our border, they were divided into two great branches, the Rind and the Lashari, and at the present day all the Baloch tribes consider themselves as belonging to one or other of these divisions.

The tribe, at least in its present form, is a political and not an ethnic unit, and consists of a conglomeration of clans bound together by allegiance to a common chief. Probably every tribe contains a nucleus of two, three, or more clans descended from a common ancestor; but round these have collected a number of affiliated sections; for, the cohesion between the various parts of a tribe or clan is not always of the strongest, and it is not very uncommon for a clan or portion of a clan to quarrel with its brethren, and, leaving its tribe, to claim the protection of a neighbouring chief. They then become his *hamsayas* or dwellers beneath the same shade, and he is bound to protect them and they to obey him. In this manner a small section, formerly belonging to the Laghari tribe and still bearing its name, has attached itself to the Kasranis. Thus, too, Rind tribes are sometimes found to include Lashari clans. So when Nasir Khan, the great Khan of Kalat, who assisted Ahmad Shah in his invasion of Delhi, reduced the Hasani tribe and drove them from their territory, they took refuge with the

Khetrans, of which tribe they now form a clan. Even str. ngers are often affiliated in this manner.

The tribe (*tuman*), under its chief or *tumandar*, is divided into a small number of clans (*para*) with their *mukadams* or headmen, and each clan into more numerous sections (*phali*). Below the *phali* come the families, of which it will sometimes contain as few as a dozen. The clans are based upon common descent ; and identity of clan name, even in two different tribes, almost certainly indicates a common ancestor. The section is of course only an extended family. The tribal names are often patronymic, ending in the Baloch termination, *ani*, such as Gurchani; or in some few cases in the Pushtu, *zai*.

An individual is commonly known by the name of his clan, the sections being comparatively unimportant. Marriage within the sections is forbidden, and this appears to be the only restriction.

The Balochis freely marry Jat women, though the first wife to a chief will always be a Balochni.

The Pathan, as already stated, presents in many respects a strong contrast to the Baloch. He is bloodthirsty, cruel, and vindictive in the highest degree; he does not know what truth or faith is, insomuch that the saying *Afghan be iman* has passed into a proverb among his neighbours; and though he is not without courage of a sort, and is often reckless of his life, he would scorn to face an enemy whom he could stab from behind, or meet him on equal terms if it were possible to take advantage of him, but never meanly. It is easy to convict him out of his own mouth. There are some of his proverbs : "A cousin's tooth breaks upon a coin",—"Keep a cousin poor, but use him."—"When he is little stay with him; when he is grown up, he is a cousin; fight him". "Speek good words to an enemy very softly; gradually destroy his root and branch".[1] At the same time he has his code of honour, which he observes strictly, and which he quotes with pride under the name of *Pakhtunwali*. It imposes upon him three chief obligations—to shelter and protect even an enemy who comes as a suppliant; to revenge by retaliation; and to give open-handed hospitality to any who may demand it. And of these three, perhaps the last is the greatest. There is a sort of charm about him, especially

1 The Pushtu word *tour* is used in differently for *cousin* or for *enemy*.

about the leading men, which almost makes one forget his treacherous nature. As the proverb says, "The Pathan is one moment a saint and the next a devil." For centuries he has been, on our frontier at least, subject to no man. He leads a wild, free, active life in the rugged fastness of his mountains; and there is an air of masculine independence about him which is refreshing in a country like India. He is a bigot of the most fanatical type, exceedingly proud, and extraordinarily superstitious. He is of stalwart make, and his features are often of a markedly Semitic type. His hair, plentifully oiled, hangs long and straight to his shoulders;[1] he wears a loose tunic, baggy drawers, a sheet of blanket, sandals, and a sheepskin coat with its wool inside; his favourite colour is darkblue;[2] and his national arms, the long, heavy Afghan knife and the matchlock or *jazail*. His women wear a loose shift, wide, wrinkled drawers down to their ankles, and a wrap over the head. Both sexes are filthy in their persons.

Such is the Pathan in his home among the fastnesses of the frontier ranges. But the Pathans of our territory have been much softened by our rule, and by the agricultural life of the plains, so that they look down upon the Pathans of the hills, and their proverbs have it—"A hill man is no man"; and again, "Don't class burrs as grass, or a hill man as a human being." The Pathans are extraordinarily jealous of female honour, and most of the blood-feuds for which they are so famous originate in quarrels about women. As a race, they strictly seclude their females; but the poorer tribes and the poorer members of all tribes are prevented from doing so by their poverty. The Pathan pretends to be purely endogamous, and beyond the border he probably is so; while even in British territory the first wife will generally be a Pathan except among the poorest classes. At the same time, Pathan women beyond the Indus are seldom if ever married to any but Pathans. They intermarry very closely, avoiding only the prohibited degrees of Islam. Their rules of inheritance are tribal and not Muhammadan, though some few of the more educated families have

1 This is not the case with the northern Pathans, who shave their heads and often their beards also.

2 The colour and cut of the clothes vary greatly with the tribe.

lately begun to follow the Musalman law. Their social customs differ much from tribe to tribe, or rather perhaps from the wilder to the more civilized section of the nation. The Pathans beyond and upon our frontier live in fortified villages, to which are attached stone towers in commanding positions, which serve as watch towers and places of refuge for the inhabitants. Raids from the hills into the plains are still not uncommon; and beyond the Iudus, the people, even in British territory, seldom sleep far from the walls of the village.

With regard to the tribal organization of the Pathans, the tribe is probably far more homogeneous in its constitution than amomg the Balochis. Saiyid, Turk, and other clans have occasionally been affiliated to it; but as a rule, people of foreign descent preserve their tribal individuality, becoming merely associated, and not intermingled, with the tribes among whom they have settled. Even then they generally claim Pathan origin on the female side, and the tribe is usually descended, in theory at least, from a common ancestor.

The *hamsaya* custom, already mentioned, by which strangers are protected by the tribe with which they dwell, is in full force among the Pathans as amongst the Balochis. But with the former, though it does protect, in many cases, families of one tribe, who have settled with another, it seldom accounts for any considerable portion of the tribe; and its action is chiefly confined to traders, menials, and other dependents of foreign extraction, who are protected by, but not received into, the tribe. The nation is divided genealogically into a few great sections which have no corporate existence, and the tribe is now the practical unit, though the common name and tradition of common descent are still carefully preserved in the memory of the people. Each section of a tribe, however small, has its leading man, who is known as *malik*, a specially Pathan title. In many, but by no means in all, tribes, there is a *Khan Khel*, usually the eldest branch of the tribe, whose *malik* is known as *Khan*, and acts as chief of the whole tribe. But he is seldom more than their leader in war and their agent in dealings with others; he possesses influence rather than power, and the real authority rests with the *jirga*, a democratic council composed of all the *maliks*. The tribe is split up into numerous clans, and these again into sections. The tribe, clan, and section are alike distinguished by patronymics formed from the name of the common ancestar by the addition of the word *zai* or *khel*; *zai* being the corruption of the Pushtu word *zoe*, meaning son, while *khel* is an Arabic word meaning an association or company. Both terms are used indifferently for both the larger and smaller divisions.[1] The stock of names being limited, the nomenclature is extremely puzzling, certain names recurring in very different tribes in the most perplexing manner. Moreover, the title which genealogical accuracy would allot to a tribe or clan is often very different from that by which it is known for practical purposes, the people having preferred to be called by the name of a junior ancestor who had acquired a local renown. The frontier tribe, whether within or beyond our border, has almost without an exception a very distinct corporate existence; each tribe, and within each tribe each clan, occupying a clearly defined tract of country, thaugh they are in the Indus valley often the owners merely, rather than the occupiers, of the country, the land and smaller villages being largely in the hands of a mixed population of Hindu origin, who cultivate subject to the superior rights of the Pathans. These people are included by the Pathans under the generic and semi-contemptuous name of Hindiki—a term very analogous to the Jat of the Baloch frontier, and which includes all Muhammadans who, being of Hindu origin, have been converted to Islam in comparatively recent times.

The original Afghans are probably a race of Jewish or Arab extraction, and the Pathans of Indian origin; but on this point there is a great conflict of opinion, and not a few deny that there is any distinction whatever between the original Afghan and Pathan stocks. But, however this may be, the nation to which the names are now applied indifferently in Persian and Pushtu, respectively, are without exception Musalmans, and for the most part bigoted followers of the Sunni sect, hating and persecuting the Shias.

The following extract from a report on the relations of the British Government with the frontier tribes in 1855, written by Mr. Temple, Secretary to the Chief Commissioner of the Punjab, is of interest as showing our estimation of their character at that time, and the manner in which we dealt with them:—

1 When our ill-fated Resident, Sir Louis Cavagnari, was living at Kabul under the Amir Yakub Khan, those who favoured the British were as known Cavagnariza and the national party as Yakubzai. The ending zai is never used by the Afridis.

Now these tribes are savages—noble savages, perhaps—and not without some tincture of virtue and generosity, but still absolutely barbarians nevertheless. They have nothing approaching to government or civil institutions. They have, for the most part, no education. They have nominally a religion, but Muhammadanism, as understood by them, is no better, or perhaps is actually worse, than the creeds of the wildest race on earth. In their eyes the one great commandment is blood for blood, and fire and sword for all infidels, that is, for all people not Muhammadans. They are superstitious and priest-ridden. But the priests (*mullas*) are as ignorant as they are bigoted, and use their influence simply for preaching crusades against unbelievers, and inculcate the doctrine of rapine and bloodshed against the defenceless people of the plain. The hill men are sensitive in regrad to their women, but their customs in regard to marriage and betrothal are very prejudicical to social advancement; at the same time they are a sensual race. They are very avaricious; for gold, they will do almost anything, except betray a guest. They are thievish and predatory to the last degree. The Pathan mother often prays that her son may be a successful robber. They are utterly faithless to public engagements; it would never even occur to their minds that an oath on the *Koran* was binding, if against their interests. It must be added that they are fierce and bloodthirsty. They are never without weapons; when grazing their cattle, when driving beasts of burden, when telling the soil, they are still armed. They are perpetually at war with each other. Every tribe and section of a tribe has its internecine wars, every family its hereditary blood-feuds, and every individual his personal foes. There is hardly a man whose hands are unstained. Every person counts up his murders. Each tribe has a debtor and creditor account with its neighbours, life for life. Reckless of the lives of others, they are not sparing of their own. They consider retaliation and revenge to be the strongest of all obligations. They possess gallantry and courage themselves, and admire such qualities in others. Men of the same party will stand by one another in danger. To their minds, hospitality is the first of virtues. Any person who can make his way into their dwellings will not only be safe, but will be kindly received. But as soon as he has left the roof of his entertainer, he may be robbed or killed. They are charitable to the indigent of their own tribe. They possess the pride of birth, and regard acestral associations. They are not averse to civilisation whenever they have felt its benefits. They are fond of tradin g,and also of cultivating; but they are too fickle and excitable to be industrious in agriculture or anything else. They will take military service, and, though impatient of discipline, will prove faithful, unless excited by fanaticism. Such, briefly, is their character, replete with the unaccountable inconsistencies, with that mixture of opposite vices and virtues, belonging to savages.

Such being their character, what has been their conduct towards us? They have kept up old quarrels, or picked new ones with our subjects in the plains and valleys near the frontier; they have descended from the hills and fought these battles out in our territory; they have plundered and burnt our villages and slain our subjects; they have committed minor robberies and isolated murders without number; they have often levied blackmail from our villages; they have intrigued with the disaffected everywhere, and tempted our loyal subjects to rebel and they have for ages regarded the plain as their preserve, and its inhabitants their game. When inclined for cruel sport, they sally forth to rob and murder, and occasionally to take prisoners into captivity for ransom. They have fired upon our own troops, and even killed our officers in our own territories. They have given an asylum to every malcontent or proclaimed criminal who can escape from British justice. They traverse at will our territories, enter our villages, trade in our markets; but few British subjects, and no servent of the British Government, would dare to enter their country on any account whatever.

In return for this, what has been the conduct of the British Government towards them? It has recognised their independence; it has asserted no jurisdiction with regrd to them; it has claimed no revenue from them, and no tribute, except in one case, and that as a punishment. But it has confirmed whatever fiefs they held within its territory; it has uniformly declared that it seeks no fiscal or territorial aggrandisement; and that it only wants, and is resolved to have, tranquillity on the frontier. It has never extended its jurisdiction one yard beyond the old limits of the Sikh dominions. Nothing has been annexed that was not a portion of the Punjab as we found it. Whatever revenue has been paid to the British Government was equally paid to its predecessors, only at a higher rate. In one solitary case has it accepted tribute in satisfaction for offences; in all other cases of misconduct it has avoided making any pecuniary demands on its own behalf. It has claimed no feudal or political ascendancy over the independent hill tribes; it has abstained from any interference in, or connection with, their affairs; it has taken no part in their contests, and has never assisted either party; it has striven to prevent its own subjects from entering into disputes with them. Though permitting and encouraging its subjects to defened themselves at the time of attack, it has prevented them from retaliating afterwards and from making reprisals. Though granting refuge to men flying for their lives, it has never allowed armed bodies to seek protection in its territory, nor to organise resistance or attack. It has freely permitted hill people to settle, to cultivate, to graze their herds, and to trade in its territories. It has accorded to such the same protection, rights, privileges, and conditions as to its own subjects. Its courts have been available, and its officers accessible, to them; its markets have been thrown open to them; all restrictions on trade and transit, all duties (exeept one)[1] which would be imposed by any native government, have been removed and remitted for them. It has freely admitted them to its hospitals and dispensaries, its medical officers have attended scores of them in sickness, and sent them back to their mountain homes cured. The ranks of its service are open to them, and they may eat our salt and draw our pay, if so inclined. What more can a civilised Government legitimately do for its rude neighbours than the above?

There is, perhaps, one method to which the Government might resort more extensively than it does at present, and that is the payment of blackmail. It does, indeed, purchase the good offices of the tribes round the Kohat pass. It does permit a section of the Mohmands to hold a fief, and more unworthy feudatories could not be found. It does also make payments to certain Derajat chiefs such as the Bozars[2]. But the other chiefs who receive money are British subjects, and really perform responsible police duties in return. In the case of the Afridis, Mohmands, and Bozdars, however, the Government only continued a concession originally granted by its predecessors. It has originated no new grants of blackmail, though it enhanced one grant. There is reason to believe that such grants would embolden rather than ward off depredation; once bought off, the hill people would molest us with greater zest than ever, in order to be bought off again. They would actually resort to plundering as a means of extorting blackmail. The appetite once gratified would become sharpened. Such concession would be regarded by the tribes as a confession of weakness, and would absolutely operate as an incitement to mischief. Certain chiefs are known to commit depredations in the hope of being bought off by fiefs, and one made of avoiding annoyance is to let it be known that under no circumstance will the Government be induced to compromise by grants of blackmail.

The character of the hill tribes given in the above report applies rather to the Pathan than the Baloch tribes. The latter are free from the religious bigotry which forms such an important element in the character of the former. Afghans are blindly subservient to their priests, and this is the chief reason that European life is so insecure in their hills, while it is safe among the Balochis, there being no instance on record of a European being assassinated

1 The Salt tax.
2 This payment was discontinued in March 1856.

by them. The absence of this religious bigotry in the Balochis makes their control comparatively easy, for there is not the perpetual fear of some outbreak of fanatical rage against the infidel which to the north, and among Afghan tribes, has always to be guarded against. Another fact which renders the control of the Baloch more easy than that of the Pathan tribes is that the former recognise the authority of their acknowledged chiefs, and pay them loyal obedience and service, and their chiefs thus become the natural channel of communication with their tribesmen, through whom control can be effectively exercised on the tribe. This manner of influencing the Baloch tribes has, for many years past, been followed in the Dera Ghazi Khan district, and generally with success. With the Pathan tribes, on the other hand, this mode of control is impossible, for every tribe is divided and sub-divided into numerous sections, each independent of the other, and yielding but small obedience to its own petty headmen; hating each other with the hatred begotten of generations of blood-feuds, and only uniting under the most exceptional circumstances against a common enemy.

With regard to the fighting qualities of the border tribes, these vary considerably in the different tribes; those on the Hazara border are contemptible as soldiers, their extreme religious bigotry alone making up for their absence of martial qualities. Between Buner and Dera Ismail Khan, the Afghan tribes are both fanatical and brave in an extraordinary degree. Courage with them is the first of virtues, and cowardice the worst of crimes. The Balochis, as turbulent, and formerly of habits quite as predatory as their neighbours, are still of a far milder and more amiable disposition. They are as brave as the Afghans; but they are animated by no fanatical hatred of the English; they have not the military genius of the Afghans, and as an enemy on the hillside they are far less formidable.

It now only remains to note the manner in which offences committed by independent tribes beyond the border are punished. The most simple way of punishing a refractory tribe, and in many cases the most effectual, is to inflict a fine and demand compensation for plundered property, or for lives lost. When the tribe is dependent upon trade with British territory, or when a portion resides within British limits, or is easily accessible from the plains to an attack of a military force, the demand for payment of fine or compensation is generally acceded to, and being paid, the tribe is again received into favour. Should the demand be refused, hostages are demanded, or members of the tribes and their property found within British territory are seized, until such time as the compensation and fine are paid. Against some tribes, as in the case of the Afridis of the Kohat pass in 1876-77, a blockade is an effective measure of punishment. It can only be employed against such tribes as trade with British territory, and while it lasts, any member of the offending tribe found within our border is at once seized and detained. This means of punishment has often been found effectual, and if effectual, it is preferable to a military expedition, which often leaves behind it bitter memories in the destruction of property and loss of life. Last, as a means of punishment, comes the military expedition, which is only resorted to in exceptional circumstances, and when every other means of coercing a hostile tribe has failed.

Mr. Davies, the Secretary to Government, Punjab, in 1864, thus alluded to the necessity for expeditions from time to time :—

Whilst any hasty exertion of physical pressure, to the exclusion of other methods of adjustment, is confessedly impolitic, there is a point beyond which the practice of forbearance may not be carried. As without physical force in reserve there can be no governing power, so under extreme and repeated provocation its non-employment is not distinguishable from weakness. In each case separately, therefore, it must be judged whether or not offensive measures have been justified. It must be noted that the despatch of an expedition into the hills is always in the nature of a judicial act. It is the delivery of a sentence, and the infliction of a punishment for international offences. It is, as a rule, not in assertion of any disputed right, or in ultimate arbitration of any contested claim of its own, that the British Government resolves on such measures, but simply as the only means by which retribution can be obtained for acknowledged crimes committed by its neighbours, and by which justice can be satisfied or future outrages prevented. In the extreme cases in which expeditions are unavoidable, they are analogous to legal penalties for civil crime,—evils in themselves, inevitable from deficiencies of preventive police, but redeemed by their deterrent effects. Considerations of expense, of military risk, of possible losses, of increasing antagonism and combination against us on the part of the tribes, all weigh heavily against expeditions; and to set them aside, there must be an irresistible obligation to protect and to vindicate the outraged rights of subjects whom we debar from the revenge and retaliation they formerly practised.

TRIBES NORTH OF THE KABUL RIVER.

CHAPTER I.

THE GILGIT AGENCY.

THE northernmost limit to which British paramountcy extends is formed by the Hindu Kush and Karakoram, or Mustagh, ranges—the great mountain barrier which divides India from Afghanistan, Russia, and China.

Immediately south of these ranges the first district to be dealt with is that now known as the Gilgit Agency, which includes :—

(1) The Gilgit Wazarat, made up of the Tehsils of Astor and Gilgit, and the Niabat of Bunji.

(2) The Punial *jagir*.

(3) The States of Hunza and Nagir.

(4) The Governorship of Yasin, Kuh, and Ghizr; and the Governorship of Ishkaman.

(5) The republican communities of the Chilas district.

Of these the Wazarat is Kashmir territory and is governed by a Wazir appointed by the Durbar. Punial is also Kashmir territory, but hitherto the Kashmir authorities have only been permitted to interfere in cases of serious crime, such as murder, which are tried in the Wazarat courts. All other matters concerning the administration of the *jagir* are dealt with by the Governor, Raja Sifat Bahadur, who is advised direct by the Political Agent. The other districts of the agency are under the suzerainty of His Highness the Maharaja, but are not Kashmir territory, and His Highness' officials are not permitted to interfere in their internal administration. Details regarding the administration of these districts will be given later in this chapter, and it will be sufficient to note here that the various chiefs, governors, and *jagirs* are interfered with as little as possible, but that all are subject to the general guidance and control of the Political Agent.

It will be seen that the Agency contains a multiplicity of forms of government. The explanation is that the peoples of the various districts differ widely in their origin and customs. It may be noted, *en passant*, that no less than four different languages are spoken within the limits of the Agency, *viz.* :—Shina, Burushaski, Khowar, and Wakhi; and that as regards religion, although all are Muhammadans, the people belong to three different sects, *viz.* :—Sunni, Shia, and Maulai.

For generations previous to the advent of British officers the different communities had been in a state of constant war with each other, and it was out of the question to attempt to bring them under one form of government. Even now the inhabitants of the various districts show little inclination to mingle with one another, and any concerted action by them against the paramount power is inconceivable.[1]

The geographical boundaries of the Agency are, on the north, the Mustagh mountains, which divide Hunza-Nagir from the Chinese New Dominions, and the Hindu Kush, in continuation of the Mustagh range, separating Ishkaman and Yasin from Wakhan. On the east lies the Skardu district of Jammu and Kashmir; and on the west the Shandur range, on the opposite side of which is the Chitral district of the Dir and Swat Agency. The southern boundaries are the Burzil pass, separating the Astor *tehsil* from the Kashmir province of His Highness the Maharaja's dominions, and the Babusar pass, by which communication is maintained with Gilgit from the Punjab, *viâ* the Kaghan valley. In the Indus valley the boundary is, on the right bank of the river, the watershed between the Hodar and Khanbari valleys, and, on the left bank, the watershed between the Thor and Harban valleys. Both Thor and Hodar are included in the Chilas district. The Hindu Raj range forms the boundary between the Agency and the independent communities of Tangir, Darel, and the Swat Kohistan.

The following are the chief passes leading into Gilgit :—

From the north, the Kilik, 15,600 feet, and the Mintaka, 15,430 feet, give entry to Hunza and Nagir from Yarkand, Kashgar,

[1] NOTE.—For an example of their incapacity for combined action, witness the failure of the Indus valley tribesmen to attack Chilas while the siege of Chitral Fort was in progress. See page 35.

and the Taghdumbash Pamir. By the Shingshal, 14,720 feet, lies a way from the Raskam valley, while the Irshad passes, 16,000 and 16,180 feet, respectively, supply routes from Wakhan. The snow and glaciers of these passes present in winter a practically insurmountable barrier to an invading force of any real strength, though small caravans of traders well acquainted with the route penetrate from Yarkand to Hunza and Nagir by the Kilik and Mintaka during the summer, and the latter pass is used by the postal service to Kashgar during the winter, when it can be crossed by small parties with some difficulty. The tracks lead over precipitous cliffs and along deep gorges, in many of which a thousand men might well be stopped by a hundred rifles at any place along the eighty miles separating Hunza from the frontier. From Hunza a good track road runs into Gilgit along the banks of the Hunza river.

From Wakhan two routes lead towards Yasin: the Baroghil pass, 12,460 feet, which is fifty-three miles from Yasin; and the Karumbar,[1] and Khora Bhort passes, which are 14,000 and 15,000 feet, respectively. The latter pass is 36 miles from Imit, and 108 miles from Gilgit.

At Gupis the main line of communication between Gilgit and Chitral is met. This, after crossing the Shandur pass at eighty-seven miles from Chitral, and sixty-five from Gupis, becomes the excellent 6-foot road which runs through Punial to Gilgit. An alternative route to the Shandur pass lies in the Chamarkand, 13,000, a shorter but rougher road. In the summer there is communication between Ghizr and Kuh on the one side and Swat Kohistan on the other by several passes; and in Punial communication with Darel is practicable by all the main *nalas* which drain into the Gilgit river on its right bank.

On the east the path from Skardu to Gilgit is perhaps the most difficult of any used means of communication in the northern Himalayas. The road by the Deosai plains, averaging from 12,000 to 13,000 feet, which crosses from Skardu to Astor, is closed by snow in all except the summer months.

1 The route from the Karumbar pass to Imit was, in 1906, rendered impracticable by the advance of the Karumbar glacier, which blocked the mouth of the Sokhta valley.

The southern routes are the most important to the Agency, for it is by these that connection with India is maintained. The present main thoroughfare from Srinagar is the 10-foot road which crosses the Rajdiangan or Tragbal pass on the northern shore of the Wular lake into the Gurais valley, from whence it leads over the Burzil pass, 13,500 feet, into the Astor valley. From here it winds down the Hattu Pir, and crosses the Ramghat bridge on to the Bunji plain. After leaving Bunji the Indus is crossed at Partab bridge and the road then follows the right bank of the Gilgit river to Gilgit, which is reached at thirty-seven miles from Bunji, 193 from Bandipur, and 228 from Srinagar. The distance from Rawal Pindi to Baramula is 162 miles, and Gilgit is therefore about 390 miles from its present railway base.

The shortest and easiest route, however, from India to Gilgit is the 10-foot road up the Kaghan valley route, *viâ* the Babusar pass. This leaves the North-Western Railway at Hassan Abdal, and, following the Kaghan valley up to the Babusar pass, drops down the Thak Nala on to the left bank of the Indus, a few miles to the east of Chilas. By this route the distance to Gilgit is 250 miles from the railway, and the road crosses only one snow pass, whereas the road from Pindi traverses two.

The whole of the Gilgit Agency is mountainous in the extreme. Lofty snow-clad peaks, rugged and barren at their base, but softening off towards their summits into pine clad slopes and grassy *maidans*, overhang deep valleys in which the heat of the summer and the cold of winter are alike intense. The rainfall is small, and the land under cultivation is chiefly irrigated by canals led from the mountain streams. The hillsides are generally too precipitous to allow of cultivation, and this is consequently mostly confined to the valleys, and to alluvial "fans," formed by deposits of stone and detritus brought down by the rivers.

The present garrison of Gilgit (1907) consists of two regiments of Kashmir Imperial Service Infantry, one Imperial Service Mountain Battery of four guns, and two companies of Sappers and Miners, which units are distributed as follows:—

Gilgit.—Five Companies, Kashmir Imperial Service Infantry.
Two companies, Sappers and Miners.

Bunji.—Kashmir Imperial Service Mountain Battery.
Three companies, Kashmir Imperial Service Infantry.
Chilas.—Two companies, Kashmir Imperial Service Infantry.
Gupis.—Two companies, Kashmir Imperial Service Infantry.

The Kashmir State maintains two brigades of Imperial Service troops of equal strength, one of which is stationed in the Gilgit Agency, and the other at Satwari, near Jammu. The two brigades relieve each other biennially. Two British officers, who perform the duties of inspecting officers for the infantry and artillery, reside at Satwari ; and three British officers are stationed in the Gilgit Agency, there being one assistant inspecting officer with the battery and one with each of the infantry battalions. The senior assistant inspecting officer, is usually stationed at Gilgit, and advises the Kashmir General Officer Commanding in all important matters.

In addition to these troops there are a certain number of levies, selected from the best material in the district, who are paid a small retaining fee on the understanding that they are liable for service whenever the Government of India may think fit to call them out.

The population of the Agency, according to the last census, is 58,358. The people are lazy and unwarlike, but are good mountaineers. Both men and women are of strong physique. The total number of men within the limits of the Agency who are considered fit to bear arms is approximately as follows :—

Wazarat	200
Chilas	800
Hunza	1,500
Nagir	2,000
Punial	300
Yasin	1,000
Ishkaman	40
Total ..	5,840

The first representative of the Government of India to visit these regions was Captain Biddulph, who was sent on a mission to Gilgit and Hunza in 1876. In 1877 the Kashmir State, which had hitherto been under the Punjab Government, was brought directly under the Foreign Department of the Government of India, and in that year Captain Biddulph was appointed Political Agent in Gilgit. He remained there till 1881, when the Government decided to abolish the Agency.

In 1886 the growth of the Imperial and Kashmir interests in and near the Mustagh and Hindu Kush ranges, and in the petty states tributary to Kashmir adjoining the northern frontiers of the Indian Empire, determined the Government of India to depute an officer to make a further report on the hitherto little known countries of Hunza, Nagir, Yasin, and Chitral. The late Lieutenant-General Sir William Lockhart, then Colonel Lockhart, was consequently sent with a mission to Gilgit, which visited the districts mentioned, penetrating as far as the valley of Kafiristan, and successfully collected a vast quantity of important information. In 1888 the unsettled state of affairs in the Gilgit district, and the frequent aggressions of the petty tribes against the Kashmir Durbar, again induced the Government of India to send an officer to visit these parts. Captain Durand was accordingly selected for this duty, and, in submitting his report on the situation, recommended the re-establishment of an Agency there. This measure was sanctioned by the Secretary of State for India in 1889.

The jurisdiction of the Agency at that time extended over Gurais, Astor, Bunji, Sai, and Gilgit, or, in other words, the present limits of the Gilgit Wazarat and the Gurais Tehsil. Chitral, Punial, Hunza, Nagir, Darel, Gor, Chilas, and Hodar were nominally tributary to Kashmir through this Wazarat. Gilgit was then garrisoned by the regular troops of the Kashmir Durbar and the outposts were held by irregulars. The former were armed with muzzle-loading weapons, and the latter with flint-locks. Military discipline was indifferent, and service in Gilgit was most unpopular with the men, who, owing to the poorness of pay, and insufficiency of rations and clothes, coupled with the fact that the district was at that time used as a penal settlement, looked upon a tour of duty there as equivalent to a term of imprisonment.

On the re-introduction of the British Agency in 1889, special service officers were sent to the district, to reorganize the force, which was soon put on a better footing and is now in a thoroughly efficient state.

The Gilgit Wazarat.

The Astor Tehsil.

Astor, or, as the Dogras call it, Hasora, was a place of some political importance prior to the permanent occupation of Gilgit by the Imperial Service troops of the Maharaja of Kashmir. Little is known of its early history, but, some fifty years ago, when the district was being torn by internal dissensions and ravaged by incessant incursions from Chilas, Ranjit Singh intervened. Astor then became an integral part of the dominion of the Maharaja of Kashmir, and the independence of the local ruler disappeared. The district developed into a large military *place d'armes*, and its Ra was made a *Jagirdar* of Kashmir. Since then the political metacentre of the Maharaja's provinces has shifted to trans-Indus territory, and Astor is now governed from Gilgit and not from Kashmir. The district has been settled and the Chilas raids have ended in the capture of that place and its incorporation into the Gilgit province.

Astor is the only part of the Wazarat where pack animals are procurable. The people have even less aptitude for military service than the Gilgitis, but their ponies, of which about 330 are available for transport, would be a valuable asset in time of trouble.

The Niabat of Bunji.

Bunji is the head-quarters of the Imperial Service Battery and one of the two battalions which constitute the garrison of the Gilgit Agency. The place is small, though, like many portions of this country, it was at one time populous. Its situation is strategically important. Placed half-way between the Ramghat and Partab bridges, over the Astor and Indus rivers, it stands at the junction of four roads, two from India *viâ* Kashmir and Chilas respectively, the third from Gilgit *viâ* the Gilgit valley, and the fourth from Skardu *viâ* Haramosh. Except for some twenty *zemindars'* houses the buildings consist of a rubble fort and the barracks. A ferry is maintained about a mile above the fort for communication with the Sai valley, which is immediately opposite on the right bank of the Indus. The fort would be of little use against modern armaments. Owing to the intense heat which prevails at Bunji in the summer, the majority of the garrison spend that part of the year at Gilgit.

Punial.

Punial is practically a portion of the Gilgit valley, and is politically included in the Gilgit Wazarat, although all local questions are decided by the Burushe Raja, who holds the post of Governor. The district extends from the plain near Shakot to Thamushki, just beyond the Hupar Pari[1] on the Gupis–Yasin road. The population amounts to about 3,000, most of whom belong to the Yaskun tribe. The people are of much the same type as the Gilgitis, but, judging from the good service rendered by the Punial levies in Chilas in 1892, and again in Chitral in 1895, they appear to have far more aptitude for a military life. The Punialis are also of a more cheerful disposition than the Gilgitis. As regards religion all are Muhammadans, three-fourths being Maulais and the rest Sunnis. The language in general use is Shina, but most of the Burushe[2] family understand Khowar, the language of Chitral.

The mass of the people live in hovels within the walls of the various forts, a custom which was no doubt necessary in the days when the country was a bone of contention between the rulers of Yasin and Gilgit, but which might now be abandoned with advantage to the public health.

With regard to communications there is a good pack road passing through the district on the right bank of the river, but the tracks on the left bank are impracticable for laden animals. Communication between the two banks of the river is maintained by numerous rafts and rope bridges, and a suspension bridge is in course of construction at Gakuch which will facilitate communication with the Ishkaman district.

Hunza and Nagir.

As the annals of Hunza and Nagir are closely intermingled, the two countries will be dealt with under the one heading.

Hunza, which lies to the north-west of Gilgit, is bounded on the north and east by the Hindu Kush and Karakoram mountains. On the west it is divided by another range from the Karumbar and Garm Chai

Hunza.

1 Gallery.

2 The Burushe is the ruling family of Punial, and is closely connected with that of Chitral and Yasin. All the males of the Burushe clan are locally called "Gushpur." They are now very numerous, and, as they pay no taxes, and have an inordinate opinion of their own importance, they are a great burden on the district.

valleys, while the southern boundary is formed by a spur running between the Shingshal and Hispar rivers, and by the Hunza river which separates it from Nagir. Hunza has also certain claims to jurisdiction over the Taghdumbash Pamir, the State of Shakshu Pakhpu, and the Raskam valley.

Hunza may be considered to consist of three parts, which are to a great extent ethnological divisions :—

(1) Hunza Proper, lying between the Bulchidas and Tashot spurs, is inhabited by people of Burush stock, speaking the Burushaski language : they are known as Birchik, or Yashkun. The population of Hunza Proper is about 6,000.

(2) Herbar, or little Gujhal, includes the main valley and all the lateral valleys north of the Bulchidas spur. All the people of this district can speak Burushaski, but amongst themselves they usually speak Wakhi. The majority of the inhabitants no doubt hail from Wakhan, but many of the families are descendants of settlers from Hunza and Chaprot. The population is about 1,600.

(3) Shinaki, the 3rd division, comprises that part of the country on the right bank of the Hunza river extending from the Tashot spur to the spur which separates Hunza territory from the Karumbar and Garmasai valleys. It contains the two fort villages of Maiun and Hini. The inhabitants speak the Shina tongue.

Nagir.

Nagir is bounded by Hunza on the north, and by the Gilgit province and Baltistan on the south ; it also includes the districts of Chalt, Chaprot, and the Buladas or Garmasai valley, on the right bank of the Hunza river. The country may be divided into two parts, namely, (1) Nagir Proper, and (2) Shinaki, or Shen Bar. The first named district extends from Hispar to Dadimal, and its inhabitants are of the same stock as in Hunza Proper, speaking the Burushaski tongue. The latter division extends from the village of Minapin as far as Chalt, and includes Chaprot, Bar, and Buladas, with a few hamlets only occupied during the summer, chiefly for grazing purposes. Shina is spoken in all the villages, but the people can also speak Burushaski. Chaprot once belonged to Hunza, and the people of Hunza intermarry with the villagers of that place, though they will not do so with any one from Nagir Proper. The population of Nagir is about 10,000.

Communications.

There are fairly good roads on either side of the Hunza river leading to Gilgit, but the country is, as a whole, exceedingly rugged and difficult, and most of the so-called roads are mere mountain tracks which are occasionally carried along the face of precipices by overhanging galleries which could be easily cut away. Serious damage has been caused to communications in Hunza–Nagir on various occasions owing to the action of a glacier in the Shingshal valley. This glacier periodically dams the Shingshal river, and a lake forms behind the barrier of ice. Eventually the water breaks through the ice and causes a flood in the Hunza river. In July 1906 a most serious flood was caused in this way which amongst other damage, wrecked the suspension bridge at Askurdas and the bridge across the Gilgit river at Chamogah, and practically destroyed the whole road between Chalt and Nomal.

Government of Hunza and Nagir.

Both states are governed by their own rajas or rulers, who are known in their own country by the name of *Tham,* though their official title is *Mir.* Each is assisted by a *wazir* or chief minister, whose office is hereditary. Murder, and other serious crimes, are dealt with by the *Mir*; other offences, except those of a petty nature, by the *wazir.* In minor cases, justice is administered by the headman of the village or group of villages. This official is called the *Trangfa* or *Jangayo,* and has one or more assistants called *Charbu.* Other minor officials assist in collecting taxes and revenue, and in providing coolies, supplies, etc., as required. Among these may be mentioned the *Ferash,* who from his duties might be called comptroller of the *Mir's* household, and the *Yarfas,* or land stewards, who superintend the cultivating and harvesting of the *Mir's* crops.

Almost all available land in Hunza and Nagir is cultivated, and the system of irrigation canals, or *khals,* is excellent.

The revenues of the *Thams* or *Mirs* are derived from taxes on cultivation, marriage and divorce, trade, live stock, and gold-washing, which latter is quite a considerable industry in these parts.

It may be assumed that in the event of invasion from outside, the two States could muster about 3,500 fighting men between them while the whole of the rest of the male population would be available for the carriage of supplies and the erection of *sangars*.

Military.

A system of levies obtains, by which all enrolled levies are called out annually for one week, and are put through a short course of musketry by the military assistant to the Political Agent. They are armed with Snider carbines which are kept in Gilgit, and only issued when the men are under training. For hardiness and activity on the mountain side the men of both States are noted throughout the Hindu Kush region. Contingents of levies from Hunza and Nagir accompanied Colonel Kelly on his march to Chitral in 1895 and rendered valuable services. As noted elsewhere the peoples of the two States are extremely jealous of each other. They have, however, been known to unite against a common foe, as for instance when they combined against Colonel Durand's force in 1891[1]; but it cannot be said that they offered each other wholehearted support on that occasion.

Although of the same race and origin, the people of Hunza and Nagir vary considerably in physique and physiognomy. The former people are of a cheerful, open disposition, and are as a rule powerfully built and of medium stature. Their complexion is rather fair, and men with reddish and sandy coloured hair are often met with. The people of Nagir, on the other hand, do not seem to posssess the fine physique which is seen in Hunza, and are generally of darker complexion. In religion the Hunza men, with few exceptions, belong to the Maulai sect, while the Nagirs are all Shias.

People.

Polo is the great national pastime in both States, as in Gilgit and Yasin, and each village has its own polo-ground where the game is played whenever time can be spared. The grounds vary from 200 to 300 yards long by 20 to 30 wide, and are surrounded by walls of stone and mud about three to four feet high. Any number of players join in the game and it is a common sight to see as many as eight and twelve a side. A description of the game appears unnecessary, but it may be mentioned that few of the English

[1] See page 17.

rules seem to be observed. Other pastimes are shooting at a mark from horseback at full gallop, and tent-pegging.

Owing to their wild and inaccessible nature the two countries, especially Hunza, have seldom been successfully invaded. Both were formerly ruled over by the same chief; but one of these princes, Lali Tham,[1] having two sons, Girkis and Moghlot, divided his territory between them, giving Hunza to the elder, and Nagir to the younger brother. These two princes quarrelled, and Girkis was killed by a servant of Moghlot. From this time forward the two countries were continually at war with each other, and even now they are far from being on good terms. The people of Nagir more than once allied themselves with the Kashmir troops against Hunza, but never with any success; and the fighting was generally of a guerilla nature. If the Hunza men took a prisoner he was sold into slavery; when the Nagirs took a captive he was killed. It is doubtful which was the less enviable fate.

The district of Chaprot used to be a constant source of strife between the two states, and was from time to time held by each in turn. In 1877, the Hunza garrison was driven out by the allied forces of Nagir and Kashmir, since when the place has belonged to Nagir. When Colonel Lockhart visited Hunza with his mission, however, the *Tham* would only allow him to enter the country on condition that he would restore Chaprot to Hunza. Colonel Lockhart consequently induced the Nagir garrison to retire, and since then the place has been solely occupied by Kashmir troops.

Expedition against Hunza and Nagir in 1891.

In February 1888 the Rajas of Hunza and Nagir rose against Kashmir, and, with a combined force of 2,000 men, expelled the Kashmir garrisons from the northern outpost of Chalt. They next threatened to attack Nomal, a fort some fifteen miles north of Gilgit. This post, however, was reinforced, and on 17th March the garrison made a successful sortie, causing the besiegers to withdraw to Chaprot. Although there were some 4,800 Kashmir troops and irregulars divided between Nomal, Gilgit, Astor, and Bunji, the force was without transport, had practically no organization, and was quite unfit to undertake military operations. Consequently

[1] The Nagir people state this man's name was Shah.

the Kashmir Durbar preferred to negotiate with the Hunza and Nagir Chiefs. An arrangement was accordingly agreed to whereby Chalt was to be garrisoned by Kashmir troops, the cultivators who had hitherto lived there being removed, and Chaprot was to be handed over to Gauri Tham (a son of Zafar Khan, Raja of Nagir), who was also furnished with an escort of twenty-five Kashmir sepoys.

Shortly after these events Captain Durand, as has already been described, was deputed by the Government of India to visit Gilgit and submit a report on the military situation with reference to the recent tribal disturbances, and the means of ensuring the security of the country up to the Hindu Kush.

Captain Durand reported that affairs in Gilgit were most unsatisfactory from a military point of view, and made various recommendations for their improvement. As a result of this report the Government of India decided to re-establish the Gilgit Agency which had been withdrawn in 1881.

The following year (1889) a Mission, consisting of Captain Durand, Lieutenant J. Manners-Smith and Surgeon G. S. Robertson, with a small escort of the 20th Punjab Infantry, was deputed to visit the States of Hunza and Nagir.

At Nagir, a place hitherto unvisited by Europeans—the Mission was cordially received. The Raja, Zafar Khan, and his son, Uzar Khan, appeared to be well disposed towards the British, and readily consented to the conditions on which the Government proposed to grant an increased subsidy, *viz.*, the exclusion of foreigners, and free passage through their territory for British officers.

The Mission next proceeded to Hunza, where the Raja, Safdar Ali, agreed to the following terms in return for the grant of subsidy, *viz.*, free passage for British officers, exclusion of foreigners, cessation of raiding on the Yarkand road, and non-interference on the part of China in the internal affairs of his country.

In 1890 the Hunza Raja, in contravention of his agreement, raided a Kirghiz encampment on the Taghdumbash Pamir. The Raja of Nagir also was reported to have kidnapped a boy in Gilgit territory late in 1889. Otherwise there was nothing to disturb our relations with these two States up to the end of 1890.

On the 25th May 1891 the British Agent at Gilgit received information that Uzar Khan of Nagir had murdered his brothers, Gauri Tham and Ding Malik, and intended to seize the outposts of Chalt and Chaprot. Raja Zafar Khan also wrote to the effect that Uzar Khan threatened to murder a third brother, Sikander Khan, then in Gilgit, should the latter return to Chaprot. Captain (now Lieut.-Colonel) Durand promptly made preparations to safeguard the Gilgit frontier, and moved to Chalt with a small force on the 29th, being joined on the way by Raja Akbar Khan of Punial and some of his men. This rapid and unexpected move surprised and disconcerted the people of Hunza and Nagir. Wazir Dadu of Hunza and Uzar Khan, who had collected their respective forces at Maiun and Nilt, tried to induce Raja Zafar Khan to join them in an advance against Chalt, but the latter refused and the attempt was abandoned.

Letters and messages were now interchanged, and, on the 15th June, *vakils* (*jirgas*) from both states came in. The Hunza *vakil* disclaimed all connection with Chalt or Chaprot, and stated that there was no intention on their part of attacking these places. The Nagir *vakil* assured Colonel Durand in Zafar Khan's name of their Chief's loyalty, repudiated all responsibility for Uzar Khan and his doings, and promised, if the troops were withdrawn, to prevent the latter from giving further trouble.

The following day at a Durbar attended by the Punial Raja, the headmen of Chalt, Chaprot, Bar, and Buladas, and the Hunza and Nagir *vakils*, Colonel Durand explained his reasons for moving to Chalt, and announced that in consequence of the assurance of the Hunza and Nagir Rajas that they would not interfere with Chalt and Chaprot in future, he would withdraw his troops. He, however, warned them that any further attack on the border villages or movement of armed men between Chalt and Nomal would be considered an act of war by Hunza and Nagir against the Kashmir Durbar and the British Government.

Having provided for the garrisoning of Chalt and Chaprot, Colonel Durand withdrew the remainder of his troops to Nomal on the 20th June. He, however, had but little hope that this settlement was final, and in a report to the Government of India he urged the complete subjection of Hunza and Nagir, the gist of the reasons on which he based his recommendation being as follows:—that, owing to their isolated position in a country extremely difficult of access, and their exaggerated ideas of their own power and importance, these people were likely to be a constant source of anxiety and trouble on the frontier; that the Hunza Chief had for some time past been guilty of intrigues with other Powers, and that it was necessary that we should have access through his country to the passes on to the Pamirs; and, lastly, that the Hunza Chief had, moreover, broken all the agreements in return for which he received a British subsidy.

In September 1891 the Government sanctioned the establishment of a garrison and fort at Chalt, and the improvement of the Gilgit–Chalt road. It was also decided to inform the Chiefs of Hunza and Nagir that roads must be made through their territories from Chalt to Hunza and Nagir, and possibly on to Gircha, the point of junction of several routes: the Chiefs were to be assured that no interference with the government of their countries was intended, but that they, as tributaries, would be expected to aid in the work, and that in the event of their objecting, our troops would enter their country and construct the roads.

In anticipation of the above-mentioned proposals leading to hostilities, a detachment of 200 men of the 1-5th Gurkhas under Captain Barrett, with Lieutenants Boisragon and Badcock, and a section of the Hazara Mountain Battery under Lieutenant Gorton, R.A., was ordered from Abbottabad to Gilgit, which place they reached about the 21st November.

In crossing the Burzil pass they had encountered very bad weather, and Captain Barrett and a number of men suffered severely from frostbite.

During the week preceding the arrival of the Gurkhas, letters were received from the Hunza and Nagir Chiefs protesting against our preparations; and the Raja of the latter State went so far as to threaten that any attempt to build a bridge at Chalt would lead to war. Both Chiefs were invited to send in their *vakils*. Their tribesmen, however, were collecting at Maiun and Nilt, and were strengthening the defences at both places. It, therefore, appeared evident that the two States were determined to combine against us.

The section of the mountain battery and half the Gurkha detachment had been pushed on to Chalt by the 21st, and the road between that place and Gilgit was strongly held. Martial law was now proclaimed in the Gilgit district, and the carrying of arms was prohibited.

	British officers.	Native officers, N.-C. officers, and men.
1 Section No. 4 (Hazara) Mountain Battery	2	76
1-5th Gurkha Rifles	2	188
Bengal Sappers and Miners	1	7
20th Punjab Infantry and gatling gun detachment	1	28
Signallers		12
1st Kashmir Infantry (Ragu Pertab Regiment)	2	257
2nd Kashmir Rifles (Body-Guard Regiment)	3	404
Punial Levy	1	159
Total ..	12	1,131

Staff,

Lieut.-Colonel A. G. A. Durand, Commanding.
Captain R. H. Twigg, 12th Bengal Infantry, D.A.A.G.
" C. T. Mackenzie, Seaforth Highlanders, D.A.Q.M.G.
" F. J. Aylmer, Commanding R.E.
" W. H. M. Stewart, Political Officer.
Lieutenant T. Manners-Smith, " "
Surgeon-Captain T. R. Roberts, I.M.S., P.M.O.
General Suram Chand, Commanding Kashmir Troops at Gilgit.

On the 28th November the troops, as shown in the margin, were concentrated at Chalt. A detachment of 200 picked Pathan road coolies, under Mr. Charles Spedding (the contractor for the Kashmir-Gilgit road) was attached to the force as an Engineer Corps. Supplies had all to be brought from Kashmir, and the complete breakdown of the contractors' arrangements caused Colonel Durand much anxiety. Lieutenant Baird, however, was despatched to Bunji in November and succeeded in forwarding sufficient supplies to enable the force to advance by the end of the month. The rations issued to the troops were nearly on active service scale, including one *chittack* of *ghi*, and meat whenever possible. This contributed much to the successful resistance of the extreme cold, especially in the case of the Kashmir troops, who had previously suffered considerably from bad and insufficient food.

On the 29th November Colonel Durand forwarded an ultimatum to the Rajas of Hunza and Nagir, of which the following is an extract :—

It is necessary for the protection of Kashmir and of your State that the troops of the Supreme Government should have free access to your country. By this means alone can the requisite arrangements be made for safeguarding here the frontier of the Empire. It is not the intention of the Supreme Government in any way to interfere with the form of rule in your State, but the arrangements for protecting its frontier necessitate on the part of

Government the making of roads which will enable it, should occasion arise, to place troops rapidly in positions guarding the passes leading from the Pamirs. The Supreme Government has, therefore, decided to make a road from Gilgit to Chalt, where a fort will be built, and from Chalt to Hunza/Nagir,[1] or so far beyond that place as may be necessary. As a feudatory of the British Government you are now called upon to give any aid in your power towards the construction of the road. I am further directed to inform you that, in so far as concerns the road beyond Chalt, which will pass through your territory, no refusal on your part to permit its construction will be accepted. The road must be made. Unless you instantly comply with the demands of the Supreme Government, troops will enter your territory, and the road will be constructed in spite of any opposition you may offer.

Three days from this date will be allowed during which your answer will be awaited, and I warn you that should it not be completely satisfactory, the troops under my command will move forward and carry out the orders of Government. The British Government has ever treated you with marked consideration and generosity. I trust that the remembrance of this fact will influence your counsels, and that by a wise compliance with the wishes of the great and magnanimous Government, whose loyal servant you have constantly confessed yourself to be, you will avoid bringing on your country and people the calamity of war.

With this ultimatum letters were sent pointing out the hopelessness of resistance and advising the Chiefs to avoid war. On the 30th November, however, our envoy returned bringing defiant answers from both the Rajas, and Colonel Durand determined to advance on the expiration of the three days' law which had been promised.

Meanwhile Mr. Spedding, with his 200 Pathans, had been rapidly improving the road from Nomal to Chalt, and 800 more coolies were at work on the road between Nomal and Gilgit.

It was considered necessary to make arrangements to safeguard the line of communications Astor-Bunji-Gilgit against any possible interference on the part of the Shinaki[2] tribes of Chilas, Gor, Tangir, and Darel. These tribes had in the past sided with Hunza and Nagir against Kashmir, and had been accustomed to look to those States for aid in the event of invasion of their countries by Durbar troops. Reports stated that they intended to give

1 Hunza or Nagir, according to the letter.

2 For the names of all the tribes to which the term Shinaki is applied, see page 30.

trouble on the present occasion, but, although there seems to have been a war party in each community, they were unable to bring over the majority to their views, and no trouble was experienced from them.

On the 1st December the force crossed the Hunza river, which had been bridged by Captain Aylmer, and entered Nagir territory. No opposition was met with on this day. On the 2nd, the force advanced nine miles to Nilt, a fort of great strength, situated at the junction of a deep ravine from the Rakaposhi glacier with the Hunza river.

Capture of Nilt.

The banks of both the ravine and the river at this place consist of precipitous and almost inaccessible cliffs, and it was on the edge of these cliffs, overlooking the ravine, that the fort had been built. The march to Nilt, along the left bank of the river, was unimpeded, except where the enemy had destroyed the path across two difficult *nalas* running at right angles to the main stream. Some road-making was necessary before the force could cross these obstacles. Here and there *sangars* had been erected, but they were not held, and no sign of the enemy was seen until Nilt was reached.

Owing to the configuration of the ground, the fort could not be properly seen until the column was within 300 yards, nor could rifle or gun fire be brought to bear on it until within even less distance. The walls of the fort, which averaged fourteen feet in height and eight feet in thickness, were of solid stone, cemented with mud and strengthened by large timbers. Towers, placed at the angles, and in the centres of the faces, afforded good flanking fire, and good head-cover was provided throughout. The main gateway which was in the south-west corner of the fort was protected, and completely hidden, by a loopholed wall, which ran along in front of the main wall. In front of this again was a deep ditch encumbered with abatis; and another broad band of abatis filled the space intervening between the ditch and a precipitous spur which projected from the hill above into the narrow strip of cultivation in front of the fort. This hill was crowned by our infantry, but their fire could not touch the defenders in the fort, who were under perfect cover, nor could the guns be taken up, until some improvement of the path was effected. The attack had, therefore, to be made straight to the front, over a space narrowing

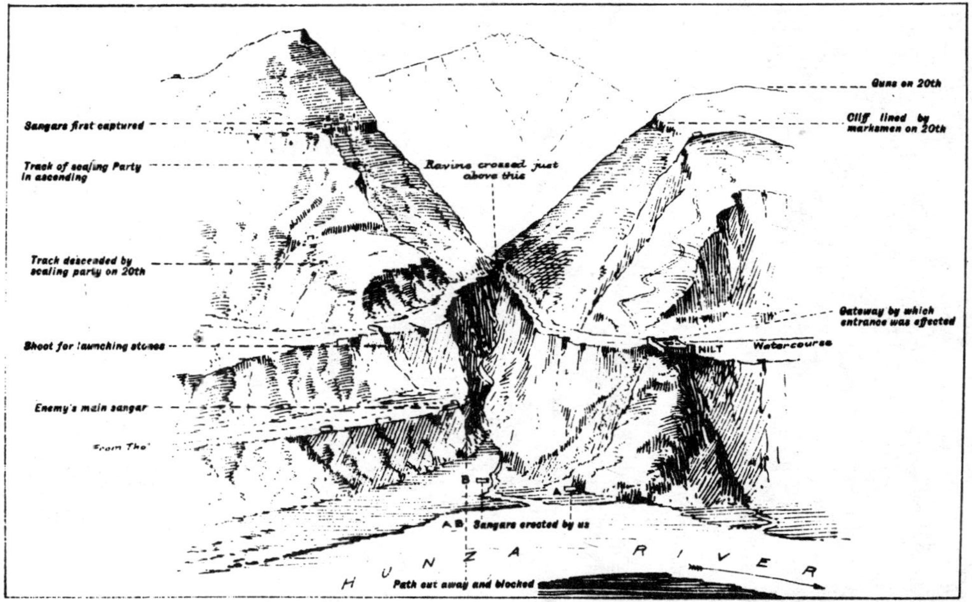

I. B. Topo. Dy. No. 6,701
Exd. C. J. A., February 1907.

VIEW OF NILT RAVINE FROM MAIUN
LOOKING SOUTH

(Sd.) J. Mc. D. BAIRD, *Lieut.*,
24th P. I.
24th January [illegible]

No. 4,061-I., 1907.

down to a width of about sixty yards. As, throughout the march, there had been no path down the steep river bank passable for animals, the force had been unable to water since leaving Chalt. Colonel Durand therefore decided to carry the fort by assault at once.

The only possible entrance was by the gateway in the south-west corner of the fort, described above. The back of the fort was situated on the edge of the cliff, with a covered way leading to the ravine below, so that the defenders could retire in safety when they saw the place was taken.

The 7-pounder R.M.L. mountain guns not being powerful enough to breach the walls, Colonel Durand ordered Lieutenant Boisragon to advance with the 5th Gurkhas. Captain Aylmer, with his small party of Bengal Sappers and Miners, was directed to accompany the Gurkhas and blow in the gate.

The assaulting party dashed forward towards the west face of the fort, on nearing which Boisragon, with Captain Aylmer and a few Gurkhas, managed to find a way through the thick abatis, and, under a heavy fire, worked round to the gate in the outer wall. This gate was promptly hacked down, and the party rushed into the courtyard of the main entrance. Captain Aylmer, assisted by Sapper Hazara Singh, then placed a charge of guncotton, tamped with stones, against the inner door, which was stoutly constructed and strongly barricaded. This point was under fire from the towers flanking the gateway and from loopholes in the gate itself. Captain Aylmer was wounded in the leg while placing the charge, but managed to withdraw under shelter of the wall to await the explosion. The fuse, however, failed, and Aylmer had to return to re-adjust and re-light it, when he was again wounded, his hand being severely crushed by a stone flung from the fort. This time the explosion was successful, and the door was blown in. At the same moment, Lieutenant Badcock, having found the gap in the abatis, came up with a few more Gurkhas, and the whole party forced their way into the porch under heavy fire, two Gurkhas being killed in the doorway, and several being wounded. Captain Aylmer, in spite of his injuries, remained in the porch, killing several of the enemy with his revolver, until, being faint with pain, he was carried by his orderly into the ditch outside. As only a few men were able to

D 2

find the gap through the abatis, Lieutenant Boisragon, leaving his little party in the porch, now went back and collected some reinforcements from the various *nalas* round the fort. The blowing in of the gateway had been carried out earlier than had been expected, and the explosion had been mistaken for the bursting of one of the enemy's guns; consequently the supporting troops continued to keep up a heavy shell and rifle fire on the fort, which added considerably to the dangers of the assaulting party, and to the difficulties of Boisragon's task. Meanwhile Lieutenant Badcock, picking up a rifle, killed several of the enemy, but was shortly after severely wounded while leading an attack into the interior of the stronghold. The enemy being unable to dislodge the party in the gateway, and seeing reinforcements coming up, now began to evacuate their position. About this time the officer commanding the force, having been informed of the successful blowing in of the gate, ordered the reserves, composed of Kashmir Imperial Service Troops, to advance, and, after a hand-to-hand fight through the maze of alleys and passages inside, the fort was taken. Colonel Durand was wounded early in the action, whilst watching the effect of the artillery fire, and the command now devolved on Captain Bradshaw.

Before the Gurkhas commenced their advance Captain Mackenzie, with the detachment of the 20th Punjab Infantry, the gatling gun, and the men of the Punial Levy, was sent to seize the hill on the right commanding the fort. It was intended that this party should cross the ravine running in rear of the fort and turn the enemy's position, and that the reserves should take up the pursuit and carry the defences on the opposite bank. The enemy, however, had destroyed the paths down the precipitous sides of the ravine, which prevented Captain Mackenzie from carrying out these intentions, and Captain Bradshaw was obliged to abandon the idea of any forward move on that day. Captain Mackenzie's party, however, accounted for a considerable number of the enemy in their flight.

Our casualties amounted to three British officers severely wounded; three men killed; one native officer, and twenty-five non-commissioned officers and men wounded. The enemy's loss was estimated at eighty killed and many wounded; among the former was the *wazir* of Nagir.

The Victoria Cross was subsequently awarded to Captain Aylmer and Lieutenant Boisragon for their gallantry on this occasion, while Lieutenant Badcock, who had also been recommended for this distinction, received the Distinguished Service Order; six men received the Order of Merit.

The capture of this stronghold with comparatively little loss was almost entirely due to the personal gallantry of the three officers—Captain Aylmer, R.E., and Lieutenants Boisragon and Badcock—and the few brave men forming the advanced party. The brunt of the fighting fell on the 5th Gurkhas, for, from the nature of the ground, the troops in support could be of little use. The Gurkhas behaved with their customary gallantry and dash, and the Kashmir Imperial Service Troops showed remarkable coolness in this their first action.

As it was found to be impossible immediately to follow up the enemy, the force halted for the night at Nilt, camping on the cultivated land outside the fort.

In front of the force lay the great ravine running from the river-bed to the glaciers some thousands of feet above. The far bank, lined with *sangars* which commanded every possible track up it, varied in height from 600 feet, where it joined the river, to 1,500 feet, and was absolutely precipitous. To the left of the fort ran the Hunza river, on the right bank of which was the strongly held fort of Maiun. Half a mile up the river, on the left bank was a fortified *ziarat*, from which to the junction with the great ravine ran one continuous line of *sangars*. During the night all the *sangars* were strongly reinforced, and those exposed to shell fire were provided with bomb-proof head-cover. The British held the edge of their side of the ravine with a line of picquets up to the snow-line, the Punial levy holding the upper positions.

On the morning of 3rd December an advance was attempted. The enemy, however, had re-occupied all the *sangars* during the previous night, and had greatly strengthened their defences. The path leading down the ravine from the fort had been destroyed, was swept by a searching fire, and was impassable for mules, and our advance was further barred by a large bomb-proof *sangar* exactly opposite, held by 100 of the enemy. After a loss of one man killed, and seven wounded, including Lieutenant Gorton, R.A., the attempt was abandoned. The situation was a difficult one. The force was very small and opposed to it was a numerous enemy, holding a well entrenched position of great natural strength. An attack on the large *sangar* on the opposite side of the ravine offered no prospect of success, while an advance up the river-bed, exposed to a cross-fire from both banks, might have involved heavier losses than the little force, with its limited number of British officers, could well afford. For seventeen days therefore the force was obliged to remain stationary. It was evident that only two courses were open, either to cross the river and storm Maiun, or to turn the enemy's defences on the opposite side of the ravine. On the night of the 12th December an attempt was made to carry out the first of these plans, but it met with no success. Night after night reconnaissances of the enemy's position were made, in the hope of finding a path up the precipice by which their defences might be turned. During all this time, the enemy were constantly on the alert, and kept up a heavy fire or rolled down avalanches of stones to prevent the approach of our men.

During this enforced inactivity, the conduct of the troops was excellent and the determination of the force seems to have disconcerted the enemy, who were unaccustomed to such continuous effort on the part of an invader. On the 9th December Safdar Ali Khan sent in a letter to Mr. Robertson, the Political Officer, who returned an answer to the effect that complete submission was a necessary preliminary to negotiation. On this the Hunza Chief apparently at once retired to Upper Gujhal and prepared for flight.

The prolonged delay had its dangers for the British force: there was always the possibility that the Shinaki tribes, encouraged by our non-success, might combine to attack Gilgit and Bunji, while the Hunza and Nagir men were already considering an attempt to cut communications with the advanced base at Chalt.

At last, on the 19th December a Dogra sepoy named Nagdu, of the Body-Guard Regiment, who had been constantly employed in the night reconnaissances, reported the discovery of a path by which the cliff below the enemy's upper *sangars* could be scaled.

Action of 20th December.

Captain Colin Mackenzie, who had assumed command on the 18th, in the temporary absence of Captain Bradshaw at Gilgit, at once decided to attack. The plan of attack was as follows: a storming party was to cross the exposed ground north of the fort under cover of darkness, and take up a position in the ravine below. On the following morning, this party was to scale the almost precipitous cliff on the extreme left of the enemy's position, and capture the four upper *sangars* on the summit. Covering parties on the ridge opposite, and in Nilt fort, were to assist this advance by directing a heavy fire on the enemy's defences, and so distracting their attention from the turning movement.

On the evening of the 19th December the storming party, consisting of 100 rifles of the Body-Guard Regiment, under Lieutenants Manners-Smith and F. H. Taylor, took up their position in the upper part of the ravine, at the foot of the cliff, unobserved by the enemy. There they remained all night, and, when daylight broke, owing to the precipitous sides of the cliff, they were still concealed from the enemy's view.

Before daylight on the 20th, the ridge facing the enemy's breastworks was occupied by the covering party, consisting of twenty-five rifles, 20th Punjab Infantry, under Mr. E. F. Knight (who had volunteered for duty), fifty rifles, 1-5th Gurkhas, under Lieutenant Boisragon, thirty rifles, Ragu Pertab Regiment, under Lieutenant Townshend, thirty rifles, Body-Guard Regiment, under Lieutenant Baird, and two guns of the Hazara Mountain Battery under Lieutenant Molony. The infantry were divided into four parties, with orders to distribute their fire on the four *sangars* opposite, at a range of 400 to 600 yards. The loopholes of the fort were also manned, and dispositions were made to, as far as possible, prevent the enemy retiring from or reinforcing any particular *sangar*.

At about 8 A.M. fire was opened on the enemy's defences, and shortly afterwards Lieutenant Manners-Smith, with his advanced party of fifty rifles, commenced his perilous ascent of the cliff, which rose almost sheer for about 1,500 feet above him. The well-directed fire of the covering party on the ridge compelled the defenders of the *sangars* to keep under cover, and prevented them from leaving this protection to fire over the edge of the cliff or to hurl down stones.

Lieutenant Manners-Smith had completed about half of the ascent, when, having moved further to his left than was originally intended, his further advance was checked by an inaccessible portion of the precipice, and he was obliged to retrace his steps to the ravine below. A fresh attempt was made at 10 A.M. and the first party reached a point about sixty yards from one of the *sangars* before they were discovered by the enemy. The defenders now began to hurl down showers of stones and rocks, but Lieutenant Manners-Smith,[1] skillfully manœuvring his men, soon reached the summit and rushed the first *sangar*. Lieutenant Taylor now followed with the supports, and the combined party cleared the other three *sangars* on the left flank, thus completely turning the position and compelling the enemy hastily to evacuate the fortified *ziarat* and the stronghold of Maiun.

The infantry were now withdrawn from the Nilt ridge, and the whole force, with the exception of the guns, was launched in pursuit. Leaving Nilt shortly after 1 P.M., the force crossed the ravine, and captured the large lower *sangar* on the opposite bank, whose defenders, to the number of about 100, threw down their arms and surrendered, their escape having been cut off by Lieutenant Manners-Smith's party.

Lieutenant Townshend, with the Ragu Pertab Regiment, now moved on to Thol, and, after clearing the neighbouring *sangars* at the point of the bayonet, captured the fort, killing twenty-two of the enemy. Sixty-five men of the Punial Levy, having crossed the river on a raft, captured and destroyed the fort of Maiun, inflicting on the defenders a loss of ten men killed. They then advanced along the right bank of the Hunza river, and levelled the defences of Hini.

Leaving a small detachment to hold Gulmit, the remainder of the force, with the 5th Gurkhas as advanced guard, and a flanking party of fifty men crossing the heights on the right, now pushed on to Pisan, seven miles from Nilt, which was reached at dusk. A strong position, known as the Yol Pari, just west of Pisan, was evacuated as our troops came up, and some of the fugitives were fired on.

Lieutenant Molony, who had been obliged to wait with the guns until the path across the Nilt Nala had been improved,

[1] Lieutenant Manners-Smith was awarded the Victoria Cross for his gallantry on this occasion.

reached Pisan, at 3 A.M. on the 21st. The baggage, which had been ordered to follow as quickly as possible, was still in rear. Ample supplies, however, were found in the fort at Pisan, and a full ration was issued to all the troops. Our casualties on the 20th were only two sepoys wounded. The enemy lost about 100 killed on the Nagir side of the river alone, and 118 prisoners were taken. These were sent back to Chalt, in charge of an escort under Mr. Knight.

Occupation of Nagir.

On the 21st, Captain Mackenzie, with the two mountain guns, 100 men of the 5th Gurkhas, and 250 of the Body-Guard Regiment, made a forced march of twenty-seven miles to Nagir. A few volleys were fired at small parties of the enemy on the opposite bank of the river; but they generally dispersed without replying. At Tuishot, a village between Pisan and Nagir, Jafar Ali Khan, the *Tham* of Nagir, surrendered to Surgeon-Major Robertson, who was now Acting Political Officer. Before reaching Nagir a deputation of Kanjutis from Hunza, headed by Muhammad Riza, brother of a former *wazir*, was received by Surgeon-Major Robertson. They announced that the people were now willing to submit, and stated that an armed party of tribesmen had been despatched in pursuit of the fugitive *Tham* and his followers. On the 22nd the troops marched back about five miles to Samaya, a village on the Nagir side of the river opposite the fort of Hunza, or Baltit, as it is locally named. Here they were joined by the remainder of the force with the baggage and rear-guard. As a proof of their complete submission, the tribesmen assisted to build a temporary bridge at Samaya, and on its completion, Captain Twigg, with the Gurkhas, crossed the river, and occupied the fort and village of Hunza.

All opposition was now at an end. Lieutenant Townshend was appointed Military Governor of Hunza, and measures were taken to disarm the population of both States.

Proclamations were issued by the British Agent to reassure the people. They were informed that they would not be subjected to oppression of any kind, but that slave-dealing, man-stealing, and brigandage must be given up at once; that they must obey the orders of the British Government, but would be allowed to live their own lives, as heretofore, without interference. The people, relying on these assurances, speedily returned to their homes and appeared to be grateful for the unexpected kindness and clemency shown to them.

On the 25th December a small flying column under Lieutenants Baird and Molony, with Lieutenant Manners-Smith as Political Officer, set out for Upper Gujhal. The object of the expedition was, if possible, to intercept the *Tham* of Hunza and other important fugitives, who had accompanied him, and also to arrange for the disarmament and pacification of that portion of the country. The column proceeded as far as Misgar, six marches from Hunza, and was well received by the people *en route*, who even pulled down their defensive towers, and offered the timbers as fuel in token of submission. It was not, however, found possible to overtake the Hunza Chief, Safdar Ali. Accompanied by Uzar Khan of Nagir and Wazir Dadu, with a following of some 500 men, women, and children he had already made good his escape and eventually found refuge on the Tagdumbash Pamir.

A small garrison of 280 men was left at Hunza, and the remainder of the force marched back to Gilgit, where it was broken up on 11th January 1892. The total British casualties in the expedition had been four Non-Commissioned Officers and men killed and four officers, one native officer, and thirty-four men wounded.

Lieut.-Colonel Durand in his despatch made the following remarks relative to the conduct of the troops:—

The conduct and discipline of the troops has throughout been admirable. As the officer to whom has fallen the honour of commanding a body of the Imperial Service Troops on the first occasion in which they have been called upon to fight in the interests of the Empire side by side with our own troops, it is with pride and pleasure that I would wish to draw the especial attention of His Excellency the Commander-in-Chief to the conduct of the Body-Guard and Ragu Pertab Regiments. I have had these regiments under my orders for two years, and have seen them grow in efficiency under the careful instructions of Captain Twigg and Lieutenant Townshend, and the steady efforts of some of their own officers. The result has been most satisfactory, and they have proved themselves fit to take their place in line with our own regiments in frontier warfare. They have shown coolness under fire, and discipline in camp. The attack by the detachment of the Body-Guard Regiment on the *sangars* crowning the side of the ravine was a task to try the best regiment; and if the Ragu Pertab Regiment had not the opportunity of showing such high qualities, yet they showed no lack of keeness, when they had the chance of meeting the enemy.

The events which followed the withdrawal of the expeditionary troops, and the subsequent arrangements for the settlement of the affairs of the two States, will now be briefly described.

In Nagir the former ruler, Zafar Khan, was appointed Governor, as it was considered that he had been coerced into opposition by his more powerful neighbour, Safdar Ali, and that he could in future be trusted to remain loyal to his engagements. This appointment was ratified by the Government of India, and Zafar Khan was granted the title of Raja. Being an old man, in feeble health, his son, Sikander Khan, was allowed to act for him, and on the death of his father in 1904, this man was confirmed as ruler of the State.

During February and March 1892, the majority of the fugitives, who had crossed into Chinese territory, were either sent back by the Chinese authorities, or returned voluntarily to their homes. Uzar Khan was also sent back by the Taotai of Kashgar, and was deported to Kashmir, where he has since remained.

Safdar Ali, on reaching the Tagdumbash Pamir, had sent letters to the Chinese Taotai of Kashgar representing himself to have been the victim of an unprovoked attack on our part. His complaints resulted in protests, first from the Taotai of Kashgar, and subsequently from the Chinese Ambassador in London and the Tsungli Yamen, against our treatment of the ruler of a State which was claimed as tributary to China.

On being informed of the true state of affairs, however, the Chinese acknowlodged that the measures taken to ensure the preservation of order and security in Hunza were just and necessary. An assurance was given that the Government of India had no desire to annex Hunza, or to upset the existing form of Government. As a further concession, Chinese representatives were invited in June 1892, to attend the installation of the new *Mir* or *Tham*, Muhammad Nazim Khan, a son of Raja Ghazan Khan, and half-brother of Safdar Ali. The selection of this member of the Hunza royal family was a matter for congratulation, because he had been recommended by the Taotai and was therefore not likely to be objected to by the Chinese Government.

Safdar Ali seems to have attempted to escape into Russian territory, but was arrested in Tashkurgan by the Taotai and taken to Kashgar. He was subsequently released and has since remained in exile in Chinese Turkistan.

Aliabad was garrisoned by a company of Kashmir troops and a political officer was stationed in the country. This garrison, however, and the political officer have since been withdrawn.

Since these events the people of Hunza and Nagir have lived peaceably, and no further troubles with them have arisen.

The Governorship of Yasin and Ishkaman.

The Yasin district, which now includes the sub-districts of Ghizr and Kuh, is separated from Wakhan on the north by the Hindu Kush, and from Chitral on the west by the Shandur range. The Hindu Raj separates it from the Swat Kohistan and Tangir and Darel in the south, while the eastern boundary is the lofty range of mountains which forms the watershed between the Hunza and Karumbar rivers.

The Ishkaman district, which was formerly included in the Yasin *Mehtari*, is now a separate charge, and includes the country on both sides of the Karumbar river from its source as far as and including the hamlet of Kuchdeh on the left bank and the Shah Choi *nala* on the right.

The chief route through Yasin is the road from Gilgit to Chitral. This is a fairly good 6-foot road from Gilgit to Gupis, whence rough tracks branch off, one through Yasin to the Baroghil, and another through Dahimal, Ghizr, and Langar across the Shandur pass. Other passes leading out of Yasin are the Chillinji, Khora Bohrt, Darkot, Thui, and Chamarkand. The first two are rarely practicable, and the remainder are only open for a period of from four to six months.

The climate of Yasin is dry and healthy. Rapid streams fed by mountain torrents water the Ghizr, Yasin, and Ishkaman valleys. The mountains are chiefly composed of sandstone, which contains a large proportion of iron, and there is much saltpetre in the soil. Slight earthquakes are frequent, while landslips and avalanches constantly occur when the snows melt in spring.

The population is about 10,000, and is almost entirely agricultural, all other labour being held in contempt. The people of

Upper Ishkaman are Wakhis, and are said to be hardy, industrious, and contented. The remainder of the people of Yasin are of a somewhat mixed race; though formerly reputed to be treacherous and unreliable, they have, by the latest accounts, settled down, and can probably be trusted to remain quiet.

The Khowar, or Chitrali language is understood by all the inhabitants, many of whom also speak two or three of the other tongues in use in this country, *viz.*, Wakhi, Shina, and Burushaski.

A few of the leading families are Sunnis, but the majority of the inhabitants are Maulai, and, though slack in their religious observances, are greatly under the influence of their *pirs.* These latter are often inclined to use their influence to foster local disturbances.

The physique of the people is probably better than that of any other district in the Agency with the exception of Hunza. It is estimated that about 1,000 fighting men could be raised in the district, of whom about 100 are worked as levies under the same system as prevails in other parts of the Agency.

Yasin, though practically independent, has always been closely connected with Chitral, and in recent times its ruler was frequently a nominee of the Chitral *Mehtar.* In 1895 when the British troops advanced through this country to Chitral, the Yasinis protested against being ruled by a representative of Chitral. Since that date the governor has been appointed by Kashmir, and in 1899 the district was transferred to the Gilgit Agency.

The district has never come directly into collision with the Government of India.

Chilas.

The district now known as Chilas is roughly the area which drains into the Indus between the point where that river is joined by the Astor stream, and the western limits of the Thor and Hodar communities. The distance from east to west is about sixty-five, and from north to south about fifty miles. The district is divided into two practically equal parts by the Indus, which throughout its course from Ramghat to Thor flows through an absolutely barren country. From Ramghat to Chilas, a distance of forty-five miles, there are only three villages on the river; the only vegetation consists of stunted shrubs; lofty mountains shut in the valley; and the whole journey gives an impression of utter desolation. The inhabitants for the most part live in the higher reaches of the ravines which drain into the main valley, and where vegetation is plentiful.

Although the name Chilas is now applied to the whole district administered by the Assistant to the Political Agent in Gilgit, it properly belongs to but one community in the country. From Ramghat down the river as far as Tangir and Jalkot the country draining into the Indus valley is known as Shinaka. Each *nala* or group of *nalas* is held by separate small republics, all professing the same language, religion, and customs, but all at enmity with each other.

The names of these different communities, from east to west, are Gor, Bunar, Thak, Chilas, Hodar, and Thor. These six republics constitute the present Chilas district. Lower down the Indus are the independent Shinaka communities, identical in language and customs with the Chilasis. These are Tangir and Darel on the right bank, and Harban, Shatial, Sazin, Somar, and Jalkot on the left. It is difficult to say where the Shinaki country stops ; for instance, the Jalkot headmen are inclined to pretend that they are Kohistanis, the general terms for the non-Shinaki tribes of the lower Indus, but as the Jalkoti all show the castes and customs peculiar to the Shinakis, they must be classed with them.

The people of the Chilas district still preserve the social distinctions of their ancestors and are separated by tradition and marriage laws into four classes, *viz.*, Shins, Yashkuns, Kamins (also called Kramins), and Doms. Of these the first two only are important. They are nearly equal in numbers, and divide the authority of the country between them.

Manual labour in the fields is distasteful to the people as a whole, and they lead a pastoral, rather than an agricultural, life. In addition to being an indolent race they are inordinately timid, and though they intrigue and quarrel amongst themselves, the tongue is a more frequent weapon than the sword. Until lately of sordid manners and customs, they are now, under the advantages of a settled and orderly government, becoming an improved and healthier race. All the people without exception are Sunni Muhammadans, and speak the Shina dialect, which differs from that spoken in Gilgit. A peculiarity of the country is a marked absence of fanaticism.

Little is known of the history of Chilas previous to the middle of the nineteenth century. At that time the people of Bunar and Gor gave a certain amount of trouble to the Kashmir troops and officials by their raids into what is now known as the Astor Tehsil. Accordingly, in 1851 a force of Kashmir troops invaded Chilas by the Kamakdari pass. The people declare that during this expedition the Dogra troops suffered heavily and were finally almost exterminated. Two years later the Maharaja's troops again invaded the country, and captured Chilas; and until the Imperial Government took over the present Chilas district in 1892 the tribesmen paid an annual tribute to the Kashmir Durbar.

Operations in Chilas, November 1892.

When the British Agency was established in Gilgit in 1889 the Shinaki tribes gave promise of causing trouble on the sole means of communication with India which the new administration possessed, namely the Gilgit-Kashmir road. At that time the Indus valley tribesmen seem to have had a reputation for ferocity, resource, and determination hardly justified by our subsequent and more intimate knowledge of their true character, but, be that as it may, they were certainly in a position to annoy us whenever they chose to raid the only line which fed Gilgit with men and stores.

During the operations in Hunza and Nagir in 1891-92 there was some unrest among the Chilasis and other Shinaki tribes, and the Commander of the British force in Gilgit had to take into consideration the possibility of a general rising of these people. But at that time an epidemic of smallpox and the want of unanimity in their councils prevented a combination of these tribesmen against us. The Chilasis, however, still remained in an unsettled frame of mind, and after the termination of the Hunza-Nagir campaign they were reported to be apprehensive of an invasion of their country by British troops.

The British Agent at Gilgit, anxious to avoid any conflict, sent a conciliatory letter to the headmen. The messenger, however, whose duty it was also to receive the tribute due to the Kashmir Durbar, was not allowed to enter Chilas. No reply was vouchsafed to the British Agent's letter, but a verbal message was sent, stating that the tribute would be paid in a month's time. In July 1892 a Chilási *jirga* visited Gilgit and was received by the British Agent. The members of this deputation expressed regret for past misconduct and promised amendment, even offering men for military service. On their return they took with them the Kashmir official who had previously been evicted. After the return of the deputation to Chilas it was soon evident that their promises were not intended to be kept. Raids into Kashmir territory recommenced, and, in reply to a protest from the British Agent, the Chilas headmen declared that they would in future receive no instructions from Gilgit, and would never permit a road to be made through their country. In consequence of this rupture the Kashmir Agent was recalled to Gilgit.

With a view to coercing the Chilasis, and preventing further raids, it was now proposed to send a small Kashmir force to occupy the tributary state of Gor.

On the 3rd November 1892, the people of Gor received a *Sanad* from Colonel Durand, in the name of the Maharaja of Kashmir, excusing them from *karbegar*, payment of revenue on kharid grain or fodder, or any addition to the tribute previously fixed, in return for which concessions they on their side agreed to open their country to officials and troops of Kashmir, to assist British officers travelling in Gor territory, and to obey all orders received from Gilgit.[1]

Having obtained the consent of the headmen to this proposal Surgeon-Major Robertson[2] proceeded to Gor on the 11th November marching from Gilgit by the right bank of the Indus. He was accompanied by an escort composed of fifty men of the Kashmir Body-Guard Regiment, fifty Punial Levies, and sixty or seventy men of the Sai valley, all under command of Major Twigg. After a cordial reception at Gor, the little force proceeded to Ges, two marches down the Indus. Here news was received of intended opposition on the part of the tribesmen. As the position at Ges was unfavourable, the force moved on ten miles down the river to Thalpin. Here a small fort was promptly put in a state of defence and the rafts belonging to the ferry just below were secured. Captain Wallace, 27th Punjab Infantry, now relieved Major Twigg, who was required at Gilgit.

1 The state of Gor was incorporated in the Chilas district in January 1896.
2 Now Sir G. Robertson, K.C.S.I.

During the march to Thalpin the *jirgas* of Chilas and Thak made some feeble efforts to render submission, but, whether from suspicion or ignorance on the part of the envoys, these overtures did not penetrate as far as the British officer. It is certain that in the subsequent fighting the people of Thak remained inactive with a flock of sheep ready for presentation to the victors, while the Chilasis, aided by the Thoris and Darelis, attacked the invaders. This diplomatic attitude of the Thak contingent was solely due to the craft of Arab Shah, their principal headman, who counselled inaction until the affair should be definitely decided. A half-hearted attempt was made by the Thak representatives on the 18th November to consult with Dr. Robertson when he was encamped at Thalpin, but as the raft sent to fetch the envoys across the river was fired on, almost all the sepoys killed, and Captain Wallace wounded, further dealings with them were dispensed with. The situation was now more clearly defined; the Chilasis seized the Thak live stock brought as an offering to the victors, and on the following day a determined attack was made on the British position at Thalpin.

After some stiff fighting the Punial levies cleared the heights above the camp, and the enemy were eventually repulsed with a loss of sixty killed and many wounded. Two days later a re-inforcement of forty rifles under Major Twigg and Lieutenant Harman arrived, having left a detachment at Ges.

On the 26th a detachment of 100 Kashmir sepoys under Subadar Hathu, marching from Ges, were attacked about two miles from Thalpin by over 2,000 Shinaki tribesmen from Darel and Tangir, Harban and Sazin. The Subadar entrenched his party during the night, and early next morning attacked and drove back the enemy with a loss of fifty killed. Seven Kashmir sepoys were wounded in this skirmish.

Surgeon-Major Robertson now assumed the offensive, and crossing the river burnt the village of Chilas and occupied the fort on the 30th November 1892. The people of Bunar and Thak immediately tendered their submission, and their example was shortly afterwards followed by most of the Chilas *jirga*.

In this fighting our principal opponents were the Chilasis and Thoris, aided by contingents from Darel, Tangir, and Jalkot, though these last were far from numerous. The Chilasis had no doubt of the result, and hoped for great spoil in the shape of arms and ammunition. A force of 300 rifles from the Kashmir Body-Guard Regiment was left in Chilas fort, and this party maintained communication with Bunji by a series of fortified posts, situated along the left bank of the Indus. The people below Thor could not understand how so small a force could have occupied Chilas, and attributed Dr. Robertson's success to the feebleness of the defence offered by the inhabitants.

For the next few months, notwithstanding constant rumours of intended risings, no disturbance occurred; but on the night of

Attack on Chilas Fort, March 1893.

the 4th March 1893, a force of from 1,200 to 1,500 Shinaki tribesmen, including some 400 Kohistanis, occupied Chilas village, which was close to the post, and opened fire on the garrison. Major Daniell, who was in command, sent out, before daybreak, Lieutenant Moberly, with thirty-five men, to clear the enemy out of the village; the attempt failed and Moberly was slightly wounded.

Major Daniell then attacked the village in front and flank with 140 men. His intention was completely to surround the enemy's position, and prevent their escape; but after having made his way round the village he was unfortunately killed close to the entrenchment. Fighting continued for two or three hours, and the enemy was severely handled. The senior native officer, Adjutant Nain Singh, who had gallantly led his men into the village, was shot dead, and Jemadar Gan Singh, finding his men running short of ammunition, withdrew in good order to the post. Lieutenant Moberly sent out a covering party to assist. The enemy kept up a desultory fire till midnight, when they evacuated the village under cover of the darkness, leaving a number of dead in and near their position.

Our losses were Major Daniell, three native officers, and nineteen men killed, Lieutenant Moberly, one Native officer and twenty-eight men wounded. The enemy's loss was about 200 killed, besides a considerable number wounded.

Reinforcements were at once despatched from Bunji, arriving at Chilas on the 9th March, and a detachment of fifty men of the 15th Sikhs, with a section of a mountain battery, were also sent up from

Gilgit. The enemy, however, evinced no desire for further fighting and dispersed to their homes. As a precautionary measure the 23rd Pioneers were subsequently ordered to Chilas, where they arrived on the 15th October *viâ* the Babusar pass.

Since that time no attempt has been made by the tribesmen against the Government. In the winter of 1893-94 the *mullas*, who resented the occupation of Chilas, tried to stir up the Shinakis to rebel, but in consequence of the refusal of the Kohistanis to join, the attempt was abandoned; and even in 1895, during the disturbances in Chitral, the whole of this country remained quiet, in spite of intrigues by Muhammad Wali in Tangir. This tranquillity was thought, at the time, to be due to the presence of a well-armed garrison in Chilas; but no one who has met those who took part in the fight of the 5th March 1893, and who has heard their account, can fail to realize that it was primarily due to the result of that engagement. Had Major Daniell acted with less determination the tribesmen would have certainly tried the fortunes of war once again; but their heavy casualty list on that day convinced these clans, for the present at least, that they dare not cope with the Government of India.

The military occupation of Chilas was followed by the appointment of an officer of the Political Department, who administers the district under the orders of the Political Agent of Gilgit.

In the beginning of 1899, at the urgent request of the people of Thor, that valley was incorporated with the Chilas district.

There is now a well built fort at Chilas, reconstructed by the 23rd Pioneers in 1894, which is quite capable of resisting any attack by local tribesmen. It is garrisoned by two companies of Kashmir Imperial Service Troops armed with Martini-Henry rifles. The ordnance of the fort consists of an obsolete brass 7-pounder gun suitable for firing case shot, and two 7-pounder R.M.L. mountain guns of 200lb, for which an ample supply of ammunition and pack equipment is kept up.

The independent tribes of Shinaka and Kohistan.

The tribes to the immediate west and south-west of Chilas are known as the independent tribes of Shinaka and Kohistan. The Government of India has no direct dealings with these people, but as many of them use the Chilas grazing-grounds in summer, a certain amount of hold could be easily exercised over them. No detailed account of the tribes appears necessary, and it will suffice to say that the Shinaka communities consist of Darel and Tangir on the right bank of the Indus, and Harban, Shatial, Sazin, Somar, and Jalkot on the left; while the Kohistan tribes comprise Khili or Kandia, Seo, Pattan, and Dobel on the right, and Palas and Koli on the left.

The only recent affair of interest between these tribes and the Giligit Agency occurred in 1902 when five men from Diamir in Tangir attacked the levy post in the Kargah Nala, killing two levies and carrying off five Snider carbines. For this act Tangir was fined Rs. 2,000, and Darel Rs. 500, the last named community being fined because they had made no efforts to arrest the raiders during their subsequent passage through their limits. As neither Darel nor Tangir made any effort to pay the fine, a blockade was established, and all Tangiris and Darelis found within the Agency limits were arrested and deported to Kashmir. The fines were paid by 1904, in which year the blockade was raised.

The fighting strengths of the various tribes, according to the latest reports is as follows :—

Shinaka.		*Kohistan.*	
Darel	700	Khili or Kandia	2,000
Tangir	700		
Harban	300	Seo	100
Shatial	200	Dobel	500
Sazin	50	Pattan	500
Somar	30	Palas	500
Jalkot	1,800	Koli	500
	Total 4,100		

The Shinaki tribes cannot be considered as formidable antagonists. They seem incapable of combining against a common foe, for any tendency to concerted action is almost invariably checked by internal dissensions and intrigues, which usually arise from the most trivial causes. Their dislike for bloodshed is most marked: where amongst Pathans the disputants would betake themselves to their rifles, Shinaki protagonists throw a few stones at each other or indulge in a biting match. If this does not settle matters, recourse is had to "Kanai," a system by which the rivals try to beggar each other by entertaining the community to dinner on alternate days. The side which spends most succeeds in enlisting the majority of his compatriots to his interests and is thought to have proved his case.

The Kohistan Republics do not seem to differ materially from their Shinaki neighbours. Though all are Sunni Muhammadans, who strive to follow the advice and orders of their *mullas*, there is nevertheless an entire absence of fanaticism. This is all the more remarkable when we consider that these *mullas* have practically all been trained in Swat or Peshawar, and that during the summer there is free and frequent communication between the Indus valley and Swat. The tribesmen's arms are knives and country guns, which are made locally; and Tangir and Dobel are reported the best at making these weapons. In winter, communication between the various *nalas* is effected by the tracks along both banks of the Indus. The river is crossed by rafts made of inflated skins or logs. These rafts are manned by gold-washers, a distinct and migratory tribe, who are allowed to wash for gold in return for keeping up a raft. In summer, the people, who all prefer a pastoral to an agricultural life, withdraw to the grazing-grounds at the heads of the *nalas* with their flocks.

CHAPTER II.

CHITRAL.

IMMEDIATELY to the west of the Gilgit Agency, and, like that district, bordered on the north by the Hindu Kush, lies the country of Chitral, also known as Chitrar or Kashkar. On the west a spur of the Hindu Kush, sometimes called the Kafiristan range, divides this country from the Afghan province of Kafiristan, and forms the British-Afghan frontier. On the east the Shandur spur and the watershed between the Chitral and Panjkora rivers divide it, from Yasin, Kohistan, and Dir. To the south, the watershed of the Arnawai stream forms the boundary between Chitral and the districts of Dir and Asmar.

The whole of this area, which is estimated at about 4,500 square miles, is of a rugged mountainous character. On the Pathan and Kafiristan borders, the habitations are usually clustered together, and sometimes surrounded by rough walls, with towers dotted here and there, thus indicating the frequency of inter-tribal fights and raids in former days. In other parts of the country, where raids were not so common, the houses are scattered, each small proprietor building on his own plot of land; and, as each house is usually surrounded by small orchards, with well-tended grassy lawns, the general effect is very refreshing to the eye. Up to an elevation of 9,000 feet, fruit is abundant and often forms the staple food of the inhabitants, much of it being dried and carefully put away for winter consumption. Beyond a radius of about twenty miles above Chitral the country is practically rainless, and the hills are bare and rugged, the only trees found being the dwarf juniper, with occasional patches of mountain birch and willow. At Chitral itself, and from thence south, the valley opens out considerably. Cultivation is more continuous, and the hills are thickly wooded with fine specimens of deodar, pine, fir, and ilex.

Chitral is watered by the Yarkhun river (also known as the Mastuj or the Chitral river), with its two main tributaries, the Torikho and the Lut-Kuf. The Yarkhun takes its rise from the Showar Shur glacier in the Hindu Kush, and flows in a south-westerly direction to Asmar, whence it continues its course, under the name of the Kunar, until it falls into the Kabul river near Jalalabad. It receives various minor affluents, which drain the valleys on either side; the most important of these are the streams from the Gazan, Chumarkhan, and Kokhsun *gols* or *nalas* above Mastuj; the Laspur river, between Mastuj and Kosht; and the streams from the Owir, Reshun, and Golen *nalas,* between Kosht and Chitral. Below Chitral it is joined by the Bashgul river, and the streams from the valleys of Oyon, Birir, Jinjoret, and Urtsun on the right, and the Shishi-Kuf, Ashreth Gol, and Arandu (or Arnawai), on the left. The river is spanned by several cantilever bridges, of fairly good construction, in addition to numerous rope bridges of the usual pattern. Since 1895, good suspension bridges have also been erected at Mastuj, Sanoghor, Chitral, Gairat, Drosh, and Naghr.

The Torikho river, which has two affluents, the Tirich and the Khot, joins the Yarkhun near Kosht. It is crossed by cantilever bridges at Drasan, Wahrkup, and Khambakhi. The Lut-Kuf, which rises near the Dorah pass, drains the country between Kafiristan and Tirich Mir, and flows into the Yarkhun, a few miles above Chitral. It is joined by two minor streams, the Arkari and Ojhor, and is crossed by cantilever bridges at Sin and Shoghot.

The rivers are usually unfordable in spring and summer; and in winter, although the fords are numerous, they are, more often than not, extremely difficult to negotiate.

There are two main routes from Chitral, namely, (*i*) from Chitral, *viâ* Drosh, to the Lowari pass, and thence through Dir and Swat to the rail head at Dargai. (*ii*) From Chitral to the Shandur pass, where it joins the Gilgit-Teru road. A third route, which, although there is no made road, is practicable for laden animals during about eight months of the year, leads up the Yarkhun valley to the Baroghil pass. Other less important passes leading from Chitral which deserve mention are:—The Shawitakh and Kankon, giving access to Wakhan: both are practicable for pack transport; the Karumbar, [1] a difficult pass leading to the Ishkaman valley; the Darkot, Thui, and Chamarkhan passes all communicating with Yasin, but more difficult than the usual route over the Shandur. All the above passes lead out of the Yarkhun valley. From the valley of the Torikho, three difficult passes lead into Wakhan, which can also be reached from the Arkari valley by the Sad-Istragh, Khatinza, Nuksan, and Agram passes; but these too are all difficult, and could only be crossed by a lightly equipped force of selected troops under favourable circumstances. A number of passes lead into Kafiristan, but only four—the Zidik and Shui from the Lut-Kuf valley, and the Shawal and Paitasun from the valleys of Bumboret and Urtsun, are practicable even for lightly laden animals. At the head of the Lut-Kuf valley, is the Dorah pass, communicating with Badakshan. Besides the Lowari, the chief outlets to the south and south-east, are the Zakhanna, Shingara, Gurin, and Atchiku passes, all more or less difficult.

Chitral is divided into the following districts: Laspur, Mastuj, Torikho, Mulrikho, Kosht, Owir, Khuzara, Chitral, and Drosh. According to a census taken about the year 1899 the total population amounted to 48,740, of which the number of fighting men was estimated at rather more than 4,200. The latest estimate of the Chitrali fighting strength is, however, 6,000.

The Chitralis are a mixed race of Aryan type, whose exact origin it is not easy to trace. The majority of the middle and lower classes are believed to be descendants of the Kalash Kafirs, who formerly occupied the whole Chitral valley below Reshun, but are now confined to the valleys of Rumbur, Bumboret, and Birir, and some villages on the right bank of the river below Drosh.

Among the people of Torikho and Mulrikho, (locally known as Kho) are descendants of Badakshis, Shignis, Wakhis, and Gilgitis. In the Arandu Gol, the people are Narsatis; and at Madaglasht, in the Shishi-Kuf valley, is a colony of Persian speaking Tajiks.

Chitrali, or Khowar, is the *lingua franca* of the people, while the Persian tongue is used by a few of the aristocracy; there are also some eight or nine other languages or dialects spoken in various parts of the country.

[1] See foot-note, page 3.

The Chitralis are divided into three classes, which are social not racial, *viz.*, Adamzadas, Arbabzadas, and Fakir Miskin. The Adamzada class is composed of (*i*) members of clans descended from the founder of the ruling family; (*ii*) families of the Zundre or Ronu caste; (*iii*) descendants of men who have been ennobled for services to the ruling family. The Arbabzada and Fakir Miskin are really of the same class; but the former are comparatively prosperous, while the latter are generally extremely poor. With the exception of the members of the Royal clan, men frequently take wives from the lower classes.

The men of Chitral are splendid mountaineers, with great powers of endurance, and, when well led, have proved themselves to be good fighters. In disposition they are a lazy, pleasure-loving people, excitable and easily led, untruthful and treacherous. Sir G. Robertson thus describes them:—

> There are few more treacherous people than the Chitralis, and they have a wonderful capacity for cold-blooded cruelty; yet none are kinder to little children, or have stronger affection for blood or foster relations when cupidity or jealousy do not intervene. All have pleasant manners and engaging light-heartedness free from all trace of boisterous behaviour, a great fondness for music, dancing, and singing, a passion for simple-minded ostentation, and an instinctive yearning for softness and luxury, which is the mainspring of their intense cupidity and avarice. No race is more untruthful, or has greater power of keeping a collective secret. Their vanity is easily injured, they are revengeful, and venal, but they are charmingly picturesque, and admirable companions.

The custom of foster-relationship, which was perhaps more prevalent under the old régime than at the present day, is worthy of mention. When a child is assigned to foster parents, the whole family or clan divide the honour of his up-bringing, and in after-life all the foster kindred share his good or evil fortune. When an Adamzada fosters a son of the Mehtar, there is always great competition among all the people, irrespective of clan or class, to share in the honour. It is thus that the factions supporting the various sons of the ruling chief are built up. It is not an exaggeration to say that as many as fifty women sometimes assist in suckling a legitimate son of the Mehtar.

Though not strict in their religious observances the Chitralis are all Muhammadans, and, in ceremonies connected with marriage, divorce, burial, etc., follow the usual practices of that faith. In the highlands the Maulai sect predominates, but in the lowlands the majority of the people are Sunnis.

The land under cultivation is rich and fertile, but very limited in area. Wheat, barley, Indian corn, rice, beans, and millet are grown, but only in quantities barely sufficient for the needs of the people. Neither fodder nor other supplies would be locally procurable for a force of any but strictly limited size.

Before 1895 the Chitralis were armed with matchlocks made by the Tajik *mistris* at Madaglasht or imported from Badakshan. Mehtar Aman-ul-Mulk also received from the British Government at various times 640 Snider rifles and carbines, and 200 muzzle-loading Enfield rifles.

Two 3-pounder brass guns also were presented to this ruler in 1884 but they were never of much use.

History.

The early history of Chitral is a record of intrigues, civil wars, and assassinations with which it is beyond the scope of this work to deal. At the time of the British occupation of the Punjab one Gauhar Aman was master of Mastuj and Yasin, while the whole of Lower Chitral was ruled by Shah Afzal II. In 1854 Gauhar Aman invaded Gilgit, and the Maharaja of Kashmir appealed to Chitral for assistance. In answer to this request, Afzal attacked Mastuj, and then followed another series of wars and intrigues, which lasted, almost without intermission, until 1880, at which time Aman-ul-Mulk, who had succeeded his father, Shah Afzal, was practically master of the whole of Chitral.

About this time, Aman-ul-Mulk, realizing that the Amir of Afghanistan desired to annex Chitral, tendered allegiance to Kashmir, and a treaty ensued, with the approval of the Government of India, whereby the former acknowledged the suzerainty of the latter and received from him an annual subsidy. At the same time a Political Agency was established at Gilgit. The objects of the policy adopted by the Government of India towards Chitral, in pursuance of which this was the first step, were, to control the external affairs of Chitral in a direction friendly to our interests, and to secure an effective guardianship over its northern passes.

In 1885-86 Aman-ul-Mulk was visited by the mission under Colonel Lockhart, who entered into negotiations with him on behalf of the Government of India. Similar visits were paid in 1888 and 1889 by Colonel Durand, and in the latter year the Political Agency at Gilgit, which had been withdrawn in 1881, was re-established, and the Mehtar of Chitral was granted a subsidy of Rs. 6,000 per annum and a large consignment of rifles.

In 1891 the Government of India, with the intention of strengthening the position of the Mehtar, decided to double this subsidy on the condition that he accepted the advice of the British Agent in all matters relating to foreign policy and the defence of the frontier.

On the 30th August 1892 Aman-ul-Mulk died suddenly of heart failure while engaged in holding a durbar. His second son Afzal-ul-Mulk happened to be at Chitral on this date while the elder brother Nizam-ul-Mulk, was absent in Yasin. Promptly seizing all the arms and treasure in the fort of Chitral, Afzal-ul-Mulk proclaimed himself Mehtar, and then proceeded to murder his half-brothers Shah-i-Mulk, Bahram-ul-Mulk, and Wazir-ul-Mulk, besides other leading men who might have endangered his position. Meanwhile Nizam-ul-Mulk fled to Gilgit, where he claimed the protection of the British Agent. Afzal-ul-Mulk was now acknowledged as Mehtar by the Government of India, but his triumph was only short lived. In November 1892 his uncle, Sher Afzal, who had been expelled by the old Mehtar Aman-ul-Mulk, suddenly crossed the Dorah pass with a few followers, and at nightfall reached Drushp in the Lut-Kuf valley. Here he surprised and slew Murid Dastgir, an illegitimate son of Aman-ul-Mulk, who was acting as Governor of the valley. Continuing his march to Chitral next day, he arrived at the fort in the dead of night and promptly attacked it. Afzal-ul-Mulk, who rushed down to repel the assailants, was shot dead in the *melée* which ensued. Sher Afzal now became master of Chitral fort and was proclaimed Mehtar. The rapidity of his advance and the secrecy which cloaked his movements after entering Chitral territory are evidence that he had many adherents in the country.

As soon as he heard the news of his brother's death, Nizam-ul-Mulk determined to proceed to Chitral and oust Sher Afzal. He announced his intentions to the British Agent at Gilgit, and as he was in no way under detention, Lieut.-Colonel Durand was obliged to allow him to depart. But in order to strengthen his own position, and to secure the tranquillity of the Gilgit frontier, Colonel Durand despatched a small force, with two mountain guns, to Gupis. Nizam-ul-Mulk, on crossing the frontier, was joined by the people of Torikho and Mulrikho; and some 1,200 men, sent by Sher Afzal to oppose his advance, also went over to him. He then continued his advance to Mastuj and Drasan, the latter place being captured on 1st December. Sher Afzal, being now persuaded that his rival was supported by the British, lost heart and fled into Afghanistan. During the following year, he was summoned to Kabul and detained there by the Amir, who subsequently gave a written assurance to the Government of India that he would not again be permitted to interfere in Chitral affairs.

Nizam-ul-Mulk having assumed the Mehtarship, and recognising the value of British support, now invited the Government to send an officer to Chitral. In accordance with this request Surgeon-Major Robertson and Captain F. E. Younghusband, with an escort of fifty rifles, 15th Sikhs, were deputed to visit the Mehtar, and arrived at his capital on 25th January 1893. The British Political Officer was authorised to promise the new Mehtar, on suitable conditions, the same subsidy and support as had been given to his father Aman-ul-Mulk. Nizam-ul-Mulk was a man of weak character, and was unpopular with the Adamzadas, who were inclined to resent his dependence on British support. Moreover, the presence in Chitral of numbers of Sher Afzal's sympathisers, armed with rifles which that Chief had distributed, was a source of no little anxiety. A rising in Yasin, headed by Muhammad Wali Khan, son of Mir Wali,[1] and the encroachments of the Jandol Chief, Umra Khan, in the Narsat district, still further aggravated the difficulties of the Mehtar's position. No disturbance arose however, and as Nizam-ul-Mulk appeared to be fairly well established, Surgeon-Major Robertson was directed to return to Gilgit in May, and subsequently he relieved Colonel Durand in charge of the Agencies, leaving Captain Younghusband as Political Officer in Chitral.

Umra Khan of Jandol.

It will here be convenient to say a few words about Umra Khan, whose actions are greatly responsible for the troublous times which now befell Chitral. This man was the grandson of Faiz Talab

1 Who had murdered an English traveller, Mr. Hayward, in 1870.

Khan, Chief of Bajaur, who fought against us in the Ambela campaign of 1863.[1] Having quarrelled with his father, Aman Khan, Chief of Jandol, Umra Khan was expelled from his villages of Mundah and Tor, and took refuge in Shamozai country, whence he made a pilgrimage to Mecca. On the death of his father in 1878, Umra Khan returned to Jandol, killed his elder brother Muhammad Zaman, and seized the Khanship of Barwa. During the next year, assisted by the Khan of Khar, he defeated the combined forces of the Khans of Nawagai, Asmar, and Dir, and made himself master of the whole of Jandol. Ten years of continuous fighting ensued in Dir, Bajaur, and Nawagai, which resulted in the complete triumph of Umra Khan, who finally expelled the Nawab Muhammad Sharif Khan from Dir, and made himself master of that country.

In 1891 Shah Tahmasp, the Khan of Asmar, died, and, in order to check the aggressions of Umra Khan, the Afghan *Sipah Salar*, Ghulam Haidar, occupied this district with his troops. The Khan of Nawagai, incited by the Afghans, now collected a force of Tarkanri tribesmen, and attacked Umra Khan, but was decisively defeated. Attempts by the Mian Gul, a supporter of the deposed Khan of Dir, and by the Khan of Lalpura, who was persuaded by the Afghan General to combine with the Nawagai Chief in a second venture, met with no better success.

In 1892 a postal road through Lower Swat and Dir to Chitral was opened by arrangement with Umra Khan. In this year the Afghan *Sipah Salar* threatened to invade Jandol from Asmar, but on this occasion Umra Khan was saved by the intervention of the British Government, and later, in June of the same year, he joined the Mamunds in a successful attack on some Afghan troops who had occupied Shurtan in the Kunar valley. Meanwhile Aman-ul-Mulk tried to induce the Yusafzai tribes to rise against the Jandol Chief, and the Khan of Nawagai was also again preparing to attack him. Umra Khan, therefore, appealed to the Government of India for assistance in the shape of arms and ammunition, but his request was refused. During the next year, however, he succeeded, by his own efforts, in maintaining his position.

[1] See page 230.

In 1893, as a result of the Durand Mission to Kabul, the disputed territory of Asmar was awarded to Afghanistan. This decision, coupled with our refusal to assist him materially in his schemes, was a cause of great offence to Umra Khan. He was, however, assured by the British Government that he need fear no interference on the part of the Afghans with his legitimate possessions, unless he himself provoked hostilities.

It is at this period that the intrusion of this ambitious adventurer into the turmoil of Chitral politics may be said to have begun.

During the confusion which followed on the death of Mehtar Aman-ul-Mulk, Umra Khan had seized the Chitrali fort of Narsat, which commands the country on either side of the Chitral river between Arandu and Bailam, and had retained it in spite of the remonstrances of the British Agent.

On the advent of Sher Afzal, he, under the pretence of assisting Nizam-ul-Mulk, moved to Drosh, but, on being informed that the Government disapproved of his action, withdrew to Jandol. About this time he was joined by Amir-ul-Mulk, brother of Nizam-ul-Mulk, and in November 1893 he declined to keep open the postal road through his territories, unless the Government acceded to his demands for arms and ammunition.

Early in 1894 Umra Khan further encroached on Chitral territory by attacking some villages in the Bashgul valley and erecting forts at Arandu and Birkot, in the valley of the Kunar. Towards the end of this year he patched up his quarrel with Safdar Khan, Chief of Nawagai, and made an alliance with him, an arrangement which left him free to turn his attention to the northern border of his possessions.

In September 1894 Captain Younghusband had moved to Mastuj, which he made his head-quarters, and in October he was succeeded by Lieutenant Gurdon. The Political Officer's escort was increased to 100 rifles, and a post was established at Gupis, in order to secure the communication with Gilgit.

The disturbance in Yasin had been allayed, and with the exception of the unrest on the southern border caused by the aggressive actions of Umra Khan described above, matters in Chitral were now fairly satisfactory. The retention of Captain Younghusband as Political Agent had the effect of ameliorating the conditions of government in the State, and of giving increased stability and popularity to the rule of Nizam-ul-Mulk; and at the same time it strengthened the ties by which that ruler was bound to the British Government.

The comparative tranquillity which had been established in 1894 was, however, not destined to continue.

On the 1st January 1895, while out hawking near Broz with his brother, Amir-ul-Mulk, the Mehtar was treacherously shot by one of the former's attendants. Amir-ul-Mulk at once proceeded to Chitral, and, having seized the fort, proclaimed himself Mehtar. He next requested Lieutenant Gurdon, the Political Officer, who happened to be on a visit to Chitral, to acknowledge him as ruler, but was informed that no action could be taken without the orders of the Government.

There is little doubt that this cold-blooded murder was instigated by the Sher Afzal faction, and that Umra Khan, if not actually a party to the plot, was nevertheless fully aware of it. Amir-ul-Mulk, who was a dull-witted youth, and merely a tool in the hands of stronger men, denied all connection with Umra Khan, but directly after the murder he sent information to that chief and requested his support. A few days later he again changed his mind and tried to dissuade the Khan from interfering, but his protest, if genuine, was of no avail. Under pretext of a religious war against the Kafirs, Umra Khan, with a force of some 3,000 men, crossed the Lowari pass into Lower Chitral, and when Amir-ul-Mulk refused to meet him, advanced to Kala Drosh.

At this time the troops of the Gilgit Agency were located as follows:—

		Effective strength.	
Astor, Bunji, and Chilas.	32nd Punjab Pioneers	821	1,424
	5th Kashmir Light Infantry	594	
	Details	9	
Gilgit	14th Sikhs	99	878
	4th Kashmir Rifles	287	
	6th Kashmir Light Infantry	344	
	Kashmir Sappers and Miners	139	
	Details	9	
	Carried over		2,302

			Effective strength.
	Brought over . .		2,302
Gilgit and Hunza	No. 1 Kashmir Mountain Battery. (4 guns)	150	481
	6th Kashmir Light Infantry .	261	
	Bengal and Kashmir Sappers and Miners . . .	70	
Gakuch and Roshan.	4th Kashmir Rifles		33
Gupis	4th Kashmir Rifles		286
Mastuj	14th Sikhs		103*
	GRAND TOTAL . .		3,205

Lieutenant Gurdon at once summoned fifty men of his escort from Mastuj, and reinforcements were promptly pushed forward to that place from Gupis and Ghizr. At this time a Mission under Mr. Udny, which had been appointed to demarcate the Afghan-Bajaur-Chitral Boundary had arrived at Birkot, a few miles south of the junction of the Arnawai stream with the Chitral river. The Afghan *Sipah Salar* and other representatives were with this Mission, but Umra Khan had declined to attend in person. News of the events in Chitral had quickly reached the British Commissioner, and both he and the British Agent in Gilgit addressed letters of remonstrance to Umra Khan and demanded his immediate withdrawal.

In reply to Surgeon-Major Robertson's demand for an explanation of his conduct, Umra Khan stated that his intention had been to support Amir-ul-Mulk, but since the Mehtar had acted in a hostile manner towards him he was compelled to retaliate; he trusted, however, that his friendship with the British Government would be in no way affected.

On the 1st February Surgeon-Major Robertson arrived at Chitral, bringing with him the remainder of the escort of the 14th Sikhs and a detachment of the 4th Kashmir Rifles.

The Chitralis had mustered about 3,000 men to oppose Umra Khan, but owing to the weakness and incapacity of their leader, Amir-ul-Mulk, and the treachery of certain of the Adamzadas,

* Less eight men with Lieutenant Gurdon, then at Chitral.

their resistance soon collapsed. On the 25th January they were driven from their position in front of Drosh, after an engagement in which both sides suffered some loss, and fell back on the fort. On the 9th February the fort of Drosh was surrendered with its garrison and some 200 rifles, and the Chitralis again fell back on Gairat.

Surgeon-Major Robertson now decided to take possession of the fort at Chitral in case of emergencies, and directed the troops to move in with all their baggage and stores, and a quantity of supplies which Lieutenant Gurdon had prudently collected.

On the surrender of Kala Drosh a number of Khuswaktis, incensed at the conduct of Amir-ul-Mulk, revolted against his authority and returned to Chitral, where they appealed to Surgeon-Major Robertson. After some discussion the British Political Agent arranged to protect the interest of the Khushwakt community, while Amir-ul-Mulk guaranteed the good behaviour of his Kators.

Towards the end of February letters were received from Government authorising the British Agent to afford the Chitral people "such material and moral support as might be consistent with the safety of his own party, and to call up reinforcements from the Kashmir regiments in the Gilgit command if necessary." Surgeon-Major Robertson, however, in anticipation of these instructions, had already allowed some of the troops to assist the Chitralis at Gairat. Rumours of desertions from Umra Khan's force were now rife and the Chief himself was believed to be on the point of retiring to Warsat. The conditions of affairs seemed to be improving, and the British Agent was able to make a favourable report. His satisfaction was, however, soon rudely disturbed by a report that Sher Afzal had arrived at Drosh. The appearance on the scene of this new claimant, probably the most popular of all the members of the Chitral royal family, was indeed an unexpected complication. As already related, this Chief had ruled Chitral for a few weeks as the successor of his victim, Nizam-ul-Mulk, and had then fled to Kabul, where he remained as the *protégé* of the Amir, who had promised that he should not again intrude in Chitral affairs. As soon as the arrival of Sher Afzal was confirmed, the British Agent entered into communication with him, and on the the 27th February received a confidential messenger, whom the former deputed to explain his intentions.

The envoy, who was overbearing in his manner, announced that Sher Afzal was willing to be friendly with the British Government on condition that he received a subsidy as Mehtar. He also added that no Europeans could be allowed to remain in Chitral, demanded the immediate withdrawal of the troops to Mastuj, and threatened that, in the event of these terms not being complied with, it would be impossible to restrain Umra Khan.

Surgeon-Major Robertson replied to the effect that Sher Afzal's message was disrespectful in tone, and that it was necessary to await the decision of the Government with regard to the Mehtarship. Meanwhile he sent a letter of protest to Sher Afzal and warned him of the consequences of any hostile act.

A few of the lower class Chitralis had joined Sher Afzal on his arrival, and by the end of February practically the whole of the Adamzadas went over to him. Gairat, being now deserted, was occupied by Sher Afzal's party, and he himself advanced to Oyon. Surgeon-Major Robertson accordingly withdrew his escort to Chitral. Amir-ul-Mulk, who was now thoroughly terrified at the consequences of his rash act, tried to intrigue with Umra Khan, with the result that the British Agent placed him in custody and formally recognized his younger brother, Shuja-ul-Mulk, as Provisional Mehtar.

The escort of the British Agent, which had been reinforced during the month, now consisted of 100 men of the 14th Sikhs under Lieutenant Harley, and 320 of the 4th Kashmir Rifles under Captain C. P. Campbell, Central India Horse.

The numbers of Umra Khan's force were not accurately known, but the original party of 3,000, which crossed the Lowari, was believed to have been largely increased by the arrival of considerable bodies of tribesmen from the south, and his total strength was estimated to be between 5,000 and 8,000 men.

Engagement of 3rd March at Chitral.

On the afternoon of the 3rd March Sher Afzal, with an armed force, reached Chitral and took up a position in some villages about two miles south-west of the fort. Captain Campbell, with 200 men of the 4th Kashmir Rifles, moved out to check the enemy's advance.

Captain Baird, with fifty men, was directed to make a flank attack along some high ground to the west, while Captain Campbell, with Captain Townshend and the remainder of the force, attacked the position in front. The enemy, however, was strongly posted and met the advancing troops with a destructive fire. An attempt to carry the village by assault failed, and as darkness was coming on Captain Campbell was compelled to retire. The enemy followed up closely and, overlapping the flanks, inflicted heavy loss on the little force, but on nearing the fort they were checked by a party of fifty men of the 14th Sikhs, under Lieutenant Harley, who successfully covered the retreat. Meanwhile Captain Baird's detachment on the right was isolated. Baird himself was mortally wounded, but was carried back by Surgeon-Captain Whitchurch. This officer and the other survivors of the party after a desperate hand-to-hand fight, during which nearly all were wounded, eventually made their way along the river to the fort.

For his gallantry in this affair Surgeon-Captain Whitchurch received the Victoria Cross, and Subadar Badri Nar Singh and twelve non-commissioned officers and men of the 4th Kashmir Rifles were admitted to the third class of the Order of Merit.

The casualties in this affair were: *Killed*—General Baj Singh, Imperial Service Troops; Major Bhikam Singh, 4th Kashmir Rifles; 1 Hospital Assistant; 21 non-commissioned officers and men, 4th Kashmir Rifles. *Wounded*—Captain J. McD. Baird, 24th Punjab Infantry (succumbed to his injuries on 4th March); Captain C. P. Campbell, Central India Horse; 1 native officer, 15th Bengal Lancers; 28 non-commissioned officers and men, 4th Kashmir Rifles;—or a total of 25 killed (including Captain Baird) and 30 wounded, out of 200 men, of whom only 150 were actually engaged. The enemy's losses are not known. During the day 15,935 rounds of Snider ammunition were expended, about 100 rounds per man.

The little British force was now beleagured within the walls of the fort, and no news of their fate reached the outside world for many weeks.

Events on the Gilgit-Chitral line of communications.

We may here conveniently turn to the events which were now taking place on the line of communications between Chitral and Mastuj.

On the 26th February, Captain Baird, who was acting as Staff Officer to the British Agent in Chitral, had issued instructions to the following effect :—

Lieutenant Edwardes was to hand over command of the troops at Ghizr, and proceed to Chitral to take charge of the Puniali levies, which had been ordered up from Gilgit ; Lieutenant Fowler, R.E., who was expected at Mastuj with a detachment of Bengal Sappers and Miners, was to continue his march to Chitral ; and a consignment of Snider ammunition was also to be despatched to that place with a suitable escort.

In accordance with the above orders, Lieutenant Moberly, who was commanding at Mastuj, sent off sixty-eight boxes of ammunition under escort of a native officer and thirty-nine men of the 4th Kashmir Rifles. On the next day, Lieutenant Moberly, hearing that the Chitral road was blocked, sent to recall the escort, but on receiving reassuring news as to the state of affairs he subsequently cancelled this order and allowed the party to proceed. At the same time he wrote to Captain Ross, who was due at Laspur on that date with 100 rifles, 14th Sikhs, requesting him to hasten on to Mastuj.

Captain Ross reached Mastuj on the 3rd March, and left again on the following day for Buni to support the ammunition escort, which had halted there owing to a break in the road beyond. On the 5th, the detachment at Buni was further strengthened by the arrival of Lieutenants Fowler and Edwardes with twenty men of the Bengal Sappers and Miners.

It should be mentioned that on the morning of the 3rd March Captain Baird wrote from Chitral to Lieutenant Moberley as follows :—

If communications with Mastuj are interrupted, the British Agent wishes the following measures taken to restore them—

The levies to move on to Drasan and take that place. The day after they leave Mastuj, Fowler will proceed to Drasan with 200 Raganaths[1] and his sappers. You go in charge of Raganaths, and as Political Officer. Make over political charge of Mastuj to Edwardes with all instructions. Ross and his Sikhs to remain in garrison at Mastuj. Order up the remainder of the Raganaths from Ghizr. Gough and 100 Raganaths to remain in garrison at Ghizr. Please inform Fowler that he is to take command, and on arrival

[1] 4th Kashmir Rifles.

at Drasan, is to reopen communications with Chitral. Above instructions depend on communications being broken.

The levies should be at Mastuj about the 12th. No British officer is to accompany them to Drasan.

It is certain, however, that these orders never reached Lieutenant Moberly.

On the evening of the 5th March, a report reached Mastuj that matters had been satisfactorily arranged in Chitral and that Umra Khan had agreed to retire.

Lieutenant Edwardes' party at Reshun.

On the 6th Lieutenants Edwardes and Fowler, with the Sappers and Miners and the ammunition escort, marched to Reshun, while Captain Ross, and the Sikhs returned to Mastuj. The next day, the two British officers, with part of the detachment, went on to repair the road, which was reported to be broken about three miles from Reshun. A native officer and guard of the 4th Kashmir Rifles was left in charge of the stores and ammunition, with instructions to entrench a position on the height commanding the bridge and approaches to the river. Immediately after leaving Reshun, the road to Chitral ascends a steep spur to the height of 1,000 feet, and, descending again to the level of the river, enters a narrow defile with the unfordable river on one side, and lofty cliffs on the other. A halt was made at the entrance of this defile, and Lieutenant Fowler, with a few men, climbed the heights, which overlooked some *sangars* on the opposite bank of the river. These *sangars* were promptly occupied by some 200 men from Parpish village, who, opening fire, killed a naick and wounded Lieutenant Fowler and two men. Lieutenant Edwardes, seeing that the enemy were too strong to permit of an advance, withdrew with his detachment to the place where the remainder of the party had been left with the stores. This position, however, proved unsuitable, and some houses near the polo-ground were accordingly occupied and put in a state of defence. The enemy, who closely followed up the retreating force, kept up a hot fire which only slackened at sunset. Eight more men were wounded during this retirement. The wounded and most of the ammunition and stores were now brought in from the abandoned position by volunteers of the Kashmir Rifles, who were reported to have behaved splendidly.

During the night the enemy, who appeared to be well supplied with rifles, made a determined attack at close quarters, but were eventually repulsed. The defenders lost four men killed and seven wounded, but, owing to the darkness, the numbers and losses of the enemy could not be ascertained. For the next five days the little garrison defended their post with great gallantry against repeated attacks from the enemy, who had managed to build several *sangars* close to the defences. Lieutenant Fowler distinguished himself by making several successful sorties to obtain water, in one of which he inflicted heavy loss on the assailants. On the 13th March the enemy hoisted a white flag, and sent Muhammad Isa, a foster-brother of Sher Afzal, to arrange a truce. This man, who was received by Lieutenant Edwardes just outside the post, stated that the fighting in Chitral had ceased, and that Sher Afzal, who was friendly to the Government, was corresponding with the British Agent. Terms were accordingly arranged whereby the besiegers agreed not to approach the walls near the post, and consented to allow access to the water and to furnish supplies to the defenders, who were meanwhile to remain in their position. At the same time, Lieutenant Edwardes wrote to the British Agent in Chitral informing him of the situation.

On the following day, another interview took place between Lieutenants Edwardes and Muhammad Isa, who was accompanied by Yadgar Beg, an illegitimate son of Sher Afzal. The latter confirmed his companion's story, and both assured the officer of their good intentions.

On the 15th, friendly relations being apparently established, the two British officers were persuaded to go and watch a game of polo. As the ground was commanded by the defensive post, the walls of which were manned, there seemed but little risk in this proceeding. When the two officers got up to return, however, they were suddenly seized by Muhammad Isa and his followers, who proceeded to bind them hand and foot. The defenders promptly opened fire from the post, but the Chitralis who were well protected by cover, which it had been impossible to demolish, succeeded in rushing the defences. A number of the garrison were killed, and the remainder were made prisoners, while some 40,000 rounds of ammunition fell into the hands of the enemy.

Lieutenants Fowler and Edwardes were taken to Chitral, where they arrived on the 19th March under escort of a party of Umra Khan's men, who had forcibly wrested them from their Chitrali guardians *en route.* At Chitral, they were received by Sher Afzal, who expressed regret for the treachery which had been practised upon them, and promised to institute a search for the survivors of their party. They were now allowed to communicate with the British garrison besieged in the fort, but permission to visit them was refused. On the 24th the prisoners were taken to Drosh, where they were met by Umra Khan, who gave them the choice of remaining at that place or proceeding to either Jandol or Chitral. As Umra Khan refused to allow the sepoy prisoners, who had joined them, to return to Chitral, the officers asked to go to Jandol. Eventually they reached Mundah on 12th April, and were shortly afterwards released and sent to the British force under Sir R. Low. The circumstances under which they obtained their freedom will be more fully dealt with in the acount of the operations of the Chitral Relief Force in Chapter XII.

Captain Ross' detachment.

To revert now to the other detachments on the Chitral-Mastuj line. Lieutenant Edwardes having sent back news of the enemy's presence beyond Reshun, Captain Ross determined to proceed to his support, and on the 7th March moved to Buni with his detachment of the 14th Sikhs, strength two officers (himself, and Lieutenant H. J. Jones), one native officer, and ninety-three men. Nine days' rations and 150 rounds of ammunition per man were taken. The next day, having left a party of thirty-three men, under the native officer, at Buni, Ross continued his march, and halted, about 1 P.M., at the village of Koragh, about half-way between Buni and Reshun. The disaster which now overtook this ill-fated detachment has been graphically described in the following words:—

About half a mile from Koragh the track enter a narrow defile, and for an equal distance traverses a succession of precipitous rocky bluffs. Between these bluffs lie great fan-shaped slopes of detritus, which fall at a very steep angle from the foot of inaccessible crags above to the river's edge below; these slopes are several hundred feet in height, and at their base have an average breadth of about 100 yards. Where the path crosses them, it can be swept from end to end by a torrent of rocks, merely by loosening the soil above, and the Chitralis, in their dispositions for an ambuscade or for the defence of a position, rely much on the deadly effect of this peculiar weapon. About one mile from Koragh, the track, leaving the level of the river, ascends a steep spur, beyond which the defile maintains an equally formidable character for several miles in the direction of Reshun.

Leaving Koragh at 1-30 P.M. the advanced party of Captain Ross' detachment ascended about half-way up this spur, when they were fired on from across the river; and, at the same time, men appeared on the mountain tops and ridges, and rolled stones down all the "shoots." At the first shot the coolies dropped their loads and bolted. Captain Ross, after an inspection of the enemy's position, decided to fall back on Koragh, and with this object ordered Lieutenant Jones with ten men to seize the Koragh end of the defile and cover his retirement. In his attempt to carry out this order, Lieutenant Jones lost eight men wounded, and was thereupon recalled by Captain Ross, who had meanwhile occupied two caves in the river bank, which afforded good cover. At 8 P.M., an endeavour was made to force a way back to Koragh, but so continuous was the fall of rocks from the cliffs above, that, fearing the total annihilation of his party, Captain Ross was compelled to retire again to the caves. After a brief halt, he next made an effort to scale the cliffs, but, after a toilsome and dangerous climb, the party was confronted by a precipice, up which they searched in vain for a practicable path. Recognising that any attempt at escape in this direction was futile, and that the only course open was to force his way, at all costs, back to Koragh by the road he had come, Captain Ross rested his men in the shelter of the caves till the morning of the 10th March. Issuing thence at 2 A.M., at which hour it was hoped that the Chitralis might be taken unawares, the Sikhs drove the enemy from the nearest *sangars*, but were then met by a very heavy fire from both banks of the river and by a deadly hail of rocks from the cliffs above. Captain Ross himself was killed in front of the *sangars*; and out of the whole detachment only Lieutenant Jones and seventeen rank and file won their way to the open ground on the Koragh side of the defile. Here they halted for ten minutes, endeavouring to silence the enemy's fire and so cover the retreat of any others of the detachment who might be near the mouth of the defile. Twice they were charged by the enemy's swordsmen, whom they repulsed with great loss; but when two more of the little party were killed, and one mortally wounded, and when the enemy began to threaten their line of retreat, Lieutenant Jones gave the order to retire slowly on Buni, which place he reached at 6 P.M.

Our losses in this affair were one British officer, forty-six men, one Hospital Assistant, and six followers killed; of the fifteen survivors Lieutenant Jones and nine men were wounded. This party having joined the detachment which had remained in the village on the 8th, now occupied a house, which they held till the 17th, when they were relieved by Lieutenant Moberly.

Lieutenant Moberly's advance from Mastuj.

Up to the 13th March Lieutenant Moberly had received reports from native sources assuring him of the safety of the detachments which had recently left Mastuj for Chitral. Becoming anxious, however, at receiving no communication from Captain Ross, he advanced on the 16th with 150 men, and reached Buni unopposed on the following day, where he found Lieutenant Jones' party. The enemy were now reported to be massing at Drasan with the object of cutting Lieutenant Moberly's communications. He accordingly decided to retire, and, after a two hours' halt at Buni, commenced his return march, reaching Mastuj before midday on the 18th. This place had been reinforced a few days previously by 166 Kashmir Rifles (who had arrived with Captain Bretherton) and the total strength of the garrison now amounted to 327 fighting men. Meanwhile the enemy advanced, and by the 23rd the British force was closely invested inside the fort. The enemy, avoiding a determined attack, kept up an ineffectual rifle fire from *sangars* and houses surrounding the fort until the 9th, on which date, alarmed at the advance of Colonel Kelly's column from Gilgit, they drew off in the direction of Sanoghar.

During this little siege the garrison expended 987 rounds of Martini-Henry and 4,603 rounds of Snider ammunition. The only casualty on our side was one man wounded, while the enemy's loss was estimated at about forty killed and wounded.

Lieutenant Moberly had abstained from attempting any counter-attack until he could co-operate with the Gilgit column; and eventually the enemy's retirement was so rapid and sudden that he was unable to collect his force in time to follow them up effectually.

Measures for relief of Chitral Garrison.

On the 7th March the Government of India had received from Gilgit disquieting reports as to the state of affairs in Chitral. The last communication from Surgeon-Major Robertson was dated 1st March and was therefore written before the action which resulted in the beginning of the siege. Although full information was not at once forthcoming, it was nevertheless apparent that communications with Chitral were interrupted and that the retreat of the British Agent and his escort was probably cut off. It was understood from previous reports that the supplies available for the garrison in Chitral, which was estimated at about 420 men, would last till about the end of April; and it was therefore necessary that its relief should not be postponed beyond that date.

In order to be prepared for the possible necessity of despatching a relief force from India *viâ* Swat, Government sanctioned the mobilisation of the 1st Division[1] on 14th March. On the same date a final letter was forwarded through Mr. Udny to Umra Khan, demanding his immediate withdrawal from Chitral territory.

Instructions, which, however, were not received, were also sent to the Agent in Chitral to warn Sher Afzal that his connection with Umra Khan was displeasing to Government.

On the 17th March the Assistant British Agent at Gilgit reported that in consequence of the disturbed state of the country he had summoned half the battalion of 32nd Pioneers to Gilgit from the Bunji-Chilas road, where they were employed on engineering work.

On the 21st March came the news of the disasters which had befallen the detachments under Captain Ross and Lieutenant Edwardes. This intelligence materially altered the situation. It was now realised that Sher Afzal and Umra Khan had already embarked on hostilities against us, and that it was no longer necessary to wait to see if the latter intended to comply with the demands of Government. Moreover, the urgency of relieving the Chitral Garrison without further delay was now evident. It was consequently decided that the 1st Division should advance as rapidly as possible, and although it was not considered that relief from Gilgit, over 220 miles of mountainous country, was practicable, instructions were sent to Colonel Kelly directing him to assume military command in that district, and authorising him to make such dispositions and movements as he thought best.

The operations of the 1st Division will be dealt with in chapter XII, and we will now return to the besieged garrison in the fort of Chitral.

1 With certain modifications as regards cavalry and artillery.

The Siege of Chitral.

The siege of Chitral commenced on the evening of the 3rd March 1895, after the action, already described, which resulted in the enforced retirement of the British garrison to the shelter of the fort.

As Captain Campbell's wound proved to be very severe, the command now devolved on Captain Townshend. The other officers were Surgeon-Major Robertson, British Agent, with Lieutenant Gurdon as his assistant, Lieutenant H. K. Harley, 14th Sikhs, and Surgeon Captain Whitchurch, I.M.S. Captain Baird, who had been mortally wounded on the 3rd, died of his injuries on the following day.

The fighting ranks numbered 99 men of the 14th Sikhs, and 301 of the 4th Kashmir Rifles. In addition there were 85 followers, and 52 Chitralis, making a total of 543 persons. It was estimated that, by issuing half rations, the supplies would last for two and a half months. The ammunition available amounted to 300 rounds of Martini-Henry, and 280 rounds of Snider per rifle.

The fort was of the ordinary local type, about seventy yards square. The walls, which were twenty-five feet high, and seven or eight feet thick, were constructed of rough stone, rubble, and mud, and were held together by a kind of cradle work of timbers. At each corner a square tower rose about twenty feet above the walls, and a fifth tower, known as the water tower, guarded the path to the river, which was further protected by a recently constructed covered-way. Outside the north-west face was a range of stables and outhouses. The fort was practically commanded on all sides, and, except on the river front, was surrounded by houses, walls, and trees, which allowed the enemy to approach under cover close to the defences.

The demolition of this inconvenient cover was at once undertaken, and was continued from time to time during the siege, as opportunity offered. Unfortunately the defenders were unable to destroy the summer house, situated opposite the south-east or gun tower, and less than fifty yards distant from it. Inside the fort, the defences were strengthened and improved. Loopholes were made, and head-cover constructed with beams and boxes filled with earth; communications were safeguarded as much as possible from the enemy's rifle fire, curtains and screens being utilised to give cover from view, where more adequate protection could not at first be provided. After the first few days, when the defenders had begun to settle down to the routine of their new duties, Captain Townshend was enabled further to improve his measures for defence. The officers, of whom only three were available for ordinary military duty, took watch and watch, as if on board ship. The garrison always slept on their alarm posts, and guards and picquet duties were necessarily very heavy. Independent firing by night was strictly forbidden. A system of extinguishing fires was organized, a very necessary precaution, owing to the great quantity of woodwork used in the construction of the fort, and the determined attempts of the enemy to set fire to it. Police were detailed to control the Chitralis, whose conduct in certain instances was a source of some anxiety. Hand-mills were made for grinding grain, and non-combatants were detailed for this and other suitable duties. Every endeavour was made to provide for proper sanitation, but this was naturally a matter of great difficulty owing to the cramped space available.

At the British Agent's request Captain Townshend ordered thirty rounds to be fired daily at a house about 1,000 yards distant, which was occupied by Sher Afzal.

Taking into consideration the small number of British officers with the force, and the fact that the Kashmir troops were somewhat shaken by their losses in the affair of the 3rd March, Captain Townshend decided not to attempt counter-attacks or sorties, unless forced to do so by the enemy's action, until he obtained news of the approach of a relieving force.

On the 6th March Umra Khan's *Diwan* was accorded an interview by the British Agent. This emissary stated that his Chief wished to remain on friendly terms with the British, and had tried to prevent the fighting against them, and that the presence of his troops at Drosh was solely due to his intention of warring against the Kafirs. He further advised Surgeon-Major Robertson to leave Chitral, and offered him, in the name of the Khan, a safe escort either to Mastuj or Asmar. The British Agent politely declined to accept these proposals, and requested that as the fort was besieged, the Khan should in future address his communications to Mr. Udny in Asmar.

On the 8th March, just before daybreak, an attack was made on the water tower, but was quickly repulsed, though not before a few of the enemy had effected an entrance to the passage beneath the tower, where they lighted a fire. This, the enemy's first attempt at incendiarism, was promptly extinguished by the *bhistis*.

By the end of the first week, our casualties amounted to five; but, owing to sickness, only 80 men of the Sikhs and 240 Kashmir Rifles remained fit for duty.

On the 11th, further futile communications were received from both Sher Afzal and Umra Khan, and the besieged officers now heard the news of the defeat of our detachments at Reshun and the Koragh defile.

On this night, the men of the Punial levy cleverly succeeded in demolishing some walls opposite the west and south faces of the fort, under a fierce but ineffectual fire from the enemy.

On the night of the 13th-14th the besiegers renewed their attack from the wooded garden on the east of the fort, with the apparent intention of rushing the waterway. They were dispersed by a few volleys, but in order to be better prepared for a similar attempt, Captain Townshend ordered the stables alongside the water tower to be loopholed and occupied by a detached post.

On the 16th, in consequence of communications received from Sher Afzal, a three days' truce was arranged, which was subsequently extended till the 23rd. Amir Ali Khan, the Agency *Munshi*, was sent to interview Sher Afzal, who was accompanied by two of Umra Khan's representatives, named Abdul Majid and Abdul Ghani. The former of these two appeared to have great influence among the besiegers, but according to the *Munshi's* report it was evident that there was considerable friction between Abdul Majid's Jandoli followers and the Chitralis. This circumstance induced the British Agent to enquire if Sher Afzal's repeatedly-expressed desire for peace was genuine, and what guarantees would be given if the garrison consented to withdraw to Mastuj.

On the 19th, letters were received from the three leaders, ignoring the question of guarantees, and offering to make peace on condition that the garrison should surrender the fort and return to India by the Jandol valley route. They also took the opportunity to inform the British Agent of the capture of Lieutenants Edwardes and Fowler. Surgeon-Major Robertson had previously been made aware by a letter received from Edwardes himself that their party was besieged in Reshun. On the 20th, the two captured officers reached Chitral, and were seen by the *Munshi*, who made unsuccessful attempts during the next two days to procure their release.

Negotiations continued without result, as Surgeon-Major Robertson definitely refused to listen to the demand that he should withdraw *viâ* Jandol.

On the 23rd, Umra Khan's *Diwan* again appeared, and truculently threatened that non-acceptance of his master's terms might unfavourably affect the treatment of the officers who were now prisoners of war. The British Agent finally declined to listen to the *Diwan's* suggestions, and sent a letter to Umra Khan, in which he stated that if the officers had been fairly captured in war, he had no complaints to make ; but, if they were the victims of treachery, he advised the Khan to hand them over at once, with a letter of apology.

On this evening the truce expired. During the time that hostilities were suspended Captain Townshend had busily employed his men in improving the defences. A semi-circular loopholed *flèche* was made outside the water gate, and the clearance of an old disused well was begun. Heavy rainfall occurred during the night of the 23rd and for the next two days, bringing down a portion of the parapet on the west face, which had to be repaired at the cost of much labour. On the 22nd, the British officers had killed and salted their ponies, and commenced to eat horse flesh.

On the 26th a few shots were fired at the enemy's *sangar* opposite the west face from one of two mountain guns found in the fort, for which an emplacement had been prepared outside the main gate. The result, however, was disappointing, and as there were no trained gunners available, artillery fire was not again resorted to. Machicoulis galleries were now constructed on each parapet, and beacon fires were lighted in these at night to illuminate the ground in front. This arrangement proved more effective and economical than the fireballs of shavings and tow soaked in oil, which had previously been used to throw over the walls when the enemy attempted night-attacks.

Meanwhile the besiegers continued to harrass the garrison by desultory rifle fire, throughout the day and night.

By the end of March, Captain Townshend had 343 men effective, of whom half were employed on guard and picquet duties, as shown in the margin. The ammunition remaining amounted to 29,224 rounds of Martini-Henry and 68,587 rounds of Snider. There was sufficient grain for another seventy-four days, and some rum and tea, but the stock of *ghi* had run low and only twelve days' supply was left for hospital use and lighting. In order to check the sickness, which was now becoming serious, a dram of rum was issued to the Sikhs every fourth day, and the Kashmiri sepoys received a ration of tea every third day.

Main gate	10
Parapets (20 on each face)..	40
Water picquet	20
„ tower	25
Stable picquet	20
Water gate	10
4 Towers, 6 each ..	24
Guard on Amir-ul-Mulk ..	6
„ „ Chitralis ..	4
„ „ Ammunition ..	6
„ „ Garden gate ..	6
Total ..	171

On the night of the 30th-31st, the enemy built a *sangar* on the far side of the river, about 175 yards from the spot whence the defenders obtained their water-supply. At the same time, the besiegers began to connect their lower *sangar* on the west with the river by a covered-way running parallel to that of the defenders, and about eighty yards distant from it. Only about eight yards of this work, however, was completed, when the rifle fire from the fort compelled the enemy to discontinue their efforts.

On the 31st Sher Afzal sent a message to the British Agent requesting him to retire to Mastuj, and offering safe conduct for the garrison, with stores and arms, as far as Gilgit; and for several days he continued to keep up a futile correspondence. During the night of the 6th April, the enemy pushed forward a *sangar* made of fascines to within forty yards of the gate in the west front, and made a palisade alongside it; they also occupied the summer house on the south-east, and made another *sangar* close to the east gate. This advance on the part of the enemy considerably increased the difficulties of the garrison, and especially harrassed the picquet in the gun tower, which was now exposed to rifle fire from very close range. The defenders replied by manning the walls which still stood outside the west gate with twelve rifles of the 14th Sikhs and some Punialis.

Attack on gun tower.

Early on the morning of the 7th the besiegers opened a heavy fire from the wooded ground on the west, while a party crept up to the foot of the gun tower and set it on fire. As there was a strong wind blowing, and the tower was largely constructed of wood, a fierce blaze soon resulted, which threatened to become dangerous. The inlying picquet, however, succeeded, after strenuous efforts, in subduing the flames; and eventually, by pouring water down through holes picked in the inside wall, the fire was extinguished, though it smoldered on during the rest of the day. The men employed in this work were exposed to fire from high ground on the south-west and from the other side of the river, and two men were killed and Surgeon-Major Robertson and nine men wounded. Subadar Badri Nar Singh and Sepoy Awi Singh, 4th Kashmir Rifles, and Sepoy Bhola Singh, 14th Sikhs, especially distinguished themselves on this occasion.

The Kashmir sentries, to whose lack of vigilance the enemy's success in firing the tower was attributed, were now replaced by men of the 14th Sikhs. At the same time the machicoulis galleries, which had been subjected to a storm of Snider bullets from the summer house, were repaired and strengthened, and the arrangements for discovering and extinguishing fires were further improved. On the 8th the Punialis completed the demolition of the walls outside the main gate, and a stone tambour was made there, which flanked the west face. As a further precaution, an officer and fourteen men were permanently posted in the gun tower.

On the night of the 10th, an attack on the waterway was repulsed with the loss of one man of the Puniali levy wounded. During the next night and the following day, a number of the enemy retired up the valley in the direction of Drasan and Mastuj to join in opposing the relieving column advancing from Gilgit under Colonel Kelly. The approach of this force, although no news of it yet reached the garrison, inspired the besiegers to redouble their efforts to capture the fort. Accordingly they began to dig a mine from the summer house to the gun tower, keeping up meanwhile a desultory fire and an incessant noise of shouting and tom-toms in order to distract the attention of the defenders, and to drown the sound of the picking of the miners. On the 16th, one of the native officers,

Enemy's mine.

becoming suspicious of the enemy's proceedings, suggested to Captain Townshend that they might be making a mine. The sentries were accordingly warned to be on the alert, and that night one of them reported that he could hear a noise of picking; but his officers failed to detect it. The next morning, however, sounds were distinctly heard, which removed all doubts as to the enemy's intentions. Captain Townshend, after consultation with the British Agent, promptly decided that the only course open to him was to make a sortie and rush the summer house, whence it was supposed the mine started.

Sortie under Lieutenant Harley.

Lieutenant H. K. Harley was selected to carry out this enterprise with a detachment of forty rifles, 14th Sikhs, and two native officers and sixty men, 4th Kashmir Rifles. Captain Townshend's orders were as follows:—Lieutenant Harley was to lead his whole party, without dividing it up, straight to a gap in the summer house wall and rush the place, using the bayonet only. He was then to hold the house with part of the detachment, while the remainder destroyed the mine. If necessary he was to rush the *sangar* opposite the east gate from the rear, sounding the 'cease fire to stop the garrison from shooting at this target, and he was to bring back a few prisoners, if possible. The party carried with them three bags containing 110lb of gunpowder, 40 feet of powder hose, a number of picks and shovels, and forty rounds of ammunition per man.

At 4 P.M. Lieutenant Harley led his men from the east gate, and rushing across the short open space between it and the summer house, captured the post with a loss of two men killed. The occupants, who proved to be some thirty Pathans, being taken by surprise, had only time to fire a few hurried shots and then fled hastily through the garden to the wall at the end, whence they reopened fire on Harley's party.

After detailing some men to return this fire, Harley led the remainder to the mine shaft, which was discovered behind the wall of the garden, just outside the house. Thirty-five Chitralis, armed with swords, rushed out and were bayoneted. Having cleared the mine, Harley arranged his powder bags and fuze, and although the charge exploded prematurely, before it had been properly tamped, the result was effective enough completely to destroy the enemy's work, which, when opened up, was seen to have reached within a few feet of the gun tower wall. The party having completed their task in a little over an hour now rushed back to the gate, under a heavy fire from the enemy at the end of the garden. Meanwhile the rest of the garrison had been engaged with a considerable gathering of the enemy who threatened to attack the east tower and waterway. The assailants were checked and driven off by the fierce fire from the fort, but their movements caused Captain Townshend some anxiety, and he had sent to urge Lieutenant Harley to complete his work as quickly as possible.

This sortie, which was most gallantly and effectually carried out, cost the garrison a loss of eight killed and thirteen wounded. The enemy's loss was estimated at about sixty, including two men who had remained inside the mine and were killed by the explosion. The expenditure of ammunition on this day was about 3,000 rounds. Two prisoners, who were brought in by Lieutenant Harley, stated that a British force had been defeated at Nisa Gol by Muhammad Isa, and had retired on Mastuj. They also added that no other mines, except the one just destroyed, had been projected; but to make quite sure, Captain Townshend decided to countermine the gun tower, and during the 18th the troops were busily employed on this work. The troubles of the little garrison were, however, now at an end. On the morning of the 19th April it was discovered that the enemy, alarmed at the near approach of the relieving forces, had abandoned the siege and withdrawn *en masse* during the night. Most of the Jandolis went to join Umra Khan in Asmar, while Sher Afzal, with a number of the Chitralis, fled towards Bashkar, where they were captured a few days later by the Khan of Dir's people. During the day, news was brought of the approach of the relief force under the command of Sir Robert Low, and a letter from Lieutenant-Colonel Kelly announced that this column would reach Chitral on the morrow.

The losses of the garrison during the siege, and inclusive of the action on the 3rd March, were, according to Captain Townshend's report, 104 killed and wounded[1] of all ranks, *viz.*—

	Killed.	Wounded.
British officers	1	2
Central India Horse	1	..
Carried over ..	2	2

[1] These figures differ slightly from those quoted in the return given in Appendix B.

	Killed.	Wounded.
Brought over ..	2	2
15th Bengal Lancers	..	1
14th Sikhs	6	9
Officers, Imperial Service Troops ..	2	..
4th Kashmir Rifles	26	44
Levies	..	2
Hospital Assistant	1	..
Followers	5	4
TOTAL ..	42	62

On the 26th April, Captain Townshend submitted a report on the defence of Chitral, in transmitting which to the Government of India, His Excellency the Commander-in-Chief in India expressed his high appreciation of the achievement. Captain Townshend's report, and the Adjutant-General's forwarding letter, were published in the *Gazette of India* of the 25th May 1895, together with a Government General Order, dated the 24th May 1895, in which His Excellency the Viceroy recorded his conviction that "the steady front shown to the enemy, the military skill displayed in the conduct of the defence, the cheerful endurance of all the hardships of the siege, the gallant demeanour of the troops, and the conspicuous examples of heroism and intrepidity recounted, would ever be remembered as forming a glorious episode in the history of the Indian Empire and of its army."

Operations of the Gilgit Column under Lieut.-Colonel Kelly.

We may now turn to the operations undertaken for the relief of Chitral from Gilgit by the force under Lieut.-Colonel Kelly.

Early in March, as has been already mentioned, Captain W. H. Stewart, the Assistant British Agent at Gilgit, requested Lieut.-Colonel Kelly to march thither with the half battalion of the 32nd Punjab Pioneers, then encamped between Bunji and Chilas. This precaution was decided upon owing to the serious news received from Surgeon-Major Robertson in Chitral, and the uncertainty as to the safety of the detachments which were known to have moved to his assistance from Mastuj.

On the 22nd March the Pioneers arrived at Gilgit, and on the same day Lieut.-Colonel Kelly received the following instructions by telegram from the Adjutant-General in India :—

In consequence of affairs in Chitral, you will assume military command in the Gilgit Agency, and make such dispositions and movements as you may think best. You are not to undertake any operations that do not offer reason able prospects of success. So long as communications with Robertson are interrupted, you will be Chief Political Officer within the zone of your military operations. On or about the 1st April a strong force of three brigades will advance on Chitral *viâ* Swat. You will report direct to the Adjutant-General at Calcutta till 28th, then to Simla, repeating to Resident, Kashmir.

Beyond the fact that the British Agent, with his escort of the 14th Sikhs and 300 Kashmir Imperial Service Troops, was besieged in Chitral by the combined forces of Sher Afzal and Umra Khan, and that Captain Ross' detachment had been cut up in the Koragh defile, Lieut.-Colonel Kelly had no certain information as to the condition of the country beyond Mastuj, which was held by a small detachment under Lieutenant Moberly. The fate of the party under Lieutenants Edwardes and Fowler was as yet unknown.

The troops at Lieut.-Colonel Kelly's disposal (excluding those at Mastuj and Chitral) were distributed as follows :—

		Men.
Astor ..	5th Kashmir Light Infantry ..	29
Between Bunji and Chilas.	32nd Punjab Pioneers ..	442
	Bengal Sappers and Miners ..	12
	5th Kashmir Light Infantry ..	466
Hunza valley ..	No. 1 Kashmir Mountain Battery (2 guns).	
	6th Kashmir Light Infantry ..	209
Gilgit ..	No. 1 Kashmir Mountain Battery (2 guns).	
	32nd Punjab Pioneers ..	403
	4th Kashmir Rifles ..	34
	5th Kashmir Light Infantry ..	108
	6th ,, ,, ..	140
	Kashmir Sappers and Miners ..	111
	Details ..	14
Gakuch	6th Kashmir Light Infantry ..	23
Roshan ..	,, ,, ,, ,, ..	10

			Men.
Gupis	..	4th Kashmir Rifles ..	34
		6th Kashmir Light Infantry ..	69
Ghizr	..	4th Kashmir Rifles 6th Kashmir Light Infantry ..	129
		Kashmir Sappers and Miners ..	52

It was necessary, besides organising a column for an advance towards Chitral, to provide for the safety of Gilgit, and the line of communications between that place and Mastuj. Moreover, although the attitude of the Hunza and Nagir people was most friendly and loyal, it was not advisable to denude the Hunza valley of troops. The Chilasis also, (though they had been submissive since their defeat in 1893), and the independent Kohistanis and Shinaki tribes on their border, required watching. Finally, the Yasinis, through whose country the column must advance, could not be trusted to abstain from active sympathy with their Chitrali neighbours.

These considerations, and the paucity of supplies and transport available, decided Lieut.-Colonel Kelly to limit his force to a small column consisting of 400 men of the 32nd Pioneers and a section of No. 1 Kashmir Mountain Battery.

The Chiefs of Hunza and Nagir, who had already furnished 100 levies employed at Ghizr, now brought 900 men with 14 days' supplies. A hundred of these were selected to follow the column to Ghizr, and another hundred were detailed to garrison Roshan, while a number of the remainder were employed in conveying supplies to Gupis.

Lieut.-Colonel Kelly was confronted by a task of very great difficulty. As far as Gupis a made road existed, which, though rough and difficult, was fit for mule transport. Beyond that place the route was a mere track, and the Shandur pass was at this time of year certain to prove a formidable obstacle. All the country beyond the pass was known to be up in arms, and there was a possibility that on the Gilgit side also the inhabitants would prove hostile and thus render the task of reaching Chitral almost hopeless; for both in the matter of supplies and transport the column must to a very great extent necessarily depend on the country through which it had to pass. It was known that the reserves stored in Gupis would suffice the column for the actual requirements of the road, and that at Ghizr there was stored enough to maintain 1,000 men for 11½ days. The actual amount, however, that had been forwarded from Gupis could not be ascertained, though it was believed that at Mastuj there were probably some sixteen days' supplies for the garrison.

Lieut.-Colonel Kelly divided the column into two parties of which the first, consisting of 200 men of the 32nd Pioneers, marched from Gilgit on the 23rd March; the remainder of the Pioneers and two guns of No. 1 Kashmir Mountain Battery followed the next day. No tents were taken, and baggage was limited to 15lb per man. The two detachments reached Gupis on the 26th and 27th. Here coolie and pony transport replaced the mules brought from Gilgit. In order to reduce the amount of transport, some stores, including Pioneer equipment, were now left at Gupis. Leaving that place on the 27th and 28th March, the column reached Ghizr on the 30th and 31st, where it was reinforced by 40 Kashmir Sappers and Miners, and 100 levies from Hunza and Nagir, led by Wazirs Humayun and Taifu. From Ghizr Lieut.-Colonel Kelly resumed his march with the whole column, intending to halt at Langar, thirteen miles distant, on the 1st April.

Crossing of the Shandur pass.

It was found that a number of the Yasini coolies and some of the ponies had bolted during the previous night, and consequently, although Lieutenant C. G. Stewart succeeded in bringing a portion of them back, only six days' supplies could be transported, instead of ten, as originally intended. Snow had been falling for five days, and about three miles from Ghizr it lay so deep that the further progress of the laden animals was utterly impossible. Accordingly, at 3 P.M. the order to retire was reluctantly given. An hour later Teru was reached, and here Lieut.-Colonel Kelly again divided his force, leaving 200 Pioneers, 40 Sappers and Miners, and 50 levies, with the whole of the coolie transport, at that place, under command of Captain Borradaile. This officer was instructed to cross the pass on the following day, and entrench himself at Laspur, whence he was to send back the coolie transport, and, if possible, open up communication with Mastuj. Lieut.-Colonel Kelly with the remainder of his force, meanwhile returned to Ghizr, but a further fall of snow prevented Captain Borradaile from leaving Teru on the next day as arranged. The men of the 4th Kashmir Rifles now volunteered to assist the gunners in making a road through the snow from Teru to Langar, and to help them in getting the guns over the pass. Having obtained permission to make the attempt, Lieutenant Stewart, with his gunners, went on to Teru on the 2nd to prepare the road, leaving the drivers and mules at Ghizr; he was accompanied by Lieutenant H. A. K. Gough, and fifty Kashmir sepoys. On their arrival at Teru, the men of 32nd Pioneers, through their native officers, asked permission from Captain Borradaile, to be allowed to assist the gunners and Kashmir Infantry men to carry the guns and ammunition over the Shandur pass. This request was acceded to. The guns arrived from Ghizr next day, and about noon Captain Borradaile, with the whole party, set out for Langar. The battery mules were soon in difficulties owing to the deep snow. A small herd of half-bred yaks was at first driven ahead, to trample down a track, but the result was disappointing, as the laden mules still sank in too deep to make any headway. Lieutenant Stewart then tried to march his section along the Langar river-bed, but men and animals soon became numbed in the icy cold water. Eventually some of the loads were slung and carried by the men, while others were dragged on sledges constructed from boxes. The Pioneers of the rear-guard and Kashmir sepoys, encumbered though they were with their own kit and equipment, manfully aided the artillerymen in their desperate task of carrying the heavy loads through the deep snow, and after a most laborious struggle the party reached Langar at 11 P.M. The guns and artillery loads were stacked on the snow and left under a guard some distance back, as the men were too exhausted to carry them further that night. They were brought on to Langar next day by the gunners and men of the 4th Kashmir Rifles, while the mules were sent back to Ghizr.

Langar is about 12,000 feet above sea-level, and the cold was intense. One small hut was found, and used for the few sick men, while the remainder bivouacked in the open, sitting round some small fires which they managed to light. Fearing to exhaust his men by a repetition of the heavy work of the previous day, Captain Borradaile left the guns and escort of 4th Kashmir Rifles at Langar, and started up the pass with the remainder of his detachment at 9 A.M. on the 4th April. Though the Shandur is considered an easy pass in ordinary seasons, the softness of the fresh-fallen snow, now from three to five feet deep, rendered the progress of the men, heavily weighted as they were with arms, ammunition, and accoutrements, intensely difficult. They suffered much from the fierce glare of the sun, which caused many cases of snow-blindness. The rate of march averaged no more than one mile an hour, and Laspur was not reached till 7 P.M. Here the villagers, who were taken by surprise at the unexpected arrival of the British force across a pass which they then believed impracticable, offered no opposition.

The next day Captain Borradaile completed the defences of some houses which he had occupied, and collected supplies and transport. Some of the villagers, who had volunteered to assist us, were sent back to bring the guns from Langar. In the evening the detachment which had been left at that place arrived with the guns, which they had carried over the pass with the aid of the Laspuri coolies. This most creditable feat was due to the indomitable perseverance of Lieutenants Stewart and Gough, and to the splendid endurance of the gunners and the men of the 4th Kashmir Rifles, who so ably assisted them. Meanwhile Captain Borradaile, who had gone out to reconnoitre, ascertained that a number of the enemy were in the vicinity.

On the morning of the 6th Captain Borradaile with 120 Pioneers and 2 guns made a reconnaissance as far as Gasht. Having obtained information that the enemy were holding the Chakalwat defile, three miles further on, with 300 to 500 men, he returned to Laspur.

Lieut.-Colonel Kelly, with Lieutenant W. G. L. Beynon, Staff Officer, and fifty Nagir Levies, reached Laspur on this date. On the 7th a halt was made in order to rest the men and give those suffering from snow-blindness a chance to recover. The artillery-men, being without goggles, were especially affected and would have been unable to lay their guns at any distance. During the day the force was further increased by the arrival of fifty Puniali Levies under Raja Akbar Khan with some ninety Balti coolies carrying supplies. On the 8th Lieut.-Colonel Kelly, rightly believing that a further delay would only allow the enemy to increase their numbers and strengthen their position at Chakalwat,

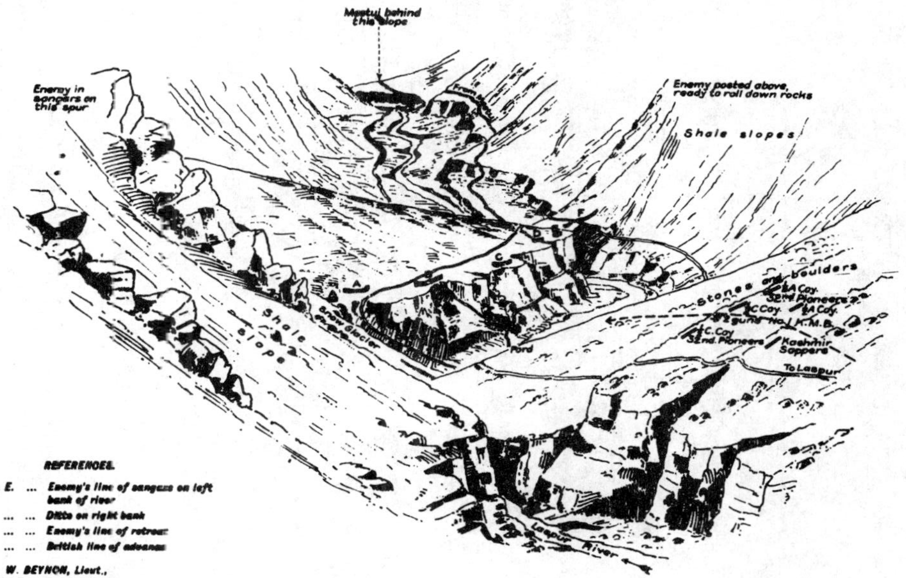

REFERENCES.

A. B. C. D. E. ...	Enemy's line of sangars on left bank of river
F.	Ditto on right bank
——→	Enemy's line of retreat
– – →...	British line of advance

(Sd.) W. BEYNON, Lieut.,
Staff Officer Gilgit Field Force,
9th April 1895.

Reconnaissance sketch of Enemy's Position at CHAKALWAT

Showing formation of attack at commencement of action on 9th April 1895

I. B. Topo. Dy. No. 6,704.
Exd. O. J. A., February 1907.

No. 4,064-I., 1907.

moved on to Gasht, without waiting for the remainder of the column. His force consisted of 200 Pioneers, 40 Sappers and Miners, 100 Hunza and Puniali Levies, and 2 mountain guns. Lieutenant Gough, with 25 Kashmir sepoys and the rest of the levies, was left to hold Laspur until the arrival of the second detachment of Pioneers.

Action of the Chakalwat defile.

On arrival at Gasht, Lieutenant Beynon, with the Hunza Levies, reconnoitred the enemy's position at Chakalwat, which commanded a ford across the Laspur stream. This position, like most of the darbands, which the Chitralis regard as impregnable, was of great natural strength. A line of *sangars* stretched across the edge of an alluvial fan some considerable height above the river, blocking the paths up the cliffs from the ford below and commanding the road on the right bank. On the enemy's right was a mass of fallen snow descending to the river, and above it a precipitous spur crowned with more *sangars*; the other flank was protected by shale slopes above which the enemy had prepared the usual stone shoots. The road from Gasht led across a boulder-strewn alluvial slope, intersected by *nalas*, and then ran along the foot of steep shale slopes opposite the *sangars*. On the 9th Lieut.-Colonel Kelly, leaving his baggage at Gasht under a small escort, advanced with the remainder of his troops in the order noted in the margin. Lieutenant Beynon, with the Hunza Levies, had already ascended the heights above the enemy's right in order to outflank the position, while the Puniali Levies had been entrusted with the task of driving the enemy away from their stone shoots on the slopes above the right bank of the river.

Advanced Guard—
Half company, 22nd Punjab Pioneers.
Main Body—
Kashmir Sappers and Miners.
Half Company, 22nd Punjab Pioneers.
2 guns, No. 1 Kashmir Mountain Battery.
One Company, 22nd Punjab Pioneers.

At about half a mile from the position, the force deployed for attack and occupied a gently sloping spur facing the enemy's two right-hand lower *sangars*. [A and B in plan.] The guns opened fire at 825 yards range, and, aided by the well-directed volleys of the infantry, cleared the enemy out of their right *sangar* [A]. Lieutenant Beynon, with the Hunza Levies, meanwhile drove the enemy back from their position on the spur above. Fire was now concentrated on the next *sangar* [B], which was soon evacuated. The occupants of these *sangars* were now joined by their comrades, who had been driven down from the hills on either side by the levies, and a general flight ensued. A few rounds were fired at the fugitives by the guns. The column then crossed the river and, having occupied the *sangars*, continued its advance for 1½ miles, when a halt was made.

The casualties on our side were one native officer and three men wounded, while the enemy, who numbered 400 to 500 men, last between 50 to 60 killed.

After a short halt, the march was continued to Mastuj, which was reached without further opposition. The garrison, seeing the besiegers retiring from their positions during the day, had come out to meet the relieving force about three miles from the fort.

Lieut.-Colonel Kelly halted at Mastuj for three days, which were spent in collecting transport and supplies, and repairing the damaged bridge over the Yarkhun river, a mile below the fort. Some ponies were also procured for the carriage of the guns. The second detachment, under Lieutenant Patterson, which had crossed the Shandur on the 9th, reached Mastuj on the 11th. Reconnaissances were made on the 11th and 12th, and the enemy were found to be holding a strong and well fortified position, blocking the advance through the narrow valley of the Yarkhun or Chitral river, where it is cleft by a deep ravine known as the Nisa Gol.

The road from Mastuj runs along the centre of an open plain, above the right bank of the river, which here flows through a valley about a mile in width, and hemmed in on either side by steep rocky hills rising several thousand feet above it. Issuing from the mountains on the right bank, the Nisa Gol, a gorge 200 or 300 feet deep with precipitous sides, cuts through the plain to the river, which here hugs the lofty cliffs on its left. The main road crosses this ravine near its junction with the river, and a rough track passes across about the centre; this second path, however, had been destroyed by the enemy.

Action of Nisa Gol.

On the far edge of the gol, the enemy had built a line of *sangars*, sunk in the ground, and well provided with head-cover. On their left, in line with these, several more *sangars* were built on the spur above, and higher still parties of men were posted to hurl down rocks on their assailants. Their right was defended by a series of

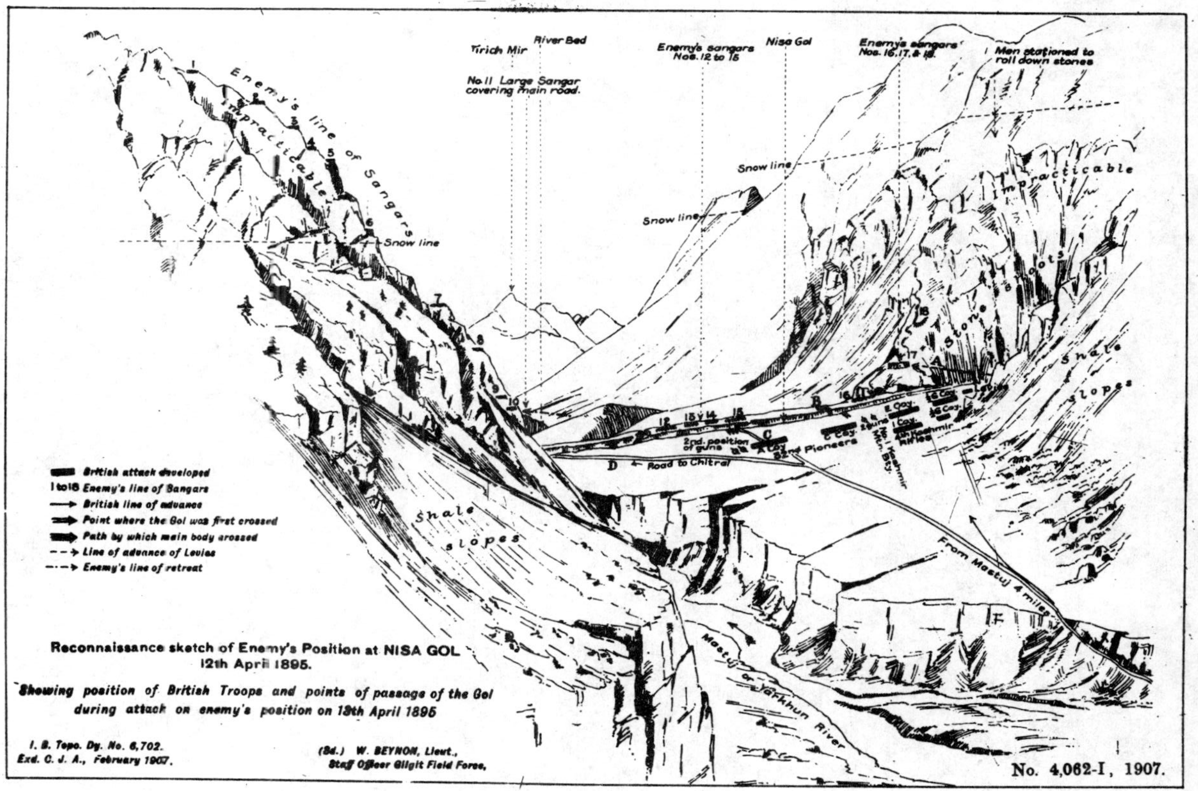

Reconnaissance sketch of Enemy's Position at NISA GOL 12th April 1895.

Showing position of British Troops and points of passage of the Gol during attack on enemy's position on 13th April 1895

I. B. Topo. Dy. No. 6,702.
Exd. C. J. A., February 1907.

(Sd.) W. BEYNON, Lieut.,
Staff Officer Gilgit Field Force.

sangars, stretching away above the snow-line, on a spur rather in front of the main position.

Lieut.-Colonel Kelly's Staff Officer had supplied him with an excellent sketch and full information as to the defender's dispositions. He accordingly decided to attack the position on the 13th, and to endeavour to turn the enemy's left. The plan of attack was as follows: The advanced-guard (one company) was, on gaining the plain, to make its way well to the right and high up the slope, where the formation of the ground favoured an advance under cover to within 500 yards of the gol. It was then to attack with well-directed volleys the lower *sangar* on the spur protecting the enemy's left flank [No. 17 in plan] until the guns and the remainder of the force came into position. After this *sangar* was destroyed, the main defences, Nos. 12 to 15, were to be attacked, while the levies made their way high up the gol in search of a path by which they might cross and turn the enemy's left.

The company forming the advanced guard came into contact with the enemy at 10-30 A.M., when, instead of working towards its right, as ordered, it deployed at about 900 yards from the gol and advanced in extended order on the centre of the position. The next company, coming up shortly afterwards, prolonged the line to the right. The two reserve companies of the Pioneers now deployed and advanced, and subsequently in turn reinforced the firing line, extending it still further to the right. Meanwhile the guns shelled No. 17 *sangar*, and temporarily silenced its fire after partially destroying the wall. The guns then moved forward to engage the *sangar* at the foot of the spur [No. 16 on plan], which was not visible till within 150 yards. This was found to be unoccupied, but the occupants of No. 17 reopened fire, and the guns accordingly silenced them with common shell and case shot. The Kashmir artillerymen, who were under a hot fire at close range, served their guns with admirable steadiness, though they lost seven killed and wounded in the section during the space of a few minutes. Of this number three were drivers, men taken prisoners at Chakalwat, and leading—under escort—ponies also captured at that place.

During this time the levies were making their way up the gol to carry out the turning movement, while the four companies of Pioneers engaged the *sangars* on the edge of the ravine, and on the spur to their right front.

After silencing No. 17 *sangar*, the guns took up a third position, whence they shelled the enemy's centre at about 900 yards' range and then switched their fire on to a large breastwork [No. 11 in sketch] further to the enemy's left, which commanded the main road. About this time, Lieutenant Beynon discovered a place where the gol could be crossed, opposite the rough track which ascended the far bank. Some sappers, under Lieutenant Oldham, R.E., and the company of the 4th Kashmir Rifles, under Lieutenant Moberly, were now called up; and the sappers, with the aid of scaling ladders and ropes, descended the ravine, and after about half an hour's work, made a practicable path down the cliff. The three officers, with about a dozen men, reached the opposite side just as the levies arrived at No. 17 *sangar*, having run the gauntlet of a stone shoot on the way. The enemy, realizing that their position was turned, now left their cover and made a hurried retreat, during which they were shelled by the guns at ranges from 950 to 1,425 yards, while the infantry poured in a few well-directed volleys. A general advance was now ordered, and a company was quickly despatched in pursuit, but the enemy's flight was rapid, and being aided by the ground, which afforded good cover till they were out of range, they were able to make good their escape in the direction of Drasan. The column bivouacked for the night opposite Sanoghar, close to the scene of action.

To quote from the official report :—

It will be observed that Lieut.-Colonel Kelly adopted the same tactics which had proved so successful in the engagement at Chakalwat. He brought his artillery fire to bear on the *sangars*, keeping up an incessant rifle fire as well, while the hardy levies climbed the precipitous hillsides high up the gol to turn the *sangars* on the enemy's left flank.

The total number of the enemy were estimated at 1,500, among whom were some 40 of Umra Khan's men; they were commanded by the treacherous Muhammad Isa, and were all armed with Martini-Henry or Snider rifles. The casualties on our side amounted to seven men killed, and one native officer and twelve men wounded, while those of the enemy were, according to native information, sixty men killed and one hundred wounded.

In reporting the above engagement, Lieut.-Colonel Kelly remarked :—

Confronted as they were by an enemy they could not see, I cannot speak too highly of the extreme steadiness and bravery of the troops during the course of the action, which lasted two hours, during which they were subjected to a very heavy and trying fire from the front and left flank.

On the 14th the wounded were sent back to Mastuj, where a field hospital was established by Surgeon Captain Luard, I.M.S. The remainder of the column resumed its march at 7 A.M. On reaching a point opposite Buni, the road along the Chitral river was reported to have been broken down, so the force, turning right-handed, ascended a spur which brought them, after a stiff climb of 2,000 feet, to a grassy plateau which sloped gradually down towards the junction of the Yarkhun and the Torikho. An easy march along this highland brought the column to Drasan, which was found to be deserted, as were all the surrounding villages. The bridge over the Torikho stream, which had been destroyed, was repaired with beams and timbers taken from the fort, so as to allow the troops to cross dry-shod. It was, however, not strong enough to bear the guns, which were carried over the ford while the animals swam across. The coolies with the baggage, who did not arrive till after dark, also preferred to ford the river rather than wait to cross the bridge in single file. Large supplies of grain were found in the fort, but, as there was no transport available to remove it, a quantity was issued to the coolies.

On the 15th the column marched to Kusht, and pushed on next day, in heavy rain to Lun.

On the 17th Lieut.-Colonel Kelly reached Burnas, having crossed the river by a dangerous ford about a mile above that place. From Sanoghar, the ordinary main road to Chitral runs along the left bank of the Yarkhun, and it was on this road that the disasters occurred to the detachments under Captain Ross and Lieutenant Edwardes. By abandoning this route, and making a détour, *viâ* Drasan and Lun, over the high ground to the west of the river, Lieut.-Colonel Kelly outwitted the enemy, and avoided the Koragh and other formidable defiles, where they had hoped to check his advance.

On the 18th, as less than three days' supplies remained in hand, foraging parties were sent out early; and on their return a short march was made to Maroi. Here it was reported that a party of the enemy under Muhammad Isa had retired during the day towards Chitral, and intended to hold a darband called the Golen Gol. The next day, although the enemy had destroyed all bridges and broken down the road in several places, no opposition was met with; and it was ascertained at Koghazi, where the column halted, that Muhammad Isa had been hurriedly recalled by Sher Afzal to Chitral.

This same afternoon a letter was received from Surgeon-Major Robertson, announcing the flight of the enemy and the end of the siege. On the afternoon of the 20th April, Lieut.-Colonel Kelly's column marched into Chitral and joined the garrison who had so gallantly defended it throughout the forty-six days' siege.

On the following day the position occupied by the combined force was entrenched, and communication was opened up, through Dir, with the Relief Force under Sir Robert Low, whose operations will be described in chapter XII.

On receipt of the news of the arrival of the column at Chitral the following telegram was sent from Simla, by the Foreign Secretary, to Sir Robert Low, for transmission to Colonel Kelly:—

I am desired by the Viceroy to express warm congratulations from himself and from Government of India to you and to your gallant troops on your admirable and successful advance to Chitral under circumstances of the greatest difficulty, arising not only from the opposition of the enemy, but also from enormous physical difficulties, which have been overcome with skill and rapidity.

On the 6th May 1895 Lieut.-Colonel Kelly submitted a despatch describing the operations of the Gilgit column, in transmitting which to the Government of India, His Excellency the Commander-in-Chief recorded his high appreciation of the skill and ability displayed in the conduct of this long and arduous advance to the relief of Chitral. Lieut.-Colonel Kelly's despatch and the Adjutant General's forwarding letter were published in the *Gazette of India* of the 25th May 1895, together with a Government General Order in which His Excellency the Viceroy expressed his deep sense of the admirable and valuable services performed by the officers and men of the Gilgit column under circumstances of extraordinary difficulty.

Surgeon-Major Robertson was made a Knight Commander of the Star of India. Captain C. V. F. Townshend received the Companionship of the Bath and a brevet majority, and Surgeon-Captain Whitchurch was awarded the Victoria Cross.

The events which followed on the relief of Chitral, and the measures adopted for the settlement of the country may now be briefly summarised.

Amir-ul-Mulk and Sher Afzal[1] were deported to India in May. On the 2nd September Shuja-ul-Mulk was installed as Mehtar of the Kator portion of Chitral, while the two Khushwakt districts of Mastuj and Laspur were placed under the rule of independent Governors, but were retained in the Chitral Agency. A garrison consisting of two battalions of native infantry, one company of sappers and miners, and one section of a native mountain battery was retained in Chitral, and has since been relieved annually *viâ* Swat and Dir. In 1899 this force was reduced by one battalion, and it is now stationed at Drosh, with a detachment at Chitral. For the defence of Lower Chitral some 200 levies armed with Sniders are now stationed at various posts.[2] They serve throughout the year, being relieved monthly, and are paid Rs. 10 *per mensem.* There are also about 150 unpaid levies employed to watch the passes leading from Dir and Kafiristan.

In 1903 the formation of a corps of Chitrali scouts was sanctioned. This force consists of 9 Native Officers and 990 Non-Commissioned Officers and men under 2 British Officers, with 8 Native instructors from the regular army. One-sixth of this force is called up at a time for two months' training, during which the men receive pay and rations. They are armed with Lee-Metford rifles.

The Mehtar Shuja-ul-Mulk receives a subsidy of Rs. 1,000 *per mensem* and an annual allowance of Rs. 8,000 as compensation for the loss of the Mastuj and Laspur districts. He has paid three visits to India and was made a C.I.E. at the Delhi Durbar in 1903. His loyalty to the British Government appears to be assured, and he seems to have become firmly established as a capable ruler. The Adamzadas and *mullas*, who were at first bitterly opposed to British interference and control, have now become more reconciled to the existing *régime*, and since 1895 nothing has occurred to disturb the peaceful relations between the British Government and the people of Chitral.

[1] Sher Afzal, with a number of the leading men in Chitral, had been captured by the Khan of Dir's *lashkar* in Bashkar, whence he was taken to the British camp at Dir.

[2] Gairat, Lower Drosh, Merkhani, Arandu, Kaoti, Ashreth, and Ziarat.

APPENDIX A.

Districts and population of Chitral according to a census taken about 1899-1900.

District.		Men, women and children.	Fighting men.
Laspur	.. .. ..	1,942	211
Mastuj Governorship.			
Mastuj	.. ..	1,142	49
Yarkhun valley	..	1,320	96
Kuh	.. ..	3,758	332
Torikho district.			
Torikho	.. ..	3,769	459
Khot valley	.. ..	1,643	237
Rech	..	819	52
Mulrikho district.			
Mulrikho	.. ..	2,525	280
Kushm and Madak	..	2,353	355
Tirich valley	..	1,654	247
Kosht district	.. ..	2,828	185
Owir district	.. ..	1,930	333
Khuzara district.			
Ojhor valley	.. ..	1,881	201
Shogot	.. ..	324	35
Lut Kuf [1]	.. ..	2,601	280
Arkari valley	.. ..	1,030	99
Chitral district	.. ..	11,587	549
Drosh district	.. ..	5,634	269
Total	..	49,770	4,368

[1] From Daral pass to Mogh.

APPENDIX B.

Casualties in action during siege of Chitral and operations from Gilgit side.

——	British Officers.		Native Officers.		Men.		Followers.		Total.	
	Killed.	Wounded.	Killed.	Wounded.	Killed.	Wounded.	Killed.	Wounded.	Killed.	Wounded.
Siege of Chitral	..	3	3	1	31	53	5	6	39	66
Captain Ross' party	1	1	1	..	45	9	6	..	53	10
Lieutenant Edwardes' party	..	1	1	..	54	..	2	..	57	1
Siege of Mastuj	..	..	..	..	1	1	..	..	1	1
Relief force from Gilgit under Lieut.-Colonel Kelly.	..	..	..	2	6	17	..	..	6	19
Total ..	1	5	5	3	137	80	13	6	156	97

Nine of the wounded subsequently died.

CHAPTER III.

CIS-INDUS SWATI AND BLACK MOUNTAIN TRIBES.

Allai.

Allai is a valley bounded by Kohistan on the north and east,[1] by the Bhogarmang valley, Nandihar, and Deshi on the south, and by the river Indus on the west. With the exception of the valley known as the Chor glen, the whole of Allai is drained by one main stream running from east to west into the Indus.

Allai is divided from Kohistan on the north by a high range of mountains, rising to a height of over fifteen thousand feet. On the south it is divided from Nandihar and Deshi by another range running from the British boundary to the Indus above Thakot. The country of the Allaiwals is conterminous with British territory to the north of the Bhogarmang valley, but they are separated from one another by a range of mountains rising from eleven to thirteen thousand feet. The main stream, known as the Allai Sirhan, which runs through the whole valley, has its source in this range, whence, running west, after receiving several lesser streams, it falls into the Indus near the village of Thandul, opposite Barkot, about eighteen miles from its source. The average breadth of the valley is about twelve miles, and the total area about two hundred square miles. Its eastern end is a succession of grass and forest-covered mountain slopes ; as the elevation becomes less, fields of wheat, barley and Indian corn begin to appear, and near the Indus extensive rice cultivation is carried on. The valley is studded by numerous hamlets, but none of them are fortified, nor is their position , as a rule, good for defence.

Politically the two principal villages are Bandi and Pokul, or Shingari. There are two leading *maliks* in the tribe, Arsala Khan and Bahadur Khan, who have an old-standing enmity with each

[1] The Chor glen to the east of Allai is geographically a part of Kohistan, but the Allaiwals have taken possession of it.

other ; the former is perhaps the most powerful, and has in his day been something of a firebrand, but he is now (1907) an old man. He has a son named Ghazi Khan. The Allaiwals are ever engaged in internal quarrels; blood-feuds are rife, and often embroil the whole tribe.

The Allaiwals are nearly all of the Swati tribe, and intermarry with the Swatis of Bhogarmang and Nandihar. It should be noted that these cis-Indus Swatis have no connection with the Yusafzai Pathans who now occupy the Swat valley. When the Pathans came eastward from Afghanistan and took possession of the Peshawar valley, they also seized the adjacent hill tracts on the north, and either drove before them the ancestors of these Swatis, or reduced them to a state of servitude, from which they released themselves by leaving their country, under the leadership of Saiyid Jalal Baba, the son or descendant of Pir Saiyid Ali, (more generally known as Pir Baba, who settled in Buner and died there), and the common ancestor of the Kaghan Saiyids, the *Saiyids* late of Sitana, and several other *Saiyid* communities who live amongst the tribes along our border. These Swatis, under their religious leader, were composed of the original inhabitants of Swat, and a few Pathans, probably, who possessed no landed property and did not belong to the conquering Pathan clan. This force went eastwards towards the Indus, and, crossing that river, took possession of the countries now occupied by their descendants. When the country had been taken full possession of, one-fourth of the whole was set aside as the share of the *Saiyid* leader and his family, and the Mada Khel and Akhund Khel religious fraternity. The Swatis are now spread over upper Hazara in British territory, and, in addition to Allai, in independent territory, Nandihar, Deshi, and Tikari are peopled by this race.

The cis-Indus Swatis appear to have all the vices of the Pathan—rankly luxuriant, and, as with them, cold-blooded murder and grinding avarice are the salt of life ; but those in British territory can only indulge the first taste at the risk of unpleasant consequences. They certainly have not any of the courage of the Pathan, and the bold, frank manner of the latter is replaced with them by a hang-dog look. They are all Sunni Muhammadans, and are very bigoted.

The population of Allai consists of 5,830 families, divided as follows :—Swatis [1], 4,100 ; *Saiyid*, Tirimzai, 430 ; Mada Khel, 440 ; Akhund Khel, 520 ; Gujars and others, 340.

The fighting men number about 8,720, [2] *viz.*—Swatis, 6,490 ; *Saiyids*, Tirimzai, 580 ; Mada Khel, 570 ; Akhund Khel, 980 ; Gujars and others, 100.

Their arms are guns, swords and shields, and pistols. About two-thirds of their fighting men are armed with guns, for the most part matchlocks, with a few muskets. They may possibly have a few rifles. Their pistols are flintlocks. Every man is supposed to be armed, and they are said to be good marksmen. They purchase their gunpowder and lead from Swat and Chakesar. In the event of their country being invaded, they might get aid from the neighbouring Swati tribes, and also from Kohistan, but the latter would be doubtful, as there is enmity between the Allaiwals and the Kohistanis, owing to the forcible seizure of Chor by the former.

In the event of a British force entering their country, the people of Nandihar and Tikari would hardly dare to give them assistance, as they are themselves open to attack from British territory. Supplies in Allai are sufficient for the inhabitants, but a force entering the country would have to take its own. These could be had from Konsh and Agror. Grass, fuel, and water are, however, plentiful. The Allaiwals are but little dependent upon British territory.

From the south, Allai may be entered either through the Bhogarmang valley, or through Nandihar, or along the bank of the river Indus. The easiest routes are those through Nandihar, and of the passes leading thence into Allai the Ghabri is said to be the most frequently used. The Ghorapher pass lies to the west of the Ghabri. The Dabrai pass, still more to the west, leads to Thakot.

During the Black Mountain Expedition of 1868 it was proposed to punish the Allaiwals for an attack on a survey party under Mr. G. B. Scott in Bhogarmang in August of that year, but the intention of entering the Allai valley was subsequently abandoned, as it was considered inexpedient to

1 The Swatis of Allai are again divided into eight sections.
2 This estimate has not been revised since 1884.—(*Editor.*)

extend the military operations at that time. A fine of Rs. 500 was imposed on the Allaiwals for the attack on the survey party; but up to the present time the fine has not been realised, and is still an outstanding claim against the tribe. In November 1874, the Allaiwals, headed by their chief, Arsala Khan, made a raid within British territory upon a party of Kohistanis, murdering three men and carrying off their flocks. This was at once punished by the seizure of some sixty Allaiwals, with flocks numbering 4,000 head, in British territory; a blockade of the tribe was proclaimed, and, notwithstanding the sympathies of our own Swati subjects with the marauders, the *jirga* of the tribe, for the first time in their history, came in and made their submission to the British Government. For the next three years the Allaiwals gave no trouble; but in November 1877 they again committed some raids on the British border, which rendered a blockade of the tribe necessary. The first raid was committed on the village of Bathal in the Konsh valley, on the 16th of November, at the instance of Arsala Khan, who was himself present in person and was the leader of the gang. In this raid two Hindus of Bathal were killed and twelve carried off. Houses were also set on fire, and property, valued at Rs. 37,000 by the owners, was carried off. The raiders were estimated to have lost thirteen killed, and twelve were taken prisoners; their numbers were about 300.

The operations of the blockade progressed but slowly. As already pointed out, Allai is but little dependent upon us, and consequently an effective blockade is most difficult to carry out. About the middle of June 1879 a *jirga* of the Allaiwals came in to the Deputy Commissioner. It was not accompanied by Arsala Khan, or by any other influential man, and it proposed that neither fine nor compensation should be demanded, and that the Allaiwal prisoners should be surrendered previous to the Hindus being given up. These proposals could not, of course, be listened to, and the *jirga* was dismissed. The Allaiwals were at the same time given distinctly to understand that no terms would be made with them until the British subjects who were in their hands were released. When this demand had been complied with they would be informed of the fine and compensation they would be called upon to pay. Up to the end of the year the Allaiwals had shown no signs of submission, and the Government of India considered that the difficulty had reached a stage at which it was highly expedient that effective measures should be taken for the punishment of the tribe. Owing, however, to the absence of so large a force on service in Afghanistan, the time was not considered opportune for an expedition. The blockade was, therefore, ordered to be continued until it should be convenient to send a punitive force into Allai.

On the 14th August 1880, the arrival of the Allai *jirga* at Abbottabad, bringing with them the Hindu prisoners, was reported. Arsala Khan, however, did not accompany the *jirga*, pleading as an excuse that he was afraid to do so. In consideration of the surrender of the Hindu captives, the twenty-nine members of the tribe, who had been seized in reprisal, were released, and the following terms, which the Government demanded, were then made known to the *jirga* :—

(1) The raiders captured in the attack on Bathal to be released on the payment of a ransom of Rs. 500.

(2) Payment of a fine of Rs. 5,000 on account of the raid on Bathal.

(3) Payment of Rs. 500 on account of the attack on Mr. Scott's survey party in 1868.

(4) Submission of Arsala Khan.

The *jirga* was then dismissed.

On the 16th February 1881, a deputation, with the ransom money, arrived at Abbottabad, and the eight surviving prisoners in the jail at Rawal Pindi were sent for and released in the presence of the *jirga*, who then departed. The other conditions, however, remained unfulfilled, and in the autumn of 1881 the necessity of a military expedition was again considered. The Brigadier-General commanding the Frontier Force was called on to submit proposals for such an expedition ; but the Government considered that the operations proposed by him would have been on a scale out of proportion to the results to be obtained, and it was, therefore, decided to defer the use of military force. The terms imposed on the tribe remained unfulfilled until 1888.[1]

On the 4th July 1887, two raids were committed simultaneously by the Allaiwals in the northern corner of the Bhogarmang

[1] See page 147.

glen above Jabar, on small grazing camps in our territory. The claim for the property carried off, together with the outstanding claim, made the total sum due from the tribe Rs. 6,500. Arsala Khan refused to refer the case to a Council of Elders, except on terms that could not be accepted, and, as no other means of recovering this amount remained, punitive measures were finally sanctioned in 1888, but these were more especially directed against Arsala Khan and his village of Pokal, as will be shown hereafter.

Nandihar.

Nandihar is a valley lying to the south of Allai, and adjoining the British valleys of Bhogarmang and Konsh on the east.

It is divided by a spur of the hills into two long, open glens, and the drainage, after joining that from the adjoining valley of Tikari, falls into the Indus at Thakot. In Nandihar, water is abundant, and rice is largely cultivated, as well as Indian corn, wheat and barley. Up the hillsides every culturable plateau, no matter how small, is brought under the plough. The area of the valley is about ninety square miles and its elevation is about four to five thousand feet. The inhabitants are Swatis, and are divided into four clans, namely :—Khan Khel, Panjmiral, Panjgol, and Dodal.

The total number of families is estimated at 1,380, *viz.*—

Khan Khel	..	326	Panjgol	..	.. 286
Panjmiral	..	394	Dodal	..	.. 374

There are about 1,000 fighting men, each clan supplying 250 men. Their arms are guns, swords, and spears. The greater part of the guns are matchlocks, with some flintlocks and a few muskets. About half the fighting men possess guns of one sort or the other. Aid could be had from Tikari, Deshi, and Thakot, as they are all Swatis, and their borders join.

The Nandiharis are constantly at feud among themselves, and cannot even unite against aggression. Supplies are plentiful, but fuel is scarce. There are routes from the Konsh glen or from Agror, which are practicable for laden mules.

Nandihar is not dependent at all on British territory, and trade carried on with us is very small; but being so easily acessible, the State is completely at our mercy. Sirdar Hari Singh, during the Sikh rule, invaded the country and made the inhabitants pay tribute.

Tikari.

Tikari is a valley lying to the south of Nandihar, and between that valley and Agror in British territory. It is about eight miles in length and five miles in breadth, and is about 4,500 feet above the sea-level, having good streams of water running through it. There is a fair amount of rice cultivation, irrigated from the main and small tributary streams, but the principle produce is Indian corn. The nature of the soil is very fertile, but the valley is singularly bare of trees. Firewood is a difficulty, even brushwood on the slopes of the hills being deficient. The valley can be entered either from Konsh or Agror, but the latter is the best and easiest road, and is the route chiefly used.

The inhabitants are Swatis and could obtain aid in case of being attacked from the neighbouring Swati tribes, and also from the Chagarzais, Akazais, and Hassanzais of the Black Mountain.

The population consists of 700 families, divided as follows :—Malkhel, or Malkals 300, Ashlor Naror 320, and *Saiyids* 80.

There are only 400 fighting men, or, roughly speaking, one to every two families. Their arms are similar to those of the Nandiharis.

Supplies within Tikari are plentiful, and water abundant. A good deal of grain is exported thence by the Black Mountain tribes. The Tikariwals occasionally bring down grain to British territory and purchase cloth from us, but they can scarcely be said to be dependent on us.

Rahim Khan of Chirmang in Tikari, with his following, joined in the Bagrian raid on the 11th July 1887.[1]

Deshi.

Deshi is the name given to the country to the north of Agror and lying to the west of Nandihar. It comprises a portion of the eastern slopes of the Black Mountain, and is a succession of bold, forest-covered spurs, with steep, rugged, intervening watercourses on the banks of which lie the hamlets of the tribe. Round each of these hamlets a few acres have been cleared of forest and cultivated.

The streams which drain the valleys of Nandihar and Tikari, after uniting three miles below the village of Trand, run along the

[1] See page 141.

foot of the Black Mountain, dividing Nandihar from Deshi, and join the Indus near Thakot, a large village, said to contain two thousand houses, including dependent hamlets. Most of the principal villages of Deshi are situated along the banks of this stream, and rice cultivation is carried on to a considerable extent; the stream is always fordable except after heavy rain.

The population of Deshi consists of some 726 families, which are apportioned among the six sections into which the tribe is divided as follows:—

Jador ..	.. 150	Khan Khel ..	.. 108
Kuchelai ..	.. 100	Warojai ..	.. 140
Rama Khel [1]	.. 120	Palolai ..	.. 108

The fighting men number about 726, or one man per family.

Their arms are guns, pistols, and swords. About three-fourths of the fighting men are armed with guns; and although cis-Indus Swatis, they bear a good name among their neighbours for fighting qualities. They seldom quarrel among themselves, and never to any great extent, and readily unite when danger threatens from without. In the event of being attacked they could get aid from the neighbouring Swati tribes. The Deshi territory could be approached by a force moving along the crest of the Black Mountain, or from Agror through Tikari, or thirdly, from Konsh through Nandihar. The second route would be most suitable for a force to adopt, and is easy throughout.

Supplies of grain, etc., are enough for the inhabitants, but would not suffice for even a small force, and these would, therefore, have to be taken with the troops. Fuel, grass, and water are plentiful. The tribe is not dependent on British territory; but, although not immediately on the British border, they are easily accessible and exposed to attack. They have a standing quarrel with their neighbours, the Saiyids of Pariari, and, in some fighting which took place in 1871, they had decidedly the best of it. They took part with the other tribes in the invasion of the Agror valley in 1868, and were fined Rs. 1,000 for their share in the disturbances of that time. Since then they have given little trouble, though a few

[1] Some authorities omit the Rama Khel and Palolai sections and substitute for them Sumla Khel and Beror.

are said to have helped Arsala Khan of Allai in some of his raids.

Tanawal.

Independent Tanawal is, roughly speaking, a square block of territory in the north-west corner of the Hazara district, south of the Black Mountain and Agror. It is drained by the Unhar and Sirhan rivers and consists of 200 square miles of hilly country, which is held as a *jagir* by the Nawab of Amb. Amb is a fort and village on the right bank of the Indus opposite the Tanawal *jagir*, and it and the other trans-Indus villages of the Nawab are entirely independent. The Tanawalis are a tribe of whose origin little is known. They appear to have crossed over from Mahaban, being expelled by the Pathans.

Black Mountain Tribes.

We now come to the Yusafzai tribes inhabiting the slopes of the Black Mountain lying to the east of the Indus, and occupying the south corner of the angle formed by that river and the British boundary.

Before describing the tribes which inhabit this tract of country, it will be well to give a brief description of the Black Mountain itself. Its total length is about twenty-five to thirty miles, and its average height about 8,000 feet above the sea. It ascends from the Indus basin at its southern end near the village of Kiara, and so up to its watershed by Baradar ; thence it runs north-east by north to the point on the crest known as Chitabat. From Chitabat the range runs due north, finally descending by two large spurs to the Indus. Thakot lies at the foot of the more eastern of these two. The Indus, after passing Thakot, runs westward along the northern foot of the mountain till it washes the western of the above two spurs, when it takes a sharp bend south, and runs below and parallel to the western foot of the range.

The Black Mountain may be described as a long, narrow ridge with higher peaks at intervals, and occasional deep passes ; the general outline of the crest is more rounded than sharp. From the sides, numerous large spurs project, which are often precipitous and rocky, with deep, narrow glens or gorges lying between them, in which lie some of the smaller villages of the tribes. The larger villages are as a rule situated on the banks of the Indus. The whole of the upper portion of the mountain is thickly wooded. The trees found are varieties of pine, oak, sycamore, horse-chestnut, and wild cherry. Along the crest frequent open glades occur in the forest, which, with the exposed slopes of higher peaks, are covered with short grass.

The following are the most important passes and peaks along the crest of the mountain from south to north, *viz.*—

Pabal Gali	..	6,370 feet.	Chitabat	..	8,710 feet.
Panj Gali	..	7,250 „	Doda	..	8,870 „
Akhund Baba-ka-Chura	..	9,150 „	Machai	..	9,817 „
Kain Gali	..	8,680 „	Khand-ka-Dana		9,429 „
Bampur Gali	..	7,640 „	Ganthar	..	9,572 „
			Kanesar	..	9,775 „

From the last peak the descent to Thakot and the Indus commences. The mountain is bounded on the south by Tanawal; on the east by Agror, Pariari, and the Swati tribes of Tikari, Nandihar, and Deshi; on the northern extremity, lies the Indus and Thakot; and on the west, between the crest and the river Indus, the slopes are occupied by Yusafzai Pathans. These slopes as a rule fall steeply for some 2,000 feet from the crest, then follows a zone of gentle slopes, all under cultivation; below this, from an altitude of about 4,000 or 5,000 feet, the hills fall precipitously to the Indus valley, which has a general fall of about ten feet a mile from Thakot to Darband. West of the Indus, from the Barandu river, which enters the Indus just north of the Mahaban range, up to Maidan, the hills rise gently and are under cultivation to their crests; above Maidan, the Duma range runs precipitously down to the river, but north of it again, at Kamach and for some distance beyond, the higher hills fall back and there is a considerable margin of cultivation on both banks of the river.

The actual valley varies in width from a few hundred yards to nearly two miles, the narrowest part being at Kotkai and the broadest at Palosi. The river runs in a well-defined channel, and in the dry season is about fifty feet below its banks, which are generally rocky and covered with large boulders. It is crossed at about eleven different points by ferries. The boats will hold from twenty to thirty passengers, but do not accommodate animals, which have to swim over alongside. They are strongly built and are worked by oars placed fore and aft; they are also assisted by ropes when necessary. The natives of the country also cross the river at nearly every point on inflated skins, and the rapidity with which this can be done was exemplified in the expedition of 1852-53, when the enemy, who had collected on the right of the Indus, crossed over to follow up our troops when they began to retire.

The routes by which troops can ascend the mountain necessarily lie along one or more of its spurs. From British territory all routes ascend either from Tanawal or Agror, and are as follows:—

1st, from Tanawal at the southern end of the mountain, by the Baradar spur, near the village of that name, there is a path—used for retirement by the 1852-53 expedition—which leads on to the watershed overlooking the Hassanzais. Near to this, on another spur, is the Chamberi outpost, a fort of the Nawab of Amb. The Baradar plateau affords room for encamping a force, and water is obtainable.

2nd, from Shingli, which lies in a gorge between two spurs, a path ascends the southern of these to Pabal Gali. In 1852 the left column of the expedition used this route.

3rd, a track goes from Chatta, a village lying on the northernmost of the above two spurs. Above Chatta it is joined by the Sambalbat spur from Agror, and then runs up to Jabai; this is one of the best routes for an ascending force. The right column of the force in 1852 moved by this route. On gaining the top, Kain Gali, a pass leading down to the Hassanzai villages, is commanded. The watershed of this spur forms the boundary between Agror and Tanawal.

4th, there is a small spur lying opposite Shingli between the two above mentioned, by which the centre column of the force in 1852 ascended to Panj Gali. It is steep and difficult, but a mule road was made up it in 1891.

5th, from Agror by the Sambalbat spur there is a path open and easy of ascent (although rather steep in parts) which joins the Chatta spur higher up.

6th, from Chajri there is a steep and exposed road, unfitted for troops.

7th, from Barchar a path rises steeply from the valley for about 1,500 feet. The village is situated at the top of this first rise, and might be held by an enemy, who could, however, be dislodged by artillery fire from below. From the village upwards the slope is more gradual and open for some distance, where thin forest commences, and on the right flank the ground gets a little steeper, with one or two knolls. The last four or five hundred feet are very steep, with dense forest on the right flank. The left is open and exposed to view from the crest. The point of junction with the top is called Bampur Gali. The levies went up this route in 1868.

8th, there is a spur running down eastward from Chitabat to the village of Kungali; thence it again ascends, still going east, and joins the Khabal mountain, which lies east of Agror. The watershed of this ridge forms the boundary between Agror and Pariari and Tikari. The main column of the force ascended from Kungali in 1868; half-way up, a large hog-backed mound, named Mana-ka-Dana, rises on the crest of the spur. The ascent to this point is easy. From Mana-ka-Dana the range dips for about 800 yards, and the forest begins, chiefly on the right flank; then the ascent starts again, and passes upwards over some steep and wooded knolls, which afford good cover for an enemy. Beyond this point the hill becomes steeper and more wooded right up to the knoll of Chitabat. On the crest a determined enemy could give much trouble. A path leads round the Agror face of Chitabat among rocks and pine trees. Mules can pass along, but it is dangerous in places. The Kungali ridge is the most northern spur ascending from British territory.

From Chitabat the path is practicable for troops and mountain artillery over Doda to the Machai peak, the highest point of the mountain, distance three and a half miles. A practicable spur runs from Machai to the Indus, dividing the Akazais from the Chagarzais on the north.

About two and a half miles beyond Machai is the Dunda peak; from it runs rather a difficult spur to the Indus, near the village of Judba, where some of the Hindustani fanatics crossed during the operations of 1868. Their encampment was at Bihar, on the other side of the river; Judba is about seven miles from the crest as the crow flies, or fourteen by the path.

From Dunda to the east runs a like practicable spur, ending at Trand; between this spur and the Kungali are the Pariari Saiyids. The distance from Dunda to Trand is about six miles. Water is found in numerous springs along the slopes; and near the crest the hillsides are covered with fields of Indian corn, affording, in the proper seasons, large quantities of forage. The range is well wooded on both sides.

The view from Machai is very extensive, embracing as it does Buner, Mount Ilam, the Hindu Kush, the mountains of Kashmir, and the Murree Hills.

The spur from Mana-ka-Dana to Chirmang, through Bilankot, is very easy, and the distance is five miles. This was the route taken by Major-General Wilde's force in 1868 on its way to the Tikari valley.

The climate of the Black Mountain is very fine in spring, summer, and autumn, but the winter is severe, and snow falls in sufficient quantity to stop communication over the crest. From the proximity of the mountain to the sultry valley of the Indus, the heat in summer, even at the highest elevation, is considerable, and along the bank of the river itself the climate is nearly as warm as that of the plains. Heavy rain generally falls in the spring and early autumn, and storms are of frequent occurrence.

The people who inhabit the western face of the Black Mountain are the Hassanzais, the Akazais, and the Chagarzais.

On the east face are the Saiyids of Pariari and the Deshiwals. The latter are Swatis, and have already been described.

The Hassanzais are a section of the Isazai clan of Yusafzai Pathans. Isa, the second son of Yusaf, is said to have had three sons, Hassan, Aka, and Mada, from whom are descended the Hassanzais, the Akazais and the Mada Khels. The Hassanzais reside on both sides of the Indus; those cis-Indus occupying the most southern portion of the western slopes of the Black Mountain, those trans-Indus living immediately opposite to them. The former are bounded on the north and east by the Akazais, on the west by the Indus, and on the south the Hassanzai border adjoins the territory of the Nawab of Amb.

The Hassanzais.

The Hassanzais are divided into ten sub-sections, which are as follows:

Khan Khel,	Kaka Khel,
Kotwal,	Mamu Khel,
Mir Ahmad Khel,	Nanu Khel,
Zakaria Khel,	Nasrat Khel,
Lukman Khel,	Dada Khel,

with a fighting strength in all of 1,895 men.

In addition to these, the *Saiyids* of Tilli could furnish a contingent of 230 fighting men, making a total of 2,125, of whom about 1,000 are trans-Indus Hassanzais, the remainder belonging to the cis-Indus portion of the tribe.

The tribe is not noted for its bravery, and is said to be very avaricious. In the event of being attacked, they could depend on getting aid from the other two sections of the Isazai Yusafzais, *viz.*, the Akazai and the Mada Khel. The latter have their settlements trans-Indus only. It is said that these three sections can concentrate their fighting men in one day.

The Hassanzais are constantly at feud among themselves, but would unite in the presence of a common danger. There are two parties among them, the *Kishardala* and *Mishardala*. The latter consist of all the men who were formerly acknowledged as headmen, but who have now been repudiated by the rest of the tribe (the *Kishardala*), because they do not divide among all, as they should, the annual blackmail paid to them by the Nawab of Amb. Thus the *Kishardala* forms the numerical majority; the *Mishardala* consists of the principal *maliks* and their dependents. This tribe is not dependent on British territory, as they procure their requirements from Chamla, Buner, Nandihar, Tikari, and Darband. A blockade would do them no harm. Supplies would have to accompany a force moving into their country.

There is a *Sahib-i-Dastar*, who has charge of the affairs of the Khan Khel, and is known by the title of "Khan of the Isazais." At the beginning of the British rule, Hassan Ali Khan was *Sahib-i-Dastar*, then his son Kabul Khan, who was succeeded in turn by his son, Malik Aman. This chief was murdered by his kinsman, Firoz Khan, and his cousin Ahmad Ali Khan became *Khan*, but he also was murdered by Firoz Khan at the beginning of 1880. The next *Sahib-i-Dastar* was Hashim Ali Khan, the brother of Ahmad Ali Khan. He was succeeded in 1891 by his cousin Ibrahim Khan, who was driven out of the country by the Hassanzais in 1906. At the time of writing the *Khanship* is vacant. The Khan Khels are the most troublesome of the Hassanzais.

During the Sikh rule, Sirdar Hari Singh, with two regiments, made an expedition into the Hassanzai country, *viâ* Darband and Baradar, and burnt some of the villages.

Akazais.

The Akazais, like the Hassanzais, are a section of the Isazai clan of Yusafzais, and inhabit a portion of the crest and western slopes of the Black Mountain to the north of the Hassanzais, having on their east a part of Agror and the Pariari Saiyids, to the north the Chagarzais, and on the west the Indus. They have no territory trans-Indus, with the exception of part of one village, which they share with the Hassanzais. Their principal villages are Kand, Bimbal, and Biliani. The first two belong to the Painda Khel sub-section, and are the nearest to the crest of the Black Mountain. They are situated on flat, open ground, but the approaches are difficult. The descent from Kand to Bimbal is very steep and rocky. The Akazais are divided into four sub-sections, as follows :—Painda Khel, Barat Khel, Aziz Khel, and Tasan Khel.

They can muster about 1,110 fighting men, in addition to which it is probable that the members of other tribes now settled in the Akazai territory would be able to furnish a contingent of about 270 more, giving a total of 1,380. Their characteristics are very similar to those of the Hassanzais, from whom they could get aid, as well as from the Mada Khels, in case of necessity.

Their territory could not furnish supplies for troops advancing into their country, and these would, therefore, have to accompany the force. They are not dependent on British territory. Since 1875 the *jirga* comes in when summoned, and on their return takes with them cloth purchased at Abbottabad. The principal hold we have over this tribe is two-fold; the power to attack them, and the knowledge we have gained of the valuable and accessible rice, wheat, and other crops cultivated by them in the Tikari valley; they hold one or two entire villages there, and shares in several others, all acquired by Pathan encroachment on the unwarlike Swatis.

During the Sikh rule they held the village of Shatut in the Agror valley, and they continued to occupy it until the expedition of 1868.

The Akazais have only in the last twenty-five years begun to give trouble. In the expedition against the Hassanzais in 1852 they afforded their neighbours but little assistance, nor did they appear openly against us in the Ambela campaign. They, however, took part in the attack on the Oghi *thana* in Agror in July 1868. They seem to have been chiefly incited to break with us by the insidious counsel of Ata Muhammad Khan of Agror, who represented that the location of a *thana* in Agror was but the forerunner of their independent village of Shatut being assessed highly like all the Agror villages.

The Chagarzais.

The Chagarzais are a section of the Malizai clan of the Yusafzai tribe of Pathans, being supposed to be descended from Chagar, the son of Mali, who was one of the sons of Yusaf. They occupy the country on both sides of the river, those cis-Indus being located on the western slopes of the Black Mountain immediately to the north of the Akazais. They are divided into the three sub-sections of Nasrat Khel, Basi Khel, and Firozais. Of these the two first mentioned are found on both banks of the river and are again subdivided as follows:—Basi Khel into Daud Khel, Shahu Khel, Khwaja Khel, Kalandar Khel, Kasan Khel and Babujan Khel; and Nasrat Khel into

Hanju Khel, Haidar Khel, Lukman Khel, and Badha Khel.[1] The Firozai are entirely trans-Indus, and occupy the slopes of the Duma mountain towards Buner.

The fighting strength of the Chagarzais is as follows:—

	Cis-Indus.	Trans-Indus.
Basi Khel	1,450	460
Nasrat Khel	620	1,180
Firozai		1,000

In addition to these numbers a religious body, the Akhund Khel, hold lands in the Chagarzai territory and are said to have about 960 fighting men, while other settlers in the district could produce about 640. The total fighting strength of the tribe may be taken as about 6,880 men.

The southern boundary of the cis-Indus Chagarzais is contiguous with the Akazais, and follows the spur of the Black Mountain which runs from the Machai peak to the Indus. The south face of this spur belongs to the Akazais, and the north to the Chagarzais. On the west and north the Indus forms the boundary, and on the east the Chagarzais are bounded by the Deshiwals and the Pariari Saiads.

The southern part of the Chagarzai country is occupied by the Basi Khel sub-division. Their principal villages are Pakban and Chamang. The best approach to the former is from the Machai peak. The descent to the Indus from Pakban is about the easiest descent from the crest beyond Chitabat, and mules could go by that route to Judba on the Indus, opposite to which was formerly a settlement of the Hindustani fanatics of Malka.

Succeeding Pakban to the north are the villages of Gugiani and Jalkai, in a small basin similar to that of Pakban, occupied by a colony of *Saiyids*. They only occupy the basin of one branch of a stream and the upper slopes. Below them the Nasrat Khels occupy Dumail and some lesser hamlets, as well as Judba on the Indus, and Bihar and the two large villages of Kabalgraon trans-Indus. Next comes another portion of the Basi Khels, occupying Kalish, rented from the Akhund Khels, but there are also some

[1] These sub-divisions of the Basi Khel and Nasrat Khel Chagarzais are not based on recent information and cannot be guaranteed as correct.—(*Editor.*)

families of Akhund Khels and Nasrat Khels. The village is on the top of a spur in the middle of a small plateau richly cultivated. This is about the largest village on that side of the Black Mountain. The descent to Kalish from the crest of the mountain is easy.

The characteristics of the Chagarzais are similar to those of the Hassanzais and Akazais already described, but they are considered braver.

In case of aggression the two sections above mentioned might be expected to afford aid, and help could also be obtained from Swat and Buner.

The chief wealth of the Chagarzais is in cows, buffaloes, and goats. Troops advancing into their country would have to take supplies with them.

No reliable information is to be had regarding the interior communications in their territory. The crest of the mountain and the Machai peak may be gained by advancing up the Kungali spur to Chitabat; but owing to the steep and rugged nature of the country, and the thick forest with which the whole of the upper portion of the hill is clad, an active enemy, well acquainted with the ground, would have every facility for annoying the troops and opposing the advance. About three miles north of Machai is the high peak of Ganthar, and the pass leading from Pariari to Pakban lies on the crest between these two points.

The ground here is broken and precipitous, flanked by thick pine forests, and in all probability is a strong position, from which the passage of a force advancing from Machai on Ganthar could be disputed. From this point, which lies in a deep hollow on the crest, the ascent to Ganthar, though steep in places and everywhere flanked by forest, is not of any great difficulty. Beyond Ganthar the advance along the crest would be easier.

The Chagarzais are in no way dependent upon British territory. They purchase cloth, copper and brass vessels, and indigo from us, but if they were under blockade they could obtain these articles through the intervention of other tribes. They have occasionally quarrelled with our subjects, and there have been some instances of forays and petty raids perpetrated by them, but we never came into hostile contact with them until 1863, when they joined the ranks of the Akhund of Swat at Ambela. They made one attack there on the "Crag" picquet, but being defeated, went straight off home again.

It was believed at first that they were principally concerned in the attack on the Oghi *thana* on the 30th July 1868, but Major F. R. Pollock, the Commissioner, stated that, as a tribe, they took no part in it, the Chagarzais who were present being some who were in the service of the Pariari Saiyids. On the occasion of the advance of the British troops in October 1868 to the Black Mountain, they, on the 4th, in company with other tribes, took part in a noisy demonstration of defence of the Mana-ka-Dana peak, but immediately retreated on the artillery opening fire, and on the 10th they gave in their submission. They also joined in the hostile demonstrations in the Indus valley in 1891.

Pariari Saiyids.

The Pariari Saiyids occupy two glens on the eastern face of the Black Mountain to the north of the Agror valley, from which they are separated by the Kungali spur; on the west side their boundary runs up to the top of the Machai peak; on the north they are bounded by Deshi, and on the east by Tikari. The whole of the land originally belonged to *Saiyids*, who are still the nominal proprietors, but a large number of the villages are held by Basi Khel Chagarzais, either by rent or mortgage. Settlers of nearly all the surrounding Pathan and Swati races are to be found in Pariari, the *maliks* of the villages being, however, invariably *Saiyids*, who, from their spiritual influence and position as original proprietors, exercise considerable influence over their tenants.

There are about 400 fighting men, *viz.*—

Saiyids	100
Basi Khel Chagarzais	200
Gujars, etc.	100

They have no reputation for bravery. They are constantly embroiled in internal feuds, but would at once unite to oppose a common enemy.

Water is plentiful, but a force would have to take supplies from Agror; this is, however, only three or four miles distant, and there is a road practicable for mules. The tribe deals and has relations with British territory, and a blockade would cause them serious injury, and an attack, *viâ* Agror, could easily be effected. A road from Mana-ka-Dana runs down the spur on to Bilankot, and so on to Chirmang and Trand. Troops passing by this route completely dominate the valley and the villages lying in it.

The tribe is most ignorant and intolerant, and has given some trouble on the border. In 1868, Major-General Wilde's force burnt some of their villages for the part they had taken in the attack on the Oghi *thana.* The leading *malik* at that time was Kudrat Shah, who was an active fomenter of disturbance against the British Government. In 1871, owing to some quarrel, the *Saiyids* were attacked by the Deshiwals and had to seek safety in flight, Kudrat Shah's own village being burnt by the enemy. Subsequently, having murdered his uncle and his uncle's children in the mosque, he was in his turn assassinated by a Chagarzai.

As the foregoing estimates of the fighting strengths of the various tribes include every able-bodied man from fifteen to fifty years of age, it is not to be supposed that the clans have been able to collect the numbers here given to oppose the various expeditions which have been despatched against them; also, most of these estimates are of recent date and, as some of the clans have increased their numbers of late years, it is possible that their actual strength was on former occasions less than here given. With regard to armament, at the time of the earlier expeditions described in this work, the weapons of the tribes were swords, shields, spears, and matchlocks. In 1891 it was ascertained that they possessed a certain number of muskets with percussion caps; and since that date they are known to have acquired a few breech-loaders.

Expedition against the Hassanzais of the Black Mountain, by a force under Lieut.-Colonel F. Mackeson, C.B., in 1852-53.

The first time the Hassanzai tribe came into notice was on the occasion of the murder of Messrs. Carne and Tapp, officers of the Customs Department. Up to this time no one (except perhaps Major J. Abbott, the Deputy Commissioner) had ever heard of their existence, but this act at once raised them to the first rank of border scoundrels.

Shortly after annexation, a preventive line was established along the left bank of the Indus, as far as British jurisdiction extended, to prevent trans-Indus salt being brought into the Punjab. In 1851 this line extended five miles beyond Torbela to a point on the Indus, where the cis-Indus territory of the Khan of Amb (Jehandad Khan) commenced.

During the autumn of that year, Mr. Carne, head of the Customs Department, desired to visit this border, with a view to any eventual extension of the line. The Board of Administration objected to the measure, and directed him not to go there.

During November, however, Mr. Carne, accompanied by one of his officers, Mr. Tapp, proceeded, against the advice of the district officer, Major J. Abbott, to reconnoitre the frontier. Having marched up the border, and returning towards Torbela, Mr. Carne dismissed all attendants, except a few of the men belonging to his own department. Shortly afterwards, the two officers, near the Hassanzai limits, but still within Jehandad's bounds, were murdered by a band of armed Hassanzais. These Hassanzais had no concern whatever in Mr. Carne's views, and even if the line had been extended, it would not have affected them. Afterwards, when called to account for the deed, they never pretended that they ever entertained any apprehension in regard to the salt line. The Hassanzais may have entertained some unjust suspicions regarding Mr. Carne's intention, but neither their bounds nor their rights were infringed, and they crossed into British territory for the purpose of murdering British officers in cold blood, because they were Englishmen, infidels, and defenceless travellers, with a little property about them.

As the murder happened in his fief, Jehandad Khan was called to account, and he at once delivered up such Hassanzais as he could find in his territory as hostages to the British authorities. The Hassanzais immediately made war upon him, and laid waste his border villages, seized his forts of Chamberi and Shingli, stirred up his subjects to rebel, and at last reduced him to considerable straits. It was evident that the whole tribe approved of the murder and sheltered the murderers. British interference became at last necessary, both to vindicate ourselves and to support Jehandad Khan, who had failed in his attempts to recover the forts of Chamberi and Shingli.

Orders were therefore given for the assembling of a force to punish the Hassanzais; and in December 1852 the troops, as per margin, were concentrated at Shergarh, under the command of Lieut.-Colonel F. Mackeson, C.B., Commissioner of Peshawar.

5th Troop, 1st Brigade, Horse Artillery (4 guns).
Mountain Train Battery (6 guns).
16th Irregular Cavalry.[1]
7th Company, Sappers and Miners.
3rd Native Infantry.[2]
Kelat-i-Ghilzai Regiment.[3]
Corps of Guides (4 companies).
1st Sikh Infantry.
Rawal Pindi Police (176 men).
Two regiments of Dogras (Kashmir).
Levies (1,760 men).

The force was formed into three columns and a reserve. The right column was placed under the command of Lieut.-Colonel R. Napier, Bengal Engineers (afterwards Lord Napier of Magdala), and consisted of 2 guns, Mountain Train Battery; 350 bayonets, Corps of Guides, under Lieutenant W. S. R. Hodson; 300 bayonets, 1st Sikh Infantry, under Captain G. Gordon; 176 bayonets, Rawal Pindi Police, under Lieutenant S. B. Cookson. The centre column, under Major J. Abbott, Deputy Commissioner, consisted of 2 companies of Police, 2 companies of Dogras and about 1,400 levies, with 5 *zamburaks*[4] and 6 wall-pieces. The left column, under Captain W. W. Davidson, 16th Irregular Cavalry, consisted of four guns, Mountain Train Battery, and the two regiments of Dogras, of the Kashmir Army. The remainder of the troops formed the reserve under Lieut.-Colonel J. Butler, 3rd Native Infantry.

On the 19th, a reconnaissance of Shingli was made, and on the 20th that fort was recovered without loss, and the next few days were spent in rendering it defensible; no attempt was made to hinder the work by the enemy, who occupied the heights above. Lieut.-Colonel Napier was at Chatta, Major Abbott at Shingli, Captain Davidson, at Shoshni, and the reserve at Shergarh.

During the rebuilding of the fort an advance might at any time have been forced upon the troops, for the posts of the Hassanzais and Akazais occupied the crest of the Black Mountain, and their picquets approached to within a few hundred yards of our posts at Chatta, whilst they waved their flags and flourished their swords in defiance, sometimes at Panj Gali, sometimes in front of Chatta, and sometimes at Pabal; and on the 21st a

[1] The present 12th Pioneers.
[2] Disbanded in 1861.
[3] Disbanded in 1882.
[4] Native wall-pieces.

reconnoitring party under Lieutenant Hodson was fired upon by the enemy's picquets near Chatta.

On the occupation of Shingli, Hasan Ali Khan, the chief of the Hassanzais, who had harboured the murderers of Messrs. Carne and Tapp, and had been the instigator of the attacks on Jehandad Khan's territory, sent in to say he had no objection to our rebuilding Shingli, but that the troops must at once be withdrawn. In reply he was informed that the force, after repairing Shingli, would march along the crest of the Black Mountain, over ground that was common both to the Hassanzais and Jehandad Khan, to the fort of Chamberi, and that on this march the troops would molest no one, unless they were molested and met with opposition; at the same time he was invited to send in a *jirga* to arrange amicably his hostilities with Jehandad Khan, which kept the British border in a state of disquiet, and which we were consequently very anxious to arrange, particularly as the cause of quarrel appeared to be Jehandad Khan having seized certain Hassanzais on our requisition. Hasan Ali Khan's answer was a refusal to send any *jirga*, and a warning that he could not restrain the thousands of allies, Chagarzais and Akazais, who had joined him, if the force moved as stated.

Plan of operations.

It was a question how the regular troops could be used as a support to most advantage. The orders of the Board of Administration were, that these troops were not to be employed on the mountain top at that late season, and at Shergarh they were in a confined, narrow valley, encumbered with impedimenta, double-poled tents, *doolies*, *palkies*, and hundreds of camels; in short, the column was equipped as if for an ordinary march and not for mountain warfare, and yet it had passed through mountain defiles to its present position and must pass through such defiles again, whatever direction it took. Lieut.-Colonel Mackeson determined, therefore, to throw off this support from his rear, and endeavour to pass it as quickly as possible into the valley of the Indus, more especially as it could there be used to turn the enemy's position on the crest of the mountain.

The heights the attacking columns would have to climb were so difficult that a hundred resolute men, not afraid to face disciplined troops, could have effectually stopped the bravest assailants.

To have attacked such heights in front without an effort to turn them would have savoured of rashness, and Lieut.-Colonel Mackeson preferred, therefore, to move the support round to the banks of the Indus, behind the Black Mountain, and thus to turn the position on the heights; and to let each column of attack trust to a small reserve of its own, and to the fort of Shergarh in the rear, if all were beaten back. Such was the plan proposed by Lieut.-Colonel Mackeson at this period of the operations.

Lieut.-Colonel Butler's column accordingly marched on the 24th and 25th December from Shergarh. Owing to the narrowness of the road through the defile to Darband, and the immense amount of baggage with the column, three instead of two marches had to be made from Shergarh to Darband, and it was fortunate that the points occupied by the irregular portion of the force at Chatta, Shingli, and Shoshni formed, with the assistance of intermediate posts, a complete screen, behind which the encumbered regular column laboriously, but securely, threaded its way through the mountain defile.

As already stated, Lieut.-Colonel Mackeson had determined not to ascend the Black Mountain till the regular brigade had been placed between the Black Mountain and the Indus, in sight of the Hassanzai villages in the plain, thereby threatening the rear of the parties who might oppose the columns on the mountain top. The weather had been very favourable; snow had not fallen and the nights were bright moonlight.

On the 27th, Lieut.-Colonel Mackeson made a reconnaissance, and from a height was enabled to obtain a view of the Hassanzai country. As a result of this he decided to alter his plans somewhat. The main force of the regular troops were to be placed at Baradar, with four companies in Chamberi, to make demonstrations on the heights in front of the latter place. It was considered that the enemy's hold of his position on the mountain would be sufficiently shaken by this disposition of the regular troops, and all idea of their movement, lightly equipped, up the banks of the Indus to a point in the rear of the enemy's position, was abandoned, as such a move would have entangled them in difficult ground; for the reconnaissance had shown that there was, with the exception of one spot below Kotkai, little plain between the Black Mountain and the Indus.

On the 28th December these dispositions of Lieut.-Colonel Butler's force were effected, and orders given for the advance of the three other columns on the 29th, Panj Gali being the point where they were ultimately to unite.

The columns were told they had nothing to fall back upon, and that the word must be "forward"; but that, in the event of a repulse, the right column should make good its retreat by Shingli towards the left column, and that all would then endeavour to reach Chamberi by keeping the road on the crest; or, failing that, to reach Baradar by the Nikapani road. The view Lieut.-Colonel Mackeson had of the Hassanzai country had convinced him that danger from a snow-storm was not insurmountable. The elevated plateau of Tilli, midway between the crest of the Black Mountain and the river Indus, would afford a resting-place, even for a month, free from snow, and nothing could have prevented supplies and reinforcements reaching that place from the plains, *viâ* Chamberi, so long as the force chose to remain there; further, the force in possession of that elevated plain could beat off all the tribes that could be collected against it.

On the 29th, the repair of the Shingli fort having been finished, the force advanced. The right column, under Lieut.-Colonel R. Napier, marched in the following order:—The advanced guard, consisting of three companies of the Guides, under Lieutenant W. S. R. Hodson, as skirmishers, with one company under Ensign F. McC. Turner as a support; the main body, consisting of 2 guns, Mountain Train Battery, and 300 bayonets, 1st Sikh Infantry, under Captain G. Gordon; the rear-guard, consisting of 176 bayonets, Rawal Pindi Police, under Lieutenant S. B. Cookson. The ground which the column had to traverse consisted of a rocky ridge rising for about a mile, and terminating in a small wooded hill which lay at the foot of the first steep ascent on which the enemy (apparently about 300 in number) were posted; shortly before daybreak a company of the Guides was sent to reconnoitre and to occupy, if undefended, the small wooded hill. This was successfully done, and proved a great advantage, as it enabled the column to advance from its position, through some difficult ground, without opposition.

The right column.

The first position held by the enemy was a steep and thickly-wooded shoulder of the mountain, rising abruptly for nearly a thousand feet, with some open ground near the summit. The enemy had made an abatis at the bottom of the ascent, from which they opened a matchlock fire whilst the guns were being brought into position. About 8 o'clock the guns opened with good effect, and, considerable impression having been made on the enemy, Lieut.-Colonel Napier gave the order to advance, whereupon the Guides rapidly ascended in skirmishing order, supported by the 1st Sikh Infantry, and cleared nearly the whole of the ascent. At this point the enemy, finding themselves unable to answer the fire, boldly charged the advanced skirmishers, whose eagerness had carried them a little too far beyond their supports, and drove them back in some confusion. Order was, however, quickly restored, and a firm advance up the hill drove the enemy from their point step by step. A bold attempt to make a second charge was checked by the guns and the leading companies of the Guides.

On the summit of the ascent was a fine piece of open tableland, upwards of a mile long and several hundred yards broad, beyond which the enemy retreated to the second steep ascent. After a short rest, the guns having closed up, the column advanced to the second hill, between which and the tableland was a hollow, studded with rocks and pine trees; the lower part of the ascent was similar to the previous one, but of a more rugged character, broken by inaccessible cliffs on one side and a dense wall of pine trees on the other, which confined the operations to a very narrow front. The enemy had felled a number of trees at the foot of the ascent to retain their assailants under fire, keeping themselves to the upper and more open ground. The skirmishers of the Guides were posted in the broken ground at the foot of the ascent, whilst the guns were being put in position; when they were ready to open, the advance was again made, covered by their fire. The skirmishers of the Guides, supported by a company of Sikhs, under Lieutenant C. H. Brownlow, on the left, and a party of Guides, under Ensign F. McC. Turner, on the right, crowned the heights. The enemy made several bold attempts to charge, coming within twenty paces of the skirmishers, but were unable to face the close fire of the rifles and the excellent practice of the Artillery, and at length abandoned their position, carrying with them their wounded.

The column had thus arrived near the summit of the Black Mountain, at a point where a broad spur, forming the top of the range occupied by the Akazais, branched off at an elevation of some 9,000 feet. By this ridge the enemy retreated. No further defence of the hill was made; a small party followed up the rear-guard, but were easily dispersed by Lieutenant Cookson. Shortly before sunset the advanced party of the Guides under Lieutenant Hodson arrived at the shoulder of the mountain above Panj Gali, where the main body of the enemy still held their position, but at the first appearance of the Guides they commenced a rapid retreat, pursued by the Kashmir troops. The main body of the right column did not reach this point till dark, when, it being too late to descend to Panj Gali, it bivouacked for the night. There was snow on the ground but the troops behaved with the utmost cheerfulness, and not a complaint was heard.

The centre column.

To turn now to the centre column. Major J. Abbott commenced his operations by sending on 500 men of the levies at 3 A.M. on the 29th to seize a hill which commanded his proposed line of advance; and, having given them three hours start, he marched about sunrise with two companies of Dogras, two Police companies, and about 900 levies, with the five *zamburaks* and the six wall-pieces. Having ascended about half-way to Panj Gali, the force came suddenly upon the main body of the Hassanzais, strongly posted upon a steep eminence in the centre of the main ravine. They formed what seemed to be a solid square of 600 matchlock men, their skirmishers lining the ravine, which could not be attacked from the front, as the forest and brushwood were so dense that the men had to cut their way at every step. Major Abbott therefore formed his line on a spur running from the hill above mentioned to the main ravine, when, after some skirmishing, he succeeded in turning the enemy's flank. The Hassanzais then fell back on a strong position at the head of the pass, followed by Major Abbott, who had been joined by the Gandghar matchlock men. At about 2 P.M., the left column, under Captain Davidson, effected a junction with this column, but the position of the enemy was so strong that Lieut.-Colonel Mackeson determined to await its being taken in reverse by Lieut.-Colonel Napier's column; on the appearance of the head of which column the Hassanzais retreated, followed by the Dogras, as already related.

The left column.

The left column, which was under the command of Captain W. W. Davidson, was accompanied by Lieut.-Colonel Mackeson. At 3 A.M. it commenced its march; on reaching the village of Agror, as the second regiment of Dogras had been detained by the guns, Captain Davidson pushed on with the first regiment, and, turning Pabal, found himself close upon a hill overlooking Tilli. Here a small picquet of the enemy fired upon the head of the column; they were immediately dislodged, and a strong party posted on the summit of the hill. At this place the column halted until the guns and the other regiment came up. About 2 P.M., the column, now complete, made good its junction with the centre one under Major Abbott, close to Panj Gali, when, as stated above, the arrival of Lieut.-Colonel Napier's column was awaited to turn the enemy's position.

On the 30th, the whole of the levies, with two companies of Dogras, were employed in destroying the Hassanzai villages. In the afternoon the different columns received orders to move to the plateau of Tilli, but, night coming on, the columns bivouacked on the hillside, and marched for Tilli the following morning in a light fall of snow; the Rawal Pindi Police being left to hold the crest of the mountain.

On the 31st, the work of destruction was continued; and the villages and hamlets in the deep glens between Abu and Tilli were destroyed. Shingri and other villages between Kotkai and Baradar, along the banks of the Indus, were burnt on the same day by Jehandad Khan and his Tanawalis, who had crossed over from Amb.

On the 1st January 1853, at daybreak, Major Abbott, being joined by Jehandad Khan and his people from Shingri, destroyed Kotkai; the enemy, aided by trans-Indus allies, following up the column as it retired. At 11 A.M., the whole force marched from Chamberi, *viâ* Panj Gali. On the following day the retirement was continued to Baradar, where the reserve under Lieut.-Colonel Butler was encamped.

The losses of the attacking columns were about fifteen killed and wounded. The enemy lost from fifteen to twenty killed, but the number of their wounded was not ascertained.

Lieut.-Colonel Mackeson, in his despatch on the above operations, said the hardships from exposure to cold and fatigue and from long fasting, were shared cheerfully and pretty equally by all the troops. He remarked that the fact of the highest summits of the Black Mountain having, when clad with snow, been climbed by British and Kashmir troops in the face of all the opposition that its mountain defenders could bring against them, needed no amplification, but would carry the conviction that those troops were resolute, and that their leaders were not easily appalled by difficulties. He particularly alluded to the Dogra regiment's equipment for mountain warfare; and their mode of carrying mountain guns, he said, was worthy of adoption. The men were ready to move at a moment's notice, and their blanket tents, which afforded sufficient protection for native troops during a few day's exposure, moved with them on the heads of coolies without causing any delay or obstruction.

The Indian Medal, with a clasp for the "North-West Frontier," was granted in 1869 to all survivors of troops engaged in the operations against the Hassanzais.

It being considered that the destruction of the Hassanzai villages, with all their grain, etc., had been sufficient punishment for the murder of the two British officers, the hostages in our hands, who had been seized by the Khan of Amb, were then sent back, and the tribe was informed "that the British Government did not covet their possessions, nor those of other neighbouring tribes, with whom it desired to be at peace; but that it expected the tribes would restrain individual members from committing unprovoked outrages on British subjects, and afford redress when they are committed; that when a whole tribe, instead of affording redress, seeks to screen the individual offenders, the British Government has no alternative but to hold the whole tribe responsible."

After this lesson the Hassanzais for a time remained quiet, and no overt act of hostility was committed by them. In April 1855 they had a dispute with the people of Agror relative to a marriage, and threatened to ravage that tract; but a message was sent reminding them of the lesson of 1852, and they desisted.

On the disturbances breaking out in 1863, which led to the expedition to Ambela,[1] complications with the Hassanzais again arose. In August of that year, instigated, it is supposed, by emissaries of the Hindustanis of Sitana, but some do not hesitate to say, incited to the movement by the Agror Chief, who was hostile to the Khan of Amb, they made a raid in force (500 to 600) on a nest of hamlets, rather than villages, in the Shingli valley on the eastern face of the Black Mountain, in which the most advanced outpost of Amb territory is situated. Seven hamlets were burnt, one man, who resisted, was killed, and some cattle were carried off. The fort of Shingli, which is in the midst of these villages, was not molested, but it was useless for the purpose of protecting them, as it had a garrison of only five men.

After this the Hassanzais appeared at one time to threaten an attack on Chamberi, and a portion of the Mada Khels crossed the Indus with the intention of assisting; but the frontier line having been greatly strengthened by the Amb authorities, the gathering broke up, and the Mada Khels re-crossed the river. Soon after an attack was made by the Hassanzais on the Amb troops on the Black Mountain border, and one jemadar and seven men were reported killed and six wounded.

In the first plan of operations, proposed in October 1863, for the expulsion of the Hindustani fanatics from Malka, it was intended that the force should afterwards cross the Mahaban mountain to the Indus, and punish the Hassanzais of the Black Mountain; but, owing to the unexpected course of events, this plan was not executed.

The Hassanzais subsequently waited on the Deputy Commissioner of Hazara at Darband, and entered into engagements which were adhered to till 1868, when they were induced by Ata Muhammad, Khan of Agror, to join in the attack on the Oghi *thana*.

Expedition against the Black Mountain Tribes by a force under Major-General A. T. Wilde, C.B., C.S.I., in 1868.

In November 1867 it was determined to establish a body of police in the Agror valley, and they were temporarily located in

[1] See Chapter VI.

the village of Oghi, until a fortified police post could be built. At daylight on the morning of the 30th July 1868, this body of police, numbering 22 men, was attacked by some 500 men belonging to the Chagarzai, Akazai, and Hassanzai tribes. The Saiyids of Pariari also took part in the raid. The enemy were, after a hand-to-hand fight, driven off, leaving six dead bodies in the hands of the police ; our casualties were, three policemen wounded, two horses killed, four carried off, besides other property plundered.

Troops were immediately called for from Abbottabad, and a force consisting of the Peshawar Mountain Battery and 350 men of the 5th Gurkhas, under Lieut.-Colonel O. E. Rothney of that regiment, marching from Abbottabad four hours after the receipt of the intelligence, reached Oghi before midnight on the 31st, having marched forty-two miles in twenty-five hours. Captain E. L. Ommanney, the Deputy Commissioner, was with Lieut.-Colonel Rothney's camp at Oghi, and on the 2nd of August he was joined by Akram Khan, the Chief of Amb, and a body of his levies. The cause of the raid was considered to be the intrigues of Ata Muhammad Khan, the Khan of Agror. This chief held a *jagir* in the Agror valley, which had been given to him by the Sikhs in 1841, and had been continued by the British Government on annexation. He was, however, discontented, and wanted to occupy a more independent position, like his neighbour the Khan of Amb. He had not disguised his dissatisfaction at the location of the police post in the valley, the establishment of which would have the effect of lessening his dignity, diminishing his influence, and repressing his unlawful exactions. He was, therefore, strongly suspected of having incited the independent tribes beyond the border to make the raid on Oghi, in order to procure the removal of the post. He was consequently seized by order of the Commissioner, and sent off under military escort to Abbottabad. His cousin, Aladad Khan, also a *jagirdar* in the Agror valley, being suspected of complicity, was likewise made a prisoner.

On the 4th August, orders were sent for the march of a squadron of the Guides Cavalry from Mardan to Abbottabad, and on the 5th the Commissioner and Brigadier-General Wilde, commanding the Punjab Frontier Force, recommended a native regiment being sent up from Rawal Pindi, and the working-parties of the

British regiments on the Murree and Abbottabad road being warned for service.

The following day a requisition was made for 200 of the men of the working-parties to be at once sent to Abbottabad, and three troops of the native cavalry regiment were asked for from Rawal Pindi. A wing of the 2nd Punjab Infantry was sent from Abbottabad to Agror, to reinforce Lieut.-Colonel Rothney, and the services of the Kashmir regiments at Muzaffarabad were also applied for.

In the meanwhile the following events had been passing in the Agror valley. On the 2nd August, as the enemy threatened the village of Dilbori, a small fort in the village was occupied by the Khan of Amb's men. The Akazais, Hassanzais, Tilli Saiyids, and the Swati clans had been ordered to send in deputations to the Deputy Commissioner, but the Akazais refused to come in, saying they had never done so to the Sikhs; the others replied they would do so, if all came in, and demanded the release of Ata Muhammad Khan. The following day Dilbori was again threatened, and the Agror and Swati levies, being sent out to support the Tanawalis, were led into a trap, and suffered rather severely.

On the 5th August, another attack was made on the village, when one or two houses were set on fire, but the enemy were driven off by the Tanawalis with some loss. On the 6th, Dilbori was again attacked, when, according to orders, the Tanawalis retired, setting fire to the fort,—their retirement being covered by Lieut.-Colonel Rothney's detachment, which had moved out from Oghi for the purpose. The enemy meantime fired six villages in the valley.

During these days the relations of the Khan of Agror had all left the valley, with the exception of his eldest son, who, on the night of the 6th, went over to the enemy, setting fire to his village before doing so. His flight was assisted by the Akazais of Shatut and others.

On the 7th, a general advance of the enemy took place, the Pariari Saiyids and Chagarzais acting in the centre of the valley, the Swati clans, who had now freely joined, acting along the Khabal hill, the Akazais and Khan Khel section of the Hassanzais acting on the Black Mountain. The Agror and Swati levies were, with very few exceptions, disorganized and untrustworthy, and

Lieut.-Colonel Rothney again moved out and withdrew the Tanawalis from a ridge in front of his camp (to which they had been withdrawn on the 6th), to the Manchura ridge, still nearer Oghi.

The whole of the Swati tribes beyond the border, except Allai, were now up and rapidly joining the ranks of the enemy, and our own Swati levies were deserting in numbers to their homes; some of the headmen of the villages had already gone off, whilst those that remained were not to be trusted. Six more villages close to Manchura had been burnt, and the rear of the position was threatened.

On the 8th, Lieut.-Colonel Rothney again moved out to cover the withdrawal of some advanced Tanawali pickets to Manchura and to the ridge to the north of Oghi, which had been shamefully abandoned by the Mansehra levies the night before. In the afternoon, when the troops, after locating the Tanawalis in Manchura, were returning to camp, the enemy moved down the hill in great numbers, and with yells charged down on the former place. The Tanawali horse made a most gallant charge up the hill, but were eventually driven out of Manchura, which was fired, as well as two other villages.

On the 9th, the force at Oghi was reinforced by a wing of the 2nd Punjab Infantry; 200 men of the working-parties (1-19th Regiment) having come down to Abbottabad. On the 10th, the villages at the foot of the Susal pass were burnt by the enemy. Lieut.-Colonel Rothney had no cavalry in his camp, and he could do little more than act on the defensive; but his great anxiety was in regard to his communications with Pakli, as the Susal pass was only held by levies, on whom no reliance could be placed. On the 11th, however, on the arrival of fresh reinforcements at Oghi, the pass was occupied by the 2nd Gurkhas from Rawal Pindi.

On the 12th Lieut.-Colonel Rothney, hearing that the enemy had determined to make a combined attack upon his camp, resolved to take the initiative. Accordingly, early on the morning of the 12th, he moved out with the mountain battery, 50 sabres of the 16th Bengal Cavalry, and 350 Infantry, in the direction of Banda, where the enemy were in strength. Two mountain guns and detachments of cavalry and infantry were left as a guard for the camp, a detachment of 50 sabres of the 16th Bengal Cavalry under Captain G. C. Ross sweeping round the valley. The enemy were in large clusters at Banda, and all along the base of the Khabal hill, and along the spur running down to Manchura. Lieut.-Colonel Rothney, having driven them from their position near Banda, forced them to retire up a spur of the Khabal mountain, where they made a stand in force on a small mound thickly covered with brushwood. He then ordered a rush to be made on this mound by two companies of the 5th Gurkhas, and one company, 2nd Punjab Infantry, supported by some Tanawali horse, and covered by the fire of the mountain guns under Major Hughes. From this position the enemy were driven with scarcely any resistance, and fled in all directions over the Khabal spur, followed by Akram Khan, the Amb Chief, with a body of his sowars. By 3 P.M., not a flag or an enemy was to be seen in the valley, although their numbers had previously been estimated at 3,000 or more. The troops were then withdrawn to camp without any molestation on the part of the enemy, and from this time no further attempts were made in the Agror valley.

The casualties in this affair had been six wounded, including Lieut.-Colonel O. E. Rothney and Major T. E. Hughes (the latter by an accident), besides six men and two horses of the levies wounded. The enemy had some thirty killed and wounded.

A few days before these events, the Deputy Commissioner had given permission to the Chief of Amb to hold communications with his partisans amongst the Hassanzais, which not only had the effect of creating suspicion of that tribe in the minds of the rest of the enemy, but caused the Hassanzais to refrain from taking any active part in the affair of the 12th.

The effects of this engagement, the arrival of British troops at Abbottabad, further reinforcements at Oghi, and the Kashmir regiments in the Pakli valley, enabled Brigadier-General Wilde on the 16th August to report that the safety of the Hazara district was secured, and that he only awaited the arrival of reinforcements to carry out any punitive measures that might be ordered.

Up to this date, twenty-one British villages, which for the most part lay in the irrigated part of the valley, had been burnt, and our total casualties had been sixty-four.

The Commissioner of the Division then recommended that a punitive expedition should be sent against the tribes of the Black

Mountain, and this proposal was strongly supported by the Lieutenant-Governor, who said that it was absolutely necessary for the security of the frontier and the vindication of the British character that the clans engaged in this outrage should be suitably punished for their invasion of British territory and their attack upon Oghi.

A feeling of uneasiness was at this time perceptible amongst the tribes trans-Indus, and news-writers from Kabul, Peshawar, and Swat agreed in prophesying coming disturbances, instigated from Swat along the Peshawar border, where for many months the Salarzai section of the Bunerwals had been blockaded for having, in February 1867, had the audacity to attack and burn the British village of Pirsai. The Commander-in-Chief therefore determined, instead of weakening the garrison of Peshawar, or drawing troops from the posts along the border, to supply the force for operations from the rear stations in the Punjab, and from the North-West Provinces; whilst the whole front of the border stations, which was held by the regular troops in Peshawar and by the Frontier Force along the border, was preserved intact.

D-F Royal Horse Artillery.
E-19th Royal Artillery.
2-24th " "
H. M. 6th Foot.
" 19th "
Two companies, 77th Foot.
16th Bengal Cavalry.
2nd Gurkha Regiment.
24th Punjab Native Infantry.

The troops, as per margin, had been already ordered from Rawalpindi to Hazara, and some of these had arrived to reinforce Lieut.-Colonel Rothney before the skirmish on the 12th August took place. On the march to Abbottabad the 6th Foot had thirty-eight men struck down by heat apoplexy, eight of whom died.

38th Foot.
2nd and 7th Companies, Sappers and Miners.
1st Gurkha Regiment.
4th Gurkha Regiment.
20th Punjab Native Infantry.
31st Punjab Native Infantry.

The troops, as per margin, were now ordered to march to Hazara. The 20th Punjab Native Infantry marched a distance to 232 miles from Lahore to Abbottabad, in ten days, in the month of August. The 38th Foot moved in like manner from Sialkot, and finally reached Darband. The 1st and 4th Gurkhas coming from the distant hill stations of Bakloh and Dharmsala emulated the exertions of the above corps and joined Brigadier-General Wilde in a wonderfully short space of time, considering the distance traversed. The 31st Punjab Native Infantry marched a distance of 422 miles, and the two companies of Sappers and Miners actually covered nearly 600 miles, by forced marches, in twenty-nine days.

Other regiments, as per margin, left their several stations of Campbellpur, Lahore, Aligarh, Amritsar, and Cawnpore, and took post at Rawal Pindi as the immediate reserve, with the exception of the 9th Bengal Cavalry, which was moved on to Darband. A line of telegraph was in the meantime ordered to be laid down to connect Abbottabad and Oghi with the general system of India.

20th Hussars.
9th Bengal Cavalry.
19th Punjab Native Infantry.
23rd Punjab Native Infantry (Pioneers).
30th Punjab Native Infantry.

The movement of these troops towards the frontier, and their gradual concentration in Hazara, had, even before any offensive movements had taken place, begun to affect most happily our political relations trans-Indus. The Akhund of Swat, conscious of past misdeeds deserving of retribution, evidently conceived that we had other objects beyond the punishment of the immediate offenders in the Black Mountain. As the direction of our objective seemed rather to threaten the valley of Swat, the Akhund immediately took action against the Wahabi Hindustanis, so long located on the slopes of the Mahaban, and headed by a chief generally stated to be Firoz Shah, son of the last king of Delhi. The expulsion of this colony, then located at Sitana on the Indus, was the cause of the expedition of 1858 under Major-General Sir Sydney Cotton (*see* Chapter V), and also, on its removal to Malka on the opposite slopes of the mountain, of the Ambela Campaign in 1863 (*see* Chapter VI); consequently it was but natural for the Akhund to look upon this hornets' nest as the possible object of further punishment. On the 26th of August a large force of the Akhund's Swat followers therefore attacked and defeated the Wahabi Hindustanis, and drove them from place to place until they sought refuge in the country of the Chagarzais trans-Indus. At the same time, at the dictum of the same high sacerdotal authority, the Salarzai Bunerwals, already referred to as under blockade for the burning of Pirsai, came in and sought terms of forgiveness from the British civil authorities in Yusafzai.

The territory of our ally, the Chief of Amb, had been frequently threatened by the trans-Indus clansmen of the hostile portion of the Hassanzai tribe, and on the 17th September the Mada Khels attacked the *Khan* in force, but were repulsed; it consequently became necessary to afford immediate support to this chief on the left flank of our front of operations. The 38th Foot, with the 9th Bengal Cavalry and the 31st Punjab Native Infantry, were therefore directed on Darband for this purpose, the whole under the command of Colonel F. A. Willis, C.B., 38th Foot.

On the 24th September the two companies of Sappers and Miners arrived at Abbottabad and completed the troops for the expedition. The force actually employed, which, exclusive of the reserve numbered 9,500 of all ranks, was disposed as shewn in the margin and was divided into two brigades, under the command of Colonel R. O. Bright, 1st Battalion, 19th Foot, and Colonel J. L. Vaughan, C.B., Bengal Staff Corps, with the temporary rank of Brigadier-Generals. The whole expedition was under the command of Brigadier-General A. T. Wilde, C.B., C.S.I., with the temporary rank of Major-General. The Maharaja of Kashmir also offered the services of 1,200 troops, and these were moved on to the Hazara Border, but did not take part in the operations on the Black Mountain.

Agror—
- D-F Royal Horse Artillery.
- E-19th Royal Artillery.
- 2-24th ,, ,,
- Peshawar Mountain Battery.
- Hazara ,, ,,
- 1st Battalion, 6th Foot.
- ,, ,, 19th ,,
- Guides Cavalry.
- 16th Bengal Cavalry.
- 2nd & 7th Companies, Sappers and Miners.
- Detachment, Telegraph Sappers.
- 1st Gurkha Regiment.
- 2nd ,, ,,
- 3rd Sikh Infantry.
- 2nd Punjab Infantry.
- 4th Gurkha Regiment.
- 20th Punjab Native Infantry.
- 24th ,, ,, ,,
- 5th Gurkha Regiment.

Darband—
- 38th Foot.
- 9th Bengal Cavalry.
- 31st Punjab Native Infantry.

With regard to the plan of operations, on the 25th August Major-General Wilde had submitted the following recommendations. The enemy, he said, were thus divided—

(1)—Hassanzais, Akazais, and Mada Khels.

(2)—Pariari Saiyids, Chagarzais.

(3)—Swatis.

With regard to the Hassanzais, they had not been as hostile (with the exception of the Khan Khel section) as the rest of the enemy. They had been defeated in 1852, and the good influence of the Khan of Amb having been brought to bear on them, they were already sending in to the Commissioner, saying they desired to treat. The Swatis, too, were also petitioning to be allowed to treat, and with the punishment of the independent tribes beyond the border, Major-General Wilde considered quiet would again be brought about. He proposed that, making the valley of Agror the base of his operations, a force should ascend to the crest of the Black Mountain which dominates all the spurs running north and west towards the river Indus, on which the lands of the Akazais and Chagarzais are situated; the Hassanzai territory being situated on the more southern slopes. At the same time, a corps of observation was to be placed at Darband as a moral support to the Khan of Amb, to distract the attention of the enemy, and to cut off, if possible, the retreat of the trans-Indus tribes if they crossed the river to aid their brethren on this side.

Major F. R. Pollock, the Commissioner, in his letter to Government recommending an expedition, had said that it would be difficult to explain how slowly the tribes accepted the fact that our long-suffering Government was really bent on coercing the border and calling them to account; and there seems no room to doubt but that the Khan of Agror had continuously led the tribes to believe that nothing would induce the Government to sanction a punitive expedition. When, however, our preparations and the formal declaration of our intentions altered their views, the people of Tikari and Nandihar spontaneously proffered payment of fines to expiate their offence, and even commenced to apportion amongst the members of their tribes, according to the means of each, the sums which they were led to suppose would be required of them; and by the time the force was prepared to advance, the representatives of these two tribes had come in and engaged to hold aloof, sending hostages to accompany our troops during their ascent of the Black Mountain.

The Hassanzais, who had, as already stated, entered into friendly communication with the Tanawali Chief as far back as the 10th or 11th of August, and had consequently held aloof from the affair on the 12th of that month, similarly sent in representatives, with apologies for those of their tribe who had offended, and with the assurance of their willingness to abide by the terms of their engagement entered into with Major H. W. H. Coxe at Darband at the close of the Ambela campaign (*see* Chapter VI).

It was true that they had not acted against us as a tribe, and there was force in what they urged, that in August they actually prevented their trans-Indus brethren, Mada Khels and others, from crossing to the Hazara bank and joining in the attack on the Agror detachment; that this was the case Major Pollock had ascertained reliably from other independent sources. Although the tribe was not, as it endeavoured to make out, free from blame, Major Pollock felt justified, looking to the importance of detaching them from the other tribes, in dealing leniently with them. They were directed, if sincere in their professions of friendship and submission, to tell off representatives to accompany the force through their country, and warned that, in the event of resistance being offered to our troops, they would be liable to the destruction of their villages and crops, and their representatives would be detained in custody.

Another significant proof of the overawing effect of the force assembling in Agror was afforded by the gradual return into British territory of the families and relations of the deported *Khans*—Ata Muhammad and Aladad Khan. The adjacent hills no longer afforded them safe asylum, and they preferred surrendering themselves to seeking shelter trans-Indus.

The troops in Hazara had, however, still to deal with the large Chagarzai and Akazai tribes; with the Deshi and Thakot Swatis; with the Pariari Saiyids and their followers; and not improbably with the Hindustani fanatics and large bodies of trans-Indus Pathans.

By the end of September the preparations for an advance were completed; the sick and weakly men were to be left at Oghi, where the camp remained standing, under the command of Lieut.-Colonel Rothney. The two Dogra regiments moved into the valley of Agror, to hold the following posts during the expedition, *viz.*, the Jalgali pass, the Susal pass, and the camp at Oghi. Preparatory to the advance of the troops into the mountains, proclamations were issued by the Commissioner, both to the cis-Indus and trans-Indus tribes, informing them that the object of Government was only to punish those guilty of committing outrages in British territory.

On the 1st October the Wahabi Hindustanis were reported to have crossed to the Hazara side of the Indus, to the village of Judba. On the same date Major-General Wilde reported that the presence of the brigade of troops at Amb, in support of the *Khan* of that place, had produced the effect of causing the Amazai and Mada Khel tribes to express a desire to make peace with that chief.

On the 3rd October the force marched out from the camp at Oghi. One day's cooked rations were carried in their haversacks by the troops, and seven days' supplies for the whole force were carried on mules.

The object of the first day's operations was to occupy the Jalgali pass, leading from the valley of Agror into those of Tikari and Nandihar, belonging to the independent Swatis, so as to secure through the Kungali village a line of communication with Oghi. The village of Kungali is situated a short distance up a spur of that name, by which it was intended one of the columns should ascend the Black Mountain. To effect these objects it was essential to carry the hills on both sides of the pass. Moreover, the movement would at once test the sincerity of the professions of neutrality which had lately been made by the Swatis of Tikari and Nandihar, as, since the commencement of hostilities, the enemy had always defiantly shown themselves on these hills.

Peshawar Mountain Battery.
H. M. 6th Foot.
2nd Gurkha Regiment.
3rd Sikh Infantry.

Brigadier-General J. L. Vaughan, C.B., commanding the 2nd Brigade, with the troops marginally noted, advanced by the direct road from Oghi as far as the village of Bagrian, situated at the foot of one of the spurs of the mountain, and the 1-6th Regiment and Peshawar Mountain Battery were there halted, whilst the 2nd Gurkhas, in skirmishing order, supported by the 3rd Sikh Infantry, advanced up the Kiarkot mountain, the crest of which was reached at 11-30 A.M., a few long shots only being fired by the enemy. In the course of the afternoon the Kiarkot mountain was occupied by the levies, and the troops then bivouacked for the night, preparatory to the ascent of the Black Mountain by the Sambalbat spur. The remainder of the 2nd Brigade joined Brigadier-General Vaughan at Kilagai.

Brigadier-General R. O. Bright moved with the marginally named troops on the village of Kungali, up to which point no opposition was offered. On arrival at Kungali, however, the enemy began to collect on a height above it. Although Brigadier-General Bright had received no instructions to proceed further than this place, he now determined to continue his advance, to prevent the enemy collecting in large numbers, and to disperse them. He consequently pushed on to Mana-ka-Dana, where he determined to spend the night.

Hazara Mountain Battery.
H. M. 19th Foot.
1st Gurkha Regiment.
20th Punjab Native Infantry.

Mana-ka-Dana is a shoulder of the Kungali spur, rising to a point in the centre, from which the ground descends to a small plateau, and then dips again at a steep angle until it joins a narrow and nearly level edge connecting it with the continuation of the ascent. The right of the ridge was very steep and broken, and thickly wooded. The high point in the centre was occupied by the 20th Punjab Native Infantry under Lieut.-Colonel C. H. Brownlow, C.B., and the small plateau beneath was held by strong picquets from that regiment. The Hazara Mountain Battery was on the ridge in rear, facing the village of Shatut. On the right rear of the peak the Bilankot spur joins the Kungali spur. This approach was held by the 1st Gurkhas under Major J. S. Rawlins, with the 19th Foot in support of them and of the guns.

The troops had not been long halted before the enemy began to fire upon the advanced picquets from the wooded and broken ground on the right flank. Some marksmen of the 19th under Lieutenant W. Bennett, Musketry Instructor, were sent to assist in dislodging them, the superior range of the Enfields and the good practice of the men having a telling effect. As dusk approached, the enemy again opened fire, and a little before nightfall made a really determined attack on the advanced picquets, but it was gallantly repulsed.

As the 1st Brigade pressed on to Mana-ka-Dana, the reserve and head-quarters moved forward and occupied the village of Kungali, with the 5th Gurkha Regiment posted in advance to maintain the communications with that brigade ; at the same time 400 of the Kashmir troops, with some wall-pieces, moved out from Oghi to hold the Jalgali pass.

From the increasing boldness of the enemy, Brigadier-General Bright supposed that, having now ascertained our line of approach, they were collecting in numbers, and really intended to dispute our advance in earnest; he accordingly applied for reinforcements, and the 5th Gurkhas under Major H. P. Close were pushed forward. reaching Mana-ka-Dana about midnight. In the meanwhile, Lieut.-Colonel Brownlow, who was with the advanced picquets, had been reinforced by two guns from the Hazara Mountain Battery, and was supported by four companies, 19th Foot. The guns did good service, as by shelling the ridge in front of the picquet the enemy were prevented from forming in force; and, although some demonstrations of renewed attacks were made, none of a really determined character took place. Our loss during the day had been two killed and six wounded.

On the 5th Gurkhas being sent forward, their place was taken by the 2nd Punjab Infantry, 200 of the Kashmir troops being brought up at the same time to Kungali.

Major-General Wilde had originally intended to ascend the crest of the mountain in three columns, the 1st Brigade advancing by the Kungali, while the 2nd Brigade and levies moved up the Sambalbat and Barchar spurs respectively, as a diversion. But the 1st Brigade having already gained the very advanced position of Mana-ka-Dana, the necessity for carrying out this operation in its entirety passed away; moreover, Mana-ka-Dana afforded an excellent temporary base for operations against the Chitabat and Machai peaks. The 2nd Brigade was therefore ordered to abandon the line of advance up the Sambalbat spur and support the 1st Brigade, leaving the levies to carry out their part in the original plan of moving up the Barchar spur.

At 2 A.M. on the 4th, the 2nd Brigade moved on to Mana-ka-Dana. As the day dawned, the enemy were observed to draw off from Brigadier-General Bright's vicinity to their own position, which was on a high grassy knoll, some 800 yards in front of Mana-ka-Dana. The approach to this knoll was along a narrow ridge connecting it with the Mana plateau, and below this ridge to the right, as well as round the knoll, was a dense forest of fir. Arrangements were made at once by Major-General Wilde to carry this position.

1st Gurkha Regiment.
5th Gurkha Regiment.
Hazara Mountain Battery.
Peshawar Mountain Battery.
20th Punjab Infantry.
1st Battalion, 19th Foot.
2nd Punjab Infantry.

Covered by the fire of D Battery, F Brigade, Royal Horse Artillery, which had come up on elephants, the 1st Brigade under Brigadier-General Bright moved out in the order marginally noted. After advancing some distance, the mountain batteries came into action on the ridge; a heavy artillery fire was thus directed on the enemy's position, and, as the 1st and 5th Gurkhas ascended the knoll and entered the abatis, few of its defenders remained to contest it. Continuing his advance Brigadier-General Bright reached Chitabat about 3-30 P.M. The last part of the road was nearly impracticable, and two mules belonging to the mountain batteries were killed by falling down the *khud*.

The casualties in the 1st Brigade were—1st Gurkhas, three men; 20th Punjab Native Infantry, two men; and 5th Gurkhas, two men, wounded.

The ground on the summit of the Chitabat peak was surrounded by thickly-wooded ravines, and breastworks were at once thrown up to resist an attack, in which work the two companies of sappers afforded material assistance.

Whilst these operations were going on, the levies under Shahzada Ibrahim Saduzai were ascending the Barchar spur. Near its summit they met with a faint resistance on the part of the enemy, from which five casualties occurred; but, the enemy retiring, the levies joined the 1st Brigade at Chitabat, and bivouacked there for the night.

On the evening of the 4th, the head-quarters and the 2nd Brigade (with the exception of the Peshawar Mountain Battery, temporarily attached to the 1st Brigade) bivouacked at Mana-ka-Dana, the 2nd Gurkha Regiment and 3rd Sikh Infantry being thrown forward to occupy the breastworks from which the enemy had been driven in the morning, and to keep open communication with the 1st Brigade.

On the morning of the 5th, the 1st Brigade, reinforced by the 2nd Gurkhas, and with both the mountain batteries, was ordered to advance from Chitabat, along the crest of the mountain, for the capture of the Machai peak.

There had been great difficulty in procuring water at Chitabat, and the rations for the British troops had been delayed owing to the badness of the roads ; so, until the men could get their breakfast, Brigadier-General Bright detached the 20th Punjab Native Infantry and 5th Gurkhas to take possession of a hill, called Doda, which intervened between Chitabat and Machai, and from which the enemy had fired upon the troops the preceding evening. At noon the remainder of the brigade marched off, and, joining these two regiments, proceeded towards Machai, the 2nd Punjab Infantry being left as baggage and rear-guard.

From Doda the road descends to the Machai Gali, flanked on each side by wooded ravines and broken ground. After descending about a mile, it opens out into a small level space, divided by a low rocky ridge from the base of the Machai mountain. The ravines and broken ground about the descent and plateau were held in considerable force by the enemy, who opened a fire upon the advancing troops; but the fire of the mountain guns, which came into action by alternate batteries, and the determined rush of the 20th Punjab Native Infantry, supported by the 5th Gurkhas, soon drove them off.

On reaching the rocky ridge at the end of the plateau, these two regiments were halted under cover, whilst arrangements were being made for carrying the Machai peak.

Major-General Wilde stated that he had never, in the border hills, seen such a naturally strong and defensible position as this peak. The ascent of the mountain was steep and rugged in the extreme. It could only be ascended with a narrow front, as the ground on the left was precipitous, and on the right thickly wooded. The following were Brigadier-General Bright's arrangements for its attack :—The two mountain batteries were brought into action in rear of the ridge where the two leading regiments were halted. The 20th Punjab Native Infantry was to lead the advance, closely supported by the 5th Gurkhas, with the 1st Gurkhas one hundred yards in rear, and the 19th Foot in reserve.

Covered by a most accurate and effective fire from the mountain batteries, the troops advanced, but the enemy retired as they came on, and with only eight casualties the position was taken, the enemy flying down the spurs into the valley bordering the Indus.

Whilst this assault was going on, the enemy, who had been dislodged from the Machai Gali, crept round the ravines to the rear, and began firing into a company of the 5th Gurkhas left in support of the guns; but these, being reinforced by four companies of the 19th, soon drove them off.

Brigadier-General Bright then made the following dispositions for the night:—The 5th Gurkhas to hold an advanced position on the Machai peak somewhat lower than the peak itself. The 20th Punjab Native Infantry, the 5th Gurkhas, and the Hazara Mountain Battery, in the centre of the position on Machai, with the 19th on a shoulder of the hill about 100 yards in rear, the plateau below being held by the 2nd Punjab Infantry and Peshawar Mountain Battery.

The whole of the troops were employed, whilst daylight lasted, in improving the defences.

The losses during the day had been—5th Gurkhas, one killed and two wounded; 20th Punjab Native Infantry, five wounded.

The remainder of the Hazara Field Force was echeloned as follows:—At Chitabat, the 2nd Gurkhas (which had been sent up there from the 2nd Brigade) and 800 levies; below Chitabat, 3rd Sikh Infantry; and at Mana-ka-Dana, the head-quarters of the force, the remainder of the 2nd Brigade, D-F Royal Horse Artillery, 2-24th Royal Artillery, and the Commissariat stores.

The night passed off with but little annoyance from the enemy. Below, rain fell; but on the Machai peak the night was bitterly cold, with snow as well as rain, and for the troops, who were without tents, it was one of great discomfort.

On the preceding evening only a scanty supply of water had been found on the Machai peak, but a good spring was discovered on the morning of the 6th on the eastern slope beneath the shoulder occupied by the 19th Foot. The supply was increased by opening fresh springs at the same spot, and by forming tanks, and eventually an ample supply for the whole force was obtained. Water was also found, but in small quantities, near the ground occupied by the 5th Gurkhas. A supply of good spring water had been obtained at Chitabat, and also at Doda, and Major-General Wilde, whose head-quarters had been moved up to Machai, was now in possession of the most commanding plateau of the range, and, with seven days' food and abundance of water, and with the line of communications with Agror secure, he was in a position to carry out any measures that might be necessary. Beyond the mere fact of our prestige among the hill-men having been considerably raised by the late events, the Major-General had in his hands the power of inflicting considerable damage and loss on all the villages of the Pathan tribes situated on the slopes near the top of the mountain; and while the troops held the ridge and upper spurs, it was easy to let loose the Hazara levies—men as light footed as the hill-men themselves—for this work of destruction.

The 6th was passed in making a road to the water, and up the crest of the mountain, to enable supplies and ammunition to be moved up; the 1st Gurkhas were also moved to reinforce the position held by the 5th Gurkhas. On the same day the Deshi *jirga* had come in to the Commissioner and submitted to the terms already given to their Tikari and Nandihar brethren, when they repeated what they had formerly asserted, that their country being so close to that of the Pathans, they had not dared to act in opposition to them until we had shown ourselves in a commanding position in the Pathan country.

On the 7th, the enemy having made no signs of submission, Major-General Wilde, with the concurrence of the Commissioner, ordered the 24th Punjab Native Infantry, under Lieut.-Colonel G. N. Cave, to move down the Bilankot spur from the camp at Mana-ka-Dana, to protect a large body of levies, who had been sent down to burn some villages of the Pariari Saiyids; this was accomplished with but little opposition, the troops and levies being back at their bivouacs before night

On the 8th and 9th October, the Pariari, Chagarzai and Akazai headmen waited on the Commissioner, leaving no tribe unrepresented, except the Thakot section of the Swatis and the Allaiwals; the latter, however, as a tribe, had held aloof from the attack on Agror.

On the 10th, assembling the *jirgas,* Major F. R. Pollock, the Commissioner, accepted their submission, and explained to the Akazais, who had taken a leading part against us, that the village of Shatut, within the British border, would in future be held by them as British subjects and assessed; hitherto, they had been allowed, as in the time of the Sikhs, to hold this rent-free and as an independent villages; in return for which they had been uniformly insolent in their tone towards us, and had for years past readily afforded an asylum to bad characters of the Hazara district. He also required their *jirga*, with the others, to accompany our force in token of submission, and as hostages for their good behaviour during our march through their country to the Agror valley, *viâ* the independent Swati tracts of Tikari and Nandihar.

With regard to more stringent conditions not having been imposed upon the tribes, Major Pollock was of opinion that the objects of Government had been fully attained when our troops, at a slight loss in killed and wounded to themselves, had gained the most commanding position in the country, and had thereby caused the enemy to submit. The *pardah* having been lifted, he thought that it was unnecessary to inflict further punishment, as so doing would only have prolonged the operations and in the end would have left the tribes sullen and discontented.

During the progress of the negotiations, a few flags belonging to the Swatis of Thakot were visible on a distant point of the mountain, and their presence gave the troops high hopes of a future encounter. The flags, however, disappeared as soon as the Swatis found that, consequent on their powerful allies, the Pathans, having concluded terms with us, the chance of opposing our troops with success was destroyed.

From the time of the first occupation of the Machai peak until its evacuation, the force remained undisturbed by the enemy, except by small parties of two or three creeping up under cover and firing at the picquets and sentries at night. The position of the 2nd Punjab Infantry on the plateau below the hill was, from the nature of the ground, most exposed to these attacks, and scarcely a night passed in which they had not a man killed or wounded. During this time the troops were continually employed in improving the defences and making roads to the other positions. The experience gained by the 19th in making hill roads during the summer months[1] here came into play, and the way in which the regiment hutted themselves gave a further proof of the benefit they had derived from being so employed.

[1] They had been employed with the working-parties on the Murree and Abbottabad road.

Terms having been made with the Black Mountain tribes, the 11th and 12th were passed in the withdrawal of the troops and commissariat stores to Mana-ka-Dana. On the 12th the Machai peak was finally evacuated. Not a shot was fired, nor was any loss incurred as long as the force was moving in Pathan lands. The deputation of the tribes accompanied the troops and remained, from that time to the end, faithful and true to their engagements. On approaching, however, to within a mile of the bivouac at Mana-ka-Dana, an attack was made on the rear-guard, consisting of a party of the 2nd Gurkhas Regiment under Lieutenant A. Battye, by some of the followers of the Pariari Saiyids, and the enemy suffered a loss of two killed and several wounded, without any casualty on our side. Except this incident, and the cowardly wounding, by the same miscreants, of a servant of the Commissariat, in the forests below Chitabat, nothing occurred to interrupt the evacuation of the Black Mountain.

It was at one time hoped by the Major-General and the Commissioner that during the course of the operations on the Black Mountain some blow might be inflicted on the Hindustani fanatics, who were known to number some 600 or 700, and were occupying the village of Bihar, on the right bank of the Indus, opposite to the Chagarzai village of Judba, whither they had moved after their expulsion from Buner. But after seeing the country on the western slopes of the Black Mountain, any such enterprise was not, in Major-General Wilde's opinion, feasible. Had the Hindustanis combined with the Pathan tribes (as there was a fair chance at one time of their doing) to resist our troops, an opportunity of defeating them would have occurred. They could not, however, come to any agreement with the tribes. To have sent a column against them was impossible, owing to the inaccessible nature of the country near the Indus where they were encamped, and, when terms had been given to the other tribes, to have attempted an attack would have been a breach of our engagement. When the Chagarzai *jirga* waited on the Commissioner, they voluntarily began by saying they would not give asylum to the fanatics, and to have made their expulsion one of the terms of peace with that tribe would have resulted in prolonging the war without any advantage, since there were no means of cutting off the retreat of these men.

During the 13th October the force halted at Mana-ka-Dana, and the *Saiyids* were called upon to make reparation for the attack on the rear-guard, and the wounding of the Commissariat servant; but without avail.

1st Gurkha Regiment.
2nd Punjab Infantry.
24th Punjab Native Infantry.
5th Gurkha Regiment.

Peshawar Mountain Battery.
Hazara Mountain Battery.
6th Foot.
3rd Sikh Infantry.
4th Gurkha Regiment.

On the 14th, therefore, when the head-quarters and the rest of the force (with the exception of four regiments, as per margin, which were sent under Lieut.-Colonel C. H. Brownlow, C.B., to occupy the village of Kungali and the Jalgali pass) moved down to Chirmang in Tikari, a flying column from the 2nd Brigade under Brigadier-General Vaughan, consisting of the troops noted in the margin, with a body of levies, and accompanied by Captain Ommanney as Political Officer, was detached for the purpose of punishing the Pariari villages.

From the villages of Bilandkot there was a descent into a deep intervening ravine, crossing which, the crest of the Pariari spur was gained by Brigadier-General Vaughan's detachment, without opposition, after a very laborious ascent. The crest was held by the troops (with the exception of a portion of the 6th Foot and the Hazara Mountain Battery, which had been left below Bilandkot to cover the retirement), whilst the police and levies were employed burning the Pariari village of Garhi; this was effected with very slight opposition, after which the troops were withdrawn to the camp at Chirmang without any attempt at molestation by the enemy.

On the 15th, the force under Major-General Wilde marched to the village of Tikari, where it was joined by two squadrons, 16th Bengal Cavalry, from Jalgali. The following day was spent in making a road over the Shabora spur, which divides Tikari from Nandihar. The troops at the Jalgali pass were employed in improving the road through it, and the 1st Gurkhas from Jalgali, and a squadron 16th Bengal Cavalry from Tikari, were sent to Chirmang to keep open the line of communications.

On the 17th, the force marched to Maidan, in the Nandihar valley, which was found to be highly cultivated, even high up on the ranges dividing Nandihar from Allai. In Tikari some little difficulty was at first experienced in reassuring the people, but as the march through it had been attended with no act of oppression or spoliation, the Nandiharis remained quietly in their villages, and firewood, forage, etc., were freely brought into camp. In his despatch Major-General Wilde specially adverted to the excellent conduct of the troops, both British and Native, on this occasion: he said that, on entering the valleys of the independent Swatis, he had announced that as they had submitted as suppliants, and as a fine of Rs. 12,000 had been imposed upon them, all supplies of food and forage were to be paid for, and no plundering could be allowed; and although the transition from war to peace in the feelings of the native soldier is no easy process, yet not a complaint was made, nor a single man punished in the force from the time it left the camp at Oghi till its return. On the 19th, the force moved to Phagora at the head of the Nandihar valley, and a shot having been fired from the hillside after dark as the rear regiment approached camp, the *maliks* of the neighbouring villages were arrested and taken on, and subsequently released at Oghi on payment of a fine of Rs. 500, as a punishment for the outrage.

The following day the force re-entered British territory, crossing a low range into the Konsh valley, and on the 22nd Oghi was reached, the troops having been absent from their baggage since the 3rd of October.

The total casualties on our side amounted to five Non-Commissioned Officers and men killed; one British officer (Lieutenant W. H. Unwin) and twenty-eight Non-Commissioned Officers and men wounded.

On the 24th October, a *durbar* was held in Agror by the Lieutenant-Governor of the Punjab, when the title of *Nawab* was conferred on the young Tanawali Khan, and on the following day the *jirgas* were dismissed to their homes and the prisoners released.

The Indian Medal with a clasp for the "North-West Frontier" was granted in 1870 to all those who actually took part in the advance under Major-General Wilde, including the force under the command of Lieut.-Colonel Rothney, which was previously engaged with the enemy at Oghi.

The Khan of Agror, at the beginning of the disturbances, had been sent into Rawal Pindi, that his conduct might be investigated, and his *jagir* had been declared forfeited on account of his treasonable conduct, and he was banished to Lahore.

In spite of the expedition narrated above, the raids in the valley did not cease. In July 1869, two hamlets in Agror—Barchar and Gulderi—were burnt by a party of raiders, consisting of Hassanzais, Pariari Saiyids, and Akazais, partisans of Ata Muhammad Khan, and four of the villagers were killed and seventeen wounded. The raiders were, however, gallantly repulsed by the men of Jaskot, a neighbouring village. In August, Jaskot itself was attacked, and several of the villagers and a police constable killed.

In consequence of these outrages, a force, as per margin, under the command of Colonel O. E. Rothney, C.S.I., was moved out from Abbottabad, a detachment of the 23rd Pioneers were ordered to march to the Susal pass to improve the road, and a blockade was established against the offending tribes.

Half Hazara Mountain Battery	..	72 men.
4th Punjab Cavalry	..	27 „
3rd Punjab Infantry	..	282 „
5th Gurkha Regiment	..	296 „
Total		677 „

On the 7th October 1869, Colonel Rothney, moving out from Oghi with the greatest secrecy at half-past two in the morning, destroyed the village of Shatut, belonging to the Akazais. The troops were delayed between Jaskot and the base of the hills by watercourses and rice cultivation, and Shatut was only reached at 6 A.M. Most of the cattle had been driven off, but a few, with a large amount of property, fell into the hands of the troops. No resistance was attempted, and the troops retired without molestation.

The lands of Shatut were then declared confiscated, and a formal proclamation was issued prohibiting the Akazais from occupying it again.

It was now determined that a force should be permanently stationed in the valley of Agror, sufficient to meet all attacks, and, if possible, to follow up raiders beyond the British border: and an order was passed by the Supreme Government removing the Agror valley from the jurisdiction of the ordinary courts and the operations of the general laws.

During the winter of 1869-70 the valley was unmolested, but as soon as the snow melted on the Black Mountain, raids recommenced. The first was on the 9th April, when Barchar was attacked by a party of Akazais, and the headman killed. On the 15th, the village of Sambalbat was burnt by Akazais and Khan Khel Hassanzais, and on the 23rd the village of Bholu shared the same fate. As the villages were all situated on the slopes of the Black Mountain, our troops, who were encamped in the valley, were powerless to prevent these outrages, nor could they avenge them without crossing the border, and committing the Government to the probability of a frontier expedition; but the presence of the troops undoubtedly prevented more extensive outrages, and secured the safety of the villages in the valley. The force in Agror consisted now of detachments of the 3rd Punjab Infantry and 5th Gurkhas, and two mountain guns, under Colonel Rothney. On the 25th April, the crops around Shatut were destroyed by him.

Meanwhile, Captain E. G. Wace, the settlement officer in Hazara, had been engaged in the preparation of the "record of rights" for the Agror valley, and had instituted a close enquiry into the nature and history of the landed rights of Ata Muhammad Khan, the ex-Khan of Agror; the result of these enquiries being that Ata Muhammad Khan was shown to have received but scant justice at the hands of the British Government with regard to his rights in Agror. He was accordingly pardoned and allowed to return.

No special responsibility for the peace of the border had devolved upon the Khan by his restoration; his responsibility was merely that of a proprietor of seven-tenths of the valley, bound to act with the utmost loyalty, and support, as far as lay in his power, the civil and military authorities. The general feeling in Agror, and even beyond the border, was one of satisfaction at the restoration of the *Khan*, and the state of the valley justified the withdrawal of the troops late in the autumn.

On the restoration of the Agror Chief, the Akazais hoped to be admitted to a share in his property, and these hopes were in all probability encouraged by Ata Muhammad Khan. The decided action of the Government, however, in absolutely refusing to permit them to rebuild Shatut, or to cultivate the land belonging to it, proved to them that their expectations were never to be realised; while the evident fear which Ata Muhammad Khan had of them encouraged them to commit raids in British territory.

The first hostile action was taken by another, though a friendly, tribe—Firoz Khan, a leading *malik* of the Hassanzais, attacking several of the Agror villages. The demonstration was, however, premature, and completely failed.

On the 4th June 1871, about 2 A.M., a raid was made on the villages of Kongu, Gulderi, and Bholu, in Agror, by a party of Akazais, numbering in all about 180 men. The raiders came down in two parties, one of which, numbering about eighty men, under a *malik* named Zarif Khan, partially burnt the village of Kongu, which is situated under the Chitabat ridge. After setting fire to this village, these raiders moved off to join the other body. This second body, numbering probably about 100 men, came down the Barchar spur and attacked Gulderi. From this village they met with little or no opposition. The men who were garrisoning the towers in the village, after having fired two or three shots, beat a hasty retreat on Jaskot. One of them was, however, wounded by the raiders. These latter then burnt the whole of Gulderi, except the *musjid*, and then proceeded to Bholu, which they also set on fire.

The raid was the act of the Akazais alone, and did not appear to excite the sympathy of the neighbouring tribes. Matters were, however, complicated by the Khan of Agror, who, without any authority, and indeed in direct opposition to the reiterated orders of Government, sent 300 men across the border to attack a small village called Ali Khan, in the Tikari country, which the Akazais held on a sort of service-tenure. This village, with two hamlets belonging to it, Ata Muhammad Khan burnt, and returned to Agror without loss.

This violent and mischievous act on the part of the Khan, who had been prohibited from carrying his quarrels across the border line, brought down upon him the grave displeasure of Government. He was well aware that there was no intention on the part of the Government to move troops across the border, yet he deliberately circulated a story to the effect that such an expedition was in preparation ; while, by his attack on Ali Khan, he hoped to force the Government to adopt active measures against his enemies.

In spite of this outbreak on the part of the Agror Chief, his conduct gradually became more reasonable and more in accordance with what was hoped would be the result of his restoration to his *jagir*. His position on the border, however, was a difficult one. He was not able to put many fighting men into the field, and, on his first restoration, found it difficult to establish his authority in such a manner as to enforce proper obedience to his calls on his tenants for service. The character of the inhabitants of Agror is such that it is difficult for any chief to use them for the defence of the border. In this favoured valley it may be truly said "man alone is vile," for a more gaunt, hungry, mean lot can scarcely be seen anywhere. Their physique is described as wretched, and their moral attributes are no better. They do not care to fight even in defence of their own villages, and, on the approach of an enemy, prefer to drive off their cattle, leaving their houses, or rather their huts, to be burnt.

During the year 1872, several offences were committed on the Agror border by the Akazais, but none of these were of a serious nature, although they showed the spirit of disaffection in the tribe on account of Shatut.

At the beginning of 1873 a section of the Hassanzais made a raid upon Nikapani (a village in the territory of the Nawab of Amb), in which four villagers were killed and six wounded. The raid was the result of inter-tribal disputes, with which the Nawab, part of whose territory lies beyond our border, was mixed up. The aggressors were punished by a retaliatory attack. On the 30th August another raid was made on the village of Harian, also in the territory of the Nawab of Amb. The raiders were Khan Khel Hassanzais, and the result was the death of one man and the plunder of a few cattle.

On the 1st July of the same year an attack was made by the Akazais, aided by the Nasrat Khel Chagarzais, on the village of Barchar, in the Agror valley; the raid was planned in revenge for the confiscation of the village of Shatut.

During 1874 the differences between the Nawab of Amb and the Khan Khel section of the Hassanzais, aided by the Tilli Saiyids continued, and raids were made by both parties, but with insignificant results. During this year the Akazais continued to give trouble on the Agror border. They threatened Agror throughout the summer, and harrassed the valley by keeping up a constant fear of raids; they carried off cattle from Ghanian, and burnt houses, and carried off property in Gulderi and Kungali, British hamlets on the slopes of the Black Mountain. On the 23rd of May, 1875, the Akazais, Khan Khels and Nasrat Khels made a combined attack upon the village of Ghanian; the village was defended by a small body of police and by Ghulam Haidar Khan (son of Ata Muhammad Khan) and some followers from Jaskot, and they succeeded eventually in beating off the enemy. On our side two villagers were killed, and two mounted men and four horses belonging to the Khan of Agror were wounded. The enemy were said to have had ten men wounded—six severely and four slightly.

After this, resort to military coercion appeared inevitable, but in September of this year (1875) the Akazai *jirga* came into the Deputy Commissioner and made a complete and unreserved submission. They renounced all claims to the disputed lands of Shatut, expressed regret for the past, and pledged their faith to respect in future British territory and British subjects. In December the Hassanzais also came in to the Deputy Commissioner at Haripur, one party through the instrumentality of the Nawab of Amb, and the other and more important body of their own free will. Both parties agreed to respect British territory in future. Accidental circumstances favoured the submission of both these tribes. An attack of the Hassanzais upon the Akazais induced the latter to come in, while the inconvenience of their consequent isolation compelled the submission of the Hassanzais themselves.

The year 1875 saw the submission to the British Government of the Black Mountain and other tribes (Chagarzais, Hassanzais, Akazais, Tikariwals, Allaiwals, and the Saiyids of Pariari) who, since 1868, had set the Government at defiance; and the arrangements made on this border received the special commendation of Her Majesty's Secretary of State. Towards the end of the year, Ata Muhammad Khan, Khan of Agror, owing to whose intrigues many of the Hazara complications had arisen, died, and was succeed by his son, then a minor.

Our further dealings with the Black Mountain tribes, subsequent to this date, will be dealt with in the next chapter.

APPENDIX A.

Hazara Field Force, 1868.

Major-General A. T. Wilde, C.B., C.S.I., commanding.

Staff.

Major C. C. Johnson, Assistant Quarter-Master General.
,, J. Morland, Assistant Adjutant-General.
Lieut.-Colonel H. C. Johnstone, in charge of the Survey.
Captain W. K. Elles, 38th Foot, Deputy Assistant Adjutant-General.
,, F. J. N. Mackenzie, Staff Officer, Punjab Frontier Force.
Major W. H. Paget, 5th Punjab Cavalry, Aide-de-Camp.
,, W. Fane, 19th Bengal Lancers, Orderly Officer.
Lieutenant L. R. H. D. Campbell, 19th Foot, Orderly Officer.
,, W. B. Holmes, Field Engineer.
,, J. A. Armstrong, Assistant Field Engineer, in charge of Telegraph.
Deputy Inspector-General of Hospitals G. E. Morton, Principal Medical Officer.
Lieut.-Colonel A. D. Dickens, Commissariat Department.

Artillery.

Colonel E. Atlay, commanding.
Major T. E. Hughes, Orderly Officer.
Lieutenant R. McG. Stewart, Adjutant.

1st Infantry Brigade.

Brigadier-General R. O. Bright, commanding.
Captain E. W. Evans, 19th Foot, Brigade Major.
Lieutenant J. E. Buller, 91st Foot, D. A. Q. M. G.
,, F. S. S. Brind, 19th Foot, Orderly Officer.

2nd Infantry Brigade.

Brigadier-General J. L. Vaughan, C.B., Commanding.
Captain J. G. Cockburn, 6th Foot, Brigade Major.
Lieutenant W. S. A. Lockhart, D. A. Q. M. G.
,, J. D. Macpherson, 3rd Punjab Cavalry, Orderly Officer.

CHAPTER IV.

BLACK MOUNTAIN TRIBES.—(Continued.)

In discussing our dealings with the various Black Mountain tribes subsequent to 1875, it will be convenient to begin by detailing the history of each tribe individually up to the time of General McQueen's expedition in 1888.

Chagarzais and Pariari Saiyids.

In 1884, the Pariari Saiyids, with their Chagarzai tenants, began to cause disturbances, and several raids were undertaken in the cause of Abdulla Khan of Dilbori. It is necessary to explain that Abdulla Khan's father, Aladad Khan, had been selected to manage part of Agror during the troubles which preceded the Expedition of 1868, and in the subsequent settlement of the valley had received from the Khan of Agror six villages on a lease, the terms of which appear to have been very disadvantageous to the latter. This arrangement, combined with other matters, eventually led to a quarrel between the successors of the two chiefs, and in April 1884 Abdulla Khan left Dilbori and crossed the border into the territory of the Pariari Saiyids, who, together with other Black Mountain clansmen, espoused his cause. On the 9th and 10th May a large body of these raided into the valley and were encountered by a force of levies. In the fighting the Khan of Agror had one man killed and four wounded, and the raiders were dispersed with three men wounded.

It was now decided in consultation between the military and the civil authorities:—(1) To leave the defence of the Agror border for the present to the Agror levies, supported by troops; (2) to occupy the Susal pass leading into Agror by levies from Mansehra, so as to set free the Khan of Agror's men; and (3) to call on Samandar Khan, *jagirdar* of Garhi Habibulla, to take measures to protect Konsh from attack. The district authorities at the same time reported that the *Khan's* levies were untrustworthy, and that most of the inhabitants of Agror preferred Abdulla Khan to the Agror Chief.

Other outrages were committed, and on the night of the 12th May 1884 the village of Belai (or Belian), in Agror, at the foot of the Barchar spur, was unsuccessfully attacked by a party of Abdulla Khan's supporters, including a few Akazais. On the 19th June, the Pariari Saiyids and Chagarzais made an attack on Dilbori, while the Akazais and Khan Khel Hassanzais attacked Belai, a second time, (*see* page 143). The attack on Dilbori was badly managed and ill-sustained, and the raiding party, under Abdulla Khan himself, was driven back over Mana-ka-Dana and out of British territory. No casualties were reported on either side.

In consequence of these repeated outrages on the Agror border orders were issued in July 1884 for the confiscation of the allowance (Rs. 592) granted to Abdulla Khan, and he was at the same time proclaimed an outlaw.

At the same time the Pariari Saiyids with their Chagarzai tenants were ordered to be placed under blockade. At the beginning of September 1884, reports were received of the arrival of a large body of Chagarzais in the Pariari country. They belonged to the Basi Khel section of the tribe and their numbers were estimated at between 300 and 400 men. In consequence of these reports advantage was taken of the relief of the Oghi post, to detain the old garrison, thus raising the strength of the post from 100 to 200 rifles.

This year and the one following it (1885) witnessed an advance in the internal defence of the Agror valley, and at the end of the latter year the Khan had a body of 100 men, armed with Enfields, who were dressed in uniform and well disciplined. The thirty police stationed at Oghi had also been armed with Enfields and seventy of these rifles had been distributed to the villagers. All the principal villages had been walled and provided with loopholed towers, the roads had been repaired, and the villagers taught to rely upon themselves.

On the 12th September 1884 some 1,000 Chagarzais, joined by Akazais and others, with standards, collected on the spurs of the Black Mountain above the villages of Ghanian and Dilbori, about four miles distant from Oghi. Accordingly the detachment, strength as per margin, under the command of Lieutenant A. A. Barrett, 5th Gurkhas, moved out from the Oghi post

	Rifles.
2nd Sikh Infantry ..	75
5th Gurkha Regiment	75
Police	25

and drove back the Chagarzais, with a few volleys, when they descended from their position about 5 P.M. The approach of darkness obliged the troops to return to Oghi for the night ; and after dark the Chagarzais made an attack on Ghanian, but were repulsed by the inhabitants, this village having been lately fortified for self-defence.

At 5 A.M. on the 13th, Lieutenant Barrett, with the same force as before, returned to Ghanian, accompanied by the Deputy Commissioner, and finding that the enemy had failed in their attack, determined to assault their position. Leaving thirty rifles in the village as a reserve, and detaching the police to a hamlet on his left flank, Lieutenant Barrett, with 120 rifles, advanced towards the spur in front of the village. In moving forward he was obliged first to descend into an intervening ravine, and, seeing this, the enemy mistook his intention and imagined he was retreating. They, accordingly, advanced down another spur, but were met by the fire of the police detachment, who had been joined by the men of Ghanian. Meanwhile the Deputy Commissioner had directed the Khan of Agror's men to advance from Dilbori towards the Kungali pass on which were a large number of standards.

On reaching the crest of the ridge, Lieutenant Barrett came in sight of the enemy ; but at his first volley they dispersed, and, seeing the simultaneous advance of the Agror levies and the police, they abandoned their whole position, and eventually disappeared from the hills, making for their own homes.

Thus, before 11 A.M., the whole force of 2,000 men were cleared off the hills by the determined conduct of the small detachment of troops, aided by the police and levies. There were no casualties on our side, and, beyond a few houses partially burnt in Ghanian, no injury was inflicted on Agror by this raid. The enemy's loss was estimated at six killed and twenty wounded.

In consequence of this raid the Chagarzais as a tribe were included in the existing blockade of the Akazais and Pariari Saiyids. On the night of the 5th November, Dilbori was attacked, but the defenders succeeded in repelling their assailants, and when the Oghi garrison and the police turned out at daylight to proceed to the assistance of the village, the raiders had disappeared. The enemy left behind them four men dead, and are said to have carried off two corpses and four wounded men. On our side four were killed and one severely wounded. The attacking party consisted of some two or three hundred Chagarzais and Pariari Saiyids, and included Abdulla Khan and his brothers.

In October 1884 full *jirgas* of the Chagarzais and Pariari Saiyids came to Abbottabad and made their submission. A fine of Rs. 800 was imposed on the Chagarzais and Rs. 600 on the Pariari Saiyids. These fines were paid on the 13th January 1886, and the thirty members of the two tribes, who had been detained, under the blockade, at Rawal Pindi since March 1885, were released. Both tribes gave hostages for their future good behaviour, and were at the same time informed that they would be held responsible for the good conduct of Abdulla Khan and his brothers across the border. The blockade against the Chagarzais was successful mainly owing to the co-operation of the Nawab of Amb.

Towards the end of 1886 it became apparent that the lenient treatment adopted in the settlement of 1885 had failed, and the Chagarzais, when they realized that Abdulla Khan and his family would obtain nothing from Government, sent insulting and menacing letters to the Deputy Commissioner.

On the 11th July 1887, a raid was made on the village of Bagrian, and some cattle, which were being carried off, were killed to avoid pursuit. The loss of the cattle was estimated at Rs. 400, and blood-money for lives lost at Rs. 600. In consequence of this raid, a *baramta* [1] was announced against the persons or property of the Pariari Saiyids and their Chagarzai tenants.

Hassanzais.

With regard to the Hassanzais, after the year 1875 they began to give less trouble on the border. In 1880 their chief, Ahmad Ali Khan, was murdered; a conflict then arose between Hashim Ali, his younger brother, supported by the Mada Khels and part of the Akazais, and Firoz Khan, the rival and murderer of the deceased chief, supported by a part of the Akazai tribe. The latter, however, was forced to seek refuge in the territory of the Nawab of Amb. In March 1882, Hashim Ali surprised the village of Kulakka, near Oghi, at night, and took the fort of one Muzaffar Khan, and his brother Samandar Khan, who were both charged by the Hassanzai *Khan* with complicity

[1] *Baramta* means reprisals, or forcible seizure of persons or property in retaliation for a wrong done to anyone.

in the murder of Ahmad Ali Khan. After a determined resistance, Muzaffar, Samandar, and one of their servants were killed, the attacking party returning unmolested to the hills. For this raid a fine of Rs. 2,000 was imposed on Hashim Ali and the Hassanzais were informed that they were responsible, as a tribe, for their chief's future good conduct. During the disturbances on the Agror border in 1884 a few of the Khan Khel section joined in the second attack on Belai (*see* next page), but the remainder of the tribe was actively hostile to this party, and up to the year 1887 their general conduct gave little cause for complaint.

On the 9th January 1889, however, a serious raid was committed by followers of Hashim Ali on Udigraon, a hamlet in the Agror valley. Two British subjects were killed and two kidnapped. The unconditional surrender of the two latter was at once demanded by Government, and the tribe was reminded of their joint responsibility. To this message some of the Hassanzai *maliks* sent a defiant answer, while Hashim Ali himself ignored it. Evidence was subsequently forthcoming, which seemed to implicate the Khan of Agror and his Agent, Fazil Ali Khan, in this raid. The charges against these two men were investigated, and as a result the latter was arrested, and the former summoned to Abbottabad, whence he was sent to Lahore.

As the Hassanzais, as a tribe, showed no intention of compelling Hashim Ali to surrender the men carried off, orders were passed on the 10th April for the whole tribe to be blockaded, and it was directed that the Pariari Saiyids and their Chagarzai tenants should also be included. The Akazais had already been under blockade since 1884. On the 1st June the Oghi garrison was reduced to 100 rifles.

Akazais.

After the settlement in 1875, the conduct of the Akazais became more satisfactory. The *jirga* at that time consented not only to a relinquishment of Shatut, but to its occupation and cultivation by others, our own subjects, amongst whom it was proposed to divide it. Action, however, was deferred in the first instance at the request of the Akazais, and the scheme was subsequently allowed to fall out of sight. It was felt that although the suggestion had been accepted by the tribe at the moment when they were inclined to submit, yet they were still likely to give trouble if its occupation should be attempted. The lands were consequently allowed to lie uncultivated, and the site of the village remained uninhabited. This state of things was considered undesirable and unsatisfactory, and in 1882 the Commissioner of Peshawar recommended that on certain conditions, the British Government should consent to the re-occupation of the Shatut lands by the Akazais.

As a preliminary to any agreement, the tribe was required to arrange for the destruction of the crops, which, in contravention of the agreement of 1875, had been cultivated on a portion of the Shatut lands by Zarif Khan, *malik* of the Painda Khel section of the tribe. This condition was fulfilled, and the crops were cut and handed over to the British authorities. A small party of the tribe, however, under Zarif Khan, refused to accept the agreement, and the offer to restore Shatut was consequently held in abeyance. Later, in 1884, this party joined the Pariari Saiyids in the attack on Belai on the 12th May, as already mentioned; and on the morning of the 19th June 400 Akazais and 40 Khan Khel Hassanzais descended the Barchar spur to attack Belai a second time. The villagers, however, came out to meet them and, after a fierce hand-to-hand fight, drove them back up the hill. The Swatis lost four killed and fourteen wounded, while the raiders left three of their number dead on the ground. In consequence of these raids the whole tribe were placed under blockade in common with the Chagarzais and Pariari Saiyids.

The Akazais aided the former tribe in their attack on Ghanian on the 12th September 1884, and took part in the fight on the following day in which the hillmen were driven back and dispersed by the small detachment under Lieutenant A. A. Barrett; further, when the Pariari Saiyids and the Chagarzais made their submission in October 1885, they were not joined by the Akazais, who, on the 3rd November and the 4th December 1885, committed raids on outlying hamlets on the slopes of the Black Mountain.

The blockade imposed upon this tribe continued in force, but did not press on them so heavily as in the case of the Chagarzais and Pariari Saiyids, no members of their tribe having been detained, and none of their property having been confiscated. They were able to obtain their supplies through the Hassanzais and Mada Khels, and the blockade really did not injure them, excepting that they had to pay a little more for salt and other supplies.

During 1886 and 1887 the Akazais continued under blockade, but did not give trouble as a tribe.

On the 18th June 1888, however, a serious affair occurred on the Agror frontier, which resulted in the death of two British officers and four men of the 5th Gurkhas. Early on the morning of the 18th June, Major Battye, 5th Gurkhas, with sixty men of his regiment and nineteen police, accompanied by Captain Urmston, 6th Punjab Infantry, left Oghi fort and ascended the Barchar spur, to make himself acquainted with the features of the surrounding country, the water-supply, etc. Shortly before reaching the crest and while still within British territory, the party was fired on by some Gujar graziers who were tenants of the Akazais. The fire was not returned, and Major Battye pushed on towards Chitabat keeping within our own territory; but, finding the enemy were becoming more numerous and their fire heavier, he decided to retreat, and accordingly the retirement of the party was ordered, covered by a small rear-guard. A havildar in the rear-guard having been wounded, the two British officers went back to his assistance with a stretcher. While they were putting the wounded man into it, the enemy charged, and in the hand-to-hand fight which ensued Major Battye and Captain Urmston were killed. The main body in the meanwhile, unaware of what had happened, continued their retirement down the mountain side. Subadar Kishenbir, who had been with the officers, though himself wounded, succeeded in escaping, and, rejoining the main body at the village of Atir, led them back and recovered the bodies of the two officers. Four of the Gurkhas were left dead on the field and six rifles were lost. Of the enemy six were killed.

Affair on the Agror frontier, 18th June 1888.

The Khan Khel Hassanzais and the Pariari Saiyids, on hearing the firing, turned out and joined in the attack on the detachment as they were retiring. The latter came to Mana-ka-Dana and fired at long ranges at our men retiring down the Chorkalam spur. Of the former, Hashim Ali with a party of some sixty men took up a position to cut off the retreat of the troops, if they should come down the Barchar spur. He was here attacked by the Jaskot villagers and driven back with a loss of two killed one being his own nephew. On our side one of the Jaskot men was killed. The Khan of Agror's levies, who occupied a tower on the Sambalbat spur, do not appear to have given any assistance.

After this affair, a large body of the Hassanzais, of nearly all sections, collected with Hashim Ali on the crest of the Black Mountain, between the Sambalbat and Chajri spurs; the Akazais assembled in force above the Barchar ridge and at Chapra, and a contingent came from Pariari. Plans were daily discussed as to how and where to attack Agror. On the 27th June, the aged Maulvi Abdulla with 120 Hindustanis from Maidan joined the Hassanzais on the crest, and it was then decided that no action should for the present be taken by the tribes; and on the 28th and 29th June the gathering dispersed. On the 7th July, the garrison of Oghi was again reduced to 100 rifles.

The Punjab Government now urged very strongly the necessity of sending a military expedition to the Black Mountain. The Lieutenant-Governor pointed out that the occurrence of the 18th of June formed a strong *casus belli* against the Akazais, and expressed his opinion that the fact that two British officers having been killed and stripped in a savage and disgraceful manner constituted an incident which must be regarded, considering our position on the border, as gravely aggravating the importance and urgency of the case. Sir James Lyall was, further, strongly of opinion that until military action had proved to the Khan Khel Hassanzais and the Akazais that their country was not beyond our reach, and that we had the power to punish them, negotiations would not lead to any satisfactory settlement with the tribes. Under these circumstances the Government of India once more took into consideration the question of punitive measures against the Black Mountain tribes, and on the 29th August an expedition was decided on.

Expedition against the Black Mountain tribes by a force under Brigadier-General J. W. McQueen, C.B., A.D.C., in 1888.

The above punitive expedition to the Black Mountain was formed on the 7th September 1888, and was officially styled the "Hazara Field Force." Brigadier-General J. W. McQueen, C.B., A.D.C., was placed in command, with the temporary rank of Major-General, and the force consisted of the marginally named troops, making a total strength of 272 officers and 9,144 men. The troops were organized in two brigades under the command of Brigadier-Generals G. N. Channer, V.C., and W. Galbraith respectively, and each brigade was subdivided into two columns. In addition to the above a field reserve was formed, consisting of one regiment of cavalry, and two battalions of infantry.* A detail of the staff is given in Appendix A.

2 Mountain Batteries, British.
1 Mountain Battery, Native.
1 Company Sappers and Miners.
4 Bns. British Infantry.
9 Bns. Native Infantry, including 1 of Pioneers.

Head-quarters and the 1st, 2nd and 3rd Columns were directed to concentrate at Oghi in the Agror valley by the 1st October and the 4th Column at Darband on the Indus by the same date. The Nowshera Brigade was at the same time ordered to be held in immediate readiness for field service. Infantry battalions were to take the field 600 strong. For baggage, staff officers were allowed half, and regimental officers one-third, of a mule. British and native non-commissioned officers and men were allowed 16lb of baggage and followers 10lb each, and no tents were taken. Seventy rounds of ammunition per rifle were carried in the pouch and thirty on mules per rifle with corps; the 4th Column taking sixty rounds with it on mules instead of thirty. A reserve of 100 rounds per rifle was established at the base. Artillery reserve ammunition was taken in full. With regard to supplies, five days', with two days' grain for all animals, were ordered to accompany the 1st, 2nd and 3rd Columns, and seven days' to accompany the 4th Column. All equipment and supplies beyond Oghi and Darband was to be carried on mules.

The Maharaja of Kashmir having offered the services of his troops to the Government of India, two battalions of these, with two guns, under the command of General Indar Singh, were ordered to join the expeditionary force.

Similarly the Khaibar Rifles having volunteered to take part in the operations, a detachment 300 strong, under Major Muhammad Aslam Khan, Sirdar Bahadur, C.I.E., were directed to proceed to Oghi to join head-quarters.

* 89 officers and 3,138 men, including the Kashmir Contingent.

By the 1st October the Hazara Field Force was concentrated at Oghi and Darband as ordered.

The instructions of the Government of India for the conduct of the operations may be summarized as follows :—

(1) To coerce into submission the Akazais and the Khan Khel Hassanzais.

(2) All other tribes and sections upon the Black Mountain not to be molested if they remained quiet.

(3) The punishment to be inflicted upon any other tribes or sections, which might join against us, to be for the consideration of the General Commanding.

(4) The march to Thakot to be reserved for further orders.

(5) When once the operations had begun, the General Commanding, while governing his operations as far as possible in accordance with the above, to have authority to act (in communication with the Chief Political Officer accompanying the force) according to his own judgment, in dealing with any development of the situation which might arise.

Subsequently, authority was received by Major-General McQueen to march on Thakot, and to visit the Allai country with the object of settling the outstanding demands against the Allaiwals.[1]

Previous to the advance, proclamations were issued to the several tribes, informing those against whom the operations were intended that their submission would be accepted up to midday on the 2nd October, while the others were told that, so long as they refrained from interfering with our columns, no damage would be done to them.

The period of grace allowed having expired on the 2nd October and the tribes not having submitted, orders were issued for the advance of the whole force; but owing to the equipment of some of the corps not being complete it was found necessary to postpone the commencement of operations for twenty-four hours.

The final orders for the advance of the different columns were as follows :—

Plan of campaign.

No. 1 Column to move on the 4th to Mana-ka-Dana, and the following day to Chitabat, leaving a sufficient force at Mana-ka-Dana to protect their line of communications

[1] *See* page 86.

No. 2 Column to advance up the Barchar spur on the 4th, occupying Barchar; thence moving on 5th to the crest of the ridge; one regiment to be at once detached to the left to meet No. 3 Column.

No. 3 Column to advance up the Sambalbat spur to the village of the same name, which was to be occupied on the 4th. The advance to be continued to the crest on the 5th. The 24th Punjab Infantry and two guns Derajat Mountain Battery to move up the Chatta spur, meeting the remainder of No. 3 Column on the morning of the 5th at the junction of the Sambalbat and Chatta spurs. The Khaibar Rifles to advance up the Chajri spur between Nos. 2 and 3 Columns on the 5th.

The 4th Column to advance on the 4th to the neighbourhood of Kotkai on the Indus.

To begin with the operations of the 4th Column under Colonel A. C. W. Crookshank, C.B.: on the morning of the 3rd October the enemy in large numbers attempted to occupy a ridge about 1,000 yards to the north of Chamb, but were anticipated by the 4th Punjab Infantry and were driven back with a loss of two killed and four wounded, there being no casualties on our side. The road down to Bela on the Indus was on this day made practicable for baggage animals.

4th Column.

Action of Kotkai.

On the morning of the 4th, the whole column crossed the frontier and advanced to the Indus by the road which had been made the previous day; the right of the advance being covered by three companies of the 4th Punjab Infantry, who occupied the ridge to the north, with orders to move over it and rejoin the column at the village of Shingri, leaving a strong picquet on the crest till the baggage and rear-guard had passed. The column advanced at 6-30 A.M. in the order noted in the margin, followed by the whole of the baggage, including seven days' supplies in regimental charge, escorted by four companies of the 29th Punjab Infantry, two of which formed the rear-guard.

- 2 companies, Royal Irish Regiment.
- Brigade head-quarters.
- 2 guns, 2-1 Scottish Division, Royal Artillery.
- 3 companies, 34th Pioneers.
- Head-quarters, 4th Column.
- Royal Irish Regiment.
- 2 guns, 2-1 Scottish Division, Royal Artillery.
- Gatlings.
- 3 companies, 4th Punjab Infantry.
- 3 companies, 29th Punjab Infantry.
- Regimental reserve ammunition.
- 1 company, 29th Punjab Infantry.
- Field Hospital.
- Telegraph.

Total strength 51 officers, 2,400 men.

At 8 A.M. the head of the column reached the river bank, and a halt was made to allow the troops in rear to form up on the open ground.

At 9 A.M. the advance was continued to Shingri, about a mile distant, which was found to be occupied by a few of the enemy. The advanced guard was accordingly halted and extended, two companies of the Royal Irish to the left of the village and two companies of the 34th Pioneers on a spur to the right, and the village was then carried with trifling opposition. A few of the enemy fired from the rocks and jungle above the village, but were driven off by a company of the 34th Pioneers, gallantly led by Subadar-Major Chattar Singh Bahadur, who was here mortally wounded.

At 10 A.M. the troops were again formed up in column of route and continued the advance across a sandy plain for a distance of about a mile, when large numbers of the enemy with many standards were discovered in position, their front line being across the open ground between the hamlet of Towara and the river, their main body holding a rocky ridge one mile long extending to the village of Kotkai, while numerous skirmishers lined the ravines and ridges of the hills on the right of the advance. At many commanding points strong *sangars* had been constructed, and similar defences on the opposite bank of the Indus were held by sharpshooters, supported by some useless guns of a reported calibre of four inches.

Having reconnoitred the enemy's position, Brigadier-General Galbraith, who was with this column, directed Colonel Crookshank to prepare for the attack by clearing his flanks. This was accordingly done; the 34th Pioneers searching the wide belt of jungle and boulders between our left and the river, while the 4th Punjab Infantry scaled the difficult heights on our right and drove the enemy from every point of vantage. In this operation Captain O. C. Radford, 4th Punjab Infantry, was severely wounded, but continued to lead his men until ordered to desist.

The advance was necessarily very slow, but at 1 P.M. the guns came into action against a wood held by the enemy some 600 yards to the front. The Royal Irish Regiment had lined a low wall, one company on the left, the remainder on the right front of the battery and machine guns.

At 1-30, the enemy's position having been well searched by artillery and machine gun fire, and the flanking parties being abreast of the line, the Royal Irish advanced, without firing a shot, and charged the enemy, Lieutenant W. Gloster distinguishing himself by rushing to the front and capturing a standard.

At this moment a body of *ghazis*, who had been concealed in a masked *nala* running diagonally towards our left front, made a desperate attempt to break through our line. All were at once shot down by the Royal Irish and the gatlings, except thirteen, who were followed and accounted for by two companies of the 29th Punjab Infantry and 34th Pioneers in the jungle near the river.

Eighty-eight dead were subsequently counted at this spot, among whom forty-eight were identified as Hindustanis.

During the advance of the Royal Irish, Brigadier-General Galbraith and his staff were between them and the leading company of the Pioneers; the latter were firing in the direction of Kotkai, and while Major J. A. Barlow, D. A. A. G., conveyed an order to the Royal Irish to fix bayonets, the Brigadier-General sent Captain C. H. H. Beley, D.S.O., D. A. Q. M. G., to direct the Pioneers to enfilade the position attacked. In pointing out what was required this officer unfortunately rode a little in front of the party, while they were emerging from a *nala*. He thus became the first object of the *ghazi* rush, and, his horse being cut down, he was overpowered by numbers and fell mortally wounded.

The enemy in and around Kotkai now began to show signs of wavering, and the guns having advanced and taken up a new position opened fire on the rocky ridge in front of Kotkai, the village itself, and the *sangars* on the both banks of river; the gatlings, meanwhile, swept the crest of the hills in front of the 4th Punjab Infantry, and, as the defenders streamed downwards, followed them with a galling fire. The enemy made little reply except from the right bank of the river, whence the Hindustani guns and sharpshooters kept up a fairly constant but ineffectual fire until nightfall.

At 3-30 P.M., the enemy was in full flight towards Kanar and four companies 29th Punjab Infantry, supported by a wing of the Royal Irish Regiment and two guns, occupied the village at 4-30 P.M. without opposition. The village is perched on the top of a high conical peak of rocks on the left bank of the river and completely closes the valley at this point.

At 5 P.M. Colonel Crookshank returned to Towara, where the remaining troops and baggage bivouacked, brigade head-quarters being established at Kotkai.

The casualties on our side during the day were five killed and ten wounded, while the enemy's loss was estimated at about two hundred.

1st Column.
Hazara Mountain Battery.
Half 3rd Company, Sappers and Miners.
2nd Battalion, Northumberland Fusiliers.
3rd Sikh Infantry.
1st Battalion, 5th Gurkhas.

We will now turn to the operations of the Agror columns. On the morning of the 4th October, the 1st Column, troops as per margin, under Colonel J. M. Sym, 5th Gurkhas, advanced at 6 A.M. from Dilbori in accordance with the plan of operations already detailed, and reached Mana-ka-Dana as 10-30 A.M., having only met with slight opposition. As soon as it was dark, parties of the enemy commenced firing into the bivouac, and this continued in a desultory sort of way throughout the night and caused a few casualties. At 11 P.M. an attack was made on that part of the bivouac where the commissariat establishments were located, and five followers were severely wounded with swords before the enemy were beaten off. Seventeen mules were also reported to have been stolen during the night.

2nd Column.
3-1 South Irish, R.A. (4 guns).
1st Battalion, Suffolk Regiment.
Wing, 34th Pioneers.
40th Bengal Infantry.
25th Sikhs.
2 Gatlings.

The 2nd Column, troops as per margin, under Colonel R. H. O'Grady Haly, accompanied by Brigadier-General Channer, V.C., and the head-quarters of the 1st Brigade, advanced up the Barchar spur from the camp at Kulakka on the morning of the 4th and reached the position assigned to them near the village of Barchar without meeting with any opposition.

3rd Column.
3-1 South Irish, R.A. (2 guns).
Derajat Mountain Battery (2 guns).
Half 3rd Company, Sappers and Miners.
2nd Battalion, Royal Sussex Regiment.
14th Sikhs.
24th Punjab Infantry.

The 3rd Column troops as per margin (with the exception of the two guns, Derajat Mountain Battery, and the 24th Punjab Infantry), under Lieut.-Colonel M. S. J. Sunderland, moved from camp at Kulakka up the Sambalbat spur and bivouacked above the village of that name. No opposition was met with during the advance. Major-General McQueen and the head-quarters accompanied this column.

The two guns, Derajat Mountain Battery, and the 24th Punjab Infantry, under Major Young, moved up the Chatta spur on the same date, and there bivouacked.

The Khaibar Rifles remained at the foot of the Sambalbat spur ready to advance up the Chajri spur the next day, their baggage accompanying the 3rd Column.

On the evening of the 4th all the columns had thus reached their appointed positions. During the early part of the night heavy rain fell, which caused considerable discomfort to the troops in bivouac.

On the 5th October, the 1st Column, leaving two companies of the Northumberland Fusiliers and two companies of the 3rd Sikhs to garrison Mana-ka-Dana, advanced at 6-30 A.M., and occupied the crest at Chitabat at 9-30 A.M., but the rear-guard did not reach camp till 7 P.M.; the path which ran along the northern side of the spur having to be made practicable for baggage animals, while the working-parties were exposed to fire from the enemy concealed among the trees. After dark the enemy continued to fire into the picquets, but without effect. Very little water was found on this day in the neighbourhood of Chitabat.

The 2nd Column continued its advance on the 5th up the Barchur spur, and, having met with but slight opposition, bivouacked on the crest to the south of Bampur Gali.

The 3rd Column moved at 6-30 A.M. on the same date from the village of Sambalbat and continued its advance up the spur. The ascent was very steep and two battery mules rolled down the hill and were killed. At the junction of the Sambalbat and Chatta spurs, the column was joined by the 24th Punjab Infantry and the two guns Derajat Mountain Battery. At 8 A.M., the Sussex advanced on a steep bluff in front, which was occupied by the enemy, and covered by the fire of the guns, took possession of it with slight loss. Pushing on, the column eventually reached the crest of the main spur at Nimal, where it was joined by the Khaibar Rifles, and where it was decided to bivouac for the night. The Chajri spur, by which the latter had ascended, proved to be steep and precipitous.

On the 6th October, owing to the difficulty of obtaining water and fodder for animals at Chitabat, all the baggage mules of the 1st Column were sent down to Dilbori under escort of six companies of the 5th Gurkhas, and arrived there without any mishap. Two guns of the Hazara Mountain Battery were sent back as a reinforcement to the four companies of infantry left at Mana-ka-Dana. At the same time a small column, strength as per margin, under the command of Lieut.-Colonel Vincent, Northumberland Fusiliers, was despatched in the direction of Doda to search for water and forage. This movement was also calculated indirectly to secure the safety of the convoy. A plentiful supply of water was discovered in the *nala* to the north of the bivouac about 450 feet below it, and some forage was found near the village of Landa. To secure both it was necessary that the Doda hill should be cleared of the enemy, who were annoying the parties at the water-supply. This was accordingly done by the two companies of the Northumberland Fusiliers, supported by the 3rd Sikhs. The former then advanced over the crest and down the other side towards Machai, leaving the 3rd Sikhs on the crest. Before the Fusiliers had returned to the crest, about thirty or forty of the enemy coming through the forest opened fire at close range on the 3rd Sikhs, who quickly advanced and drove them down the hill, and the Fusiliers, coming round, took them in flank and killed several of their number. The advance was then continued down the spur to the east by the 3rd Sikhs, supported by the Northumberland Fusiliers, as far as the village of Landa, which was burned. The crops about the village were cut and sent back to camp, and the water-supply was thoroughly opened up. The total loss to the enemy was estimated at thirty killed and wounded. A quiet night was the result.

Northumberland Fusiliers, 2 companies.
3rd Sikhs, 3 companies.

The 2nd Column, on the 6th October, moved along the crest to Nimal and occupied the bivouac vacated by the 3rd Column, which advanced from Nimal towards Seri, the 14th Sikhs leading. The road lay along the crest for about $1\frac{1}{2}$ miles and then turned abruptly to the right down a steep spur. It had to be made by the Sappers and working-parties nearly the whole way, and consequently progress was extremely slow. The path lay through thickly wooded forest, in which the enemy carried on guerilla warfare, but did not appear in any large numbers.

The 14th Sikhs, with Major-General McQueen and the head-quarters staff, reached the hamlet of Kaima at midday, and, as it was impossible for the baggage to get further than this point before darkness set in, it was decided to bivouac here for the night. Kaima consisted of two small plateaux with a few huts. The map of this part of the country, which had been compiled from native information, was found to be altogether incorrect, and the country in front to be far more difficult than had been supposed. From Kaima smoke could be seen ascending from the Seri villages, which had been set on fire by the Khan Khel Chief, Hashim Ali Khan, and his people, probably in the hope of thus avoiding a visit from our troops and also to save himself from the disgrace of having his villages burnt by us. Our casualties during the day were one killed and eight wounded.

On the following day, the 7th, having found that the nature of the country rendered it difficult to move a large body of transport animals till the roads had been improved, and the water-supply at Kaima being scanty and difficult of access, Major-General McQueen decided to return to the crest of the Black Mountain; the 3rd Column was accordingly withdrawn. The enemy emboldened by our retirement followed up the rear-guard of the column and we lost three men killed and one severely wounded. The column bivouacked on the northern slopes of Akhund Baba, the General and head-quarters being at Kain Gali, close to the 2nd Column.

During the 7th, the 1st and 2nd Columns remained at Chitabat and Nimal.

To return now to the doings of the 4th Column on the Indus. From the 5th to the 10th October, daily reconnaissances were made from Kotkai; but no forward movement was possible, the road from Towara to Kotkai being so bad that it was necessary to bring up supplies by hand. On the afternoon of the 5th a party under Colonel Crookshank, consisting of the 29th Punjab Infantry, and two guns, reconnoitred in the direction of Kanar, but, after advancing along the left bank of the river for one and a half miles, it was found impracticable to proceed further, owing to the fire kept up by the enemy from the opposite bank of the river, which it was impossible to silence; the party accordingly returned to camp. During this reconnaissance Colonel Crookshank received a wound, from the effects of which he subsequently died. Colonel Beddy, 29th Punjab Infantry, as next senior officer, now assumed command of the 4th Column.

Tilli, Kunari, and Garhi, were also visited by reconnoitring parties, and during the retirement from the latter place, which is on the right bank of the Indus, a determined attack was made at dusk on the rear-guard of the 4th Punjab Infantry under Captain Gray. This was beaten off with some loss to the enemy, our casualties being two men wounded. The column then advanced on the 11th to Kanar, and on the 12th to Ghazikot, the Royal Irish with brigade head-quarters remaining at the former place. The rate of progress was necessarily slow, owing to the bad state of the road, which had to be improved as the column advanced.

On the 11th signalling communication was opened with the Oghi force at Panj Gali.

On the 13th Brigadier-General Galbraith crossed the river with a force of 1,450 rifles and 3 guns and destroyed the settlement and fort of Hindustani fanatics at Maidan. A gathering, on the hills above the fort watched the proceedings of the column, but with the exception of a few stray shots no opposition was offered by the enemy.

On this date Brigadier-General Channer and staff with an escort of some 300 rifles arrived at Kanar from Betband, and thus joined hands with the 4th Column.

The fact that the Hindustanis offered no resistance to the destruction of their stronghold seems to show that the losses they sustained in the affair near Kotkai on the 4th October had completely broken their spirits. Maulvi Abdulla and his following subsequent to their defeat had dispersed among the Chagarzais and neighbouring tribes, wherever they could find a refuge.

The destruction of Maidan may be considered to have brought to a close the active operations of the 4th Column, as its subsequent operations, which included reconnaissances to places on both banks of the river, were entirely unopposed. Later on in the month, in order to bring pressure to bear on the Hassanzais, a hamlet on the right bank of the river opposite Kanar was destroyed on the 24th,

Garhi and Bakrai were burnt on the 25th, and on the 29th October Kotkai was also destroyed. The following day the tribe gave up the remaining prisoner in the hands of Hashim Ali Khan, (the other had previously made his escape), and paid their outstanding fine of Rs. 7,500. Orders were accordingly given to cease destroying the villages and cutting the crops of this clan, and their *jirga* was then sent to Oghi, where it arrived on the 2nd November.

The operations of the Agror columns, which have been described up to the 7th October, will now be continued up to the end of the first phase of the operations.

During this period the three columns remained in occupation of the crest of the Black Mountain above the Hassanzai and Akazai territories, and numerous reconnaissances were made to explore the country or destroy the villages of the offending clans.

The Hassanzais as a tribe were informed that their fine had been increased on account of the opposition they had offered to our columns, and they were given a certain period of grace in which to submit, with the result which has been shown above.

A message was also sent to Hashim Ali Khan, that if he did not deliver up himself and his three relatives, Sheikh Ali Muhammad, Turabaz, and Sikandar Khan, unconditionally, the remaining Khan Khel villages would be destroyed. The only assurance given was that their lives would be spared.

The Akazais were at the same time informed that it was proposed on the following day to destroy certain of their villages, unless they submitted in the meantime; and in accordance with this notification a force of 500 men and 2 guns from the 1st Column proceeded from Chitabat on the morning of the 10th and burnt Biran, an Akazai village concerned in the attack on Major Battye's party.

The following were also destroyed by various small columns:—

Akazai villages: Kan, Meraband, Maira and Darai; Khan Khel Hassanzai villages: Selle, (or Tsil), Karwai, Sabo, and Ril; Pariari villages: Kangan, Baffa, Siada, and Saidra.

This punishment had the desired effect as regards the Akazais; and their *jirga*, having arrived at head-quarters on the 19th, accepted unconditionally all the terms that had been imposed, and were given seven days in which to collect the fine, leaving five selected hostages in our hands. Orders were accordingly issued that no more Akazai villages were to be destroyed during the period of grace thus allowed.

The opposition offered by the enemy during these operations was almost a negligeable factor, and our losses were proportionately small, but some casualties were occasioned by parties of the enemy creeping up to the picquets and sniping them at night. In consequence of this, orders were issued that all fires and lights in bivouac should be extinguished at sunset, and that trees should be fired at a distance of from 50 to 100 yards in front of the bivouac, so as to prevent the unseen approach of the enemy.

With the submission of the Akazais and the cessation of hostilities on the part of the Hassanzais, the first phase of the operations may be said to have been completed, and we will now turn to the second phase. This may be considered to have begun on the 21st October, the object being to coerce into submission the Pariari Saiyids and the Tikariwals. The scope of the operations was subsequently extended; on the 23rd October permission was received for a movement on Thakot, and on the 31st, the despatch of a force into the Allai country was sanctioned.

Account of operations. Second phase.

On the evening of the 20th October, the troops of the Hazara Field Force were distributed as follows:—

Divisional head-quarters } Mana-ka-Dana.
Head-quarters, 1st Brigade }

No. 1 Column, reinforced by a wing, 34th Pioneers. Mana-ka-Dana.

No. 2 Column, occupied Chitabat, having relieved No. 1 Column.

No. 3 Column, distributed between Karun, Akhund Baba, Nimal and Tilli.

No. 4 Column. Ledh, Kanar, Kotkai, Shingri, and Darband.

A fifth column composed of four guns, 3-1 South Irish Division, Royal Artillery, Head-quarters and wing of the Seaforth Highlanders, wing, 40th Bengal Infantry, the Khaibar Rifles and two gatlings, under the command of Colonel A. Murray, Seaforth Highlanders, was moved up to Dilbori with a view to taking part with No. 1 Column in the ensuing operations. On the 21st, the 1st Column moved on Trand.

The 5th Column moved forward from Dilbori and bivouacked at night about a mile short of Chirmang. This village had been found deserted by the troops in the morning, and in the evening Rahim Khan, the headman, and chief of the Malkal section of the Tikariwals, came into camp and agreed to pay up the share of the fine demanded from him. The other two leading men of Tikari, *viz.*, Ghafar Khan of Trand and Nawab Khan of Darian, had made their submission before their country was entered and thus the whole fine of Rs. 1,000 imposed on the Tikariwals had been realized. As, however, Rahim Khan had delayed his payment and attendance, he was further punished by having forage for the force for one day taken from his lands, and wood taken from his village.

On the 22nd, Major-General McQueen reconnoitred the Pariari glens from the Bilandkot spur, to arrange his plan for attacking the villages of the Pariari Saiyids. Brigadier-General Channer at the same time made a reconnaissance in the direction of Maidan over the Shabora spur, and strong working-parties were ordered out to improve the road. In the evening a *jirga* of the Pariariwals came in, but the principal men were not present. An ultimatum was accordingly sent to the tribe warning them that if these men did not attend by the following evening their villages would be destroyed. On the 23rd, the 5th Column moved forward two miles in advance of the 1st Column to Sufian, at the foot of the Shabora spur. The Pariari headmen not having come in, the incomplete *jirga* was dismissed, and orders were issued for punitive measures to be carried out on the following day.

Sanction having been received on the 23rd for the force to visit Thakot, letters were sent to the Thakoti *maliks* giving them notice of this and stating that our intentions were friendly, as long as no opposition was offered, and inviting them to send in their *jirga*.

At 8 A.M. on the morning of the 24th, a force moved into the Pariari country. On the left 2 guns, 3-1 South Irish, with an escort of 100 infantry, took up a position on the spur under Bilandkot, to cover the advance. In the centre a column, composed of 300 men of the 3rd Sikhs, advanced up the Machai spur and destroyed the village of Kopra with slight opposition, while a small force of 200 men and 2 guns from Chitabat co-operated down the spur from the direction of the Machai peak. On the right the main column, consisting of 800 rifles and 2 guns, moved up the principal Pariari glen, past the villages of Machai and Pariari direct on Garhi, which the Khaibar Rifles, supported by the Seaforth Highlanders, destroyed after some opposition from the enemy. There were no casualties on our side.

On the 25th and 26th Brigadier-General Channer, with the 5th Column, moved to Dabrai, making the road as he advanced; and the 1st Column, with Major-General McQueen and the head-quarters staff, moved to Maidan, leaving a detachment at Chirmang. Messengers arrived from Arsala Khan of Ailai to beg that the force might not visit his country, and a reply was sent, stating the terms on which the Government was prepared to accept the submission of the tribe.

On the 27th Brigadier-General Channer advanced from Dabrai *viâ* Paimal and Serai to Chanjal—about two and a half miles. The road just beyond Dabrai and also between Serai and Chanjal was very steep and difficult, and strong working-parties, assisted by the corps of coolies, were employed during the day in improving it. The Major-General moved from Maidan to Serai with a portion of the 1st Column, leaving detachments to hold Maidan and Dabrai.

Up to this point there had been no opposition, but the attitude of the Thakotis was uncertain and their *jirga* had not come in. It was, moreover, reported that their women and cattle had been sent away, and that their lower villages were deserted; and on the 27th a message was received by the Chief Political Officer asking for twenty days in which to collect their *jirga*.

Under these circumstances the General Officer Commanding decided to make an immediate advance so as not to allow time for any combinations of the tribes to oppose the advance. Orders were accordingly issued for a lightly equipped force to proceed to Thakot the following day.

At 6-30 A.M. on the 28th, a force under Brigadier-General G. N. Channer, V.C., having left all baggage behind under a guard, and taking only one blanket per man, great coats, and one day's rations, marched to Thakot.

Visit to Thakot.

3-1 South Irish, Royal Artillery	2 guns.
Seaforth Highlanders	259 rifles.
3rd Sikhs	250 "
34th Pioneers	269 "
Khaibar Rifles	200 "
2 gatlings.	

The path led down from Chanjal to the Nandihar (or Thakot) stream, whence it ascended the opposite spur to Karg, from which hamlet there was a descent of about 1,500 feet to Thakot. The path was steep and bad, and had to be improved as the troops advanced. The force reached Karg at 8-30 A.M., and Brigadier-General Channer, leaving here a small detachment with the two guns, descended by a steep path to Thakot, which was reached without opposition soon after noon. The village proved to be an insignificant place, and from its position at the bottom of a valley surrounded by hills it was of no military importance. The distance from Chanjal was somewhat over five miles. Thakot had not been visited by the force in 1868, owing chiefly to the difficulties of the country, and this had given an exaggerated importance to the place, and had caused the inhabitants to regard it as inaccessible to our troops. After marching the whole force through the village, Brigadier-General Channer returned to the village of Lora on the left bank of the Nandihar stream. During the afternoon the inhabitants of the village of Daut, across the Indus, opened fire upon our troops, and shots were also fired from the heights to the south, in rear of the bivouac, but a few rounds from the gatling guns cleared the ground in front, and the Khaibar Rifles and 34th Pioneers, gaining possession of the heights to the south soon cleared those parts of the enemy. The casualties on our side were two men wounded.

Owing to the opposition which had been offered, and which was traced to the headmen of Lora, that village with its tower was destroyed before the force retired on the morning of the 29th. Thakot itself was spared, as its inhabitants had not opposed our troops. The two guns, which had been brought down from Karg, shelled the village of Daut on the other side of the river, whence the enemy had opened fire the previous afternoon. The tower of this village was destroyed by the guns, and the village itself set on fire. The force then returned to Serai which was reached the same evening.

Colonel Gatacre, with a detachment of the 3rd Sikhs and Khaibar Rifles, withdrew from Thakot by a path running along the right bank of the Nandihar stream, and some opposition was experienced by this party during their return near the small village of Mirazai, the inhabitants of which rolled down stones on the troops.

Colonel Gatacre accordingly ordered the few houses composing the hamlet to be destroyed. On the 30th October the whole force returned to Maidan.

The period of grace given to Arsala Khan of Allai to come in and make his submission having expired on the 30th, and there being no signs of any intention on his part to accept the terms offered by the Government, orders were issued by Major-General McQueen for an advance towards the Allai country on the following day.

Accordingly, on the morning of the 31st, a force composed of the troops of the 1st and 5th Columns, as per margin, under Colonels J. M. Sym and A. Murray respectively, marched towards the Ghorapher pass. The other troops of these columns remained at Maidan.

Advance into Allai.

1st Column.	
Hazara Mountain Battery, 2 guns.	
Half No. 3 Company, Sappers and Miners.	
Northumberland Fusiliers ..	540 rifles.
Detachment, Suffolk Regiment [1]	50 ,,
Detachment, Royal Sussex [1]	50 ,,
Detachment, 24th Punjab Infy. [1]	50 ,,
Wing, 34th Pioneers ..	246 ,,
5th Gurkhas	479 ,,
5th Column.	
3-1 South Irish Division, R.A. ..	4 guns.
Wing, Seaforth Highlanders ..	248 rifles.
3rd Sikh Infantry [2] ..	445 ,,
Khaibar Rifles	253 ,,

Brigadier-General Channer accompanied the 1st Column and the whole force bivouacked at Mazrai [3] for the night.

At Mazrai, which was over 7,000 feet, little water was obtainable, and there was no forage to be had except from a distance. During the day Brigadier-General Channer reconnoitred towards the Ghorapher pass which was found to be occupied by the enemy.

A detachment of Kashmir troops had in the meantime moved into Nandihar from the Chattar plain.

Capture of the Chaila ridge.

On the 1st November the advance on the Ghorapher pass, leading into Allai, was continued by the 1st Column, supported by the 5th Column. The path led along a gentle spur, rising some 1,000 feet in about 3½ miles, to the foot of a precipitous ascent, very much broken with rocks and cliffs. The enemy held the crest and the forest

[1] Fifty marksmen from each of these regiments had been sent up to join the force in Nandihar.

[2] This regiment had been transferred from the 1st to the 5th Column.

[3] This was the name given officially to this camping-ground, but the place is called Bhagsir by the people of the country.

on the left of the advance, and the position they occupied was naturally so strong that, if it had been held by a determined opponent, it would have been almost impregnable.

The crest of the Chaila mountain is here protected by immense masses of precipitous granite slates, behind which, as the force ascended the spur, clusters of men could be seen. The first shots were fired in the thick forest at the foot of the ascent at 10-30 A.M., and as the advance progressed, with the Northumberland Fusiliers and Khaibar Rifles leading, the firing was for a short time very brisk. The guns, at a range of 2,000 yards, covered the advance, throwing shells amongst the granite crags and into the thick forest. The enemy at first beat drums, played their pipes, and yelled in defiance, but these sounds soon died away as our men pushed up the steep slopes and scrambled over the crags. Before noon the position was taken, the Fusiliers and Khaibaris reaching the crest almost simultaneously. Our loss was only one man killed and one wounded. A few bodies of the enemy were found on the crest, and also some blankets, food bags, etc., shewing they had gone off in a hurry.

On the crest being gained Brigadier-General Channer pushed on with the Northumberland Fusiliers, 5th Gurkhas, and Khaibar Rifles to Kage Oba,[1] two and a half miles further on, the total distance from Mazrai being six and a half miles. Here a plentiful supply of water was found and a good camping-ground, and there was a track fit for mules leading to it along the crest. The path up to the crest, however, for the last 500 feet was found to be quite impracticable for mules. The Pioneers and the Sappers and Miners, assisted by the coolie corps, which had been brought up from the rear, were employed all day in trying to improve it, but it was not till dusk that it was reported practicable. Only a very few mules could be got up this day, and the night was one of great discomfort for the troops, who were for the most part without food or blankets. There was, moreover, a hard frost during the night, the elevation being over 9,000 feet. Fortunately wood was plentiful, the bivouac being in partially cleared forest. The baggage was massed, as far as possible, at the foot of the ascent to the Chaila crest, with the guns ; and the

[1] This means "the winding stream."

Seaforth Highlanders with the 3rd Sikhs held the line of the crest with picquets. Five hundred men of the Kashmir troops moved from Batgraon to Mazrai to take the place of the force that had advanced, and to keep open the communications. A letter was received this day from Arsala Khan, the point of which was contained in the last sentence "kindly wait and stay a little." His object was evidently to gain time, being aware that owing to the lateness of the season operations might at any time be stopped by snow.

At daylight on the 2nd, the baggage commenced to ascend the steep part of the road from the bivouac below. In places the road was very difficult. The last mules did not reach the crest till dark, and the rear-guard did not arrive in camp till 9 P.M. The difficulty of the road may be imagined from the fact that the baggage took twelve hours to make the ascent—about one mile in length. During this ascent some fourteen mules were killed by falling over the precipice. The enemy fired occcasional shots from the forest and caused a few casualties among our troops.

During the morning Brigadier-General Channer made a reconnaissance in the direction of Pokal, the head-quarters of Arsala Khan, returning to camp about 3 P.M. The reconnoitring party met with some slight opposition and three of the enemy were killed and two wounded. A report was now brought in that Arsala Khan had fled across the Indus, but that his eldest son Ghazi Khan was holding out with a following. Orders were accordingly issued for a small force under Brigadier-General Channer to proceed to Pokal the following day, and after destroying it to return to the bivouac on the crest. During the day slight snow was falling.

On the 3rd, the force, as per margin, proceeded to Pokal. The path ran with a gentle gradient till within two miles of Pokal, from whence the descent was steep and over open ground. The enemy offered some opposition to the advance and suffered considerable loss. On reaching the village the detachments

Destruction of Pokal.

3-1 South Irish Division, R.A. ..	2 guns.
Northumberland Fusiliers ..	160 rifles.
Suffolk Regiment	40 ,,
Royal Sussex Regiment ..	40 ,,
Seaforth Highlanders ..	160 ,,
24th Punjab Infantry ..	50 ,,
5th Gurkhas	200 ,,
Khaibar Rifles	150 ,,

of Suffolk and Royal Sussex Regiments (all picked marksmen) fired volleys on the retreating bodies of the enemy at long ranges with great effect. The village of Pokal was entirely destroyed, with the exception of the mosque, and the force at 1 P.M. began to retire, detachments of the Seaforth Highlanders and Khaibar Rifles forming the rear-guard. The enemy followed up most persistently, to the number of about 300, to within a mile of the camp, but were driven off by the steady fire of the troops. One company of the Northumberland Fusiliers occupied a knoll, and, waiting for the enemy to collect in groups, soon had an opportunity of pouring in a volley, which effectually drove them back, leaving a good number killed. Our loss during the day had been one killed and four wounded. Brigadier-General Channer in his despatch estimated the enemy's loss at from 80 to 100 killed, and he considered that the small number of casualties on our side was largely due to the admirable manner in which the troops skirmished during the advance and performed rear-guard duties during the retirement. The troops all returned to camp before dark after a very heavy day's work. The distance to Pokal was seven miles and the descent 4,300 feet. The Allai valley was found to be open, highly cultivated, and dotted about with numerous large villages.

Late on the evening of the 3rd, an Allai *jirga*, representing five out of the eight sections, and comprising the faction opposed to Arsala Khan, arrived in camp, and on the 4th November the whole force withdrew from the Allai country to Mazrai. The Pioneers, Sappers and Miners, and Hazara Mountain Battery moved back the same day to Maidan, and the Kashmir troops returned to Batgraon.

It may be mentioned that on the 28th the Chitabat peak had been evacuated, and the head-quarters of the 2nd Column had been transferred to Chirmang, in order to bring pressure to bear on the Pariari Saiyids by taking grain, forage, and wood from their country.

This had the desired effect and their *jirga* came into Maidan on the evening of the 4th, paid up Rs. 479, and gave five headmen as hostages. They were then dismissed, being allowed two days to collect the remainder of the fine of Rs. 1,500 imposed upon them.

This they subsequently brought in to the Major-General at Chirmang on the 7th November.

On the 5th Brigadier-General Channer's force was withdrawn from Mazrai to Maidan. The Allai *jirga* which had accompanied the force to Maidan was this day dismissed, as it was considered impossible to deal with any but a full *jirga*, or one bringing in the whole fine, which the present deputation was not prepared to do. It was explained to them that all Allai would be held responsible for the hostile action of any of its inhabitants, and that the whole fine must be paid within a reasonable time, in cash or cattle, otherwise a blockade would be re-imposed. It was also pointed out to them that we had punished Arsala Khan, had seen the Allai country, and could at any future time visit it again if we wished; moreover, if such a visit were forced on us, our stay would be a longer one, and we should live on the country.

From Maidan the troops were gradually withdrawn to British territory, and on the 10th the whole force (with the exception of the 4th Column on the river side, and the Kashmir Contingent, which had been withdrawn on the 8th to the Chattar plain), was concentrated in the Agror valley. The head-quarters of the 2nd Column had been withdrawn from Chirmang to Kulakka on the 5th November, and the 3rd Column from Karun had reached the same camp on the 4th, being rejoined there by the 14th Sikhs and the half company of Sappers and Miners from Tilli on the 7th November. Orders were received on the 11th for the force in the Agror valley to be broken up, and the necessary instructions were at once issued.

On the same date orders were received by Brigadier-General Galbraith to withdraw his force to British territory. This was carried out without a shot being fired, and on the 13th the whole of the 4th Column was concentrated at Darband, whence they were dispersed to their several destinations.

Results of expedition.

The immediate results of the expedition may here be briefly recapitulated. The Khan Khel section of the Hassanzais had been severely punished and had had all their principal villages burnt. The Hindustani settlement had been completely destroyed. The Pariari Saiyids, after bringing heavy punishment on themselves, had eventually submitted and fulfilled the Government terms; and Arsala Khan of Allai had been punished by having his village and tower destroyed. The fines imposed were all duly paid, for the most part in cattle. Of the two British subjects carried off into captivity by Hashim Ali Khan, one escaped and the other was released. The Akazais and Hassanzais gave hostages for future good behaviour, and admitted their responsibility for the conduct of the *khan* of the Khan Khels, who is the chief of all the three divisions of the Isazais, the clan to which they both belong. They undertook that in future the troops, or servants, of the British Government should not be molested if they marched on the Black Mountain anywhere within British territory, or along the crest of the mountain on the boundary between British and independent territory. The Akazais promised for the future to lay no claim to the Shatut lands, to make no buildings, and to graze no cattle to the east of the watershed of the Black Mountain on the Agror side. The Hassanzais undertook not to injure any roads which had been made within their territory during the operations, and a similar promise was made by the Tikariwal and the Nandihar *jirgas*.

Major-General McQueen, in his despatch on the operations of the Hazara Field Force, noted in addition to the above political results of the campaign, the opening up of the Thakot and Allai countries by the formation of good mule roads into the heart of these tracts; the completion of a thoroughly good camel road from Oghi to Dabrai and a mule track from Darband to Kanar; and the detailed survey of 177 square miles of unknown country.

The measures of a permanent kind which should be taken to facilitate intercourse with the Black Mountain tribes, to give us a better and quicker command of the approaches to that region, were postponed for subsequent consideration and settlement; but Major-General McQueen recommended—

(1) The construction of a good camel road between Agror and Darband down the valley of the Unhar stream.

(2) The maintenance of a good road from Darband along the Indus to our frontier, and if possible beyond, as far as Kanar.

(3) The maintenance of the camel road from Oghi *viâ* the Jal pass and Chirmang to Maidan in Nandihar, and if practicable to Paimal.

(4) The construction of a good camel road from the Chattar plain *viâ* Phagora and Batgraon to Maidan.

(5) The establishment of a post on the Jal Gali to be held by men of the Agror valley who have done good service for Government

The casualties sustained by our troops during the operations were: two officers (Colonel A. C. W. Crookshank, C.B., Commanding 4th Column, and Captain C. H. H. Beley, D.S.O., D.A.Q.M.G.,) died of wounds; three officers (Captain O. C. Radford, and Lieutenants F. J. S. Cleeve and C. F. S. Ewart) wounded; twenty-three men killed, and fifty-four wounded. It is difficult to give the enemy's losses with any approach to accuracy, owing to their custom of carrying away their dead, but they were estimated to be about 400 killed and wounded. The losses from disease on the side of the British were slight, as the health of the troops remained good throughout, in spite of, or perhaps in consequence of, the hard work and hardships undergone.

One peculiar feature of this expedition was the large number of British subjects who went from Hazara, and, it is said, even from the Rawal Pindi and Jhelum districts, and fought against us, many being killed and wounded; the greater number no doubt went from the first named district and especially from the Tanawali tract. The fact of the Hindustanis being engaged against us may be accepted as the cause that led to the rising of this wave of religious feeling. No other reason has been put forward, and no other can be suggested as at all likely to have induced men thus to sacrifice their lives. Such being the motive, it may be assumed that the continued residence of the Hindustanis at Maidan, so close to our border, had led to the spread of their doctrines in the neighbourhood. The expedition, therefore, on this ground, was not a day too soon to show the people on this border our power, capability, and determination to punish when necessary.

Events on the Hazara border subsequent to the expedition of 1888.

During the year subsequent to the Hazara expedition of 1888 affairs on the Agror border remained quiet. By the removal of the Khan of Agror a salutary warning had been given to other *Khans* within our frontier, whose intrigues and machinations had been the fertile cause of trouble with the clans on this border. Police control over Agror was strengthened, and several criminals who had fled from justice in past years were arrested, brought to trial, and punished.

After the submission of the tribes and withdrawal of the troops, the Government of India took into consideration measures to secure control for the future over these clans and to give easy access to their country. Among these measures the Supreme Government, in March 1890, ordered the construction of several roads leading from Agror up to the crest of the Black Mountain, and at the same time called for the opinion of the Punjab Government, whether, in order to reap the full benefit of these roads, troops should not use them and visit the border periodically. After some correspondence it was decided to send a small force to make a route march in a peaceable manner along the crest of the range during the autumn of 1890.

In the meanwhile, as the roads near the crest could not be safely made without the co-operation of the neighbouring tribes, the Hassanzais, Akazais, and Pariari Saiyids were invited to send in their *jirgas* to arrange for the peaceable completion of the work on the upper slopes of the mountain. They replied objecting to the construction of the roads and refusing, or evading, the invitation; and when they were subsequently ordered to send in deputations to accompany troops on their march along the crest, and were warned at the same time that opposition would be severely punished, they returned evasive replies. The column detailed to march along the crest was placed under the command of Brigadier-General Sir J. W. McQueen, K.C.B., A.D.C., commanding the Punjab Frontier Force, to whom the object of the operation was notified in the following terms by the Quarter Master General in India in a telegram, dated the 10th October 1890:—

His Excellency wishes to impress on you that the operations this autumn are merely intended to prove our right under the treaty to march along the crest, and are not intended to develop under any circumstances into a large expedition. Should the tribes oppose the promenade this autumn you should not push forward, but, having clearly put upon the tribes the odium of not having carried out their obligations, reserve their punishment for an expedition in the spring, which they will be told will be sent against them.

No. 2 (Derajat) Mountain Battery.
500 rifles, 4th Sikh Infantry.
350 „ 1-5th Gurkhas.
350 „ 2-5th „

Accordingly the marginally noted force marched from Abbottabad, and arrived at Oghi on the 19th October, on which date Brigadier-General Sir John McQueen took over command. The attitude of the tribes, except the Pariari Saiyids who had sent in their *jirga*, was doubtful, and numerous gatherings of tribesmen were reported at Nimal, Kain Gali, and other places, where they had been induced to collect by Hashim Ali, the Khan of the Isazais, a man who has been consistently hostile to Government since he first came into notice as successor to Ahmad Ali Khan.

Heavy rain and snow on the crest of the hill prevented an advance for some days, and it was not until the 23rd October that Sir J. McQueen moved up the Barchar spur with a column of 1,000 rifles and 4 guns, bivouacking above the village of Barchar, with picquets about a mile below the crest. There was a considerable amount of firing at the bivouac that night, but owing to its position on the reverse of the slope no damage was done.

On the morning of the 24th information arrived that the Akazais as well as the Hassanzais had determined to join Hashim Ali in opposing our advance, and at daylight large numbers of tribesmen were seen to be assembling on the crest of the hill. Under these circumstances Sir J. McQueen withdrew his troops in accordance with his instructions.

Expedition against the Hassanzai and Akazai Clans of the Black Mountain by a Force under Major-General W. K. Elles, C.B., in 1891.

In consequence of the opposition offered to our troops, it was now decided by the Governor-General in Council to despatch a force into the Hassanzai and Akazai territories, and the Commander-in-Chief was called upon to submit proposals for carrying out the necessary operations.

The objects of the expedition were stated in the Government letter to be, first, to carry out the purpose for which the movement of troops in October had been made, namely,—to assert our right to move along the crest of the Black Mountain without molestation; and next, and more particularly, to inflict punishment on the tribes concerned for the hostility practised on that occasion. The occupation of the country to be entered was to be prolonged until the tribes concerned had made complete submission and had carried out whatever conditions had been imposed upon them. The whole of the Hassanzai and Akazai clans were held to be responsible for the hostility displayed towards our troops.

It was decided that the expedition should take place whether or no the tribes in the meanwhile offered submission; and the Punjab Government was authorized to inform the tribes of this decision, and also that the Government of India demanded their unconditional submission; they were further to be informed that, if they submitted, not only would Government be disposed to treat them leniently, but would undertake to settle all outstanding cases by tribal *jirga* in accordance with the custom of the country, and would be prepared to discuss with them in the same fashion the future mangement of their country.

In consequence of the experience gained during the 1888 expedition, it was decided that the advance should be made only by the Indus line. The reasons which led to this decision were that the large villages and most valuable lands of the Hassanzai and Akazai clans are situated along the Indus, or at no great distance from it, and could be easily reached by an advance up the left bank of the river, while, on the other hand, the ascent of the mountain from the east and south-east is difficult; that the crest line is our boundary, and for some way down the western side there are no villages or property the destruction of which would be much felt; and finally, that in the forest which clothes the upper part of the mountain the conditions of fighting are in favour of an active enemy well acquainted with the ground, while the superior armament and discipline of our troops might be partially neutralized. It was accordingly decided that while Oghi should be occupied by a small force, this should be merely placed there as a precautionary measure, and not in view to an advance from that side of the Black Mountain, except as far as the occupation of Pabal Gali and Tilli.

The force was directed to advance from Darband into the enemy's country in two columns, one moving *viâ* Baradar and Pailam to Tilli, and the other along the river route *viâ* Kotkai and Kanar; and the troops were ordered to concentrate at Darband and Oghi by the 1st March 1891, as shown in the margin.

Left or River Column, at Darband.
No. 1 M. Battery, R. A., 3 guns.
No. 2 (Derajat) M. Battery, 3 guns.
2nd Bn., Seaforth Highlanders.
H.-qrs. and wing, 32nd Pioneers.
37th (Dogra) Bengal Infantry.
Guides Infantry.
4th Sikh Infantry.

Right or Tilli Column, at Darband.
No. 9 M. Battery, R. A.
1st Bn., Royal Welsh Fusiliers.
11th Bengal Infantry.
Wing of 32nd Pioneers
2nd Bn., 5th Gurkhas.
Khaibar Rifles.

Divisional Troops at Darband.
11th B. L. (one squadron).
No. 4 Coy., Bengal Sappers and Miners.

To occupy Oghi.
11th B. L. (one squadron).
No. 2 (Derajat) M. Battery, 3 guns.
28th Bengal Infantry.

Reserve Brigade at Rawal Pindi.
11th B. L. (one squadron).
1st Bn., King's Royal Rifle Corps.
19th Bengal Infantry.
27th " "

The total strength, exclusive of the Reserve Brigade, was 169 officers, 7,120 native officers, non-commissioned officers and men (British and natives), and 15 guns. There was also with the force a Coolie Corps, 200 strong, for road-making, under the charge of Lieutenant Birdwood, R.E. The detail of commands and staff will be found in Appendix B. Full political authority was conferred on the General Officer Commanding the Expeditionary Force, and Mr. F. D. Cunningham, C.I.E., C.S., was appointed Chief Political Officer under his orders. Direct communication between the General Officer Commanding and the Foreign Office was sanctioned on all matters connected with that Department.

The advance was delayed by bad weather, but on the 11th March Major General Elles reported that the force was assembled and ready to move forward on the following day. In the meanwhile good roads had been completed on the Tilli line to near the frontier, and on the river line to Bela. Phaldar and Bela were both occupied by our troops, the telegraph line being completed to these points. On the 11th the boats for a bridge, which had been brought up from Attock, arrived at Bela. On the same date four days' supplies for the right column had been collected at Phaldar, and four days' for the left column at Bela. A few shots had been fired from the opposite side of the river at working-parties, but beyond this, there were no signs of opposition. The news received of the intentions of the tribes was conflicting, but it was reported that the Hassanzai and Akazai were both pressing Hashim Ali Khan, the nominal chief of both clans, to submit and join them in a deputation to the British authorities. On the 10th March it was notified to the Hassanzais that, if they remained peaceably in their villages when the force advanced into their country, they would not be injured in person, and their villages would be protected from harm. The terms of submission would be made known after the country had been occupied.

On the 11th March a Bunerwal *jirga* arrived at Amb, and a native official Ibrahim Khan, Khan Bahadur, was sent by the General to assure them that the Government had no quarrel with them, and no intention of interfering with them or their country. A Mada Khel *jirga*, which had also gone to Amb, were at the same time informed that we had no quarrel with them, if they behaved peaceably and neither offered opposition to our troops nor permitted others to attempt hostility from their country. They were further told that their *jirga* would be received at Kanar, or at some convenient place in the Hassanzai country.

In view of the attitude of the Bunerwals, the garrison of Mardan was increased, so that pressure might be brought to bear on the tribe from the Peshawar side, if necessary

Plan of operations.

The plan of operations proposed by Major-General Elles was, after the occupation of Kanar and Tilli as directed, to push forward both columns; the left column to occupy the lower Hassanzai country on both banks and the Diliarai peninsula of the Akazai country, and the right column to pass through the middle levels of the mountain by Ril and Kungar and occupy the Khan Khel country. Thereafter the two columns to work up and down on the north of the Shal Nala, through the Akazai country, till they met. On a junction being effected, the occupation of the whole country of the two tribes would be completed. As regards punishment, the Hassanzais, who had submitted, were in the event of their return to their villages to be mulcted in one-fourth of their standing crops. In other cases the troops would subsist on the country, as far as their requirements could be met, until submission took place.

On the morning of the 12th March the Tilli Column marched from Darband at 8 A.M., and the River Column (accompanied by the General Officer Commanding and the divisional head-quarters)

at 8-30 A.M. The former occupied Pailam and the latter Kotkai without opposition. There was some desultory firing at the River Column from the opposite side of the Indus, from a point where the Hassanzai and Mada Khel boundaries meet; and when the boats were coming up the river, shots were fired from this point at the boats' escort. A company of the Guides crossed over the river and dislodged the men who were firing, without any casualties on our side. Villages along the river bank passed *en route* were found deserted, and all property and grain had been carried off.

The River Column bivouacked for the night at Towara, on the site where the action of Kotkai had been fought in 1888.

At daybreak on the morning of the 13th, two companies of the Guides, who had been sent over to the right bank the night before, moved to take up fresh ground, and found the village of Nadrai occupied. A brisk fire was opened by the enemy, and the Guides rushed the village, which was carried with a loss to the enemy of three killed and three wounded, there being no casualties on our side. The same morning, a reconnoitring force, consisting of a half battalion of the Seaforth Highlanders and a half battalion of the Guides, crossed to the right bank of the river at the Marer ferry, and proceeded to Doshkand, and thence to the Palosi plain, visiting Garhi, Nawekili, and Palosi, which were found deserted. Maidan, the Hindustani settlement which had been destroyed in 1888, was still in ruins. At Garhi the force was met by two companies of the Guides, who had marched direct to that place along the right bank of the river. Under cover of this movement the road between Kotkai and Kanar was examined, and it was ascertained that it could not be made practicable until the evening of the following day, and it was therefore decided that the column should remain at Towara. All the villages visited during the day (except Nadrai, which had been fired by the Guides after its capture) were left untouched. On this date the boats were all collected at Kotkai.

The right column, which had marched to Tilli, remained halted at that place.

On the 15th, a reconnaissance was made to the Palosi plain, for the purpose of selecting ground for a bivouac, and also to ascertain the nature of a tribal gathering reported at the western end of the plain. On nearing Palosi the party was fired on from both sides of the river, but the enemy were driven off, and the reconnaissance was then pushed about a mile beyond the ruins of Maidan, where a considerable gathering of armed men was seen on both sides of the river on the surrounding hills. The party then returned to Towara. On the same day a detachment of the 4th Sikhs, proceeding along the left bank of the river from Kanar, surprised the enemy under the cliffs beyond Ghazikot, and inflicted some loss on them. Brigadier-General Hammond, who commanded the right column, now reported to the General Officer Commanding that he was experiencing great difficulties at Tilli on account of lack of forage. General Elles was consequently obliged to change the original plan of operations, as is shown in the subjoined telegram from him to Army Head-quarters.

I find that the difficulty in supporting the transport of the Tilli Column at that level is very great at this early time of the year. Fodder would either have to be taken up from here[1] or brought in from Phaldar. The crops at Tilli are only just above ground. Seri was reported under snow. I therefore decided on the spot to make other dispositions for the present; first, to open out Tilli-Kanar road; second, to establish permanent posts at Tilli, Ril, and Makranai; third, to bring down Tilli Column with all its transport to join River Column at Palosi; fourth, to establish one advanced depôt at Kotkai and supply the whole force from this. The circuit round upper posts will be completed by a track from Makranai to Kanar, which can be made practicable for laden mules. Before transferring his brigade to Palosi, General Hammond will probably make a flying advance to Seri, stay one night, and blow up any defences there. As for this, I am now awaiting his report.

I expect to have all the above dispositions completed in four days at latest. As to the future, I intend right column to operate *viâ* Bakrai upwards through Akazai country, and left column through Trans-Indus Hassanzai.

During the 14th and 15th, reports were received by the Chief Political Officer of armed men and flags crossing over the Baio range to Karnar and Kamach, and on the 15th it was reported that the aged Maulvi Abdulla, the leader of the Hindustani fanatics, had reached Kamach.

[1] Namely, the Indus valley.

On the 16th Kanar was strengthened by a wing of the 4th Sikhs to facilitate work on the road to Tilli from that place. The bridge-of-boats at Kotkai was completed, span 110 yards, with easy approaches ; and a camel road to Palosi opened out.

The Hassanzais and Akazais were now reported to be anxious to submit, and notice was sent to them that, if they returned peaceably to their homes, no harm would be done to them, and that not more than one-quarter of their crops would be taken for the supplies of the army. The surrender of Hashim Ali and his family was demanded.

On this day (the 16th) it was ascertained that the Hindustanis under Maulvi Abdulla were collecting at Didal and that there were a number of Chagarzais at Kamach. It was also reported that Hashim Ali, Khan of Seri, had been travelling about exciting the people, and had then gone off to Swat to ask Mian Gul to join and lead a holy war. A small gathering, 400 men or so, was reported in villages about Darbanai, Surmal, etc., but it appeared that the tribes were assembling for the most part in the Trans-Indus Chagarzai country.

Attack on Ghazikot.

Early in the morning of the 19th March the outpost at Ghazikot, a small straggling village on the left bank of the Indus, about three-quarters of a mile north of Kanar, was attacked. A narrow street ran up the middle of the village; a small *musjid* was at its south-east corner; while north and south of it, at a distance of about 200 yards, were two narrow *nalas* running at right angles into the river. The outpost consisted of the Dogra company of the 4th Sikhs, under Subadar Dheru, and was composed of two native officers and sixty-seven men. The picquet was placed behind some stone walls half-way between the northern *nala* and the village, while the remainder of the company bivouacked in rear of the *musjid*.

On the evening of the 18th some shots were fired by the enemy at the picquet, and at about 3 A.M. on the 19th, the havildar in charge of this picquet reported to Subadar Dheru that the enemy were collecting in force in the *nala* to his front. When they arrived close enough to be seen, the picquet fired four volleys at them, on which the swordsmen of the enemy, with shouts, rushed past the right of the picquet straight for the *musjid* in the south-east corner of the village. The enemy being in this way in rear of the picquet, the latter retired and joined the main body of the company. A hot fire was then commenced on both sides, the enemy firing from the roofs of the houses and charging with swords out of the *musjid*. At about 3-20 A.M., reinforcements, consisting of a company of the 4th Sikhs under Lieutenant Maconchy, followed by a second company of the same regiment under Lieutenant Manning, arrived on the scene. Closely following on these, under Colonel Sir B. Bromhead, C.B., came two companies of the 32nd Pioneers.

At that time a very hot fire was going on, the enemy being in the *musjid* and on the roofs of the houses. Half a company of the 4th Sikhs, under Lieutenant Maconchy, rushed through the centre of the village and occupied the right front of it, but in getting through the narrow street, Lieutenant Maconchy and three sepoys were wounded. Colonel Bromhead with the Pioneers now joined this party, having swept round the right flank of the village, while a company of the 4th Sikhs at the same time went round the left flank. Under orders of Colonel Bromhead, all firing was then stopped, and orders given to rely on sword and bayonet only. By that time the main body of the enemy had evidently retired, but *ghazis* kept creeping from various places, firing and using their knives in the dark. When day broke the Pioneers and 4th Sikhs cleared the village, and Captain DeBrath, with one company of the former regiment, advanced about a mile along the path on the left bank of the river in the track of the enemy's line of retreat, when four men were seen crossing to the right bank on a raft, and about eighty returning to Bakrai at the mouth of the Shal Nala. The ravines and caves in the vicinity of Ghazikot were searched, but no more of the enemy were discovered.

Lieutenant Maconchy was subsequently awarded the D. S. O. and Subadar Dheru, Havildar Waziru, Naik Ganesha Singh, Lance-Naik Alam Khan and Hospital Assistant Ahmadulla Khan received the 3rd Class of the Order of Merit for their gallantry on this occasion.

The number and loss of the enemy, who were reported to have consisted almost entirely of Hindustani fanatics, could not be estimated, but they left twenty-five bodies in and near the village. Of these, twenty-two were Hindustanis, two were

Pathans, and the remaining body was that of a Hindu *baniah*, who had been for some days previously at Kanar, and was probably made to act as guide to the attacking party. Our casualties were four killed and twenty-one wounded.

During the night of the 19th there was some firing at Kanar, and two companies of the Guides were sent from Towara to reinforce the detachment there. Two companies of the Seaforth Highlanders were also sent to reinforce the wing of the 37th Dogras at the bridge head. In this fighting the enemy lost three killed, and our casualties were three sepoys of the 32nd Pioneers wounded and one mule-driver found dead in a ravine to the south of the village.

The River Column, accompanied by divisional head-quarters, moved on the 20th from Towara to Pirzada Bela. The enemy was seen in considerable numbers on the surrounding hills, and Bakrai and Makranai were shelled.

On the 21st the River Column marched from Pirzada Bela to Palosi, where a defensive position was formed so as to include the village. On this day the Right Column occupied Ril, and having destroyed Seri on the 22nd, it returned to Tilli.

Affair on Diliari Heights.

On the 23rd March, a flying bridge was established at Bakrai under cover of a party of the 4th Sikhs, who were sent across the river to occupy that place. This led to a large gathering of the enemy on the Diliari hill overlooking Bakrai, who shortly after advanced down the spur towards the position. The Sikh picquet was now thrown forward to check this advance, and a wing of the Guides was sent across the river by the General Officer Commanding, who had observed the enemy's movement, to act as a support.

By about 5-30 P.M., the Sikhs had succeeded in driving the enemy from the hill and had occupied the crest, where they were joined by the Guides. Shortly after, however, orders were given for the whole party to withdraw to a breastwork which had been built about half-way up the slope from Bakrai.

In order to understand the position of affairs at this juncture it is necessary to explain that the hill on which Diliari stands is situated about one mile to the north-west of, and some 1,800 feet above, Bakrai, and is an offshoot of the large spur that bounds the Shal Nala on the north and north-west. The top of the hill is terraced and, although commanded at about 800 yards by the main spur, forms a good position for a strong picquet.

Immediately the rear party of the 4th Sikhs quitted the crest of this hill, the enemy, in Pathan fashion, began to collect again and press upon them, so that it was necessary to bring up supports and hold on to a ridge that afforded a good defensive position. It was now about 6-45 P.M. The enemy, who appeared to number about 50 or 60 men with firearms and 200 swordsmen, were receiving reinforcements every minute, so that not only would it have been very difficult to retire, but the position of the 4th Sikhs at Bakrai would have become more or less untenable at night. Under these circumstances Lieut.-Colonel Gaselee, commanding the regiment, decided to re-occupy Diliari, and, posting one company to a flank, to fire on the crest, he advanced with the other two companies which were at hand, and cleared the hill. The enemy at once evacuated the position, which was then occupied for the night by one company of the 4th Sikhs and two companies of the Guides, the remaining two companies of this regiment being sent back to camp at Palosi.

Thus was driven home the lesson that, even with the tribal firearms of those days, it was necessary to occupy all commanding ground within range, and that a position for a picquet on the slope of a hill is not to be thought of, unless it is absolutely impossible to hold the crest. The forwardness of a Pathan enemy during a retirement from an awkward position and the rapid collapse of their opposition before an energetic advance are characteristics that are too well known to need comment.

The enemy were Chagarzais and Hindustanis, and they owned to having lost twelve killed and sixteen wounded. Our losses were one officer (Lieutenant Harman) and four men wounded, mostly in hand-to-hand fighting.

On the 24th March, Brigadier-General Hammond, with the troops as per margin, marched from Tilli to Palosi, leaving a detachment of the Gurkhas at the former place and also a detachment of that regiment and the left wing of the 32nd Pioneers at Ril and Makranai. On arrival at Palosi the Khaibar Rifles were

No. 9 Mountain Battery, R.A. (2 guns).
1st Battalion, Royal Welsh Fusiliers.
Half Battalion, 2-5th Gurkha Regiment.
Khaibar Rifles.

sent across the river to Bakrai, while the remainder of the troops joined the River Column.

The occupation of the Diliarai heights at nightfall on the 23rd by the 4th Sikhs had been followed by the retirement of the enemy, and no attempt had been made on the picquets during the night. On the morning of the 24th, ground to the north-west was occupied up to a point overlooking Didal and Kamach on the right bank of the Indus, and three guns of No. 2 (Derajat) Mountain Battery were sent from Palosi to join the 4th Sikhs. A movement of the enemy southwards along the Indus valley from Kamach and Didal was observed, about ten standards crossing to Darbanai and the same number proceeding towards Karnar and Baio.

On this date the General Officer commanding reported that the political situation was as follows :—

The lower Hassanzai, including all the clans except the Khan Khel, have submitted. They have offered no opposition to our advance, and they are anxious to be allowed to return to their villages. The Akazai would probably submit on the occupation of Darbanai, but are intimidated by *mullas* and others from Chagarzai territory. With regard to the Chagarzai themselves, their country is overrun by a horde of *mullas*, *talibs*, and such like from Kohistan, Batkul, Kana, Ghorband, Chakesar, etc.; and they are unable, even if willing, to maintain a peaceable attitude. The Bunerwals, who have been for some days at Baio, appear to be maintaining a watchful attitude, but there is up to this time no general gathering of the tribe. Mr. Cunningham reports from information received by him, that the armed gathering at Baio is composed of men brought there by Mulla Faizi of Bajkatta, in upper Buner, and the Akhund Khel of Kuria, in the Chamla valley.

On the morning of the 25th March the force, as shown in the margin, under Brigadier-General Hammond, advanced up the Shal Nala, covered by the 4th Sikhs and the three guns of No. 2 (Derajat) Mountain Battery on the Diliarai spur. The objective of the movement was Darbanai, a village situated on a knoll jutting out from the main spur into the Indus valley. It is about 1,500 feet above the Indus and is a most commanding position, dominating the course of the river northwards as well as

No. 9 Mn. Battery, R. A., 4 guns.
1st Bn., Roy. Welsh Fus.
11th Bengal Infantry, 2 companies.
2-5th Gurkhas wing.
Khaibar Rifles.

the northern slopes of the main spur, and the whole of the right bank of the Indus from below Didal to above Kamach. A *kotal* on the same level as the village connects the Diliarai heights with the upper portion of the spur. The track up the Shal Nala was a most difficult one, but at 1 P.M. Brigadier-General Hammond was in possession of the *kotal*. Before attacking, however, he waited for his guns, which had ascended the bed of the *nala* through a very rough track. Directly the advance began the enemy opened fire from the village and from the spur above Ledh. The Khaibar Rifles ascended the hill on the right, the Gurkhas advanced on the left, and the Royal Welsh Fusiliers and the 11th Bengal Infantry in the centre. The enemy abandoned the village before it was reached, and made off down the slope of the hill towards lower Surmal, the Royal Welsh Fusiliers following them closely. The Khaibar Rifles meanwhile had cleared the hills on the right for a long distance, doing a hard day's work. The troops bivouacked for the night in and about Darbanai. Our losses during the day had been Lieutenant Doughty, Royal Welsh Fusiliers, and one man of the Khaibaris wounded. The enemy's losses were estimated at about forty.

The water-supply at Darbanai, which was brought by a channel from a ravine about a mile distant and 800 or 900 feet above the village, having been cut by the enemy, Brigadier-General Hammond sent word to the village of upper Surmal, where a number of armed men were collected, that, if the firing into camp did not cease, and the water was not turned on, he would attack and destroy their village.

On the 27th, as the enemy in the neighbourhood of Darbanai had taken no notice of the warning sent to them, and a force had collected at lower Surmal in a threatening attitude, Brigadier-General Hammond, having posted No. 9 Mountain Battery in a position commanding that village, advanced down the spur towards it, sending the Khaibar Rifles up the hills on the right. The guns of No. 9 Mountain Battery were ordered to open fire on Surmal and the spurs above it, and the 2-5th Gurkhas were directed to make a flanking movement to the right; whilst the Royal Welsh Fusiliers, with the 11th Bengal Infantry in reserve, dropped down into the *nala*, and then ascended on the other side. There were 400 or 500 of the enemy in and about the village, and they had almost perfect cover from the guns under the brow of the spur.

The Gurkhas and Royal Welsh Fusiliers arrived about the same time, and the enemy at once bolted under a heavy fire from both these regiments. As orders had been received not to advance further than necessary into Chagarzai territory, the troops were not allowed to go beyond the ferry, and only two houses in lower Surmal were burnt as a warning to the Chagarzais. The Khaibar Rifles and a company of the Gurkhas, which had gone up the hill, had in the meanwhile met and dispersed an almost equally large number of the enemy, who in the same way had not attempted to come to close quarters. Our loss was 3 men wounded, while that of the enemy, most of whom were Chagarzais, was estimated at 120.

On the 29th, the number of armed men at Baio increased, and the village of Wale was occupied by their advanced picquets. The gathering was being swelled from various quarters—from Buner, Chamla, and from the Amazai and Gadun country.

On this date, owing to the threatening attitude of Buner, the 9th Bengal Lancers and the 22nd Bengal Infantry were ordered to move from Nowshera to Mardan to strengthen the garrison of that place, which consisted of the Northumberland Fusiliers and the Guides Cavalry. These troops were to be held in readiness for service towards the Buner frontier, and Brigadier-General F. J. Keen, C.B., was ordered to proceed from Peshawar to Mardan and assume command.

Three guns of No. 2 (Derajat) Mountain Battery were ordered to march on the following day from Oghi to Darband, and a wing of the 28th Bengal Infantry to move to Pabal Gali. Orders were also given for the road from Pabal Gali to Tilli to be constructed as soon as possible by civil labour.

On the 31st the whole of the Reserve Brigade, troops as per margin, under the command of Brigadier-General Sir William Lockhart, were concentrated at Darband.

No. 1 Mn. Battery, R.A., 3 guns.
No. 2 (Derajat) Mn. Battery, 3 guns.
1st Bn., King's Roy. Rifles.
19th Bengal Infantry.
27th " "

The designations of the Brigades were now altered to 1st, 2nd, and 3rd Brigades, commanded respectively by Brigadier-Generals Williamson, Hammond, and Lockhart.

On this date the Chief Political Officer reported that there were in the neighbourhood of Baio, or in the Chagarzai country to the north, a coalition against us of all the clans from the Peshawar border to Thakot, and the General Officer Commanding wired to the Government to know whether, in the event of the *lashkar* not dispersing, he might be allowed to make them do so by force.

On the 1st April Brigadier-Generals Lockhart and Hammond came to Palosi for a conference with the General Officer Commanding, but no instructions were issued for any movements pending the final orders of Government.

Mian Gul was reported to have arrived at Baio, but there was no ostentatious display of standards. The gathering at that place was now a large one and included all sections of the Bunerwals.

A letter was sent to Mian Gul and the Buner *jirga* by the Commissioner of Peshawar, under the orders of the Punjab Government, who had been in communication with the Commander-in-Chief, to the effect that we had no intention of invading the Chagarzai country, and that we wished for peace with the Bunerwals; but that we should consider ourselves at liberty to attack them from both sides in their own country of Buner if after this explanation their *lashkar* did not retire.

This communication, together with other correspondence that took place between the Government and Mian Gul had the desired effect and on the 4th April it was reported by an old sepoy of the 5th Punjab Infantry (a Bunerwal) that the *lashkar* was dispersing. A reconnaissance was now made along the right bank of the Indus, as far as the limits of Hassanzai territory.

There was no opposition from Baio, near which only a small gathering was seen. A few standards with a collection of armed men were observed on the spur dividing the Hassanzai from the Chagarzai territory, but these moved off as the troops approached, and their movements were hastened by a few shells from the left bank below Diliarai. The right bank south of Karnar was found to be quite impracticable for animals and difficult for foot men; and any improvement would have required much time and labour, as the road ran over solid rock.

The village of Bimbal was burnt this day as a reminder to the Akazai that they had not made their submission.

On the 7th April, owing to a sudden outbreak on the Miranzai border, the troops of the Reserve, or 3rd, Brigade were withdrawn from the Hazara Field Force, and marched from Darband for

Kohat with transport complete. Brigadier-General Sir William Lockhart and staff had started for the same destination on the preceding day.

On this date the Mada Khel and Hassanzai *jirga* deputed to Baio returned and reported that the place was absolutely deserted, not even the usual inhabitants being there. Steps were at once taken, in accordance with orders received from Army Head-quarters, to withdraw all troops to the left bank of the Indus. It was reported that Mian Gul had advised Hashim Ali to surrender, but that the latter had refused to accept this advice, and had gone off to Teri in the Makki Khel country.[1] At 6-30 A.M. on the 8th the Guides Infantry, accompanied by the divisional head-quarters, marched from Palosi to Ril *viâ* the flying bridge at Bakrai, and thence by the road through Makranai. This road was very steep and caused delay to the mules, the rear-guard not arriving at Ril till 7-30 P.M.

The Seaforth Highlanders with three guns of No. 1 Mountain Battery and the head-quarters of the 1st Brigade moved to Tilli, *en route* to Seri, *viâ* the bridge-of-boats at Kotkai, and the detachment of the 11th Bengal Infantry joined the head-quarters of the regiment at Lashora. By noon Palosi and Nawekili were entirely evacuated, and the inhabitants were seen returning to their villages. The only troops remaining on the right bank of the river were the 37th Dogras at the Kotkai bridge head.

Arrangements were now made for a change of base from Darband to Oghi, the abandonment of all river posts except Bakrai, the dismantling of the bridge and return of the boats down river. Orders were issued for various moves, and from about this date until the termination of the expedition in June, the troops remained in occupation of the Black Mountain in the following positions :—

Divisional and 1st Brigade Head-quarters at Seri, with detachments at Kan, Abu Kotal, Ril, Kungar, Karun, Maira, and Pabal Gali. 2nd Brigade at Darbanai with detachments at Diliari, Peza, Tilli, China, Abu Kotal, and Panj Gali. A road connecting the two brigades through Maira was taken in hand, and opened on the 17th April.

[1] The Makki Khel are a small clan supposed to be descendants of Akhund Salak Baba by a slave girl. They are settled on the western side of the Duma range, between the Hassanzai, Chagarzai, and Buner borders.

Active operations were now practically over. The Hassanzais, with the exception of the Khan Khel section, had long ago submitted and in fact had never really opposed us, but certain further punitive measures were necessary to bring the Akazais to reason.

On the 16th of April the village of Moratta was destroyed for having resisted a foraging party, and a little later a similar treatment was meted out to Darai and Larai for being concerned in a raid on the commissariat enclosure at Seri.

On the 24th April the whole of the Akazai country was visited by a combined movement from Seri and Kan. One party proceeded from Kan to the crest of the ridge dividing Akazai from Chagarzai territory; another party proceeded from Seri to the crest of this ridge *viâ* Kan, Sokar, and Toram; a third party visited Doda and Machai from Seri *viâ* Saudagara and Biran. The whole of the country was found deserted, but sixty-five head of cattle were captured, and a large amount of grain was found concealed in some of the villages.

On this date Darband was evacuated, and the transfer of the base to Oghi was completed. Communication was then established across the Pabal Gali pass, and through Tilli and Ril. Pabal Gali had been occupied, as soon as the state of the snow permitted, by a detachment of the 28th Bengal Infantry from Oghi. The new route proved unsatisfactory owing to its length and the difficulty of the sections of road passing under and around the cliffs of Abu. Accordingly, as soon as the snow cleared, a shorter and much more convenient line was opened through Panj Gali. This route was made practicable by the 1st May and opened for regular traffic on the 7th, and the distance between Oghi and Seri was reduced from thirty to seventeen miles. As this is in every respect the best line of route across the mountain from Oghi to Seri, considerable labour was expended on the road. It is probable that in ordinary winters it could be kept clear of snow by working-parties.

On the 30th April a party went out from Darbanai and Diliari and, crossing the Indus on a raft, captured some sheep belonging to Akazais. Bilianai was destroyed on the return march. On the 13th May the villages of Biran and Zanlui were destroyed by a party from the camp at Seri for a raid made by Gujars from those villages on a convoy.

On the 26th May the Hassanzai and Akazai *jirgas*, who had arrived in camp, were interviewed at Seri; and the latter, influenced by the fear of losing their autumn crops as well as the spring harvests already forfeited, tendered the unconditional submission of the tribe. They were thereupon given permission to re-occupy their lands and villages on the same terms as had been accorded to the Hassanzai at the commencement of the expedition. On the first condition to be imposed on the tribes, namely, the surrender of Hashim Ali, being brought up, the united *jirgas* declared their inability in this respect, and the matter was referred to Government, the conference being suspended.

Agreements made with the Hassanzai and Akazai on the 29th May.

On the 28th the approval of Government was received to terms of settlement proposed by the General Officer Commanding, and on the 29th the *jirgas* of the Hassanzai and Akazai agreed to these terms, which were subsequently also accepted by the Mada Khels and the Pariari *jirga*. The text of the agreement may be summarized as follows :—

The three Isazai sections—Hassanzai, Akazai, and Mada Khel—and the Saiyids and Chagarzai of Pariari bound themselves to the perpetual exclusion and banishment of Hashim Ali and his family ; to be of good behaviour ; to be responsible for all offences by their clansmen in British territory ; to protect our subjects in their country ; to refer claims against them to the Deputy Commissioner ; and to refrain from the time-honoured custom of *baramta*, by which a clansman, having a fancied claim against one British subject, seizes the person or property of any other he can lay hands on. They also bound themselves not to permit any settlement of Hindustani fanatics in their country.

The Hassanzai, Akazai, and Pariariwals further promised to accompany troops marching on their borders, and, with due notice given, to escort and arrange for the safety of officials and British subjects who may visit their country. The three Isazai clans admitted their joint responsibility for the conduct of any Khan of Seri whom they might elect.

Failing the actual surrender of Hashim Ali, which, as he ran away before our troops advanced, these clans could not effect, the next best arrangement which could be secured was his perpetual banishment.

The *maliks* were also informed that a force would be kept in their country, until Government was satisfied that they were strong enough to prevent the return of Hashim Ali, and to preserve order.

On the 9th June sanction was received from Army Headquarters for the return to India of all troops except those named in the margin, who were to remain in occupation of the crest of the Black Mountain, and at Seri and Oghi, under the command of Brigadier-General Hammond, V.C., D.S.O., with Captain Bradshaw, 35th Sikhs, as Brigade-Major.

No. 9 Mn. Battery, R. A.
1st Bn., Royal Welsh Fus.
No. 4 Coy., Bengal S. and M.
1-1st Gurkhas.
4th Sikh Infantry.
28th Bengal Infantry.

Our losses during the expedition were nine killed and thirty-nine wounded, the latter including three officers, *viz.*—Second-Lieutenant C. H. M. Doughty, Lieutenant E. W. S. K. Maconchy, and Lieutenant R. Harman.

Cause of the hostile coalition of Yusafzai clans in 1891.

The widespread coalition against us, which led to the hostile gathering at Baio and to actual opposition to our columns on several occasions by tribes with whom we were not at war, is almost without a precedent on this border, and can only be compared to the Ambela outbreak in 1863, although it did not lead, as on that occasion, to serious fighting.

The political officer was of opinion that this hostile demonstration was due to the fact that all the Yusafzai clans of the Indus valley believed that it was intended that the force should march through Chagarzai territory to Thakot. To quote from his report :—

There is no doubt that Hashim Ali Khan and his friends spread rumours among the tribes between Palosi and Thakot which made them dread the same treatment.[1] In order to realize this, it must be remembered that these people are fanatical, ignorant, and suspicious to a degree which those who have no personal experience will not readily conceive. Intensely jealous of their independence, they dread the visit of an army as possibly preluding subjugation and certainly involving a risk of general punishment if some misguided men fire at a camp or cut a telegraph wire. Such prejudices have, of course, no right to survive in face of a forward policy and the necessity

[1] Namely, the same treatment as that meted out to the clans who had offended us.

of extending our influence beyond our border. All that seems advisable is that it should be understood that they exist in a form which makes it difficult for us, in the absence of special arrangements, to make friendly marches in a peaceful way among some of these clans, or to get them to co-operate for the management of their country upon lines which they dislike. When they have been well beaten, they will be more malleable, and, once annexed, they would soon make peaceable subjects.

To make this account of the 1891 Hazara expedition complete, a brief record is necessary of the events subsequent to the withdrawal of the main portion of the Hazara Field Force in June 1891. As already mentioned, a brigade under Brigadier-General Hammond remained at Seri and at Nimal in order to maintain quiet and ensure the banishment of Hashim Ali. On the 13th July a fully representative *jirga* of the Akazai came to Seri and elected Ibrahim Khan, the cousin and rival of Hashim Ali as their chief, tying the turban on his head with all due formality. In August the two other Isazai clans, the Hassanzai and Mada Khel, followed this example, and formally elected Ibrahim Khan as their chief.

With a view to increase our control over the clans on this border, to assist in the maintenance of peace, and to secure the continued expulsion of Hashim Ali, the levy of a small force of 200 Border Police, to be recruited from the independent clans and posted at suitable places on the frontier, was sanctioned. The Swatis of Nandihar, Tikari, and Deshi, and the Saiyids and mixed population of Pariari freely accepted service in this force. The Hassanzai and Akazai at first refused the offer of allowances and of service in the police, but finally agreed, in order to shorten the occupation of their hills by our troops.

In addition to the Border Police, for which (including the old Agror Police) a sum of Rs. 29,000 was allotted yearly, Government sanctioned allowances for leading men of the clans on this border—to the Hassanzai, Akazai, and Mada Khel, on condition of maintaining the compacts made by them in 1891; to the others on condition of general friendship, good behaviour, and assistance in preserving peace on this part of the frontier.

By the end of November the evacuation of the Black Mountain by our troops was complete.

Expedition against the Isazai clans by a force under Major-General Sir W. S. A. Lockhart, K.C.B., C.S.I., in 1892.

At the end of March 1892 Hashim Ali, the ex-Chief of the Isazai clan, visited Baio, and later on his supporters and sympathizers among the trans-Indus Hassanzais and Mada Khels agreed to his family settling at Baio and Doba. Baio is a Hassanzai and Doba a Mada Khel village. On the 8th April he brought his family to the former place, escorted by a following of Makki Khel and Sundar Khel sections of the trans-Indus Chagarzai, who live on the slopes of the Duma range; and here his supporters built him a house.

In thus allowing Hashim Ali to return to Baio, the Hassanzais and Mada Khels were guilty of a breach of the agreement, to which they had subscribed at Seri in 1891. The clans were warned of the consequences of their action, and efforts were also made, but without avail, to induce Hashim Ali to surrender himself, a place of residence with a monthly allowance being offered him in British territory. Finally in September orders were issued for the assembly of a Field Force to expel the ex-chieftain and to punish the villages which had harboured him. In accordance with these orders a force of two brigades, numbering with divisional troops 6,250 of all ranks and 24 guns, advanced from Darband on the 2nd October under the command of Major-General Sir W. S. A. Lockhart, K.C.B., C.S.I., with Brevet-Major A. R. Martin as Assistant Adjutant-General.

As the tribes on this occasion offered no resistance to the march of troops through their territory, the operations of the Isazai Field Force will be very briefly described.

Crossing the Indus at Marer, Sir W. Lockhart ordered the 1st Brigade and divisional troops, with one maxim gun,[1] to assemble at Palosi on the 5th October, and to move on to Wale the same night; the 2nd Brigade was ordered to Manja Kot.

At daybreak on the 6th October the divisional artillery moved into position on the ridge in front of Wale, within range of Baio; and the advance of the two brigades—the 1st from Wale and the 2nd from Manja Kot—was then carried out. The crest was reached

[1] This gun had been sent up from Bombay in charge of a small party of the Yorkshire Light Infantry, and had arrived at Darband on the 3rd October. This is the first record of a maxim having been sent with troops on field service in India.

almost at the same time on the right and left by the advanced parties of each brigade at 7-30 A.M.; and on approaching Baio the place was found to be deserted. The towers and defences were then destroyed, the former being blown up.

Before the demolition of the Baio defences was carried out, the troops which had not reached the crest were ordered to retire—those of the 1st Brigade and the divisional troops to Palosi, and those of the 2nd Brigade to Manja Kot. On the demolitions being completed, the whole of the troops were withdrawn. The 2nd Brigade, before retiring, destroyed the village of Doba. This brigade was ordered to march back to Towara on the following day (the 7th) after carrying out certain demolitions in the villages of Manja Kot and Karor, in accordance with the suggestions of the Chief Political Officer.

The defences of the villages of Garhi and Nawekili were destroyed on the 8th, and orders having been received for the return of the expedition, the force was marched back to Darband on the 11th and there broken up.

The health of the troops, which on former expeditions in the Black Mountain area had been good, was on this occasion indifferent. This was chiefly due to the prevalence of malarial fever and to an outbreak of cholera, which resulted in twenty-four deaths out of fifty-five cases.

Subsequent events.

Since the expedition in 1892 the Black Mountain tribes and their neighbours have given no serious trouble; and the arrangements sanctioned in 1891, *i.e.*, the granting of certain allowances and the establishment of the Border Police, have been found to be efficacious in keeping the Hazara border quiet.

In 1899 it was found necessary to divert a portion of Ibrahim Khan's allowance for direct payment to the headmen of the various sections of the clan, owing to the chief's parsimonious habits.

On the 9th November 1901 Hazara was included in the North-West Frontier Province which was then formed.

In 1902 a dispute about some debatable land led to a raid being made by the Saiyids of Tilli into Tanawal. This dispute had not been settled in 1905 when the last report was received.

Hashim Ali has still a considerable number of sympathizers among his clansmen, and in 1902 an abortive attempt was made to get up an agitation on his behalf; the Hassanzais continued to sulk until 1903, when they apologized for their behaviour and are now again in receipt of their allowances.

In 1904, for some unexplained reason, the Akazais refused to accept their allowances.

In November 1905 Ibrahim Khan's brother, by name Isa Khan, was murdered at Seri. The latter had formerly been a subadar in the Border Military Police but had been dismissed for misconduct, and he was at this time, under the orders of Government, in receipt of an allowance from Ibrahim Khan, with whom he had always been on the worst of terms.

This crime, which the Isazais believed to be the work of Ibrahim Khan and his son, put the finishing touch to the former's unpopularity, and in April of the following year the Hassanzais drove him out of Seri and stated, in *jirga* before the Deputy Commissioner of Hazara, that they disowned him and would only recognize as their *Khan* a son of Hashim Ali.

Ibrahim Khan's faction was, however, at the time, strong enough to bring him back to Seri and partially rebuild the village, which had been burnt down; but within a month or two he was again forced to fly for his life, and this time he took refuge in Agror, his crops having been destroyed and his tower dismantled. It would have been better for him if he had remained there, for, having returned to tribal territory, he and some of his retainers were killed in a *musjid* near Karun, on the 4th November 1906, by a band of Hassanzais led by Sikandar Khan and Torabaz Khan, brothers of Hashim Ali. The Hassanzais acted against their agreements with Government in admitting these proscribed persons into their territory.

At present, 1907, the Isazais are without a *Khan*, but it is probable that they will try to bring in Hashim Ali's elder son, a youth seventeen years of age, named Sher Ali Khan, who was a mere child in 1891, when the agreement excluding Hashim Ali from the *Khanship* was made. No mention was made in this agreement of any son of Hashim Ali. The latter is still living and has another son aged five years.

APPENDIX A.

Command and Staff, Hazara Field Force, 1888.

A. D. C., McQueen, Major-General J. W., C.B., S.C. ...	Commanding.
Western, Lieutenant J. S. E., 1st Punjab Cavalry ..	Aide-de-Camp.
Gatacre, Colonel W. F.	D. A. Q.-M. G.
Egerton, Major C. C., 3rd Punjab Cavalry ..	A. A. G.
Elles, Major E. R., Royal Artillery	A. Q.-M. G.
Mason, Captain A. H., Royal Engineers	D. A. Q.-M. G. (Intelligence.)
Lovett, Colonel B., C.S.I., Royal Engineers ..	Commanding Engineer.
Goold-Adams, Captain W. R., 1st Dragoon Guards ..	Superintendent, Army Signalling.
Thornton, Deputy Surgeon-General J. H., C.B., M.B., I.M.S.	P. M. O.
Keighley, Major C. M., Staff Corps	Chief Commissariat Officer.
Yielding, Captain W. R., Staff Corps	Divisional Transport Officer.
Wahab, Captain R. A., Royal Engineers	Survey Officer.

Artillery.

Deshon, Lieut.-Colonel C. J., Royal Artillery ..	Commanding.

First Brigade.

V.C., Channer, Brigadier-General G. N., S.C. ..	Commanding.
O'Gorman, Major N. P., Lincolnshire Regiment ..	D. A. A.-G.
Money, Major E. E., 11th Bengal Lancers ..	D. A. Q.-M. G.

Second Brigade.

Galbraith, Brigadier-General W.	Commanding.
Barlow, Major J. A., Manchester Regiment ..	D. A. A.-G.
Beley, Captain C. H. H., D.S.O., 25th Bengal Infantry	D. A. Q.-M. G. to 4th October 1888.
Grierson, Captain J. M., Royal Artillery	D. A. Q.-M. G. from 9th October 1888.

APPENDIX B.

Command and Staff, Black Mountain Expedition, 1891.

Elles, Major-General W. K., C.B., British Service ..	Commanding.
Shakespear, Colonel G. R. J., 10th Bengal Lancers ..	A. A.-G.
Carter, Captain F. C., Northumberland Fusiliers ..	D. A. A.-G.
Mason, Captain A. H., R.E.	D. A. Q.-M. G.
Keith, Lieut.-Colonel J., R.A.	C. R. A.
Greenstreet, Major W. L., R.E.	C. R. E.
Hamilton, Captain E. O. F., Royal West Surrey Regiment	Superintendent, Army Signalling.
Bradshaw, Deputy Surgeon-General A. F. M. S. ..	P. M. O.
Lyons-Montgomery, Captain H. F., B. S. C. ..	Chief Commissariat Officer.
Tulloch, Lieutenant J. W. G., B. S. C.	Divisional Transport Officer.
Wahab, Captain R. A., R.E.	Survey Officer.

Left or River Column.

Williamson, Brigadier-General R. F., Royal Welsh Fusiliers	Commanding.
Bradshaw, Captain L. J. E., 35th Bengal Infantry ..	Brigade Major.

Right or Tilli Column.

V.C., A.D.C., Hammond, Brigadier-General A. G., D.S.O., 3rd Sikh Infantry	Commanding.
Colleton, Captain *Sir* R. A. W., *Bart.*, Royal Welsh Fusiliers	Brigade Major

Oghi Column.

Hills, Colonel G. S., 28th Bengal Infantry	Commanding.

CHAPTER V.

YUSAFZAI AND GADUN TRIBES BETWEEN THE BLACK MOUNTAIN AND SWAT.

THE tribes occupying the British border from the Black Mountain to the Utman Khel territory belong, with the exception of the Gaduns, to the important tribe of Yusafzai Pathans, of which the Hassanzis, Akazais, and Chagarzais, occupying the western slopes of the Black Mountain, and described in the previous chapter, are also branches.

The Yusafzais inhabit the division of that name in the Peshawar district, as well as independent territory beyond the border. They are descended from one Mandai, who had two sons, Umar and Yusaf. Umar died, leaving one son, Mandan; and from Mandan and Yusaf are the two primary divisions of the Yusafzais, from which are sprung all the sub-divisions. The relations of the different branches of the Yusafzai tribe will be understood by referring to the table given in Appendix A. at the end of the chapter.

First in order of the independent tribes on the British border between the Black Mountain and the Utman Khel territory, come the Mada Khels and Amazais, adjoining the territory of our feudatory the Nawab of Amb; to the south of the Amazais lie the Utmanzais, to their west the Gaduns, and beyond them the Khudu Khels. To the north of the Khudu Khel territory is the Chamla valley, inhabited by members of different tribes, and separated from Buner by the Guru range of mountains. Next come the Nurizai and Salarzai tribes of Buner, which march with our border. Between Buner and the Utman Khel limits is the district of Swat, and the portion adjoining British territory is inhabited by members of the Baizai and Ranizai tribes of Swat.

Before describing these tribes, a few words are necessary with regard to the position of the Nawab of Amb on this border, as it is, in some respects, a peculiar one. His territory may be described roughly as a square block in the north-west corner of the district of Hazara, separated on its west from the independent Pathan country by the Indus, and having the Black Mountain and Agror to the north. The Tanawal Chief has also two or three villages beyond the Indus, the largest of which is Amb, which contains 300 houses, flat-roofed and built of stone and mud, but ill-adapted for defence. The Nawab of Amb holds his cis-Indus territory as a *jagir* from the British Government on a perpetuity tenure. His villages trans-Indus are independent, but the *Nawab* is responsible that he does not misuse his power. He administers the *jagir* himself, subject to no interference from us, except in heinous criminal cases, which are comparatively few. The existence of this little principality is in many ways convenient; and the *jagir*, while really no expense to the Government, forms a stronghold upon the loyalty of the chief. Tanawal lies between Hazara and some of the more turbulent independent tribes of the frontier, with which the Tanawalis have old feuds that render coalition with them scarcely possible; moreover, his trans-Indus villages, formerly the property of the wild tribes of the Mahaban, keep the chief ever in hot water with them, and his only safe policy, therefore, is to be faithful to British interests. At the same time, he is more than a match for any of the tribes on his border, and is consequently able to keep them in order. Muhammad Akram Khan, the present chief, is a very old man who has shown his loyalty on more than one occasion, and did good service in 1868, for which he was granted the title of *Nawab* as already stated, and was also made a Companion of the Order of the Star of India. He is one of the most reliable chiefs on the border.

Mada Khel.

The Mada Khels are a section of the Isazai Yusafzais, and occupy the northern slopes of the Mahaban mountain down to the right bank of the Indus. They are bounded on the north by the Hassanzais, on the east and south by Amb territory, and on the west by the Amazais. Their country may be described as lying between the Indus on the east, and the watershed of the northern portion of the Mahaban on the west, the eastern slopes of the range being Mada Khel, and the western Amazai.

The Mada Khel are divided into three principal sub-sections, with 1,460 fighting men—

Mada Nama	.. .. ..	750 fighting men.
Hasan Khel	.. .. ..	340 " "
Bazid Khel	.. .. ..	370 " "

In addition to these, the Dilazaks, Gujars, etc., who live within the Mada Khel limits, could furnish a contingent of 565 men, making the total fighting strength of the Mada Khel 2,025 men. They are armed with guns and swords. The guns are matchlocks and flintlocks, for the most part the former. They purchase their powder and their lead from Chamla, Buner, and British Yusafzai.

The Mada Khels have no great name for bravery. In the event of being attacked they could obtain aid from the Hassanzais and Akazais, as they all belong to the Isazai clan, and their borders join.

A blockade would give them little trouble, as they are not dependent on British territory. Their country is poor and barren, and supplies would have to accompany a force entering their hills. The majority of their villages are situated in the Mahaban range, and only two or three are on the banks of the Indus. The easiest approaches to the Mada Khel territory lie through the Hassanzai country, and this tribe would, therefore, have to be coerced, and the Nawab of Amb would have to give assistance. There is, however, a route which avoids the Hassanzai country, and crosses the river lower down, but this is hilly and impracticable for laden animals.

The Mada Khels can scarcely be said to be on our border, as the territory of the Nawab of Amb intervenes, and their dealings are for the most part with him. The *Nawab* is, as a rule, left to manage his own affairs with them. Their grand *jirga* has, however, twice been summoned, in 1863 and 1868, on both occasions in matters connected with Amb.

The Amazais are a section of the Usmanzai Yusafzais. About half of their country is settled within, and the rest beyond, the British border. The section has two sub-sections—1. Daulatzai; 2. Ismailzai. Within British territory the Daulatzai inhabit the Sudum valley, and their chief villages are Chargolai and Rustam. The Ismailzai

Amazai.

occupy a strip of country in the sub-division of Yusafzai, in the Peshawar district, south of the Karamar range, and on the road from Mardan, east. Their chief village is Kapur-ka-garhi. The Amazais beyond the border are divided into the Saiyid Khel and Mobarak Khel, two sections constantly at feud with one another. They are bounded on the south by the trans-Indus territory of the Nawab of Amb, and by the Gaduns; on the west by the Khudu Khels and the Chamla valley; on the north by Buner; and on the east by the Mada Khels. From the village of Birgalai, where the Amazai meets the Gadun territory the border runs parallel with the Indus to Betgali, including the village of Faruza in its course. From Betgali it takes a north-west direction to the main north spur of the Mahaban mountain; it runs down this to the Barandu river, and follows that stream as far as its junction with the Chamla. Thence it follows the course of the Chamla for about four miles, after which it runs in a generally south-east direction back to Birgalai.

The Amazai country is divided into two districts by a northern spur from the Mahaban. All the villages lying to the east of this spur, and between it and the Indus, are called Pitao Amazai, and all to the west, Surai Amazai. The first belongs to the Saiyid Khel, and the second to both sections. The Amazai country is narrow and rough, and is drained by many mountain torrents, all of which, except the Ashera stream, drain to the Barandu, and are perennial. It contains about thirty villages, situated along the courses of the different hill streams. Cherorai is the chief village. The whole of this district is well wooded with pines; cultivation is consequently scanty. Cattle are plentiful, and *ghi* is the product of the country.

The strength of the trans-border Amazais is about 1,500 fighting men. They are considered one of the best fighting clans of all the Yusafzais. They still intermarry and communicate with their brethren under British rule, but in matters of internal government are quite distinct from them. In matters affecting the politics of the tribe, in connection with their neighbours, they side with the Bunerwals, the authority of whose chiefs they acknowledge to some slight degree.

The Amazais are not dependent on British territory, and like the Mada Khels, they can hardly be said to be on our border, as all their dealings are with the Nawab of Amb. Their relations with this chief have generally been of a friendly nature, though there is a party in the tribe who are hostile to him. The nearest approach to the Amazai country from British territory is through Amb, but there is another road starting from Panjman on the Gadun border to Nagrai in Amazai territory (a distance of twenty-seven miles), which is well supplied with water, and is practicable for laden camels. This road, however, passes through the independent territory of the Gaduns and of the Khudu Khels.

The only occasion on which we have come into direct contact with the Amazais was in the Ambela campaign of 1863, and our dealings with them at that time will be described in the account of that expedition in the next chapter.

Utmanzai.

The Utmanzais are a clan of the Mandan Yusafzais. They are divided into four sections, *viz.*, Alazai, Kanazai, Akazai, and Saduzai. The first three are beyond the British border, and occupy the eastern slopes of the southern portion of the Mahaban mountain on the right bank of the Indus. The Saduzai section consists of five sub-divisions, *viz.*,—Aba Khel, Umar Khel, Mir Ahmad Khel, Bihzad Khel, and Khudu Khel. The first four of these are located within British territory, and occupy the south-eastern corner of the Peshawar district. The Khudu Khels are beyond the border, and occupy the western slopes of the Mahaban between the Gaduns on one side and the Chamlawals on the other. They will be described separately further on.

The Utmanama division of Yusafzai takes its name from this tribe. A considerable portion of the original Utmanzai territory, about two-thirds, is now occupied by the Gaduns, who were in former times invited to come over from across the Indus as military mercenaries, and in reward for their services were granted the lands they now hold on the western and southern slopes of the Mahaban mountain. The Utmanzais are considered better soldiers than the Gaduns, but they are numerically weak, and cannot muster more than 400 fighting men.

Alazais	60	Akazais ..	125
Kanazais ..	150	Saiyids ..	50
	Gujars, etc. ..	15	

About two-thirds of the fighting men are armed with guns, of which the greater part are matchlocks. They also possess one piece of ordnance.

There are several routes into the Utmanzai country, and owing to the fact that members of the tribe are settled in Yusafzai and Haripur, and own lands within our border, they may be said to be dependent upon us. This tribe harbours outlaws from our territory, and Government has not insisted on their surrender, possibly because they could easily send them further beyond the border. The principal villages of the Utmanzais are Kaya and Kabal. The village of Sitana was also within their territory, but was given by them as a *muafi* grant to the Saiyids of Tiringi on their first arrival. These Saiyids are related to the Saiyids of Khagan and Swabi, as well as to those of Jumla and Buner.

The Gaduns are a tribe of Pathans who reside partly on the southern slopes of the Mahaban, and partly in the Hazara district. Their origin is not very clear, but they are not Yusafzais, like the tribes around them. By some they are supposed to be a branch of the Kakar tribe, which was in the first instance driven to take refuge in the Safed Koh, and afterwards in Hazara and Chach in the Rawal Pindi district. The divisions of the Gaduns are :—

Gaduns.

(*i*) Salar, sub-divided into Mathkhwazai, Utazai, and Sulimanzai.

(*ii*) Mansur, sub-divided into Khadrzai, Daulatzai, and Musazai. The whole of these clans, but especially those of the Salar division, are settled along the banks of the river Dor in the Hazara district, as far as the Urash plain; and own a fertile prosperous tract, which they gradually possessed themselves of from the Dilazaks,[1] when the latter threw off their allegiance to the Emperor Jehangir.

Another portion of the tribe is settled trans-Indus, and owns territory on the southern and western slopes of the Mahaban mountain. They are bounded on the east by the Utmanzais, on the north by the Amazais, on the west by the Khudu Khels, and on the south by British territory.

1 A people of Scythic origin who inhabited the Peshawar valley before the Pathan invasion. Scattered families of them are found in Hazara and the Rawal Pindi district.

Of the clans into which the tribe is divided, the Matkhwazai live in Babinai, in Yusafzai, in British territory. The Utazai principally inhabit Gandap. The Sulimanzai are a small clan, and are scattered about Mahaban; their principal villages are Bada, Kalagar, and Atchailai. The Khadrzai own Malka Kadi, Kadura, and Thakail. The Daulatzai own Dawal, Kaghbanai, Gadjai, and half of Bisak. The last is the principal village of the Mansur division. The Musazai own the other half of Bisak, Sukailai, and several smaller hamlets.

The villages near the foot of the hills, such as Ganda, Bisak, Malka Kadi, are chiefly dependent on rain for their cultivation, and their land is indifferent in quality. The land, however, belonging to the villages in the hills is more fertile; and wheat and rice are grown in large quantities on the slopes of Mahaban. The tribes are all cultivators or cattle-owners, and their buffaloes are celebrated. Considerable quantities of *ghi* and timber are exported by them to Yusafzai, and, cloth, indigo, and salt taken in return. The only level ground in the Gadun country is in front of Gandap, Bisak, and Malka Kadi.

The trans-Indus Gaduns number about 2,000 fighting men. They are not, however, considered a fighting tribe.

There are two ways of coercing the trans-Indus portion of this tribe—(1) by blockade; as their cultivation is carried on in a great measure by our permission, and they depend much on their trade with the plains, this would soon render them quite helpless; (2) by invasion; if this was chosen, an expedition should start on the 1st September or 1st October, when their cattle are collected and their autumn crops cut, or early in April, when their spring crops are ready. At these seasons they could be punished by the loss of property to the value of Rs. 80,000, *viz.*, crops Rs. 30,000, cattle Rs. 25,000, houses and property Rs. 25,000. Unless they were surprised, however, they could send their cattle into Amazai territory. Their country could be overrun without other tribes being molested or approached too nearly. The hill portion would, of course, be the more difficult, as they have a retreat open to them. Two days would suffice for an expedition to surprise their villages and return. A blockade has on several occasions proved successful against this tribe, and a seizure can always be made. They cannot cultivate their lands in the open plain when blockaded, and they fear attack.

The Gaduns do not appear to have given any trouble on the border till 1861, when they failed to act up to their engagements to prevent the Hindustani fanatics from returning to Sitana, and were in consequence subjected to a blockade. Our subsequent dealings with the tribe will be related in their proper place.

Khudu Khels.

The Khudu Khels are a sub-division of the Saduzai section of the Utmanzai Mandan Yusafzais. Their territory is bounded on the north by Chamla, a spur from the Sarpatai peak of the Mahaban intervening, on the west by Yusafzai, on the south by Utmanama, and on the east by the territory of the Gaduns and Amazais. Its greatest length from the Sarpatai spur to Panjman is twenty-two miles, and its breadth from Narinji to Dargalai fifteen miles.

Their country is drained by the Badrai Nala, which is dry, except after rain in the hills, when it rushes down with great violence. It rises in the Sarpatai range, and at Dandar it receives a branch from the east, and a little lower another branch from Chinglai joins it from the west; it then passes the site of Panjtar, the villages of Gurgushti, Khalai Kala, and Jehangir Dara, and issues into the plains north-east of Salim Khan, and thence passes through British territory, and joins the Indus near Hund.

The Khudu Khels are divided into Usman Khel and Bam Khel. The former own half the village of Chinglai, as well as Dagi, Totalai, Sanarwai, and minor hamlets, and the latter inhabit the other half of Chinglai, Bam Khel Totalai, Dargalai, and other villages. Mangal Thana is occupied by a colony of *Saiyids*. Baja and Bam Khel, in British territory, also belong to this tribe.

The Khudu Khel are now divided among themselves, and therefore are easy to manage; but, if united, they could give a good deal of trouble. In former times, when united under Fateh Khan, and aided by the Hindustani fanatics, they were able to bring 3,000 men into the field; but at the present time, probably, they could not furnish more than 1,600 fighting men. They are not a martial people, and are dependent on British territory for their supplies and wants.

The crops are, for the spring time, wheat, barley, and mustard; for the autumn, Indian corn, *bajra*, *mash*, *kangani*, beans, and *moth*. The dress of the residents, their food, marriage, and other customs are in no way different from those of Utmanama. Adultery is much more stringently dealt with than in Yusafzai. Hindus are obliged to pay Rs. 20 at each marriage, and they are charged three rupees annually for protection by the *malik* of the *kandi*. The inferior class pay one rupee, and have to turn out, in case of a feud, to the aid of their respective *maliks*.

A blockade would inconvenience them very much, more especially as they have intimate relations with the people in our territories. The villages are, moreover, for the most part in the open, and exposed to attack, which gives us a greater hold over them than even the fear of a blockade. A good seizure could always be made.

Our connection with this tribe dates as far back as 1847, and in July of that year a detachment of Guides Cavalry, with a troop of Sikh Regular Cavalry, marched from Yusafzai to surprise the village of Moghdara, in Khudu Khel territory. Half an hour before daybreak they arrived at the mouth of a narrow defile, three-quarters of a mile long, leading to the village, and along which only one horseman could go at a time. The Guides, under Lieutenant H. B. Lumsden, pushed rapidly through the defile; but the Sikhs, for some unaccountable reason, did not follow. The village, however, was surprised, the inhabitants disarmed, and the headmen and 300 head of cattle were brought away by the Guides.

Again, on the 26th June 1849, a detachment of the Guides (69 sabres and 177 bayonets), under Ressaldar Fateh Khan, marched during the night from Peshawar to Yar Husain in Yusafzai, and the next morning attacked and destroyed the Khudu Khel village of Bagh and returned to Yar Husain by noon.

On the whole, however, the tribe has given little trouble. We perhaps owe this good conduct to its openness to attack from our territory; and there can be no doubt, should it be necessary to punish them, it would be very simple to do so, as the approaches to the country are easy.

From the year 1820, the history of the Khudu Khels has been mixed up with, and comprises the vicissitudes which have befallen,

Fateh Khan of Panjtar and his no less remarkable son, Mukarrab Khan, who for years has been an exile and a wanderer from his tribe, but who still is an important political factor on this part of the border. Mukarrab Khan is the representative of a family which is acknowledged to be the foremost amongst the different sections of the Mandan clan, which inhabit this part of the frontier, and more will be said of him later on.

Chamlawals.

The Chamlawals are a mixture of Mandan clans, and inhabit the small valley of Chamla, to the south-east of Buner. This valley is bounded on the north by Buner, on the west by Yusafzai, on the south by Khudu Khel territory, and on the east by the lands of the Amazais.

The valley runs east and west, its extreme length from Ambela to Garhi being ten miles, and its greatest breadth two-and-a-half miles. A spur of the Guru mountain separates it from Buner, another from the Sarpatai peak of the Mahaban range intervenes between it and Khudu Khel territory, whilst a somewhat similar spur from the same range divides it from the country of the Amazais. In former years, when, after subjugating the country, the Yusaf and Mandan clans began to quarrel amongst themselves for their possessions, the latter located their families in the Chamla valley pending the settlement of the disturbances. The contest terminated in the Yusaf clans occupying Swat and Buner, whilst the Mandan race appropriated the plains of the Peshawar district. Chamla, though nominally a *daftar* of the Mandans, is completely subservient to its powerful neighbour Buner.

The political importance of Chamla is very small, and as soldiers the inhabitants are held in the lowest estimation.

A stream with a firm bottom runs down the middle of the valley, the water flowing on a level with the surface of the ground as far as Kuria, but beyond that the ravine deepens gradually, and the valley ceases to be open and easy. Between Ambela and Kuria, cavalry and horse artillery could manœuvre, as there are no obstacles except the stream, which could be crossed without difficulty. The elevation of the valley is little over 2,000 feet. The country produces during the spring crops, wheat, barley, peas and *masur*; during the autumn, *mash*, *moth*, rice, Indian corn, *dal*, and *kangani*. The soil is good, water abundant, and the country generally most favourable for agricultural purposes. The customs of the people are similar to those of other Pathan races; the Khudu Khels, Amazais, etc., all conforming more or less to their own peculiar tribal customs.

There are about twenty villages in the valley, of which the largest is Koga, followed probably by Sura and Garai. These villages are all built with the houses joining, so as to leave few entrances, and most, if not all of them, have towers also, for musketry. The Chamlawals could probably muster about 1,300 fighting men.

The Chamla valley can be approached from the north from Buner by several passes; the easiest of these is said to be the Buner pass, which leads from Bar Kilai to Ambela; its length is only about two miles through the Guru range, and, according to native reports, is practicable for laden camels. The valley can also be approached from the east by the valley of the Barandu river; through the Khudu Khel country by Chinglai to Koga; and from British territory by the Ambela, Sherdara, and Narinji passes, the first mentioned being the easiest.

During the campaign of 1863 the Chamlawals were at first friendly, but were afterwards forced to join against us by pressure from the other tribes.

Bunerwals.

The Bunerwals inhabit the Buner valley, which is bounded on the north-west by Swat; north-east by the Puran valley; south-east by the Mada Khel, and Amazai territory; south by the Chamla valley; and south-west by Yusafzai. It is a small mountain valley, dotted with villages and divided into seven sub-divisions. The Morah hills and the Ilam range divide it from Swat, the Sinawar range from Yusafzai, the Guru mountain from the Chamla valley, and the Duma range from the Puran valley. From these ranges run smaller spurs, meeting one another and forming a small nucleus of inferior valleys, richly cultivated and well populated. The valley is drained by the Barandu, a perennial stream which falls into the Indus above Mahabara, after receiving the drainage of Chamla and the country of the Amazais. Its general width is about sixty feet, and has, in summer and winter, water to a depth of three or four feet, and is never less than two feet. There are about a dozen villages on its right bank, but the left bank is mostly covered with jungle, having a few hamlets at a distance. Buner is inhabited by the Iliaszai and Malizai clans of the Yusafzais,[1] which are sub-divided into seven sections as follows:—Salarzai, Nasozai, Ashazai, Gadaizai, Nurizai, Daulatzai, and Chagarzai.

There is no finer race on the north-west frontier of India than the Bunerwals. Simple and austere in their habits, religious and truthful in their ways, hospitable to all who seek shelter amongst them, free from secret assassinations, they are bright examples of what good materials a Pathan tribe can be developed into, clinging with the fondest affection to their country and ancient customs handed down to them by their forefathers. Ignorant by nature, they hold trade in the very lowest estimation; excessively under the control of *mullas* and others of the priestly class, they are often deluded with precepts and orders said to emanate from some high religious authority, such as the late *Akhund* of Swat. They are still perfectly upright in their dealings with enemies and strangers. Their word once given through the general council of the tribe, may be depended on with greater certainty than that of any other border race, even when unaccompanied with the usual security for the fulfilment of the contract. Though poor, they are free from those thievish propensities which disgrace nearly every other tribe on the Peshawar border. This is a curious and, at the same time, a most exemplary trait in their character.

The Bunerwals have always been inimical towards us, and stand aloof, generally speaking, from intercourse with British officers; but they do not allow bands of robbers to come into our limits for the purpose of annoying the British border villages nearest to them; and though they harbour outlaws from our territory, they never join with them in committing depredations. We seldom hear of a raid in which they are participators, and when they are, it is generally found that they were instigated to it by men in our limits, receiving grants from Government and holding influential positions in Yusafzai. Men from British territory used sometimes to be seized and detained because of some debt due by another in our limits, but they were immediately released on the amount being liquidated, or security given for payment. The Bunerwals, if well united and prompted by a common

[1] The term Bunerwal strictly only includes these two clans; but it should be pointed out that all trans-border tribes, bordering on Buner proper, frequently call themselves Bunerwals.

cause, could bring 7,000 fighting men against us in the field, independent of those which other tribes could send to their assistance in case of need.

The climate of Buner is said to be very severe in winter, snow falling to a considerable extent on the surrounding hills and continuing for some time, but in the valleys it seldom remains longer than a week or ten days. The hot weather sets in later than in the plains, but is more oppressive and continuous, owing to the confined nature of the valley. The frequent storms that burst over these hills do not cool the air, but on the contrary produce a hot, steamy atmosphere in the valley below. It is said to be unhealthy in summer, from the coarse, gravelly soil becoming heated and radiating its heat during the night, making the air very close and oppressive. In the spring and autumn malarious exhalations rise from the porous soil, and fevers become rife during both these seasons.

The autumn crops consist of Indian corn, rice, and *mash* ; the spring crops of wheat and barley. The grain cultivated is not, however, sufficient to meet the wants of the inhabitants of the valley, and has to be imported from other quarters. A force would, therefore, have to bring its own supplies if it entered Buner. The inhabitants are rich in cattle, especially buffaloes, and are almost entirely occupied in the tending of their herds and the cultivation of the soil.

The betrothal and marriage ceremonies are similar throughout all the sub-divisions, varied in some places, with reference to the lower classes, at the will of some *malik*, whose authority may be more arbitrary and oppressive than that of his neighbours. A poor man has generally to pay Rs. 50 to Rs. 60 for his bride, the middle Rs. 120, the others from Rs. 200 to Rs. 300, the man being further bound to feed the relations of the girl, both at the betrothal and the marriage, with rice, *ghi*, and sugar. The musician receives a fee of Rs. 2 at the betrothal and Rs. 5 at the marriage, the shortest interval between the two events being two months and the longest two years. The age of the bridegroom usually ranges from twenty to twenty-two, that of the girl being fifteen to seventeen. This seems a move in the right direction, the girl being older than custom usually permits in Muhammadan countries where parents allow their daughters of twelve or thirteen to marry and cohabit with their husbands. The punishment for adultery with the higher classes is death, and nothing short of this will satisfy them. The lower orders, if poor, are sometimes satisfied, after a period of two or three years, with a *surra*. This means that the man who has enticed away the daughter or wife of another gives a sister or other female relation to the aggrieved party in exchange. There is no fixed rule as to what the father is to give on the birth of a child.

All *hamsayas*, such as Gujars, have to pay Rs. 5 annually; but of this number, those who are not artisans, have to take up arms in time of necessity, and fight for their *maliks*, being fed by them as long as the feud lasts.

With regard to the communications between Buner and the surrounding countries, there are three passes leading from Buner into Swat, the Kalel, the Jowarai, and the Karakar. Of these the last named is the only one practicable for mule transport. On the east, the Indus being crossed at Mahabara, Buner can be entered, but with difficulty, by the defile of the Barandu. From British territory, the Malandri pass and the Ambela pass lead into Buner, and are both practicable for laden animals. There are several other routes from Yusafzai, but they are difficult.

The trade of the country is principally in the hands of the Hindus of Rustam and Bazar in British territory, with agencies at the principal villages in Buner. *Ghi* is exported in large quantities, also honey, timber, etc., the imports being chiefly cotton fabrics and salt. Goats, sheep, and cattle are annually purchased in Buner for the Peshawar market.

The Bunerwals are independent of us for the necessaries of life, and fear a blockade less than any of the other tribes. For villages adjoining our border a blockade has been found to be successful; but for others it is impossible.

Having discussed the country, customs, etc., of the Bunerwals, it is now necessary to notice briefly the different sections of the tribe. The two which border on British territory, and therefore most nearly affect us, are the Salarzais and the Nurizais.

The Salarzais are a powerful section, and are said to be able to bring 1,600 men into the field. Sub-divided into the Mali Khel and the Aib Khel, they have fourteen villages, of which Jowar is the largest and most important. The residents of this village belong to both sub-divisions. The Salarzais have more communications with our subjects than any other section of the Bunerwals.

The Nurizais adjoin British territory to the south-east of the Salarzais, and are separated from the Chamla valley by the Guru range. They communicate with British territory by the Malandri and Ambela passes, which lead direct to their country. They are divided into two sub-sections, the Panjpai and the Ali Sher Khel. The former have always been favourably disposed towards the British. Their *maliks* have invariably attended to the summons of the Assistant Commissioner of Yusafzai, when called upon to do so, and have done their best to smooth any difficulties that might arise between them and us. The Ali Sher Khel *maliks*, on the contrary, are the most troublesome people we have to deal with in Buner. The Nurizais were not implicated as a whole in the attacks on the Malakand and Chakdara in July 1897. The principal villages of the Panjpai section are Kharappa and Nawa Kala, and of the Ali Sher Khel, Rega, and Bar Kala. The *maliks* of the last two places have the greatest influence in the Nurizai country. The section is said to be able to turn out 1,100 fighting men.

The Ashazais are located at the base of the isolated Jafir hill, having the Salarzais on their west and the Nurizais on the south. They are the most warlike men in Buner, and owing to their central position play a prominent part in the politics of the country. They are divided into four sub-sections, the Khadin Khel, Aya Khel, Musara Khel, and the Khakizai. The first live in Anghafur ; the Aya Khel and Musara Khel divide Tursak, which is the largest village of the Ashazai ; and the Khakizai are settled in Ilai. The section numbers about 1,000 fighting men.

The Gadaizais occupy the southern slopes of the Ilam and Dosiri mountains, and are too far located from our border for their chiefs ever to be brought into political contact with our officers. They are divided into four sub-sections, Ibrahim Khel, Hasan Khel, Ali Sher Khel, and Seni Khel.

The Nasozais occupy the western slopes of the Duma mountains to the south-east of the Gadaizais. They are divided into two sub-sections, the Panjpai and the Makhozai. Their most important village is Bagra, and, during the Ambela campaign, the Khan of that place and the Khan of Daggar, also belonging to the Panjpai sub-section of the Nasozais, were considered the most important chiefs in Buner.

The Daulatzais occupy a portion of the valley on both banks of the Barandu stream to the north of the Chamla valley. They are divided into three sub-sections, Ismailzai, Mandazai, and Barkazai. The principal village of the first is Kalpani; of the Mandizai, Bajkatta; and of the Barkazai, Shal Bandai. Some of their villages are flourishing places, and have an extensive trade through Hindus with Sudum, more especially Bajkatta and Kalpani. The *maliks* of this section, in case of any dissensions among the Chamlawals and Chagarzais, obtain large sums of money for helping and assisting the rival pretenders to power.

The Chagarzais have already been described under the heading of the Black Mountain tribes. Of the three sections into which they are divided, *viz.*, Nasrat Khel, Firozai, and Basi Khel, the second only is located in the Buner valley, and inhabits the western slopes of the Duma mountains; its principal villages being Tangora and Batora. This section numbers about 1,000 fighting men.

Affair with the Hindustani fanatics at Kotla in January 1853.

About the year 1823, there arrived on the Yusafzai frontier one of those famous saintly adventurers, who have at all times managed to beguile the credulous and simple Pathan race for their own ends, and have been the means of creating discord, upheaving society, and fomenting rebellions, which have been checked and crushed with the utmost difficulty. This man was Saiyid Ahmad Shah of Bareilly. At one period of his life he was the companion-in-arms of the celebrated Amir Khan Pindari, who was himself a Pathan, born in the valley of Buner. Saiyid Ahmad studied Arabic at Delhi, and then proceeded to Mecca by way of Calcutta. It was during this journey that his doctrines obtained the ascendancy over the minds of the Muhammadans of Bengal, which has ever since led them to supply this colony with fresh recruits. Although the *Saiyid* in after life attempted to disguise the fact, his doctrines were essentially those of the *Wahabi* sect, inculcating the original tenets of Islam, and repudiating commentaries on the *Koran*, the adoration of relics, etc.

It was in 1824 that the adventurer arrived by way of Kandahar and Kabul amongst the Yusafzai tribes of the Peshawar border, with about forty Hindustani followers. This was an opportune moment to raise the spirits of the Yusafzais and other Pathans (which had been lowered by the crushing defeat they and the Peshawar *Sirdars* had received from Ranjit Singh at the battle of Nowshera), by religious exhortation. Saiyid Ahmad gave out that he was a man of superior sanctity, and divinely commissioned to wage a war of extermination, with the aid of all true believers, against the infidel. Amongst a race so simple and superstitious, the mission of all enthusiasts, such as Saiyid Ahmad, is eminently successful. Animated by a spirit of fanaticism, and with the desire of freeing themselves from their Sikh oppressors, a numerous, although ill-disciplined, army was soon at his disposal. His own Hindustani followers had been increased by recruits till they now numbered 900 men. In addition to this, the Peshawar *Sirdars*, feeling the influence of the movement, and hoping to break the Sikh rule, joined in the crusade.

Collecting his army together, and strengthened by the contingents of Khadi Khan of Hund, Ashraf Khan of Zaida, and the followers of the Peshawar *Sirdars*, the *Saiyid* proceeded to Nowshera with the intention of laying siege to the fort of Attock. He, however, found Ranjit Singh forewarned. Hari Singh with a large army awaited him on the Indus, and Budh Singh was sent across the river with a considerable force. Moving up to Saidu to meet the fanatics, Budh Singh entrenched his army, who were thereupon surrounded by the fanatics and in time reduced to great distress. Budh Singh at length determined to fight; and warning the Peshawar *Sirdars* of the near approach of Ranjit Singh and the fate that awaited them if they acted with Saiyid Ahmad, he commenced the battle. The *Sirdars*, with Yar Muhammad at their head, accepting the warning, fled immediately. This act of treachery had the desired effect, and the Muhammadans were routed with great slaughter by the Sikh soldiery. Yar Muhammad, however, derived little benefit from his act, for Ranjit Singh doubled the amount of the Peshawar tribute, desecrated the mosques, despoiled the country, and ultimately retired, taking Yar Muhammad Khan's son as hostage. It subsequently transpired that the *Saiyid's* attempt on Attock had been a failure owing to the treachery of Kadi Khan of Hund, who had disclosed his intentions to Ranjit Singh.

Saiyid Ahmad, after this defeat, which occurred in the spring of 1827, escaped with a few followers, *viâ* Lundkhwar, to Swat. Thence he proceeded to Buner, and ultimately, at the invitation of some of the *Khans*, returned to Yusafzai. The Pathans, who still believed in his miraculous powers, swarmed in thousands round his standard, and being joined by Mir Baba the Sudum chief, and others, he determined to chastise the Khan of Hund for his misconduct. The parties met, with no decisive result; but by an act of treachery, in which he was aided by the late Akhund of Swat, the *Saiyid* induced Khadi Khan to visit him in a friendly way, and instantly had him seized and slain. After this he proceeded to Panjtar, and was heartily welcomed by Fateh Khan, the chief of the Khudu Khels, a connection which strengthened his position among the Pathans. Aided by Fateh Khan and his own bands of Hindustanis, the *Saiyid* now commenced a series of exploits which eventually placed the whole of Yusafzai and Peshawar under his control. He subdued the Khans of Hund and Hoti, and levied tithes from the Yusafzai clans. In 1828, by a night attack he defeated the Barakzai force, which had advanced against him as far as Zaida, and subsequently he took possession of Amb. In 1829, having again defeated the Barakzais at Hoti, he occupied Peshawar. But his successful career was now brought to a close. His exactions had become oppressive to the Pathans, and an attempt on his part to put a stop to their taking money on the betrothal of their daughters was still more distasteful. There was a general insurrection against him, and many of his followers, including the deputy left at Peshawar, were massacred. Fateh Khan also, having derived every advantage from the *Saiyid's* presence at Panjtar, was now desirous of getting rid of his obnoxious ally. He therefore joined heartily in the scheme for the assassination of his followers; but when the beacon was lighted on the top of Karamar, which was the arranged signal of slaughter, he found that Saiyid Ahmad and his compact little army of 1,600 Hindustanis under Mulla Ismail, was a force which he dared not attack openly. Finding the Mahaban no longer a safe asylum, the Hindustanis now crossed the Indus and proceeded to Balakot. Here the followers of the *Saiyid* again rallied round him, and an army under Sher Singh marched against him. In spite of the disparity of numbers, and the warning of his friends, the *Saiyid* determined to fight. Three times did his small band of Hindustanis beat back the Sikh regiments, but at last, overpowered by numbers, they were defeated and destroyed, only three hundred of their number escaping and the *Saiyid* himself being amongst the slain.

Of his disciples who escaped with their lives a portion found their way to Sitana. This village, as already stated, had been given as a *muafi* grant by the Utmanzais to the Saiyids of Tiringi on their first arrival, and belonged to one Saiyid Akbar Shah, a man who was held in great veneration by the Utmanzais, Gaduns, and neighbouring tribes, and who was a declared enemy of the Sikhs. It was at that time the refuge for outlaws and offenders from Yusafzai and Hazara, and was the rendezvous of all the discontented *Khans* and their followers. Saiyid Akbar had served as a treasurer and counsellor to Saiyid Ahmad, and on this account he willingly allowed the Hindustanis to gather round him. Here they settled, and established a colony, and also constructed a fort near Sitana, which they called Mandi. After the British annexation of the Peshawar valley, Abdul Ghafur, the well-known Akhund of Swat, prevailed on the people of Swat to receive Saiyid Akbar as their king, and he was accordingly proclaimed King of Swat.

The first occasion of our coming into collision with this Hindustani colony, occurred in 1853, after the expedition against the Hassanzais, related in a previous chapter. The Hindustani fanatics had co-operated with the Hassanzais against Jehandad Khan of Amb, and had actually seized a small fort of his, named Kotla, in the Amb territory, on the right bank of the Indus, and it was necessary that it should be recovered and restored to the Amb chief. Accordingly, after the conclusion of the operation in December 1852 and January 1853, under Lieut.-Colonel Mackeson, C.B., a force was moved down to the left bank of the Indus, opposite Kotla.

None of the tribes around, the Amazais, Mada Khels, or Gaduns, had joined the Hindustani fanatics; but the latter, in answer to the warning to them to withdraw from Kotla to their own settlements, gave no written reply, and according to some verbal reports, sent a defiance—Maulvi Inayat Ali Khan, the leader of the Hindustanis, declaring he had come to die.

Feeling confident, after seeing the ground, that the crossing and re-crossing could be well protected, and the garrison reduced to extremity if they offered opposition, Lieut.-Colonel Mackeson determined to send a force across, though there were only two boats available for the passage, each capable of carrying 100 men at a time.

Mountain Train Battery, 2 guns.
1st Sikh Infantry.[1]
3rd " " [2]
Two regiments of Dogras of the Kashmir Army.
6 wall-pieces.
6 Zamburaks.

On the 6th January, the troops, as per margin, were crossed over from Kirpilian under the command of Major J. Abbott, to retake the fort. As there were doubts if the mountain guns would suffice to reduce the stronghold, two Horse Artillery guns were held ready to be sent across in addition; the other two guns were kept on the left bank to cover the crossing and retirement.

The village of Ashera is on a spur of the mountain about 200 feet above the Indus and the fort of Kotla is higher up on the same spur, at an elevation of 1,000 feet or more from the river. It was known that there was no spring or well in the fort, and it was intended that Jehandad Khan's men should assault the village under cover of the Horse Artillery guns on the left bank of the river, whilst Major Abbott's column should move round and gain possession of the heights above it, the crossing opposite Sitana being threatened by the regular troops from their encampment at Rargarh. Directly the two Sikh regiments and mountain guns began to ascend the hill, the Hindustanis fled incontinently from the fort of Kotla and village of Ashera, and, being pursued by Jehandad Khan's people, some thirty or forty were cut up.

The troops bivouacked for the night at Ashera, and re-crossed the Indus the following day.

Affairs at Shekh Jana and Narinji under Major J. L. Vaughan, in July and August 1857.

The only portion of the Peshawar district in which advantage of the Sepoy Mutiny was taken by the people to disturb the country was on the Yusafzai frontier, and this was principally due to the presence of the Hindustani fanatics, who were supported by contributions of men and money from traitorous princes and private individuals in Hindustan.

The Yusafzai country was controlled by the fort of Mardan which was usually garrisoned by the Corps of Guides; but in the

[1] Now the 51st Sikhs (Frontier Force).
[2] Now the 53rd Sikhs (Frontier Force).

middle of May 1857, this regiment moved down to form a portion of the Punjab Moveable Column, its place being taken by the 55th Native Infantry. At the end of May the 55th Native Infantry broke into mutiny, when about 100 sepoys were put to the sword, and 150 taken prisoners by a column which had moved out from Peshawar under Lieut.-Colonel John Nicholson, some 600 sepoys of the regiment making good their escape to Swat.

Two powers had hitherto reigned in Swat—the *Akhund*, or priest, and the *Badshah* or king, whom the *Akhund* had set up for carrying on the temporal government. Had these two been united in harbouring the 55th Native Infantry, and at that moment proclaimed a *jehad* against us, there can be no doubt that it would have set fire to the valley of Peshawar, and placed us in considerable difficulties. But Saiyid Akbar, the king, had just died. He had long survived his popularity, and had he then been alive, would not have been allowed by the *Akhund* and chiefs of Swat to entertain a disciplined army of Hindustani sepoys. The crisis roused these chiefs to the preservation of their liberties, and they first expelled Saiyid Mubarak Shah, the son of the late king, and lastly, the refugees of the 55th Native Infantry, who were conducted by disciples of the *Akhund* through mountain paths to the river Indus, which they crossed at a point far above our territory, with the desperate design of making their way to Kashmir and seeking an asylum with Maharajah Golab Singh. They were, however, destroyed before they arrived at their destination.

A few of the sepoys of the 55th Regiment had, however, shrunk from encountering the perils of the journey to Kashmir, and had joined the young Saiyid Mubarak Shah, who had taken up his abode at the village of Panjtar. Not far from this village, at a place called Mangal Thana, a settlement of Hindustanis under some *maulvis* of the *Wahabi* sect had sprung up, being a branch of the parent colony at Sitana.

Mukarrab Khan, Chief of Panjtar, was also hostile to us. In order to understand the cause of his hostility it is necessary to refer briefly to his history since the death of his father, Fateh Khan, in 1841, when he succeeded to the position of *Khan*. For the first eight years he seems to have managed the Khudu Khels well, and the tribe remained quiet and contented. Dissensions did now and then break out, but the parties were appeased, till at last Mukarrab Khan seized, deprived of his sight, and slew Sirkar, *malik* of Bam Khel Totalai, a man who had been his father's, Fateh Khan's, agent. This act seems to have been the beginning of all the troubles which afterwards overtook him. It was about this time that he rendered himself useful to Major James Abbott, who was then holding Hazara; and on the annexation of the Punjab he presented himself to our officers. Even then his oppression had made him at variance with his subjects, and the object of his visit was to obtain British aid against them, which it is needless to remark was refused. Nothing particular was done by him for several years after this, but in 1855 he made a petition claiming our aid against the Hindustani fanatics at Mangal Thana who had assembled there to the number of 420 men under Saiyid Abbas, with the intention of attacking the *Khan's* villages. The sincerity of Mukarrab Khan was considered doubtful, and it appeared probable that the agitation was got up by the *Khan* himself, who was at variance with his subjects, the Totalaiwals, and wanted the fanatics to help him against them. The cause of this difference was that the *Khan* claimed a house and tithe tax at the rate of Rs. 2 per harvest, whilst the Totalaiwals declined to pay anything beyond Rs. 2 a house per annum.

The dispute was referred to the British authorities, and a decision was given against Mukarrab Khan, and he was informed at the same time by the Chief Commissioner that he would be held responsible for the good conduct of the Hindustani colony at Mangal Thana. This so displeased him that from that time he did not hide his hostility to the British. Matters continued in an unsatisfactory state, and it was apprehended that there would be an armed movement into British territory. In October 1856 sanction was given by the Supreme Government for a force to be employed against the *Khan* should necessity warrant such a measure. On the 30th August 1856, previous to the receipt of the above sanction, a raid on Swabi and Salim Khan being expected, a detachment of Guide Cavalry and 200 Infantry, under command of Major H. B. Lumsden, moved out to protect the threatened villages. But the force soon returned, as it appeared that the fanatics were to be used against the Totalaiwals and not against the British villages.

On the 5th October 1856 the *maliks* of Totalai and Mobaraz Khan of Chinglai, cousin of Mukarrab Khan, having joined together, determined to raise the whole of the Khudu Khels against Mukarrab Khan, if he did not instantly dismiss the fanatics. On the 7th October 1856 the *Khan* wrote to the Assistant Commissioner at Mardan, informing him that the Hindustanis had been dismissed, and he had made peace with his subjects. During the troubles of 1857 Mobaraz Khan invited the Hindustani fanatics under Maulvi Inayat Ali Khan to his village without consulting his cousin; the Khudu Khels joined him, and Mukarrab Khan found himself isolated at Panjtar.

It was at this time that some of the western villages began to give way to the influences by which they were tempted to disaffection, and, having refused to pay their revenue, they appealed to Mobaraz Khan of Chinglai and to the Hindustanis to come down and begin a war for Islam. The defaulting village of Shekh Jana was accordingly occupied by 200 men from Chinglai under Baz Khan, the nephew of Mobaraz Khan, and by 50 horsemen under a partisan soldier, named Jan Muhammad, besides men from the neighbouring villages.

The fort of Mardan, after the mutiny of the 55th Native Infantry, had been garrisoned by the 5th Punjab Infantry and two guns of the Peshawar Mountain Train Battery, the whole under Major J. L. Vaughan, 5th Punjab Infantry. The Assistant Commissioner, Lieutenant J. C. Horne, having called upon that officer to act, he moved out on the afternoon of the 1st July with the detachment as per margin, and the next morning attacked Shekh Jana. A considerable number of matchlock men, with the horse, were drawn up along the the eastern bank of the *nala* on which the village is built. A few rounds from the guns speedily threw them into disorder; when the skirmishers of the 5th Punjab Infantry cleared the village, and the 2nd Punjab Cavalry, pursuing the fugitives over the open plain in its rear, drove them into the adjoining village of Spinkana.

Peshawar Mountain Train Battery, 2 guns.
2nd Punjab Cavalry, 80 sabres.
5th Punjab Infantry, 270 bayonets.

This village was then attacked and carried, and the enemy pursued to the hills by the cavalry and some levies, under Lieutenant G. A. Graham, when several were cut up and some twenty-five taken prisoners. The only casualties on our side were two sowars, 2nd Punjab Cavalry, and three of the levies, wounded.

Major Vaughan stated that the conduct of the troops had been admirable, and the pursuit by the cavalry very spirited. Baz Khan was amongst the slain, and Jan Muhammad, having been taken prisoner, was tried and executed, as were, subsequently, seven of the villagers.

A fortnight after the affair of Shekh Jana, the Hindustani fanatics, under the leadership of Maulvi Inayat Ali Khan, crossed the border and raised the standard of religious war at the mountain village of Narinji. Narinji is on the extreme border, and, being very difficult of access, had become an asylum for bad characters, and had several times defied the authorities in Yusafzai; at the last moment, however, the *maliks* had always hitherto saved the place from destruction by submission and reparation. The villagers were proud that the place had more than once been attacked by a Sikh force without success.

The number of Hindustani followers with the *maulvi* was about 150, and he had also some 30 or 40 of the men of the late 55th Native Infantry. The fighting men of Narinji were about 400, and 40 horsemen had joined the party from Panjtar, under the brother of Mukarrab Khan. A few horsemen had also come down from Swat, and several of the fugitives from Shekh Jana were with the *maulvi*. Mobaraz Khan of Chinglai remained aloof, and refused to give assistance.

Peshawar Mountain Train Battery, 4 guns.
2nd Punjab Cavalry, 1 troop.
4th Punjab Infantry, 400 bayonets.[1]
Mounted Police, 40 sowars.
Multan Levy, 100 „

On the night of the 18th July, a force, as per margin, marched from Mardan under the command of Major J. L. Vaughan, 5th Punjab Infantry, and accompanied by Captain H. R. James, the Deputy Commissioner, to Yar Husain, thirteen miles. The 4th Punjab Infantry, under Captain A. T. Wilde, had marched from Nowshera on the 18th, but had been so much delayed in crossing the Kabul river that it was necessary to halt on the 20th to give them a rest.

This route was adopted in order to conceal the object of the movement, which was further effected by the laying in of supplies at Salim Khan, as if the troops were proceeding to Panjtar, the people in the vicinity of which commenced to remove their property. On the night of the 20th the troops marched to Parmali, nine miles, and, after a short halt, advanced towards Narinji, five

[1] Now the 57th Wilde's Rifles Frontier Force.

miles, which was sighted at daylight. The surprise was complete though the enemy made such hasty preparations as were possible after the troops were seen.

The position of the village was very strong. It was built in terraces, and situated at the foot of a precipitous hill, the rocky spurs of which surrounded it on three sides ; but in the front the ground was open and practicable for cavalry. A broad sandy *nala* ran along the foot of the hill, on the other side of which *nala*, facing Narinji, was another range of heights. The slopes of the hill above Narinji were very steep, though practicable for infantry.

Major Vaughan's force was not strong enough to enable him to crown the heights above the village before attacking it in front ; moreover, the men had had a long night's march, the season of the year was very trying, and it was unadvisable to attempt such a laborious operation, or, whilst the enemy's strength was undeveloped, to divide the force. Consequently a position favourable for artillery fire was seized upon, from which the mountain guns began to bombard the village.

The *maliks* had been previously called upon to give up the *maulvi*, but as in their reply they ignored his presence, the infantry advanced in skirmishing order, and after a tenacious resistance on the part of the enemy, made themselves masters of the lower part of the village, and of the rocks which flanked it. There were several strong breastworks in the upper part of the village, and the enemy, who were very numerous, then pressed down to try and drive the infantry out of the position they had won ; but though they fought with great bravery, they were driven back with loss, and the village was then destroyed.

About 8 A.M., Major Vaughan determined on retiring, as it was not probable that further injury could be inflicted that day. The troops had been severely worked, and would soon have become exhausted from the almost intolerable heat.[1] The supply of water, too, would have become scarce, as it had to be brought from the villages in rear, on donkeys.

The retirement was effected without the slightest opposition on the part of the enemy, although the ground was most favourable for them, and the troops reached their camp at 10 A.M.

[1] Forty men, of whom nine succumbed, had been struck down by the sun the previous day.

The losses of the enemy had been very severe. Independently of those who must have been killed or wounded by the guns on the higher slopes above the village, which the infantry did not reach, fifty of the enemy fell in the lower village alone; many of these were Hindustanis. The wounded were estimated at about fifty more. Our loss had been five killed and twenty-one wounded.

The people of Narinji, nevertheless, remained stubborn, and would not expel the *maulvi.* Soon afterwards a raid was made on cattle in British territory, and nothing remained but to renew the attack on the refractory village. It was known that Mobaraz Khan of Chinglai, and Alam Khan, brother of Mukarrab Khan of Panjtar, had taken money from the *maulvi,* and succeeded in purchasing the aid of the chief men of Buner, who promised to bring assistance three days after the festival of the *Eed.* Chamla had already sent seven standards (probably 200 men), and other parties were daily arriving. Promises had been made from Swat, and reinforcements of Hindustanis had arrived from Mangal Thana and Sitana.

Major Vaughan's camp had been established at Parmali after the affair at Narinji, but on the 31st it was moved to Shewa, as affording better shelter for the European troops, and partly to conceal our intentions. On the morning of the 2nd August, reinforcements were received from Peshawar, but the force had been previously weakened by the departure of the 4th Punjab Infantry.

At 1 A.M. on the 3rd August, a column of the strength marginally noted marched from Shewa, under Major J. L. Vaughan, with Captain H. R. James as Political Officer, on Narinji. Captain James had information that there was a bye-road branching off about one mile and a half before reaching Narinji, by which a column could ascend to the rear of the village.

24-pr. Howitzers (2 guns).
Peshawar Mountain Train Battery (4 guns).
H. M. 27th Foot, 50 bayonets.
" 70th " 50 "
" 87th " 50 "
2nd Punjab Cavalry, 150 sabres.
21st[1] Native Infantry, 50 men.
5th[2] Punjab Infantry, 400 "
6th[3] " " 200 "
16th[4] " " 150 "
Police and levies, 225 mounted, 100 foot.

A force of 300 bayonets, 5th Punjab Infantry, and 50 bayonets, 87th Royal Irish Fusiliers, was therefore detached under the command of Lieutenant W. D. Hoste, 5th

[1] The present 1st Brahmans.
[2] The present 58th Vaughan's Rifle (Frontier Force).
[3] The present 59th Scinde Rifles (Frontier Force).
[4] The present 24th Punjabis.

Punjab Infantry, to take the enemy in flank and rear. The existence of this road was known when the first attack was made, but the force was then too weak to detach any portion of it.

The main body came in sight of Narinji soon after sunrise. Rumours which had exaggerated our weakness now turned our hundreds into thousands, and as the force approached many of the auxiliaries fled. Maulvi Inayat Ali Khan was among the first to leave the village.

As soon as the main body had come into position opposite the village, fire was opened upon it, and upon the clusters of men observed upon different parts of the mountain. This was feebly replied to by a matchlock fire from the *sangars* above the village and along the heights.

After about half an hour, the column which had been detached to ascend the hill made its appearance far away on the right. Its progress was vigorously opposed by the enemy, but the latter were dislodged from every point where they attempted to make a stand, and the column passed on in the most brilliant manner, and without a check, until the rear of the village was gained. The upper portion of the village, which is very strong and commanding, was then rapidly taken possession of at the point of the bayonet by a portion of Lieutenant Hoste's men, whilst the remainder continued their advance in pursuit of the enemy.

As soon as the success of Lieutenant Hoste's column was no longer doubtful, a detachment of the 6th Punjab Infantry, under Lieutenant G. N. Saunders, was sent to ascend the heights which enclose the village to the left, and intercept the retreat of the fugitives. This service was well performed, and twenty-five or thirty of the enemy were killed. Amongst the slain were several *purbeahs,* believed from their arms and accoutrements to be men of the late 55th Native Infantry. Simultaneously with the movements last described, the 16th Punjab Infantry and fifty bayonets of Her Majesty's 70th Regiment entered the village from the front and found it deserted.

The work of destruction then began, and not a house was spared. The towers were blown up under the direction of Lieutenant F. S. Taylor of the Engineers, and the village was soon a mass of ruins. The troops were then withdrawn. Three prisoners were taken—

one a Bareilly *maulvi*, the second a Chamla standard-bearer, and the third a vagrant of Charouda: they were all subsequently executed.

Though not actively engaged, the large force of cavalry gave security to the movements of the guns and infantry in the bed of the *nala*, and the foot levies were useful in occupying the heights opposite the village, from which possible annoyance was anticipated. Our losses were one killed and eight wounded.

Expedition against the Khudu Khels and Hindustani fanatics by a force under Major-General Sir Sydney J. Cotton, K.C.B., April–May 1858.

At the end of October following the destruction of Narinji related above, Lieutenant J. C. Horne, Assistant Commissioner of Yusafzai, whilst encamped at Shekh Jana with a small escort, was attacked by the Hindustanis and Chinglai Khudu Khels, aided by the Narinji and Shekh Jana people. Lieutenant Horne was forced to take refuge in a ravine, and being favoured by the darkness, he saved his life. All his baggage was, however, taken, and five of his servants were killed. There is no doubt that Mukarrab Khan, Mobaraz Khan, and nearly all the *maliks* of Shekh Jana were in league with the fanatics.

To punish this outrage, Lieut.-Colonel H. B. Edwardes, the Commissioner of Peshawar, strongly urged that as soon as troops were available, due punishment should be inflicted for these wanton and unprovoked hostilities. Accordingly, on the 22nd April 1858, a force, numbering 4,877 men of all ranks, assembled on the left bank of the Kabul river, opposite Nowshera, under the immediate command of Major-General Sir Sydney J. Cotton, K.C.B., where it was joined by Lieut.-Colonel H. B. Edwardes, C.B., the Commissioner. The force was divided into two brigades, commanded respectively by Lieut.-Colonel H. Renny and Major A. T. Allan, both of Her Majesty's 81st Regiment.

On the 25th of April, the frontier village of Salim Khan was reached, and reconnoitring parties, one under Captain T. Wright, and the other under Lieut.-Colonel H. B. Edwardes, C.B., were at once sent forward.

The approaches to Panjtar were held by the people of Totalai, who had for several years been resisting the payment of tithes demanded by Mukarrab Khan, as already stated. When, therefore, the Totalai people saw the reconnoitring parties approaching, they not only turned out to welcome them, but rushed ahead with all their men to try and seize Mukarrab Khan. That chief, imagining that the reconnoitring parties were followed by a column of attack, abandoned his position, and fled with about sixty horsemen to Chinglai; seeing which, the people of Totalai dashed in and set fire to Panjtar before our troops had come up. Our first object was thus unexpectedly and easily attained.

1st Column.

Peshawar Lt. Fd. By.,[1] 4 guns.
Peshawar Mt. Trn By., 2 „
H. M. 98th Foot, 260 bayonets.
7th Irregular Cavalry,[2] 100 men.
Guides Cavalry, 200 sabres.
Peshawar Light Horse,[3] 30 men.
Sappers and Miners, 100 men.
21st Native Infantry,[4] 300 men.
Guides Infantry, 300 men.
9th Punjab Infantry, [5] 400 men.
18th „ „ [6] 400 „

2nd Column.

31st Foot, 200 bayonets.
18th Irreg. Cav.[7] 100 men.
Sappers and Miners, 47 men.
Kelat-i-Ghilzai Reg.[8] 200 „
8th Punjab Infantry,[9] 450 men.

3rd Column.

81st Regiment, 105 bayonets.
98th „ 10 „
7th Irregular Cavalry, 25 men.
18th „ „ 25 „
Guide Cavalry, 60 sabres.
Kelat-i-Ghilzai Regt., 254 men.
21st Native Infantry, 155 men.
Guide Infantry, 76 bayonets.
8th Punjab Infantry, 54 men.
9th „ „ 137 „
18th „ „ 185 „

Before crossing the frontier the force was divided into three columns, as per margin. Salim Khan was made the base of operations, where the camp remained standing. The Major-General was to proceed, accompanied by Lieut.-Colonel Edwardes, with the first column, with two days' provisions, so as to enter the Khudu Khel territory by the Daran (or Darhan) pass, whilst Lieut.-Colonel H. Renny, 81st Regiment, proceeded in command of the second column direct to Panjtar; the third column, under Major A. T. Allan, 81st Regiment, remained in charge of the

[1] The Peshawar Light Field Battery was raised on the 5th June 1857. It was manned by the 4th Company, 2nd Battalion, Bengal Foot Artillery (now the 35th Field Battery R.A.) and had a company of European drivers composed of volunteers from the companies of Foot Artillery at Peshawar. The horses and syces were taken from the 5th Bengal Light Cavalry which had been dismounted and disarmed. This was one of the Regular Cavalry Regiments, and the horses were the property of Government.

[2] Now the 5th Cavalry.

[3] The Peshawar Light Horse, raised on 3rd June 1857, was formed of men from His Majesty's 27th, 70th, and 87th Foot, mounted on horses taken away from the disarmed native cavalry. Captain F. Fane, 87th Foot, was commandant, and the strength was 2 officers, 4 sergeants and 84 men.

[4] Now the 1st Brahmans.

[5] Now the 21st Punjabis.

[6] Now the 26th Punjabis.

[7] Now the 8th Cavalry.

[8] Now the 12th Pioneers.

[9] Now the 20th Duke of Cambridge's Own Infantry (Brownlow's Punjabis).

standing camp at Salim Khan. No tents were taken by the advancing columns.

At one o'clock on the morning of the 26th April, the first column left camp for Chinglai, and at daylight entered the Daran pass, a remarkably narrow defile, of about two miles in length, but with heights on either side easily crowned to cover the passage of troops. The enemy made no attempt to dispute the passage of this pass.

Near the entrance of the Chinglai valley, in a wooded nook of the hills, stood the village of Bagh, inhabited by *Saiyids*. A stream of water ran through its shady groves of mulberry trees, and it was a favourite halting-place for marauders when making raids on our territories. The Major-General and the Commissioner visited the *Saiyids* to call them to account, but on their pleading their real inability to refuse a shelter to the robbers, their village was not destroyed; a fine of one rupee a house was taken from them, with an injunction in future to give information of any raids that were contemplated.

The column, after reaching the top of the Daran pass, proceeded at once to the village of Chinglai, which was a large village and contained about 1,000 houses, very substantially built. Here resided Mobaraz Khan, who had a substantial little fort of wood and stone. No resistance, however, was attempted.

During the day it was observed that some of the village people with their property had endeavoured to secrete themselves in ravines on the mountain side, overlooking the village of Chinglai; and the 9th Punjab Infantry, under Captain J. B. Thelwall, was accordingly ordered to ascend the mountain by a circuitous route, with a view to cutting off their retreat into the Chamla valley; whilst a party of the 98th Regiment, under Captain L. S. Cotton, proceeded straight up the hill to dislodge them from their position. A few shots only were exchanged, and then the enemy hastily retired, leaving several killed on the ground. During the day the troops were employed, under the direction of Captain H. Hyde, of the Engineers, in destroying the fort, village, and crops, and at night they bivouacked on a ridge near Chinglai.

On the 27th April, the force, having completed its work at Chinglai, returned to Salim Khan, *viâ* Panjtar and the Jehangirra

Darra. As an approach to Chinglai this route proved to be much more difficult than the Daran Pass route. The track is chiefly through broken country, and at one point passes through a rocky defile called Taralai, a very formidable obstacle if disputed.

Mukarrab Khan's horsemen and footmen were seen lurking about our line of march during the day, but apparently only in hopes of preying on stragglers from the force. Nothing, in fact, could more strongly mark the badness and unpopularity of the *Khan's* character than his total inability to work up his own clan to defend what had hitherto been considered a strong country.

The second column meanwhile had thoroughly destroyed Panjtar, and returned to Salim Khan.

It was now necessary to destroy Mangal Thana, a stronghold of Mukarrab Khan's, on one of the chief spurs of the Mahaban mountain, whither he had removed his property on the approach of the troops to Chinglai, and whither he himself was in the habit of resorting in the last extremity. It had also been the resort of Maulvi Inayat Ali Khan, who had so perseveringly endeavoured, at Narinji and other places, to raise Yusafzai in rebellion in 1857.

The road from Panjtar to Mangal Thana was reported to be practicable, though difficult, and the people of Totalai expressed their willingness to act as guides to the troops.

The force was again divided into three columns: the first to act against Mangal Thana, the second to proceed to Panjtar as a support, and the third to remain in reserve at Salim Khan.

1st Column.
Peshawar Lt. Fd. By. 2 guns
Peshawar Mt. Tn. By. 2 „
81st Regiment, 200 men.
Guide Cavalry, 50 men.
Sappers and Miners, 50 men.
Kelat-i-Ghilzai Regt. 400 „
Guide Infantry, 400 bayonets.
8th Punjab Infy. 400 men.
18th Punjab Infy. 400 „

On the 28th April, the 1st column, strength as per margin, under the command of the Major-General, left camp at Salim Khan, and pushed on by moonlight towards Mangal Thana. The ascent of the hills was very arduous, and half the column had to be left at Dukarai. The advance guard reached the heights about 11 A.M. Not a shot had been fired at the troops, and on entering Mangal Thana the fort was found to have been recently abandoned.

Mangal Thana consisted of two villages, upper and lower. The lower comprised thirty or forty houses, and was occupied by peaceful *Saiyids*, while the upper part consisted of strong fortifications made of large stones and timber. In this part stood the citadel of Saiyid Abbas, the leader of the fanatics, with enclosures for his Hindustani followers. The position was about 5,000 feet above sea level and the neighbourhood was densely wooded.

The advanced troops bivouacked at Mangal Thana for the night, and the next day the fort was blown up by the Sappers and Miners.

On the 30th April, the troops returned to their camp at Salim Khan, and halted there on the 1st May.

It now only remained to deal with the colony of fanatics at Sitana, for which purpose the force marched towards Khabal, distant from Sitana about four miles, where it encamped on the morning of the 3rd May.

Between Amb, on the right bank of the Indus, and our frontier village of Topi, lies a narrow strip of land which forms part of the Utmanzai territory. It contains, in addition to the two or three small hamlets of Topi, the villages of Upper and Lower Khabal (exactly opposite Torbela), Upper and Lower Kai, and Sitana, Mandi, and Upper Sitana. The Utmanzais of this strip had, previous to this date, had feuds with the *Saiyids* and Hindustanis of Sitana, and consequently welcomed our troops as allies against a common foe.

Peshawar Mountain Train Battery, 2 guns.
Hazara Mountain Train Battery, 3 guns.
2nd Sikh Infantry, 300 men.
6th Punjab Infantry, 450 men.
12th Punjab Infantry, 300 men.

By previous arrangements Major J. R. Becher, the Deputy Commissioner of Hazara, moved to the left bank of the Indus with the marginally noted troops with a view to crossing the river so as to co-operate with General Cotton in the attack on Sitana.

The Major-General having, on the evening of the 3rd May, reconnoitred the hills and villages of the enemy, determined the following morning to make a general attack. Major Becher, therefore, crossed the Indus early on the morning of the 4th, and advanced against the villages from the east, while the main column moved against them from the south. At the same time, the Chief of Amb, Jehandad Khan, who was our ally, occupied the hills to the north.

As the main force approached Lower Sitana, skirmishers were thrown forward and the 2nd Sikhs and the 6th Punjab Infantry were detached from Major Becher's column to move up the mountain in rear of Sitana. The 18th Punjab Infantry, under Lieutenant J. Williamson, supported by the 9th Punjab Infantry, under Captain J. B. Thelwall, were the first to gain contact with the enemy, and drove them from their main position with considerable loss. The enemy now retreated to their second position, but were met by the 6th Punjab Infantry who drove them back on to the bayonets of the 18th. A hand-to-hand struggle now ensued till every Hindustani in the position was either killed or taken prisoner. The fanatics had Pathan allies from the neighbouring Gadun tribe, but their heart was not in the business, and they fled precipitately.

Whilst these operations were going on, Upper Sitana was held by a wing of the 81st, under Lieut.-Colonel H. Renny, and the Sappers and Miners, under Captain H. Hyde, were employed in destroying the village.

The position of the enemy having been carried at all points, and their villages destroyed, the Major-General determined to retire. In the afternoon, the enemy, chiefly Pathans, rallied again upon another height; but it was determined to adhere only to the object in hand, and not advance further into the hills, where the troops would have come into collision with the Gadun and other independent tribes.

As the troops withdrew, the enemy followed up closely, but were kept in check by a detachment of the 98th Foot, the Guide Infantry, and two 5½-inch mortars. This was the first time that the Enfield had been used in the hills; its fire was most effective, and evidently made a great impression on the minds of the enemy and also on the native chiefs who accompanied the force.

It was dusk before all the troops had descended the hill, and the force encamped for the night on the Sitana plain by the bank of the Indus, whence they proceeded next day to Khabal. The British losses amounted to six killed and twenty-nine wounded, while the enemy lost sixty killed, including fifty Hindustanis. The number of their wounded was not ascertained.

The Hindustanis, expelled from Sitana by the Utmanzais, had taken refuge with the Upper Gaduns, and it was feared that on our retiring the Gaduns would come down and compel the Utmanzais to re-admit the fanatics. To prevent this, a force was sent to surround the Gadun villages of Gandap and Bisak, which are close to the Yusafzai border. The headmen came in at once, but declared their inability to coerce the Upper Gaduns; they were therefore sent to them to say that, unless our terms were agreed to, coercive measures would be adopted. This threat took immediate effect, and on the night of the 8th May, the Upper and Lower Gaduns sent in their representatives, and signed an agreement, in full conclave of Utmanzais and Gaduns, by which both sides bound themselves to unite in expelling and keeping out the *Saiyids* and Hindustanis, and in resisting any third tribe which should endeavour to bring them back.

The objects for which the troops had taken the field being now fully accomplished, the force marched back to Nowshera, where it was broken up.

The Indian Medal, with a clasp for the "North-West Frontier," was granted in 1869 to all survivors of the troops engaged in the above operations under Major-General Sir S. J. Cotton.

APPENDIX A.

Table showing the relationships of the different branches of the Yusafzai Pathans.

- MANDAN
  - *Usmanzai*
    - Kamalzai
      - Mishranzai.
      - Kishranzai.
    - Amazai
      - Daulatzai.
      - Ismailzai.
  - *Utmanzai*
    - Alazai.
    - Kanazai.
    - Akazai.
    - Saduzai
      - Aba Khel.
      - Umar Khel.
      - Mir Ahmad Khel.
      - Bibzad Khel.
      - Khudu Khel.
  - *Razar*
    - Ako Khel.
    - Malikzai.
    - Khidrzai.
    - Mamuzai.
    - Manizai.
- YUSAF
  - *Isazai*
    - Hassanzai.
    - Akazai.
    - Mada Khel.
  - *Iliaszai*
    - Salarzai
      - Mali Khel.
      - Aib Khel.
    - Gadaizai
      - Ibrahim Khel.
      - Hassan Khel.
      - Ali Sher Khel.
      - Seni Khel.
    - Ashazai
      - Khadin Khel.
      - Aya Khel.
      - Musara Khel.
      - Khakizai.
    - Nasozai
      - Panjpai.
      - Makhozai.
  - *Malizai*
    - Daulatzai
      - Ismailzai.
      - Mandizai.
      - Barkazai.
    - Chagarzai
      - Nasrat Khel.
      - Ferozai.
      - Basi Khel.
    - Nurizai
      - Panjpai.
      - Ali Sher Khel.

YUSAF—*contd.* .. *Akozai* .. ..

- **Baizai** .. ..
  - **Kuz Sulizai.**
  - **Babuzai.**
  - **Bar Sulizai.**
- Ranizai .. ..
  - Ali Khel.
  - Utmanzai.
  - Khawazo Khel.
  - Bahram Khan Khel.
  - Usman Khel.
  - Sultan Khan Khel.
- Khadakzai.
- Abazai.
- Khwazazai .. ..
  - Adinzai.
  - Shamozai.
  - Nikbi Khel.
  - Sibujni.
  - Shamizai.
  - Malizai.

APPENDIX B.

Sitana Field Force, 1858.

Major-General Sir Sydney J. Cotton, K.C.B., Commanding.

Staff.

Captain T. Wright, Deputy Assistant Adjutant-General.

Lieutenant G. R. Greaves, Acting Deputy Assistant Adjutant-General.

Captain W. Cooper, Deputy Assistant Quarter Master General.

„ L. S. Cotton, Aide-de-Camp.

„ H. Hyde, Bengal Engineers, Field Engineer.

Artillery.

Captain T. Brougham, Commanding.

Lieutenant E. Tierney, Staff Officer.

Cavalry.

Lieut.-Colonel W. E. Mulcaster, Commanding.

Lieutenant H. R. Osborn, Staff Officer.

1st Infantry Brigade.

Lieut.-Colonel H. Renny, Commanding.

Captain V. Tonnochy, Brigade Major.

2nd Infantry Brigade.

Major A. T. Allan, Commanding.

Captain E. J. Ellerman, Brigade Major.

Hazara Column.

Major J. R. Becher, Commanding.

Lieutenant M. J. White, 12th Punjab Infantry, Staff Officer.

CHAPTER VI.

YUSAFZAI AND GADUN TRIBES BETWEEN THE BLACK MOUNTAIN AND SWAT.—(Continued.)

The Ambela Expedition, 1863.

THE Hindustani fanatics, after being prevented, by the agreement mentioned in the last chapter, from re-occupying Sitana, settled at Malka on the north side of the Mahaban mountain. In 1861, however, they came down to a place named Siri, just overhanging their old haunt at Sitana, and commenced sending robbers into Hazara to carry off Hindu traders. The Gaduns, in contravention of their agreement, allowed free passage to the Hindustanis through their territory when proceeding on and returning from these kidnapping and marauding expeditions.

The nature of these outrages was thus described by Lieut.-Colonel R. G. Taylor, the Commissioner of Peshawar :—

> A trader loads his mules at one of our chief towns, and starts across country to a village he hopes to reach by nightfall. On the road, in some lonely spot, he is seized, gagged, and taken aside into the jungle, and there kept close till dark, when the whole party starts by well-known, but unfrequented, tracks to the mountainous river bank, where he is ferried across the Indus, and is detained till his relations pay up the required ransom. His chief danger lies in the day dawning, or other obstruction occurring, before the kidnapping party reach the Indus, in which case the encumbrance, in the shape of a gagged idolator, must be got rid of. The robbers might, perhaps, let him go if they could afford it, but the locality and route would be described by him, and individuals perhaps recognised, and so he is knocked on the head, and thrown into a mountain crevice.

Owing to the mountainous nature of the country it was found impossible to deal with these crimes merely by protective police measures, and the Commissioner urged that the only way to check their occurrence was to punish both the tribes who sent out the brigands, and those who gave them passage through their lands.

In order therefore to bring them to a sense of their responsibilities, the Utmanzais and Gaduns were now placed under blockade, and on the 2nd October 1861 they came in and made their submission, and consented to enter into fresh engagements to exclude the *Saiyids* and Hindustanis.

During the winter of 1862, there was a marked absence of these kidnapping practices; but in the spring of 1863 two murders were committed, which were generally attributed to Mubarak Shah's men, and on the 5th July it was reported that the *Saiyids* and Hindustanis had suddenly re-occupied Sitana. No attempt to prevent their doing so was made by the Gadun or Utmanzai tribe, and some of their members actually invited them. These tribes, being called upon for their reasons for having thus broken their engagements, only afforded evasive replies; and as the Hindustanis were sending threatening messages to our feudatory, the Chief of Amb, a blockade of the Gadun and Utmanzai tribes was again imposed, and militia were entertained for the defence of the territory of the Amb Chief.

It should here be stated that after the expedition to Sitana in 1858, a somewhat remarkable man, named Amir Shah, who had for years been the chief counsellor of Saiyid Akbar, the late king of Swat, had waited on Lieut.-Colonel H. B. Edwardes, (then Commissioner) soliciting that some employment should be given to the remaining *Saiyids* and Hindustanis. If a *jagir* could be given to Mubarak Shah, the son of the late Saiyid Akbar, "he and his people could come in and settle peaceably within the British dominions." Lieut.-Colonel Edwardes told him that it was impossible to bestow lands on *Saiyids* as such, but offered to give Mubarak Shah military service. This contingency had, however, been already discussed between them, and Mubarak Shah had instructed Amir Shah to decline such an offer on his own part, but to accept it for his uncle, Saiyid Amran, and about sixty horsemen, for whom there was no longer any means of subsistence. The Commissioner had accordingly given these men service to the extent of one troop. On the reduction of the troops, this party was disbanded, and about this time (July 1863) Colonel R. G. Taylor, C.B., the Commissioner, heard that they had returned to Sitana.

The dispositions for the blockade were as follows :—

Shergarh .. .. Shingli .. .. Chamberi .. .. Chamba	On the Hassanzai border of the Amb territory held by Amb troops.	Left bank of Indus.
Darband	50 Police and mounted levies .. 100 Foot levies	,, ,, ,,
Kirpilian	Hazara Mountain Train Battery. 50 sabres, 5th Punjab Cavalry 1st Punjab Infantry .. 50 Police over the boats ..	,, ,, ,,
Naogiran .. .. Tawi .. .. Khanpur .. .. Torbela .. .. Dalmohat	85 Foot levies .. .. .. 37 Police and levies .. .. 55 Levies .. .. .. One company, 5th Gurkhas .. 20 Police over the boats ..	,, ,, ,,
Amb	100 Amb mounted levies .. 300 Amb foot levies .. .. 135 Hazara levies	Right bank.
Topi	150 Cavalry of the Guides .. 300 Infantry of the Guides ..	,, ,,
Swabi and Maneri ..	2 9-pounders from Kohat Head-quarters of the Guides ..	,, ,,

The 101st Royal Bengal Fusiliers[1] were also ordered to Hazara.

The *Saiyids* and Maulvi Abdulla were now acting with their Hindustani followers in the bitterest spirit against the British Government; the leaders of the colony expressly declared they were embarked in determined opposition to the infidel, and called upon all good Muhammadans to quit the friendship of the unbelieving, and join the would-be martyrs of the faith. A letter to this effect was sent to the Chief of Amb.

On the night of the 3rd September, Maulvi Abdulla, with his Hindustanis, and accompanied, it was said, by Malik Esau, Gadun, attempted to attack the camp of the Guides at Topi. The attacking force had arrived within a short distance of the camp, when they came upon a cavalry patrol of one duffadar and four sowars,

[1] Now the 1st Battalion, Royal Munster Fusiliers.

of the Guide Corps. The duffadar had been previously warned of the neighbourhood of a body of men, and on coming on an advanced party he immediately attacked them. Two of the enemy were cut down, and the rest, rushing back on the main body, communicated a panic, which ended in a general flight. The Hindustanis then erected a breastwork on the right bank of the Indus, from which they continued to annoy the picquet held by the levies at Naogiran.

About the middle of September, the Hassanzai tribe, instigated, it was supposed, by the Maulvi of Sitana, made an unprovoked attack on the hamlets in the little Shingli valley of the Black Mountain, in which the most advanced outpost of the Amb territory is situated. The fort was not molested, but some six or seven hamlets were destroyed, and one man, who resisted, was killed.

The Hassanzais then threatened an attack on Chamberi, and a portion of the Mada Khels crossed the Indus with the intention of assisting; but the frontier line having been greatly strengthened by the Amb authorities, the gathering broke up, and the Mada Khels recrossed the river. Shortly afterwards, the Hassanzais made an attack on the Amb levies on the Black Mountain border, in which one jemadar and seven men were killed, and several of the levies wounded.

It was now considered absolutely necessary to have recourse to military operations. Hitherto the hostilities and provocations had been offered by detached tribes, but now, for the first time, the majority, if not the whole, of the Hazara border tribes were arrayed against the British Government. In the opinion of the Lieutenant-Governor of the Punjab, it was perhaps possible, though very doubtful, to avert a campaign by making use of the feuds and factions of the different tribes to sow discord in their councils; but this could only put off the day of reckoning a little further. Delay, which with these tribes is little understood, might encourage other tribes to action, and a favourable opportunity might thus be lost for putting an end to the chronic frontier irritation which existed. That an expedition against these tribes would be forced on the British Government sooner or later appeared inevitable, and condonation without chastisement would only be an inducement for them to repeat their offences.

An expedition was accordingly sanctioned by the Supreme Government, the first object of which was effectually to rid the frontier of the chronic cause of disturbance,—the Hindustani fanatics. Their mere expulsion from the right bank of the Indus back upon their old posts at Malka and on the south bank of the Barandu, was not considered enough; nor was it thought advisable that they should find shelter in Swat, and make that powerful tribe the future focus of disturbance on the frontier. If possible, the line of retreat of the fanatics towards the Barandu was to be cut off; and although their extirpation might not be possible, yet if the co-operation of the well-disposed sections of the tribes could be obtained, their dispersion would be on lines of direction favourable to their capture. The punishment of the Gaduns was to be a secondary consideration to the primary one of crushing effectually the small, but troublesome, horde of fanatics.

Plan of operations.

In a memorandum drawn up by Lieut.-Colonel A. T. Wilde, C.B., commanding the Corps of Guides, it was stated that the expedition of 1858, although successful, had not been conclusive as to its results. The Gadun tribe had not felt the power of the British Government; and although the Hindustanis had been turned out of Mangal Thana and driven from Sitana, they had retreated on Malka, more from the pressure put upon them by the Gadun tribe than from the defeats they had sustained from our troops. For the future peace of the border, Lieut.-Colonel Wilde said the destruction of this colony of priests and fanatics was a necessity, and that they must be removed by death or capture from the hills, and a treaty made with the hill tribes not to allow them to reside in their territories. The force to be employed would have to be a strong one, and it would be necessary to occupy temporarily the country to the north of the Mahaban; the military object in view being to attack the Hindustanis from the north, and force them to fight with their backs to the plains: operating, in fact, on their line of retreat, instead of, as in previous expeditions, advancing from the plains, driving them out of Mangal Thana and Sitana, and allowing them a safe retreat and passage into the hills. To effect this, two columns would have to be employed, the base of operations of one column being in the Peshawar valley, and that of the other in Hazara. The detailed movements proposed for these two forces was as follows:—

The Peshawar column was to be assembled at Nawa Kala and Swabi, with the avowed object, as in 1858, of moving on Mangal Thana (which would be naturally expected); but, when ready to march, the column was to pass through the Ambela or Surkhabi pass and occupy the village of Koga, in the Chamla valley, thirteen miles by a camel road chiefly over our own land and stated then to be "easy in the extreme." The next day the force was to march to Chirori, sixteen miles, an open plain near the river Barandu, when, simultaneous with the occupation of that place, the Hazara column was to drop down the Indus and drive the enemy out of Sitana, the Peshawar column moving on the third day to Malka.

No hostilities were anticipated from the Bunerwals, as, holding different tenets, and forming part of the religious constituency of the Akhund of Swat, they were known to have no sympathy as a body with the Hindustani party. Further, they had, for fifteen years, given us no trouble, and were generally judged to be peaceable. Secrecy regarding the line of proposed operations was of the utmost importance, and it was consequently considered inadvisable to communicate our intentions to the Buner *jirga*, or to question them or the Chief of the Sudum valley about the country on our line of advance.[1] With regard to the Chamla valley, it was known to be inhabited by mixed clans, some of them settlers from our own Yusafzai plains, some from Buner, others belonging to the Khudu Khel tribe, who were known to be desirous of remaining friendly with us, and the rest being Amazais, who were in some measure implicated as enemies, from the fact of the Hindustani colony at Malka being in their territory. The valley was not claimed by, or considered as under, the protection of any large clan, and it was known to be divided from Buner by a lofty range of mountains called the Guru. Of its advantages as a military position, it was said that a force would be here able to take its stand in open ground, in rear of the whole of the enemy's tract, which it would fully

1 This precaution, though unavoidable, was most unfortunate, as, on the approach of our troops to the border, the suspicion of the Bunerwals of an intended invasion into their country was raised, and they ultimately joined in a coalition of other tribes against us.

command, and from which, by rapid excursions, it would be able to do all its work and deal with all difficulties, returning, when convenient, to its standing camp; such a position would render the tribes on the southern slopes of the Mahaban mountain well-nigh powerless, as they would be surrounded, and would be at the mercy of an army which could descend upon their strongholds, and carry out its ends with irresistible advantage.

Brigadier-General Sir Neville B. Chamberlain, Commanding the Punjab Irregular Force, who had been selected by the Commander-in-Chief for the command of the expedition, decided upon adopting this plan of operations, with the exception that the Hazara column was not to take any active part in the movements against the Hindustanis, but simply to remain stationary at Darband, with the sole object of overawing the Hassanzais and other tribes on both banks of the Indus, and protecting the Hazara frontier from attack; the active operations against Sitana being confined entirely to the column under his personal command.

The following troops were to hold the line of the Indus, Hazara, and Yusafzai:—

Darband ..	3 guns. 350 European infantry (51st Regiment). 250 native infantry.
Torbela ..	1 squadron of native cavalry. Details of native infantry.
Topi ..	2 guns. 150 native cavalry. 250 native infantry.
Abbottabad ..	3 guns. One company of European infantry (93rd Highlanders). 50 Native cavalry. Depôts of two regiments of native infantry.
Rustam Bazar	300 native cavalry. Details of native infantry.
Mardan ..	Depôt of the Guide Corps.

To form the expeditionary force, all the northern stations had been considerably weakened, and there was no reserve nearer than Lahore.

On the 13th October, Brigadier-General Sir Neville Chamberlain arrived at Swabi, the place at which it had been arranged that the troops proceeding from Hazara were to assemble, and on the 18th October a force, as per margin, marched to the mouth of the Darhan pass. This is the pass by which the column under Major-General Sir S. J. Cotton entered the hills in 1858; and the impression was, of course, conveyed that the force was about to enter the hills by the same route as before. The other troops of the expedition moved up at the same time to Nawa Kala from their camps in the rear.

Peshawar Mountain Train Battery.
Hazara Mountain Train Battery.
1st Punjab Infantry.[1]
5th Gurkha Regiment.

On the afternoon of the 19th, when it was too late for the Chamla or other tribes to make any preparations on a large scale for impeding the march of the troops through the Ambela pass, a proclamation was forwarded by the Commissioner to the Chamla, Khudu Khel, Gadun, Amazai, Mada Khel, and Buner tribes, stating the object for which the force was about to enter the Chamla valley, and assuring them that it was with no intention of injuring them or of interfering with their independence, but solely because it was the most convenient route by which to reach the Hindustani fanatics, and to effect their expulsion from the Mahaban.

At 9 P.M., on the 19th October, the troops marginally noted, marching from Nawa Kala, effected a junction at Parmalao with the troops which had been sent on before to the mouth of the Darhan pass, and the united detachments, under Lieut.-Colonel A. T. Wilde, C.B., moved upon the Ambela pass, which they reached at sunrise the following day. The *maliks* of our own village of Surkhabi were then taken on by the force, and told Colonel Taylor, the Commissioner, who was accompanying the column, that opposition was to be expected in the pass the following day. About 9 A.M., the baggage being left at the entrance of the pass, under an escort of the 11th Bengal Cavalry, the troops advanced, the Guide Infantry and the 1st

100 sabres, Guide Cavalry.
100 „ 11th B. C.
Guide Infantry.
5th Punjab Infantry.[2]
20th „ N. I.[3]

[1] Now 55th Coke's Rifles (Frontier Force).
[2] Now 58th Vaughan's Rifles (Frontier Force).
[3] Now 20th D. C. O. Infantry (Brownlow's Punjabis).

Punjab Infantry leading, supported, respectively, by the 20th Punjab Native Infantry and the 5th Punjab Infantry. The 5th Gurkhas remained as an escort to the two mountain batteries.

When about a third of the defile had been traversed, information was received to the effect that our further progress would be disputed, and that the head of the pass was being held by the people of Buner. At 12 o'clock the enemy opened fire from the rocks in the vicinity of the road, but were gradually dislodged by the advanced guard; in this manner two-thirds of the pass was traversed, when the end of the defile, called the Ambela Kandao, appeared in sight. The hills on both sides were high, covered with low brushwood and jutting rocks, but perfectly practicable for good light troops. On many of the most prominent rocks small parties of the enemy showed themselves, and fired occasional shots.

The infantry of the Corps of Guides, under Lieutenant F. H. Jenkins, were directed to take the crest of the hills to the right, and the 1st Punjab Infantry, under Major C. P. Keyes, to move up the valley slowly; and it was left to Major Keyes to act as his judgment directed. Lieut.-Colonel J. L. Vaughan, with his regiment, the 5th Punjab Infantry, protected the flank of the column, which some parties of the enemy threatened. By 2 P.M. the top of the pass was secured. The number of the enemy was estimated at from 200 to 250 men, and their loss amounted to two killed and three wounded, besides one captured. On the side of the troops there were no casualties.

One of the *maliks* of Ambela had been made prisoner while opposing the advance, and informed us that the slight opposition met with in the pass was made by the people of his own village (situated at the mouth of the pass in the Chamla valley, and therefore belonging geographically to Chamla, but paying tribute to one of the Buner tribes), and by a few of the Chamla villagers. He was sent to his people by the Commissioner, together with a wounded man, and they were allowed to take away the bodies of their men who had been killed. The *malik* was charged with a verbal message corresponding with the terms of the proclamation, and informing the Chamla people that if they would bring supplies they would be liberally paid for them.

The main column, composed of the troops as per margin, marched from Nawa Kala at 1 A.M. on the 20th October, and reached Rustam at 7 A.M. The road was a mere village track, and as any attempt to improve it earlier would have revealed our intended route, it had only received such repairs as the sappers could hastily give it. Late in the afternoon of the 19th, when concealment was no longer necessary or practicable, the civil authorities aided in removing obstructions by employing large parties of villagers, who worked at the road by torchlight; and a line of fires further helped to mark the route. After a short halt at Rustam the advance was again resumed. From that place to Surkhabi, the track was tolerably good; but in the Ambela pass it again deteriorated, often lying in the bed of a stream, and at other times being overgrown with jungle and low trees. The hills on either side of the pass rise to some height, but for the most part with a gradual slope, so that infantry can ascend them without difficulty, except for the obstacle presented by thick, thorny jungle. The guns were drawn by horses as far as possible, and then transferred to elephants. The progress of the force was, of course, extremely slow, as in most parts it was only practicable to move in single file, and it was not till late in the afternoon that the rear of Lieut.-Colonel Wilde's column was reached.

Half C Battery, 19th Brigade, R.A.
71st H. L. I. (550).
101st Roy. Bengal Fus. (500).
Coy. of sappers and miners.
3rd Punjab Infantry.[1]
6th " "[2]
32nd " Native Infantry.[3]

The last named force had not been strong enough to post flanking parties at more than a few of the most important points in the pass. Detachments were, therefore, posted from the main column wherever it seemed necessary, and the entire 5th Gurkha Regiment, which had advanced with the main body, was left about three-quarters of a mile from the crest of the pass in a commanding position, where it served as a support to the small flanking parties, and also protected the baggage. The 32nd Punjab Native Infantry formed the rear-guard, but did not get beyond Surkhabi on the night of the 20th.

Lieut.-Colonel Wilde had encamped the advanced column, on and beyond the crest of the pass, on tolerably open and level

[1] Disbanded in 1882.
[2] Now the 59th Scinde Rifles (Frontier Force).
[3] Now the 32nd Sikh Pioneers.

ground, which afforded sufficient room for the main column also to bivouac as it came up. The whole of the cavalry had been sent on with the advanced column, under the idea that the pass was much easier and shorter than it proved to be, with the idea of pushing them forward, supported by some infantry and mountain guns, to reconnoitre the road down the pass and the head of the Chamla valley. But when it was found what difficulties the pass presented even to the march of the troops, and how long it would necessarily be before the whole of the baggage could come up, it was thought prudent to make no further movement in advance. The ammunition mules of the infantry had with difficulty managed to keep up with the rear of their respective regiments, but with this exception not a single baggage animal reached the camp during the night of the 20th.

The position which the troops occupied on that night was thus described by Brigadier-General Chamberlain:—

On the left the position was enclosed by the Guru mountain, which divides the Ambela pass from Buner. This mountain, which is estimated roughly to be 6,000 feet, rises in a succession of ridges, steep but not precipitous, running generally parallel to the pass; occasional plateaux and knolls are found on its sides, which afforded convenient and safe situations for our picquets; and about 1,000 feet above the camp was a very remarkable heap of enormous granite rocks, which formed a conspicuous object from the entrance and throughout the pass, and marked the point at which the crest or watershed is reached, which separates Yusafzai from Chamla. The sides of the Guru mountain were clothed with fir trees of large growth, interspersed on the lower slopes with the wild fig and the date trees: a remarkable mixture of the vegetation of a cold and of a tropical climate. To the front of the camp the pass widened as it descended, and opened out into little plateaux, which at last met the plain of Chamla. The latter was distant about three miles from the camp, and had the appearance of being well cultivated, with a stream flowing through the middle of it, the head of which gave water to the camp. A range of hills, much lower than the Guru, was on the right, and was crowned by our picquets. To the rear, but far below, was seen the plain of Yusafzai.

Up to the evening of the 21st, only a small portion of the baggage had reached the camp, partly in consequence of the difficulties of the road, and partly from the inferior nature of much of the transport and the incompetence of the drivers. Time had not sufficed, after the assembly of the troops, for the arrangement of all details, such as the careful distribution of loads according to the strength and efficiency of the cattle, and the large amount of mule and pony transport necessary had resulted in the presence of a good many animals very little fitted for their work. Loads had been thrown off all along the line, and the attempts, as night fell, to push on necessary stores for the European troops, increased the existing difficulties in narrow places to such an extent that the result was a stoppage of the whole train.

The Ambela *malik*, who had been allowed to go back to his village the day before, returned the following day with the other *maliks* of Ambela and Koga, who were earnest in their professions of a full intention to assist the force. Later in the day other headmen from the principal Chamla villages came into camp with supplies and promises of assistance; but all these friendly sympathies subsequently received a check when Buner threw itself into opposition.

It has already been stated that on the 19th a proclamation had been sent to the Buner and other tribes; to this a reply was received by the Commissioner from the two chief Buner *maliks*, saying that the force was at liberty to follow its own enemies, and that the Buner people would only be prepared to defend their own country should it be attacked; in return, an agent was sent to them by Colonel R. G. Taylor to explain fully our intentions.

On the morning of the 22nd, the rear-guard being then at no great distance from the camp, it was considered that the preliminary steps might be taken for moving the force forward, and a detachment of sappers was accordingly set to work to improve the descent of the pass. The road was fair, and the pass, about two miles in length, was unoccupied by the enemy. The sappers were supported by the 20th Punjab Native Infantry, under Major C. H. Brownlow, and, as soon as the road was reported tolerably good, were followed by the cavalry shown in the margin under Lieut.-Colonel D. M. Probyn, V.C., C.B. The sappers were then sent back to camp, and the cavalry proceeded to reconnoitre, supported by the 20th Punjab Infantry.

Guide Cavalry, 50 sabres.
11th Bengal Cavalry, 100 sabres.

From the foot of the pass there were two roads through the Chamla valley: one passed by the village of Ambela, and lay under the hills which divided Chamla from Buner on the north side of the valley; the other road was by Koga and along the south side of the valley; and as Ambela, though actually in Chamla, was regarded by the Buner people as one of their own villages, the orders to Lieut.-Colonel A. Taylor, commanding the reconnoitring party, were to proceed by the Koga route, to guard in every possible way against giving offence to the Buner people, and to prove to them our desire to hold entirely aloof from them and their country.

As the cavalry passed the *kotal* leading into Buner, which was on their left, distant about two-and-a-half miles, it was seen that it was occupied in force by the Bunerwals; but from all that could be learned, none had descended into the valley. On arrival at Koga (four miles from camp), the reports that the valley was quite unoccupied were confirmed, and Colonel Taylor consequently pushed on for seven miles to Kuria, returning to Koga camp the same afternoon. From Ambela to Kuria the surface of the valley was level, free from obstructions, and quite practicable for field artillery. The *nala* banks were all low, water was abundant, and the land highly cultivated. Fuel, however, had to be supplied from the hills, as there was no jungle in the valley. Beyond Kuria the country was rugged and difficult.

On regaining the foot of the Ambela pass, it was found that the Bunerwals had been, and were still, descending in considerable numbers, with the view of preventing the return of the reconnoitring party. They now attempted to gain possession of a patch of very broken ground at the extreme end of the valley through which the road lay, but were driven back by a spirited charge by the cavalry. Major Brownlow then occupied the broken ground with two companies, and the cavalry returned to camp.

The rear-guard duties now devolved on Major Brownlow. Emboldened by the continued retreat of the party, the enemy recovered from the effects of the cavalry charge, and, by the time the pass was fairly entered, had assembled in great numbers, and had surrounded a picquet under Lieutenant G. M. Richmond, which it took some time to withdraw. By this time daylight had quite gone, and the remainder of the retirement was effected in dim moonlight. The enemy pressed Major Brownlow very closely, and several times came in amongst his men sword in hand. Eventually, as the troops drew into camp, the picquets became engaged, and there was a general attack upon them in the front and on the flanks of the camp, which continued at intervals until midnight. The loss on the British side was however trifling, and only one officer, Lieutenant W. A. Gillies, R.A., was killed. The enemy lost about fifty killed including some men of influence.

At this time a very remarkable paper fell into the hands of he Commissioner, *viz.*, a letter from Maulvi Abdulla, the military leader of the Hindustani fanatics, and Saiyid Amran, an uncle of Saiyid Mubarak Shah, to the Buner chiefs, warning them that, with reference to the assembly of troops in Yusafzai, we might probably assert it was to punish the Hindustanis, but it was in reality to lay waste and annex Chamla, Buner, and Swat. The letter was not dated, but had evidently been written before the proclamation, and must have roused the worst suspicions of the Buner people, as the predictions contained in it anticipated, almost word for word, portions of the proclamation.

That the Buner people should thus have taken a decidedly hostile part against us was extremely serious, and not only altered our position in the hills, but required a change in the plan of operations. The security of the communications of the force with the rear had first to be arranged for ; the wing of the 14th Native Infantry [1] was consequently ordered up from Nawa Kala to Rustam, and application made for another native infantry regiment to be sent from Peshawar. Sir Neville Chamberlain requested the Commissioner to arrange for the occupation of the lower portion of the pass with his foot levies, and thought it probable that he would have to ask for more native infantry before the communications with the rear could be considered secure, even while the force occupied its position on the crest of the Ambela pass.

The plan of operations, as already shown, was to use the Chamla valley as a route to reach the Hindustani settlement on the Mahaban, but it now became doubtful if it could be adhered to. With a powerful tribe like the people of Buner in declared hostility on the left flank of the proposed line of march, and in a position to which they could always return, even though once dislodged and beaten, it would perhaps be impossible to persevere in this plan of operations. Moreover, as information had been received that

[1] Now the 14th (P. W. O.) Sikhs.

the Buner people had summoned the Hindustanis to their aid, and that at least a portion of them had obeyed the summons, it was probable the fanatics would either be encountered in our present position, fighting with the people of Buner, or have to be sought elsewhere than on the spurs of the Mahaban.

On the 23rd October the strength of the Yusafzai Field Force was about 6,000 men, of whom about 450 were sick. On the morning of the 24th, the sick, both British and Native, all baggage except that absolutely necessary for efficiency, and all transport rendered spare by this arrangement, were sent to the rear under a strong escort; whilst an infantry regiment occupied a spur of the Guru mountain, thereby preventing any attack by the Bunerwals on the convoy as it filed down the pass. At the same time, parties from the camp were employed in improving the road and in removing the worst of the obstacles. The enemy remained quiet, but large bodies of Hassanzais, Chagarzais, Mada Khels, and Hindustanis, with numerous standards, were observed approaching the mouth of the pass.

On the night of the 24th, the 1st Punjab Infantry, under the command of Major C. P. Keyes, occupied the advanced picquets of the right defence. A little after daylight on the morning of the 25th, the enemy showed on a ridge of hills opposite, and close to, these picquets; and Major Keyes advanced to dislodge them. Of the 200 troops under his command, he sent 100 to take the enemy in flank, while with the remainder he made a frontal attack. The enemy quickly retired, and Major Keyes took up a position on a ridge commanding the plain over which they had retreated. On the other side of this plain was a conical hill, the summit of which commanded the ridge at a range of 700 yards. On this the enemy were collecting from the plain by the villages of Lalu and Koga. As they appeared to be coming in considerable force (eventually between 2,000 and 3,000 men), Major Keyes asked for reinforcements of a mountain battery and another regiment, and ordered the 1st Punjab Infantry to keep under cover, and not to return the fire of the enemy.

Owing to the distance from camp and the nature of the ground, these reinforcements did not arrive till 2 P.M.; 150 men of the 71st Highland Light Infantry and 101st Royal Bengal Fusiliers being the first to arrive. The marksmen of this party were selected and placed along the ridge, the men of the 1st Punjab Infantry being recalled and drawn up out of sight of the enemy, as also the 5th Gurkha Regiment, which joined shortly afterwards. As soon as the Peshawar Mountain Train Battery arrived, they were brought up as near the ridge as possible without showing themselves to the enemy. The guns were then man-handled into position, and immediately opened fire with shrapnel at a distance of 600 yards, the marksmen opening fire at the same time.

The "Conical" hill was rocky and very precipitous, but essentially a weak position, having a line of retreat that would expose the retiring enemy to great loss if closely pursued.

After the guns had fired two rounds, the 1st Punjab Infantry were advanced at the double, supported by the 5th Gurkha Regiment, the whole of the British troops keeping up the fire from the ridge. The enemy did not stop to defend their position, but, after firing a few shots, retreated at their utmost speed. To the admirable practice of the guns, and the withering fire of the marksmen, may be attributed our obtaining the hill without any loss. The enemy left several bodies on the ground, and their total loss was afterwards ascertained to have been thirty-three killed and upwards of forty wounded.[1] Our loss was only one sepoy, 1st Punjab Infantry, wounded on the first advance from the picquets. As soon as the enemy were seen to have repassed the village of Lalu on their way to the plains, the troops were dismissed to their quarters.

Whilst this affair was being conducted by Major Keyes on the right, the heights above the left flank picquets were crowned by large bodies of the enemy, and it afterwards became known that a simultaneous attack on both flanks of the camp had been arranged; but the Buner people who were to have attacked the left flank failed to keep their agreement. This gave great offence to the tribes engaged in the right attack; and the Mahaban tribes were so disgusted by this reverse that they trooped off the same day down the valley to their homes, and did not rejoin the enemy for some weeks.

The camp arrangements at this time were as follows (*see* Sketch of British position). The front picquets were under command of Colonel W. Hope, C.B., 71st Highland Light Infantry, those on the right

[1] Amongst the killed was the brother of a *Saiyid* of some note, residing in Chamla, although this tribe had sent in a deputation to the Commissioner.

under Lieut.-Colonel A. T. Wilde, C.B., Corps of Guides, and those on the left under Lieut.-Colonel J. L. Vaughan, 5th Punjab Infantry. The heights which commanded the camp were occupied by strong parties of infantry and stockaded picquets. The approach to the camp from the gorge was defended by a breastwork and guns in position, and the rear was also secured from attack.

The defences consisted of loopholed stone walls, abatis, and branches of trees pointing upwards. As will be afterwards seen, the enemy generally singled out one position at a time for attack; and, owing to the nature of the ground, which was broken and wooded, they were enabled to get close up and attack in such large numbers, and with such boldness, that in some instances they pulled down the stone walls and threw the stones at the defenders.

Reports were now rife that the Buner people had solicited the aid of the Akhund of Swat. If he joined in the war, bringing, as he would doubtless do, an immense accession of material as well as moral strength, an advance by the Chamla valley would become still more difficult; but Sir Neville Chamberlain considered that in the meantime the halt of the force at the crest of the pass was not without its advantages. The situation was a menacing one; it obliged the enemy to keep a large body of men together whom they found it difficult to feed, and it made it indispensable for them to become the attacking party, when all the advantage was on our side.

It has been mentioned above that a simultaneous attack upon both the right and left flanks of the camp had been arranged by the enemy to come off on the 25th, but that the Buner men failed in their agreement to carry out the attack on our left. But as large bodies of men had then been seen collected upon the Guru mountain, it was necessary to provide against the threatened attack on that flank, and also against the possibility of the enemy making an attempt from the spurs of the Guru upon a convoy of sick, baggage, etc., which was about to be sent to the rear. Accordingly, on the morning of the 26th, the left picquets, under Lieut.-Colonel J. L. Vaughan, were reinforced with the troops noted in the margin.

Hazara Mountain Train Battery.
30 marksmen, 71st and 101st Regiments.
200 men, 71st Regiment.
5th Punjab Infantry.
6th " "

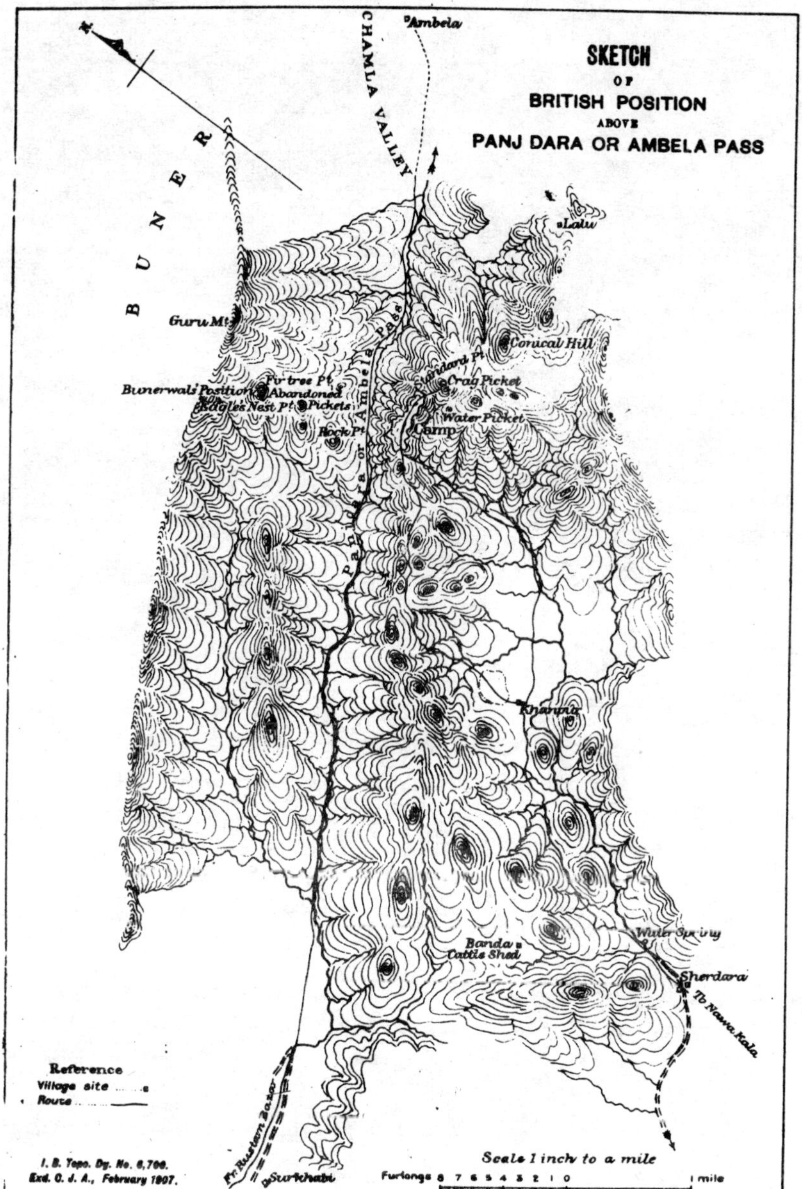

No. 4,060-I., 1907.

The troops proceeded to the neighbourhood of the "Eagle's Nest" picquet. This picquet occupied the top of a very steep, rocky knoll, which rises out of the southern face of the Guru, and was the apex of that portion of the mountain which overlooked the left flank of the camp.

It was necessary to hold this position with a picquet by day in order to give security to the grasscutters, etc., of the camp; but its distance from camp, and the consequent difficulty of reinforcing it quickly, had made it unadvisable to hold it by night until the ground below had been securely occupied, and the picquet had been consequently withdrawn at sunset to a lower position. The knoll had been hastily prepared for defence, the preceding afternoon, by the erection of a breastwork of stones on high ground, showing a semi-circular front of about ninety feet. In front of this the ground was level, and commanded by the work, but beyond the plateau, the hill, which was well wooded and studded with rocks, rose again, and its crest (distant about 500 yards from our breastwork) was protected by a similar work of the enemy.

Lieut.-Colonel Vaughan now made the following dispositions. The "Eagle's Nest" was held by thirty marksmen of the 71st Foot and 101st Fusiliers, under Lieutenant G. V. Fosbery, 104th Fusiliers, and eighty marksmen of the 20th Punjab Native Infantry, the whole being under the command of Major C. H. Brownlow, 20th Punjab Native Infantry.

As the picquet itself was only capable of holding about 110 men, some large rocks at the base of the knoll were made to shelter 120 men, *viz.*, fifty men of the 3rd Punjab Infantry, and seventy men of the 20th Punjab Native Infantry. The rest of the force was drawn up on and about a small knoll, 400 yards west of the "Eagle's Nest" picquet, in the following order from right to left:—Detachment 71st Highland Light Infantry under Major A. C. Parker, the 6th Punjab Infantry under Captain W. D. Hoste, Hazara Mountain Train Battery under Captain F. R. DeBude, and the 5th Punjab Infantry under Lieutenant C. E. Stewart. The last regiment in extended order lined the crest of the knoll, with three companies in support of the guns. The 71st Highland Light Infantry was in connection with the "Eagle's Nest" picquet.

The breastwork on the crest of the hill opposite the picquet was occupied by about 2,000 of the enemy, and at about noon on the 26th the Bunerwals, who had hitherto fired only an occasional shot, began to move down from their position by the different spurs, and with loud shouts attacked the picquet. The steady fire, however, with which they were received, rendered their very gallant efforts to enter the defences unavailing. In attacking the picquet, the matchlock men of the enemy posted themselves most advantageously in the wood, and opened a galling fire, while their swordsmen and others advanced boldly to the attack, charging across the plateau in front in the most determined manner. The nature of the ground prevented the guns from being brought to bear at first upon those who assailed the picquet, and they were thus able to swarm up the steep sides of the knoll, and to plant their standard close under the breastwork. All the efforts of the garrison failed to dislodge the enemy from this position for some time, notwithstanding that the direct fire from the breastwork was aided by a flanking fire from the mountain guns and from the Enfield rifles of the 71st Highland Light Infantry. The enemy were ultimately driven back, leaving the ground covered with their dead; their matchlock men only maintaining the fight, and continuing to harass the picquet.

Whilst this was occurring at the "Eagle's Nest," an attack was also being made on the rest of the troops on the Guru mountain. The mountain guns, opening fire with shrapnel, common shell, and round shot, soon checked those of the enemy who were advancing against them, though not those moving against the "Eagle's Nest" picquet. This check of the enemy by the Hazara Mountain Train Battery affording a favourable opportunity, the 6th Punjab Infantry, which was in reserve, made a very bold charge upon the tribesmen, headed by their commander, Captain Hoste; but unfortunately, carried too far in the ardour of pursuit, this regiment lost heavily in its retirement, *viz.*, four native officers and forty sepoys wounded, and two non-commissioned officers and nine sepoys killed.

On the advance of the 6th Punjab Infantry, the enemy had again come down the hill, and with loud yells rushed, sword in hand, to the assault of the "Eagle's Nest," but were again finally repulsed.

During the course of the action, Lieut.-Colonel Vaughan, seeing how desperate were the attacks on the "Eagle's Nest," and how hardly pressed was its garrison, sent one company of the

71st Regiment and one company of the 5th Punjab Infantry to reinforce the picquet. In one of the sallies made by the troops who were holding the rocks below the "Eagle's Nest," Lieutenant R. Clifford, Adjutant of the 1st Punjab Cavalry, who was on leave when the force was formed, and joined it as a volunteer with the 3rd Punjab Infantry, was killed whilst gallantly leading his men.

After the repulse of the enemy's second attack on the "Eagle's Nest," no further attempt was made on Lieut.-Colonel Vaughan's position. During the rest of the day they kept up a heavy fire from the low hills and broken ground in front of the troops, but the ground affording excellent cover, little damage was done to our men.

While this attack was going on at the left defences of the camp, a demonstration was also made by the enemy in the front, when Lieutenant T. H. T. Drake of the 32nd Punjab Native Infantry was wounded.

The determined attack on the "Eagle's Nest" had, of course, been productive of severe losses, our casualties amounting to two officers, one native officer, and twenty-six men killed, and one officer, seven native officers and eighty-four men wounded. The enemy lost about 250 killed, whilst numbers of the wounded had been carried to their homes, or crawled to the nearest Buner villages.

The attacks had been made by the Hindustanis and the Bunerwals, and as amongst the killed were large numbers of the Salarzai, Daulatzai, and Gadaizai sections of the Bunerwals, it was apparent how general was the combination of that tribe against us.

It had been originally intended to bring the troops back to camp by sunset, and to withdraw the "Eagle's Nest" picquet at the same time; but the enemy were in such force on the mountains, and the importance of continuing to hold the position was so apparent, that Lieut.-Colonel Vaughan determined to stay there during the night. The troops under him, therefore, bivouacked on the ground they had held during the day, the Bunerwals, who had evidently suffered severely, making no further hostile demonstrations of any kind, although there was some firing by Hindustanis and others.

On the following day, the 27th, the "Eagle's Nest" picquet was strengthened, and another, called "Vaughan's" picquet, on an adjoining eminence, which supported the "Eagle's Nest," was erected, and it was determined that these positions should be held permanently,—the "Eagle's Nest" by 40 British infantry and 300 native infantry; "Vaughan's" picquet by the Hazara Mountain Train Battery, 60 British and 300 native infantry.

When, on our invitation, the Bunerwals came down to carry off their dead who had fallen the previous day, opportunity was taken to try and reason with them as to the unnecessary loss they were causing to their tribe, but with little effect. Their demeanour was courteous, and they conversed unreservedly with Sir N. B. Chamberlain and the Commissioner, Colonel R. G. Taylor; but it was evident from their manner that they were not in the least humbled.

Upwards of thirty bodies of the Hindustanis were counted upon the ground during the short truce. It was observed that both the wounded and dead bodies of the Hindustanis on this and subsequent occasions were left by their allies, who seemed to look upon the Hindustanis as they might upon earthen vessels, to be thrown at our heads in the day of battle, when no doubt their utility was appreciated, but of which it was quite superfluous to think of picking up the fragments if they happened to get broken in the fray. But what their allies would not do was performed by the British soldiers, for, under the orders to Sir Neville Chamberlain, these mutilated rebels of our own territories, together with some wounded Bunerwals, were taken into our hospitals and carefully and tenderly treated. Two of the wounded Hindustanis were apparently soldiers of the late 55th Native Infantry, and many of them young men, apparently from Bengal; they used the old pattern musket and Government ammunition.

The duty of the troops was now very heavy, the effective strength of the regiments' having been considerably reduced by casualties and by sickness. The camp was this day, the 27th, however, reinforced by the arrival of the 14th Native Infantry under Major C. C. G. Ross.

News was now received that the Akhund of Swat had actually joined the Bunerwals, and that he had brought with him from Swat 120 horsemen and upwards of 100 standards, each standard representing probably from thirty to forty footmen. Besides the tribe with which he was more immediately connected, *viz.*, the

Yusafzais of Swat, he had summoned the people of Bajaur, the Malazais of Dir under their Chief, Ghazan Khan, and other distant tribes whose names at that time were hardly known, except to officers who had served long on the frontier.

In chapter VIII the country of Swat and its inhabitants will be described, and some account will then be given of the rise of this remarkable man, known as the Akhund of Swat. Suffice it here to say that originally a *Saiyid* of Buner, he had passed his life in close study and asceticism, and at this time must have been about seventy years of age. He had gained an immense ascendancy over the minds of Muhammadans in general, and more particularly over the tribes on the Peshawar frontier, and his position towards them at this time can best be illustrated by comparing it with that of the Pope of Rome.

It is remarkable that up to the present time the *Akhund*, with the solitary exception of forcing a king upon the people of Swat, had always held himself aloof from worldly affairs, and had, even in 1857, counselled peace to his disciples, who flocked to him for advice. He also was ostensibly opposed to the tenets of the Sitana fanatics. The previous year, it was said, he had been unusually busy in attempting to refute some religious views held in Peshawar which were opposed to his own. For the time, however, all sectarian differences were now forgotten; the *Akhund* and the Sitana *Maulvi* were said to be on the most friendly terms, and it was known that the whole Hindustani colony were either at, or on their way to, Ambela. Colonel R. G. Taylor believed (and his belief was shared by the native chiefs best able to judge, who were in the camp at the time) that the *Akhund* had moved in fear that if he did not show sympathy with Buner on the occasion, he might lose influence with the tribe, who were his natural constituents; and possibly to this was added anxiety lest Mubarak Shah, who was an aspirant to his father's position of King of Swat, might, by having joined the war with the Hindustanis, gain some of the influence which he, the *Akhund*, would lose. It was also known that the adjurations of the Buner Chiefs and people had been most passionate, all the *mullas* of the country, with many of the women, having been deputed to beseech him to adopt their cause.

The *Akhund* was accompanied by the two Chiefs of Swat, Sobat Khan and Sherdil Khan, usually at bitter feud with each other, but now, for the time being, the best of friends.

The Hindustani fanatics were under the leadership of Maulvi Abdulla. They numbered at the beginning about 900 men, most of whom had been wrought up to a pitch of fanaticism, and were all prepared to lay down their lives. It is, indeed, only men animated by this spirit who can be found willing to leave their homes in India, and to take up their residence in these rugged mountains. Widely separated in language, manners, and interests from the people amongst whom they dwelt, receiving only a bare subsistence from the *Maulvi*, who entertained them, and paying exorbitantly for all the supplies they consumed, their life was passed in a manner by no means congenial to natives of Hindustan. They were drilled on our system, and some were clothed like the sepoys of the old Indian army. Three of their jemadars had been non-commissioned officers in the late 55th Native Infantry. The *Maulvi* himself had been about four years in these parts. He was the nephew of that Maulvi Inayat Ali Khan who gave so much trouble in 1857 at Narinji, and was a man of good ability. He it was who appropriated all the contributions received from India for the colony, from which he derived a rich income.

With these Hindustanis were associated the family of the Sitana Saiyids. The only one, however, who took a prominent part against us was Saiyid Muhammad Shah, who had been in our service for some time. For, after the expedition of 1858, the eldest representative of the family, Mubarak Shah, took no active part in the proceedings.

An account of the Bunerwals has been given in the previous chapter. Their chiefs at this time were Zaidulla Khan, Ahmad Khan, and Nawab Khan, the two first named being closely allied by marriage to our own chiefs of the Sudum valley, Ajab Khan, of Chargulai, and his brother Aziz Khan. They were said to be able to bring 12,000 to 15,000 men into the field, but this was probably an exaggeration.

The village of Chamla likewise sent their quota—the Amazais of Chirori being well represented—and the Mada Khels also came in force.

In addition to these, there were small parties of men from other tribes who had joined the enemy. In fact, there was a general combination of almost all the tribes from the Indus to the boundary of Kabul; and the total number of men in arms against the force at this time was computed at about 15,000. Old animosities were for the time in abeyance, and, under the influence of fanaticism, tribes usually hostile to each other had joined, or were hastening to join the *Akhund's* standard, and to fight for the sake of their common faith.

Independently of these, however, was a mischievous gathering of our own subjects, who associated with bands of the enemy in infesting our lines of communication. Chief amongst these were the Utman Khels, an Afridi clan, long settled in the upper parts of of the Lundkhwar valley, but who had retained all the wild habits and plundering propensities of their race. They were joined by men from Narinji, and by bigots and malcontents, who, individually, or in parties of two and three, slipped away from a great number of our villages. They numbered only a few hundreds in all, but were of great use to the enemy in harassing our rear.

Such being the state of affairs, it is easy to understand how entirely the situation had altered since the force entered the Ambela pass. Instead of having to deal with the Mahaban tribes, with a view to the expulsion of the Hindustanis from that tract, the force was now engaged in a contest with the enormous coalition above mentioned. Brigadier-General Chamberlain felt certain that it would not be advisable to make any advance into the Chamla valley with his present force against such numbers. He could only do so by giving up the Ambela pass. If the force moved into the valley, with a view to continue its advance towards the Mahaban, to carry out the original views of Government, it would be exposed to the enemy's incessant attacks, both by day and night, in flank and rear, and it would be impossible, in the face of such numbers, to protect adequately a long line of laden animals, to which would be daily added an ever-increasing number of sick and wounded. On the other hand, if the force merely moved into the valley, with a view to take up a position in open ground, it would still lose its communications with the rear, and whenever it required fresh supplies of provisions or ammunition, or to clear the camp by sending sick and wounded to the rear, it would have to retake the pass, and to re-occupy, at great sacrifice of life, the very ground from which it had advanced. Further, if the force was seriously compromised by a hazardous movement in advance, there were not, within a reasonable distance, the troops necessary to meet any difficulty which would under such an eventuality be certain immediately to arise, either within or beyond the border. In fact, Sir Neville Chamberlain considered that, with the present numbers, the only way to uphold the honour of our arms and the interests of the Government was to act on the defensive in the position the force now held, and trust to the effect of time and of the discouragement which repeated unsuccessful attacks were likely to produce upon the enemy, to weaken their numbers, and to break up their combination.

To continue now the narrative of the operations. During the 27th a demonstration was made by the enemy in front of the camp, but without any result, and news was received that the *Maulvi* had sent for more Hindustanis.

On the 28th the sick and wounded were sent back to Rustam, and the breastworks were stengthened to enable the force to move out to attack the enemy below. Many of the enemy's skirmishers who endeavoured to annoy the picquets were killed daily by the British marksmen. News was received in camp that some 280 Hindustanis, with treasure and more men from Swat, had joined the enemy, and that the *maliks* of Buner and Swat had elected the *Maulvi* to command the united force. There was little firing during the day, but a night attack was threatened.

On the 29th it was reported that the *Akhund* had called upon the Utmanzais, Ranizais, Mohmands, and people of Bajaur, for support. The 4th Gurkhas and two guns of No. 3 Punjab Light Field Battery[1] joined the camp on this day. This was a Thursday—the Muhammadan day commences at sunset—and an attack in force by the enemy was reported as intended either during the night or the next morning. From the nature of the ground, the position held by the troops was both extensive and difficult, and required half the native troops to guard it.

[1] This battery belonged to the Punjab Irregular Force. The artillery attached to the force at this time consisted of three Horse Light Field Batteries, one garrison company of artillery, and the Peshawar and the Hazara Mountain Train Batteries.

On the 30th October the first result of the combination between the *Akhund* and the *Maulvi* showed itself. The advanced picquets of the right defence were held by the 1st Punjab Infantry and a company of the Guide Corps, and were under the command of Major C. P. Keyes. Above the main picquets was a high rock, subsequently always known as the "Crag." The ascent to this was most precipitous, the path leading to its top narrow and difficult, and when the summit was reached there was but little level ground to stand upon; it was, however, necessary to occupy it, as it commanded the lower picquets, and Major Keyes placed a small party of twelve men in it, which was as much as it would conveniently hold. About half an hour before daylight heavy firing commenced on the "Crag," and it soon appeared that the picquet was hard-pressed by the enemy. All the men from the lower picquets that could be spared were immediately detached in support, and accompanied by Lieutenant H. W. Pitcher, Adjutant of the 1st Punjab Infantry, Major Keyes himself, with about twenty picked men, advanced to their assistance; but before the top of the "Crag" was reached, the small party holding it had been overpowered and driven off the rock, though they were still holding the ground lower down the hill.

First capture of the Crag Picquet by the enemy.

Finding this important position lost, the men were ordered to take cover from the enemy's fire beneath the overhanging rocks, about twenty paces from the summit, and Major Keyes determined to wait till daylight should enable him to distinguish friends from foes, and reinforcements should arrive from Lieut.-Colonel Wilde, who was commanding the right defences.

As the day broke, the 20th Punjab Native Infantry, under Major C. H. Brownlow, entered the main picquet, and Major Brownlow became the senior officer on the ground. Major Keyes now, feeling convinced of the danger of allowing the "Crag" to remain even for a short time in the hands of the enemy, and foreseeing that, should the enemy (many hundreds of whom were in the rear) once understand that their advanced party had gained an advantage over our troops, they would quickly occupy the position in force, and render the lower picquets untenable from their raking fire, suggested to Major Brownlow that he should advance by a ridge which ran to the right of the "Crag," and threaten the enemy in rear, while he (Major Keyes) attacked the position in front. To this Major Brownlow at once assented, and there is no doubt that this flank movement most materially aided the success of Major Keyes's attack, though it deprived Major Brownlow of the opportunity of sharing in the actual conflict at the "Crag."

From the nature of the approach to the top of the "Crag," owing to the large rocks, one or two men only could advance at a time. Ordering his men to fix bayonets, Major Keyes ascended with his party by one path, while Lieutenants G. V. Fosbery and H. W. Pitcher were directed to push up different paths, each at the head of a few men. The party under Major Keyes was led to the assault with a perseverance and intrepidity seldom surpassed, and Major Keyes spoke in equally laudatory terms of the way in which Lieutenants Fosbery and Pitcher led their respective parties. Lieutenant Fosbery, 104th Bengal Fusiliers, was the first man to gain the top of the "Crag." Lieutenant Pitcher had led his men up to the last rock, when he was knocked down and stunned by a large stone. As soon as our men had reached the top, a most exciting hand-to-hand fight ensued, in which Major Keyes was wounded; the enemy, however, were driven out at the point of the bayonet, the position recovered, and three standards taken. No sooner had the "Crag" been recaptured than a panic seized the remainder of the enemy who were attacking on the right, and they quickly disappeared down the mountain.

This attack had been made by the Hindustani fanatics, who lost fifty-four killed on the spot, and seven wounded.

Lieutenants Fosbery and Pitcher subsequently received the Victoria Cross for their gallantry on this occasion.

Almost simultaneously with the attack by the Hindustanis on the right defences, an attack was made on the front of the camp by the Swat contingent, which was repulsed without difficulty, under the personal superintendence of the Brigadier-General, by the good practice of the artillery under Captain J. S. Tulloh, and the fire of the 71st Highland Light Infantry and the 101st Royal Bengal Fusiliers under Colonel W. Hope, C.B., and Lieut.-Colonel F. O. Salusbury, respectively. Some of the enemy behaved with considerable boldness, making an attempt to assault the 9-pounder battery in the gorge. This afforded the 5th Gurkha Regiment an opportunity of making a spirited charge, and they quickly drove the assailants down the slope.

The enemy left forty-five dead bodies on the ground, which were recognised as men from Swat and Ranizai, and they must have lost heavily in addition; though, according to custom, they carried off as many of their dead as they could.

At the same time a demonstration was made against the upper left flank picquets, where the 5th Punjab Infantry lost three killed.

By 10 A.M. the enemy had been driven off at all points, and the effect of their defeat was so great that they proceeded at once to the village of Ambela, and from thence fled with the *Akhund* to the other side of the Buner pass. The *Akhund* was, in fact, in full retreat to Swat when he was overtaken by the Buner chiefs and induced to return, as they represented that, if he deserted them, their country would be lost.

Our losses during the day had been fifty-five killed and wounded.

Between the 31st October and the 5th November, the enemy attempted nothing more serious than firing as usual at our exposed breastworks and picquets, and advancing from time to time with standards, as if to attack the camp; these demonstrations were met with alacrity by the marksmen and the field guns in position, with some loss to the enemy, and little or none to the troops. In the meanwhile, the inactivity of the enemy enabled the troops to improve the breastworks and defences generally, as well as the interior communications of the camp, and a 24-pounder howitzer was sent up to strengthen the "Eagle's Nest" picquet.

During this time communications were entered into with the Buner tribe by means of the Sudum chiefs, and by the agency of two Buner *maliks*, residents of the Malandri pass in our own territory.

New line of communications.

From the moment that the Buner tribe had declared hostilities, it was evident that the line of communications by the Ambela defile could no longer be depended upon, and it became indispensable to seek some new line further removed from the Guru mountain, thereby enabling communications to be kept up with British territory beyond the reach of the Buner tribe. A line of road between the villages of Khanpur and Sherdara had accordingly been selected by Lieut.-Colonel A. Taylor, the Commanding Royal Engineer, for this purpose, and its construction was begun. The base of operations was changed, after its completion, from Rustam to Parmalao, the nearest village in the plains where water was obtainable. Working-parties had also been employed for some days in making a road in the direction of Ambela along the western slopes of the right ridge. This road was to supersede that by the gorge, which was extremely bad, and commanded on both sides, and would enable the troops, whenever the time came, to march forward without coming under fire from the Guru mountain.

On the 28th October the march of the 93rd Highlanders from Sialkot, and of the 23rd and 24th Punjab Native Infantry from Lahore, was ordered. The last two regiments were on escort duty with the Viceroy's camp at that place. On the 5th November the 7th Fusiliers, which also formed part of the escort. marched towards the frontier.

Foreseeing the demand that would arise for transport suitable to the hills, the Punjab Government at this time ordered its collection, and during November and the beginning of December 4,200 camels and 2,100 mules were assembled from all parts of the Punjab at Nowshera.

In the absence of regular troops, a party of police, 200 foot and 75 horse, were sent to Nawa Kala to aid in protecting the rear communications which had been threatened.

On the morning of the 6th November Sir Neville Chamberlain had gone down with the troops covering the working-parties on the road which was being made towards Ambela; on his return to camp he placed this covering party under command of his orderly officer, Major G. W. Harding, 2nd Sikh Infantry, whose conduct on previous occasions had led the Brigadier-General to place entire confidence in his coolness and judgment. Major Brownlow, who was commanding the advanced picquets on the right, had detached 100 men of the 20th Punjab Native Infantry, under Lieutenant J. Bartleman, to cover the immediate front of the working-parties, and had posted a similar number of the 1st Punjab Infantry, under Lieutenant W. H. Unwin, on the head of the ridge beyond that at the foot of which the parties were at work. Lieutenant Unwin was instructed to send patrols down the ridge as far as he could with regard to their safety, and Lieutenant Bartleman's orders were to keep two or three hundred yards in front of the working-parties.

About eleven o'clock Lieutenant Bartleman's party had been pushed forward to a spot low down the ridge, the top of which was in possession of Lieutenant Unwin's party. At half-past twelve, hearing that Major Harding was anxious lest the enemy should get above him, and wished the party of the 1st Punjab Infantry strengthened, Major Brownlow sent a company of the Guides, under Lieutenant W. Battye, to join Lieutenant Unwin. About the same time instructions were received from Lieut.-Colonel A. T. Wilde, commanding the right defences, for the working-parties to be withdrawn, and the covering parties to retire up the hill. These instructions were forwarded at once to Major Harding, who was at the time on the top of the hill with a detachment of the 1st Punjab Infantry, he having gone up to see the positions of the detachments holding his line of retreat. The working-parties were at once withdrawn; but why the lower covering parties were not withdrawn at the same time can never be known, Major Harding having been subsequently killed. There appears no doubt, however, that he found it difficult to bring away some of his party who had been wounded, and that consequently, remaining too long, he permitted himself to be surrounded; probably on his return from the top of the hill he found his lowest detachment involved with their assailants, and encumbered with killed and wounded.

At about two o'clock Major Brownlow, observing that the enemy were moving in considerable numbers, sent all the available men he had as reinforcements for Major Harding, *viz.*, two companies of the Guide Corps, under Lieutenant F. H. Jenkins, and eighty bayonets of the 1st Punjab Infantry, under Lieutenant J. P. Davidson.

At about half-past three, Lieut.-Colonel Wilde, receiving information that Major Harding was being attacked in force by the enemy, proceeded to the advanced picquets, sending to head-quarters for reinforcements. In about an hour the Peshawar Mountain Train Battery and 350 bayonets of the 4th and 5th Gurkha Regiments arrived at the main (Major Keyes's) picquet.

Only one hour of daylight remained, and it became necessary to endeavour to cover Major Harding's retreat by the shortest route; accordingly Captain C. W. R. Chester, commanding the

4th Gurkha Regiment, was ordered to proceed across the lower spurs in the direction of the beleagured picquet, whilst the guns of the mountain battery, protected by the 5th Gurkhas, took up a position on one of the lower spurs, checking the advance of the enemy on the picquet, and covering Captain Chester's advance to its assistance.

Whatever error Major Harding may have committed in too long delaying his retirement, when he found himself overmatched and in difficulty, he behaved like a gallant soldier, and probably saved his detachment by his coolness and determination. Colonel R. G. Taylor writes: "It was on seeing the approach of the 4th Gurkhas that Major Harding finally resolved on retiring. I saw myself the detachments fall in very steadily for retirement and move off, a portion being engaged all the time with an enemy we could not see." Major Harding was the last man to leave the picquet. "After the detachment had passed out of our sight, the enemy appear by a rush to have broken in between two of the detachments. Major Harding had been previously shot through the neck, and was being carried by a Gurkha sepoy, and it was at this time that he and Lieutenant T. B. Dougal, of the 79th Regiment, were killed." The latter officer had left the advanced breast-works without leave, and accompanied by a single sepoy had gone down to join the covering party. During this time Captain Chester, with the 4th Gurkhas, had advanced as far as the nature of the ground and light permitted, and some of his men had reached the spur upon which Major Harding's detachment were fighting; a movement which enabled the remainder of the covering party, which was fighting its way up the ridge, to reach the crest, and the troops to get back to camp, though not till after dark.

The losses in this affair were seventy-eight officers and mer killed and wounded.

Peshawar Mountain Train Battery.
101st Fusiliers.
Corps of Guides.
4th Gurkhas.
32nd Punjab Native Infantry.

As already stated, night had come on before the covering party got back to camp, and it had been impossible to recover the bodies of the killed on the previous evening. Accordingly, early on the morning of the 7th, the troops, as per margin, moved out under the command of Lieut.-Colonel A. T. Wilde, C.B., for this purpose. Small parties of the enemy appeared on that portion of the ground where Major Harding's picquet had been situated; these were quickly dispersed and driven into the plain, and, having collected the bodies of seven British and twenty-eight native officers and men, the force returned to camp without any casualty. It appeared that the enemy had suffered severely the day before, as they were seen by this column removing many of their slain, and they showed no inclination to meet the troops, although they had displayed great boldness on the previous day, charging sword in hand. They consisted of the Ranizais of Swat, under Sobat Khan, assisted by some of the Mahaban tribes—the chief *malik* of the Mada Khels being amongst the killed.

On the 8th, the new road to the rear being reported practicable, and easier than the Ambela pass, it was decided to cease using the latter route, and the supplies and supports were moved to Parmalao. At the same time, as it was intended shortly to concentrate the whole force on the south side of the pass, which would save much picquet duty, and give a stronger position, preparations were made to move the commissariat stores to the new site.

The nights were getting colder, and Sir Neville Chamberlain considered it necessary to sanction a moderate issue of meat, rice, and rum, at fair prices, to the native troops, to keep away sickness.

Two more roads had been opened up to the ridge on the right of the camp, and the Peshawar Mountain Train Battery, the 5th Gurkha Regiment, and the 14th Native Infantry, had been moved up to strengthen that flank.

At this time, as uneasiness was felt, owing to sympathy evinced by the border villages of the Lundkhwar valley for the Akhund's cause, the 11th Bengal Cavalry, then at Parmalao, was ordered to Mardan, so as to hold a more central position in Yusafzai.

On the 11th the enemy showed in large numbers about Ambela, whence considerable bodies ascended the hills in the direction of Lalu, on our right front, evidently with the intention of attacking the picquets on that flank of the camp. These picquets were accordingly reinforced, and their breastworks and defences strengthened. The "Crag" picquet in particular had been much enlarged and strengthened since the occasion of its being attacked on the 30th October, and was now capable of containing a garrison of 160 men. It was also supported by the guns of the Peshawar Mountain Train Battery, which were placed in position in the main picquet.

Major C. H. Brownlow assumed command of the "Crag" picquet at 4 P.M. on the 12th; the garrison then consisted of 160 marksmen of the following regiments,—15 men of the 101st Fusiliers, 30 of the 14th Native Infantry, and 115 of the 20th Punjab Native Infantry.

Two of the four guns of the Peshawar Mountain Train Battery which were in the main picquet had been placed in position to command the left shoulder of the hill on which was the "Crag" picquet, as well as the front of the "Centre" picquet below. The enemy occupied a level ridge, about 250 yards in front of the "Crag" picquet, and their position extended more than half a mile in a direction facing our own. Between the two positions lay a smooth hollow intersected by a ravine. The ground on the right and rear of the "Crag" was precipitous, and almost unassailable in any force. The left face of the post was its weak point, rocks and trees affording shelter to an attacking party till within a few yards of it.

Anticipating an attack, Major Brownlow had urged Lieutenant J. Bartleman, 20th Punjab Native Infantry, who commanded the picquet during the day, to use his utmost exertions in improving the position as much as he could, by heightening the breastwork, constructing an abatis, etc.; a duty which was admirably performed by that officer.

Before dark every man was in his place for the night, with strict orders as to the nature of his duties, and the direction of his fire in case of attack. About 10 P.M. the enemy's watch-fires showed that they were in movement, and descending in great numbers to the hollow in front of the picquet, which in half an hour was full of them. Their suppressed voices soon broke into yells of defiance, and they advanced in masses to the attack, their numbers being, as far as could be judged, at least 2,000. They were allowed to approach within a hundred yards of the picquet, when a rapid and well-sustained fire was opened upon them from the front face, which did great execution, and soon silenced their shouts and drove them under cover, some to the broken and wooded ground on the left, and the remainder into the ravine below. In half an hour they rallied, and, assembling in increased numbers, rushed to the attack, this time assaulting both the front and left of the picquet. They were received with the great steadiness, and again recoiled before our fire. These attacks continued until 4 A.M., each becoming weaker than the last, many of them being mere feints to enable them to carry off their dead and wounded.

The post was at one time in great danger of being forced at its left front angle, which, from its position, was badly protected by our fire. The enemy clambered up, and assailing its occupants with stones from the breastwork, stunned and drove them back; at this critical moment the gallantry of five men of the 20th Punjab Native Infantry, saved the post. Answering Major Brownlow's call when others wavered, they followed him into the corner, and hurling stones on the enemy, who were close under the wall, and sheltered from musketry, they drove them back, and rebuilt the parapet, holding that point for the rest of the night.

The Peshawar Mountain Train Battery rendered Major Brownlow very valuable assistance during the night. From its position, about 250 yards below and in the right rear of the "Crag," it made most successful practice, being guided as to direction and range by voice from the picquet. Two shells were pitched by it into the watch-fire of the enemy before the attack began, and must have done considerable damage.

In the morning not more than eight or ten of the enemy were in sight. The British casualties in the attack were only slight, as owing to the darkness of the night the enemy's fire had been ineffective.

Major Brownlow's men having been forty-eight hours on picquet duty, during which time they had worked all day and watched all night, were completely worn out, while their muskets were so foul that they could scarcely load; they were, therefore, relieved at 8 A.M. on the 13th by a detachment of the 1st Punjab Infantry under Lieutenant J. P. Davidson.

2nd capture of the "Crag" Picquets.

A short time after Lieutenant Davidson had taken over the "Crag" picquet from Major Brownlow, he sent a note to Major C. P. Keyes, commanding the 1st Punjab Infantry, asking for reinforcements, as he did not consider the ninety men he had with him enough for its defence. At this time Major Keyes was on the "Standard" hill with Lieutenant E. R. Conolly of the Peshawar Mountain Train Battery, who was preparing a platform for his guns on the side of the hill. Constant firing had been heard at the "Crag," but it did not attract any particular attention, as heavy firing had been kept up there all night, and was continued at intervals after the relief of the picquet. On Lieutenant Davidson's requisition being received, Major Keyes immediately sent him up a reinforcement of thirty bayonets under a native officer, being all that could be spared, as a serious attack was expected on the "Centre" and "Cliff" picquets.

Shortly after this reinforcement reached the "Crag" picquet, Major Keyes observed, as he was descending the "Standard" hill, the men of the "Crag" picquet rushing down in confusion. He did not see the beginning of the retreat, as the position was not visible from the platform where he was at the time. Proceeding immediately to the breastwork across the road by which the main post was approached from the "Crag," he rallied all the men that could be got together, and kept up a heavy fire, which was taken up by the guns of the Peshawar Mountain Train Battery. This checked the advance of the enemy; but, as many wounded soldiers and others who had been garrisoning the "Crag" rushed past the breastwork and could not be stopped, a panic was communicated to the camp followers, who took to flight and increased the confusion. These men retreating had a visible effect upon all, and Major Keyes felt the necessity for an advance to reassure those that were wavering, and further to check the enemy until reinforcements should arrive; he therefore directed a few men to remain in the breastwork, and ordered the rest to charge. Considering that his presence at the breastwork was absolutely necessary to keep the men together, the duty of leading the charge devolved upon Lieutenant H. W. Pitcher, 1st Punjab Infantry, who was accompanied by Lieutenant H. R. Young of the same regiment. The assaulting party were supported by a small detachment of the Corps of Guides, under Lieutenant W. J. Forlong of that regiment; but in spite of the coolness and daring with which the assault had been conducted (in which Lieutenant Pitcher had been severely wounded), the detachments were too weak to be able to retake the "Crag," and they had to fall back upon the rocks beneath it.

Major C. C. G. Ross, commanding the advanced picquets, on seeing that the "Crag" had been carried by the enemy, who were pouring a heavy fire into the camp, which was in great confusior collected as many men of the 14th Native Infantry and the other regiments as possible, and advanced in front of the camp, where he was joined by Lieutenant A. D. C. Inglis, 14th Native Infantry, and Lieutenant H. R. Young, 1st Punjab Infantry, who assisted him in getting men together to try to retake the lost position. Owing to the confusion this was not immediately possible, but on Major Ross reaching the steep rocks of the picquet itself, a heavy fire, which was taken up by the mountain guns, was opened on the top of the rock until reinforcements could arrive.

On receiving the news of the disaster which had occurred at the "Crag," Lieut.-Colonel A. T. Wilde, commanding the right defences, asked for the 101st Royal Bengal Fusiliers, and proceeded immediately from his camp with three companies of the Guide Corps towards the "Crag," meeting on his way the head of the 101st, which the Brigadier-General had already ordered to move at once to the advanced picquets.

Sir Neville Chamberlain was in the camp below when the "Crag" fell into the hands of the enemy, and his attention had been accidentally drawn to the dust and confusion caused by the unusual rush of camp followers and animals down the hill. Feeling convinced that some reverse had occurred, he immediately ordered the 101st, which was fortunately under arms for another purpose, to move towards the "Crag"; and, shortly afterwards receiving information from Lieut.-Colonel Wilde of what had occurred, he gave orders to Lieut.-Colonel F. O. Salusbury to move his regiment up the hill as fast as possible, and retake the position at any sacrifice.

The "Crag" from its locality was the key of the whole position, and its loss rendered the lower picquets untenable. On Lieut.-Colonel Wilde's arrival at the advanced picquets the state of affairs was as follows—Major Ross was half-way up the "Crag" hill, gallantly holding the enemy in check, but unable, with the few men he had rallied round him, to advance and retake the lost picquet. Parties of the enemy were attacking the lower picquets, but were kept back by the steadiness of the fire of Captain T. E. Hughes's mountain guns. The 1st Punjab Infantry, 20th Punjab Native Infantry, and two companies of the Corps of Guides still held the breastworks, but numerically the garrison was too weak to resist the numbers of the enemy advancing to its capture.

Crag picquet retaken by the 101st Fusiliers.

Lieut.-Colonel Wilde then directed Lieut.-Colonel Salusbury to assault the "Crag" with his regiment, leaving one company as a support in the main position. Fatigued as they were by their rapid march to the relief of the troops in advance, the 101st never halted nor broke till they had gallantly stormed the height and secured the picquet, driving the enemy over the hills beyond. Lieutenant F. H. Jenkins, commanding three companies of the Guide Corps, leading his men up the "Crag" hill, drove the enemy back from the right of the position, whilst the detachments of the 14th Native Infantry and 1st Punjab Infantry, which, with some of the Guides, had held their ground until the arrival of the 101st, joined in with the British regiment in the attack. With this success on the part of the Fusiliers all opposition ceased, and order was as quickly restored as it had been previously disturbed by the suddenness and force of the enemy's attack.

In their retreat, the enemy, who chiefly consisted of Bunerwals, under Zaidulla Khan, with men of Swat and some of the Hindustanis, suffered so much that they desisted from all further attempts that day along the whole line of defences. Their loss was 57 killed and left on the ground, 32 killed and carried off, and 140 wounded; amongst the first was a Bajauri *malik* of consequence.

Whilst the attack was going on on the right, the enemy made demonstrations both against the front and left defences of the camp; but these were not of a serious nature, and were only made as diversions.

The defenders of the "Crag" appear to have been seized with an unaccountable panic, but the nature of the ground and the thickness of the brushwood enabled the enemy to concentrate a large force upon the weak picquet, unobserved; Lieutenant J. P. Davidson, who commanded, behaved in a most heroic manner, and, after endeavouring in every way to recall his men to a sense of their duty, was killed at his post.

From the 14th to the 17th November no serious attempts were made by the enemy, and in anticipation of the change of position already alluded to, by which the whole force was to be concentrated on the south side of the pass, the commissariat stores, reserve ammunition, etc., were gradually removed to the eastern ridge.

On the 15th the defences were strengthened, and the 101st Fusiliers were ordered up to the ridge on the right flank. The enemy had sent marauders to harass the line of communications to the rear; it was therefore unsafe, except for strong, armed parties. A demonstration was made by the enemy in front of the camp, but they soon withdrew. Half the Bajauris were said to have returned to their homes after the action of the 13th, but the *Akhund* was reported to be trying to stop these desertions. The enemy were also said to be much depressed at their losses and want of success.

On the 16th the *Akhund* was on the top of the Buner pass to prevent his followers going home. Owing to the communications with the rear being unsafe, the mules, which had come up with a convoy the day before, were sent back by the Ambela pass, getting down unmolested, the enemy not expecting this movement. The Sappers and Miners, Pioneers, and fatigue parties were employed daily, under engineer officers, in strengthening the defences, but the tools were deficient in number and of bad quality.

On the 17th, the *Akhund* was still on the summit of the Buner pass, where he had built a temporary mosque for shelter. News was received that the Haji Sahib of Kunar, a valley to the north-east of Jalalabad, had been sent for. He was reputed to be very holy, and gifted with the power of counteracting the effect of bullets. Intimation was received that a party of the Utman Khels of the Lundkhwar valley had been told off to intercept convoys between the camp and Sherdara. Battery horses, being in the way and consuming the camp supplies of grain and forage, were on this day sent to the rear. An attempt to impede their march resulted in loss to the marauders only. Late on the evening of the 17th, the guns of Captain Griffin's battery (C-19th R. A.) were removed from the advanced breastworks in front of the camp to a new position, to cover the withdrawal of the picquets from the Guru mountain, two guns of the Hazara Mountain Train Battery being sent down from the Guru temporarily to take their place.

At daylight on the morning of the 18th, the whole of the troops on the Guru mountain, under the command of Lieut.-Colonel J. L. Vaughan, consisting of the Hazara Mountain Train Battery, and the 3rd, 5th, and 6th Punjab Infantry, were withdrawn, and the entire camp and troops transferred to the heights on the south of the pass. Every precaution had been taken to prevent the enemy from suspecting the intended movement, and the troops both on the Guru and in the front line of defence continued to strengthen up to the last moment their breastworks and defences. These precautions were successful, and though the enemy's picquet on the Guru was not 400 yards distant, the withdrawal was effected without their knowledge, and in the most perfect order.

The concentration of the whole of the troops on the eastern heights made it necessary to extend the position, and particularly to secure the full command of the water, on which the whole force was now dependent. With this view, the troops, as per margin, moved out under the personal command of Sir Neville Chamberlain, as soon as the change of position was completed, to drive the enemy from what was afterwards known as the "Water" ridge. This was very quickly effected by the advance of the 1st and 6th Punjab Infantry, with a loss on our side of three men wounded, whilst some of the enemy were killed. The troops were then placed in position to protect the 5th Punjab Infantry and 32nd Punjab Native Infantry, employed as a working-party under the direction of Lieut.-Colonel A. Taylor, C.B., Commanding Royal Engineer, in stockading a picquet to command the water. These troops were withdrawn to camp in the evening under the direction of Lieut.-Colonel Vaughan, 5th Punjab Infantry, the new work having been completed and occupied.

Peshawar Mountain Train Battery.
Wing, 101st Fusiliers.
1st Punjab Infantry.
6th " "

On discovering the camp and picquets on the Guru to have been vacated by the troops, the enemy seemed to have supposed that the force was in retreat, and with this idea came into the gorge in great numbers, both from Ambela and from the Guru, and thence, about 11 A.M., began an attack upon what had now become the left front of the position. The defences at the point principally attacked consisted of some small breastworks thrown up on the side of the hill to cover the picquets connecting the advanced right picquets with the camp in the gorge below. It was not intended to hold these breastworks permanently after the camp had been removed from the gorge; but it was necessary to hold them this day to prevent the enemy from pressing upon the camp and firing into it before the troops were thoroughly established in their new position. These picquets were rather advanced and exposed to be taken in flank, and they were, from natural features, not easily defensible.

Major Ross commanded at this point, and the breastworks were held by 130 men of the 14th Native Infantry, who being greatly outnumbered by the enemy, were, in the first instance, compelled to give way, but being reinforced by the troops as per margin, retook the post and drove back the enemy.

Two companies, 71st Highland Light Infantry.
One company, 101st Royal Bengal Fusiliers.
One company, 5th Punjab Infantry.
Three companies, 5th Gurkha Regiment.

The enemy, however, being reinforced, again attacked the picquets, when it became necessary for the two lowest down on the hill to fall back on the third, which was nearer the camp breastworks. The picquet upon which the lower picquets had retired was withdrawn after dark. On its withdrawal the enemy pressed on, and some few of them endeavoured to annoy the camp until a late hour of the night, but without making any serious attack.

Our loss on this occasion was 43 killed and 75 wounded, while the enemy were known to have lost 130 killed and upwards of 200 wounded.

Among the killed were Captain C. F. Smith of the 71st Highland Light Infantry, Lieutenant T. S. G. Jones, attached to that regiment, Lieutenant H. H. Chapman, Adjutant of the 101st Fusiliers, and Lieutenant W. F. Mosley, of the 14th Native Infantry. Among the wounded was Lieutenant A. D. C. Inglis, of the 14th Native Infantry.

On the 19th, it was found that the picquet posted the day before to command the water, was more advanced than necessary, and it was therefore abandoned, and a new position chosen and stockaded about 300 yards to the rear.

During the day the enemy kept up a fire upon the "Crag" and "Water" picquets, when Captain R. B. Aldridge, 71st Highland Light Infantry, was killed at the latter, and Ensign C. M. Stockley, 101st Royal Bengal Fusiliers, severely wounded at the former post.

The troops had now been very hard-worked, day and night, for a month. Having continually to meet fresh enemies, it was difficult to repel the attacks and at the same time to provide convoys for supplies and wounded sent to the rear. There were at this time 166 wounded and 286 sick men in the camp, and every animal not urgently needed had been sent to Parmalao.

The *Akhund* about this time issued a proclamation that any deserter from his camp should have his property confiscated. He was averse to the proposal of the Buner tribe to treat, and said he would not be bound by any engagement they might make; he also abused the tribes for want of success. At this time some men were reported to have joined him from Kabul.

Major H. R. James, C.B., Commissioner of Peshawar, having returned from furlough, took over political charge from Colonel R. G. Taylor, C.B., on this day, the 19th; but Colonel Taylor, at his own request, remained with the force, to be of any use he could.

"Crag" picquet.
101st Fusiliers, 100 bayonets.
20th Punjab Native Infantry, 100 bayonets.
"Water" picquet.
71st Regiment, 100 bayonets.
3rd Punjab Infantry, 100 bayonets.

On the 20th November the garrison of the "Crag" and "Water" picquets were as marginally noted. About 9 A.M. the enemy began to collect in great numbers near these picquets, the "Crag" being, as before, the point principally threatened. They were, however, checked in some degree by the fire of the Peshawar Mountain Train Battery; Captain T. E. Hughes, from previous experience and his acquaintance with the ground, knowing exactly on what points to bring his fire with most effect, even though the enemy were not visible from the battery. The "Crag" and "Water" picquets also mutually supported one another by their cross-fire at 450 yards.

3rd capture of the Crag Picquet.

Up to a late period of the afternoon the enemy had made no impression upon the "Crag" picquet, though numerous standards had been gradually advanced under cover to within a few yards of the breastworks; but about 3 P.M. the unaccountable conduct of an officer on the left of the picquet, who suddenly ordered the troops in his part of the position to retire, gave the enemy possession of the post. This was not, however, accomplished without affording the officers and men who held the lower portion of the picquet the opportunity of distinguishing themselves by the resolute way in which they endeavoured to hold their portion of the post under very discouraging circumstances, abandoning it only when it was no longer tenable. These officers were Major H. G. Delafosse[1] of the 101st Fusiliers, who commanded the picquet, Captain R. G. Rogers, of the 20th Punjab Native Infantry, and Ensign A. R. Sanderson and Assistant Surgeon W. Pile, both of the 101st Fusiliers. The last two officers were killed at the breastwork whilst endeavouring to rally their men. The above officers were well supported by some men of the 101st Fusiliers, and by some of the 20th Punjab Native Infantry.

On the fall of the "Crag" coming to the notice of Sir Neville Chamberlain, he immediately ordered the 71st Highland Light Infantry and the 5th Gurkha Regiment to be got under arms and proceed to the upper camp; and at the same time directed Captain Griffin's half battery (C-19th R.A.), and the two 24-pr. howitzers of No. 3 Punjab Light Field Battery, under Captain Salt, to open fire upon the "Crag"; this they did in so efficient a manner (joined to the fire of Captain Hughes's mountain guns) that they effectually prevented the enemy from attempting to occupy the post in anything like large numbers.

Crag Picquet retaken by the 71st Highland Light Infantry.

On the 71st and 5th Gurkha Regiments reaching the upper defences, Colonel W. Hope, C.B., commanding the former, was ordered to storm the "Crag" in front, and Lieut.-Colonel J. L. Vaughan, with the 5th Gurkhas and 5th Punjab Infantry, to go round the hill, so as to take the lower portion of it in flank. The 71st discharged their duty in the most steady and soldier-like manner, and the work was retaken without much loss on our side. The 5th Gurkhas, with detachments of the 5th and 6th Punjab Infantry, supported on the left.

Thus for the third time the "Crag" picquet was lost and won—a spot which, from the heavy losses sustained there on both sides, had become known in the country as *katlgar* or the place of slaughter. Lieut.-Colonel J. L. Vaughan and Major J. P. W. Campbell, commanding the 5th Gurkhas, were both wounded.

Brigadier-General Chamberlain accompanied the storming column, and when near the crest of the slope received a severe wound, which, though it did not prevent him pressing on and entering

[1] One of the two British officers who survived the massacre of the Cawnpore garrison in 1857.

the work at the time, subsequently obliged him to relinquish the command of the force; Lieutenant W. C. Anderson, 3rd Punjab Cavalry, his orderly officer, was also wounded.

Colonel Hope then pushed forward in pursuit of the enemy, having been joined by Lieut.-Colonel Vaughan's column, and drove them for some distance over the heights in the direction of Lalu. After continuing the pursuit as far as seemed prudent, Colonel Hope withdrew the troops towards the "Crag," and was severely wounded whilst superintending the re-occupation of the picquet, which, at his special request, was garrisoned for the night by 200 men of his own regiment.

The British casualties on this day amounted to 2 officers and 25 men killed, and 5 officers, 1 native officer and 104 men wounded, while the enemy's losses were reported to be 120 killed and 200 wounded. Large reinforcements were stated to have joined the *Akhund* this day.

The action of the 20th seemed to have had a depressing effect upon the enemy, notwithstanding that they had gained a temporary success, and had wounded the Brigadier-General, which last injury it would have been natural for them to make and think a great deal of. From the 20th November to the 15th December, however, they made no further attack in force, and at one time their gathering had dwindled down so much that there appeared a possibility of their giving up the war altogether.

Early on the morning of the 21st, Lieut.-Colonel Vaughan, commanding the advanced picquets, moving out, drove off a few of the enemy in the vicinity, and recovered without any casualty all the bodies of our men slain on the 18th. Twelve of the enemy were killed. The "Crag" picquet defences had been improved, and the troops were in the same position they occupied before the previous day's attack.

On the 22nd the enemy came, at the invitation of the Commissioner, and removed their dead. The sick and wounded officers and men were safely escorted to Parmalao. The defences of the "Crag" picquet being now completed, that post was occupied by 200 bayonets of a British regiment, held on alternate days by the 71st and 101st Regiments. The health of the troops was good, and the weather mild.

On the 23rd, 24th, and 25th, the enemy still remained quiet, but on the last of these dates large numbers appeared in the plain near the village of Ambela, and an attack was expected either on the 26th or 27th. The defences of the "Crag" and "Water" picquets had been much strengthened by Lieut.-Colonel A. Taylor, Royal Engineers. Communication with the rear had also been greatly improved by the completion of a second line of road to Khanpur, by a low ridge of hills easily occupied by our troops. The men were hutting themselves, and as the nights were getting very cold, arrangements were being made for getting up tents.

Sir Neville Chamberlain's wound proved more serious than he had expected, and it was with the greatest regret he had to request to be relieved of the command of the force, which devolved temporarily on Lieut.-Colonel A. T. Wilde, C.B., who had been in charge of the camp since the Brigadier-General was first wounded.

On the 26th November the enemy assembled in small parties on the ridge above the advanced picquets, and reinforcements were sent to the upper camp, with orders to attack, should the enemy attempt to descend. No collision, however, took place, and the day passed off quietly. This day was Friday, a day on which, owing to the superstitious reverence of the enemy (it being the Muhammadan Sabbath), it had hitherto been customary with them to attack in force.

Although, since the 20th, there had not occurred anything of importance in the field, the work of the political officers had been steadily going on. Major H. R. James had done all that was possible by negotiations to weaken the enemy, and met with considerable success, due in some degree to the losses they had sustained. He had succeeded in drawing off Ahmad Khan, with the greater portion of the Ashazai and Salarzai sections of the Buner tribe; the Ranizais of Swat were also induced to return to their homes, to the number of 2,000; Sobat Khan sent home his immediate followers; minor personages acted in a similar manner; and amongst those who remained a mutual mistrust prevailed. These desertions were becoming so numerous that the *Akhund* issued denunciations, as already stated, against all who should leave the field, and the *Maulvi* redoubled his efforts to bring back the wavering.

On the 25th a deputation had been received from the Buner *jirga*; and both from conversation with those composing it, and with men who arrived at intervals by permission to take away their slain, it was evident that the main body of the Bunerwals were really inclined for peace. It was hoped that the *jirga* would now come to terms, and agree to a brigade passing up the Chamla valley to Malka. The greater portion of them were certainly inclined to do so; but the negotiations were broken off by Zaidulla Khan, who was informed by the *Maulvi* that his rival, Ahmad Khan, had received large sums of money from the Commissioner. However, the negotiations resulted in the retirement of Ahmad Khan, with two important sections of the tribe.

Meanwhile, the above desertions were more than counterbalanced by the arrival of large reinforcements to the enemy. Some 3,000 men arrived at intervals from Bajaur, under Faiztalab Khan, the chief of that country. The Haji of Kunar arrived with about 500 men; and his repute for sanctity rendered his advent a matter of great rejoicing to the war party. Still it was noted that, notwithstanding these accessions, the enemy were so divided and mistrustful of each other, that they were unable to resume the attack, even on a Friday, as previously stated.

On the 30th November, Major-General J. Garvock arrived in camp, and assumed command of the force, which was now organized into two brigades, the details of which are given in Appendix B.

Some time previous to this it had been in contemplation to create a diversion on the Swat border, and for this purpose the Commander-in-Chief, Sir Hugh Rose, ordered a column under Colonel R. Y. Shipley, consisting of the troops as per margin, to advance to Shergarh on the Swat frontier, and threaten the Malakand pass. But Major James had meanwhile, unknown to Major-General Garvock, promised the Swat chiefs that no British troops should enter their country, and he now wished this force to be used to punish the villages of British Baizai for their recent misconduct. This use of the force was, however, not considered advisable by the military authorities, as the object was considered inadequate.

Battery Royal Horse Artillery.
A-19th Royal Artillery.
7th Hussars.
7th Fusiliers.
Guide Cavalry.
3rd Sikhs.[1]

[1] Now the 53rd Sikhs (Frontier Force).

Owing, therefore, to the misunderstanding caused by Major James having kept his negotiations with the Swat leaders secret from the General Officer Commanding, the arrival at Ambela of the 7th Fusiliers and the 3rd Sikhs, which were destined to reinforce Major-General Garvock's force, was much delayed. The other reinforcements which arrived to strengthen the Yusafzai Field Force consisted of the 93rd Highlanders and the 23rd Punjab Native Infantry Pioneers.[1]

Although the enemy had been so disheartened by their defeats that after the 20th November they had made no further attempts on the camp, and the Bunerwals were really desirous for peace, the reinforcements which they had received made them still believe they could successfully oppose our advance; and as the 93rd Highlanders, the last of our reinforcements, marched into the camp, the bands playing them in, the plains below and around Ambela were covered with formidable masses of armed men, evidently as a counter-display to ours.

The force had at this time two parties in its front to deal with—

(1) The Buner and Chamla tribes, originally fighting for their country, but now crediting our repeated assertions that we had no intention to invade them; weary of the war, divided amongst themselves, and subject to innumerable vexations and inconveniences by the presence amongst them of so large a host.

(2) The *Maulvi* and his fanatics, with the *Akhund* and his allies, a mixed assemblage of men from far and near, whose ranks had been reinforced by Ghazan Khan, the chief of Dir, with 6,000 men, and who imagined they were beginning to realise their dream of years, *viz.*, the expulsion of the British from the country trans-Indus.

Major James's communications with the tribes were now beginning to have effect. On the afternoon of the 10th December a deputation from the Buner tribe had come into camp, where they remained all that night. Every chief of influence was there, and after several lengthy discussions they had agreed—

1st.—That they would accompany the Commissioner with a force and destroy Malka.

2nd.—That they would expel the Hindustanis from their country.

[1] Now the 23rd Sikh Pioneers.

They left on the morning of the 11th, to obtain the sanction of the *Akhund* and his allies to these arrangements.

At first, by the complete silence of the enemy, the withdrawal of some of their picquets and other indications, a pacific reply was anticipated; but on the 13th, the day fixed for a decision, repeated firing of musketry, welcoming fresh arrivals, and the reports of proclamations issued by the *Akhund*, fulminating anathemas against anyone who spoke of peace, prepared the Commissioner for the message which arrived early in the morning of the 14th, to the effect that the *jirga* had been overruled by Ghazan Khan and other newcomers, and that they were therefore unable to return to the camp. It was further intimated that a general attack on the camp was to be made on the 16th, and they advised our taking the initiative, when they, the Bunerwals, would take no prominent part in the action.

Offensive measures for the next day were, therefore, at once decided on by the Major-General, in communication with the Commissioner, in order to anticipate further reinforcements expected by the enemy.

At this time there was a force of some 4,000 of the enemy at Lalu, including some 300 Hindustanis; and as no attack could well be made on Ambela with that force on its flank, it was determined to attack the former place.

After the arrival of the 7th Fusiliers, 93rd Highlanders, 3rd Sikhs, and 23rd Punjab Native Infantry, the force consisted of about 9,000 men.

First Column.

Hazara Mn. Train Battery.
7th Royal Fusiliers.
1 Co. Sappers and Miners.
3rd Punjab Infantry.
4th Gurkha Regiment.
23rd Punjab Native Infantry.
32nd „ „ „

Second Column.

Peshawar Mn. Train Battery.
101st Royal Bengal Fusiliers.
1 Co. Sappers and Miners.
Corps of Guides.
3rd Sikh Infantry.
5th Gurkha Regiment.

On the 14th, orders were issued for the attack on Lalu to be carried out on the following day. The attacking troops were to be formed into two columns, as per margin, and were under the command of Colonel W. W. Turner, C.B., 97th Regiment, and of Lieut.-Colonel A. T. Wilde, C.B., Guide Corps respectively. Rations for two days were served out to the troops. Lieut.-Colonel J. L. Vaughan was to be left in camp with 2,900 men.

At daybreak on the 15th December the attacking force, consisting of 4,800 men, unencumbered by tents or baggage, was ready to move.

The first column assembled at the base of the "Crag" picquet, and on receiving the order to advance, it moved off in the marginally-named order. The advance was made from the right flank of the "Water" picquet; on reaching the crest of the heights overlooking that position, the enemy's picquets were encountered, and driven with some loss to the "Conical" hill.

Advance Guard.
4th Gurkhas.
3rd Punjab Infantry.

Main Body.
7th Royal Fusiliers.
Sappers and Miners.
Hazara Mountain Battery.
23rd Pioneers.
32nd "

From the "Conical" hill the first column was separated by a valley about 200 yards wide, and Colonel Turner therefore directed the troops to line the crest of the heights overlooking it from our own side, and to await the arrival of the mountain guns, which, on coming up, were forthwith brought into action. Under cover of their fire, the 23rd Pioneers, supported by the 32nd Pioneers, were moved up into a valley on the right, and secured a height which enabled the left of the enemy's position to be turned.

As soon as the first column had passed out of the main position of the upper camp, the second column was formed as noted in the margin, the rear being brought up by a detachment of the 3rd Sikh Infantry. Colonel R. G. Taylor accompanied Lieut.-Colonel Wilde throughout the operations. This column advanced under the "Crag" picquet, the skirmishers of the 5th Gurkha Regiment quickly reaching the low ridge of rocks immediately in front of the enemy's position, which was held in strength behind stone breastworks. The following dispositions were made for the assault: the Peshawar Mountain Train Battery moved up and opened sufficient fire to keep down the matchlock fire from the heights; the 101st Royal Bengal Fusiliers and Corps of Guides were formed in line of quarter columns out of fire beyond the ridge; the other two regiments being held in reserve, in column of sections, to protect the left flank during the coming attack.

5th Gurkha Regiment.
101st Royal Bengal Fusiliers.
Peshawar Mountain Train Battery.
Sappers and Miners.
Corps of Guides.
3rd Sikh Infantry.
Artillery reserve ammunition.
Infantry reserve ammunition.

Both columns were now ready to assault the "Conical" hill, which was a most formidable position. The hillsides were rocky, precipitous, and scarped by nature, and the summit, strongly occupied, was strengthened by stone breastworks offering no ordinary obstacle. The ascent would have been a matter of considerable difficulty under any circumstances. Below it, and to its proper left, was the hamlet of Banda, strongly protected by artificial defences. Beyond it stretched a narrow ridge, terminating in a hill of lesser elevation; and then came a small, picturesque level, backed by a lofty range containing the village of Lalu.

Assault on the Conical Hill.

On the bugle sounding for the assault, under cover of the mountain guns, which were admirably served, the two columns advanced to the assault. The first column advanced down the hill, across the valley, and in ten minutes was driving the enemy down the opposite side of the heights. At the same time the 101st Fusiliers, the leading regiment of Wilde's column, without even loading their rifles, dashed straight for the almost perpendicular sides of the highest peak, a strong work crowded with the Hindustani fanatics and their Pathan allies. The Corps of Guides made for a point a little below, with the object of taking the pressure off the 101st, to whom the most difficult part of the assault had been safely assigned. The Fusiliers, leaping into the breastwork amidst a shower of bullets and huge stones, bayoneted some thirty of its defenders, and the Corps of Guides, turning the position, shot and cut down numbers as they retreated; while the reserve, under the personal direction of Lieut.-Colonel Wilde, secured the line of hills on the left overlooking the Chamla valley, and drove small parties of the enemy before it.

The enemy, some 2,000 in number, were now in full flight towards the hamlet of Banda, and were rapidly pursued by the men of both columns; the Guides and the 23rd Pioneers having the honour of reaching the hamlet at the same time.

The village of Lalu now appeared about a mile and a half on the right flank of the first column. Colonel Turner therefore pressed the pursuit in that direction, leaving five companies to guard and bring up the guns, and followed the enemy so closely that they retreated in the utmost confusion down the hills towards Ambela.

As soon as the main position of the enemy had been gained by the second column, Lieut.-Colonel Wilde moved the Peshawar

Mountain Train Battery to the end of the ridge, and placed the two regiments which were in reserve in position to watch the spurs of the mountain leading up from the Ambela plain. The enemy, evidently under the impression that the force had pressed on too far, leaving its left unguarded, came out in large numbers from the village of Ambela, and threatened both the left of the camp and the communications of the second column. Ascending the spurs of the heights, they then commenced a vigorous assault on Lieut.-Colonel Wilde's position.

In the meanwhile, having secured possession of the village of Lalu, Colonel Turner found himself on a line of heights flanking the approach to the "Conical" hill, and seeing the attack which was now being made on the second column, he directed the fire of the guns of the Hazara Mountain Train Battery on to the flank of the enemy.

As soon as the enemy's attack was developed, Lieut.-Colonel Wilde sent for reinforcements. The Major-General had already despatched two companies, 7th Fusiliers, to support the second column, and, on receiving this requisition, the 101st Fusiliers, with the exception of four companies left at the "Conical" hill and on the ridge beyond it, were sent back to Lieut.-Colonel Wilde's support, who was at this time rejoined by the Corps of Guides.

Passing these troops along the rear, Lieut.-Colonel Wilde re-occupied all the ground close up to the "Crag" picquet, and thus received the enemy's attack. A gallant attempt to force the line of communications with the camp was made at the point held by the 3rd Sikhs, under Lieut.-Colonel R. Renny, but was successfully beaten back by that regiment.

Shortly afterwards, Major-General Garvock directed a forward movement to be made, and the Guides, and a portion of the 5th Gurkhas and of the 3rd Sikhs, charged down one of the spurs, and the 101st down another, when the enemy were driven off with great slaughter, leaving a standard in the hands of the Gurkhas, and in their flight coming under the fire of the guns of Colonel Turner's column.

Whilst these operations were being carried on at the front, a desultory attack was made by a considerable number of the enemy upon the front and left flank of the upper camp. Being met by the fire of the only one of Captain Griffin's guns (C-19th R.A.)

which could be brought to bear upon them from the "Standard" picquet, and by the musketry fire from the breastworks, the enemy were reduced to taking cover amongst the rocks and broken ground, from which they caused, from time to time, considerable annoyance to the upper camp, also to C-19th Royal Artillery, and to the adjoining breastworks.

Later in the forenoon, successive bodies of the enemy endeavoured to approach the camp by the gorge from the direction of Ambela, but coming under the fire of the guns of C Battery, in the lower camp, they broke away to the left, and, ascending the ravines and spurs to the front of the position, joined in the attack upon the upper camp. The advanced picquet upon the ridge below and in front of the "Crag" (consisting on this day of fifty men, 1st Punjab Infantry) had been threatened from early morning by a constantly increasing body of the enemy. The ground occupied by the advanced picquet, from which the whole of the centre of our position could be commanded, and on which the "Crag" picquet could not, from the nature of the ground, maintain an effective fire, was the point the enemy strove to gain. This point was so important to the safety of the main position that Lieutenant W. H. Unwin, 1st Punjab Infantry, was instructed by Major C. P. Keyes, commanding that regiment, to hold it as long as he could with any degree of safety. The enemy repeatedly crept up under cover of the rocks, within a few yards of the picquet, having driven in a small party placed there for observation. Lieutenant Unwin was then reinforced, and subsequently had 200 bayonets at his disposal, including sixty men of the 5th Punjab Infantry, under Lieutenant E. S. Fox,—all that could be spared from the reduced force. The enemy made two vigorous attempts, in considerable strength, to take the position, but were repulsed on each occasion by the picquet, who charged down upon them, and inflicted a loss of forty killed.

At this time (about 2 P.M.) Major C. H. Brownlow, 20th Punjab Infantry, who had command of the right defences of the upper camp, observing that the enemy seemed much dispirited by the ill-success against Lieutenant Unwin's picquet, determined to assume the offensive from the camp, and accordingly about 100 men of the 1st Punjab Infantry, led by Major Keyes, advanced from the breastworks and by a succession of well-executed charges upon the different points occupied by the enemy, completely cleared the whole front and left flank of the defences, driving the enemy in great confusion into the plain below, leaving their dead on all sides.

All opposition having now ceased in every part of the field, and the enemy being in-full retreat, arrangements were made for bivouacking for the night. Colonel Turner occupied the ground he had gained in the vicinity of Lalu, and Lieut.-Colonel Wilde that between the camp and the "Conical" hill. Not a shot was fired during the night. Our losses were 16 men killed, and 2 officers, 5 native officers, and 60 men wounded. Those of the enemy were 400 killed and wounded.

Early on the morning of the 16th, 400 sabres of the 11th Bengal Cavalry and Guide Corps, under the command of Lieut.-Colonel D. M. Probyn, V.C., C.B., were brought from camp, and the order was given to advance towards the plain.

Lieut.-Colonel Wilde's column, which was accompanied by Major-General Garvock, passed down by the spurs in its immediate front, the mountain guns attached to it descending with the cavalry by a steep path, which ran down a hollow on the right. The plain was reached about midday, and the column having been formed as per margin, Lieut.-Colonel Wilde advanced across the valley towards the Buner pass, the troops in high spirits confidently hoping for an engagement on ground comparatively easy to what they had been previously accustomed.

Advanced guard.
One company Guide Corps.
Main column.
Guide Corps.
101st Royal Bengal Fusiliers.
Peshawar Mountain Train Battery.
Sappers and Miners.
5th Gurkha Regiment.
3rd Sikh Infantry.
Ammunition *dandies.*
Rear-guard.
1 coy., 3rd Sikh Infantry.

As the column debouched into the open country, the enemy appeared in great force on a low ridge of hills, which completely covered the approach to Ambela, and numerous gay standards of all colours were visible on the prominent hillocks. Major-General Garvock determined, after a careful examination of the ground, on attacking the enemy's position, and turning their right.

The position occupied by the enemy was singularly well chosen; it was of great strength, and peculiarly capable of defence. The enemy, however, seeing that his left would be effectually turned by Colonel Turner's column, which was now advancing, and by the cavalry, abandoned this position, and, almost without firing a shot, retreated slowly towards the pass leading to Buner.

As soon as the second column had begun to descend from the "Conical" hill, the first column, having the shortest line to pass over, had moved in echelon of regiments from the left. The 3rd Punjab Infantry passed down the spur which ran parallel to that by which Lieut.-Colonel Wilde's column was descending, and protected the right flank of that column; the 4th Gurkhas marched down the next parallel ridge, and the main body, consisting of the 23rd Pioneers in advance, left wing Royal Fusiliers, Hazara Mountain Train Battery, Sappers and Miners, and right wing, Royal Fusiliers, proceeded down the gorge leading from the village of Lalu to that of Ambela and to the Chamla valley; while the 32nd Pioneers crowned the heights and effected a parallel movement, covering the right flank. The pathway was steep, and in parts precipitous and rocky, and it was with great difficulty that the mountain guns could be brought down; but Captain F. R. DeBude, by his energy and perseverance, overcame all obstacles, a company of Sappers and Miners, under Lieutenant L. H. E. Tucker, rendering most valuable service. At 2-30 P.M., Colonel Turner found himself able to debouch into the plain with the leading regiments, and the left wing of the Royal Fusiliers.

The 3rd Punjab Infantry and the 4th Gurkhas had now effected their junction with the right of Lieut.-Colonel Wilde's column, and with it were in possession of the extreme right of the enemy's position, which was about a mile and a half from, and facing the entrance to, the Buner pass.

Up to this time the cavalry had remained concealed behind a projecting spur; they were now ordered to advance, and passing on at a gallop, under Lieut.-Colonel D. M. Probyn, and Captain C. W. Hawes of the Guides, passed round the left of the enemy's position, now in our possession, swept into the valley beyond, and halted to the eastward of Ambela. The village, which had been previously abandoned, was immediately fired, large stores of grain falling into our hands.

The main portion of the second column had deployed immediately opposite the village of Ambela, and Colonel Turner was now ordered to try and cut off the rear of the enemy from the pass as they were retreating before Lieut.-Colonel Wilde, but at the same time not to compromise himself in the pass. He therefore formed a line of the 23rd Pioneers and left wing of the 32nd Pioneers, with the right wing of that regiment in support, and directed their advance along the south-western face of the village of Ambela, the left wing of the 7th Royal Fusiliers forming the reserve, in quarter column, in rear of the centre of the line. After passing the village, which was in flames, the right wing of the 32nd was brought up in prolongation of the line to the right, thus bringing the right near the base of the hill which shut in the mouth of the pass. The advance was steadily continued in the same order to within about 800 yards of the mouth of the pass, when the enemy opened a furious fire of matchlocks and *zamburaks*, which was returned by the line as it continued to advance. As a large body of the enemy were observed moving to their right and beyond the left flank, Colonel Turner moved two companies from the reserve of the Royal Fusiliers, and placed them in an oblique position covering the left, whilst at the same time Lieut.-Colonel Probyn moved a body of his men into a position which still further covered the left flank.

Seeing these movements, the enemy made a furious onset, sword in hand, upon the left flank of the line, which was now in broken ground covered with jungle. The 23rd and 32nd Punjab Native Infantry were staggered for the moment by the suddenness of the onslaught, but turning quickly on their assailants, they destroyed the whole of them, not allowing one to escape. Upwards of 200 of their bodies lay upon the field, 40 of whom were Hindustanis. Lieutenant G. Alexander, of the 23rd, was killed, and Captain C. F. F. Chamberlain and Lieutenant C. D. P. Nott, of the 23rd, and Major T. Wheeler and Lieutenant F. H. B. Marsh, of the 32nd, were wounded.

Flushed with success, the Pioneer regiments now pushed forward into the pass, driving the enemy before them. But the day was far spent, the hostile position was occupied in great force, and Major-General Garvock was moreover aware that the Government did not desire to invade Buner. The withdrawal of the troops was therefore ordered. This was effected in echelon of regiments from the right under cover of the fire of the guns of the Hazara Mountain Train Battery, and C-19th R. A. The guns of the latter battery had been brought on elephants from the camp, and were now fully horsed. No molestation whatever was offered by the enemy, who, in immense numbers and in sullen silence, lined the heights above.

The number of the enemy in the field during these two days, *viz.*, the 15th and 16th, was 15,000. The Bunerwals gave signal proof of their sincerity by taking no prominent part in the action, the men who fought having been chiefly Hindustanis, Bajauris, and the men of Swat and Dir. Thus the punishment inflicted fell, as the Commissioner had hoped, on those who had in such an unprovoked manner joined in the contest, and overruled the Bunerwals in their desire for peace.

On the night of the 16th the columns bivouacked in the neighbourhood of Ambela. During the night Faiztalab Khan and the Bajauris, Ghazan Khan and his clansmen from Dir, with the miscellaneous gatherings from more distant parts, were all in rapid flight towards their homes. The *Akhund*, with the *khans* and people of Swat, alone remained on the crest of the Buner pass, not as before, with flaunting standards, but behind the hill, out of sight, and all prepared to run in the event of the troops advancing. Thus enabled to act independently, the Buner *jirga* returned to Major James on the morning of the 17th, not even talking of terms, but simply asking for orders.

There were two plans, either of which could be adopted. The first was to send a strong brigade to Malka to destroy it, and to return by the Chamla valley to Ambela. But in this case it would be necessary to call up another convoy from Parmalao, and this would necessitate a delay of seven days in the advance of this brigade, during which time the *Akhund* and *Maulvi* would have time to collect their scattered forces and to receive reinforcements of fresh men on their way to join them; this delay also would give the Amazais, Mada Khels, Hassanzais, and other northern tribes, time to collect and organise resistance; and, moreover, on the retirement of the brigade there would be no guarantee that the Hindustanis would not be allowed to return to Malka by the neighbouring tribes stirred up by these proceedings. This plan was not therefore approved.

The second plan was to require the Buner men to destroy Malka without any aid from our troops. Its advantages were, that the success already gained would be at once completed, collision with distant tribes in a rugged country would be avoided, and the Hindustanis would be cut off from every hope of a resettlement on the spurs of the Mahaban; for the Buner men would be obliged to associate with themselves the Amazais, and Mada Khels; and if these tribes committed themselves thus openly against the fanatics, it would be a sure guarantee that they would not re-admit them.

The destruction, however, was to be real, not nominal; and it would be necessary that some British officers should accompany the *jirga* to see the work carried out. This would necessitate the sending of an escort with them sufficient to protect them from any individual or factious acts of treachery: of more extended faithlessness Major James had not the slightest anxiety. Half the *jirga* were to remain with the Commissioner. The force was in possession of the Chamla valley, and Buner itself was at our mercy. At the same time it was known that Malka was deserted, and that there could be no opposition which the Buner tribes would be unable to overcome. Major-General Garvock concurring in the Commissioner's views, the following requisitions were made on the Buner *jirga*, to which they unanimously consented:—

(i) To dismiss the army of all kinds on the Buner pass.

(ii) To send a party to destroy Malka completely, to be accompanied by British officers and such escort as might be considered necessary.

(iii) To expel the Hindustanis from the Buner, Chamla, and Amazai lands.

(iv) To leave as hostages the whole of their chief men till the above requirements should be fully carried out.

Leaving the greater part of their number with the Commissioner, a few returned to the pass, and by the next morning the army on its crest, including the Swat *khans* and people, were hastening to their homes.

Colonel R. G. Taylor, from the first, had been unremitting in his inquiries regarding the nature of the country, and to no safer hands could the important and delicate duty about to be undertaken have been entrusted. He was, therefore, deputed to proceed with the Buner *jirga*. Escorted by the Corps of Guides, under Lieutenant

F. H. Jenkins, and a body of levies, under the Sudum chief, Aziz Khan, and accompanied by the officers marginally noted, the party advanced from Ambela on the 19th, and reached Kuria, at the upper end of the Chamla valley, that evening. Here they were detained on the 20th by heavy rain, and it then became apparent, from the diminished number of the Bunerwals, that the *jirga* intended rather to carry out their engagements by friendly overtures to the Amazais than by coercion. Colonel R. G. Taylor, fully appreciating the policy which had been adopted, and, supported by the evident frank determination of the Buner *maliks* to fulfil their engagements, determined to acquiesce in this plan of operations.

Col. J. M. Adye,[1] C.B., R.A.,
Lieut.-Col. A. Taylor, C.B., R.E.
Major F. S. Roberts,[2] V.C., R.A., Assistant Quarter Master General.
Major H. C. Johnstone, Revenue Survey.
Major T. Wright, A.A.G.
Lieut. T. T. Carter, R.E.

On the morning of the 21st, the weather having cleared, the march was continued. On turning to the southward, the party entered Amazai territory. From Kuria to Nagrai is seven miles. Soon after leaving the former place, a narrow defile, which could be easily rendered defensible, was entered. The road, for about a mile, followed the stony bed of the *nala*, and then turned up over a spur of the ridge, which, though not a very stiff one, would have been a good place to offer opposition to an advance. On arrival at Nagrai, a party of the Amazais appeared on a hill commanding the onward march, under their chief, Mouza Khan, in full warlike array, with standards and drums, and it became known that they had been joined by parties of the Mada Khels.

To those unacquainted with the real nature of the case, it must have seemed a critical moment, and undoubtedly it was one requiring the utmost tact and firmness on the part of the political officer; but Colonel R. G. Taylor, fortunately, was an officer who eminently possessed those qualities. It appeared that the Mada Khels were either marching to join the war, and had only heard, on reaching the Mahaban tract, of the complete collapse of the tribes, or that Mouza Khan, having heard that the Bunerwals had given in, and were going to force the burning of Malka on the

[1] **Afterwards General Sir John Adye, G.C.B.**
[2] **Now Lord Roberts.**

Mahaban tribes, had called them up to see what aid they could afford to mitigate the evils.

The Buner chiefs, advancing, held council with those of the Amazais, and, after a long conference, the *lashkar* of the latter withdrew. Mouza Khan and their other headmen now joined Colonel R. G. Taylor, and with this accession of strength, the party proceeded to Malka, where it arrived late in the afternoon, and where, owing to the delay caused by the above interruption, it took up its quarters for the night.

Malka was situated on an elevated plateau, on a northern spur of the Mahaban range. It was a much larger and more substantial place than any known in those hills, containing several large edifices, among which the *Maulvi's* hall of audience, barracks for the soldiers, stabling, and a powder manufactory, formed conspicuous objects. There were no regular fortifications, but the outer walls of the houses were connected, and formed a continuous line of defence with posterns. There was also a tower at the gateway.

The place was found deserted, and on the morning of the 22nd December the Bunerwals and Amazais began to burn and destroy it. An effort was at first made by the Amazais, and afterwards by the Buner *khans*, to save a large portion of the place, on the plea that it had been occupied by men of their tribe, and not by the Hindustanis; but Colonel R. G. Taylor was firm, and determined to destroy the whole town, which was completely done by noon. The escort witnessed the burning, but were in no way employed in the work of destruction. Whilst this was going on, information was brought that the Amazais were going down the valley to join the Mada Khels, who had remained at Nagrai. This, of course, caused Colonel R. G. Taylor much anxiety.

The Shergarh pass, by which the column had to return, was a difficult one, and if the smouldering sparks in the minds of the hillmen had blown up into a flame, the position would have been most critical; but Colonel R. G. Taylor never wavered in his determination. Shortly afterwards, Aziz Khan, the Sudum chief, who was in a manner in general charge of the proceedings, sent word that he wished for leave to go down the valley to look after what was going on, and Colonel Taylor agreed at once, putting full trust in the honest intentions of the Bunerwals to carry out their engagements. Matters were speedily arranged by Aziz Khan, who ordered the baggage, which had begun moving towards Kuria, but had been stopped on the above untoward report, to continue its march.

Colonel R. G. Taylor spoke to the Amazais who were present, but they were sullen, and not inclined to answer in good spirit; they were, however, saved the trouble by Zaidulla Khan, one of the Buner chiefs, who stepped in front of them, and, grasping his beard with his one remaining hand, said—"I am answerable for these men, both for their conduct now, and for their excluding the Hindustanis in future." This incident illustrates the fact that the Mahaban tribes, though strong, and not to be despised with their stiff country, are yet powerless to resist the will of Buner.

If things at times looked a little lowering and uncertain, it was but the natural result of the position in which this force was placed; their task had taken them through a narrow defile into a cup of wild, mountainous country, never previously visited by our troops. The force found themselves in the presence of strong tribes, certainly not over well pleased with their visitors, or the errand on which they had come; but from the first, Colonel R. G. Taylor felt confident that the representatives of the stronger tribe that accompanied him could carry out their engagements, and overcome the would-be recusants.

Colonel Taylor said the spectacle of a tribe like the Bunerwals doing our bidding and destroying the stronghold of their own allies in the war, at a distant spot, naturally under the protection of other tribes of well-known prowess and strength, with British witnesses looking on, must have been a thoroughly convincing proof to the surrounding country of the reality of our success, and of the indubitable prostration felt by the powerful Buner tribe, which had been the foremost in opposing us.

The party returned to Kuria that evening, and on the morning of the 23rd marched to the camp in the Ambela pass, accompanied by some of the Amazai *maliks*.

On the departure of Colonel R. G. Taylor's party, the troops had returned to their former position in the pass; and the 1st, 5th, and 6th Punjab Infantry and the 20th Punjab Native Infantry, had begun their march towards their different cantonments. The remainder of the force now began its return to the plains, all being assembled at Nawa Kala on the 25th December.

The British loss during the whole of the above operations had been 15 British and 4 native officers, 34 British and 185 native rank and file—total 238, killed; 21 British and 27 native officers, and 118 British and 504 native rank and file—total 670, wounded; grand total 908. The total loss of the enemy was estimated at 3,000.

The Indian Medal, with a clasp inscribed "Umbeyla," was granted in 1869 to all survivors of the troops engaged in the operations of the Yusafzai Field Force.

Coercion of the Gaduns and Utmanzais after the Ambela Expedition.

The attitude of the Gaduns during the campaign had been, on the whole, satisfactory. Most of their chiefs were present in camp with the political officers, and there was no general collection of any part of the tribe against us. Individuals, undoubtedly, joined the enemy, but not nearly to such an extent as did our own subjects in Yusafzai. Only two men of the tribe were killed or wounded. One of the headmen, Malik Isa, of the Mansur section, however, did not present himself the whole time, and it being considered necessary to require security from the Gaduns generally after the Ambela campaign was over, a brigade, consisting of the troops noted in the margin, under the command of Lieut.-Colonel A. T. Wilde, C.B., marched from Nawa Kala to Meni on the 28th December 1863, being accompanied by Major H. R. James, C.B., as Political Officer.

Peshawar Mountain Train Battery.
Hazara Mountain Train Battery.
101st Royal Bengal Fusiliers.
One company of Sappers and Miners.
Corps of Guides.
3rd Sikh Infantry.
3rd Punjab Infantry.
5th Gurkha Regiment.

Ten days' supplies were carried with the force, with ammunition at 200 rounds per native soldier, and 140 rounds per British soldier.

The remainder of the troops of the Yusafzai Field Force marched back to their respective cantonments.

The Gadun tribe, as already stated, is divided into two chief clans, the Mansur and the Salar. The former had generally formed the recusant party in dealings with us, under the leadership of Isa Khan; but associated with him had been Jehangir Khan, of the Salar clan.

On the 30th December the troops arrived at Meni, and on the following day all the chiefs of the tribe had assembled in the villages of Bisak and Gandap, the head-quarters of the Mansur and Salar clans respectively, and both situated about four miles distant. Isa Khan was with them, but, actuated by fear, he did not come in to the Commissioner with the rest, though he counselled them to perfect submission. However, on Major James again sending for him, he came in and joined the *jirga*.

On the 1st of January the Commissioner had a discussion with them on the subject of their offences, which they admitted, at the same time pleading certain things in extenuation; it only remained, therefore, to take guarantees for the future.

When the *Saiyids* and Hindustanis had returned in the previous July, they had occupied Mandi, a place adjacent to Sitana, and had built there a kind of fort of lcose stones. The village itself belonged to *Saiyids* not connected with Mubarak Shah's family, and it had been spared in 1858, as they were considered to be blameless for what had then happened. As the Hindustanis had, however, again found the place ready to their hand, and occupied it, it became as necessary to remove a powerless as a disloyal colony. By requiring the Gaduns and Utmanzais to perform this work, a guarantee in their case would be obtained similar to the security we had in regard to the Bunerwals and Amazais at Malka. Believing this to be a more complete and satisfactory termination than the taking of hostages, regarding which there were several difficulties, Major James made a demand on them for its execution, to which they expressed their consent.

During the night, however, worked on by interested parties, and at the instigation of Jehangir Khan, the men of Gandap left the camp, and declined to be parties to the agreement. The ostensible cause was declared to be that it was proposed to take the force *viâ* Gandap, the direct road to Khabal, which portended mischief to the village. It was a case to be promptly met, and Lieut.-Colonel Wilde, therefore, moved out on the morning of the 2nd, and occupied the low hills in rear of, and over, the village of Gandap. The ascent was steep and difficult. The village was a strong one, situated among low hills, and consisting of about a thousand houses full of cotton and other property. The place was completely at our mercy; but being most anxious not to be forced to extremities, the Commissioner sent men of the Gadun *jirga* (all of whom, together with those of the Utmanzai *jirga*, had accompanied him) to reason with the Gandap people, with the result that they all came in, and agreed to join in the allotted work. The troops accordingly returned to camp at sunset without a shot having been fired.

The following day the force proceeded to Khabal, where the Utmanzais were formally associated with the Gaduns. Leaving the camp there, Major James proceeded on the 4th to Mandi, accompanied by Lieut.-Colonel Wilde and a portion of the troops. The whole village, which had been much improved and contained some substantial houses, was then destroyed and burnt by the *jirgas*, and the walled enclosure, denominated a fort, was levelled. Sitana was found still a ruin, as it had been left by Sir J. S. Cotton in 1858. On the 5th the troops returned to Pihur, where the Gaduns and Utmanzais executed fresh agreements, individually and collectively, and, at their intercession, the Gandap men were pardoned for their foolish conduct on the 2nd of January.

All the objects of the expedition trans-Indus having been thus accomplished, and the season being too far advanced for any active measures against the Hassanzais of the Black Mountain, Lieut.-Colonel Wilde's force was broken up, and the troops returned to their respective cantonments.

On the 9th January 1864 the *jirga* of the Mada Khels came in to Major Coxe, the Deputy Commissioner of Hazara, who was with the troops watching the Hassanzais and protecting the Amb territory, and asserted that they had entertained no hostile feeling towards the British Government, but had been compelled by pressure of the neighbouring tribes, which they were unable to resist, to join the hostile movement organized by the Bunerwals and the Akhund of Swat. They then executed an agreement to maintain in future friendly relations with the Tanawali chief, and on no account to grant the Hindustanis countenance or habitation within the limits of their country.

Two days afterwards, that section of the Amazais which had not previously waited on the Commissioner at Ambela, came in to Major H. W. H. Coxe, and also executed an agreement to exclude the Hindustanis altogether from their limits. Later on, he also received the submission of the Hassanzais, with the exception of Kabul Khan, the son of the chief. The subsequent misbehaviour of the Hassanzais and their misconduct in 1868 has already been related in Chapter III.

APPENDIX A.

YUSAFZAI FIELD FORCE, OCTOBER 1863.

Brigadier-General Sir N. B. Chamberlain, K.C.B. (Commandant, Punjab Irregular Force), commanding.

Staff.

Major T. Wright, Assistant Adjutant-General.
Lieut.-Colonel G. Allgood, Assistant Quarter-Master General.
Lieutenant F. J. N. Mackenzie, Staff Officer, Punjab Irregular Force.
Lieut.-Colonel A. Taylor, C.B., R.E., Commanding Royal Engineer.
Surgeon W. Simpson, Principal Medical Officer, British Troops.
,, H. B. Buckle, ,, ,, ,, Native ,,
Captain J. H. Jenkins, Principal Commissariat Officer.

Artillery.

Captain J. S. Tulloh, commanding Royal Artillery.
,, F. C. Griffin, ,, half C-19th Royal Artillery.
,, T. E. Hughes, ,, Peshawar Mountain Train Battery.
,, F. R. DeBude, ,, Hazara Mountain Train Battery.

Cavalry.

Lieut.-Colonel D. M. Probyn, V.C., C.B., commanding 11th Bengal Cavalry
Captain C. W. Hawes, commanding Guide Cavalry.

Engineers.

Lieut. L. H. E. Tucker, commanding Sappers and Miners.

Infantry.

Colonel W. Hope, C.B., commanding 71st Highland Light Infantry.
Lieut.-Colonel F. O. Salusbury, commanding 101st Royal Bengal Fusiliers.
,, A. T. Wilde, C.B., commanding Guide Corps.
Major C. P. Keyes, commanding 1st Punjab Infantry.
,, P. F. Gardiner, commanding 3rd Punjab Infantry.
Lieut.-Colonel J. L. Vaughan, commanding 5th Punjab Infantry.
Captain W. D. Hoste, commanding 6th Punjab Infantry.
Major C. C. G. Ross, commanding 14th Native Infantry.
,, C. H. Brownlow, commanding 20th Punjab Native Infantry.
,, W. D. Morgan, commanding 32nd Punjab Native Infantry (Pioneers).
Captain C. W. R. Chester, commanding 4th Gurkha Regiment.
Major J. P. W. Campbell, commanding 5th Gurkha Regiment.

Political Officers.

Colonel R. G. Taylor, C.B., Commissioner.
Captain A. A. Munro, Deputy Commissioner.
Lieut. R. G. Sandeman, Assistant Commissioner.

Survey Officers.

Major H. C. Johnstone, Survey Department.
Lieutenant W. Barron, Survey Department.

With the troops which subsequently joined.

Captain T. H. Salt, commanding No. 3 Punjab Light Field Battery.
Colonel R. Y. Shipley, commanding 7th Fusiliers.
Major F. W. Burroughs, commanding 93rd Highlanders.
Lieut.-Colonel R. Renny, commanding 3rd Sikhs.
Captain C. F. F. Chamberlain, commanding 23rd Punjab Native Infantry (Fioneers).

APPENDIX B.

DISPOSITION OF THE YUSAFZAI FIELD FORCE AT AMBELA ON MAJOR-GENERAL J. GARVOCK ASSUMING THE COMMAND, 30TH NOVEMBER 1863.

First Brigade.

Colonel W. W. Turner, C.B., 97th Foot, commanding.
Lieutenant J. H. Campbell, 71st Highland Light Infantry. Brigade-Major.

Half C-19th Royal Artillery.
Peshawar Mountain Train Battery.
71st Highland Light Infantry.
1st Punjab Infantry.
3rd " "
5th " "
20th " Native Infantry.
32nd " " " (Pioneers).
5th Gurkha Regiment.

Second Brigade.

Lieut.-Colonel A. T. Wilde, C.B., Guide Corps, commanding.
Captain C. W. R. Chester, 4th Gurkhas, Brigade-Major.

Half No. 3 Punjab Light Field Battery.
Hazara Mountain Train Battery.
101st Royal Bengal Fusiliers.
14th Native Infantry.
Guide Infantry.
6th Punjab Infantry.
4th Gurkha Regiment.
23rd Punjab Native Infantry (Pioneers.)

CHAPTER VII.

YUSAFZAI AND GADUN TRIBES BETWEEN THE BLACK MOUNTAIN AND SWAT.—(Continued.)

Dealings with the tribes subsequent to 1864.

THE history of the Hindustani fanatics subsequent to the Ambela campaign is not very easy to follow, but it appears that after their expulsion from Malka, the greater number of them, led by Maulvi Abdulla, retreated into the Chagarzai country, north of the Barandu river. After a time they obtained from the Chagarzais grants of the villages of Tangora and Batora, where they made permanent settlements, and remained undisturbed up to the commencement of 1868. Their position was, however, by no means comfortable. The people amongst whom they dwelt made them pay dearly for the protection afforded them, and for the supplies they received; and it was only by the greatest efforts that their agents in Hindustan were enabled to forward to them enough money for their support. They were, moreover, frequently threatened with expulsion by their hosts, who forcibly prevented the completion of two towers which the *Maulvi* had commenced to erect in Batora. The *Akhund* also looked upon them with no friendly eye: their *Wahabi* inclinations were abhorrent to him, and their position in the country was a standing menace; for their leaders maintained their position only by intrigue, and were ready tools in the hands of the rival faction in Buner and elsewhere, followers of the Kota Mulla. [1]

The Hindustani fanatics.

It is not surprising that, with this constant pressure on them, both at home and abroad, the community was several times on the point of dissolution. During the autumn of 1866, Muhammad Isak and Muhammad Yakub, two of their leaders, made several attempts

[1] Kota is a village in the south-west corner of Yusafzai. Saiyid Amir, better known as the Kota Mulla, was at this time one of the rivals of the *Akhund* in the religious world.

to open communications with Colonel J. R. Becher, C.B., the Commissioner of Peshawar, through the instrumentality of Saiyid Muhammad (formerly in our service); their letters were received and messages sent to them, but their plans were entirely frustrated by the vigilance of Maulvi Abdulla, who appears to have gained an entire ascendancy over all the other leaders. Matters remained thus until the beginning of 1868, the fanatics being too much engaged with their own quarrels and intrigues to annoy us or continue the system of highway robbery in our territories, which at first led to the recommendation by the Punjab Government for punitive expeditions in 1858 and 1863.

In February 1868 news was received that the fighting men of the Hindustanis, numbering 400 or 500, had moved from Tangora and Batora to Bajkatta, in Buner, on the invitation of Azim Khan of Bajkatta, an opponent of the *Akhund* and firm supporter of his rival, the Kota Mulla. Azim Khan offered to give the Hindustanis houses and lands in his village if they would bring over their families and settle there permanently; his offer was accepted, and the fanatics accordingly abandoned Tangora and Batora. Nothing more was heard of them until the 18th of April, when the arrival of Feroz Shah, the son of the last King of Delhi, at Bajkatta was reported by Azim Khan himself, who wrote to the Commissioner of Peshawar to make his excuses for harbouring men whom he knew to be mortal enemies of the British Government. Feroz Shah had arrived some months before at Saidu, the residence of the *Akhund*, in great poverty, and with only four attendants; he was well received, and reported to be in high favour, until the evil news of the arrival in Buner of his countrymen reached the Akhund.

The movement of the fanatics into Buner was fatal to them; at a distance they might have been tolerated, and in time possibly have regained their prestige. The *Akhund* now lost no time in exerting all his influence to get rid of what he well knew would be a fruitful source of trouble to him. By skilful management he was enabled to conciliate and bring over all the Buner tribes of the opposite faction; Azim Khan, Zaidulla Khan, Nawab Khan, and a few other chiefs alone holding aloof. On the 25th of May, at a large meeting of all the Buner tribes convened by Mirji Khan, the most trusted of the itinerant *Shekhs* of the *Akhund*, it was determined that the Hindustanis should be expelled from Buner, their presence being displeasing to the *Akhund* and contrary to the terms of the treaty made with the British Government. In consequence of this resolve, the fanatics, to the number of about 700 fighting men, accompanied by Feroz Shah and Azim Khan, made a precipitate retreat to Malka, where they commenced to rebuild their houses, and made arrangements with the Amazais for supplies. In the meantime Maulvi Abdulla in person visited the *Akhund*, and found means to turn away his anger, for Mirji Khan was recalled, and permission given to the Hindustanis to resettle in Buner; the greater portion of them returned to Bajkatta, but had not been there very long before the intrigues of their leaders again brought them into trouble. Maulvi Abdulla was induced to join a league that had been founded by Azim Khan and other Buner chiefs, together with the Amazais and Mukarrab Khan, ex-chief of the Khudu Khels, to oppose the influence of the *Akhund*, and obtain for Mukarrab Khan recovery of his former possessions and reinstatement at Panjtar. Mukarrab Khan, who, after his expulsion from the Totalai villages and the destruction of Panjtar and Mangal Thana by our troops, had come in to the Commissioner of Peshawar, and been allowed to reside in British territory, was the prime mover in this plot, by which he sought to regain his former position; his money cemented the various alliances and purchased the neutrality of some of the Buner chiefs. On the 2nd of August Zaidulla Khan committed the first overt act of hostility by seizing a number of Swat traders passing through his lands. The *Akhund* immediately mustered his followers, and directed the Buner tribes to break up the league by expelling the Hindustanis and putting to death the refractory chiefs. In pursuance of his orders, Zaidulla Khan was treacherously assassinated in his own house. On the 12th they arrived, together with the *Akhund's* followers, before Bajkatta, and sent a message to the *Maulvi*, giving him one day to remove all his followers, women, and children.

The fanatics at first thought of resistance, and exchanged a few shots with the Salarzais, but were induced by Azim Khan to give in and commence preparations for a retreat. The next day the whole body evacuated Bajkatta, the women and children being sent on ahead, and the rear brought up by a guard of fifty or sixty men armed with rifles. For the first few miles all went well, the Buner men being occupied in plundering and burning the deserted settlement; but as the fugitives neared the pass between Bajkatta and Batora they saw that the hills on both sides were held by the *Akhund's* followers. The mass of the fugitives, including Maulvi Abdulla, Azim Khan, and the Buner chiefs, pushed on through the pass, and made their escape with slight loss, but the rear-guard was cut off, and, after a gallant stand, entirely destroyed. From Batora the fugitives fled to Gulima Bori, in Chagarzai territory; here they obtained a short respite, and even conceived hopes of being able to establish themselves permanently, being promised support, in the event of an attack, by the Amazais and one section of the Chagarzais.

The power of the *Akhund*, increased by his complete triumph over the rival faction in Buner, was, however, too great for them. The Chagarzais, in obedience to his orders, expelled the fanatics, who continued their flight through Tangora to Bihar, on the right bank of the Indus, where they arrived about the 18th of September, with some twenty or thirty wounded men. Later accounts of them are very conflicting, but it is certain that the *Maulvi*, with some hundreds of followers, came over to Judba, and that many of them remained there till the British force arrived on the crest of the Black Mountain in 1868. The fanatics were welcomed and given the grant of a hamlet in Judba, and were enabled to purchase several rafts, thus getting the command of the river, and making themselves independent of the extortionate Pathan ferrymen whilst at that place. The *Maulvi*, it is said, received letters in 1868, from the Tikari chief, who offered to give the whole body of fugitives an asylum in his fort, and land in the Tikari valley, and also from the Allai *jirga* and the chief of Thakot, who promised to come to Judba to hold a great council and discuss measures of resistance against the British. Mubarak Shah was also summoned, and the war party, cis-Indus, was daily increasing. It seems probable that a month later, the force under Major-General Wilde would have found a powerful coalition and some organised plan of defence, but our rapid approach disconcerting them, the fanatics hastily recrossed the river, deserting their Chagarzai hosts, thereby departing from their profession as soldiers of the faith, and destroying the last remnant of their former prestige, already injured by the treatment they had met with at the hand of the *Akhund* and his disciples.

The main body of them then went to Palosi, a village of the trans-Indus Hassanzais, who refused, however, to allow them a permanent settlement. From Pālosi, they went to Thakot, but, finding no resting-place there, moved up the river to Bihar and Judba of the Chagarzais, and being obliged to abandon this refuge also, they at last threw themselves on the mercy of the Hassanzais. Here they received some land called Maidan, near the village of Palosi, and remained there till 1888, paying a rent of Rs. 800 per annum for the buildings and land they occupied.

In 1880, with the permission of the Mada Khels, they established a small outpost at Smatsai, a cave village of Gujars, dependent on the Mada Khels, their object apparently being to use this as a stepping-stone towards obtaining a position again in Malka, or on the Mahaban; but the Amazais, acting up to their agreement with the British Government at the conclusion of the Ambela campaign, refused to give shelter to them and the colony was withdrawn in 1881, the garrison retiring to Palosi. During 1882, an internal dispute arose, which resulted in some of them leaving the settlement for a time, and in the following year they vainly negotiated with the Nurizai Bunerwals for a settlement within their territory. In their letter to the Nurizai leaders, they stated that their wish was to raise a religious war, but their real reason appears to be that they wanted to avoid the high rent which the Hassanzais charged them.

During the Buner complications in 1885,[1] the Hindustani colony was not actually hostile, but their missionaries were very active, and it is probable that, had an expedition been sent into Buner they would have joined the Bunerwals against the Government, and they made the probability of such an expedition a reason for asking for contributions from their supporters throughout India. In May 1885, Maulvi Abdulla sent a letter to the Deputy Commissioner of Hazara, complaining that there was a debt due the colony of Rs. 8,000 from two men residing in British territory, requesting that the claims might be settled by the Government, and threatening that, if this were not done, reprisals would be undertaken. As it appeared on enquiry that there was no ground for this claim, the Commissioner was directed, if he

[1] See page 309.

considered it necessary to reply at all to the *Maulvi's* communication, to inform him that letters accompanied by threats could not receive attention.

A contingent from Palosi joined Hashim Ali in a defiant demonstration on the Black Mountain in 1888[1], and from 100 to 200 of the fanatics took part against us in the fight at Kotkai in the autumn of the same year. After this they allowed their fort and settlements to be demolished without offering any resistance, and then sought refuge among the Chagarzais and Akhund Khels, amongst whom they were still residing during the Black Mountain Expedition of 1891. The night attack on our picquet at Ghazikot on the 10th March, which has already been described in the account of that expedition, was the work of some sixty followers of Maulvi Abdulla, backed up by an equal number of clansmen from the neighbourhood; and the loss they sustained on this occasion is said to have greatly disheartened the community. Soon after this they sought and found asylum among the Amazais, where they remain up to the present time, in spite of the agreement entered into by the Amazais in 1864 to exclude the fanatics altogether from their limits.

The most recent reports place the number of men in the colony at 900. Although residing among the Amazais, they do not appear to take any active part in the feuds of their hosts, nor have they been shown to be implicated in recent disturbances, although considerable pressure was brought to bear on them by the Amazais to induce them to do so.

Maulvi Abdulla died in 1902 and was succeeded by his son Abdul Quddus.

The Gaduns.

The Gaduns entirely failed to act up to the engagements into which they entered in 1864. In 1866 a meeting was held, with their sanction and in their country, to consider whether the fanatics should be permitted to re-occupy Sitana. In January 1867, they permitted one of the leaders of the fanatics to occupy Siri, and in April they made a request that he might be permitted to remain. Being refused, they reiterated their request, but with no better success. They then, on the 27th of April, came down and

[1] See Chapter IV.

attempted to build a tower near our border, but, being attacked by the Utmanzais, were worsted, and obliged to desist, having lost thirteen killed and fourteen wounded.

Their conduct continued to be so unsatisfactory that, on the 15th of June 1870, a blockade was declared against them. Thereupon, they began raiding in our territory, attacking the villages of Bara, Gazai, and Pihur. They were, however, in every case, driven off by the men of Topi and Meni. On the 14th of July it was reported that they had sent for aid to the Hindustanis at Palosi.

On the 16th of July 1870 they assembled in considerable force in a ravine called the Kondel, and erected a high and stong barricade apparently for the purpose of shelter, in the event of their being driven back in any attack on Panjman, Jhanda, and Boka. At this barricade 300 men were stationed. In the course of two or three days, however, it was swept away by heavy rain, and was not rebuilt.

On the 17th of July 1870, a party of Gaduns made a feint of a night attack on Panjman. Shots were exchanged, but without loss on either side; and the Gaduns retired at noon of the same day. Four or five Gaduns, headed by Mirbaz, an outlawed British subject, made an attempt to drive off by stealth a herd of cattle belonging to the village of Jhanda. The manœuvre was discovered in time, and the plunderers got away to the hills, but without their booty.

On the 18th July a night attack was made on Meni by some fifty Gaduns, but the villagers, being on the alert, drove off the assailants without loss.

On the 19th July one Akhtarai, a chain-carrier employed in the settlement, was met, as he was going in the evening from Topi to Bara, by a roving band of Gaduns, and murdered, his body being afterwards blown up with powder.

On the 20th July some *zamindars* of Meni, out ploughing, were threatened by fifty Gaduns, who made a descent on them. The armed escort of the *zamindars* accompanying them fired on the Gaduns, who returned the shots, but fled as the villagers came moving out to the rescue. Later in the day, the watchmen of Datugrah were fired at by a small band of Gaduns, who retired before they could be attacked. The Gadun head-quarters were now moved from Gudjai to Malka Kadi, and preparations were made for a grand assault on Meni, Topi, and Panjman.

On the 22nd July an attempt was made during the night to surprise and do some damage to Pihur, but failed, as the police were on the look-out. The outlying picquets of Jhanda and Boka were fired at by straggling parties, but without effect.

On the 25th July it was reported that, notwithstanding these numerous petty attacks, no large force had entered British territory, but they were collected in large numbers at the village of Gudjai in a threatening attitude. Their application for assistance to the Bunerwals, Swatis, Amazais, and Hindustanis was said to have met with a promise of compliance in case they should be attacked.

On the 26th the Deputy Commissioner visited the border to see the arrangements made for the defence of the villages. Two towers were built at Panjman, and were constantly manned with a force of 125 men.

On the afternoon of the 28th, about 4 P.M., some 300 Gaduns came down and established themselves in a strong position on a mound near Meni, and thence began firing at long ranges. The villagers got together, and went out to attack them, but they were largely reinforced, and it was not until near 10 P.M. that the Meni men, reinforced by reliefs from Topi, were able to attack. Four men of the attacking party were wounded; the Gaduns fleeing at once. Their loss is not known. One of the wounded, Saidulla Khan, a *malik* of Meni, afterwards died. His death caused a great sensation amongst the Utmanzais, to the family of whose *khans* he belonged.

On the 4th September 100 Gaduns came to Bara, in British territory, on pretence of taking part in the funeral obsequies of Aslam Ali Khan, a man of some influence, who had died there. After the *fatiha*, they made a feint of attacking Pihur, but, after firing a number of shots without harm, retired. On the same date Shahdad Khan of Hund and Ibrahim Khan of Zeyda, both of whom with their levies were guarding Panjman, at the desire of the Gaduns, met their *jirga* on the boundary, they having been authorised by the Deputy Commissioner to open communications with them. The Gaduns expressed their desire for peace, and readiness to come in and hear on what terms they could again be admitted to our friendship. At the same time they expressed their readiness to return cattle and other property taken from any British subjects, except Utmanzais, and did, in fact, in several cases return such property. As to the exceptions, it is to be remarked that, owing to the position of the Utmanzais immediately on the Gadun frontier, the collisions that had taken place had been, so far as British subjects were concerned, almost entirely with Utmanzais, and the deaths that had taken place on either side had caused a bitter feeling between the two; to which may be added that Khabal, with which the Gaduns had long had a feud, was Utmanzai. It being deemed desirable to get in the *jirga*, the two *khans* were directed to encourage their attendance, if they were in reality disposed to come to terms. A guarantee of safe conduct was with the same view forwarded, and the Utmanzais were strictly prohibited from hostile demonstrations of any kind; at the same time careful watch was enjoined, lest all this should be a mere feint to throw us off our guard, and enable them to make a damaging attack on some of our frontier villages—a not uncommon trick of these people. The Deputy Commissioner was at once informed of the aspect of affairs, and instructions requested as to the terms that should be offered in case the *jirga* came in. It was suggested that—

1st.—A fine of at least Rs. 1,000 should be imposed, in addition to the Rs. 1,000 forfeited on account of violated engagements, the refusal to pay which had caused the present complications.

2nd.—All property destroyed should be compensated for, and all carried away returned.

3rd.—Fresh engagements taken from the principal men, binding them, under a fine, to respect British territory, and not enter it at any time with an armed force.

On the 9th August a great number (reported as 6,000 or 7,000, but no doubt greatly exaggerated) of Gaduns came into the Meni lands with flags, etc., and remained some hours, expecting the villagers to come out and attack them; a body of some 500 advanced to within a few hundred paces of the village and fired upon it. The villagers, interpreting too strictly the orders prohibiting them from aggressive hostilities, remained in their village, and after a time the assailants withdrew. No injury was inflicted.

On the 15th August Captain W. G. Waterfield, Deputy Commissioner, reported that the Gadun council desired to make terms. They were ordered to pay Rs. 3,285, and give security for Rs. 500 more, and also to bind themselves for Rs. 1,000 not to violate British territory.

On the 22nd August the Assistant Commissioner of Yusafzai reported that Shadad Khan of Hund and Ibrahim Khan of Zeyda had brought in the *jirga*, 115 in number, fully representing every section and interest in the tribe; and on the 10th September it was finally reported that the above terms had been accepted.

After the settlement thus effected, the tribe continued to behave well. In December 1873, however, several robberies were committed in British territory by the Salar Gaduns of Gandap, and a *baramta* was therefore ordered, the tribe being placed under blockade until they paid a fine of Rs. 500, which they did at once. In 1881 they were again fined Rs. 200 for a raid on the village of Salim Khan, from which they carried off some cattle, which were subsequently returned, and the fine was paid without demur.

In September 1888 some Gaduns made an impudent attack on Mr. Hastings, Deputy Superintendent of Police, who was travelling between Topi and Meni. The Gaduns *jirga* admitted responsibility and paid a fine of Rs. 1,000. In 1897 the Gaduns were implicated in the attacks on the Malakand and Chakdara garrisons.[1] On the 22nd December their *jirga* assembled at Swabi, and stated that they were ready to comply with any terms which might be imposed; and subsequently, at Mardan they paid a fine of Rs. 2,500 and surrendered 200 guns and the standards of Gandap and Bisak.

Khudu Khels.

With regard to the conduct of the Khudu Khels subsequent to the Ambela expedition. Although they do not seem to have joined, as a tribe, against us during that campaign, yet there is no doubt that many members of the tribe were opposed to us. Mukarrab Khan, the chief of the tribe, at the commencement of the operations was a refugee in British territory, and living at Baja; but during the campaign he was present with the British troops, and remained in attendance on the Commissioner, receiving a subsistence allowance

[1] See page 367.

of Rs. 3 a day. On the termination of hostilities he begged for some provision being granted him, and requested that his *daftar* in Baja should be held by him rent free. This was granted on the understanding that if he left British territory and returned to his own country, he would forfeit the asylum granted him. In 1868, owing to his disobedience of orders, his lands in British territory were resumed by the Government. In 1874 he returned to his own country, and attempted, with the aid of the Amazais, to recover his Khanship in the tribe; and in August of that year he was guilty of a base crime in the assassination of the Khudu Khel *jirga*, eighty in number, whom he had entrapped into his power. After varying fortunes, which it is not necessary here to follow, being deserted by his allies, he had at length to abandon the attempt to recover the Khanship. In August 1879, however, he succeeded in regaining his power among the Khudu Khels, and for two years his relations with the tribe seem to have been fairly amicable; but in March 1881 he quarrelled with some of the leading men of the Bam Khel section, and, in the fighting which ensued, he lost his only son, Akbar Khan. This event led to extraordinary exertions on his part, and, spending money freely, he called in the Gaduns and Amazais to his assistance, and with them and a small contingent from Amb, invested, in June 1881, the village of Bam Khel Totalai, the stronghold of his opponents, but without success. His auxiliaries then dispersed, and the Bam Khels summoned the Nurizai Bunerwals to their aid, and burnt Panjtar. Fruitless negotiations and desultory skirmishes followed throughout July and August, in which the Nurizai and Daulatzai Bunerwals alternately offered to assist the contending parties, but confined themselves to accepting subsidies without committing themselves to anything more than promises. Eventually, with the connivance of a few of the Bam Khels, Mukarrab Khan and the Gaduns occupied Totalai on the 30th of August, and immediately burnt the village. The traitors among the Bam Khels were themselves seized by Mukarrab Khan, and only escaped with their lives owing to the intercession of a local *mulla*. The Bam Khels having now fled to British territory, arrangements were made to intern them at a safe distance from the border. In the flush of this success the Gaduns and Mukarrab Khan were tempted to commit excesses. The former carried off some cattle belonging to the

British village of Salim Khan, which were grazing near the border, and detained a messenger despatched to demand their release; but subsequently the messenger was released and the cattle were returned; and Mukarrab Khan instigated two attacks, one of which proved fatal, within British territory, upon Bam Khel refugees. For these offences a fine of Rs. 200 was imposed upon the Gaduns, which was paid, as already stated, without demur, and a fine of Rs. 800 was imposed on Mukarrab Khan, which was also paid. In January 1882 the Bam Khels left British territory and began to collect in the villages of Chamla and Buner, contiguous to the Khudu Khel country, preparatory to an attack on the *Khan*, with the explicit understanding that, if unsuccessful, they would not be permitted to seek refuge again in our territory. The *Khan* had, however, failed to learn moderation and prudence from the reverses of many years, and he had succeeded by his tyrannical and oppressive behaviour in thoroughly alienating his own party, who began secretly to encourage his enemies. In July the Bam Khels had succeeded in gaining possession of some Khudu Khel villages with the connivance of Mukarrab Khan's faction, and, by the end of the month, he was again in flight, and seeking protection in British territory. As he continued to intrigue against the Bam Khels, making arrangements to renew hostilities, he was directed to recross the frontier, and took up his residence in a Gadun village. Half of that tribe were inclined to assist him; but, by judicious management, the Bam Khels contrived to neutralise their influence. Unable to procure help from the Gaduns, Mukarrab Khan next turned to the Bunerwals. By liberal gifts of money and promises he induced a body of Ashazai, Daulatzai, and Nurizai Bunerwals to move in March 1882 on the village of Chinglai. The Bam Khels in turn bribed the men of Buner to retire, which they were not loath to do, after fleecing both parties among the Khudu Khels; and Mukarrab Khan, after an eventful feud with his tribe, which had extended over a period of thirty years, found himself an exile in his old age. Major H. R. James and Sir H. B. Edwardes placed on record their opinion regarding the character he bore in days gone by; and in his declining years—one might say on the brink of the grave—, oppressed with cares and want, the old septuagenarian did not belie the evil reputation which clung to him, and which his own race attributed to him twenty-eight years before, *i.e.*, that he was a man whom no ties would bind, and on whose word no reliance could be placed. In 1897 the Khudu Khels participated with the Gaduns, Bunerwals, Chamlawals, and Amazais in the attacks on the Malakand and Chakdara garrisons, see page 367, and in the fight at Landakai, see page 383. They subsequently consented to the Government's demand for complete submission, and on 15th December paid a fine of Rs. 2,000 and surrendered 150 fire-arms, 200 swords, and the standards of Dogi, Ialate, and Chinglai.

Bunerwals.

It now remains to notice the conduct of the Bunerwals subsequent to the Ambela campaign. In March 1868 a party of the Salarzais came down and burnt the village of Pirsai, in the Sudum valley, in British territory, in the prosecution of a private feud. A blockade was established, but in April 1869 they came to terms, rebuilt the destroyed village, and paid a fine to the British Government. During the above complications it was proposed to try and surprise Chor Banda and burn it, but the idea was never carried out.

The tribe continued to behave well till 1877, when a serious raid was committed on the border villages of the Sudum valley in the month of July. Considerable damage was done, both in burning villages and property and killing several of the peasants. The raiders, however, were so severely punished by the villagers themselves, supported by the British police post, that they retired, with the loss of twenty-one killed, thirty wounded, and fourteen prisoners.

The cause of the raid was traced to Ajab Khan of Chargulai, the chief, who, with his brother Aziz Khan, had done us such good service, as already shown, during the Ambela campaign. Through this chief all matters connected with the Buner frontier had been managed, but, finding that his personal importance had become much lessened in the eyes of the political authorities, in consequence of his intriguing conduct across the border, he determined to create complications which should have the effect of bringing himself to notice, as he fully expected that he would be employed in restoring order, and would acquire credit for so doing. It was with this object that he incited the Bunerwals to send a raiding party against the Sudum villages, but in doing this it is probable that he never intended that more than a demonstration should take place, accompanied with the burning of a few huts and stacks in the outlying hamlet of Baringan. The results which followed, ending in much loss of life and property, could only be viewed as the natural consequences of the incitement given, and Ajab Khan was therefore tried on the criminal charge of abetment of *dakaiti*, accompanied with murder. He was convicted and sentenced to death, and was publicly executed in front of the Peshawar jail on the 27th of June 1878. With regard to the Bunerwals, they were placed under blockade; but, in consideration of the powerful instigation under which they had acted, and also in consequence of the severe punishment they had met with during the raid, the Government was pleased to sanction that no further demand should be made from the tribe beyond requiring the restoration of the property carried off. Towards the end of September, the Nurizai and Daulatzai sections made their submission; but the third section implicated in the outrage, the Ashazai, continued contumacious, and a fine of Rs. 700 was accordingly imposed upon them. At length, in consequence of the military punitive measures adopted on other parts of the border of the Peshawar district at this time, the Ashazais discovered that it was to their interest to submit to the terms ordered by the Government, and accordingly they came in to the Assistant Commissioner of Yusafzai in April 1878, and a final settlement with the Bunerwals was effected. The execution of Ajab Khan is said to have produced a very marked impression on the tribe, who never for a moment expected that a *khan* of such local importance would be hanged as a common malefactor.

During December 1878 and January 1879 the excitement was very great in Buner, owing to the fanatical preaching of certain *mullas*, who were trying to create a *jehad*. At one time it was feared that nothing could prevent a disturbance on our border, and the Gadaizais and Salarzais had actually sent their quota to Tursak for a move by the Malandri pass. The friendly attitude of certain Buner chiefs, however, and the resolute behaviour of the Sudum villagers, prevented a rupture.

In January 1880 reports were received that a raid on Sudum was being organised by one faction of the Bunerwals. Their intention, however, was frustrated by the opposition of their enemies at home, and by the prompt measures taken to reinforce the border by the movement of some native cavalry from Mardan to Rustam.

The action taken by the Nurizai and Daulatzai clans in the Khudu Khel troubles has been noticed above. The proceedings in connection with the decennial *vesh*, or redistribution by lot of holdings among the Ashazai, Salarzai, and Gadaizai clans of the Bunerwals absorbed the attention of the tribe about 1883.

On the 16th May 1884, a party of Salarzai Bunerwals raided and burned the frontier village of Pirsai, carrying off twenty-six Government rifles, thirty-five muskets and some cattle and other property. One villager was killed and another wounded in the affray. Reparation was demanded from the section, but to no purpose. Subsequently the Ashazai and Nurizai sections also committed acts of hostility, raiding the villages of Barock and Surkhabi. In October a blockade of the Salarzai was ordered, which was shortly afterwards extended to the other sections of the Bunerwals. The duties involved by this blockade were performed by the inhabitants of the frontier villages, who were supplied with Government arms for their own defence. They were assisted by a few men of the border militia, and on one or two occasions, when the Bunerwals, who constantly attempted reprisals, became particularly aggressive, they were supported by a detachment of regular troops at Rustam.

The blockade was maintained throughout the year 1885.

Attack on Bunerwals at Surai Malandri by a column under Colonel Broome in January 1887.

In January 1887 a small column, consisting of 10 sabres, 12th Bengal Cavalry, and 450 rifles, Guides Infantry, was sent to attack Surai Malandri, in order to put a stop to the incursions of raiding parties from the Malandri pass. Colonel Broome, 12th Bengal Cavalry, who was in command, marched his troops from Rustam and Mardan on the night of the 7th-8th January, intending to surprise the village at dawn. But about 4 A.M., while the force was halted some three miles beyond Baringan, a raiding party of the enemy suddenly fired a volley from close range, and charged down upon the head of the column. Lieut.-Colonel Hutchinson,[1] Commanding the Guides Infantry, fell mortally wounded, a havildar was killed, and three men were wounded. The Guides speedily dispersed the tribesmen, who disappeared in the darkness. All hopes of a surprise were now at an end, but Colonel Broome pushed

1 Lieut.-Colonel Hutchinson and one sepoy died of their wounds the next day.

on at daylight and cleared the village of Surai Malandri, driving the enemy into the hills with considerable loss. This village was then burned, but the hamlet of Patao Malandri, which lay some two miles beyond, and was also held by considerable numbers of the enemy, was not attacked. The troops now returned to Rustam, which they reached at 2 P.M. on the 8th; the Guides Infantry, who had come from Mardan, having marched thirty-four miles in twenty-one hours. The gathering of the Bunerwals present at this affair was estimated to be between 4,000 and 5,000 strong; and, although the village of Patao was not dealt with, the punishment received by the tribesmen at Surai was sufficient to make a lasting impression on them, and they were careful in future to avoid exposing themselves to our attacks.

The Bunerwal *jirgas*, however, were still recalcitrant, and insolently refused to comply with the demands of the Punjab Government. In the spring the Government of India considered the advisability of despatching an expedition to coerce the tribe; but at that time it was not deemed convenient to undertake military operations in Buner, and accordingly the question was deferred.

Small raids continued, and in August three murders were committed; but the border villagers were on the alert, and with the assistance of the border militia succeeded in inflicting some loss on the enemy. Meanwhile the blockade was maintained as strictly as possible, and finally the Bunerwals decided to submit. A representative *jirga* attended at Mardan, where they surrendered all the arms captured by the Salarzai tribesmen at Pirsai, and paid a fine of Rs. 1,500; all the property captured from the tribesmen during the blockade was also confiscated. A few days later some sixty leading men of the *jirga* proceeded to Peshawar and tendered formal submission to the Commissioner, on behalf of the tribe.

During the Black Mountain Expedition of 1888 there was considerable unrest in Buner, but no actual disturbance resulted. In 1891, while operations were in progress against the Hassanzai and Akazai tribes of the Black Mountain, a number of Bunerwals and men of the neighbouring clans collected at Baio, in the hills above the British camp at Palosi. They dispersed, however, as soon as they were assured that no invasion of their country was intended.

On the advance of the Chitral Relief Force in 1895, the Bunerwals sent a contingent to assist their neighbours in the defence of the passes leading into the Swat valley. They arrived too late, however, to take part in the fighting at the Malakand, and on hearing of the defeat of the Swatis, they returned to their own country. Later in the year some excitement was caused by the Kabuli Mulla Haji Ahmad Ali, who endeavoured to persuade the people of Buner that the British meant to annex their country. The Bunerwals were so far impressed by the *mulla's* harangues that they sent away their women and children, and collected to defend the passes which give access to their territory. Major Deane, however, forwarded a letter explaining that no interference with their country was intended, and the gathering dispersed. In consequence of the doubtful attitude of the Bunerwals, the Reserve Brigade of the Chitral Relief Force had been moved from Rawalpindi to Mardan early in April. No serious trouble, however, was given by the tribe throughout the operations of 1895.

The events which culminated two years later in a sudden outbreak of fanaticism in Swat, and led to a general uprising of most of the Pathan tribes on the North-West Frontier, will be found related in Chapter IX. During that rising the following tribes participated in the attacks on the Malakand and Chakdara garrisons, and in the fight at Landakai in Upper Swat; *viz.*, the Bunerwals, Chamlawals, Gaduns, Khudu Khels, and Amazais. The Government accordingly demanded the complete submission of each of these tribes.

The Gaduns and Khudu Khels, as has already been related, and also the Amazais, at once testified their willingness to submit, but the Bunerwals and Chamlawals made no move to comply with the demands of Government. The Mian Guls, in order to prove the sincerity of their own submission, had volunteered to induce the former tribe to sue for peace; but their efforts met with no success. Accordingly an ultimatum was sent to each of these tribes informing them of the terms imposed, and allowing seven days for compliance. This period of grace expired in the case of the Chamlawals on the 5th January 1898, and in the case of the Bunerwals on the following day. The Chamlawals made no reply; but defiant answers on behalf of the Nasozai and Daulatzai Bunerwals were sent by Hukmat Khan of Dagar and Mubaras Khan of Shalbandai, and reached Mr. Bunbury, the Political Officer on the 3rd January.

Two days later, a representative of the Ashazai section came to Rustam, and stated that this people were willing to submit, and requested an extension of the period of grace for another week in order that they might persuade the rest of the tribe to follow suit. As however there was no reason to suppose that the other sections were inclined to agree, this request was refused.

Meanwhile Major-General Sir Bindon Blood, Commanding the Malakand Field Force, had been engaged in preparations for an advance into Buner, and an expedition into the country at once took place.

Expedition against the Bunerwals and Chamlawals, by a force under Sir B. Blood, in January 1898.

Sir Bindon Blood was placed in command of the Buner Field Force, and was given full political charge, while Mr. Bunbury, I.C.S., Deputy Commissioner of Peshawar, and Lieutenant C. P. Down were appointed Assistant Political Officers. The troops forming the expedition are shown in the margin.

On the 6th January, the disposition of the force was as follows:—At Pirsai, the 31st Punjab Infantry, Guides Infantry and a section of No. 4 Company, Bengal Sappers and Miners. At Rustam, three squadrons, 10th Bengal Lancers, and two squadrons, Guides Cavalry. The Headquarters and the remainder of the Force concentrated at Sanghao. The Base Supply Depôt was at Nowshera and a staging godown, with fifteen days' reserve supplies, was formed at Mardan. Ten days' supplies for the whole force were forwarded to an advance depôt at Sanghao. The first Brigade and the Pirsai

1st Brigade.
(Brigadier-General W. H. Meiklejohn, C.B., C.M.G.).
1st Bn. Royal West Kent Regiment.
16th Bengal Infantry.[1]
20th Punjab Infantry.
31st ,, ,,[2]

2nd Brigade.
(Brigadier-General P. D. Jeffreys, C.B.)
1st Bn. East Kent Regiment (The Buffs).
21st Punjab Infantry.
Guides Infantry.

Divisional Troops.
10th Field Battery, Royal Artillery.
No. 7 Mountain Battery, Royal Artillery.
No. 8 (Bengal) Mountain Battery.
10th Bengal Lancers (1 squadron).
Guides Cavalry.
2nd Battalion, Highland Light Infantry.
3rd Bombay Light Infantry, 6 companies.[3]
No. 4 Company, Bengal Sappers and Miners.[4]
No. 5 ,, Madras ,, ,, ,,[5]

1 Now the 16th Rajputs (The Lucknow Regiment).
2 Now the 31st Punjabis.
3 Now the 103rd Mahratta Light Infantry.
4 Now the 1st P. W. O. Sappers and Miners.
5 Now the 2nd Queen's Own Sappers and Miners.

column were equipped entirely with mule transport, and carried seven and three days' supplies respectively. The second Brigade had five days' supplies and was furnished with camel transport.

The plan of operations was as follows: Sir Bindon Blood, with the troops at Sanghao, intended to force the Tanga pass, about a mile to the northward, while the Pirsai column was to capture the pass of that name. The cavalry from Rustam were then to move over the Pirsai pass, and cut across the enemy's line of retreat from the Tanga.

The various passes leading into Buner had been previously reconnoitred, and the Tanga was selected as affording the most suitable route for the main advance. The ground on the Buner side of the pass was most unfavourable to troops retiring from it before a successful attack, as there was practically no cover whatever in the valley below the pass, or on the spurs of the hills on either side, for a distance from it considerably exceeding distant rifle range. On the 6th January it was ascertained that this pass was held by about a thousand of the enemy, and twenty-seven standards were counted on their position. The Ambela and Mal ndri passes were each guarded by about the same number of tribesmen, but only some forty or fifty men had collected to defend the Pirsai pass.

One Squadron, 10th B. L.
10th Field Battery, R. A.
No. 7. M. Battery, R. A.
No. 8 Bengal M. B.
1st Bn., East Kent Regt. (The Buffs).
3rd Bombay Light Infantry, (5 companies).

During the night a few harmless shots were fired into the camp at Sanghao. At about 8-30 A.M., on the following morning the advanced troops and artillery, under Brigadier-General Jeffreys, moved off in the direction of the Tanga gorge. Half an hour previously, the 20th Punjab Infantry had started to ascend a steep spur further to the east, which led to a high peak overlooking the position. From here they were to deliver an assault on the enemy's right flank and rear, as soon as the frontal attack was sufficiently advanced.

At 9 A.M. the Field Battery came into action on a knoll near the mouth of the gorge leading to the pass, and opened fire at 2,200 yards' range on the *kotal* ridge. This position was now seen to be defended by at least 2,000 tribesmen with some thirty standards. Under cover of the artillery fire the Buffs, after a difficult climb, ascended a parallel spur facing the ridge held by the enemy, and some 250 feet below it. From this position the Buffs fired volleys at an average range of 1,500 yards, and shortly afterwards the two mountain batteries came into action on the same spur. During this bombardment the Sappers and Miners were sent forward to improve the track through the defile.

1st Bn., Rl. West Kent Regt.
2nd Bn., Highland Light Infantry.
16th Bengal Infantry.
21st Punjab "

Meanwhile the remainder of the troops, as per margin, under the command of Brigadier-General Meiklejohn pushed forward through the ravine in front of the Field Battery.

By noon the 20th Punjab Infantry were seen to be nearing their objective, and a few minutes later Brigadier-General Meiklejohn was ordered to commence the frontal attack. The Royal West Kent Regiment and 16th Bengal Infantry, preceded by a detachment of the Bengal Sappers and Miners, moved up the pass by the track. The 21st Punjab Infantry ascended two very difficult spurs on their left, while the Highland Light Infantry climbed another spur still further to the left. As the assaulting troops made their way up the steep slopes, the enemy opened fire with matchlocks and a few rifles, and tried to check the advance by rolling rocks down the hillsides. But they were demoralized by the artillery fire and the long range volleys of the supporting infantry, which forced them to keep under shelter. About 1-30 P.M., the 20th Punjab Infantry, led by Lieut.-Colonel Woon, captured the peak above the enemy's right flank, driving the defenders back with a loss of two standards and some fifteen killed. Half an hour later General Meiklejohn's battalions crowned the *kotal* ridge within a few minutes of each other. Before this, however, the tribesmen, finding that they could not repel the frontal attack without exposing themselves to a murderous fire from the artillery and infantry on the opposite ridge, and being pressed by Lieut.-Colonel Woon's battalion on their right, had begun to abandon their position. Without waiting for the troops to close with them, they fled in haste down the valley towards Kingargali and the hills beyond, suffering some loss during their flight from the rifle fire of the infantry, who had reached the summit of the pass.

Brigadier-General Meiklejohn now pushed on to Kingargali with the three battalions of the 1st Brigade, and bivouacked there for the night. This village was found to be deserted, the enemy having sought refuge in the hills to the north. The 16th Bengal Infantry and the Sappers, who were at work on the road till dark, spent the night on the top of the pass. The remainder of the troops returned to Sanghao. The track over the pass proved impracticable for animal transport, but a few mules were brought over, and the greatcoats and blankets of the troops at Kingargali and on the ridge were conveyed to them by 500 coolies, who had been collected at Sanghao to meet this contingency.

The only casualty on our side during this action was one man of the Highland Light Infantry mortally wounded.

The enemy, who numbered about 2,000, were composed of Salarzai and Asharzai and men from the villages of Sultanwas, Kalakhela, Bai, and Ghazi Khan. Considerable reinforcements were on their way to help the defenders of the Tanga pass, but they retired without taking any part in the action. The enemy's loss was estimated at about fifty killed.

While the operations above described were in progress, the marginally named troops from Pirsai and Rustam, under the command of Lieut.-Colonel Adams, had entered Buner by the Pirsai pass. Early on the morning of the 7th, the infantry under Lieut.-Colonel McRae captured the pass without loss, meeting with but slight resistance from a party of Salarzai tribesmen of Kuhai and Chorbanda. The enemy were completely taken by surprise, and were unable to collect reinforcements from the other passes in time to offer any serious opposition. At 11 A.M., the cavalry began to cross the pass, which proved exceedingly difficult, owing to the extreme roughness of the track, now rendered slippery and dangerous by ice and hoarfrost. Leading their horses in single file, the troopers eventually overcame all obstacles, and Lieut.-Colonel Adams pushed on up the narrow valley between the Sukara and Ali Sher spurs. Meeting with no opposition, he reconnoitred the country as far as Kuhai, and then returned to Chorbanda, two miles north of the Pirsai pass, where the column bivouacked for the night. The troops were without baggage, as the

Guides Cavalry (two Squadrons).
10th B. L. (three Squadrons).
31st Punjab Infantry.
Guides Infantry.
No. 4 Company, Bengal Sappers and Miners (one section).

transport animals could not cross the pass; indeed it was not until after three days' very hard work that all of them were brought over. On the 8th the cavalry pushed on to Tursak, where a hostile gathering was seen on the neighbouring hills; and having reconnoitred the country to the south-east proceeded to Kingargali. On the 10th the infantry marched from Chorbanda to Bampokha, where they joined Brigadier-General Meiklejohn's force.

Commenting on the operations of this column Sir Bindon Blood remarked in his despatch—

The movement thus successfully carried out by Lieut.-Colonel Adams, V.C., was of very great value, as the sudden appearance of five squadrons and two battalions in the middle of the Buner country, in addition to the brigade which came over the Tanga pass, helped most effectually to prevent the enemy from being encouraged to make fresh resistance, as they might otherwise have been, in consequence of the delay which necessarily took place before I could bring enough supplies over the pass to enable me to advance.

On the 9th the *jirgas* of the Salarzai and Asharzai sections came in to Kingargali, and tendered their submission.

Although, as a general rule, it is desirable to deal with a tribe as a whole collectively, and not with its various sections separately, yet in the present instance it was deemed advisable to depart from this rule, since it was of the greatest importance that, as the troops marched eastwards through Buner, no section should be left in rear that had not made complete submission. It was, moreover, found that the expression Buner was merely a geographical, and not an ethnographical, term, and that the distinction, not merely between the main clans of Iliaszai and Malizai,[1] but also between the various sections comprised in each clan, was plainly marked. Accordingly the Salarzai and Ashazai sections were informed that payment of ther sectional shares of the Government demands would be accepted from them, while the force was in their limits; and that troops would visit the territory of each section in Buner, and would live free while in the country, but that no damage would be done to their villages, provided the tribesmen were not guilty of hostile behaviour or misconduct. This same announcement was made to the other sections as the force advanced.

1 It should be noted that the Malizai of valley, though both are divisions of the Buner and Chamla are distinct from the Yusafzai. Khwazazai Malizai of Dir and the Panjkora

The threat to destroy their property had an excellent effect, and not a single shot was fired into camps at night while our troops were in Buner. The force remained at Kingargali till the 10th January, while a mule road was being constructed over the Tanga pass by the Sappers and Miners. As there was no prospect that this route could be made practicable for camel transport, Brigadier-General Jeffreys received orders on the 9th to march with a portion of the 2nd Brigade and the 10th Field Battery from Sanghao to Katlang, whence he was to proceed by easy stages to the Ambela pass.

Two squadrons, Guides.
No. 7. M. Battery, R. A.
Section, Bengal S. and M.
Highland Light Infantry.
20th Punjab Infantry.

On the 10th Brigadier-General Meiklejohn marched with the small column shown in the margin to Jawar in the Bazargai valley. On the next day Sir Bindon Blood and the Head-quarters staff, with No. 8 Bengal Mountain Battery and a half company of Bengal Sappers and Miners, arrived at Kingargali.

Owing to a report that the enemy were collecting near Tursak to oppose him, Sir Bindon Blood now ordered Brigadier-General Jeffreys to hasten his march to the Ambela pass, and to make a demonstration there. The Bunerwals, however, abandoned their intention of offering further resistance, and on the 12th January the 10th Bengal Lancers and Guides Infantry were sent to join the 2nd Brigade,[1] as they were no longer required for operations within Buner limits.

On the same date Sir Bindon Blood, leaving a wing of the West Kent Regiment to hold Kingargali, marched to Tursak, where he was joined by General Meiklejohn's column from Jawar.

No. 8 Bengal Mountain Battery.
Half Battalion, H. L. I.
Half Battalion, West Kent Regiment.
Half Battalion, 20th Punjab Infantry.
Half Battalion, 31st Punjab Infantry.
Half No. 4 Company, Bengal Sappers and Miners.

On the 13th the marginally-named troops, under Brigadier-General Meiklejohn, proceeded to Bai in the Gadaizai valley, about two miles from the tomb of the famous saint, Pir Baba, which was visited by the Mussulman soldiers. The other half battalion of the West Kent marched to Tursak on this day, escorting a supply column from Kingargali, and the latter post was evacuated. The 1st Brigade being now provisioned

[1] Three sections of No. 5 Company, Madras Sappers and Miners had been sent from the Tanga pass on the previous day to join this Brigade.

up to the 24th January, the line of communications *viâ* Sanghao and the Tanga pass was abandoned.[1]

On the 14th Brigadier Meiklejohn's column marched from Bai to Hildai, and next day moved to Rega, where the troops destroyed the house belonging to the Mad Fakir, and demolished two towers in order to punish the *maliks* who had given him shelter there after his retreat from Swat. On this date Sir Bindon Blood, with the remainder of the force, visited Dagar in Nasozai territory, where that section and the Daulatzai paid in their fines. The Asharzai, Salarzai, and Gadaizai had made their settlement in full on the previous day at Tursak, and Hukmat Khan of Dagar with other leading men had also come in to tender their submission.

On the 16th the troops under Brigadier-General Meiklejohn marched to Barkeli, where they were joined by the Head-quarters staff. The Nurizai section were settled with at this place, and on the following day, this portion of the Brigade crossed the Buner pass to Ambela village in the Chamla valley. The other column, now under the command of Lieut.-Colonel Adams, marched to Bajkatta on the 16th. The troops halted here for two days, in order to obtain the surrender of certain rifles still due from the tribesmen. Some of these had been taken by Mubarak Khan, ex-chief of Dagar, who had fled to the Chagarzai hills. A cash deposit of a thousand rupees and one hostage were accordingly accepted as security for the missing rifles, and all outstanding cases were satisfactorily settled. On the 18th the last of the troops left Buner territory, and marched to Ambela.

Operations of the 2nd Brigade against the Chamlawals.

To return now to the movements of the 2nd Brigade. On the 11th January Brigadier-General Jeffreys reached Rustam. Leaving the 10th Field Battery and two companies of the Buffs at this place, he proceeded on the following day to Surkhabi, at the foot of the hills below the Ambela pass. The construction of a road fit for camel transport was at once begun. Some slight resistance was offered by a party of tribesmen on the pass, who were driven off with

[1] The advanced depôt was transferred to Rustam, where 5 days' supplies were forwarded, and the staging godown at Katlang was moved to Kulakhet. The 16th Bengal Infantry and 5 companies, Bombay Light Infantry, came on to the new line of communication.

a loss of five men killed and wounded. The road was completed by the evening of the 16th, and on the following day the 2nd Brigade crossed the pass, and occupied the villages of Koga and Nawagai, while the cavalry reconnoitred the Chamla valley.

On the 18th the Chamlawals complied in full with the terms imposed, paying a money fine of rupees 1,500, and surrendering a number of arms and the standards of Koga and Nawagai.

The complete submission of the Bunerwals and Chamlawals having thus been obtained, Sir Bindon Blood re-crossed the Ambela pass with the whole of his force, and reached Mardan on the 20th of January. Three days later he relinquished the command of the Buner Field Force, which was then broken up.

Since the expedition described above the tribes dealt with in this chapter have given little or no trouble to Government.

APPENDIX A.

Commands and Staff of the Buner Field Force.

Major-General Commanding ..	Major-General Sir B. Blood, K.C.B.
Assistant Adjutant General ..	Major H. H. Burney, Gordon Highlanders.
Assistant Quarter Master General ..	Lieut.-Colonel A. Masters, Central India Horse.
Deputy Assistant Quarter Master General (Intelligence).	Captain H. E. Stanton, D.S.O., Royal Artillery.
Commanding Royal Engineers ..	Lieut.-Colonel W. Peacocke, C.M.G., R.E.
Superintendent of Army Signalling ..	Captain E. V. O. Hewett, Royal West Kent Regiment.
Chief Commissariat Officer ..	Major H. Wharry, Assistant Commissary-General.
Divisional Transport Officer ..	Captain C. G. R. Thackwell, Assistant Commissary-General.
Principal Medical Officer ..	Surgeon-Colonel S. C. G. Carmichael, I.M.S.
Senior Veterinary Officer ..	Veterinary Captain H. T. W. Mann.
Commanding Royal Artillery ..	Colonel W. Aitken, C.B., R.A.
Commandant, Line of Communications.	Colonel V. A. Schalch, 11th Bengal Infantry.
Deputy Assistant Adjutant General, Line of Communications.	Brevet-Major L. Herbert, Central India Horse.
Base Commandant	Colonel Bingham, 13th Bengal Infantry.

1st Brigade.

Commanding	Brig.-Gen. W. H. Meiklejohn, C.B., C.M.G.
Deputy Assistant Adjutant General	Major E. A. P. Hobday, R.A.
Deputy Assistant Quarter Master General.	Captain C. F. H. Dillon, 40th Bengal Infantry.

2nd Brigade.

Commanding	Brigadier-General P. D. Jeffreys, C.B.
Deputy Assistant Adjutant General..	Captain A. B. Dunsterville, East Surrey Regiment.
Deputy Assistant Quarter Master General.	Major C. H. Powell, 21st Gurkha Rifles.

CHAPTER VIII.

SWAT TRIBES.

THE district of Swat proper[1] comprises the valley of the river of that name, from its junction with the Panjkora river northwards to the village of Ain. Above this village the country is known by the general term of Swat Kohistan. The upper portion of the valley from Ain to the Landakai spur, five miles above Chakdara, is known as Bar (upper) Swat, while Kuz (lower) Swat comprises the country from Landakai downwards to the village of Kalangai. The average width of the valley, a length of some seventy miles, is about twelve miles from crest to crest of its watersheds, and comprises a continuous series of tracts of rich alluvial lands of varying extent along the river banks. The river is fed by glaciers and snow, and during the summer months swells to considerable size. During the winter it shrinks considerably, and in mid-winter is fordable almost anywhere. It begins to rise about the middle of April and soon becomes unfordable, commencing to fall again in the middle of September. There are no other rivers of importance in the district, and the only canals are those for irrigation purposes.

The climate of Swat, though differing from that of the Yusafzai plain, is described as resembling that of Buner in most points. The hot weather sets in later than in the plains, but it is more oppressive and continuous, owing to the surrounding mountains preventing the free circulation of the winds. The frequent storms that burst over these hills do not cool the air, but, on the contrary, produce a hot, steamy atmosphere in the valleys below. The district is unhealthy in summer, for, owing to the extensive surface under cultivation of rice, malaria is exhaled in great abundance. This circumstance has given the country an unenviable notoriety

[1] In addition to what is here called Swat proper, there are tracts of country to the south of the Malakand and Morah mountains, and between them and the British border, which are dependent on Swat, and inhabited by the same tribes, and of which more will be said hereafter.

for its peculiar and obstinate fevers, which affect all ages alike. The malaria, it appears, is of universal distribution throughout the valley, and very poisonous in its effects. It has impressed its mark on the people, who, in their general physical condition, are more or less fever-stricken and unhealthy. In Swat, shut in as it is by lofty snow-clad mountains, the winter is a milder season than in the open plain; for the air is less disturbed by winds, and the frosts are also less severe. Snow does not always fall at the lower levels. At intervals of three or four years the valley everywhere receives a coating of snow; but it seldom remains longer than a week or ten days.

There are no camels to be found in Swat; but there are horses, mules, asses, bullocks, oxen, cows, and buffaloes; oxen, mules, and asses are the beasts of burden.

The total population of the valley is estimated at about 96,000. The bulk of the people are husbandmen, who live on the produce of their cattle and fields, and whose domestic wants are supplied by a minority of merchants, petty traders, mechanics, and artisans.

The Pathan tribes generally have a great respect for the last resting-places of their own dead, but the inhabitants of Swat seem to feel little compunction or respect on this head. The strip of land lying between the villages and the rise of the mountains is set apart for the cultivation of wheat and barley, and in that land their burying-grounds are also situated. After a few years they allow these fields to lie fallow for some time, plough up all the burying grounds, and bury the dead in the fallow land. This may be consequent on the small quantity of land available for purposes of agriculture, but it nevertheless appears a very unwholesome custom.

In character the people appear to differ but little from other Pathans. They possess all the vices common to that race, and are not behind them in pride, cupidity, revengefulness, or treachery. In the last-named vice, indeed, they may indisputably be given the first place among Pathan tribes. They do not compare unfavourably with others of their race in manliness, bravery, or hospitality. It was the custom until recent times to disparage their martial instincts, but the events of 1895 and 1897 have taught us that in this respect they have been curiously misjudged. In religion they are all Sunni Muhammadans. They are by no means individually fanatical, but owing to an innate spirit of discipline, which they have in a marked degree, their leaders are able to rouse a spirit of collective fanaticism which is a remarkable trait in their character.

The language of the country is Pushtu, except in Swat Kohistan, where Torwali and Garhwi are spoken.

The houses of Swat generally consist of walls built of mud; on the top of these are a few rafters with dry grass spread over them, and over this a layer of plaster is laid, of the same materials as the walls.

The Swat valley is highly cultivated and densely populated throughout its extent along the course of the river, whilst each glen and gorge has its hamlets or collections of shepherd's huts. The general surface of the ground is rough and stony, and there is a considerable slope from the foot of the hills to the bed of the river. Owing to this, the fields are laid out in strips or terraces, one above the other, the boundary walls being formed of the stones collected from the surface. By this arrangement the soil is cleared of stones, and made level to retain the water led on to it for irrigation. The chief crops are rice, wheat, barley, lucerne, peas, and beans; but sugarcane, Indian corn, cotton, and tobacco are also cultivated. The spring crop of *khasil*, affording excellent fodder for animals, is procurable from March to June, by the end of which month there is abundant grass, provided there is labour to cut and bring it in; no grass is stored by the inhabitants. The villages of Thana and Mingaora are the most important trading centres.

There are few or no trees in the lower parts of the valley, save in the smaller glens running at right angles to it, but on the mountains, on either side of the valley, trees are numerous. On the southern range are pines principally, while on the northern are magnificent forests of deodar.

The exports from Swat to British territory are, rice in large quantities, fruits, honey, glue, and timber; and the imports are salt, cotton goods, indigo, spices, sugar. The people of Swat are quite independent of British territory for the necessaries of life, but they dread a blockade, on account of the loss their trade would suffer.

The best road from the south to Swat is over the Malakand pass; and the next best is by the Shakot pass, which is shorter than the Malakand route, but the ascent is steeper. There is also another by the Morah pass, which is still more difficult.

In the valley there are roads, tolerably well defined, leading from village to village on both sides of the river, which, during the cold season, is fordable almost everywhere, and during the hot weather is crossed by the natives on rafts of inflated skins. During the latter season they can flood the whole valley, which is thereby splendidly irrigated, and is a luxuriant sheet of rice culivation; but owing to the noxious exhalations caused thereby, making the country extremely unhealthy, the cold weather is the best season for military operations.

The valley of Swat is divided into five districts, *viz.*—

1. Baizai. 3. Khadakzai.
2. Ranizai. 4. Abazai.
5. Khwazazai.

Of these, Baizai and Ranizai are situated to the south, and Khadakzai, Abazai, and Khwazazai to the north, of the river Swat.

The inhabitants of Swat are the Akozais, a division of the powerful tribe of Yusafzai Pathans, of which the Bunerwals, Black Mountain tribes, etc., described in previous chapters, are also branches (see Appendix A, Chapter V). The five districts above mentioned receive their names from the five clans of the Akozais by which they are held. Of these the two clans, the Khadakzais and Abazais, are far inferior, both in power and extent of territory, to the other clans.

The Baizais.

The Baizais inhabit the country on the left bank of the Swat river, from the borders of Kohistan as far as, and including, Thana. The different sections of the clan are as follows, beginning from the lower end :—

		Population.	Fighting men.
Kuz Sulizai ..	1. Khan Khel	11,800	3,000
	2. Musa Khel	5,500	1,500
	3. Aba Khel	8,000	2,000
Babuza. ..	4. Barat Khel	4,000	1,000
	5. Aba Khel	5,000	1,200
	6. Akamaruf	5,000	1,500
	7. Bami Khel	3,000	800

		Population.	Fighting men.
Bar Sulizai ..	8. Maturizai	4,500	1,300
	9. Azzi Khel	3,500	900
	10. Jinki Khel	4,000	1,200
		54,300	14,400

In addition to the above there are, beyond the limits of the Swat valley, in the Ghurban, Kana, Puran, and Chakesar valleys, the drainage of which finds its way into the Indus, the following :—

	Population.	Fighting men.
Babuzai	2,500	750
Azzi Khel	4,000	1,200
Jinki Khel	11,500	3,000
	18,000	4,950

Making the total for the tribe in rough numbers, population 72,000. Fighting men 19,400.

The principal villages in Baizai are :—

	Section.
Thana	Khan Khel.
Abuwa	Musa Khel.
Barikot	Aba Khel.
Ghalegai	Aba Khel.
Mingaora	Akamaruf.
Manglaor	Bami Khel.
Charbagh	Maturizai.

Like the rest of the Swat valley the portion occupied by the Baizai consists of a belt of irrigated ground on the river bank which is chiefly devoted to the cultivation of rice. This portion is much cut up by irrigation channels and is always difficult and at times impossible for the movement of troops. Above this is the *barani* or *lalmi* ground, which produces wheat and barley. In the lateral valleys are hamlets and *bandas* occupied by tenants and servants belonging to the villages below, while in the hills are numerous Gujar villages with herds of cattle and buffaloes.

In addition to the Baizai above described are the Sam Baizai, who occupy the land from our border to the foot of the hills below the Morah pass. The villages in this territory formerly belonged to the Baizai *maliks,* and were occupied by their tenants and servants. These, however, have now become independent—and among them will be found many Utman Khels, Khattaks, etc., who assisted them to obtain their independence.

The Ranizais.

The Ranizai tribe occupy the left bank of the Swat river, from the district of the Khan Khels (the lowest section of Baizais) at Thana, to the Utman Khel boundary, which is about three miles above the junction of the Swat with the Panjkora. To the north their territory extends to the river, and includes the islands between the different channels. The southern boundary is formed by the watershed of the hills on that side. The importance of the tribe lies a great deal in the fact that the Malakand and Shakot passes are in their territory. The Digar pass, which is further to the west also leads into the Ranizai country, but the pass itself is partly in the hands of the Utman Khels.

Formerly the whole of the country from the hills to the British border, which is now held by the Sam Ranizais, belonged to the Ranizai tribe, as the people known as Sam Ranizais, though now independent, were originally servants and tenants of the various Ranizai sections. The sections of the Sam Ranizais still correspond in name with those of the Ranizai tribe.

The Ranizais consist of the following sections :—

	Population.	*Fighting men.*
1. Ali Khel	3,000	800
2. Utmanzai	2,500	700
3. Bahram Kha Khel	3,500	800
4. Usmani Khel	2,000	600
5. Sultan Kha Khel	2,500	700
	13,500	3,600

The principal Ranizai villages are Aladand, (at the mouth of the Shakot pass) whose *Khan* is the most important man in the tribe, Butkhela, Dheri, and Totekhan.

The Khwazazai, the last of the three powerful clans into which Swat is divided, occupy the valley on the right bank of the river from Kohistan to Chakdara.

The Khwazazais.

The following are the different sections of the clan:—

	Population.	*Fighting men.*
Shamizai	16,000	3,750
Sebujni	8,000	1,750
Nikbi Khel	11,000	2,750
Shamozai	6,000	1,500
Adinzai[1]	7,000	1,750
	48,000	11,500

Chakdara, an Adinzai village, is important as being the crossing place of the river on the main route to Chitral and Bajaur. The river here runs in six channels, covering about three quarters of a mile of ground. The village is on a bank 60 feet high and some 600 yards from the nearest branch of the river, the intervening ground being irrigated. An iron girder bridge crosses the river three-quarters of a mile below the village, and a fort, garrisoned by regular troops, forms a bridge head on the right bank. To the north of Chakdara is an open cultivated plain extending seven and a half miles to Kotigram. There is a good camping-ground to the north of the village but after the month of May it is surrounded with irrigation.

The Abazais[1] occupy a small valley on the right bank of the Swat river below the Adinzais, and are said to number about 250 fighting men.

The Abazais and Khadakzais.

The Khadakzais,[1] also on the right bank, extend from the Abazais to the country occupied by the Dusha Khel. Hemmed in as it is by rocky spurs, all the paths out of this district are difficult. The principal village is Barangola. The Khadakzais are said to number about 500 fighting men.

In addition to the above-mentioned tribes must be mentioned the Dusha Khel, a division of the Sheikh Khel, Ausa Khel, Malinzai, Yusafzai, whose territory lying south of the Talash valley and east of the

Dusha Khels.

[1] This section has been handed over to the Khan of Dir.

Panjkora, runs down in a narrow wedge between that river and the Khadakzai country to the banks of the Swat. Probably owing to the mountainous nature of their district these people seem to be more independent than their neighbours, and bear an evil reputation as marauders and thieves. Communications in Dush Khel are nothing but mere mountain tracks. The district has now been made over to the Khan of Dir.

The government of Swat is, like that of all Pathan tribes, a most complete democracy. The country is split up into almost as many factions as there are villages. Each sub-division of each section of each clan has its separate quarrels and supports its own chief, who is generally at mortal feud with either his own relations or his neighbours, and who is seldom obeyed one instant longer than is convenient; so that nothing short of pressing danger to the whole community from without could ever bring together all the divisions into which Swat is divided. But that which could not be effected by ordinary means, has, in a measure, been brought about by the influence of one individual working on the religious feelings of a mass of grossly ignorant and proportionally bigoted people, such as the inhabitants of Swat are; this man was the late Akhund of Swat.

The *Akhund* exerted such a powerful influence, as already seen in the Ambela expedition, not only over the district of Swat, but over the whole of the Yusafzai border, that an account of him somewhat in detail will not be out of place. His original name was Abdul Ghafur, and he was born about the year 1794 at Jabrai, a small shepherds' hamlet in Bar Swat. His parents, of whom nothing certain seems to be known, were poor and obscure people. His boyhood was passed tending his father's cattle, but it is related of him, even at that early age, that he was remarkable amongst his neighbours as a sober, thoughtful lad, with a decided predilection for a life of religious seclusion. As a shepherd-boy, it is related of him that he refused to drink of the milk of any of the cows of his herd save his own, which he led daily to pasture by a halter to prevent its trespassing on the crops of others, and thereby rendering its milk unlawful. In his later life it is said that he ordered his goats to be muzzled when driven out to graze, lest they should take a sly nibble at a neighbour's crop in passing.

The late Akhund of Swat.

At the age of eighteen he proceeded to Barangola, where he first learnt to read and write, and became acquainted with the first rudiments of his religion.

Thence, after a time, he set out as a *talib-ul-ilm* or "enquirer after wisdom," and arrived at Gujar Garhi, a village about three miles from Mardan. Here he took up his abode in the mosque of one Abdul Hakim Akhundzada, and, after a few months' stay, again set out on his travels. At Tordhair he became the disciple of one Sahibzada Muhammad Shwaib, who was held in high repute for sanctity in those parts. His tutor was a *fakir* of the Kadiriya order, to which most of the Sunni *maulvis* on the North-West Frontier belong, and the *Akhund* there resolved to exchange the mosque for the hermitage, and to become a recluse of the same order as his master.

He accordingly, about the year 1816, retired to a lonely spot on the bank of the Indus, below the small village of Beka (some four miles east of Tordhair), where he led a life of austerity, religious seclusion, and meditation, according to the rules of his order, for twelve years. His diet during the whole of this time is said to have been confined to *shamakha*—a very inferior species of millet, which grows in rice-fields, and is only eaten by the very lowest classes—and water. This grain is said to have been his chief food for many years after he left Beka, but the water was replaced by buffalo's milk, and more lately by strong tea, in which he indulged freely, with the view to keeping himself awake at night, so that he might duly perform his religious exercises. His first fame as a saint dates from his sojourn at Beka, for there the people of the surrounding country first flocked to his cell to solicit from him a blessing or an intercessory prayer, and therefore it is that he is now known, even in the most distant parts of Persia, as "the Hermit of Beka," and that some persons erroneously regard it as the place of his birth.

Owing, however, to his unwise interference in the quarrel between Khadi Khan of Hund and Saiyid Ahmad, which has already been referred to,[1] he was forced to abandon his retreat at Beka. For some years he wandered about the country unknown and uncared for, but at length settled down in a *ziarat*

[1] See page 210.

at Ghulaman, a village of British Yusafzai, where he soon recovered his former name for sanctity and piety, and was resorted to by crowds of eager worshippers.

Thence, in time, he, at the invitation of the inhabitants of Salim Khan,[1] removed to their village, and, being regarded by the people at large as a saint (*wali*), had the title of *Akhund* conferred on him by the learned Moslem doctors of the day.

Meanwhile, his fame had reached the ears of Dost Muhammad Khan, the Amir of Kabul, who, in the year 1835, invited him to join his camp at Shekhan (near the present fort of Bara, in the Peshawar district), and bring with him a body of fanatical religious disciples to attack the Sikh camp. This the *Akhund* promptly did, and his small army of champions had one or two smart encounters, in conjunction with other *ghazis* in the Amir's army, with the Sikh troops. But the arrival of the Maharaja Ranjit Sing to command the Sikh force in person soon changed the aspect of affairs, and the Amir, finding himself surrounded, retreated precipitately on the 11th May 1835, through the Khaibar, the *ghazis* in his force being the foremost to plunder the bazaar of his army.

The *Akhund* fled panic-stricken to Bajaur, with a few followers, who also, in a short time, deserted him. He, therefore, once again resumed his former ascetic and secluded life, and after a while, settled down in the village of Kaldara, in the Utmanzai canton of lowland Ranizai.

After a few years' residence there, he removed to the village of Saidu Mandz, in the Babuzai canton of the Baizai district of Swat, where he resided till his death, that is, for a period of over thirty years.

During his residence in Saidu, the *Akhund* married a woman of the Akhund Khel of the neighbouring village of Salampur, by whom he had issue two sons—Abdul Manan, *alias* Mian Gul, and Abdul Khalik—and one daughter.

The *Akhund* was consulted in all difficulties, but frequently (though in his later years such cases became more rare), after his opinion had been given, a chance of procuring plunder proved too powerful for religious reverence, and led the chiefs to follow the bent of their inclinations, though opposed to his expressed

[1] In the south-east of British Yusafzai, and on the frontier of the Khudu Khel tribe.

command. The following are instances of this sort :—When the inhabitants of Babuzai and Palai in 1847 drove Major Lawrence, in charge of the Peshawar valley, to destroy those villages, the *Akhund* strongly advised the people of Swat not to support the rebels ; nevertheless, they flocked to Palai in great numbers. Again, in 1849, the *Akhund* exerted his utmost influence to persuade the headmen of Palai to discontinue their depredations, and to discharge the gangs of professional highwaymen then in their pay ; this counsel being disregarded, they brought on themselves the punishment inflicted by Lieut.-Colonel Bradshaw, which will shortly be narrated.

The *Akhund* gained such an ascendency over the minds of Muhammadans in general, that they believed all kinds of stories about him ; for instance, that he was supplied by supernatural means with the necessaries of life, and that every morning, on rising from his prayers, a sum of money sufficient for the day's expenditure was found under the praying carpet. He was in the habit of keeping open house for the pilgrims who thronged to consult him, and had never been known to receive a present since his arrival in Swat.

Up to the year 1895, the only Swatis with whom the British had any direct dealings were the Baizais and Ranizais who inhabited the country south of the Morah mountains.

The first time we came into contact with these people was the occasion mentioned above, in 1847. In October of that year, Major George St. P. Lawrence, who was then holding the Peshawar valley for the Sikhs, was fired on from the village of Babuzai, when reconnoitring with Lieutenant H. B. Lumsden, of the Guides ; and as the *maliks* would not come in to tender their allegiance, Major Lawrence determined to attack the village. Babuzai contained about two hundred houses, and was situated in a deep *cul-de-sac*, formed by two short, steep, and rugged spurs from the lofty ridge of hills which divides Lundkhwar from Sudum. The village was situated at the further extremity of this *cul-de-sac*, which was about 500 yards long and 300 yards broad. A direct attack was therefore unadvisable ; indeed, the village had the previous year successfully repulsed a superior force under Sirdar Sher Singh.

Operations by Major Lawrence in 1847.

Major Lawrence's force consisted of a brigade, composed of cavalry and infantry, with six guns, Horse Artillery, of the troops of the Sikh Durbar, aided by the newly-raised Corps of Guides. A reconnaissance, made by a duffadar of the Guides, showed that the heights above the village could be occupied, and it was therefore determined to turn the position from this direction. Mir Baba,[1] the chief of Sudum (whom Major Lawrence had released from captivity in the fort of Attock), had tendered his services, which were accepted on account of his expressing great anxiety for an opportunity of evincing his gratitude.

On the 10th October Major Lawrence detached a small party (one native officer and thirty bayonets of the Guides), with orders to join Mir Baba's men in the Sudum valley, under pretence of collecting cattle, the property of the enemy, and from thence to ascend the range during the night, so as to gain the heights in time to co-operate with the main attack at daybreak. This party, as soon as they saw the main column in position, was to descend the spurs and clear the village of its defenders.

Major Lawrence struck his camp on the night of the 10th, and, after placing his baggage in a convenient and defensible position under a suitable escort, moved with the main body over an open country along the base of the hills. At 6 A.M. the troops advanced to the attack, covered by skirmishers from each of the regiments under Lieutenant Lumsden, the infantry in two divisions, with the cavalry in reserve—the infantry under Colonels Mehtab Singh and John Holmes, and the cavalry under Khan Singh Rosa. A detachment was sent to the left to cut off any assistance from the neighbouring villages.

The action commenced by the enemy opening a sharp fire from the right on the skirmishers, when the guns opened without much effect. The skirmishers were then ordered to occupy the spurs on each side of the defile. In trying to effect this, the left column was driven back; but the head of the rear attack being now seen descending on the village, a general assault was ordered, and the village was soon carried,—the Sikhs, under Lieutenant Lumsden, ascending and clearing the heights, and the Guides pursuing the discomfited foe.

[1] This chief was the father of Ajab Khan of Chargulai, whose ignominous end was related in the previous chapter.

The village had been deserted, the enemy having previously removed their families and property; and as there was no other means of punishing the villagers of Babuzai, and of deterring others, Major Lawrence was reluctantly compelled to order it to be fired.

The Guide Corps in this, their first skirmish, did good service, and Major Lawrence advocated their being armed with rifles.

The casualties on our side had been only one killed and thirteen wounded.

In this affair it appears that the village of Babuzai was assisted by the men of Palai, in Sam Baizai, and accordingly, on the 14th, the force under Major Lawrence proceeded to that village. The Guides, under Lieutenant Lumsden, crowned the heights on the left, while the Sikhs occupied those on the right, and a detachment of the Guide Cavalry, making a successful charge along the valley, cut up several of the enemy with the loss to themselves of only two horses wounded. Having destroyed the village, the force then retired. A few days after this, ten villages made their submission, several of which had never before tendered allegiance to the Durani rulers or to the Sikhs.

Expedition against certain refractory villages in Sam Baizai by a force under Lieut.-Colonel J. Bradshaw, C.B., in December 1849.

After the annexation of the Peshawar district in 1849, the inhabitants of Swat uniformly proved themselves bad neighbours to the British. They seemed to regard the plains of Peshawar, especially Hashtnagar, as a hunter does his hunting grounds. Plunderers and marauders, sometimes on foot, and sometimes mounted, issued from Swat, passed through Ranizai, and proceeded to the plains of Hashtnagar and Yusafzai. They would not usually make regular raids, and they would refrain from molesting Pathans, their fellow clansmen; but they would attack persons of all other classes—cultivators, petty traders, cattle-graziers, wayfarers, and the like. They would carry off Hindus in particular, for the purpose of putting them to ransom. Again, the inhabitants of Swat harboured renegades, refugee criminals, internal malcontents, and external enemies, the names of whom are too numerous to mention. For years the valley was a rendezvous for any and every person hostile to the British Government; and among them were several persons who had been dismissed from the British service, and one man in particular, named Mukaram Khan, who had been dismissed from the Peshawar Police, was received with great favour, and enjoyed a large landed grant in Swat. Not only did Swat receive and support enemies of the British, but encouraged them to commit depredations in British territory. Further, the people of Swat took every opportunity of inciting British villages to set authority at nought. They invited their fellow Pathans to throw off the British yoke and acknowledge a nominal allegiance to Swat. For this purpose they would not only assemble troops in Ranizai or Baizai, but they would even send horsemen into British villages, partly as emissaries, and partly as representatives of authority.

In October 1849 it was reported by Lieutenant H. B. Lumsden, Assistant Commissioner of Yusafzai, that the whole of the Utman Khel villages of Sam Baizai had positively refused to pay revenue; that they had warned the native revenue collector against sending any Government servants into the country; and that the people were all busy preparing for war. In reporting this matter to Government, and urging the despatch of a military force, Lieut.-Colonel G. St. P. Lawrence, the Deputy Commissioner of Peshawar, said the Sikhs were in the habit of sending yearly from 1,200 to 1,500 men, with some guns, to collect the revenue in Yusafzai, which, though it harassed the country, had a salutary effect; and as no troops of ours had up to that time been seen beyond the cantonment of Peshawar, an impression had got abroad among the ignorant hill tribes throughout the frontier that we had either no force or were afraid to approach their fastnesses.

In sanctioning the employment of such a force, the Governor-General recorded that in "all ordinary cases the employment of British troops for the mere collection of revenue is a measure to be avoided. But the refusal of the villages in Lundkhwar to pay the little revenue demanded of them is not merely a denial of the revenue which they owe, but is, in fact, a test and trial of the British power, and of the authority which is to be exercised over them. It is, therefore, quite indispensable that the demands of the Government shall be fully enforced, and a conspicuous example made of these men, the first in this newly-conquered province who have dared to resist the orders of the British officers." It was further ordered that if resistance should be attempted, it was to be put down severely, but without any unnecessary harshness; but, under any circumstances, the headmen of the villages were to be brought prisoners to Peshawar, there to await the pleasure of the Government. It was added, that if any foreigners should aid these villages in force, they were of course to be dealt with like any other enemy, and punished with a severity proportioned to the unjustifiable and predatory nature of the attack they might make.

Immediately after Lieut.-Colonel Lawrence had sent in his report, two forays on British territory were made by horsemen from the village of Palai.

On the 3rd December 1849, the force, as per margin, moved from Peshawar, under the command of Lieut.-Colonel J. Bradshaw, C.B., 60th Rifles; Captain H. Richards, 3rd Bombay Native Infantry, acted as Staff Officer to the force; and Lieutenant F. A. St. John, 60th Rifles, as Orderly Officer to Lieut.-Colonel Bradshaw. The force was accompanied by Lieut.-Colonel G. St. P. Lawrence, the Deputy Commissioner, as Political Officer. Lieutenant H. B. Lumsden, with 200 men of the Guides, was sent on ahead of the troops to lay in supplies, and, on his approach, nearly all the recusant villages waited on him, and paid up their revenue.

2nd Troop, 2nd Brigade, Horse Artillery.
200 bayonets, 60th Rifles.
300 „ 61st Foot.
13th Irregular Cavalry.[1]
One company, Bombay Sappers and Miners.[2]
3rd Bombay Native Infantry.[3]

On the 11th December, Lieut.-Colonel Bradshaw, with the whole of his force, which had been strengthened by the Guides and 100 men of the 1st Punjab Infantry, attacked and destroyed the insurgent village of Sanghao which had refused to submit. This village was situated in a very strong position, immediately beneath an apparently precipitous rock about 2,000 feet high, from which two spurs projected some 900 yards into the plain, forming a *cul-de-sac.*

The position had been reconnoitred the previous day by Lieut.-Colonel Bradshaw, who determined to attack it on both flanks and in front simultaneously. The cavalry were to protect the baggage and the left flank of the operations. The detachment

[1] Became the 14th in 1847 and mutinied in 1857.

[2] Now the 3rd Sappers and Miners.

[3] Now the 103rd Mahratta Light Infantry.

of the 60th Rifles, supported by four companies of the 3rd Bombay Native Infantry, was to crown the spur on the left of the village, covered by two guns of the Horse Artillery; while the Guide Corps, supported by the detachment, 1st Punjab Infantry, were to turn the spur on the right, with a view of cutting off the only apparent retreat the enemy possessed.

When these arrangements had been partially effected, the main body, consisting of the detachment, 61st Foot, supported by the remainder of the 3rd Bombay Native Infantry, and covered by the fire of four guns, charged and took the village. The left attack was met by a heavy fire and showers of stones, the precipitous nature of the ground rendering the advance very difficult; but the heights were gallantly crowned, and the enemy driven off.

The enemy, finding his retreat on both flanks cut off, retired up the height in rear of the village by a path not noticed by the reconnoitring party the day before, and which was inaccessible to the troops beyond a certain height.

The strength of the enemy was estimated at 2,500 men. The villages had been reinforced by large bodies from the Buner country, and their loss must have been very considerable. The British casualties amounted to four killed and eighteen wounded.

On the 13th December Lieut.-Colonel Bradshaw moved his camp to a position at the mouth of the valley of Bazdara, within three miles of the insurgent village of Palai, and of Zormandai and Sher Khana, in Sam Baizai.

A reconnaissance being made, the villages were found situated as nearly as possible in echelon—Palai being the most advanced. On the right of this village rose a hill of some 1,500 feet, which completely commanded it, and was evidently the key of the enemy's position; this was occupied by a mass of not less than 5,000 men, and the hills to the right and to the rear of the other villages were also occupied by large bodies. The enemy also held the valley in front of Palai in force, his right resting on the hill first mentioned, and his left stretching across to a range of hills which bounded the valley on the left, about a mile distant. From these, hill-spurs projected at right angles into the valley, which were also strongly occupied.

Finding that the principal strength of the enemy lay on the hill to the right of Palai, Lieut.-Colonel Bradshaw determined on seizing it, and on the 14th the operations were carried out.

The detachment, 60th Rifles, six companies of the 3rd Bombay Native Infantry, and a troop of the 13th Irregular Cavalry, were detached against this hill, and supported by four Horse Artillery guns, which opened fire on it with great effect. The Guide Infantry and detachment, 1st Punjab Infantry, supported by three companies of the Bombay Native Infantry, were detached to the right, to turn the enemy's left. Lieut.-Colonel Bradshaw, seeing that the movement aginst the hill on his left was likely to prove successful, pushed forward the remaining two guns, supported by the detachment, 61st Foot, and the remainder of the 13th Irregular Cavalry against the left of the enemy's position. The light company of the 61st moved in extended order to the right of the guns, and the enemy's left was now completely turned.

Having thus succeeded in turning one flank, and holding the other in complete subjection, Lieut.-Colonel Bradshaw advanced with four guns up the centre of the valley (the other two being left in support with the troops, which had now gained, and were holding, the hill to the right of Palai), carrying and destroying the villages in detail, and driving off the enemy, who made for the hills in their rear and on their left. The ground being tolerably favourable, Lieut.-Colonel Bradshaw directed the 13th Irregular Cavalry to charge, which they did with great effect.

All that the Deputy Commissioner desired having been carried out, and the enemy dispersed on all sides, Lieut.-Colonel Bradshaw withdrew from the valley without a shot being fired.

The inhabitants of these villages had been assisted by people from Swat proper to the extent of from 5,000 to 6,000 men, and they had literally been driven like sheep across the frontier, leaving their dead on the field—a great disgrace amongst these tribes—and there had been nothing to prevent our troops pursuing them into their own country, if it had been deemed necessary to do so.

Our losses amounted to three killed and twenty-two wounded.

The force, with the exception of the Guides Corps, then returned to Peshawar, *viâ* Hashtnagar and Doaba, crossing the Kabul river by a pontoon bridge, and reaching Peshawar on the 22nd December. The Guides remained behind to cover the erection of a fortified post, the sanction for which had been accorded. Lieut.-Colonel Lawrence, in his report, stated that he had been unable to carry out that part of the Governor-General's instructions requiring that the headmen should be brought into Peshawar, as the nature of the country precluded the possibility of surprising them, and there was no opportunity of seizing them either during or after the action. He added that a most severe punishment had been inflicted on them, not the least of which was the capture of a quantity of grain, roughly estimated at 3,000 maunds.

Only one prisoner had fallen into our hands—a priest from Bajaur—from whom it was ascertained that the combination against us among the hill-tribes had been very great; it was afterwards known that reinforcements of 15,000 men were *en route* to join the insurgents when intelligence was received of their total defeat.

The Indian Medal, with a clasp for the "North-West Frontier," was granted in 1869 to all survivors of the troops engaged in the above operations under Lieut.-Colonel Bradshaw.

After the expedition above described, the villages of Sam Baizai continued to give trouble. Crime was not to be stopped at once, and Hindus were carried off, property stolen, and outrages committed. Lieutenant W. S. R. Hodson, then in charge of Yusafzai, demanded security for the future, and one Ghulam Shah Baba, who seems to have been held in considerable estimation, and who owned property in our territory and in the Bazdara valley, became responsible for them.

The arrangement seems to have been successful to a great extent. No open aggression was offered; but occasional affrays and some cases of exaction occurred, when parties who had received some real or fancied injury would endeavour to right themselves by seizing the person or property of one of their neighbours. This was not, however, more than might have been anticipated. Between the Palaiwals and the people of Kharkai there continued to be constant disputes about the right of grazing, cutting grass, wood, etc., on the hill which formed the boundary between the two.

In 1855, the Kuai people gave an asylum to a number of refugees from Palai, which nearly led to an attack on Kuai by the people of Sherkhana, Zormandai, etc., assisted by a force from Buner.

Arrangements were, however, made by the British authorities, by which a breach of the peace was avoided, and an amicable settlement effected. The headmen bound themselves by oath to abstain from all acts of aggression, and, should cause of complaint arise, to refer the matter for the decision of the British civil authorities at Mardan.

In the same year the village of Sanghao was fined Rs. 200 on account of its robberies and molestations of traders from Buner, and, as a further punishment, the village was ordered to be removed from its hill position. The measure of removal was carried out by a good deal of pressure, and after a considerable time; but in the confusion of 1857 the villagers crept back again, and this fact was only discovered by Lieut.-Colonel H. B. Edwardes, the Commissioner, in 1858, after the success against Panjtar and Sitana, when, thinking there was an opportunity for leniency, he imposed a small fine, and allowed the old site to be re-occupied. During the operations at Ambela in 1863, the Utman Khels of British Baizai flocked to join the combatants, and gave a deal of trouble by cutting up stragglers between the British position and the rear. Major H. R. James, the Commissioner, recommended that a force, destined by Sir Hugh Rose, the Commander-in-Chief, for a diversion against Swat, should be sent to punish the people; but, as stated in chapter VI, this was not considered advisable by the military authorities. After the campaign, the *maliks* of this tract were summoned, and a fine of Rs. 2,500 was imposed upon them.

It appears that the deputation which came in represented only a portion of the tribe, many of the principal men standing aloof, partly from a sense of their culpability, and partly from a disagreement among themselves and the *malik* through whom they were summoned. The fine was paid by all, but it may be assumed that those who presented themselves were generally of the party disposed towards our rule.

Soon after their return home, dissensions broke out among them. There were many latent causes, especially that of the fine; the party who stayed away reproaching the party which presented itself. The spirit of jealousy and faction ran high, the villages being divided into two parties, and the two villages of Kuai and Pipal, situated in the plains, comprising the majority of those well disposed towards the Government, found themselves opposed to Barmul and Mian Khan, joined by Sanghao.

Intimation of approaching hostilities was given to the Assistant Commissioner of Yusafzai at the beginning of July 1864, and he sent to warn the tribesmen against committing themselves. On 21st August, however, a regular fight with matchlock and sword occurred between the villages of Kuai and Barmul, in which several lives were lost on both sides, and several men wounded. In this the aid of villages beyond our border was brought in, and a regular warfare between these villages went on for some time. At the end of the year attempts made by the civil officers failed to bring matters to a peaceable solution.

In February of the succeeding year, 1865, a heavy fine was inflicted, and certain of the *maliks* were retained as hostages. These measures were not, however, successful, as in 1866 quarrels broke out afresh, and it was evident that this state of lawlessness among our subjects must be at once suppressed, or it would infect others, and encourage them to revert to their original Pathan condition, which had only disappeared under a knowledge of our power to maintain peace and order. It was therefore determined to move out a force to compel the attendance of all the principal men, and to destroy and remove the villages of Barmul and Sanghao to a more accessible position in the plains, these villages being then situated in a difficult part of the country. As three of the villages beyond our border had assisted and fomented all these disturbances, it might be necessary that they also should be punished; the position of these villages was naturally strong, and (though this was not anticipated by the Commissioner) aid might be furnished, as it had been in 1849, by Swat and Buner; it was necessary, therefore, in determining the strength of the force, to be prepared for all contingencies.

On the 7th January 1866, 100 sabres of the 13th Bengal Cavalry and 200 bayonets of the 27th Punjab Native Infantry were detached from Peshawar to Mardan, to enable the Corps of Guides to take the field. The 20th Punjab Native Infantry had been moved up from Rawal Pindi, and a mountain battery and the 2nd Punjab Infantry from Abbottabad, and on the 15th January a force of 4,000 men and 12 guns was assembled at Nowshera, under the command of Brigadier-General H. F. Dunsford, C.B., with Colonel J. R. Becher, C.B., the Commissioner of Peshawar, as Political Officer.

The native troops had brought with them five days' supplies, which were to remain intact until their arrival at Mardan; the Commissariat carried twelve days' supplies for the British troops. All were supplied with sepoys' tents, and the baggage was cut down as far as possible.

On the 16th the force moved to Mardan, when the Commissioner reported that, of the four recusant villages, the headmen of Kuai and Barmul had come in, that the village of Sanghao had been abandoned, and that it only remained therefore to deal with Mian Khan and the independent villages. On the 17th the force marched to Likpani, where it had to halt the following day, owing to heavy rain. The Khan of Palai then presented himself to the Commissioner, and agreed to pay certain sums that had been obtained from our subjects, at the same time binding himself not to interfere with any British villages, to submit all claims against British subjects to the proper authorities, and expressing penitence for the past.

On the 19th the force marched to Mian Khan. No opposition was met with; so, leaving half the force to destroy the place, Brigadier-General Dunsford proceeded with the remainder to Sanghao, which was also destroyed. The inhabitants of both villages had been warned to remove their property, and it had been intended to spare the wood, that it might be used in building the new villages; but, notwithstanding the efforts to prevent it, some houses were burnt. The Khan of Palai was made to witness this destruction.

As only representatives of the chiefs of the independent villages of Sher Khana and Zormandai had come in, the chiefs themselves were summoned, under threat of their villages being burnt; whereupon they waited on the Commissioner. On the 21st the camp was moved to Tanaki, a strong column proceeding to the villages of Kuai and Barmul. As the former was situated in the plains, and as the inhabitants sued for pardon, it was not destroyed, but a fine of two years' revenue was levied instead from the Pathan inhabitants. Barmul was then destroyed, the inhabitants unroofing the houses themselves, and the walls being destroyed by the sappers and the elephants.

The force halted at Tanaki on the 22nd whilst the Commissioner made arrangements with the *Khans* of Palai, Sher Khana, and

Zormandai; the principal *maliks*, and those concerned in the late disturbances of our own villages, were placed in confinement for judicial investigation. On the following day the force was broken up.

Colonel Becher said, the most favourable feature in the matter had been the absence of all interference with our right to punish our subjects, although the tract lay close to the Swat and Buner borders. The Akhund of Swat, recognizing the justice of the measures taken from first to last, proclaimed that the duty of subjects was "to obey their rulers and abstain from internecine strife"—a commendable sentiment, but doubtless prompted to some extent by a reminiscence of the Ambela campaign.

After the destruction of the three villages of Sanghao, Mian Khan, and Barmul, the villagers were directed to re-establish themselves on certain sites that were fixed at reasonable distances from the hills, and arrangements were made to expedite the building of the new villages by making all the inhabitants of British Baizai assist in the work.

On the 13th of February following, the Assistant Commissioner visited the new villages which had been erected, the old sites having been completely levelled by the villagers.

The leniency shown towards these villages had not however been fully appreciated by them, for, in 1872, disturbances arose consequent on the settlement operations, when troops were moved out from Mardan, and the village of Kuai was made over to Afzal Khan, a Khattak chief, who promised to hold it with levies of his own tribe. This he did for a short time; but the position was not altogether a pleasant one, and he soon asked to be relieved. The houses of the ringleaders of the outbreak at Kuai were pulled down, and the people of the three villages of Kuai, Barmul, and Mian Khan, who had abandoned their villages, being given to understand that their refusal to return would lead to the confiscation of their lands and houses, gave in, and afterwards gave little cause for complaint.

After 1866, the villages of independent Baizai also continued to behave fairly well. In 1871, the Khan of Palai was fined Rs. 500 for the murder of a British subject, and the following year had to pay another fine for interfering with men of British territory. At the end of 1873 reprisals were made on the men of Palai for robbing and wounding our subjects when returning from visiting the *Akhund*. After the expedition against the Ranizai village of Shakot in 1878 (see page 359), the villages of Palai, Sher Khana, etc., in Baizai became much alarmed, and feared similar punishment, in consequence of the outlaws they were harbouring. They accordingly made overtures to the Assistant Commissioner of Yusafzai, and entered into satisfactory arrangements for settling all claims that might be proved against them. Between that date and 1884, they gave little cause of complaint to the British Government.

We will now turn to an account of our early dealings with the Ranizais.

Expedition against the Ranizais by a force under Brigadier Sir Colin Campbell, K.C.B., in March and May 1852.

The rapidity and success of Lieut.-Colonel J. Bradshaw's operations in 1849 against the Sam Baizais opened the eyes of the Swat chiefs to the possibility of a British force one day visiting their own valley, and filled all classes with alarm. In this exigency the oracle was again consulted, and advised that the only chance of making a stand would be by appointing one chief to command the whole disposable forces, all other chiefs being sworn on the *Koran* to obey him implicitly; and that the land tax of one-tenth of the produce, authorised by the Muhammadan law, should be at once collected to provide the sinews of war.

This proposal being agreed to, the chiefs commenced a scramble for the command, which threatened to end in a general *mêlée*. Ghazan Khan of Dir left the council, declaring that he could never obey any man save the *Akhund*. To end this broil, the *Akhund* proposed that a chief hitherto unconnected with Swat should be chosen, and, among other nominations, pointed out Saiyid Akbar of Sitana, as a man of energy and true Muhammadan principles, qualified for the position, with the advantage of being a *saiyid*. Saiyid Akbar was accordingly invited to become King of Swat, under the patronage of the *Akhund*, and shortly afterwards was duly installed, with the usual accompaniments of prayers from the priesthood and *nazrana* from the chiefs.

This chief was, as already related, a follower of the famous Hindustani fanatic, Saiyid Ahmad; and when the latter held temporary possession of Peshawar, Saiyid Akbar joined him in the double capacity of treasurer and prime minister. He was thus thrown in constant contact with the Hindustani soldiers in that chief's camp, and formed a friendship for them which lasted ever afterwards.

The moment his authority was a little established by the *Akhund's* good offices over the Swat chiefs, and the first year's revenue collected, Saiyid Akbar sent for his Hindustani levies; but they refused, under some pretext, to join him, when he set about collecting a standing army and guns, by the aid of which he hoped to put down any chief who should afterwards dispute his authority. He so far succeeded as to collect five or six guns of sizes, 800 sowars, and 3,000 footmen, all receiving pay in grain direct from himself.

Towards the end of 1851 the Swatis moved bodies of troops, several thousand strong, to the foot of the Morah mountain, and into Sam Ranizai, for the purpose of creating disaffection on our border. On the night of the 6th March 1852, a party of 180 horsemen, under the leadership of Mukaram Khan, assailed a detachment consisting of thirty sabres of the Guide Corps stationed at the British village of Gujar Garhi, under Ressaldar Fateh Khan, as an escort to a party of the Great Trigonometrical Survey. The attack was very sudden, it being believed that the approaching party were the survey officers coming into camp, and the enemy were into camp before the men had time to form. But the assailants were gallantly repelled, leaving one dead body and six disabled horses in the camp; the Guides losing one sowar killed, and two wounded. The gallant conduct of this detachment afterwards received the approbation of the Governor-General in Council.

Mukaram Khan, the leader of the attacking party, as already mentioned, had been dismissed from the Peshawar Police, and had been given a *jagir* in Swat. Half of this grant was on this side of the Malakand pass, half on the other; and, when wishing to plunder, he used to come into British territory, retiring to Swat when danger threatened. It was therefore determined to treat the Sam Ranizais as a tribe, and to punish them in such a way as to make them feel they could not afford to allow refugees from our territory, or bad characters from their own, to embroil them with the British Government.

A force under the command of Brigadier Sir Colin Campbell, K.C.B., was accordingly despatched into the valley. This force, which consisted of the troops noted in the margin, marched from Peshawar on the 11th March 1852 towards Tangi, accompanied by Lieut.-Colonel F. Mackeson, C.B., the Commissioner of Peshawar.

1st Troop, 1st Brigade, Horse Artillery.
600 bayonets, 32nd Foot.
15th Irregular Cavalry.[1]
Wing, 29th Native Infantry.[2]
66th Gurkha Regiment.[3]

On the 14th March, the people of Sam Ranizai sent in to Lieutenant H. B. Lumsden, the Deputy Commissioner, offering to submit to any terms imposed, and to pay revenue; the force under Sir Colin Campbell was accordingly halted at Turangzai, and the *maliks* of Ranizai summoned. This delay had the advantage of enabling two heavy howitzers with elephant draught to join Sir Colin Campbell from Peshawar. But the *maliks* afterwards refused to come in, declaring their intention of opposing us, and that they expected assistance from Swat. It had been now clearly ascertained that Saiyid Akbar's nephew, accompanied by a following, had been with the party that had attacked the detachment of the Guides, and the force therefore moved on towards Ranizai, arriving at our frontier village of Sherghar, about eight miles from Shakot, on the 21st of March.

On the march to Shergarh from Gujar Garhi much rain fell on the hills around, and, just after the troops and guns had crossed a very deep *nala* a body of water like a wall came down it suddenly, and for a short time a portion of the baggage and its escort and the rear-guard were separated from the main body of the troops.

On the evening of the 21st, the *maliks* of the Lundkhwar valley had brought the intelligence to Lieutenant Lumsden that the Sam Ranizai *maliks* wished to tender their submission, when they were told that the troops would not be halted, but would march at daybreak to Shakot. It was further intimated to them that if they came in on the road, and paid the fine originally demanded of them, and gave satisfactory security for the safety of our frontier

[1] Became the 16th in 1847. Disbanded in 1861.

[2] Mutinied in 1857 at Moradabad.

[3] Now the 1st (P. W. O.) Gurkha Rifles.

from the depredations of marauders from Swat, and our own bad characters who had taken refuge in Swat, their villages would not be destroyed, nor their crops injured on this occasion by encamping the force in their valley, but that the troops would, in any event, be marched into the valley of Ranizai, to enable the Brigadier to see as much of it as was desired.

On the morning of the 22nd, Sir Colin Campbell's force marched towards Shakot, of which a reconnaissance had been made the previous evening. On the road the Ranizai *maliks* came in, introduced by their neighbours, British subjects of the Lundkhwar valley. They tried to obtain an abatement of the fine imposed, and on two occasions, when it was refused, broke up their council and walked towards their villages. The force then advanced again, when some of the party would return to offer to pay their own share if their particular crops were spared. This farce continued till the force was drawn up within range of their village, when they were all sent away, and given half an hour to bring an unanimous submission to the terms offered, or abide the consequences. In the meantime, the road across the deep chasm in front of the village was made practicable for guns.

After a while, the Ranizai *maliks* returned with a full submission to the terms, and with ten *maliks* as hostages for their fulfilment. They then pointed out a practicable road into the heart of the Ranizai valley—indeed, the high road to Swat, which passed to the right of the drainage chasm, and only crossed a small branch of it higher up the valley, where it was no obstacle.

It was now about 1 P.M., and Sir Colin Campbell gave orders for the camp to be pitched at Shergarh, where it had remained ready laden, awaiting orders. The ten prisoners, as security for payment of the fine, were made over to the civil authorities, and the force moved on, conducted by one of the *maliks* of Ranizai. The road was found to be excellent, although a little narrow, nearly all the way to Dargai; and to reach Dargai, nearly the whole breadth of the valley had to be traversed. This village was situated at the extreme western end of a spur, which from this point ran up for a distance of three miles to the foot of the Malakand pass, forming, with the Malakand range, a narrowing valley. The ground was covered with cultivation, the whole valley being closely tilled.

On reaching Dargai, it was reported that Mukaram Khan had just left that village, and, on turning the spur of the hill, some of our cavalry, seeing two or three horsemen in the distance, galloped on towards the Malakand pass. Sir Colin Campbell also ordered a party of the 15th Irregular Cavalry up from the rear and two guns from the troop of Horse Artillery. Subsequently, five men with standards were seen skulking away up ravines towards the pass with about one hundred footmen. From the direction in which the men were first seen, there is no doubt that they had been at Dargai all the morning, and had only left when they saw the force approaching.

The troops might, had they advanced towards the foot of the Malakand pass, have driven those people off and over the hill, and looked down into Swat; but it was late in the day, and they would have had to encamp in Ranizai, and thereby broken the engagement with the *maliks,* whose hostages were in our camp. Sir Colin Campbell would thus also have engaged in hostilities against the people of Swat proper without having orders from Government to prosecute them to an issue. He therefore waited till he saw, with the aid of a telescope, these standards borne on their way steadily up the pass in open flight, and then returned to camp, without a shot having been fired during the day.

Lieut.-Colonel Mackeson had fixed, with the sanction of Government, the fine to be paid by the Ranizais at Rs. 5,000; he might have increased his demand, in consequence of the message of defiance sent by the Ranizai *maliks* after they had actually given Lieutenant Lumsden to understand they would come in, but he considered their position a difficult one. The Ranizais on the south of the Malakand range, as has been seen, are only a portion of the tribe, and the majority live in Bar Ranizai, above the passes. They were, therefore, too weak to control the whole of Swat, when bent on hostility, although they were strong enough to check parties of marauders, not exceeding 300 or 400 men, from going through their country (which is the principal road from Swat) to commit raids in our territory. Lieut.-Colonel Mackeson might, too, have kept a larger number of the principal men as hostages, and have concluded no terms until he heard from the Board at Lahore as to whether it was desirable to prosecute hostilities into Swat proper;

but then the force must have remained out well into April, with an attendant expense. Great injury would have occurred to the crops of our own subjects near our encampment ; the Swat river and the Kabul river were on the rise ; the one might become unfordable, and the other might carry away our bridge, when the Mohmand tribes would not have neglected to make raids on the Doaba, seeing the communications of the force with Peshawar cut off. Under these circumstances the Commissioner thought it wiser to make a settlement of the question at once.

On the morning of the 23rd, Sir Colin Campbell's force marched to Jalala, where it remained on the 24th, in consequence of heavy rain, and resumed its march to Turangzai on the 25th, *en route* to Peshawar. The ten prisoners were sent, under a guard of the 15th Irregular Cavalry, towards Peshawar, where they arrived safely on the 27th of March.

Immediate payment of the fine could not be exacted from the Ranizais, as the first intimation they had of the demand was on the morning of the 22nd, and they asked some little time to collect it, which was accordingly granted them.

In the following month some men of the Ranizai tribe were implicated in the attack on the village of Charsada,[1] and letters, believed to be genuine, were subsequently taken, which proved the complicity of Swat. One letter from the *Akhund* authorised the leader of the raid, one Ajun Khan, to destroy all Europeans and Hindus in the Peshawar valley, and all Muhammadans in the British service ; but enjoined him to spare all other Muhammadans.

On the conclusion of the terms with the Ranizai people, a conciliatory letter had been sent to the King of Swat, to which not only was no reply received, but it was reported that the killing of the messenger had been debated, to mark the King's determination not to hold any intercourse with the infidels.

The Ranizais, moreover, withheld the payment of the fine which had been imposed upon them, repudiated the hostages, and expelled their families from their territory, declaring their reliance on Swat. Further coercion, therefore, became necessary.

[1]See Chapter X.

1st Troop, 1st Brigade, Horse Artillery, (6 guns).
Detachment 3rd Company, 4th Battalion, Artillery, and No. 19 Light Field Battery attached, (2 guns).
H. M.'s 32nd Regiment.
2nd Irregular Cavalry.[1]
Guide Cavalry.
1st Punjab Cavalry.[2]
2nd Company Sappers and Miners.
28th Native Infantry.[3]
66th Gurkha Regiment.
Guide Infantry.
1st Punjab Infantry.

On the 15th of May, the force, as per margin, consisting of 3,270 of all arms, was assembled at Shergliar, under the command of Brigadier Sir Colin Campbell, K.C.B.

On the 16th and 17th the force halted at Shergarh, and it was reported that considerable numbers were flocking from Swat and elsewhere to the village of Shakot to defend the Ranizai valley, and that many *ghazis* had come over the passes to fight in this cause; and it was evident that the people of Swat proper regarded an attack on Ranizai as one made on themselves. The *Akhund* and the King were at variance on the subject of the non-payment of the fine by the people of Ranizai,—the one being in favour of the payment, the other opposing it,—as his influence would be diminished by such a course.

On the 18th the camp was struck, and the baggage moved two or three miles to the rear, under a strong escort. The force then marched to dislodge the enemy, who had taken up a position in the neighbourhood of Shakot, and afterwards to proceed with the punishment of the Ranizais.

Shakot was situated between a very deep and broad *nala* on the east, and some hills on the west. About an hour after daybreak, when two miles had been accomplished, Shakot being then distant two more, the enemy were discovered on one side of the *nala*, stretching away in one continuous line to the village, which was the left of their position, the ground they held on the margin of the *nala* being about a mile and a half in length.

The troops were now formed in line of quarter columns, the cavalry being sent to the left to watch the extreme right of the enemy. The advance then took place in echelon of regiments from the right, in column, Sir Colin Campbell's design being to break the enemy's centre with the Horse Artillery, and attack their left, which was on their line of retreat.

A sharp cannonade was opened by Captain R. H. Baldwin's troop of Horse Artillery on the centre of the enemy's position, which,

[1] Now the 2nd Lancers (Gardner's Horse).
[2] Now 21st Prince Albert Victor's Own Cavalry (Frontier Force).
[3] Mutinied at Shahjahanpur in 1857.

however, they stood with great firmness, availing themselves of the broken ground for protection. The two leading regiments on the right, the Guide Corps and 66th Gurkhas, now "left-wheeled into line" and stormed the *nala*, covered by the fire of the two 9-pounders, and supported by the light company of Her Majesty's 32nd Regiment and the 1st Punjab Infantry, under Captain J. Coke. The attack was well executed by the troops, the first assailants having to encounter a heavy fire and much resistance. A company of the 66th Gurkhas were engaged in a hand-to-hand fight, a party of the enemy having charged into the centre of them.

The Horse Artillery now rapidly changed position, and galloped to the edge of the *nala*, which they enfiladed with great effect whenever they could fire without injuring our own men. As soon as the two 9-pounders could be spared, they were moved rapidly to the right, and brought into action opposite the village, and a large burial-ground at right angles to it, which were both full of the enemy. The 32nd Foot covered the guns, and the 28th Native Infantry were kept in reserve, ready to move on any required point.

The fire of the guns was sharp and telling, and they were advanced closer and closer to the enemy as the attack on the *nala* showed itself to be successful. The enemy at length broke, a large body swarming up the hills to the rear of the village, and another making for the Malakand pass,—the 9-pounders playing on those retreating up the hills, the Horse Artillery going in pursuit up the valley. Three miles from the scene of resistance, the Guide Cavalry, directed, at Sir Colin Campbell's request, by Lieut.-Colonel F. Makeson, C.B., the Commissioner (who had accompanied the force as Political Officer), sabred a considerable crowd trying to make their escape. The pursuit had been so rapid that this had happened before the 9-pounders had succeeded in clearing the face of the opposite hills, although no time was lost by the fugitives in that direction.

In addition to the armed villagers, about 4,000 infantry and 500 cavalry, all from Swat, had been opposed to the force, and the King and *Akhund* had stationed themselves on the crest of the Malakand pass, overlooking the valley, to view the fight.

Great slaughter had been committed on the enemy, with comparatively trifling loss to our troops,[1] and large numbers of dead bodies were found all over the ground where the enemy had fought, and on their line of retreat.

The amount of ammunition expended by the troops was 20,613 rounds.

Arrangements were now made for the destruction of Shakot, a large village numbering some 600 houses, many of which appeared to be of much pretension. It was thoroughly burnt, as well as the crops around.

Having echeloned various parties to prevent the possibility of further annoyance, Sir Colin Campbell proceeded to destroy Dargai, about three miles higher up the valley. This was also a very considerable place, being full of houses of the better sort, and, according to rough calculation, having some 400 altogether. No opposition was offered by the enemy, and the troops returned to Shergarh about 3 P.M.

A day's rest having been given to the troops on the 19th, the force marched round the Ranizai valley on the 20th destroying the villages named in the margin, together with much grain.

Warter.
Dobandi.
Sandasur.
Kadam Khel.
Harkai.
Usman Khel Garhi.
Musamena.
Mirdai.

On this day no opposition was encountered, and but few of the inhabitants of the valley were to be seen. The troops were under arms and in movement from 4 A.M. till 6-30 P.M.

On the 22nd, a detachment, as per margin, marched about nine miles to destroy the village of Hiro Shah. This place had been represented to be in an open valley. It was found, however, to be situated in close ground, within matchlock range of the hills, at the head of a ravine, some two miles in extent, up which the troops moved. Besides being so strong by nature, it was surrounded by a loopholed wall. The inhabitants had retreated to a distant range of hills, and the troops were not molested till after the destruction of the village had been effected,

1st Troop, 1st Brigade, Horse Artillery, (3 guns).
200 sabres, 1st Punjab Cav.
2nd Company, S. & M.
200 bayonets, 28th N. I.
300 " 66th Gurkha.
200 " Guide Infantry.
300 " 1st P. I.

[1] Our casualties only amounted to eleven killed and twenty-nine wounded.

and they had begun to retire towards camp. They were then followed by a matchlock fire till quite clear of the hills and ravines. The retrograde movement having been conducted very slowly and in perfect order, no loss was sustained.

The force then marched back through Lundkhwar to Gujar Garhi, where it was broken up.

The Indian Medal, with a clasp for the "North-West Frontier," was granted in 1869 to all survivors of the troops engaged in the above operations against the Ranizai villages.

In June, the month following Sir Colin Campbell's operations, the Ranizai people, finding themselves houseless and unable to rebuild their dismantled villages, made overtures for peace. Shortly afterwards, they tendered unconditional submission, offered to pay revenue to the British, and to allow a fortified post to be erected in their valley. The supreme Government declined to accept any tribute or revenue from them, only requiring them to behave as friendly and peaceable neighbours. They were accordingly excused from payment of the original fine, and they bound themselves to permit no marauders from Swat or elsewhere to pass through their lands to cross the British frontier, and also to live at amity with the neighbouring British villages, Lundkhwar, and others. These arrangements were completed in September 1852.

The following is the agreement entered into on this occasion with the British Government:

1st.—If the Government require us to pay revenue, we will do so.

2nd.—If the Government desire to build a fort in Ranizai, they are at liberty to do so.

3rd.—If we are left by the Government to re-settle by ourselves, we will do so.

4th.—The *khans* agree that they will always be ready to do service for the Government, and will not receive in to their country any person evilly disposed to the Government, nor give such person a road through their country.

5th.—If any army comes against us too strong for us to cope with, we will come with our families into British territory.

That Swat had been the fountain head of all this offending was evident; we had never interfered with them, but they had chosen to make war upon us. Our chief fault in their eyes was that we were infidels by religion, and that we were the lords of a fair and fertile valley within reach of plunder. It was at one time thought that a good opportunity presented itself of dashing up the Malakand pass and down into the Swat valley. A separate expedition, on a considerable scale, was also being organized during the summer of 1852. The military authorities at that time, however, considered that various difficulties existed in the execution of the plan, and the Government consented to postpone the expedition until the cold season of 1852-53, when it was eventually abandoned altogether. The Swat Government seem to have taken to heart the punishment inflicted on the Ranizais, and to have dreaded similar operations in their valley; for they subsequently abstained from annoyance or hostility against the British, and the Peshawar valley enjoyed immunity from marauders from Swat.

It might naturally have been expected that the King of Swat would have been at the head of all mischief when the troubles of 1857 overtook us. It is a remarkable fact, however, that he died on the 11th of May, the very day that the first news of the Mutiny reached Peshawar, so that Swat itself was simultaneously plunged into civil war, and entirely pre-occupied with its own affairs. The question was as to the succession—king or no king. Saiyid Mubarak Shah, son of the deceased Saiyid Akbar, wished to succeed his father; but the people of Swat had grown tired of tithes, and called on the *Akhund* to excommunicate the heir-apparent; both sides called in their friends and allies, and prepared to settle it with arms. It was at this juncture that 500 of the fugitive sepoys of the 55th Native Infantry, who had escaped from Lieut.-Colonel John Nicholson's pursuit, burst upon the scene, and were at once taken into the young king's service.

Had the Akhund of Swat at this time, standing forward as the champion of the faith, preached a holy war against us, and, hushing intestine strife, moved across the passes and descended into the Peshawar valley with all the prestige of the 55th sepoys in his favour, Lieut.-Colonel H. B. Edwardes, the Commissioner, said he did not doubt that he would have excited among our subjects that spirit of religious zeal which may be overlaid for a while, but which is never extinguished by material prosperity. Instead of this, he suddenly sided with the popular party, dismissed the

55th sepoys, with guides to conduct them across the Indus, and expelled the young king from Swat.

After this we do not appear to have again come into collision with the inhabitants of Swat until the Ambela campaign.

The important part played by the *Akhund* and his followers in that memorable campaign has been shown in a previous chapter. On the 27th of October 1863 he joined the ranks of the enemy, with 100 standards (between 3,000 and 4,000 footmen) and 120 horsemen, under the leadership of Sherdil Khan, the chief of the Ranizais, and his nephew, Sobat Khan. Later on, the priestly influence of the *Akhund* had brought to his standard large bodies of men from Kunar and Bajaur, the latter under their chief, Faiztalab Khan; and in the beginning of December, 6,000 more men, under Ghazan Khan, the Khan of Dir, had joined the enemy.

The reasons which, in the opinion of Colonel R. G. Taylor, the Commissioner, may have influenced the *Akhund* in throwing in his lot against the British Government have already been given.[1]

It is now well known that, ever since the English obtained possession of the Peshawar valley, the *Akhund* was suspicious and apprehensive lest the valley of Swat, his adopted home, should fall into our power. "It was his policy," writes Major James, "during the whole of the reign of Saiyid Akbar, to keep up, in concert with him, a system of marauding on our frontier, for which purpose they offered maintenance to men of lawless habits and to influential refugees from our districts, whom they settled in villages about Ranizai, and incited to constant deeds of depredation and violence, thus keeping up the fear of our invasion by encouraging acts which might be expected to lead to it—a fear upon which they originally founded their authority, and which is their best security for its preservation."

This policy was, however, much modified, if not entirely reversed, after the Ambela campaign. The *Akhund* no longer incited the people of Swat or Buner, or other independent tracts, to raid on British territory; but, on the contrary, as far as it is possible to judge, advised them to behave as good neighbours, and, if they offended and were called to account by us, to meet such demands as might be made, and comply with such terms as might be imposed.

1 See page 251.

This policy was, doubtless, the result of his experience of our power and of the faintheartedness and want of persistent energy of his own disciples, as witnessed by himself at Ambela. Feeling he could not trust to the tribes of Swat or Buner to resist the force of the British arms, he was not anxious to provoke a second attack on either country. Not that he openly avowed this. On the contrary, he gave out that it was the result of his miraculous power as a saint, and steadfast maintenance of his position on the crest of the Buner pass, which prevented the British troops, in the high tide of success, from advancing on both Buner and Swat, and bringing them under their sway. And these assertions were believed by the majority of his credulous disciples, who saw in this continuous forbearance of ours further and most convincing proof of the ***buzurgi***, or saintly reputation, of the *Akhund*.

A very noticeable feature in the Ambela expedition was the alliance of the *Akhund* with the Hindustani fanatics of Sitana, whose tenets he abhorred, and whom he stigmatised as *Wahabis*. It is simply to be accounted for by the fact that the *Akhund* was really alarmed for the independence of his disciples in Buner and Swat, and considered it the wiser policy to sink, for a time, all sectarian differences. Hardly, however, had our troops withdrawn from the Chamla valley, before the religious disputations between them broke out afresh, and in August 1868 we find the *Akhund* stirring up the whole of Buner, as already described, against a small party who had given some of these fanatics an asylum in the village of Bajkatta, in the Daulatzai canton, and not only expelling them, but encompassing the death of the fine old chief, Zaidulla Khan, who had befriended them, and raising up the Bunerwals to harass them in their retreat, and prevent their finding a resting-place until they had reached the banks of the Indus.

There can be little doubt that this expulsion was the result of the *Akhund's* suspecting that our preparations, then being made for the expedition against the tribes of the Black Mountain, were intended to be made use of also against the Hindustanis, and he was most unwilling to be again himself, or have the people of Buner, embroiled with us on their account.

During the later years of his life the *Akhund* desired very much to see his elder son, Mian Gul, elected King of Swat; for he saw that after his death he was not likely, owing to his want of force of character, and the number of his enemies, to acquire for himself any position of influence in the country. At the same time he never directly proposed him for the office, although on two occasions he attempted indirectly to bring it about by a plebiscite of the people of Swat. The first occasion was in May 1871, when he suggested that Saiyid Mubarak Shah, the son of the former King of Swat, who had died fourteen years before, should be elected king in his father's place; but the suggestion was not received with favour, and nothing came of it. The second occasion was in June 1875, when he appointed one Ahmad Shah, a *saiyid*, living in the Nikbi Khel canton of the Khwazazai district, King of Swat; but deposed him again in the following month, giving as an excuse that a *ghaza* (holy war) not being imminent, a king was not required; whilst he also asserted that he had doubts as to the integrity, as a ruler and judge, of his nominee. On both occasions the *Akhund* hoped that his candidate would be indignantly rejected by the people, and a unanimous offer of the crown be made by them to his son, Mian Gul. He simply desired, when making the above proposals, to gauge public opinion, and give the people of Swat an indication of his own views.

On the 12th January 1877, the *Akhund*, who was then about eighty-three years of age, died. During the last year of his life, in spite of great pressure from without, urging him to adopt a hostile attitude towards the British Government, he persistently refused to depart from the neutral and almost friendly demeanour he had adopted for some years past.

With regard to the real feelings of this man towards ourselves, conflicting accounts are given; but, if he be judged by the actions and the sentiments expressed by him on certain important occasions, he will be found to have, as a rule, used his influence more to support than to frustrate or hamper our action, so long as we refrained from aggressive measures against any of the tribes in his neighbourhood, who looked up to him as their spiritual guide. The best proof of the *Akhund's* wise restraint of the evil spirits of Swat and Buner is the almost total immunity, for many years previous to his death, of that portion of our border from raids and other serious offences.

The three main objects of the *Akhund's* policy seem to have been, in his later years—

1st.—To preserve the independence of Swat for at least his own lifetime.

2nd.—To silence all his religious rivals.

3rd.—To bring about the election of his son, Mian Gul, to the Kingship of Swat.

In the first two he was successful; in the last he was not.

When the *Akhund* died, there were two great factions in Swat, one of which was headed by Sherdil Khan, the chief of the Ranizais, supported by Rahmatulla, the son of Ghazan Khan, who had succeeded his father as Khan of Dir; the other was headed by Abdul Manan, better known as Mian Gul, the elder son of the *Akhund.* All the principal men of Swat and the surrounding countries sided with one or other of these parties. Sherdil Khan, however, had an opponent in his own district of Ranizai in the person of his nephew, Saadat Khan, whom, as might have been expected, Mian Gul supported. These men had both, at various times, been supreme in, and *Khans* of, their clan; but, at the time of the *Akhund's* death, Sherdil Khan held that position, and had done so, with the exception of a short interval in December 1875, for the past four years.

Expedition against the Ranizai village of Shakot in March 1878.

After the death of the *Akhund*, the Ranizais began again to give trouble on our border. Subsequent to the operations of Sir Colin Campbell's force in 1852, this part of the frontier had remained undisturbed, and the Ranizai people had fulfilled satisfactorily the engagements then entered into with the British Government. Our border was not molested by marauders from that direction, nor did any cause for dissatisfaction on our part arise. Indeed, so anxious were the Ranizai people to maintain peace with us, that afterwards, when some of the leading men, who had brought about their submission in 1852, were killed in an internal feud, a deputation came from Ranizai to the British authorities expressly to explain that, although these men were dead, the tribe still adhered to their agreements. This good behaviour continued during the lifetime of the *Akhund*, but in 1877 the village of Shakot, by harbouring outlaws, and not restraining them from committing offences within the

British border, had become troublesome, and appeared disinclined to obey the orders of the Assistant Commissioner of Mardan to attend and adjust the claims recorded against the village. It was considered unadvisable to allow this state of things to continue, and a proposal was therefore sanctioned to use the Guides and the Hazara Mountain Battery at Mardan to coerce the village.

Hazara Mountain Battery.
Guide Cavalry—249 men.
„ Infantry—428 „

A force, as per margin, under the command of Major R. B. P. P. Campbell, of the Guides, accordingly marched from Mardan at 8-45 P.M. on the evening of the 13th of March 1878, to punish the inhabitants of Shakot.

The force was accompanied by Captain P. L. N. Cavagnari, as Political Officer, and by Captain R. Warburton, as his assistant. The object was to surprise the village and capture as many of the fighting men as possible. In order to avoid giving any notice of the approach of the troops, a detour was made to avoid the village of Jalala, and the force arrived within two miles of Shakot about 2 A.M. on the morning of the 14th of March.

Shakot, at this time, was a village of about 500 houses, and was reported to possess about 400 fighting men. It is situated, as already stated, on the right bank of a deep ravine, which, running north and south at this place, is the main drainage channel of a great portion of the Sam Ranizai country. The ground between the ravine and the hills on the east is practicable for cavalry, and to the north-west there is a small detached hill which commands the village, which, if held, would prevent any assistance being given by the independent villages to the north. The first object being to gain possession of this hill, Major Campbell sent two companies of infantry, under Major G. Stewart, against it. This movement was successfully carried out, and the party reached the crest of the hill without having alarmed the inhabitants of the village. The main body of the infantry, under Major Campbell, followed about a quarter of an hour later, and, having crossed the *nala* took up a position in front of Shakot just as day was breaking.

The artillery and the cavalry remained on the left bank of the ravine, at a distance of about two miles from the village, with orders to wait till daybreak, when the artillery was to take up a suitable position to the south, and the cavalry, under Captain W. Battye, was to move rapidly forward and cut off the retreat of the enemy to the north and east of the village. The first thing which made the enemy aware of the presence of our troops was hearing the cavalry trotting past to take up the position assigned them. They then began beating drums, and it appeared as if they intended to offer resistance. At the same time, the inhabitants, chiefly women and children, began to flee towards the hill to the north-west of the village, but stopped on seeing that it was occupied by our troops. Captain Cavagnari then sent forward a man to summon the village to surrender, or take the consequences. When sufficient time had been allowed for the messenger to reach the village, the advance was sounded, and the infantry began to move forward in skirmishing order.

Seeing that resistance would be hopeless, the headmen came out and made an unconditional surrender, without a shot having been fired on either side. The troops then entered the village, and the following terms were demanded :—

1st.—That they should pay a fine of Rs. 500 for past misconduct.

2nd.—That they should at once adjust all claims of British subjects for compensation for losses inflicted on them within British territory.

3rd.—That all outlaws should at once be expelled from Shakot, and suitable guarantees should be given by the headmen, binding them to refuse such persons an asylum in future.

4th.—That hostages, or other suitable guarantee for the good behaviour of the village in future, should be furnished.

The headmen agreed to these demands without demur, and thirty-three hostages were selected from the inhabitants, and accompanied the force on its return. The neighbouring villages had made no attempt to assist Shakot, and they now sent in their headmen to pay their respects to the British officers.

The village was occupied till 10 A.M., when the return march was begun, and the whole force arrived at Mardan the same evening, having marched nearly fifty miles within twenty-four hours.

In December 1878 the two sons of the late *Akhund* endeavoured to create a *jehad*, and *mullas* were sent in all directions to raise up the *khans* and the people. Fortunately, just then the powerful party of Sherdil Khan had been turned out of power. These were persuaded to discourage the fanatical movement in Ranizai, and, through their adherents, in Upper Swat also ; and, in consequence, the movement was an utter failure. In April 1880, Sherdil Khan of Aladand, who had been ill for some time, died in British territory, where he had come for medical treatment. After his death the chief political power in Swat passed into the hands of Rahmatulla Khan, the Khan of Dir. During the later months of the occupation of Afghanistan in 1880, the well-known Mulla Khalil, with other *mullas* from the Mohmand hills, worked hard to incite the tribes of Dir and Swat to commence a holy war, by an attack on the British line of communications near Jalalabad. Their efforts were, to a great extent, neutralised by the passive attitude of Rahmatulla Khan, and ere long the cry for a *jehad* died away.

In 1883 a desultory contest was carried on between Mian Gul and the Khan of Dir, for the supremacy in Swat, but in March 1884 these two came to terms. By this agreement, Mian Gul acknowledged the authority of Dir over Malizai ; Rahmatulla Khan, on the other hand, pledging himself not to interfere unasked in the affairs of Swat proper.

The history of our subsequent dealings with the Swat Tribes will be reserved for a new chapter.

CHAPTER IX.

SWAT TRIBES.—(Continued.)

BETWEEN the years 1884 and 1890 the Swat valley was kept in a ferment of intrigues and factional feuds by the ambitious actions of Umra Khan of Jandol, whose career has been described in the preceding chapters. The Mian Guls sided now with Muhammad Sharif, who had succeeded his father Rahmatullah as Khan of Dir, and now with the Jandol Chief.

In 1887 Abdul Manan, the elder Mian Gul, died, and was succeeded by his brother Abdul Hanan, also called Abdul Khalik or Shirin. The Swatis were now still further split up into factions, some supporting Abdul Hanan while others urged the claims of the two young sons of the elder brother, aged three and five. In 1888 much unrest was caused among the Swat clans by the conduct of the Amir, and by persistent rumours that he was aiming at the annexation of Bajaur, Dir, and Swat. Hitherto the Government of India had consistently refrained from all interference with the internal affairs of these countries, but since the policy of the Amir now appeared to threaten our interests, in that it would isolate the northern outposts of Chitral, a firm remonstrance was sent to Kabul. On being informed that no interference on his part in Dir and the adjoining territories could be tolerated, the Amir at once acknowledged that Swat was outside his sphere of influence, though he asserted claim to the other countries. Nevertheless, Afghan intrigues were continued with more or less persistence until 1893, when the Durand Mission to Kabul brought about a better understanding. During the year 1889, a number of Afghan refugees, headed by General Faiz Muhammad Khan, Ghilzai, came and settled in Swat. Soon after this, the Swatis became divided on the question of the administration of their country—some advocated the intervention of the Government of India, others wished to call in the headmen of the Hindustani fanatics at Palosi, and a third party suggested making the Afghan General Faiz Muhammad Khan their chief. All seemed to be agreed as to the necessity of opposing Umra Khan, who had threatened to attack Thana and might attempt to overrun all Swat.

In 1890 Muhammad Sharif Khan of Dir was finally driven out by Umra Khan, and took refuge in Upper Swat. During the next few years, the Swatis assisted the ex-chief of Dir in various attempts to regain his possessions and oust Umra Khan, but their efforts met with little success.

In 1892 arrangements were made with the Swat *khans* and *maliks* for the opening of a postal service through the Swat valley, which was continued through Umra Khan's territories in Dir to Chitral.

In 1893 the Mian Gul Abdul Hanan died, and after some debate it was decided that the succession should remain in abeyance for a few years, after which Saiyid Badshah, son of Abdul Manan, should be recognized as the senior Mian Gul. In this year Umra Khan, after a successful attack on the Dusha Khel, moved into Swat and compelled the submission of Barangola and Badiyan, two villages belonging to the Khan of Aladand. Having taken a heavy fine he expelled the chief, and installed his own nominee, Saadat Khan, in his place.

For the next two years there was continual faction-fighting in Swat, and at one time considerable pressure was put upon the *khans* of Thana to induce them to forego the allowances which they received for the postal service, and to break off all relations with Government. The *khans*, however, strove their utmost to remain loyal to their engagements.

It may not be out of place to add a word of explanation as to the attitude of the *mullas* and other religious leaders during the period which preceded the establishment of direct relations between the Government of India and the Swat clans.

After the Afghan war of 1878-80, the *mullas* of Swat and the adjacent countries were for some years openly hostile to the Amir, and sedulously denounced him as a friend of the British and therefore not a true follower of Islam. They also fostered the opposition to his intrigues and advances in Swat and the countries on its borders. In 1889, however, the Amir issued a proclamation to the inhabitants of Swat and other neighbouring tribes calling on all Mussulmans to acknowledge him as King of Islam, and to obey him as leader of the Muhammadan religion. Some years later, in 1896, he published several religious books, in which he impressed upon all Muhammadans the duty of *jehad* in defence of their country against invasion by an infidel. The *mullas*, who were by this time incensed at the increasing influence of Umra Khan throughout Dir and Swat, now directed their energies against him and in turn denounced him for his supposed reliance on British support. At the same time they agreed to recognize the Amir's claims to be the leader of their religion; and, henceforward proclaiming themselves his emissaries, they quoted his authority in their mischievous preachings against the British.

The first occasion on which British troops entered the Swat valley was in 1895. The events which led to the despatch of a force through the valley in that year for the relief of Chitral, and the operations undertaken by Sir R. Low for the coercion of Umra Khan of Jandol will be described in a subsequent chapter.[1]

Notwithstanding the assurances of the Government that, in demanding a free passage for our troops through Swat no interference with their country was intended, and in spite of the efforts of their *maliks* and *khans* to restrain them, the Swatis allowed their fanaticism to carry them away and opposed our entrance to the valley. After the advance of the troops beyond Chakdara, however, the Swat clans remained quiet, and, after the withdrawal of the force in September 1895, they raised no objections to the presence of our garrisons at the Malakand and Chakdara, which were established to guard the communications with Chitral.

An agency was instituted, with head-quarters at the Malakand, to conduct the political business between the Government and the tribes, but interference in the internal affairs of the country was as far as possible avoided. The postal service to Chitral was reopened, and a levy[2] system established, and increased allowances were granted to the *khans* of Swat and Ranizai, a special sum being added in lieu of tolls, which were henceforth to cease.

After the defeat and flight of Umra Khan in 1895[3] the Khan of Dir regained possession of the territories which he had lost five years

1 See Chapter XII.

2 The Swat levies guard the road from Dargai to the Chakdara bridge; their strength is 281 infantry and 35 *sowars*, and they are composed of Sam and Bar Ranizai with a small percentage of other mixed Pathans.

3 See page 541.

previously and took over practically all the conquests of the exiled chief of Jandol. His southern boundary was now the Swat river, and consequently he claimed as his subjects the following Swat sections who inhabit the right bank, *viz.*, Adinzai, Shamozai, Nikbi Khel, Sebujni and Shamizai, all of whom belong to the Khwazazai branch of Akozai-Yusafzai. These sections, however, are essentially Swatis and have therefore been dealt with in this chapter, instead of being included in the Dir tribes mentioned in Chapters XII and XIII.

The new arrangements appeared to be entirely satisfactory, trade increased rapidly, and all signs of hostility on the part of the people quickly disappeared.

In 1896 continual faction-fights took place in Upper Swat, and some unrest was caused by the interference of the Khan of Dir with the subject clans on the right bank of the river. The *mullas* and other religious leaders attempted to stir the fanaticism of the people, but no serious disturbance resulted; and the condition of the valley was on the whole satisfactory. The increase of trade along the Chitral road was very noticeable :—

Value of imports and exports through Swat.

	Imports. Rs.	Exports. Rs.
April-September 1894	2,91,929	2,22,744
,, .. 1896	16,15,892	10,43,424
October 1896 to March 1897 ..	20,10,669	7,70,684

Early in 1897, the *khans* of Aladand, Palai and Thana, who had grown rich and prosperous, began to oppress their poor neighbours; but the ringleader Sharif Khan of Aladand was punished, and matters finally quieted down. In June the rivalry between the Mian Guls and the Khan of Dir was causing much friction, and the latter was permitted to put a stop to the intrigues of the fanatical faction by coercing the tribes on the right bank of the river over whom he claimed authority. Early in the following month, the combined *jirgas* representing the clans of Upper Swat met Major Deane at Chakdara, and requested that he would "settle matters between them and the *khan*." Between 1,400 and 1,500 *maliks* attended the meeting, representing the four Khwazazai clans on the right bank, and the Musa Khel, Babuzai, and Jinki Khel on the other side of the river.

Major Deane reported that the *jirgas* accepted the fact of their being under Government influence in a good spirit, and looked to us now to have their country on the same footing as that already under us. They said that they wanted peace, they were ready to perform service if required, undertook to furnish fighting-men for Government, if called on to do so, and declared that the friends of the Government should be their friends and the enemies of Government their foes. Their principal petition was that they might not be called on to perform unpaid labour, and that exiles, convicted by them of murder, might not be put back on the land against the wish of the *jirgas*. Major Deane explained to them that Government had no desire to interfere with their internal administration, but would assist them in settling their disputes if they brought them before the Political Agent; that Government did not intend to impose revenue on them, and that all that Government wanted was to secure peace and order in Upper Swat, as had been done in Lower Swat and Ranizai. The main regret expressed by the tribesmen was that they had not entered into friendly relations with us before, so as to have excluded any interference by the Khan of Dir.

The authority of the Khan of Dir over the tribes on the right bank was now acknowledged; the power of the Mian Guls was broken; and their mischievous intrigues with the Hadda Mulla[1] and Palam Mulla received a severe check.

Throughout the early part of this year the Swat tribes had been to some extent affected by the general spirit of unrest which had spread throughout the Pathan tribes on the north-west frontier. This had been due in a great measure to the exertions of the Hadda Mulla and other priests, in Mohmand territory and in Dir and Bajaur, who had everywhere been spreading false reports and trying in every possible way to inflame the people against the British. After the settlement with the Swat *jirgas*, however, affairs in the valley seemed to have quieted down, and it appeared not unreasonable to accept the assertion of the Swatis themselves that "they had made up their minds to lay hold of the skirt of Government for good and all."

The progress made in the settlement of the Swat valley, since the establishment there of the Political Agency, and the apparently

[1] See page 471.

satisfactory attitude of the Swat tribes, have been alluded to at some length, in order to emphasize the very unexpected nature of the sudden outbreak of fanaticism which now occurred.

About the middle of July some strangers arrived in Upper Swat from Buner, where they were known to have lately been intriguing against the Government. Although it was not feared that any serious trouble would result from the presence of these men in the valley, a close watch was nevertheless kept on their actions.

At about the same time, some excitement was caused in Lower Swat by the appearance of a *fakir* named Sadullah (also called Mulla Mastan or Fakir Sartor) who took up his abode at Landakai. This man, who came to be known as the 'Mad Fakir,' was a Bunerwal, and was said to have been mad since the death of his son, who was accidentally killed some fifteen years previously. Having failed in his endeavours to incite the people of Buner to join in a *jehad* against the British, he now set himself to work to arouse the fanaticism of the Swat tribes. He distributed copies of the Amir's book [1] on the righteousness of *jehad*, promised heavenly rewards to all who would join, and assured his superstitious listeners of all kinds of miraculous assistance. At first he seems to have been regarded as a mere harmless lunatic, but news of his preaching soon spread, and began to attract large numbers of people from all parts of the country.

On the 25th July, Major Deane, the Political Agent, had an interview with the *khans* of Thana, who had asked him to prohibit the *fakir's* assemblies. Major Deane had, however, declined to interfere, and the *khans*, who were accompanied by the headmen of Khar and Keh, now stated that there was no cause for alarm. They also produced a letter from the Pisani Mulla, the chief adviser of the Mian Guls, stating that the latter would expel the madman should he continue to cause any trouble. It was reported later that the Mian Guls had actually ordered the *fakir's* removal, and as it was believed that the Swatis themselves were prepared to prevent the *fakir* from causing any disturbance, interference on the part of the Government officials appeared to be inadvisable.

[1] The Takvim-ud-Din.

Attack on the Malakand and Chakdara posts, by a fanatical gathering under the Mad Fakir.

On the afternoon of the 26th July the officers from the Malakand and Chakdara posts played polo on the ground near Khar village, without being in any way interfered with by the people, whose attitude was apparently quite friendly. Towards evening, however, disquieting reports of the Mad Fakir's proceedings reached the Political Agent at Malakand, and he accordingly requested Colonel Meiklejohn to hold the troops in readiness for immediate action in case of necessity. At the same time the Officer Commanding the Queen's Own Corps of Guides at Mardan was requested by telegram at once to reinforce the Malakand garrison with all available men.

Lieutenant Minchin, the Assistant Political Officer, was sent to Chakdara to report on the situation there, and to reassure the levies, who were thought to be unreliable. Shortly after his arrival there, this officer telegraphed to Major Deane that the *fakir* had been joined by the people of Thana, and was moving down the valley with a following of 400 or 500 men.

About 7 P.M., Major Deane informed the officer commanding the troops at the Malakand that the Mad Fakir had reached Aladand with a large gathering, and that the intervention of the troops would be necessary. Accordingly Colonel Meiklejohn arranged to despatch a column under Lieut.-Colonel McRae, at midnight, to seize the Amandara pass, while he himself proposed to follow three hours later with the remainder of the troops. But shortly before 10 P.M., news was received from Chakdara that the *fakir* had already passed Khar, and was on his way to the Malakand. Almost immediately after this, a Jemadar of Levies arrived, and reported that the *fakir* had been joined by the people from all the villages through which he had passed, and was now close at hand with a large force.

The Malakand Brigade under the command of Colonel W. H. Meiklejohn, C.B., C.M.G., was distributed as follows :—

MALAKAND.

Fort.—200 rifles, 24th Punjab Infantry.

Crater Camp.—6 companies, 24th Punjab Infantry.
6 companies, 45th Sikh Infantry.
No. 5 Company, Madras Sappers and Miners.

North Camp.—1 squadron, 11th Bengal Lancers (less 20 sabres).
No. 8 Bengal Mountain Battery.
6 companies, 31st Punjab Infantry.

CHAKDARA.

20 sabres, 11th Bengal Lancers.
180 rifles, 45th Sikh Infantry.

DARGAI.

200 rifles, 31st Punjab Infantry.

The Malakand position was somewhat extended (see plan). The fort was built on a spur running down from Guides Hill on the south-west to the *kotal*; north of this, in an irregular hollow known as "the crater" were the camps of the 24th Punjab Infantry, 45th Sikhs, and Sappers and Miners, with the Engineer park and Commissariat office and stores. The various enclosures were surrounded by abatis and wire entanglements, and picquets were posted on the high ground to the north. About three-quarters of a mile to the north-west was a second camp, called North camp, which was situated on a piece of flat open ground, and protected by a breastwork and obstacles. The two camps were connected by a well-made road. From the *kotal,* the newly made Chitral road, (known as the graded road) ran through the Crater Camp, and passing between the Castle Rock spur and Gibraltar Hill, led down to the Swat valley. Further east, the old Buddhist road, of which only a rough track remained, ran in a more or less parallel direction through a succession of narrow gorges.

About 10 P.M., on the receipt of Major Deane's report of the near approach of the fanatical gathering, Colonel Meiklejohn ordered the alarm to be sounded; the troops had hardly reached their posts when the enemy began an attack on the camp, advancing along the graded and Buddhist roads. Lieut.-Colonel McRae and Major Taylor, having promptly collected a few men of the 45th Sikhs, hurried off to seize the gorge through which the old Buddhist road descends from the *kotal.* This party was only just in time to check the rush of a large body of tribesmen, who tried to force an entrance to the camp through the defile. Driven back from the gorge by the steady fire of this handful of Sikhs, the enemy now climbed the rocky hills on either side. Colonel McRae being now reinforced by a second party under

Lieutenant Barff, responded by withdrawing his men to more commanding ground a little further back, where he was joined by the remainder of the regiment. Here he took up a position and held the enemy off till 2 A.M., when the tribesmen, foiled in their attempt to reach the camp on that side, beat a retreat, leaving many of their dead behind.

Just before the retirement of the Sikhs from the gorge, Major Taylor fell mortally wounded.

In his report on this affair Colonel Meiklejohn said—"There is no doubt that the gallant resistance made by this small body in the gorge against vastly superior numbers, till the arrival of the rest of the regiment, saved the camp from being rushed on that side, and I cannot speak too highly of the behaviour of Lieut.-Colonel McRae and Major Taylor on this occasion."

As soon as the alarm sounded, the picquets in front of the Crater camp had been doubled; one company 24th Punjab Infantry held the walls of the enclosure on either side of the entrance from the north camp road, while another under Lieutenant Climo, manned the wall of the bazaar facing the gorge through which the graded Chitral road passes. The remaining companies of this regiment were held in readiness to support any part of the line when required, and the central portion of the camp was defended by the Madras Sappers and Miners.

The enemy, advancing in large numbers along the graded road, drove back the picquets and spread out over the ground surrounding the camp. The *serai*, which was held by levies, was quickly rushed; the civil treasurer was killed, and all the property in the enclosure was looted or burned. A Nikbi Khel prisoner, who had been arrested a short time previously as a suspicious character, and who was undoubtedly implicated in the rising, was found here and liberated by his kinsmen. The enemy next attacked the bazaar, and some of them, getting on to the high ground behind the commissariat enclosure, kept up a heavy fire on the defenders; while a number of the tribesmen forced their way into the store godown, where they killed Lieutenant Manley. Colonel Meiklejohn, who had taken up his position in the central enclosure, now recalled the company from the bazaar, and sent for another company from the reserve to reinforce this portion of the defences. The tribesmen repeatedly charged the position held by the Sappers and Miners, and twice succeeded in forcing their way through the abatis which surrounded it. In one of these rushes, they captured the guard tent and a quantity of ammunition, which had been loaded up on mules for removal to the fort. After a sharp hand-to-hand struggle, in which Captain Holland was wounded and several men killed, the enemy were eventually driven out of this enclosure.

At about 2-30 A.M., Lieutenant Rawlins succeeded in making his way to the fort, and brought down 100 men to reinforce the Crater camp, which was now being hard pressed.

The enemy kept up the attack with great vigour till 4-30 A.M., when they retired, carrying off most of their dead and wounded.

During the attack, Lieutenant E. W. Costello had crossed the ground in front of the defences under heavy fire and, with the assistance of two sepoys, brought in a non-commissioned officer who was lying wounded about sixty yards away. For this gallant action, Lieutenant Costello was awarded the Victoria Cross.

The casualties in the Malakand garrison during this night attack were one officer and twenty-two non-commissioned officers and men killed; five [1] officers and thirty-one men wounded.

Next morning the troops in North camp, which had not been seriously attacked, were despatched in pursuit of the enemy. The cavalry advanced along the Chakdara road, but when the infantry reached a small knoll called Bedford Hill, opposite Khar village, a large hostile force was seen on the surrounding hills, and in the valley beyond. The guns and infantry were accordingly ordered to retire, covered by a wing of the 24th Punjab Infantry, which had been sent out to support them. As some of the enemy on the hills to the east of the Buddhist road threatened to cut off the retreat, Lieutenant Climo boldly attacked them with two companies, and drove them off, capturing a standard and inflicting heavy loss.

Meanwhile the squadron of the 11th Bengal Lancers [2] under Captain Wright had reached the Amandara defile. Finding the heights on either side strongly occupied, the cavalry skirted the hill on their left, and, fording the river with great difficulty, reached a small island in midstream. Pushing forward along this they soon

[1] Lieut.-Colonel J. Lamb, 24th Punjab Infantry, and Major W. W. Taylor, 45th Sikhs, subsequently died of their wounds.

[2] Captain D. Baker, Brigade Transport Officer, accompanied the cavalry to Chakdara.

THE MALAKAND POSITION.

Scale 1 Inch = 1600 Feet.

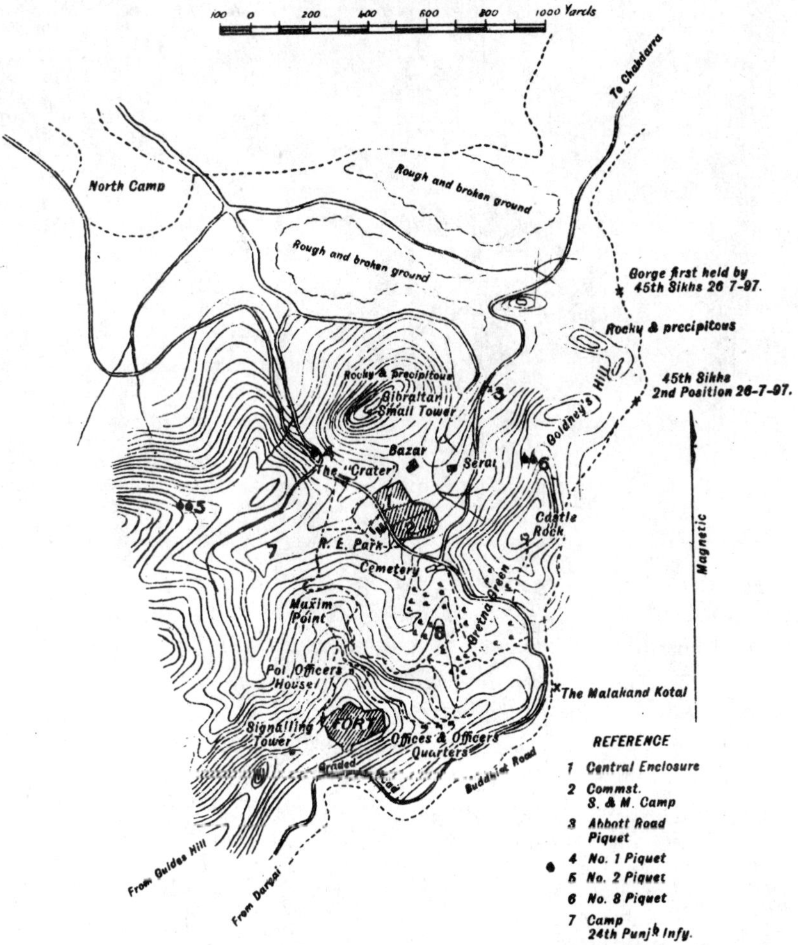

REFERENCE

1 Central Enclosure
2 Commst. S. & M. Camp
3 Abbott Road Piquet
4 No. 1 Piquet
5 No. 2 Piquet
6 No. 8 Piquet
7 Camp 24th Punjb Infy.
8 45th Sikhs

NOTE.—The line of the enclosures as here shown is only approximately correct as it was altered from time to time.

I. B. Topo. Dy. No. 6,698.
Exd. C. J. A., February 1907.

No. 4,058-I., 1907.

again came to the river, and re-crossed to the left bank. Here two men were wounded and some of the horses were hit, so Captain Wright dismounted a few of his troopers to hold the enemy in check until the rest of his party had forded the stream. He then continued his march to Chakdara, where he took over command from Lieutenant Rattray.

It was now plainly seen that the enemy were receiving reinforcements from various directions, and it was evident that the rising was not confined to the Swat tribesmen. Instead of being a merely local disturbance it appeared indeed to be a combined attempt on the part of the neighbouring clans to drive the British troops out of the valley. Information as to the state of affairs was telegraphed to the Government, and steps were taken to improve the defensive arrangements in preparation for a renewal of the attack.

Colonel Meiklejohn having decided to concentrate all his troops in the Crater and on the Malakand kotal, issued orders for the evacuation of North camp. Stores and baggage were sent up early on the 27th, but it was found impossible to move the large E. P. tents with the transport available, so these, together with a quantity of heavy baggage, had to be abandoned, and fell into the hands of the enemy. During this withdrawal, the troops were harassed by the tribesmen, about 1,000 of whom eventually charged down from the western heights, and tried to rush the Crater camp. They were however driven off by two companies under Lieutenant Climo, and the retirement was completed just before dark, when the last of the North camp troops reached the Crater, covered by the fire of the supports.

On this day the force at Colonel Meiklejohn's disposal was strengthened by the arrival of the Corps of Guides.[1] The cavalry had started from Mardan at 12-30 A.M. and reached the Malakand eight hours later, while the infantry, who left their station at 2 A.M., arrived at 7-30 P.M., having covered the distance of thirty-two miles in seventeen and a half hours. The Officer Commanding the Corps had only received his orders at 9 P.M. on the 26th, and the promptness with which the Guides responded to the call, and the forced march in the intense heat, reflected the greatest credit on the regiment.

1 Guides Cavalry, 160 sabres under Lieut.-Colonel Adams.
Guides Infantry, 250 rifles under Lieutenant P.C. Elliot Lockhart.
Guides Infantry, 50 rifles remained to reinforce Dargai post.

On the night of the 27th-28th July, the disposition of the troops was as follows:—On the right flank, holding a position about fifty yards in rear of that finally occupied on the previous night, were the 45th Sikhs, 100 rifles of the Guides, and 2 guns. In the centre the 31st Punjab Infantry, the Guides, No. 5 Company, Madras Sappers and Miners, and two guns defended the enclosures containing the Sappers' camp, and the commissariat and engineer stores. The 24th Punjab Infantry and the remaining two guns held the hill on the left (marked No. 2 picquet in the plan).

At 8-30 P.M., the enemy began a fresh attack, which was maintained throughout the night all along the line. The *serai*, overlooking the graded road, which was held by twenty-five men of the 31st Punjab Infantry under Subadar Saiyid Ahmad Shah, was most gallantly defended against tremendous odds until 3 A.M. The enemy then succeeded in partially demolishing the building and set it on fire, whereupon the survivors of the little garrison retreated to the enclosure in their rear, carrying their wounded with them. During their defence of the *serai* this party had lost nine men killed and ten wounded. Owing to the darkness and the noise of the firing all round, their need for assistance had not been realized by the troops in rear and consequently no reinforcement had been sent to them. Just about dawn, Lieutenant Climo with two companies of the 24th Punjab Infantry, supported by the fire of the two guns on the left, made a counter-attack on the enemy, who were closely pressing that flank from the high ground on the west. The tribesmen, many of whom were armed with Martini rifles, at first made a determined stand, but were resolutely driven back by Lieutenant Climo's men, losing forty killed and as many more wounded. The enemy had also closely pressed their assault on the centre and right of the position, but had everywhere been repulsed with heavy loss.

The casualties during the night amounted to eleven men killed, one British officer and forty-five men wounded.

Though the enemy had again been repulsed with considerable loss, they were by no means discouraged, and the news of the pillage of North camp, which was accepted as evidence of a defeat of the British troops, attracted large numbers of the tribesmen to come forward and join in the rising. Prompt measures, however, had already been taken to reinforce the beleaguered garrison.

Orders were issued on the 27th July for the immediate despatch of the marginally noted troops to the Malakand, while two squadrons, 10th Bengal Lancers and the 22nd Punjab Infantry were ordered from Jhelum to Mardan, and the Royal West Kent Regiment was held in readiness at Peshawar.

1 squadron, 11th Bengal Lancers.
No. 7 Mountain Battery, Royal Artillery.
35th Sikhs.
38th Dogras.

During daylight on the 28th, the enemy kept up a desultory fire on the camp. As any attempt to assume the offensive or to undertake the relief of Chakdara was out of the question until the arrival of reinforcements, the troops were employed throughout the day in strengthening the defences. At 10 P.M., the enemy renewed their attack on the camp with great energy; but, being repulsed at all points, they withdrew shortly before daybreak in the direction of Khar. As the day broke, they could be seen on the neighbouring hills, carrying off numbers of killed and wounded men; pursuit, however, was impossible, owing to the exhausted condition of the troops. On our side the casualties were two men killed, three British officers and thirteen men wounded.

On the 29th the defences were further improved, and the ground in front cleared. Bonfires were also prepared, to illuminate portions of the ground over which the enemy would have to advance.

Signalling communication was reopened with Chakdara, which was reported to be successfully holding out against continual attacks. During the afternoon one squadron, 11th Bengal Lancers, arrived at the Malakand, escorting a supply of 12,000 rounds of ammunition. The same evening the 35th Sikhs, 38th Dogras, and some men of the Guides, all under command of Colonel A. J. Reid, reached Dargai. The troops were greatly exhausted by their trying march in the intense heat; and the 35th Sikhs, who had pushed forward as quickly as possible from Nowshera, lost twenty-one men from heat apoplexy. Brigadier-General Meiklejohn accordingly ordered Colonel Reid to halt at Dargai the next day in order to rest his troops.

On the night of the 29th-30th, the enemy again attacked the camp, and avoiding the centre, where they were exposed to the light of the bonfires and the fire of the 9-pounder guns in the fort, they directed their main efforts on the flanks. A fierce assault was made on the water picquet in rear of the position held by the 24th

Punjab Infantry, and several of the enemy were bayoneted inside the *sangar*. At 2 A.M., the tribesmen made a final desperate effort to break through the defence, and even succeeded in cutting through the wire entanglement, and tearing down portions of the *sangars*; but their attack was everywhere repulsed with great loss, and half an hour later they suddenly abandoned the attempt and dispersed. It was afterwards reported that the Mad Fakir, who personally led the last assault, had retired to Landakai, having been wounded in the hand. His chief companion and second-in-command was found dead outside the line. This man was identified as a native of India, and it was said that the *fakir* had intended to crown him King of Delhi, when he had completed the overthrow of British rule in India.

The casualties on our side during the night had been two British officers severely wounded, one man killed, and seventeen of the native ranks wounded.

Early on the morning of the 30th, 200 rifles of the 31st Punjab Infantry, who had formed the garrison of Dargai, were sent up to the Malakand camp. Here the troops were again employed in repairing the damage done during the previous night, and further improving the defensive arrangements. There was less interference than usual on the part of the enemy, who were apparently discouraged by the non-success which had hitherto attended their determined and costly attacks. During the afternoon, however, it was observed that they were being largely reinforced, which tended to confirm a report received from Chakdara that the Mian Guls had joined the enemy, and had obtained the assistance of a contingent from Buner.

At night the tribesmen renewed their attack, and kept up a continual fire till daybreak, but the garrison, being well protected behind their improved defences, suffered little loss. The enemy did not show the same reckless spirit that they had displayed in their former attacks; one party, however, taking advantage of a sharp thunderstorm which broke over the camp, tried to rush the east flank held by the 45th Sikhs, but were repulsed with the bayonet.

On the next morning Colonel Reid, having left a garrison of 400 men and some cavalry at Dargai, reached the Malakand unopposed with the remainder of his reinforcements, numbering in all 707 rifles. Large numbers of the enemy occupied the surrounding hills, and kept up a desultory fire during the day; but no night attack followed, though a few shots were fired into the camp.

On the 1st August, Brigadier-General Meiklejohn decided to despatch a portion of his troops to relieve the garrison at Chakdara, which was known to be running short of ammunition and supplies.

Accordingly at 11 A.M., the Guides Cavalry under Lieut.-Colonel Adams were sent off by the North camp road with orders to reconnoitre the Amandara defile, and if possible seize the pass. The enemy however promptly detected the General's intentions, and hastily collected in large numbers to oppose the advance of the troops. As they reached the plain, the cavalry charged a considerable body of the tribesmen and killed at least a hundred of them, but the broken ground, which was very rocky and much cut up by *nalas*, greatly impeded their progress. In this skirmish the Guides lost one man killed, two officers and twelve men wounded. Brigadier-General Meiklejohn now realised that, owing to the lateness of the start, there was small prospect of being able to push through to Chakdara that day, in face of the opposition which was certain to be encountered. He accordingly decided to postpone the attempt till the next morning, and directed the troops to withdraw to camp.

On this date Major-General Sir Bindon Blood arrived at the Malakand and assumed command. Brigadier-General Meiklejohn's proposals for the immediate relief of Chakdara having been approved by Sir Bindon Blood, a column consisting of the marginally noted troops, bivouacked on Gretna Green, preparatory to moving out at daybreak. The enemy meanwhile remained collected in large numbers on the hills to the north, and firing was kept up all day and throughout the night. Several parties of tribesmen advanced to within a few hundred yards of our picquets, and shortly before midnight the column on Gretna Green got under arms in expectation of a determined attack. The enemy however declined the attempt, and at 3 A.M. firing ceased.

2 squadrons, Guides Cavalry.
2 ,, 11th Bengal Lancers.
4 gun, No. 8 Bengal Mountain Battery.
½ No. 5 Company, Madras Sappers and Miners.
400 Rifles, 24th Punjab Infantry.
400 ,, 15th Sikhs.
200 ,, Guides Infantry.

At 5 A.M. on the 2nd, Brigadier-General Meiklejohn moved off with the relieving column, and Sir Bindon Blood, who directed the operations from Castle rock, at the same time ordered Lieutenant-Colonel Goldney

The relief of Chakdara.

with a detachment of the 35th Sikhs and 38th Dogras to advance and seize a spur[1] about half a mile further north. This party approached to within a hundred yards of the position without being perceived, and suddenly rushing forward captured the hill without loss. The tribesmen, who had been completely taken by surprise, dispersed in all directions, leaving seven dead bodies on the ground. The infantry now took up their position on Goldney's hill, and with two mountain guns in action on Castle rock covered the advance of the column for some distance along the graded road.

As the column reached the open ground and deployed, a number of the enemy hurriedly occupied a position on high ground near the junction of the main road with that leading from North camp, and opened a heavy but inaccurate fire on the troops. The Guides Infantry and 45th Sikhs were at once ordered to attack, and, carrying this position with slight loss, drove the defenders off at the point of the bayonet before they could be reinforced. Abandoning sixty or seventy dead, the enemy now fell back to a second position on a cluster of knolls known as Bedford hill, on which is the village of Malakot. Here they were again speedily attacked by the 24th Punjab Infantry and 45th Sikhs, who advanced on the left and centre, while the Guides carried the heights on the east. Driven back a second time with considerable loss, the tribesmen were now thoroughly disheartened, and large numbers of them took to flight across the Khar plain. Here they were intercepted by the cavalry, who vigorously pursued them, spearing and cutting them down in all directions.

As soon as the squadrons had reformed, Lieut.-Colonel Adams, who was in command of the cavalry, pushed on to Amandara and seized the pass. Meanwhile the infantry, after a short halt, continued their advance; and on arrival at Bat-Khela, the 45th Sikhs drove out a number of the enemy who had just before fired on the cavalry. These men made a stubborn resistance, and eighty of them were bayoneted in the village. The cavalry now pushed forward to Chakdara whence the sound of heavy firing could be heard, and reached the bridge over the Swat river at 9 A.M. On the advance of the relieving troops the enemy who were collected round Chakdara abandoned their attempt to capture the fort and

[1] Afterwards called Goldney's hill—see plan.

began to retire. Thereupon Lieutenant Rattray, collecting a few men of the garrison, made a sortie, drove off about thirty of the assailants who were holding the Civil hospital, and shot them down as they tried to escape along the river bank. Some more men were now collected from the fort by Captain Baker, and the combined party ascending the hill overlooking the river, cleared a number of *sangars* whence the enemy were trying to oppose the advance of the cavalry.

Meanwhile the cavalry, having crossed the river, started in pursuit of the fugitives, who fled in several parties up the Adinzai valley; but as the men and horses were already fatigued by their exertions and the excessive heat, they were soon recalled.

The remainder of the column reached the fort at 10 A.M., when the village of Chakdara was destroyed and the hills surrounding the post occupied without opposition. The garrison of the fort were found in excellent health and spirits after their six days' siege, and had only lost three men killed and nine wounded throughout their spirited defence.

The casualties of the relieving column amounted to five men killed and twenty-eight wounded, while the cavalry lost twenty horses killed and wounded.

The defence of Chakdara.

It has previously been mentioned that a fortified post was constructed at Chakdara in 1895 for the protection of the suspension bridge across the Swat river. This fort, which was built of stone, was situated on a small rocky knoll on the right bank of the river, and about 150 yards from the end of a spur which descends from the high hills on the west. On the north-west and west faces were double-storeyed barracks with rows of loopholes and arrangements for flanking fire. The north-east side of the knoll was steeply scarped and protected by a wall and barbed wire fence, while on the south was a small hornwork, enclosed by a stone wall and surrounded by wire entanglement. About 500 yards away, on the spur to the west, was a small one-storeyed blockhouse, used as a signalling tower, from which communication was maintained with the Malakand. On the left bank of the river the entrance to the bridge was guarded by a loopholed iron gate with a blockhouse on either side.

When the outbreak occurred in July 1897 the Chakdara garrison was under the command of Lieutenant H. B. Rattray, 45th Sikhs. On the afternoon of the 26th July this officer was playing polo at Khar, when he received an urgent message from 2nd-Lieutenant Wheatley, at Chakdara, stating that large numbers of tribesmen with standards were approaching along both sides of the river. Lieutenant Rattray at once rode back to his post, without being in any way interfered with by the people along the road, and having ascertained that the information as to the hostile gathering was correct he promptly telegraphed the news to the Malakand. News of the rising was first brought to Chakdara by a Sikh havildar who was employed on survey work, and who reported that he had been robbed by a party of tribesmen, and prevented from sketching. Shortly afterwards Inayat Khan of Thana arrived at the fort, with a few personal followers, and stated that the rest of the people of his village had joined the Mad Fakir.

A little after 10 P.M., a signal fire was lighted on a neighbouring hill by a man of the Dir Levies, who had arranged to give warning of the enemy's approach. The alarm was instantly sounded and, almost immediately after, the attack[1] began. The enemy, who consisted chiefly of men from the Adinzai valley and Khwazazai-Shamozai, made their first assault on the west face, and when that failed tried to scale the east side by means of ladders procured from the civil hospital. They next attempted to force an entrance to the hornwork, but were everywhere repulsed, and withdrew shortly before dawn to Chakdara village and the hills on the north and north-west. From these heights, which completely commanded the fort at ranges varying from 500 to 1,000 yards, the tribesmen opened a desultory but harassing fire. Early on the morning of the 27th, Captains Wright and Baker, with forty lances of the 11th Bengal Lancers, reached the fort from Malakand as already described. Captain Wright now

[1] It may be interesting to note here that at 2 A.M. after the attacks had been made on the Malakand position, the troops at Chakdara saw a fire balloon with a scintillating ball of intensely white light sent up from the top of a hill, about four miles off, adjoining the Swat valley. This was of course a pre-arranged signal for the tribes to rise. As such a signal was quite different to the usual tribal custom of signalling by means of lighting fires on the hilltops, and as moreover the balloon must have been an imported article, this strange occurrence is a proof that the idea of a rising did not originate in the Swat valley itself, but was instigated elsewhere.

assumed command of the post, and the sowars were detailed to defend the hornwork, which had been held on the previous night by the original detachment of cavalry, assisted by a few men of the Sikhs. In the forenoon the attack was renewed with great energy; under cover of a heavy fire from their riflemen, successive parties and even single men carrying standards charged recklessly up to the very walls, only to be mown down by the hail of bullets from the fort. When at last the assailants fell back to the hills, the garrison set to work to strengthen their defences, improvising headcover where the walls were not loopholed, and erecting cover for the gun detachments, who had been somewhat exposed.

Communication with the Malakand was now interrupted; the telegraph wire had been cut, and the enemy had built *sangars* all round the signalling tower, and kept up an incessant fire, which prevented the signallers from carrying on their work. The party in the tower, which consisted of ten men of the 45th Sikhs, was reinforced by six more rifles, and supplies and water were sent up under cover of fire from the fort. Water had to be sent up daily in this manner, as unfortunately the tank in the tower had not been kept filled. The *bhisties*, who had to carry their water-skins up the steep face of the ridge, where they could get no cover from the enemy's fire, performed this dangerous duty with the unflinching courage which men of this caste have so often displayed in Indian warfare.

During the night the tribesmen made two attacks, and attempted to scale the north-east face, but were driven off with heavy loss. On the evening of the next day and throughout the night the enemy, who had now been joined by contingents from the Abazai, Khadakzai, and Musa Khel clans, continued their fruitless attacks, but were invariably beaten off.

On the afternoon of the 29th a determined attempt was made to capture the signal tower, but the enemy only succeeded in setting fire to a thatched shed outside the wall, and retreated at dusk, having suffered severely from the fire of the troops in the fort. Their losses on this occasion were so heavy that they were unable to carry off all their dead during the night, and on the following day some fifty bodies were left lying round the foot of the tower.

On the 30th July the besiegers were reinforced by some men from Bajaur, but they only made a somewhat half-hearted attack in the evening, and were easily defeated; the assault however was renewed on the following night, but with no better success, for the tribesmen again lost very heavily from the effective fire of the maxim and 9-pr. guns. During this night too, the enemy occupied the civil hospital, and, having loopholed the walls facing the hornwork, manned them with a number of riflemen. Other parties of tribesmen had also built *sangars* on the west spur between the signal tower and the fort, but defiladed from the fire of the defenders in the former post. From this position they were able to bring a close rifle fire to bear on the fort.

On the 1st August it was evident that the numbers of the enemy were rapidly increasing, and they were believed to have been joined by men from the Malakand, and by a number of Malizai clansmen. The increased numbers of the enemy, and the cautious manner in which they were now pushing forward under cover of entrenchments, in contrast to the frenzied recklessness of their former open attacks, greatly augmented the difficulties of the garrison. Matters looked so serious that Captain Wright decided to send an urgent message to the Malakand asking for assistance. Signalling was difficult, as the men had to come outside the tower and expose themselves to fire from close range; they however succeeded in sending a short message containing only the words "help us," but the reply, stating that relief would be sent the next day, was not received. Meanwhile the garrison were kept continually at their post throughout the day and the following night. On the 2nd August the enemy, whose strength was now estimated at about 8,000 men, advanced to the attack in a most determined manner. They carried ladders and bundles of grass, and evidently intended to make a last effort to capture the post at all costs. A very heavy fusilade was maintained on both sides but, though large numbers of the tribesmen were seen to fall, the combined fire of the small arms and the maxim and 9-pr. gun was barely sufficient to check the onward rush. Just as the position of the defenders was becoming critical, the cavalry of the relieving column appeared on the Amandara ridge. The enemy continued to press their attack until the squadrons were near at hand, when they beat a hasty retreat, their rearmost detachments being severely handled by the gallant little band from the fort, which made the dashing sortie already mentioned.

The casualties among the garrison during the siege and final sortie amounted to five men killed, one officer and ten men wounded. This comparatively slight loss was in a great measure due to the excellence of the defensive arrangements and to the effective cover which had been provided under the superintendence of Captain Baker. Sir B. Blood concluded his report in the following terms :—

During the fighting above described, the conduct of the whole of the garrison, whether fighting-men, departmental details, or followers, is reported to have been most gallant. Not the least marked display of courage and constancy was that made by the small detachment in the Signal Tower who were without water for the last 18 hours of the siege. The signallers, under Lance-Naick Vir Singh, 45th Sikhs, who set a brilliant example, behaved throughout in a most courageous manner ; one of them, Sepoy Prem Singh, climbing several times out of the window in the Tower with a heliograph, and signalling outside to the Malakand under a hot fire from *sangars* in every direction.

On the 3rd August Brigadier-General Meiklejohn's column marched back to Amandara, where they were joined by a column under Colonel Reid, who was conveying supplies and ammunition to Chakdara. The two columns, accompanied by Sir Bindon Blood, visited Aladand and Thana, and thoroughly searched the villages, meeting with no opposition. On the following day Sir Bindon Blood returned with Colonel Reid's column to the Malakand, while the troops under Brigadier-General Meiklejohn remained at Amandara, where the 1st Brigade of the Field Force was to be formed.

Operations of the Malakand Field Force under Major-General Sir Bindon Blood, K.C.B.

In order to crush the rising, and to punish the Swatis and other clans who had joined them in the attacks on our posts, which have just been described, the Government of India sanctioned the despatch of a force under the command of Major-General Sir Bindon Blood, K.C.B. This force which was known as the Malakand Field Force, included the troops which originally formed the garrisons of the Swat posts, and the units which had been sent to reinforce them on the first outbreak of hostilities.

The composition of the force is given in Appendix A.

An advanced supply depôt was established at Khar on the 9th August and subsequently reserve supplies were arranged for as follows :—

At Malakand	30 days' supplies for the		1st and 2nd Brigades.
„ Rustam	15 „	„ „ „	3rd (Reserve) Brigade.
„ Nowshera	30 „	„ „ „	1st and 2nd Brigades.
	45 „	„ „ „	3rd Brigade.

The 1st Brigade was ordered to concentrate at Amandara, the 2nd Brigade at Khar and Malakand, while the Reserve troops were to be held in readiness at Rawalpindi and Mardan.

The divisional troops, with the exception of detachments detailed to hold posts on the line of communication at Jalala and Dargai, were also to concentrate in the Swat valley, and were attached to brigades as required. Concentration was completed on the 8th August, but meanwhile the punishment of the Lower Swatis had already been begun by the force then in the valley, and cavalry reconnaissances had been made for some distance into Upper Swat.

On the 7th August, Brigadier-General Jeffreys with a force of two battalions and four guns visited Jalalkot, Dherai, Jolagram, and some other villages to the west of Khar. These were all found to be deserted, and their defences were demolished without opposition. On the following day, in consequence of a report that some Bunerwals and Hindustani fanatics were moving into the valley, the Shakot, Morah, and Charat passes were reconnoitred. Only a few of the enemy were met with, and these were easily dispersed by the cavalry.

On the 9th the Ranizai and Khan Khel *jirgas* came in, and tendered their submission, which was accepted on the following terms [1] :—Payment of a fine of Rs. 47,000; surrender of all arms, and all Government property in their possession; forfeiture of *maliki* allowances and compensation in lieu of tolls. The destruction of their villages and the prospect of losing their rice crops, the value of which was estimated at a lakh and a half of

[1] Additional penalties were imposed in the case of Sharif Khan of Aladand and certain other leading men who were not included in the general terms arranged with the *jirgas*.

rupees, doubtless convinced these clans of the folly of further resistance. The terms having been agreed to, the inhabitants were permitted to return to their villages.

On the 12th August the Khwazazai clans (Shamozai, Nikbi Khel, Sĕbujni and Shamizai) on the right bank of the Swat river, who are nominally subject to the Khan of Dir, sent in their *jirgas* to Chakdara to sue for peace. Their submission was also accepted on terms similar to those imposed on the Lower Swatis, and in addition they agreed to the passage of troops through their country whenever the Government should consider it necessary.

Advance into Upper Swat and action of Landakai.

Sir Bindon Blood now decided to advance along the left bank of the river into Upper Swat, and in order to guard his force against a flank attack from Buner, the Reserve Brigade under Brigadier-General Wodehouse was ordered to remain in observation at Mardan and Rustam. This latter place is situated at the foot of the passes leading from the Yusafzai plain into Buner, and consequently the troops which concentrated there were in a position to hold the Bunerwals in check.

Guides Cavalry.
11th Bengal Lancers.
Royal West Kent Regiment.
24th Punjab Infantry.
31st ,, ,,
45th Sikhs.
10th Field Battery, R. A.
No. 7 Mountain Battery, R. A.
No. 8 Bengal Mountain Battery
No. 5 Company, Madras Sappers and Miners.

Sir Bindon Blood's movement had been delayed by bad weather, but on the 16th he marched with the troops noted in the margin from Amandara to Thana. This force was without tents; twelve days' supplies for men, and two days' grain for animals were carried. The cavalry, who were sent forward to reconnoitre towards Landakai, obtained information that a large force of the enemy was holding the hills above that village.

The position at Landakai, which is one of great natural strength, is locally known as "the gate of Swat." Here, just west of the village, a steep rocky spur runs down from the mountains on the south and ends abruptly at the river's edge, where it commands the road from Thana, which is the only entrance to the upper valley. The road through the gorge leads for about a mile along a narrow stone-paved causeway, only wide enough for men to advance in single file. The enemy's main position lay along the crest of the Landakai ridge, which was fortified with *sangars.* About a mile or more to the west another ridge, descending from a peak which overlooks the Landakai spur, ends at the village of Jalala. Between this village and Landakai is an open valley about half a mile across, with a *nala* running through it, and then another spur divided off from the Landakai ridge by a deep ravine.

At daybreak on the 17th August, some excess baggage was sent back to Khar under escort of a squadron of the 11th Bengal Lancers. The remainder of the baggage and stores was left at Thana, guarded by two squadrons, 11th Bengal Lancers, two companies, 45th Sikhs, and 400 rifles, 35th Sikhs.[1]

The advanced guard, headed by the Guides Cavalry under Lieut.-Colonel Adams, marched from Thana at 6-30 A.M., and on reaching Jalala found the enemy's scouts holding some Buddhist ruins on the spur above the village. Two companies of the West Kent Regiment at once engaged them, and on the arrival of the main body they fell back.

A few minutes before 9 A.M. the 10th Field Battery and No. 7 Mountain Battery came into action on the Jalala ridge, along which the West Kent Regiment was already extended, and opened fire on the Landakai spur, where some two or three thousand tribesmen were strongly posted in an ancient Buddhist fort and numerous *sangars.* Meanwhile Brigadier-General Meiklejohn, with the remainder of the infantry and No. 8 Bengal Mountain Battery, moved to his right along the rear of this position, and ascended a spur leading up to the crest of the main ridge, which commanded the enemy's left flank. The enemy had evidently prepared to meet a frontal attack, and had posted their main force and reserves along the northern end of the position to defend the causeway. But as soon as they realised that a turning movement was in progress, which not only endangered their weakly-held left, but also menaced the line of retreat towards the Morah pass, they made an effort to reinforce the threatened flank from their right and centre. This move however was frustrated by the fire of the artillery and the long range volleys of the West Kent Regiment, which held the defenders in check and drove them under cover behind the ridge.

[1] This detachment of the 35th Sikhs was sent from Khar for this duty.

The enemy now began to waver, and before the flanking column could intercept them a considerable number made off towards the Morah pass. On the summit of the ridge, a few of the bolder spirits covered the retreat of their comrades, and checked the leading infantry until they were dispersed by the shrapnel fire of the supporting guns. The ascent at last accomplished, the flanking troops turned left-handed and pushed forward along the crest, clearing the enemy out of a cluster of ruined buildings in their front, and gaining touch with the West Kent companies, which had moved further up the Jalala spur. The enemy were now everywhere retiring, and at 11 o'clock the left wing of the West Kent moved forward, and, seizing the Landakai ridge, drove the defenders from their last *sangars*. As soon as the sappers and miners had repaired the causeway, and removed the obstructions placed there by the enemy, the cavalry were launched in pursuit. The track along the causeway was so rough and narrow that the troopers had to advance in single file leading their horses. As the leading files debouched into the open, Captain Palmer hastily collected a few men and dashed on in pursuit. He was followed at no great distance by Lieut.-Colonel Adams and another troop in loose formation, while the other squadrons came on in succession as quickly as they could. The majority of the enemy had meanwhile reached the foot hills above Nawakila, a village lying about a mile and a half to the eastward of Landakai. Seeing that it was too late to charge, Lieut.-Colonel Adams ordered his sowars to hold a small *ziarat* close to the village and open fire. Unfortunately this order was not heard by Captain Palmer or by Lieutenant Greaves,[1] who was riding beside him, and the two officers galloped on. Coming up with a few stragglers, Captain Palmer cut down one of the enemy, but, immediately after, his horse was shot under him and he himself was disabled by a wound, and was with difficulty rescued by two of his men. At the same moment Lieutenant Greaves was struck by a bullet, and losing control of his horse was carried on to the foot of the slope, where he fell to the ground and was instantly surrounded by the enemy's swordsmen. Seeing this,

1 Lieutenant R. T. Greaves, Lancashire Fusiliers, accompanied the force as a newspaper correspondent, and Lieutenant Viscount Fincastle, 16th Lancers, was present in the same capacity.

Lieut.-Colonel Adams and Lieutenant Viscount Fincastle, followed by Lieutenant Maclean with a few of the Guides Cavalry, immediately dashed forward under a hot fire from the tribesmen on the hill, and, scattering the swordsmen, saved the wounded officer from their clutches. As he was being lifted on to a horse, however, Greaves was shot dead, and an instant later Maclean was killed at his side. Under cover of the fire of the dismounted cavalry the rest of the little party reached the shelter of the *ziarat*, carrying with them the bodies of their comrades.

For this gallant action Lieut.-Colonel Adams and Viscount Fincastle received the Victoria Cross,[1] while Jamadar Bahadur Singh and four men of the Guides Cavalry were awarded the Order of Merit.

While the cavalry pursuit was taking place, the infantry and mountain batteries, continuing their advance, descended from the Landakai spur and pushed forward through the Kota hamlets towards the hills. On their appearance, the tribesmen moved off into the higher hills, firing a few shots at impossible ranges as they retreated. When the main body came up, Lieut.-Colonel Adams remounted his men and continued the pursuit about a mile further up the valley to Abuwa, on the Barikot road. Here about 150 of the enemy who were holding the village were driven off, 8 of them being killed, and the cavalry returned to camp near Landakai, which they reached at 6-30 P.M.

While these operations were going on a number of the tribesmen, who had retreated in the direction of the Morah pass, came down towards Thana with the intention of cutting off the baggage. But, seeing the camp well guarded, they did not press the attack and were easily dispersed, losing some twenty men killed. The British casualties during the day were two officers killed, two officers and seven men wounded. The enemy's losses were subsequently ascertained to have exceeded 300.

The small loss incurred by the troops, and the comparative ease with which the enemy were dislodged from their strong position at Landakai, was in a great measure due to the skilful dispositions of the General Officer Commanding; and the discomfiture of the enemy was completed by the admirably executed

[1] A recent announcement (1907) in the *London Gazette* states that Lieutenant Maclean would also have received the Victoria Cross had he survived, and the decoration has been handed to his relatives.

turning movement, and by the effective fire of the artillery—especially of the 12-pr. B.L. field guns, which this year made their first appearance [1] in Indian frontier warfare.

On the 18th August the column marched along the left bank of the Swat to Ghalegai. No opposition was met with, and all the villages along the road were found to be deserted. At Ghalegai, however, the *maliks* and other inhabitants had remained in their village, and on the arrival of the troops they promptly complied with the General's demands, and surrendered all arms and Government property in their possession, and furnished supplies and transport. On the following day the troops moved on by a fairly good road to Mingaora. Many of the inhabitants had returned to their villages, and the people everywhere seemed to have abandoned all ideas of further resistance, and were evidently anxious to propitiate the troops by offering supplies. A few shots were fired into the camp during the night, but the villagers themselves turned out and quickly dispersed the snipers.

The force remained at Mingaora until the 24th August, during which time Major Deane was engaged in enforcing the terms of submission on the various sections of the tribes implicated in the rising. Reconnaissances were made up the valley to Manglaor, Charbagh, and Gulibagh, and eastward as far as the Kotkai pass, which gives access to the Jinki Khel valley of Ghurband.

Steps were taken to disarm the country up to the limits of Kohistan, and forty-one breech-loading rifles and some 800 other fire-arms were collected; a number of standards, and some Government property, including transport animals and equipment, were also surrendered. A considerable quantity of grain, fodder, and fuel was taken without payment; and the tribesmen were compelled to demolish the defensive towers in their villages. They were also required to protect the post service between Thana and Mingaora.

Submission of the Upper Swatis.

On the 22nd August, the Upper Swati *jirgas* agreed to unconditional surrender, and signed a document to that effect. They were assured that Government had no desire to interfere with them or their country, but that peace must be maintained on the border. In

1 The Field Battery equipped with 12-pr. B.L. guns, which took part in the Chitral relief expedition of 1895 did not come into action.

his interviews with the tribesmen, Major Deane had persistently endeavoured to ascertain the true reasons for the outbreak, and from the replies received to his questions it appeared that, in the case of the Swatis at any rate, fanaticism was the sole motive. They had no complaint to make against the action of the Government, or the conduct of the officials, and when asked direct why they had attacked our post on the Malakand, they naively replied that they were "not aware that Government had issued any orders forbidding them to do so."

The Mian Guls had sent letters some days previously in which they expressed their desire for peace and willingness to submit, but they had not ventured to attend in person, and they now withdrew to Ilam on the border of Buner. As they were already discredited in Swat, it was not considered worth while to take any further steps to procure their surrender. The Mad Fakir was at this time reported to be at Mahaban in Buner, but he too had completely lost the extraordinary influence he had so rapidly acquired over the Swatis, and they now bitterly reproached him for the misfortunes which he had brought upon them.

On the 24th August the force under Sir Bindon Blood marched back to Barikot, where a halt was made in order to reconnoitre the Karakar pass leading into Buner. The column continued its return march to Thana on the 26th, and on the following day the troops moved on to Khar and Malakand.

Movements of the troops in Lower Swat.

During the operations in Upper Swat, the 2nd Brigade under Brigadier-General Jeffreys had remained at Khar to enforce the submission of the Lower Swatis. With a view to an advance into Utman Khel country, a passable road had been made by a difficult route *viâ* Jolagram to Matkanai, and on the 24th August Brigadier-General Jeffreys visited the latter place with a portion of the 2nd Brigade. Thence he reconnoitred the Mekhban valley belonging to the Sultan Khel, and advanced as far as Pir Khel, in the direction of the Digar pass; a reconnaissance was also made up to the junction of the Swat and Panjkora rivers. The inhabitants were everywhere submissive, and were evidently much disturbed by the presence of the troops.

On the 27th August the 2nd Brigade marched to Thana, whence Sir Bindon Blood intended that Brigadier-General Jeffreys should advance into Buner by the Karakar pass. But the condition of affairs in other parts of the frontier, and the extension of the rising to the Afridis and Orakzais[1] induced the Government to postpone the coercion of the Bunerwals to a more favourable time. Sir Bindon Blood was however authorised to proceed at once with the punishment of the Utman Khel on the left bank of the Swat river if he considered such action desirable. Accordingly the 2nd Brigade returned to Jolagram on the 28th, and two days later moved on through Kalangai, the last village in Swat, and encamped at the foot of the Inzargai pass. On the following day however the orders for the operations against the Utman Khel were suddenly countermanded and the 2nd Brigade was recalled to Khar.

On the 30th Colonel A. J. Reid with the marginally noted troops, moved from Chakdara to Uch, in order to support the Nawab of Dir in dealing with the Adinzai and the Khwazazai clans of Upper Swat on the right bank of the river. These people were nominally subjects of this chief, and he had accordingly been deputed to collect the fines in money and rifles which had been inflicted on them.

2 squadrons, 11th Bengal Lancers.
10th Field Battery R.A.
38th Dogras.
22nd Punjab Infantry.
½ No. 5 Company, Madras Sappers and Miners.
Section, No. 13 British Field Hospital.
Section No. 35 Native Field Hospital.

The Government of India now decided to despatch two brigades under Sir Bindon Blood through Dir and Bajaur in order to co-operate from Nawagai with the Mohmand Field Force, and completely crush the Hadda Mulla's gathering. The 2nd and 3rd Brigades were selected for these operations[2] and the 1st Brigade remained in the Swat valley.

On the 24th September Major Deane had a satisfactory interview with the Upper Swat *jirga*, which was accompanied by the younger Mian Gul, Gul Badshah, son of the late Abdul Hanan.

On the 2nd October the Mian Gul Amir Badshah, younger son of Abdul Manan, also came to visit Major Deane at Malakand, and was attended by several *maliks*, *mullas*, and *sheikhs*. The senior Mian Gul, Saiyid Badshah, elder son of Abdul Manan, had written to say that he, too, was on his way to attend the meeting,

1 See Volume II.
2 Sir Bindon Blood, with 2nd and 3rd Brigades, advanced from Chakdara, on 6th September. The further operations of these brigades being against the Mohmand tribes, will be dealt with in Chapter XI.

but was prevented by illness from completing his journey, and would come on as soon as he recovered. He kept his promise on the 30th October, when he came in with his brother and the Pisani Mulla to attend an important meeting at which some 600 *maliks* and representative men from Upper Swat were present. The attendance of the Mian Guls was significant, and proved that the religious leaders, as well as the tribal representatives, were sincere in their expressed willingness to submit to the terms imposed and complete the settlement. The *jirga* raised the question of the future administration of their country, and a large majority of the tribesmen expressed themselves in favour of direct control by the Government of India, stating that by no other means could they obtain justice or settle their interminable disputes.

About a fortnight later Major Deane was able to report that the fanatical feeling in the country generally had subsided, and that the people were engaged in repairing damage done to villages, and in their ordinary occupations.

On the 27th October all the troops of the Malakand Field Force (with the exception of the 3rd Brigade which had remained with the Mohmand Field Force) were again concentrated in the Swat valley. A few days later the 2nd Brigade moved into the old North camp, while the remainder of the troops were withdrawn to Jalala.

The Indian Medal, 1895, with clasp and medal inscribed "Punjab Frontier, 1897-98" was granted to the troops which proceeded beyond Jalala and took part in the operations above described. An additional clasp inscribed "Malakand, 1897" was awarded to those who took part in the defence and relief of Malakand and Chakdara between the 26th July and the 2nd August inclusive.

In November 1897 and January 1898, the Malakand Field Force was employed in operations against the cis-Swat Utman Khel and against the Bunerwals, a description of which will be found in the chapters dealing with those tribes. On the conclusion of the latter expedition, the force was broken up, but a moveable column (consisting of three squadrons, one mountain battery, two companies of Sappers and Miners, and six battalions) remained in the Swat valley.

Events in Swat after the operations of 1897-98.

In February 1898 some unrest was caused in the valley by the *mullas*, who tried to rekindle the fanticism of the tribesmen. The latter, however, showed little enthusiasm, and were easily restrained by their headmen. Towards the end of the year more trouble was caused by the action of the Mad Fakir, and the moveable column was sent up from Khar towards Landakai; but the *fakir's* attempt failed, and his gathering, which had moved into Dir territory, was dispersed by the *Nawab's lashkar.*

For the next three years nothing occurred to disturb the peace in the Swat valley, and trade was continually on the increase. In January 1901 the light railway from Nowshera to Dargai was opened for traffic. In 1902 some excitement was caused on the Yusafzai border, owing to mischievous reports which were circulated regarding the concentration of troops for the Yusafzai manœuvres. The apprehensions of the tribesmen were however soon allayed, and the moveable column at Khar was broken up.

In 1903 Saiyid Badshah, the eldest Mian Gul, was murdered, and a faction fight ensued between his brother Amir Badshah and his cousin Gul Badshah, who disputed the succession; but the quarrel led to no serious disturbance. In the following year the clans on the right bank of the Swat river became greatly incensed at the tyranny and oppression of the Nawab of Dir, and it was feared that they might be provoked to call upon the Mad Fakir and their kinsmen on the other side of the valley to assist them in throwing off their allegiance to their hated ruler. Had this disturbance come to a head, it might have entirely upset the arrangements made by Government to preserve our communication with Chitral, but fortunately Major Deane was able to effect a settlement and to restrain the *Nawab* from taking aggressive action against his Swati subjects.

In April 1905 the Mian Guls and chief men of the Upper Swatis attended a durbar held by the Chief Commissioner of the North-West Frontier Province, at which Badshah Khan was formally installed as Khan of Dir, in succession to his father, who had died in December of the previous year.

In May 1905 the Political Agent at the Malakand accepted an invitation from the Upper Swat *jirgas* to visit their country. Travelling *viâ* Thana and Kota, he visited the *Akhund's* grave at Sadu, and then proceeded to Minglaor and Charbagh. The good result of our political influence in Upper Swat was demonstrated by the cordial reception given to the British representative on this occasion; and the extraordinary sense of discipline prevailing, and the power of the tribal parliaments over the masses, was exemplified by the attitude of the tribesmen, the cessation of all tribal feuds during the tour, and the arrangements which were made for the safety of the visitor.

Although for the moment the prospects of peace and prosperity are bright, there is nevertheless one matter which deserves attention, and that is the acquisition by these tribes of arms of precision. This arming of the tribes with long range rifles is a most serious question. Under our benign influence the trade and general prosperity of the country has in recent years increased by leaps and bounds, and large sums are disbursed annually as allowances and compensation. In spite of this, however, there are no indications that the tribes are attempting to apply their increased affluence to improving their country or themselves according to western ideas, and they still continue to live in the same primitive way as they have done for hundreds of years. One can only think, therefore, that the bulk of the money which finds its way into the country is expended in the purchase of arms and ammunition.

APPENDIX A.

COMPOSITION OF THE MALAKAND FIELD FORCE, 1897.

In Command.—Major-General Sir Bindon Blood, K.C.B.

1ST BRIGADE (BRIGADIER-GENERAL W. H. MEIKLEJOHN, C.B., C.M.G.).

1st Battalion, Royal West Kent Regiment.
24th (Punjab) Regiment of Bengal Infantry.
31st („) „ „ „
45th (Rattray's Sikh) Regiment of Bengal Infantry.

2ND BRIGADE (BRIGADIER-GENERAL P. D. JEFFREYS, C.B.).

1st Battalion, East Kent Regiment (The Buffs).
35th (Sikh) Regiment of Bengal Infantry.
38th (Dogra) „ „ „ „
Guides Infantry.

DIVISIONAL TROOPS.

1 squadron, 10th Bengal Lancers.
11th Bengal Lancers.
Guides Cavalry.
No. 1 Mountain Battery, R. A.
No. 7 „ „ „
No. 8 (Bengal) Mountain Battery.
22nd (Punjab) Regiment of Bengal Infantry.
2 companies, 21st (Punjab) Regiment of Bengal Infantry.
No. 4 Company, Bengal Sappers and Miners.
No. 5 „ Madras „ „ „

RESERVE (3RD) BRIGADE (BRIGADIER-GENERAL J. H. WODEHOUSE, C.B., C.M.G.)

1st Battalion, Royal West Surrey Regiment (The Queen's).
2nd „ Highland Light Infantry.
6 companies, 21st (Punjab) Regiment of Bengal Infantry.
39th (Garhwal Rifles) Regiment of Bengal Infantry.
No. 10 Field Battery, Royal Artillery.[1]
No. 3 Company, Bombay Sappers and Miners.

[1] The 10th Field Battery joined Divisional Troops at Khar on 6th August.

APPENDIX B.

COMMANDS AND STAFF OF THE MALAKAND FIELD FORCE.

General Officer Commanding the Force (with the temporary rank of Major-General).	Brigadier-General Sir B. Blood, K.C.B.
Aide-de-Camp	Captain A. B. Dunsterville, East Surrey Regiment. (Replaced by Lieutenant Viscount Fincastle, 16th Lancers.)
Assistant Adjutant-General	Major H. H. Burney, 1st Battalion, Gordon Highlanders.
Assistant Quarter Master General	Lieut.-Colonel A. Masters, Central India Horse.
Deputy Assistant Quarter Master General (Intelligence).	Captain H. E. Stanton, D.S.O., R.A.
Field Intelligence Officer ..	Captain H. F. Walters, 24th Bombay Infantry. (Replaced by Captain J. K. Tod, 7th Bengal Cavalry, 2nd October 1897.)
Superintendent, Army Signalling..	Captain E. W. M. Norie, 2nd Battalion, Middlesex Regiment. (Replaced by Captain E. V. O. Hewett, Royal West Kent Regiment.)
Principal Medical Officer ..	Surgeon-Colonel G. Thomson, C.B., I.M.S. (Replaced by Surgon-Colonel J. C. G. Carmichael, M.D., I.M.S.)
Commanding Royal Artillery ..	Lieut-Colonel W. Aitken, C.B., R.A.
" " Engineer ..	Colonel J. E. Broadbent, R.E. (Replaced by Lieut.-Colonel W. Peacocke, R.E., 17th October 1897.)
Adjutant, Royal Artillery ..	Captain H. D. Grier, R.A. (Replaced by Captain H. Rouse, R.A.)
Adjutant, Royal Engineers ..	Captain H. J. Sherwood, R.E.
Field Engineer	Major E. Blunt, R.E.
Ordnance Officer	Captain W. W. Cookson, R.A. (Replaced by Captain L. G. Watkins, R.A., 26th December 1897.)

Chief Commissariat Officer	..	Major H. Wharry.
Divisional Transport Officer	..	Captain C. R. J. Thackwell.
Inspecting Veterinary Officer	..	Veterinary Captain H. T. W. Mann.
Commissariat Officer, Advance Depôt.		Captain A. R. Burlton, I.S.C.

1st Brigade Staff.

Commanding (with the temporary rank of Brigadier-General).		Colonel W. H. Meiklejohn, C.B., C.M.G.
Orderly Officer ..	..	Lieutenant C. R. Gaunt, 4th Dragoon Guards.
Deputy Assistant Adjutant General.		Major E. A. P. Hobday, R.A.
Deputy Assistant Quarter Master General.		Captain G. F. H. Dillon, 40th Pathans.
Brigade Commissariat Officer	..	Captain C. H. Beville.
" Transport Officer	..	Captain J. M. Camilleri, 13th Bengal Infantry.
Veterinary Officer ..	..	Veterinary Captain W. R. Walker.

2nd Brigade Staff.

Commanding ..	..	Brigadier-General P. D. Jeffreys, C.B.
Orderly Officer ..	..	Lieutenant J. Byron, R.A.
Deputy Assistant Adjutant General.		Major E. O. F. Hamilton, Royal West Surrey Regiment. (Replaced by Captain A. B. Dunsterville, East Surrey Regiment.)
Deputy Assistant Quarter Master General.		Major C. H. Powell, 2nd Battalion, 1st Gurkhas.
Brigade Commissariat Officer	..	Captain G. A. Hawkins.
" Transport Officer	..	Captain D. Baker, 2nd Bombay Grenadiers.
Veterinary Officer ..	..	Veterinary Lieutenant G. M. Williams.

For Base and Line of Communication.

Base Commandant	..	Lieut.-Colonel V. A. Schalch, 11th Bengal Infantry.
Staff Officer at the Base	..	Captain H. Scott, 2nd Battalion, The Royal Sussex Regiment. (Replaced by Brevet-Major A. Cadell, 38th Dogras, 30th November 1897.)

Section Commandant ..	Captain O. B. S. F. Shore, 18th Bengal Lancers. (Replaced by Captain C. E. Belli-Bivar, 7th Bombay Lancers, 5th October 1897.)
Base Commissariat Officer ..	Captain W. S. Lincoln.
Commandant, Depôt, British Troops.	Captain H. d'E. Vallancey, 2nd Battalion, Argyll and Sutherland Highlanders.
Adjutant and Quarter Master ..	Captain A. F. Burdock, 2nd Battalion, South Lancashire Regiment.
Commandant, Depôt, Native Troops.	Captain R. R. Renton, 18th Bengal Infantry.
Adjutant and Quarter Master ..	Lieutenant H. L. Tomkins, 28th Punjab Infantry (appointed 7th January 1898).
Engineer Field Park ..	Major M. C. Barton, R.E.
Ordnance " " ..	Lieutenant J. Henry R.A.
Veterinary Officer ..	Veterinary-Lieutenant W. A. McDougal.

Command and Staff, 3rd (Reserve) Brigade.

Commanding	Brigadier-General J. H. Wodehouse, C.B., C.M.G., R.A.
Orderly Officer	Captain R. I. G. Elkington, R.A.
Deputy Assistant Adjutant-General.	Captain A. H. G. Kemball, 5th Gurkhas.
Deputy Assistant Quarter Master General.	Captain H. R. B. Donne, Norfolk Regiment.
Field Intelligence Officer (attached to Divisional Head-Quarters).	Captain J. K. Tod, 7th Bengal Cavalry. (Replaced by Lieutenant A. C. M. Waterfield, 11th Bengal Lancers, 11th October 1897.)
Veterinary Officer	Veterinary-Lieutenant T. W. Rudd.
Brigade Commissariat Officer ..	Captain A. Mullaly.
" Transport Officer ..	Captain E. deV. Wintle, 16th Bengal Lancers.

APPENDIX C.

Genealogy of the Akozai Yusafzai (Swat tribes).

AKOZAI.

- *By first wife Rani.*
  - Ranizai. *by 3 sons Utman, Halim, and Mukka*
    - (1) Sultan Kha Khel — Lower Swat, left bank.
    - (2) Usmani Khel — Lower Swat, left bank.
    - (3) Bahram Kha Khel — Lower Swat, left bank.
    - (4) Utmanzai — Lower Swat, left bank.
    - (5) Khawaza Khel — Lower Swat, left bank.
    - (6) Ali Khel — Lower Swat, left bank.
    - (7) Khan Khel — Lower Swat, left bank.
- *By second wife Gauhara.*
  - Baizai.
    - Kuz Sulizai
      - Aba Khel
        - (7) Khan Khel
        - (8) The 4 other sub-sections of the Aba Khel. — Upper Swat, left bank.
      - (9) Musa Khel — Upper Swat, left bank.
    - Babuzai
      - Aka Khel, Maruf Khel — (10) Akamaruf — Upper Swat, left bank.
      - (11) Barat Khel — Upper Swat, left bank.
      - (12) Bami Khel — Upper Swat, left bank.
      - (13) Aba Khel — Upper Swat, left bank.
    - Bar Sulizai
      - (14) Azzi Khel — Upper Swat, left bank.
      - (15) Jinki Khel — Upper Swat, left bank.
      - Maturizai
        - (16) Allah Khel — Upper Swat, left bank.
        - (17) Bahlol Khel — Upper Swat, left bank.
  - (18) Khadakzai — Lower Swat, right bank.
  - (19) Abazai — Lower Swat, right bank.
  - Khwazazai.
    - (20) Shamizai — Upper Swat, right bank.
    - Sibat Khel, Juna Khel — (21) Sebujni. (*Adopted families, not real Yusafzai in origin.*) — Upper Swat, right bank.
    - (22) Nikbi Khel — Upper Swat, right bank.
    - (23) Shamozai — Upper Swat, right bank.
    - Adinzai
      - (24) Utmanzai — Lower Swat, right bank.
      - Babu Khel.
        - (25) Mir Hassan Khel. — Lower Swat, right bank.
        - (26) The other 4 sub-sections of the Babu Khel. — Lower Swat, right bank.
    - Malizai. (*Sub-sections shown in Appendix A (ii), Chapter XII.*) — Dir and Panjkora valley.

CHAPTER X.

THE UTMAN KHEL TRIBE.

THE Utman Khel are a tribe of Pathans who occupy the hills to the north of Peshawar, between the Mohmands and Ranizais of Swat. They appear to be of the Kodai branch of the Kalanri, who attached themselves to the Yusafzai and Mandanar tribes during the migration of the latter from their earlier homes north-west of the Suleiman range, and have in course of time found themselves in possession of their present country, which they occupied about the same time as the Yusafzais conquered Swat and the Tarkanris took possession of Bajaur. The tribe is a large one, numbering some 40,000 persons and being able to muster some 9,300 fighting men. They have always maintained complete independence and pay tribute to no one.

Their country, which is, with the exception of a small tract in the north, barren and unfertile, lies on both banks of the Swat river until the limits of the Mohmand territory is reached; here the river bends to the south and forms the boundary between the two tribes.

The country to the north of the river, which is the larger portion, consists of a series of valleys between spurs of the hills radiating from the lofty Koh-i-Mohr, a mountain 8,200 feet high. To the south and south-east of this peak are the important divisions of Barang, and Ambahar, while to the north-east lies that of Arang. South of the Swat river again, and between it and British territory, lies the narrow hilly tract known as the Laman,[1] which is traversed by the Sulala range, rising to its highest point in Mount Khanora, north of the village of Pranghar. This portion is under the political administration of the Peshawar district.

[1] The word Laman strictly denotes only the country between the watershed of the Sulala range and the plain. The portion intercepted between that and the river has no special name.

The chief divisions of the tribe, a detailed table of which is given in the Appendix, are :—

1. Ismailzai.	5. Gorai.
2. Mandal.	6. Peghozai.
3. Alizai.	7. Bimmarai.
4. Mutakkai.	8. Sinazai.

Of these the most important, both from their numbers, their situation, and their consequent connection with the British Government, are the Ismailzais, who are divided into three principal branches—Shamozais, Asils, and But Khels. The Shamozais inhabit Arang, and the Asils Barang, while the But Khels live in the valley of Ambahar. Colonies of the Asils have also settled in the Laman.

Of the other clans, the Mandal, Alizai, and Mutakkai live on the northern slopes of the Koh-i-Mohr mountains; none of these have much intercourse with British territory. The Sinazai, Peghozai, and Bimmarai live in Totai, a district included in Sam Ranizai and separated from the Laman by the valley of the Jhindai, a small perennial stream.

The Laman proper is held by a variety of tribes, Utman Khel and others. The Shahdad and Pakhai sections of the Umar Khels live in Prangarh, Rangmiana, and Nasir; and the Dini Khel in Nawadan. Besides these there are a few non-Utman Khel tribes—the Zirak, who are said to be the original inhabitants of the country, in Tarakai and Bucha; and the Mullagoris, in Sapri and Nawakili. This settlement of the Mullagoris [1] is an offshoot of the Mullagoris of Tartara, who inhabit a tract of country to the north of the Khaibar pass, and who will be described in another chapter. The men of the Laman being our immediate neighbours, have continual intercourse with British territory. In ordinary times they may be seen in numbers in Abazai and Tangi with grass and firewood for sale, and they cultivate a large portion of the land of these two villages north of the road from Abazai to Gandera.

The intercourse of the people of the Laman with British territory, and the fact of so many of their villages cultivating land and rearing valuable crops far within the British border, make a *baramta*,

[1] Generally known as the Eastern Mullagoris, to distinguish them.

or reprisals, on them easy, and the existence of these crops is, until the end of the harvest, a kind of security for their good behaviour.

The roads leading into the Utman Khel country from British territory are difficult. There are three roads, or rather tracks, leading through the Laman and across the river to Ambahar and Barang, but these are all difficult and impracticable for horsemen. There is a road to Arang through Totai, by the Agra pass, which is practicable for laden animals.

In the whole course of the Swat river through Utman Khel territory there are only five rope or swing bridges ordinarily kept up. There are no other means of crossing the river, which is a swift, deep torrent, between high, precipitous banks. By going through Mohmand territory the difficulty of crossing the river could be avoided. The road from Matta, on the Mohmand border, through Pandiali to Ambahar is a good one, and practicable for laden animals.

During the lifetime of the Akhund of Swat, the Utman Khels did not recognise his influence to any great extent, and he had not so much power among them as among other Pathan tribes.

The Utman Khels are in no way connected with any of the Afghan tribes which surround them, such as the Mohmands, Ranizais, Bajauris, etc., but look upon the Shinwaris as their best friends. Taking into consideration the geographical position of each, however, and the fact of the Mohmands having been originally their enemies, it is difficult to understand how this friendly intercourse could have been established and maintained.

The Utman Khels have twice waged war with the Mohmands, once in 1827, and the second time at the commencement of 1850, on both of which occasions the Mohmands showed proof of their superiority. They are now on terms of peace, and the people of the one tribe mix with the other; but there is no great friendship between them.

Expedition against the Independent [1] Utman Khels by a force under Brigadier Sir Colin Campbell, K.C.B., in May 1852.

During the first few years after the annexation of the Peshawar valley the Utman Khels gave a great deal of trouble on the

[1] So designated to distinguish them from the Utman Khels of Sam Baizai, mentioned in the previous chapter.

border, by constant raids in the Hashtnagar division, and on the *maira* to the south of their hills, and at last, in 1852, they capped their misdeeds by giving an asylum to, and aiding, Ajun Khan, the fugitive Khan of Tangi. This chief was a young man of a restless, proud, and bigoted character, and, at the beginning of the British rule, was residing at Tangi, a large and important village in the Peshawar district.

A large part of the village was held by him rent-free, but he desired the whole of it, and also exemption from personal attendance at our courts, and from the interference of our revenue and police officials in his village. Finding that these demands were not likely to be complied with, he adopted the course, not unfrequent during the Durani and Sikh rule, of removing to the hills, calling around him a band of adventurers, and leading them in acts of aggression upon British villages, in the hope that the Government would be induced to yield to such pressure, and grant him the privileges he sought. A native officer of the Guide Corps was sent to induce him to return, but he refused to do so unless his villages were given to him rent-free and he was exempted from attendance at any of our courts.

This step led him to believe that we feared him, and ever after he caused annoyance to the Government. To do this most effectually, he aimed at striking fear into our villagers, and causing them to leave their lands uncultivated, by which not only a loss of revenue was to be anticipated, but a general feeling of disaffection and disquietude, leading to internal disturbances. He took up his quarters in the Utman Khel villages, to the north of the district, and received some villages in *jagir* from Saiyid Akbar, the King of Swat, who was himself anticipating the advent of the British, and willingly received such fugitives, locating them in his border villages to act as an advanced guard.

On the night of the 20th April 1852, Ajun Khan, with a band of 200 horsemen, attacked the large village of Charsada, which was the head-quarters of the Hastnagar division.

The party came from the Utman Khel villages of the Laman, and were aided by men from Ranizai (see page 348).

The revenue buildings had not then been constructed, and the establishments were located in native houses, with mud enclosures, which could offer but slight resistance. The *tehsildar*, himself a *saiyid*, was murdered and cut to pieces. Several other officials were similarly treated, and the *tehsil* treasury was plundered. On the following day, in furtherance of his plans, Ajun Khan came down and occupied the village of Abazai, where he remained twenty-four hours. He then desired the *maliks* to leave the village with their cattle, and killed one man who refused to do so. Ajun Khan next proceeded to Pranghar and Nawadan, where he took up his quarters.

On the receipt of the report of this outrage, orders were at once given for a punitive expedition to be carried out against the Utman Khel villages, and on the 28th of April 1852 troops began to move out from Peshawar.

The force was under the command of Brigadier Sir Colin Campbell, K.C.B., who established his head-quarters at Abazai. Lieut.-Colonel F. Mackeson, C.B., the Commissioner, and Captain H. R. James, the Deputy Commissioner, accompanied the force. On the 2nd of May a picquet of twenty men of the Guide Cavalry, under Lieutenant G. N. Hardinge, in advance of the line of outposts, observed the enemy advancing in force. They were at once ordered to charge, which they did with great gallantry, checking the advance of the enemy. The latter had many of their number cut up, besides losing a standard. On our side, Lieutenant Hardinge and two sowars were wounded.

On the 11th May, the Commissioner having called on Sir Colin Campbell to destroy the Nawadan group of villages, the Brigadier moved out with the troops noted in the margin.

1st Troop, 1st Brigade, Horse Artillery.
Detachment, 2nd Company, 4th Battalion, Artillery (two 8-inch howitzers).
Her Majesty's 32nd Foot, 300 bayonets.
One squadron, 2nd Irregular Cavalry.
One squadron, Guide Cavalry.
2nd Company, Sappers and Miners.
28th Native Infantry, 300 bayonets.
66th Gurkhas, 300 bayonets.
Guide Infantry.

Nawadan was about four miles from Abazai, the last mile of the approach to it leading over hilly and broken ground. On the arrival of the force the villages were found deserted, but many of the hillmen were seen on the neighbouring heights. As the burning proceeded, the enemy gradually gathered at different points, and began skirmishing with the advanced picquets of the Guides. This lasted whilst the work of destruction went on, the Guides having one jemadar and four men wounded. The ground was too broken to admit of the guns being brought up near the village.

As the troops withdrew, the numbers of the enemy appeared slightly to increase, but the retirement was conducted without loss, the village and large quantities of grain having been destroyed.

During the operations, the 1st Punjab Infantry, under Captain J. Coke, and two squadrons of the 1st Punjab Cavalry, under Lieutenant W. T. Hughes, joined Sir Colin Campbell.

These troops had made an extraordinary march. The letter from the Commissioner, sent by express to Captain Coke at Kohat, calling for his services, had miscarried, and that officer only got his orders in a second letter sent by post. The 1st Punjab Infantry, and the two squadrons of the 1st Punjab Cavalry, marched from Kohat at 2 A.M. on the 8th, and reached Peshawar, forty miles, the same day. On arriving at the bridge-of-boats over the Kabul river, Captain Coke found it had been swept away, and the boats carried down stream. On the evening of the 10th the troops had got across, and on that night marched for Abazai, halting for two hours under the Shabkadar fort; and when, on reaching Abazai at daybreak, it was found the force under Sir Colin Campbell had gone out to attack Nawadan, Captain Coke pushed on, joining the force as the attack was begun, having marched more than forty miles when Abazai was reached after the operations.

On the 12th the force under Sir Colin Campbell moved about seven miles to Gandera, with a view to attacking Pranghar which was generally looked on in the country as the stronghold of the Utman Khel tribe.

1st Troop, 1st Brig., H. A.
Detachment, 2nd Co., 4th Bn., Artillery (two 8-inch howitzers).
Detachment, 3rd Co., 4th Bn., Artillery, and of No. 19 Light Field Battery attached, (2 guns).
Her Majesty's 32nd Foot, 300 bayonets.
One squadron, 1st P. C.[1]
2nd Coy., S. and M.
28th[2] N. I., 300 bayonets.
66th Gurkha Regiment, 300 bayonets.
Guide Infantry, 300 bayonets.
Six coy.s, 1st P. I.[3]

On the 13th, a force, of the strength given in the margin, marched a little before daybreak about five miles to the foot of the hills, which were broken and very stony, but not inaccessible to artillery. Pranghar was a large village, with its rear resting on high hills, and flanked by spurs and lower heights. Preparations had been made for defence, and both the place, which was surrounded by good walls, and the adjacent eminences, were crowded with men.

1 Now 21st Prince Albert Victor's Own Cavalry.

2 Mutinied at Shahjahanpur in 1857.

3 Now 55th Coke's Rifles (Frontier Force).

The enemy quickly opened fire on the advanced guard, which was then halted until the guns were in position.

The guns having opened fire, cleared the road, and the men of the 1st Punjab Infantry, the 66th Gurkha Regiment, and the Guide Corps immediately advanced to the attack, Her Majesty's 32nd and the 28th Native Infantry remaining with the guns as a reserve. The only fault committed was the too great impetuosity of the men, which caused the artillery fire to be stopped sooner than Sir Colin Campbell desired.

The village was carried at a run, the enemy retreating to the hills behind, whence the skirmishers drove them from rock to rock, far up the side of the high mountain, rendering the destruction of village easy and safe. The artillery made good practice, effectually aiding the skirmishers. A desultory fight was then carried on, until the object for which the Brigadier had received the Commissioner's requisition was effected, *viz.*, the destruction of the village and grain. Of the latter, a large quantity, which had been stacked in a supposed place of security, high up the mountain, was destroyed by our skirmishers. The troops then retired.

Considering that no less than ten pieces of artillery opened on their devoted village, it must be owned that its inhabitants made a gallant defence. But for our guns we should have sustained heavy loss, the walls and flanking defences above alluded to being formidable. As it was, the number of our casualties was small.[1]

The enemy, who numbered perhaps 1,000 matchlock men, were led by Ajun Khan and his father, Hamid, and were assisted by the Utman Khels of the Totai villages. They only left three dead on the ground, but it was believed that they had many casualties. Three prisoners were taken; one was a servant of Ajun Khan, who was concerned in the murder of the *tehsildar*, and another was a student from our own village of Tangi.

Some Persian letters were found in the village by a sepoy of the Guides, one from the *Akhund*, and one from the King of Swat to Ajun Khan, promising him assistance, assigning to him all the property of the Hindus and servants of the British in Hashtnagar as lawful prey, and desiring him not to spare them, but to keep his hands from Muhammadans not in our service.

[1] Three killed and fifteen wounded.

On the 14th the force halted at Gandera to make various arrangements, and to allow of more crops being destroyed.

The Indian Medal, with a clasp for the "North-West Frontier," was granted in 1869 to all survivors of the troops engaged in the above operations.

The result of the chastisement of the Utman Khels was to restore order and security to the Hashtnagar division, and to put a stop to the flight of the chiefs on the border.

At the end of 1852, for the better security of this part of the border, the fort of Abazai was erected.

After the destruction of the village of Pranghar, Ajun Khan fled from Utman Khel territory, and wandered about from place to place,—Kabul, Jalalabad, Lalpura, Swat, etc. In 1857 he was at Pranghar, threatening to attack British territory, but was checked by a force moving out from Peshawar, accompanied by Lieut.-Colonel J. Nicholson, the Deputy Commissioner. In 1872 he suddenly returned, and, with the aid of the men of Totai and some of the Ranizai villages, built two towers and several houses at a place called Spankhara, five miles and a half north of Gandera. On this the Deputy Commissioner sent a warning to the Council of the Ranizais, and to the various men of influence in proximity to our territory, when a hundred men of Pranghar, moving out suddenly, surprised Spankhara, killing six men, and burning the hamlet. Ajun Khan died in 1877.

Operations against the Independent Utman Khels in February and March 1878.

After the expedition against the Independent Utman Khels under Sir Colin Campbell in 1852, the conduct of the tribe had been for many years uniformly good, and in June 1875 the outstanding cases against them, all of a minor character, were settled.

On the 9th of December 1876, however, an offence of the gravest description was committed by this tribe, a number of the ill-disposed members of which, instigated by persons of influence in British territory, attacked a body of unarmed coolies engaged in the preliminary operations of the canal about to be taken from the Swat river at Abazai. It appears that the party, consisting of about 100 men under the leadership of Mian Rakan-ud-din of Sapri, at about

2 A.M. on the morning of the 9th December, surrounded the tents in which the coolies were sleeping, and, at a given signal, having cut the ropes of the tents, threw them down simultaneously. The unfortunate men inside were caught like birds in a net, and, as each cried for mercy or help, he was slashed at through the tent-cloth. After the butchery, the camp was robbed of almost everything it contained. Some of the dead and wounded were stripped of the very clothes on their backs. Of the sixty-five men in the tents, six were killed and twenty-seven wounded, some dangerously. After plundering the camp, the raiders successfully effected their escape to the hills before any assistance from the Abazai fort could reach the spot.

The party consisted principally of the But Khels of Ambahar, in concert with the people of the Laman. The former were induced to come down by hopes of the plunder of the treasure in the camp, which was given out to be very great; but with the latter there were several other causes at work, the principal of which was the suspicion and dislike of the people on this part of border to the project of the new canal, and especially to the taking up of land for that purpose. The land near the villages of Abazai and Tangi was cultivated by men of independent territory. The people of Sapri, headed by Mian Rakan, cultivated the land near Abazai which had been taken up for the canal. The *Mians* of Sapri had a bitter feud with the *Mians* of Abazai, and, at the time of the outrage, the state of factions on this border was on the one hand Sapri, with the adjoining hamlet of Nawakili, aided by Mir Hassan, the Khan of Tangi, in British territory, and, on the other, Nawadan, Pranghar, and the *Mians* of Abazai. The reason why the last gave no warning of the raid, which they must have known was going to take place, is not very clear, but they probably hoped by their silence to compromise their enemies, the men of Sapri, with the Government.

After the occurrence of the raid, the *maliks* of Abazai, and also Mir Hassan of Tangi, who was suspected of complicity, were apprehended, and sent into Peshawar under a military escort. It is probable that this raid would never have taken place at all if proper care had been taken for the protection of the workmen employed on the canal works, and it cannot be denied that sufficient precautions were not taken by the officers responsible, to prevent an attack of this sort, when the work was being carried on so near the frontier. It could not, however, have been anticipated that a Muhammadan tribe would, without provocation or without quarrel with the British Government, attack and kill an unarmed band of Muhammadan workmen—a dastardly outrage, which brought down on them the virtual excommunication of the aged Akhund of Swat.

In consequence of the Swat canal outrage, the Utman Khel tribe was excluded from British territory, but, owing to the exigencies of other Imperial considerations, it was not possible at that time to take more active measures against them.

At the beginning of 1878 the sanction of the Government of India was asked for an attempt being made to surprise the village of Sapri, in which it was known that Mian Rakan was residing. It was felt that while this man, who was the instigator of the outrage, was still at large, any satisfactory settlement with the tribe would be next to impossible; and with the object of his capture the proposal was sanctioned.

The village was situated close to our border, and thus offered great facilities to an operation of this kind. The success of the expedition depended on the correctness of the information obtained by the Deputy Commissioner, the secrecy of the preparations made by the officer in command, and the rapidity of the march of the troops to a distant point.

At seven o'clock on the evening of the 14th of February 1878, the troops, as per margin, belonging to the Corps of Guides, marched from Mardan. The infantry were mounted on ponies, and each man carried sixty rounds of ammunition. Captain Wigram Battye, of the Guides, was in command, and Captain P. L. N. Cavagnari, the Deputy Commissioner of Peshawar, accompanied the troops as Political Officer.

Cavalry.
4 British Officers.
9 Native "
255 Sabres.
Infantry.
1 Native Officer.
11 Bayonets.

The route taken was by the main road to Tangi and Abazai, skirting the village of Jalala. On arriving within a short distance of the village of Tangi, the column left the main road and passed through some low detached hills to the north, and then, after crossing the line of the Swat canal, proceeded to within about two miles of Abazai, and there dismounted, the horses being left in charge of sixty-three men of the party, with orders to take them to Abazai fort at daybreak. The distance traversed to this point was about thirty-two miles. The object of making this detour, and avoiding the villages of Tangi and Abazai, was to prevent the chance of the news of the approach of the troops being conveyed across the border.

After dismounting, the force proceeded on foot through some very heavy ploughed land for about two miles to the Swat river, and thence along its left bank for four miles to Mada Baba Ziarat, where a mountain torrent joins the river. Here the party ascended a narrow, steep path by the side of the torrent for about a mile, till they arrived at the *kotal* leading to the village of Sapri. The *kotal* was reached about 4 A.M., and from this point the village lay within easy rifle range. An attempt was made to reconnoitre the village, but the village dogs becoming alarmed, began to bark, and it was thought best to wait till daylight. From information received, the Political Officer was of opinion that Mian Rakan would be found either in the village mosque, or in his own tower, which was in the centre of the village, and which could be commanded from a spur of the hill on the west overlooking Sapri. Captain Battye, therefore, arranged to post a picquet on this spur, and with the remainder to attack the village.

Immediately daylight broke, the assault was made, and our men, rushing into the village, seized the mosque. The surprise was a complete success, and the inmates awoke to find soldiers with drawn swords standing over them. Having secured the mosque, the party proceeded to the tower, which was, however, found deserted. Hearing that the *Mian* had taken refuge in a small building behind the mosque, the party returned there, and called upon the people inside to surrender, threatening at the same time to burn the roof and force them to come out if they refused. A duffadar of the Guides, named Turabaz, here distinguished himself by his gallantry, and succeeded in shooting Mian Rakan's nephew and wounding another man, when the door of the building was partially opened for a moment. The *Mian* was now called upon to surrender quietly, or he would have to take the consequences. Thereupon the door was opened, and he stepped out, apparently with the intention of surrendering himself; but probably the sight of his enemy, Tehsildar Ghulam Mohi-ud-Din (through whom this misfortune had come upon him, and who had accompanied the troops), was too much for him, and he made an attempt to stab him with a dagger; the attempt failed, and the next moment he was shot down by our men. The others inside the house, seeing the fate of Mian Rakan, surrendered quietly.

The object of the Government having been thus obtained, arrangements were made to retire. It had been intended to blow up the tower, but the powder unfortunately did not come up in time. At the request of the Political Officer the village was not burnt.

The men who had made good their escape from the village had, in the meanwhile, ascended the heights above, and kept up a desultory fire on our troops. A party of them having taken up a position on a high hill to the south-east of the village, commanding the line of our retirement, were attacked by Captain Battye, and driven off with a loss of three killed, whose bodies were left on the ground. The movement to the rear was then effected without any hurry or confusion, the enemy making no further attempt to harass the retiring column. The number of the enemy opposed to our troops was estimated at 300. Their loss was seven killed (the number of wounded could not be ascertained), and six taken prisoners, three of whom were relatives of the *Mian*. Our casualties were eight wounded.

The troops reached Fort Abazai at 11 A.M., on the morning of the 15th. Brigadier-General C. C. G. Ross, C.B., commanding at Peshawar, had previously sent secret orders to the officer commanding the Doaba outposts to have the garrison at Abazai in readiness to afford the Guides any assistance that might be required, but, as has been seen, there had been no occasion to ask for aid.

After the successful attack upon Sapri, the representatives of the Utman Khel tribe were summoned to hear the terms the Government required from them as a punishment for their conduct in the Abazai outrage. These terms were as follows:—

1st.—Rs. 200 blood-money for each coolie killed, and Rs. 100 wound-money for each coolie injured and recovered.

2nd.—Restitution of, or compensation for, property plundered by raiders.

3rd.—A fine of Rs. 1,000.

4th.—Settlement according to border rule of all recent pending cases.

5th.—Hostages to be given for one year as a guarantee for the good conduct of the tribe generally, but especially with reference to the canal works.

The gravity of the offence would have justified far heavier penalties, but the object was to impose terms that could not reasonably be refused, and to put matters on a satisfactory footing for the future prosecution of the canal scheme. The headmen of Pranghar, Nawadan, and Sapri attended in obedience to the summons, but the representatives of the Zirak and Pakhai villages refused to come in, and, as an incomplete settlement would not have been of much advantage, the *jirga* was dismissed.

After the successful surprise of the Ranizai village of Shakot in March 1878, described in chapter VIII, the attitude of the Utman Khel villages changed, and they became most desirous of a speedy settlement. The pecuniary demands against these villages amounted to Rs. 5,000, as per detail in the margin, and of this amount the representatives of Pranghar, Nawadan, and Sapri agreed to pay Rs. 5,000, leaving the balance to be recovered from the recusant Zirak and Pakhai villages. On this understanding the submission of the *jirga* was accepted, and proposals for the coercion of the Zirak villages of Tarakai and Bucha, and the Pakhai villages of Rangmiana and Nasir, were submitted to Government, and sanction to these proposals was received on the 19th March 1878.

	Rs.
Blood-money ..	1,600
Wound-money ..	2,200
Fine ..	1,000
Value of property carried off ..	200
Total ..	5,000

At noon on the following day (20th) the force, as per margin, under the command of Lieut.-Colonel F. H. Jenkins, commanding the Corps of Guides, marched from Mardan, and reached the Utman Khel border early on the morning of the 21st. The force was joined at a spot about two miles from the frontier by the Deputy Commissioner, Captain P. L. N. Cavagnari, who accompanied the troops as Political Officer. The column entered the hills just as day was breaking. No opposition was offered by the hamlet of Tarakai, which was passed on the left as the force entered the valley in which are situated the three villages of Bucha. These villages lie in a kind of horse-shoe shaped amphitheatre, formed by the Sulala range of hills, and this amphitheatre is divided by the Tor Tam hill in the middle into two parts, one of which contains

Hazara Mountain Battery—	
2 British Officers.	
4 Guns.	
Guide Cavalry—	
2 British Officers.	
243 sabres.	
Guide Infantry—	
9 British Officers.	
11 Native "	
442 Bayonets.	

the Zirak villages of Bucha, the other being occupied by the Pakhai villages of Rangmiana and Nasir.

A small party having been left to look after Tarakai, the main body pushed on to Bucha. Messengers had been sent on to this place to inform the inhabitants that if no resistance were offered, the villages would be spared. This allowed time for the women and children to escape, and, as our troops approached, the inhabitants were seen driving off their cattle into the interior. The first village was deserted, but a company of the Guide Infantry, under Captain A. G. Hammond, which had gone round to the eastern village, was fired on, and one man dangerously wounded. At the same time parties of the enemy showed themselves in the third village, and in the broken ground beyond and on our left. Captain Hammond, advancing with his party, at once cleared the eastern village and drove the enemy off the ground on to the tops of the Sulala range. At the same time, Lieutenant F. D. Battye, with a party of Guide Infantry, cleared the third village. The operations against the Bucha villages were materially assisted by the fire of the mountain guns, which was directed on the enemy whenever they tried to assemble to oppose the advance of the infantry.

Leaving the cavalry to secure the position, Lieut.-Colonel Jenkins now ascended the Tor Tam hill with four companies of infantry and the mountain guns. The enemy offered little opposition, and the force, on gaining the ridge, marched along it to a point abreast of Rangmiana. This placed the remaining villages entirely at our mercy, and Captain Cavagnari now sent to summon the Zirak and Pakhai headmen to submit, as there was no desire on our part to destroy their villages and crops. This summons, after some delay, they obeyed, and they then agreed to pay the fine of Rs. 2,000 after twenty days, and in the meantime to give good security for the amount.

The cattle (about 150 head) which had been captured during the attack on the villages were then restored—a piece of moderation on our part which the tribesmen had hardly expected. The demands of Government having thus been obtained, and the objects of the expedition fulfilled, the troops were ordered to retire, which they did, entirely unmolested, and bivouacked for the night at the Jhinda outpost of the Swat canal-works, having marched over forty miles since noon of the previous day. The day following the force returned to Mardan. The loss of the enemy could not be ascertained, but twelve bodies were left on the ground about Bucha and the Tor Tam hill, and two men severely wounded were brought into the village while our troops were there, after the engagement. Our casualties had been only one man wounded.

The rupture on account of the Swat canal outrage having been brought to a satisfactory termination, the head-works of the canal, which had been stopped pending the submission of the Utman Khel villages, were continued.

During 1882 the men of Sapri committed a series of thefts of cattle employed on the head-works of the canal, and in order to check their misconduct, it was necessary in December 1882 to levy a fine of Rs. 300 on the village, and to enforce the restoration of the stolen property.

After the payment of this fine, the Utman Khel caused no serious trouble until 1895. In that year, some sections of the tribe, particularly the Shamozai, joined the neighbouring clans of Swat, Dir, and Bajaur in opposing the passage of the Swat river at Chakdara by the troops of the Chitral Relief Expedition. They also fired on our baggage columns on the march through the Talash valley to Sado; and some of their fighting-men took part in the actions of the 13th and 17th of April.

No special punitive measures were, however, taken against the tribe for their hostility on this occasion.

Participation of the tribe in the Swat rising, 1897.

In 1897 large numbers of the Cis-Swat and Laman Utman Khel were implicated in the attack on the Malakand post. Many of them also joined the Mohmands, under the leadership of the Hadda Mulla, in the raid on Shankargarh, and took part in the subsequent fight at Shabkadar (on the 9th August), which will be found described in chapter XI. The Shamozai section (trans-Swat) were also implicated in the rising in the Swat valley, and joined in the assault on Chakdara; and later they made a move to seize the Panjkora bridge in order to oppose the advance of our troops into Bajaur. Their intention was, however, frustrated by the prompt action of General Meiklejohn, who arrived at the bridge with a brigade of the Malakand Field Force on the 4th September.

Punishment of the trans-Swat Shamozai section.

On the arrival of Sir Bindon Blood (with the 2nd Brigade of the above-mentioned force) at Ghosam five days later, the Shamozai Utman Khel *jirga* came in and sued for peace.[1] The tribesmen at once agreed to the terms imposed, but by the following day had only surrendered a few of the arms demanded from them. There was then no time available for coercive measures against these people, to enforce full compliance with the terms of submission, as Sir Bindon Blood was obliged to continue his advance into Bajaur.

About 100 tribesmen of the Shamozai joined the Mamunds in the attack on Brigadier-General Jeffreys' camp at Markhanai on the 14th September.[2] A few men of the But Khel sub-section of the Ismailzai were also supposed to have been present on this occasion, but no special action was taken against them. Supplies were, however, taken from Markhanai village belonging to the Mandol Utman Khel who were also implicated in the fighting in Swat, but who had hitherto not submitted.

With the exception of this outbreak at Markhanai, the Shamozai Utman Khel kept the peace during all the time that our troops were employed in Bajaur; and they even assisted to protect the line of communication along the border of their territory. In consideration of this latter service a portion of the fine of arms originally imposed was remitted; and on the return of Sir Bindon Blood's force on the 21st October, the Shamozai *jirga* came to Jhar, and surrendered the balance of the rifles and guns still due.

It has been mentioned in chapter IX that Sir Bindon Blood intended to despatch a brigade under General Jeffreys from Lower Swat, which was to enter Utman Khel country by the Inzargai pass. But as these troops were required for the operations in Bajaur at the end of August, the coercion of the Utman Khel had to be postponed. Meanwhile the Government imposed terms on the various sections who had been implicated in acts of hostility, and demanded the complete submission of the tribe.

Expedition against the Cis-Swat Utman Khel in 1897.

Up to the 21st November the only Cis-Swat Utman Khel who had submitted were the inhabitants of the Kuz Totai villages of

[1] See Chapter XIII. [2] See page 571.

Kot, Myana, and Bar. Three hundred fire-arms were due from the villages of Bar-Totai and Agra; and the Laman Utman Khel had made no move to comply with the terms. It was accordingly decided to send a portion of the Malakand field force to compel their submission.

On the 22nd November 1897 the marginally noted troops, under the command of Colonel A. J. F. Reid, concentrated at Usman-Khel Garhi near Dargai. The 16th Bengal Infantry, under Lieut.-Colonel A. Montanaro, was sent to Abazai to protect the head of the Swat canal and to strengthen the hands of the political officers who were to deal with the Laman Utman Khel. On the 23rd November Colonel Reid's column marched to Hariankot at the foot of the Bar-Totai pass, which was crossed the next day, when the troops advanced to Kot. Here the combined *jirgas* of Agra, Bar-Totai and Khanauri, with the *maliks* of Bar and Myana, came in and were interviewed by Colonel Reid, who had been given full political charge.

1 squadron, 10th Bengal Lancers.
No. 8 Bengal Mountain Battery.
No. 5 Company, Madras Sappers and Miners.
1st Battalion, East Kent Regiment.
21st Punjab Infantry.
35th Sikhs.

The *jirgas* were most anxious to make peace, and agreed to comply with the following terms:—

- the surrender of 300 guns, and every rifle in their possession, (50 from Khanauri, 100 from Bar-Totai, and 150 from Agra);
- to be responsible, within their own limits, that our troops were not opposed when traversing the country;
- to permit a complete survey of their country;
- to provide supplies for the transport animals, and wood, etc., for the troops while in the limits of their country;
- to permit the troops to make such roads as might be found necessary.

On the 24th and 25th November reconnaissances were pushed forward in the direction of the Agra and Kelo passes. On the following day, the column marched up the Jhindai stream to Siloipatai; the people of this village and the neighbouring hamlet of Badami were perfectly friendly and furnished all the supplies demanded. On the 27th the troops moved on four and half miles by a very difficult track to Bargholai. Thence Colonel Reid pushed forward with four companies, two mountain guns and a party of sappers and miners to reconnoitre the Agra pass, and improve the track which led up to the *kotal.* As this route proved to be impracticable for camels, Colonel Reid crossed the pass on the 28th with a portion of his brigade, equipped with mule transport. On the next day a reconnaissance was made to the Inzargai, Yardiali, and Ormullo passes; the people were everywhere submissive, and during the stay of the troops at Agra the villagers picqueted the approaches to the camp in order to prevent any interference on the part of their trans-Swat kinsmen. On both days a party of Shamozai clansmen, with a few standards, were seen on the hills on the opposite bank of the river; but they abstained from any act of open hostility. Having collected the arms due from the Agra people, and surveyed the country up to the Swat-Panjkora junction, Colonel Reid returned on the 29th to Bargholai.

By the 1st December the Bar-Totai people had surrendered all the arms due, and the force marched back to Kot. Here some representatives of the Asil sub-section of Ismailzai from Khanauri informed Colonel Reid that one Gujar Khan, *malik* of the Umar Khel sub-section in their village, had fled the country in order to avoid his share of the penalty, and had thus prevented them from complying in full with the terms imposed. They, however, brought in some of the arms demanded, and next day a detached column visited Khanauri and obtained the balance, and destroyed Gujar Khan's house.

On the 4th December all the terms having been fully complied with, and the survey work completed, Colonel Reid's force evacuated the Cis-Swat Utman Khel country, returning by the Bar-Totai and Kaga passes to Hariankot and Hiru Shah, and was broken up on the following day. The Bar-Totai and Agra *jirgas* proceeded to the Malakand, and there made their formal submission to the Political Agent.

Submission of the Laman Utman Khel, December 1897.

On the 27th November, the Laman Utman Khel *jirga* assembled at Gandera, where they were met by Mr. C. Bunbury, I.C.S., and Mr. Stuart Waterfield. The following terms were imposed:—

payment of a money fine of Rs. 2,000;

surrender of 300 fire-arms, 300 swords, and all rifles in their possession;

assistance to British officials in making a survey of their country;
free forage and fuel for troops visiting their country, should it be found necessary to employ them to enforce compliance with the terms.

By the 4th December the Laman Utman Khel had complied in full with the above conditions, except that they surrendered no rifles. The sworn statement of each headman of every village or quarter to the effect that they had no rifles in their possession was accepted, and that portion of the penalty was remitted. Within the next few days the whole of Laman Utman Khel country was thoroughly reconnoitred and surveyed, the inhabitants abiding by their agreement to render assistance in this operation.

Certain Utman Khel villages within the British border, whose inhabitants had taken part in the fighting against our troops, were also punished by fines and the forfeiture of allowances.

Since the disturbances in 1897 this tribe has caused no sérious trouble to the Government.

APPENDIX A.

Genealogy of the Utman Khel.

UTMAN KHEL.

- Ismailzai
  - Shamozai
    - Umar Khel (1).
    - Sarni Khel (2).
    - Sarkanri Khel (3).
    - Painda Khel (4).
  - Asil
    - Bada — Madak
      - Zado (5).
      - Parshai (6).
      - Anam (7).
      - Painda (8).
    - Balu — Abar (9).
  - But Khel (10).
  - Takur (11).
  - Mandanr (12).
- Mandal
  - Suari (13).
  - Mata (14).
  - Gadu (15).
  - Dabar (16).
- Alizai
  - Mahmunzai (17).
  - Isozai (18).
  - Adrizai (19).
  - Marchozai (20).
- Mutakkai
  - Shahdad Khel (21).
  - Walidad Khel (22).
  - Turi Khel (23).
- Peghozai (24).
- Bimmarai (25).
- Gorai
  - Khushal kor (26).
  - Rahman kor (27).
- Sinazai (28).

APPENDIX B.

Composition of the Utman Khel column under Command of Colonel A. J. F. Reid, 22nd November 1897.

	Officers.	Other ranks.
1st Battalion, East Kent Regiment,—Lieut.-Colonel A. E. Ommanney	19	534
One squadron, 10th Bengal Lancers,—Captain W. L. Maxwell	2	121
No. 8 (Bengal) Mountain Battery,—Captain A. H. C. Birch, Royal Artillery	4	253
The 21st Punjab Infantry,—Lieut.-Colonel W. C. Faithful	9	688
The 35th Sikhs,—Colonel T. H. Goldney	11	635
No. 5 Company, Queen's Own Madras Sappers and Miners, Captain E. P. Johnson	4	130

Staff.

Deputy Assistant Adjutant-General,—Captain A. B. Dunsterville, East Surrey Regiment.

Deputy Assistant Quarter Master General,—Major L. Herbert, Central India Horse.

Orderly Officer,—Lieutenant H. A. Vallings, 29th Punjab Infantry.

Intelligence Officer and Assistant Political Officer,—Lieutenant A. C. M. Waterfield, 11th Bengal Lancers.

Commissariat Officer,—Captain A. R. Burlton, Staff Corps.

Transport Officer,—Lieutenant R. S. Weston, Manchester Regiment.

Senior Medical Officer,—Surgeon-Lieut.-Colonel P. F. O'Connor, Indian Medical Service.

Senior Veterinary Officer,—Veterinary-Lieutenant G. M. Williams, Army Veterinary Department.

CHAPTER XI.

THE MOHMAND TRIBE.

THE Mohmands are a tribe of Pathans who reside, partly in the Afghan province of Ningrahar, partly in the Peshawar district, and partly in the hills between the Peshawar plain and the Kunar valley.

This work has no concern with the first-named section, and but little with the second, though, as will be seen, they were involved in some of the disturbances that have occurred on that part of the border.

The Mohmands are closely allied, in dress, language and customs, to the Yusafzais.

The independent, or hill, Mohmands are divided into eight clans, namely the Khwaezai, Baezai, Halimzai, Tarakzai, Isa Khel, Burhan Khel, Dawezai, and Utmanzai. The last two of these are usually considered "affiliated clans," and not true Mohmands.

The Safis, a clan residing in the northern portion of the Mohmand country, are vassals of the Mohmands.

The boundaries of the independent Mohmand country are, roughly, as follows:—On the east, the Peshawar district from near Jamrud to Abazai, and the Utman Khel country; on the north, Bajaur; on the west, Kunar; and on the south, the Kabul river.[1]

This whole tract consists of rows of rocky hills, scantily clothed with coarse grass and dwarf palm, and broad dry ravines. In summer the heat is intense, and water is everywhere scarce. Springs are infrequent, and the water-supply of many of the villages consists of rain water collected in tanks.

From the days of Ahmad Shah the Mohmands as a whole were more or less subject to the Kabul rulers until 1893, when the Durand agreement divided their country between the British and Afghan Governments. The boundary drawn on the map

[1] The Mohmands of Shilman, south of the Kabul river, and also the Mullagoris, who are claimed as vassals by the Mohmands, will be referred to in Volume II.

attached to that agreement runs through the centre of the Mohmand hills, but this boundary has never been demarcated, and has, on various occasions, been disputed.

There are numerous roads through the Mohmand country, as the hills, though rugged and rocky, are nowhere impassable. The clans residing on the bank of the Kabul river have from time immemorial, enjoyed the right to levy tolls on rafts of timber, etc., coming down the river.

The Mohmands do not enjoy a great reputation for bravery, and do not possess very many modern fire-arms. The Baezai are the most warlike clan, and also the best armed. The fighting strength of the various clans was in 1906, as follows :—

Clan.	*Fighting men.*	*Clan.*	*Fighting men.*
Khwaezai	2,000	Halimzai	3,500
Baezai (excluding Musa Khel)	9,000	Burhan Khel	700
Baezai Musa Khel	3,000	Isa Khel	700
Tarakzai	1,600	Dawezai	700
Utmanzai	350		

Operations against the Mohmands by a force under Brigadier Sir Colin Campbell, K.C.B., in 1851-52.

The first occasion on which the British Government came into contact with the Mohmand tribe was during the first war in Afghanistan, in 1838–42. At that time, Saadat Khan was chief of Lalpura. On the news of the approach of the British army, Turabaz Khan, his cousin, and enemy, immediately started off to meet the army at Jhelum. Saadat Khan thereupon espoused the cause of the Barakzais, and Turabaz Khan was installed as Khan of Lalpura by Colonel Wade. He seems to have done loyal service for Mackeson while we held Afghanistan. After the disasters at Kabul, the whole country rose, and Turabaz Khan, at risk to himself, saved an English lady and her child from the Pesh Bolak garrison, and took her down the river on a raft to Peshawar. The officers of the *jazailchis* stationed at Pesh Bolak escaped over the Tartara hills, and Turabaz Khan himself took refuge in British territory. He returned with General Pollock's force, but was ousted by Saadat Khan on the withdrawal of our troops. He subsequently made his peace with the Amir, and received a *jagir* in Kama.

The Mohmands, during the early years of British rule in the Peshawar valley, gave more trouble than almost any other tribe.

The Michni Mohmands, after annexation, were allowed to hold a fief in the Doaba (the fertile triangle near the junction of the Swat and Kabul rivers) from the British Government, of which they collected the revenue. A portion of the lands they cultivated themselves, the remainder they farmed out to other tribes of the plains as tenants. Many of their clansmen dwelt in the plains of Michni, and some in the neighbouring hills, and they traded largely in the Peshawar valley. The Halimzai Mohmands also held Panjpao in British Doaba as a fief, chiefly cultivated by tenants. A few of their men lived in the plains, but the majority in the hills. These also traded in the valley. The Pandiali Mohmands at a former period had held a similar *jagir* in the Doaba, but not since British rule. They had few relations, either with the Government or the people of the Peshawar valley, and inhabited a very strong locality in the hills. The fiefs were originally granted by preceding Governments to the Mohmands, as blackmail, to buy off depredations.

The first inroad of the Mohmands occurred in December 1850, in an unprovoked attack on the village of Shabkadar, organised by Fateh Khan, the son of Saadat Khan, who was still the chief of Lalpura, and who was naturally not well disposed towards us, and did his best to incite the tribe to hostilities.

In March 1851, Lieutenant H. R. James, Deputy Commissioner, reported an intended raid on the Doaba by Saadat Khan of Lalpura from Pandiali, and in March and April two attacks were actually made on Matta by Nawab Khan, the chief of Pandiali; but both were gallantly repulsed by detachments of the Guide Corps, under Lieutenant H. N. Miller and Ressaldar Fateh Khan, respectively.

In the first affair, hearing of the intended raid, Lieutenant Miller placed two companies of the Guides, under Lieutenant H. J. Hawes, in ambush, when the enemy were attacked on their way back, Lieutenant Miller coming up with the few cavalry he had with him. The enemy lost five killed and six wounded, and the Guides had one man killed.

In the second affair, the Guides had three men wounded, the Mohmands losing three killed and several wounded.

To these attacks minor depredations succeeded in July 1851, headed by one Nur Gul of Panjpao.

In August 1851, Rahimdad, a headman of Michni, deserted, and collecting 600 matchlock men, sent them to dam up the water of a village on the border, but they were driven off by the villagers, with some loss.

In October 1851, the Mohmands of Michni made a more serious attack on several British villages, and, though opposed by the villagers, they succeeded in destroying many of the crops. At length, on the 15th of October, the Supreme Government deemed it necessary to direct that the Mohmand fiefs in the Doaba should be confiscated, that the defensive posts should be strengthened, and that British troops should operate against the offending Mohmands, and destroy their chief villages.

Accordingly, on the 25th of October 1851, a force, as per margin, numbering 1,593 of all ranks, marched from Peshawar under the command of Brigadier Sir Colin Campbell, K.C.B., towards the Mohmand frontier. Lieutenant H. W. Norman was Brigade-Major and Lieutenant H. B. Lumsden accompanied the force, as Political Officer.

Detachment, 3rd Co. 1st Bn., Artillery, with No. 17 Light Field Battery attached.
2 companies, 61st Foot.
2 „ 98th „
2nd Irregular Cavalry.
2nd Co., Sappers and Miners.
66th Gurkha Regiment.
Wing, 71st Native Infantry.

The first day's march was to a village, eight miles, where a bridge-of-boats had already been constructed over the Kabul river by Lieutenant H. B. Lumsden, at Sir Colin Campbell's suggestion, in anticipation of orders for these operations; here the force was joined by Lieutenant Lumsden, with four companies of the Guides, about 250 bayonets.

The next day the force continued its march to Mian Khel, close to the border, having crossed the Adizai branch of the Kabul river by a ford. Sir Colin Campbell might with ease have pushed on to where he intended to operate, but it appeared to him more advantageous to allow time for the Deputy Commissioner to communicate with the influential people of the country, and for the moral effect of the expedition to be felt, rather than to advance with greater haste. On the following day the force halted, and Sir Colin Campbell reconnoitred the villages of Dab, the inhabitants of which had been most active in causing annoyance.

The villages were flanked by mud towers, commanding the river and the surrounding country. The approach to them was over a succession of low, stony hills, which increased in height and precipitousness in their immediate vicinity. The villages were found deserted. On the 28th the camp was moved to within two miles of the villages, when news was received that a considerable body of hillmen were collecting in the hills in front of Matta.

Captain G. Jackson was therefore detached with the 2nd Irregular Cavalry to Matta, to protect our villages in the plains—a measure which had the desired effect, as no attempt was made by the enemy to advance into the open.

During the 28th and 29th, the Dab villages were destroyed by a fatigue party of the Guides, and the towers, some ten in number, blown up, under the direction of Captain J. R. Oldfield, Bengal Engineers. The fatigue party was covered by the remainder of the force, and, both in advancing and retiring, each range of hills was successively occupied. A desultory matchlock fire was kept up by the enemy during these two days, to which Sir Colin Campbell did not think it worth while to reply; the retirement on both days was unmolested, and the villages were destroyed without any casualty on our side.

The force now remained in the position that it had taken up, in order that Sir Colin Campbell might fix the site of the present fort of Michni, and to cover the workmen engaged in its erection. The 2nd Irregular Cavalry was posted at Shabkadar and Matta. For the first two nights after the demolition of the villages the picquets were molested, and on the second the hill people seemed to have increased in number; but arrangements had been made for their reception, and, after being driven off, they were followed for some distance by the Guides, without any loss to us.

Annoyance then ceased; the people of the newly-annexed valley of Michni seemed to be returning to their homes, and matters to be taking a pacific turn.

But on the 23rd November Sir Colin Campbell reported that, although the picquets had been unmolested, which he attributed to the fact that the ground for some distance round the camp had been cleared and levelled, the people had not really returned to their villages; those that had come down having done so merely to pluck the heads of their Indian corn, and having then gone off again to the hills.

On the 22nd, a party of Mohmands murdered four of the contractor's butchers in the Peshawar cantonment, wounding three others, and carrying off some bullocks; and on the following night they set fire to a Government building and killed a man. These outrages had been planned by Saadat Khan, the chief of Lalpura, who was then about six miles from the camp, in the Tartara hills, on the right bank of the Kabul river, where he had been joined by eighty *jazailchis*, and by Daria Khan, the partisan leader who had conducted the operations against us in the Kohat pass the year before (see Vol. II, Chap. III). He had also sent a threatening letter to Lieutenant H. B. Lumsden.

As an attempt by the Mohmands from the hills on some of our villages seemed probable, 120 sabres of the 15th Irregular Cavalry, under Major S. Fisher, were ordered out from Peshawar, and posted at Mian Khel, four miles to the east of the camp, to which place two companies of the Guides were also sent, and the bridge-of-boats over the Kabul river was protected by the throwing up of bridge heads.

The chief, Saadat Khan, had been busily engaged in arranging differences which had existed amongst the Mohmands. On the 26th he had moved to Gandab, twenty miles north-west of Shabkadar, where a meeting took place to decide on the plan of operations, and on the 30th of November he was joined by the chief of Bajaur, with a large following.

On the nights of the 28th and 29th November, eluding our cavalry patrols, the Mohmands attacked respectively the villages of Uchwala and Marozai—at the former only carrying off some bullocks, but killing two men; at the latter, wounding others, besides carrying off some property and on the 29th November they burnt a village in the Khalil district, between Peshawar and the hills.

On the 27th a number of the enemy, creeping down from the hills, got into the sugarcane around Matta, but were quickly driven out by two companies of the Guides, under Lieutenant H. N. Miller.

At this time heavy patrols of cavalry were nightly on the move from Mian Khel, Shabkadar, and Matta along the frontier, but the numerous *nalas* and the broken nature of the ground rendered it impossible to prevent parties passing through to our villages along such an extended line of hills, throughout which were numerous bodies of Mohmands. Besides, the people of the hills were so similar in dress, appearance, and language to those of the plains that they could at all times resort to the plains ; whilst no party could at any time leave our camps without information being immediately given in the hills.

Strong fatigue parties of the troops were at this time employed carrying on the heavy work necessary for the construction of the fort.

At the beginning of December the gatherings of the Mohmands had increased so considerably, that Sir Colin Campbell deemed it right to draw in Major S. Fisher's detachment, which had been reinforced by two guns and two companies of infantry, from Mian Khel, keeping up his communications with Shabkadar by strong cavalry patrols. At the same time, Captain G. Jackson at Matta was reinforced by three companies of Gurkhas and two of the Guides, having in all 415 bayonets, 320 sabres, and 2 guns.

On the 7th, without any previous information having been received, Saadat Khan suddenly moved out of a gorge in the hills to the right front of camp, quickly occupying a range of hills in front with 4,000 foot and 80 or 100 horse. Sir Colin Campbell at once moved out with a troop of the Guide Cavalry, two guns, and two companies of infantry, to cover the return of Major Fisher, who was guarding the camels at graze.

Having seen Major Fisher safely in with his charge, Sir Colin Campbell waited till sunset, and then retired very slowly, to prevent the enemy taking up his ground with the advantage of daylight: the latter, however, declined to follow. During this time the hills to the westward, in the neighbourhood of Dab, had also been strongly occupied by the enemy; and a party of 200 men came down to the left bank of the Kabul river, immediately in rear of the camp.

The Brigadier had, on seeing the force displayed, sent orders to Lieut.-Colonel W. R. Mansfield, Her Majesty's 53rd Regiment (who was to be at Peshawar the next day), to march on in the afternoon with the 2nd Troop, 1st Brigade, Horse Artillery, under Major R. Waller, and six companies, 53rd Regiment, and to advance to the bridge-of-boats on the Kabul river.

On the night of the 7th December a patrol of one native officer and thirty sabres of the 2nd Irregular Cavalry, from Matta, fell in with upwards of 500 horse and foot close to the village of Banda. After a short skirmish the enemy retreated to the hills, followed by the patrol; two sowars were killed and two wounded.

At noon the following day, the Mohmands, numbering from 4,000 to 5,000, under Saadat Khan, advanced in line on Matta. On the enemy coming within 900 yards, the artillery opened, when the Mohmands, inclining to the left, tried to get to the rear of Captain Jackson's position, but were well stopped by the Guides, under Lieutenant H. N. Miller. A company of the 66th Gurkhas and one of the Guides then advanced in skirmishing order, supported by two squadrons of the 2nd Irregular Cavalry, and the enemy fell back to his original position on the low hills. The two guns at Matta were in position, and the enemy in heavy masses on the hills, with a *nala* in their front, and Captain Jackson could not therefore attack them. All endeavours to draw them on to the plain again proved useless, and nothing further occurred. There were no casualties on our side, but the enemy suffered from the artillery fire.

Sir Colin Campbell, in reporting this affair, especially alluded to the conduct of Sikandar Khan, the headman of Matta, who turned out with 300 matchlock men, and rendered the most efficient assistance, thereby thoroughly compromising himself on our side.

All this day reports were rife that the chief of Bajaur was collecting men in Pandiali in great numbers, and orders were therefore sent to Lieut.-Colonel Mansfield to collect what troops he could to meet this, and to send in to Peshawar for a detachment of Her Majesty's 61st Foot. His force accordingly bivouacked for a few hours, and then marched at 4 A.M., to Shabkadar, on which the enemy altered their intentions, and the point of attack was to be Sir Colin Campbell's camp, near Dab.

Orders were now sent to Lieut.-Colonel Mansfield to detach a company to Matta, and to march with the remaining five companies, 53rd, and Major Waller's troop, Horse Artillery, and take the enemy in flank, while Sir Colin Campbell engaged them till his arrival. Lieut.-Colonel Mansfield joined at 3 P.M. on the 9th, the 53rd having marched forty-two miles in thirty hours, and the Horse Artillery thirty miles in twenty-four hours. This accession of strength at once told on the enemy, and after much consultation, instead of attacking, the gathering broke up, Saadat Khan decamping to Gandab and then to Lalpura.

After this, nothing of moment occurred; the enemy appeared to have entirely dispersed, and the only offences were some cases of robbery with violence in the neighbourhood of the camp.

On the 25th of December the Guide Corps was detached to Yusafzai, as hostilities were threatening in the direction of Swat, and as the fort was now completed. On the 28th of December the detachment, 61st Foot, with four guns of the field battery, returned to Peshawar, followed on the 2nd of January by the remaining two guns and detachment 98th Foot.

On the 1st of January Sir Colin Campbell established his head-quarters at Mian Khel, leaving the marginally-named garrison of the fort under Captain R. H. Hicks, 15th Irregular Cavalry. On the 2nd the Brigadier moved to Panjpao, where the civil authorities were engaged in settling various points connected with the lands around belonging to individuals of the Mohmand tribe, and the presence of the force had a good effect in hastening the desired settlement.

12 European gunners.
50 sabres, 15th Irregular Cavalry.[1]
2nd Company, Sappers and Miners.
Three companies, 71st Native Infantry.[2]

On the 3rd of January the detachment 15th Irregular Cavalry returned to Peshawar. Matta was at this time held by the head-quarters 2nd Irregular Cavalry, and a company of Her Majesty's 53rd and of the 66th Gurkhas.

On this date (3rd) a picquet of twenty-three sabres, 2nd Irregular Cavalry, were posted about a mile beyond the village of Panjpao, when the enemy showed in considerable force, driving in two of the videttes. Lieutenant W. T. Hughes, second-in-command of that regiment, therefore proceeded at once to the picquet with twenty more sabres. Advancing to reconnoitre, he came suddenly upon a party of some fifty of the enemy, who, from the cover of rocks and brushwood, opened a matchlock fire upon his party.

Lieutenant Hughes displayed great decision and gallantry, and, setting an example which was well followed by his men, immediately charged and pursued the enemy to the foot of the first range of hills, not fewer than fifteen of their number being left dead on the ground, many more creeping away badly wounded, and one being taken prisoner. The 2nd Irregular Cavalry lost one man killed and three wounded.

[1] Became the 16th in 1847. Disbanded in 1861.
[2] Mutinied in 1857 at Lucknow.

The ground over which the charge has been made was ill-suited to the operations of cavalry, being much broken and intersected by ravines; and, as the enemy was mustering in masses on the heights above, Lieutenant Hughes did not think it advisable to attempt a further pursuit.

On the 15th of January, Lieutenant A. Boulnois, Bengal Engineers, in command of the 2nd Company, Sappers and Miners, was killed near Michni. It appears that he had ridden out in company with other officers of the garrison to a considerable distance, and, leaving them, incautiously cantered up to a tower near the entrance of a gorge into the hills, nearly three miles from the fort. Upon his approaching the tower, some men, who had been previously concealed, fired a volley and killed him. His body was carried off, but was recovered through the instrumentality of the *Thanadar* of Mian Khel, and was interred in one of the bastions of the fort. The murderers were never punished.

On the 3rd of February Sir Colin Campbell returned to Mian Khel, to blow up some eleven or twelve towers and several fortified enclosures, the safety of the road to Michni requiring their destruction.

On the 7th the force changed ground to Shabkadar, to be present whilst the villages of Panjpao, close to the hills, were being levelled, as the inhabitants had been made by the civil authorities to remove to a site nearer the fort of Shabkadar, and consequently more under our control,—these villages having been generally the point of rendezvous of the parties who from time to time had started on plundering expeditions into the plains.

A police post had now been established at Matta, and the troops were therefore withdrawn from that place.

It was said that Saadat Khan was at a village a few miles from Pandiali, but that he had failed to obtain assistance from the chief of that tract, who had kept quite aloof from him; and that the Halimzais, who had entered into terms with Captain H. R. James, the Deputy Commissioner, early in the previous month, had also refrained from assisting him.

With the additional police arrangements that had been completed, and with the military posts at Shabkadar and Michni, the civil authorities considered there was no longer any necessity for the force remaining out, and it accordingly returned on the 14th of February to Peshawar.

Affair at Panjpao under Brigadier Sir Colin Campbell, K.C.B., in April 1852.

On the 30th of March news was received at Fort Shabkadar that the Mohmands had collected in the hills in front, and detachments were held ready to turn out at a moment's warning. About 3-30 A.M. on the 31st, a shot being fired at the village of Shabkadar, Captain J. L. Walker, of the 71st Native Infantry, commanding the outpost, immediately moved out with sixty bayonets, but the enemy were in retreat before he could come up with them.

Lieutenant F. R. Tottenham, commanding a troop of the 7th Bengal Light Cavalry, had at once detached a division (forty sabres) of the troop, under Subadar [1] Bulwant Singh, to cut off the retreat of the enemy, whilst he followed with the remainder.

The position taken up by this division was most favourable for the purpose, and as 250 of the enemy were advancing on it with a brisk matchlock fire, Lieutenant Tottenham, who had joined it with eight men, after posting the second division to cut off the enemy's retreat in another direction, advanced to charge, but, with the exception of the subadar, and a havildar, Shekh Husain Baksh, and a trumpeter, Karram Ali, not a man followed him. Riding back, he entreated his men to follow him as the enemy passed their flank, but in vain ; and although Lieutenant Tottenham subsequently induced this detachment to follow the enemy to the foot of the hills, no order, no entreaty, no example, could get them to charge. Both the subadar and the trumpeter had their horses wounded. The second division appear to have behaved well, killing one man and having themselves several horses wounded.

The enemy, who numbered 400 foot and 60 horse, had two killed and several wounded, and left several stands of arms on the ground, with two prisoners. Two of their horses were killed ; one was recognized as belonging to Nauroz Khan, a son of Saadat Khan. Nothing was carried off by the Mohmands from the village, but a policeman was wounded.

1 In the old Bengal Light Cavalry regiments, the native officers and non-commissioned officers held the same ranks as in the infantry, *viz.*, subadar, havildar, etc. In the Irregular Cavalry this was not the case, and the ranks were the same as at present in the cavalry, *viz.*, ressaldar, duffadar, etc.

Our casualties had been two horses killed, and two sowars and eighteen horses wounded.

From the end of the month of March, reports had been rife that Saadat Khan had been making great efforts to conciliate differences among the various Mohmand tribes, in view of again attempting the recovery of the lands we had annexed; and about the middle of April it was said that he had succeeded in his endeavours, and that large bodies of men had collected for the purpose. But the Commissioner, Lieut.-Colonel F. Mackeson, C.B., doubted the truth of these reports, and was averse to the display of force unless actually required, under the apprehension of investing hostile chiefs with notions of importance as to their power to draw troops out and give trouble.

However, as Captain H. R. James, the Deputy Commissioner, who was at Shabkadar collecting information, believed the intentions of the hillmen were serious, Brigadier Sir Colin Campbell, Commanding at Peshawar, bearing in mind his responsibility for the posts held by detachments of regular troops, determined to strengthen Shabkadar, but not to any great extent, in deference to the Commissioner's views. Two Horse Artillery guns and 150 sabres were accordingly sent out, and Sir Colin Campbell proceeded to Shabkadar, to judge for himself of the intentions of Saadat Khan.

On the 15th of April, about 3 P.M., the Mohmands debouched from the hills, in numbers certainly not less than 6,000 matchlock men, with about 80 sowars. They moved along the foot of the first range of hills, in front of Shabkadar, in very fair order, their cavalry and a crowd of matchlock men coming across a tableland, the summit of which overhung the ruined villages of Panjpao. The direction of the movement of the main body was towards Matta.

The troops at the disposal of Sir Colin Campbell numbered only 600 of all ranks. Before displaying a single soldier, the Brigadier allowed this movement to become quite pronounced. He then issued from the fort with the troops, as per margin.

2nd troop, 1st Brigade, Horse Artillery (2 guns).
7th Light Cavalry, 87 sabres.
15th Irregular Cavalry, 179 sabres.

The enemy's cavalry, with a crowd of matchlock men, occupied the edge of the tableland, thus screening the movement towards Matta. Having dispersed this party with a few rounds from the guns, Sir Colin Campbell crowned the low hills at a gallop, and established the guns in rear of the enemy. He was confident that this was the most certain method of averting mischief from Matta. The practice of the two guns was excellent, and the enemy soon began to shake in their purpose, and to forsake the tableland. The Brigadier followed them, but they showed great dexterity in availing themselves of the ground to avoid the artillery fire. Their masses were now broken and the pursuit lasted for about a mile and a half, being brought to a termination by some low ravines near the foot of the hills, which were strongly held.

The gallantry and determination shown by the enemy, when on account of approaching darkness it was deemed prudent for the force to retire, were admirable. The guns were hardly limbered up, the gunners had actually not mounted, when a shout ran down their whole line, and swarms rushed forward, taking advantage of every accident of ground, and evidently thinking their turn was now come. But the guns were instantly unlimbered, and double charges of grape checked the wild, but gallant, attack. It must be remembered that these mountaineers had been for two hours exposed to a cannonade to which they had no means of replying.

The force then retreated across the tableland at a foot's pace, the guns taking up successive positions at every 300 yards, and keeping up a fire of grape; loss was thus avoided, and the most perfect order preserved, while the casualties suffered by the enemy were considerable.

The infantry from the fort had been sent for by Sir Colin Campbell, thinking they might be useful in passing the ruined villages of Panjpao, but they were not found necessary.

The losses of the British in this affair only amounted to two killed and eight wounded. The action had, on our side, been entirely one of artillery, the duties of the cavalry having been restricted to covering the guns in the face of the very large bodies of the enemy opposed to the force.

For some days previously, 500 bayonets of Her Majesty's 53rd Foot had been held in readiness at Peshawar to move at an hour's notice. The Deputy Commissioner having made earnest representation of the fear pervading the country in consequence of the paucity of the troops, and the number of armed enemies in the immediate neighbourhood, six companies of that regiment and four guns, 2nd Troop, 1st Brigade, Horse Artillery, were ordered out on the 16th. The enemy, however, had been so disheartened by their defeat on the 15th, that on the 17th news was received of their having dispersed, and on the 18th the troops which had been sent for, returned to Peshawar.

The approbation of the Governor-General in Council, and the sense entertained by the Government of the political value of striking such a blow, were subsequently conveyed to Sir Colin Campbell and the officers and troops which were under his command, "when the combined Mohmand tribe had been defeated by so small a British force."

The Indian Medal, with a clasp for the "North-West Frontier," was granted in 1869 to all survivors of the troops engaged in the above affair at Panjpao.

Expedition against the Michni Mohmands by a force under Colonel Sydney J. Cotton, in 1854.

In the month of July following the affair at Panjpao, the Michni and Panjpao Mohmands, exiled from house and lands, and cut off from trade, and such like relations in the plains, tendered their submission, and prayed for restoration to their fiefs. They were restored on condition of paying a yearly tribute of Rs. 600 for Michni, and Rs. 200 for Panjpao. The amounts fixed were merely nominal; but, for example's sake, it was necessary to demand some payment, lest immunity in this respect should encourage our own subjects to misbehave, in the hope of avoiding the just dues of Government, or should embolden our neighbours to harass the border in the hope of extorting landed grants. On this, as on other occasions connected with the independent tribes, the Punjab Government declared that revenue was not wanted, but only a quiet frontier.

The Halimzai Mohmands of Panjpao, after this, did not give any cause for dissatisfaction, and remained in the enjoyment of their fief. Their good behaviour may, however, have been due to the fact that they were within range of the guns at the Shabkadar fort.

The conduct of the Michni Mohmands was not so good. In the autumn of 1854 two years tribute was due, and the chief, Rahimdad, fled from Peshawar, whither he had been summoned.

Under such circumstances flight was tantamount to rebellion. The greatest patience and forbearance had been shown by Captain H. R. James, the Deputy Commissioner, in regard to the payment of these arrears; but it was now evident that there remained nothing but attaching their property to the amount of the tribute due, with the addition of a fine for giving so much trouble. The Commissioner, Major H. B. Edwardes, C.B., therefore requested that a force might be sent out to Michni, to support the Deputy Commissioner in case the Mohmand should resist the civil power; that a company of infantry might be placed in Mian Khel for its protection; and that patrols might be sent to seize all cattle moving off to the hills.

1st Troop, 3rd Brigade, Horse Artillery, (4 guns).
One squadron, 1st Irregular Cavalry.[1]
2nd Company, Sappers and Miners.
Three companies, 1st Native Infantry.

On the evening of the 22nd of August, a column, of the strength detailed in the margin, moved out from Peshawar under the command of Major C. T. Chamberlain, 1st Irregular Cavalry. On the orders reaching the fort of Michni for the capture of cattle, Lieutenant C. H. Brownlow, 1st Sikh Infantry, who was in command there, succeeded in capturing 1,100 head, in the act of being driven off across the frontier.

On the 23rd, as it was known that some 200 armed men had come down to the village of Sadin at the invitation of Rahimdad Khan, Major Chamberlain moved out with the artillery and cavalry, and, the guns opening on them, they dispersed.

The capture of Rahmidad's cattle secured a much larger amount than the tribute—Rs. 600—due to Government. But it was necessary to make arrangements for the lapsed shares of the Michni *jagir*. The *zamindars* of the plain, our own subjects, were quite willing to become responsible for the revenue, provided that they were secured from the constant raids from the independent border villages of the fugitive hill chiefs, *viz*., Dab, Sadin, and Shahmansur Khel. The two former belonged to Rahimdad; and Dab, as already related, had been destroyed by Sir Colin Campbell's force in 1851. Shahmansur Khel was just beyond them, on the left bank of the Kabul river, five miles from the Michni fort, and beyond it there was no other Mohmand village for many miles. If these villages

[1] Now 1st Duke of York's Own Lancers (Skinner's Horse).

were left close to our border, in the hands of hostile Mohmands, they would become nests of robbers, and convenient depositories for plunder. Major Edwardes, the Commissioner, concurred in the Deputy Commissioner's opinion that the villages should be destroyed, and never allowed to be re-occupied. The extra military measures to effect this were therefore ordered, it being necessary that the force should be strong enough to meet any resistance the Lalpura chief might send to Rahimdad.

2nd[1] Company, 2nd Battalion, Artillery, with Mountain Train Battery attached, (2 howitzers and 4 guns).
Two companies, 42nd Foot.
One squadron, 10th Light Cavalry.
9th Native Infantry.
1st Sikh Infantry.

On the 27th, the troops, as per margin, commenced to move on Michni. This force, which was to co-operate with that already at Michni, was commanded by Colonel Sydney J. Cotton, 22nd Foot.

The fort of Abazai was temporarily occupied by three companies, 62nd Native Infantry, and one squadron, 14th Irregular Cavalry; that of Shabkadar by three companies, 4th Native Infantry, and one squadron, 16th Irregular Cavalry. Sixty bayonets were detached to the *thana* at Mian Khel, three companies of the 1st Native Infantry relieving them at Michni.

Mountain Train Battery.
Two companies, 22nd Foot.
One troop, 10th Light Cav.
2nd Company, S. and M.
9th Native Infantry.
1st Sikh Infantry.[2]

At daylight on the morning of the 31st August a force, as per margin, under the command of Colonel S. J. Cotton, moved from Michni along the left bank of the river in the direction of Shahmansur Khel.

1st Troop, 3rd Brigade, Horse Artillery, (2 guns).
2nd Company, 2nd Battalion, Artillery, (two 24-pr. howitzers).
One squadron, 1st Irreg. Cav.
Three companies, 1st N. I.

Major Chamberlain's column, consisting of the troops detailed in the margin, had been previously encamped on the right of the river, ready to co-operate with the Peshawar column.

The 1st Sikh Infantry, under the command of Major G. Gordon, in skirmishing order, formed the advance of Colonel Cotton's column; but no opposition was offered at the villages of Sadin or Dab, the enemy falling back on Shahmansur Khel.

Major Chamberlain had now advanced his guns, under Major J. Brind, to an elevated plateau commanding the village of, and

[1] The Mountain Train Battery at this time was drawn by mules, and was attached to the 2nd Company of the 2nd Battalion, Artillery, at Peshawar, with four 3-pr. guns and four 12-pr. howitzers.

[2] Now the 51st Sikhs.

approaches to, Shahmansur Khel, and their fire had partially cleared the village; but this necessarily ceased as the head of the other column approached it, and the 1st Sikh Infantry were met by a sharp matchlock fire from the towers, walls, and houses: however, they quickly cleared the village, driving the enemy to the heights above.

Before the destruction of the village and towers could be started, it was necessary to seize all the commanding positions; for which purpose a strong party of skirmishers of the 9th Native Infantry, under the command of Captain J. Murray, together with two companies of the 1st Sikh Infantry, under Lieutenant C. H. Brownlow, were ordered to drive the enemy from their several positions, and to crown the heights. In carrying out this order the infantry were ably assisted by a well-directed fire from the mountain guns, under Captain T. Brougham. The hills to the north-east of the village were occupied and held by some companies of the 1st Sikh Infantry, under Major G. Gordon.

The village and towers were now completely destroyed, under the direction of Lieutenant H. Hyde, of the Engineers, and Ensign A. U. F. Ruxton, commanding the Sappers and Miners; about 500 maunds of grain were either carried away or destroyed, the houses were levelled by elephants, and all the timber work burnt.

Although the enemy only numbered some 200, the heights had not been occupied without a struggle, and the troops holding them were, during the whole time, exposed to an unceasing and galling fire from the neighbouring ridges, causing a loss of one killed and sixteen wounded, including Lieutenant C. H. Brownlow, of the 1st Sikh Infantry, and Lieutenant C. A. McDougall, Adjutant, 9th Native Infantry, who were both dangerously wounded, and whose gallantry in holding the heights had been most conspicuous. As soon as the village had been completely destroyed, these covering parties were withdrawn, under cover of the mountain guns.

The force then retired from Shahmansur Khel, covered by the guns on the right bank of the river, and the camp was reached at 4-30 P.M.

As far as could be ascertained, the loss of the enemy had been four killed and twelve wounded.

On the 2nd September, the troops, under Colonel S. J. Cotton, advanced on Dab and Sadin, supported by Major Chamberlain's detachment on the right bank of the river. No opposition was offered by the Mohmands, although they were in as great force as at Shahmansur Khel, the guns on the right bank keeping them in check. The total destruction of these villages having been effected by 2 P.M., the troops returned to Peshawar.

Colonel Cotton, in his despatch, reported most favourably of the conduct of the troops, who had shown throughout the greatest activity, gallantry, and zeal. The heat had been at times excessive, and the exposure great.

The Indian Medal, with a clasp for the "North-West Frontier," was granted in 1869 to all survivors of the troops engaged in the above operations.

Immediately after these operations, the well affected Mohmands of Michni, who had remained on the *jagir* when Rahimdad fled, deposited their quota of tribute with the Deputy Commissioner, as a proof of their adherence to the original terms pending the final orders of Government.

A settlement of the Michni fief was then made. The faithful Mohmands, who stood by their lands, continued to pay their share of the tribute. The lands of those who fled were farmed out and assessed with revenue. Rahimdad was not restored, and he continued to give trouble on this part of the border. Towards the close of 1854 he appeared at Peshawar, under a safe conduct, to pray for restoration to his fief; but as he did not, and indeed could not, offer any security for good conduct, he was sent back across the frontier, and forbidden to re-enter British territory.

After the expedition above narrated, under Colonel Sydney Cotton, the Mohmands continued to commit outrages on our territory, and on the 24th March 1855, a party, numbering 300, came down and carried off seventy-seven bullocks. Troops, consisting of detachments of the regiments as per margin, under the command of Major G. Gordon, 1st Sikh Infantry, were moved out, and a skirmish ensued, in which one duffadar of police and one villager were killed, and Ensign G. S. Bradford and four sepoys of the 62nd Native Infantry were wounded.

10th Light Cavalry.
16th Irregular Cavalry.[1]
62nd Native Infantry.[2]
1st Sikh Infantry.

[1] Now the 7th Hariana Lancers. [2] Mutinied in Mooltan in 1858.

On the 5th May 400 Mohmands issued from the hills, but were met by the troops and driven back with the loss of two sepoys killed on our side. Between this date and the 16th of September 1855, ten outrages were committed on this border. On the latter date a party of Mohmands came out, but were driven back, with the loss on our side of two sowars and one sepoy wounded. In these outrages the offenders had been, for the most part, Mohmands of Pandiali. At last, Lieut.-Colonel H. B. Edwardes, C.B., the Commissioner, brought this persistent misconduct to the notice of Government, and recommended that, instead of restoring to them their allowances, we should endeavour to punish them.

He recommended that the Amir of Kabul should be called upon either to inflict summary punishment on the Pandiali Mohmands for the past, and restrain them for the future, or else to intimate that he left them to be dealt with as we thought proper. With this report he submitted a memorandum, showing how he would propose to carry out these operations in the Pandiali valley. In this memorandum he said that nothing less than the complete destruction of every village of the Pandiali Mohmands would be sufficient to meet the case, and for this purpose he considered a force of 5,000 effective men would be required.

Sir John Lawrence, the Chief Commissioner, supported the recommendations of Lieut.-Colonel Edwardes; but the Government of India, while recognising the necessity of punitive measures, considered that the time was inopportune, and that immediate action should be postponed.

Nothing further was therefore done except remonstrating strongly with the Amir on the indifference shown by his government to these raids and annoyances. These remonstrances, however, had no effect, and raids on our border continued as before, and between September 1855 and July 1857, no less than twenty-four serious outrages were committed, with the object of plunder and murder.

This continued misconduct was made the subject of conversation by Sir John Lawrence with the Amir Dost Muhammad, during his visit to Peshawar in January 1857, but no satisfactory result followed.

It was evident that the Mohmand chiefs hoped that the British Government would at last be driven, by perpetual annoyances on its border, to grant them some rich fiefs. Preliminary arrangements were under discussion for the advance of a punitive force to Pandiali, when the Mutiny broke out in India, and our attention was more pressingly directed to other quarters.

Although the sepoy outbreak gave the Mohmands an excellent opportunity of increasing their annoyances, yet they showed no signs of profiting by it; their raids continued, it is true, but they were not of a more formidable nature. In the middle of August, however, a fanatical Kunar *saiyid*, named Saiyid Amir, after vainly endeavouring to raise the Khaibar tribes against us, betook himself to the Mohmands of Michni. They received him with open arms, and gave him protection, while he sent incendiary letters and arms to the troops at Peshawar.

On the 9th of September, with the aid of the Shahmansur Khel Mohmands and forty or fifty rebel sepoys, he made a night attack on the fort of Michni, but the garrison, being composed of a party of the Kelat-i-Ghilzai Regiment, were staunch, and beat them off.

The Mohmands were now in a state of the highest excitement, and sent the "fiery cross" to all their neighbours, being evidently determined to strike a blow for the recovery of their fiefs.

As there were no troops to move out against them, Lieut.-Colonel Edwardes had to yield with as good grace as possible. He sent them word that they were going the wrong way to work, and that if they wanted to regain their confiscated privileges, they must render some marked service to Government, instead of adding to the embarrassments of a passing crisis. For instance, if they sent the *Saiyid* away and gave hostages for good conduct till the war was over, Lieut.-Colonel Edwardes said he would gladly ask Government to consider their case, but not on such favourable terms as formerly. The Mohmands then sent in their hostages to Peshawar, packed off the *Saiyid* unceremoniously, and sat down quietly to wait for the return of peace in Hindustan. A few days after, the news of the capture of Delhi having arrived, the crisis passed over without any further serious danger. Nevertheless, in spite of their professions, the Mohmands evidently did not consider themselves bound to refrain from raiding, and this went on as before.

From the beginning of September 1857 to March 1860, 39 serious outrages were committed by members of this tribe, and the question of a punitive expedition was again submitted for the consideration of the Government. Within five years there had been 85 raids committed by parties of an average strength of 75 men, in which 14 British subjects had been killed, 27 wounded, and 55 carried off, and over 1,200 head of cattle plundered. This was exclusive of 40 minor raids, in which 35 British subjects had been killed or wounded, and 267 head of cattle plundered. The Government still refused, however, to sanction an expedition, and determined to wait and see what would be the result of resolutely refusing to restore the confiscated *jagirs* of the Tarakzais, the cause of these complications.

About the 20th of March, the first really hopeful sign of a satisfactory issue to this policy occurred, when Nauroz Khan, the son and adopted heir of Saadat Khan of Lalpura, sent in, asking for permission to come into Peshawar, and stating that he had been engaged punishing the Shinwaris for an attempt made by one of that tribe on the life of Fateh Khan, Khattak, when carrying despatches from Peshawar to Kabul. Nauroz Khan was accordingly invited to come in.

In seeking to make peace with us, Nauroz Khan's great aim was to get back the forfeited *jagirs*; but, finding that Lieut.-Colonel Edwardes was firmly opposed to this ever being brought about, and knowing that the Kabul Government had signified their intention of interfering to stop the misconduct of the tribe, the young *Khan* only asked that mortgages on lands held by some of the Michni Mohmands in the Peshawar district, who were in rebellion, might hold good if peace was made, and that prisoners might be released; this was promised in regard to political prisoners, but not in regard to criminals, who, it was declared, must be dealt with according to law.

The result of this conference was the granting of the following terms to the Mohmands:

1st.—That Government should accept the assurances of Saadat Khan, chief of Lalpura, and his son, Nauroz Khan, of their desire to live on good terms with the British Government, and to be responsible for the peace of the frontier, and overlook all past causes of hostility.

2nd.—That the blockade against the Mohmands should be raised, and the tribe be free to resort to our territory, individual notorious criminals being, of course, responsible to the tribunals.

3rd.—That Nawab Khan, chief of Pandiali, and all his branch of the tribe, be included in the amnesty.

4th.—That such of the Mohmands as went out with Rahimdad Khan be also included on the same terms.

5th.—That no confiscated land or *jagir* be given to any one.

6th.—That all Mohmands who may have been apprehended during the blockade merely because they belonged to a hostile tribe, but not taken in the commission of crimes or raids, be released on payment of the reward given for their capture.

Lieut.-Colonel Edwardes's letter to Saadat Khan regarding these terms is given in full, and was as follows :—

I have received your letter, and, as I have no desire to injure you in any way, I can assure you that the coming in of your son, Nauroz Khan, was a great pleasure to me. From all he said, and from all you write, I believe you sincerely desire to put an end to the disturbances on the Mohmand frontier, and to come to friendly terms. I have this day addressed my own Government in your favour, and asked that your past offences may be forgiven, and bygones be bygones; and as your son, Nauroz Khan, undertakes to be responsible for the rest of the Mohmand *maliks*, such as Nawab Khan of Pandiali, and others, I have recommended that the pardon be extended to all other Mohmands (except such individuals as may be known to have committed a murder or other serious crimes, of which justice must take notice), and that the blockade be taken off, and the Mohmands be admitted to come and go, and trade in the Peshawar valley. For I conceive it is beyond my discretion to forgive and condone an old-standing enmity like this, though I have every hope that Government will listen to my representations.

As to any *jagirs* that have been confiscated, I do not think it at all advisable that they should be released; for they will only be a future bone of contention. Whoever sits on a barren hillside and enjoys a fine estate in the plain below for doing nothing, must necessarily get wind in his head. He thinks he owes it to his own strength, and the fears, not the generosity, of Government. So after a year or two he gets full and proud, and rebels; and then the whole fight comes over again, and the tribe is plunged into war to please him, and many lives are lost. In short, *jagirs* in the plain are not good for the men on the hills, and they will never be given with my consent. Don't think I say this for the sake of the money. To a great Government the sum is of no consequence; but it is bad for the administration. If there be any Mohmand mortgages in the hands of our subjects, the Mohmands will be free to sue in our courts, where every justice will be done them. And as to the prisoners in our jails, to please you I will release every

Mohmand who has been seized merely because he was a Mohmand, on consideration that he pays whatever reward was given for his own seizure. But no highwayman, or murderer, or other criminal, will be released; justice must take its course with such offenders.

My friend, I have spoken my mind out, for it is best to be plain. For the rest, I desire the honour, and welfare, and strength of you and your family, and I conceive that they will be better served by the friendship than by the enmity of the British Government.

Soon after this, Saadat Khan of Lalpura and Nawab Khan of Pandiali came in to Peshawar in person, and made their submission to the Commissioner.

Affairs with the Mohmands, near Shabkadar, December and January 1863-64.

After the submission of their chiefs, the Mohmands desisted from troubling our border until the occasion of the Ambela expedition in 1863, when the emissaries of the Akhund of Swat were sent all over the hills bordering on the Peshawar valley, but were only successful in exciting disturbances among the Mohmands. Sultan Muhammad Khan, son of Saadat Khan, owned the *Akhund's* religious supremacy, and was, moreover, ill disposed towards us. He was a man of bad character altogether; he began life by murdering his eldest brother, and was often at feud, even with his own father. Collecting a body of Mohmands, who were joined by a miscellaneous rabble of Safis, Bajauris, and the like, he came down to the British frontier on the 5th December 1863.

Captain J. M. Earle, who was commanding the fort of Shabkadar, hearing firing on the Abazai road, moved out with fifty-five sabres, 6th Bengal Cavalry,[1] and ninety-six bayonets, Native Infantry. The enemy were estimated at about 500, of whom 300 were posted on the summit of a slight eminence. Captain Earle advanced against them with his infantry in skirmishing order, and the cavalry on the flanks. On nearing the enemy, the cavalry charged from both flanks, and succeeded in killing seven or eight of their number, and wounding some twenty. Lieutenant St. G. M. Bishop, 6th Bengal Cavalry, who was gallantly leading the division on the left, was mortally wounded, and a sowar was also wounded during the charge.

[1] Now the 6th King Edward's Own Cavalry.

Before the infantry could come up, the enemy had gained the crest of one of the hills in the first range, when Captain Earle, having accomplished his object by driving the enemy beyond our frontier, retired leisurely towards the fort. The enemy made no attempt to follow up, but came down immediately afterwards to collect their killed and wounded.

The Shabkadar garrison was then reinforced by troops from Peshawar, under Lieut.-Colonel G. Jackson, 2nd Bengal Cavalry. On the 7th of December, the enemy having advanced from the hills and taken up a position on the ridge in front of Shabkadar, Lieut.-Colonel Jackson moved out with his force. As he gained the ridge, the enemy fell back, and were driven in half an hour to the end of the plateau into the ravines and broken ground at the foot of the hills, from the sides of which they kept up a heavy fire ; Lieutenant A. FitzHugh, with a detachment of the 4th Sikhs, was closely engaged on the left front of the line, and kept the enemy at bay for some time. Evening setting in, Lieut.-Colonel Jackson recalled that officer, and retired the force. As it fell back, the enemy followed, keeping up a fire the whole way, but at a long distance ; it was dark when the troops reached the fort, and a party of the enemy having got into the village about 800 yards from the fort, they were shelled out.

Our loss was, two sepoys of the 4th Sikhs killed, one jemadar and one sepoy of the 4th Sikhs and two sepoys of the 8th Native Infantry, wounded.

Towards the end of December, Sultan Muhammad Khan took up a menacing position at Regmiana, a small village in the hills about five or six miles distant from Shabkadar. Nauroz Khan, son of Saadat Khan, had recently joined his brother, but Saadat Khan himself remained in the hills to the westward of Michni, pretending inability to restrain his sons, but really affording them countenance by his presence in the neighbourhood.

When Sultan Muhammad Khan arrived at Regmiana, the number of his followers did not exceed 400 men. Nauroz Khan brought an accession of 300 more, and occupied the Mohmand village of Chingai, north-east of Regmiana.

Sultan Muhammad Khan was accompanied by a band of *mullas* from Ningrahar and other parts of Afghanistan, who assisted him in collecting the tribes, with the avowed object of carrying on a religious war. Their success in stirring up the Mohmands after the affairs of the 5th and 7th December was not great at first. Occasional accessions of small bodies under Muhammadan priests, and a few absconded leaders of robbers from Government territory, were received ; but it was not until the 31st of December that the importunities of the priests and the efforts of Sultan Muhammad Khan, had collected a miscellaneous assemblage, estimated at 3,800 men, as per margin.

Mohmands of the Baezai clan ..	.. 600	men.
" " Khwaezai clan ..	.. 1,000	"
" " Halimzai " ..	.. 1,500	"
" " Tarakzai " ..	.. 200	"
Safis, Ghilzais, etc. ..	.. 500	"
Total	.. 3,800	"

On the evening of the 1st January these numbers were augmented by the arrival of 800 more Baezais, under Sultan Muhammad Khan, 500 Halimzais, and 500 others under Nauroz Khan, making the total strength of the enemy 5,600.

Having thus assembled this force, Sultan Muhammad Khan, after consultation with his brother and other leaders, and more particularly at the pressing instigation of the priests, resolved to move out to meet the British force stationed at Shabkadar. This force had been considerably increased, and was now under the command of Colonel A. Macdonell, C.B., of the Rifle Brigade, and consisted of the troops noted in the margin.

	Officers.	Non-commissioned Officers and men.
D Battery, 5th Brigade, Royal Horse Artillery, (3 guns)	.. 2	49
7th Hussars	.. 5	140
3rd Battalion Rifle Brigade	.. 27	691
2nd Bengal Cavalry [1] ..	.. 5	231
6th " " ..	.. 1	95
2nd Gurkha Regiment [2] ..	.. 7	453
4th Sikh Infantry [3] ..	.. 1	93
Total	.. 48	1,752

At about eleven o'clock on the morning of the 2nd January 1864, the Mohmands and others who had gathered at Regmiana made their appearance, debouching from the gorge north-west of Fort Shabkadar, and gradually forming under their leaders on the plateau in front of it, to the number of some 5,000 matchlock men and 40 horsemen.

By 2 P.M., the enemy being fully collected, their formation presented the appearance of a crescent. Having reason to believe that they would not venture far from their line of retreat, Colonel

[1] Now 2nd Lancers (Gardner's Horse).

[2] Now 2nd King Edward's Own Gurkha Rifles.

[3] Now 54th Sikhs (Frontier Force).

Macdonell, with a view to tempt them down, occupied with two companies of riflemen the village of Badi Shamberi in front of his centre, posting a squadron on the Michni road to attract their skirmishers to the plain, which partly succeeded in drawing forward the enemy's right.

One company, Rifle Brigade.
" " 2nd Gurkhas.

On this, the cavalry dashed forward, turning and gradually folding the enemy's right on the centre. Simultaneously the three guns of the Royal Horse Artillery, having taken up a position in front of Badi Shamberi, raked the retiring wing of the enemy with some effect.

The cavalry continued the turning movement (three times were the Mohmands charged by the 7th Hussars), and Colonel Macdonell then advanced the 3rd Battalion of the Rifle Brigade in skirmishing order, when the enemy were driven beyond the border, and the troops returned after sunset, unmolested.

Our loss was two killed and seventeen wounded, while the enemy were believed to have sustained about eighty casualties.

Many Mohmands of the Tarazkai section proceeded straight to their homes after their defeat, and a defection of at least 1,000 men took place the next morning, on the plea of scarcity of provisions, and the necessity of burying the dead at the usual places of interment. The result of the action also had the most dispiriting effect on the leaders, and, notwithstanding the endeavours of the priests, the gathering gradually dispersed.

The Indian Medal, with a clasp for the "North-West Frontier," was granted in 1876 to all survivors of the troops who took part in the above affair.

On the requisition of the Commissioner of Peshawar, the Amir of Kabul now interfered in Mohmand affairs, and Sher Ali Khan sent his son, Sirdar Muhammad Ali Khan, to eject Saadat Khan, and to replace him by Riza Khan, the son of his former rival, Turabaz Khan. Saadat Khan and his son, Nauroz Khan, were carried off prisoners to Kabul. The old *Khan* was subsequently released and died soon afterwards.

Riza Khan, having taken possession of Lalpura, considerably strengthened it. He was attacked by Sultan Muhammad Khan, son of Saadat Khan, and a large gathering; but he repulsed them with heavy loss, and Sultan Muhammad Khan then wandered about amongst the Mohmands, trying to invite them either to assemble and retake Lalpura, or to commit raids upon the British border. In August 1866 he was joined by some of the chiefs of the Khwaezai and Baezai sections, who had lost friends in the former attack on Lalpura. Their object in coming together appears to have been twofold ; 1st, to retake Lalpura ; and, 2ndly, in the event of failure, to punish some of the Mohmand Tarakzai villages above Michni, and close the caravan routes by Kharappa and Tartara to Peshawar. When some 4,000 or 5,000 men had collected, dissensions broke out, fomented by our ally, Nawab Khan, chief of Pandiali, and the gathering dispersed.

Eventually, the Amir, finding Riza Khan useless, removed him, and placed Sultan Muhammad Khan in the office of his father, at the same time releasing Nauroz Khan, who, with his son, Muhammad Sadik Khan, went off to join Sirdar Yakub Khan, the Amir's son, at Herat.

In 1870, Sultan Muhammad Khan was shot dead in the Lalpura bazaar by the son of Riza Khan, who was instantly killed by the *Khan's* followers. Nauroz Khan having returned from Herat, then assumed the chieftainship, and marked his tenure of office by great vigour and energy, and endeared himself to the tribe by his generous hospitality.

After the affair near Shabkadar in 1864, the Mohmand border was not disturbed by any serious outrage until the beginning of 1873, when Major H. Macdonald, the Commandant of Fort Michni, was murdered in a most dastardly manner. Major Macdonald and Captain R. M. Clifford, of the 16th Bengal Cavalry,[1] were strolling unarmed and unattended on the bank of the Kabul river, about a mile above the fort, when they were suddenly attacked by armed men. Both officers attempted to escape ; Captain Clifford succeeded, but Major Macdonald was wounded in the thigh by a matchlock ball, and fell, and was thereupon pursued, and hacked to death with swords. Captain Clifford would also have probably lost his life if it had not been for the intervention of a party of villagers in a hamlet near the scene of the outrage, who, hearing the shots, turned out and fired upon the murderers.

[1] This regiment, formerly the Rohilkhand Horse, was disbanded in 1882 and re-established in 1885. Now the 16th Cavalry.

From inquiries made into the circumstances of the outrage, it was established that the murder was committed under the direction of Bahram Khan, half-brother of Nauroz Khan, chief of Lalpura. Bahram Khan had been for some time in charge of an outpost at Nasir Kot,[1] about two miles above Michni, and had the reputation of being a wild and restless character. No adequate motive for the crime was discovered, but it was proved that Bahram Khan had for some time previously formed the intention of making himself notorious by the murder of a British officer. After the murder, Bahram Khan fled to Ningrahar, and evaded all attempts at capture; but in 1879 those of his retainers who had actually cut down Major Macdonald were seized at Dakka, and met with their well-deserved, though long-delayed, fate. For this outrage a fine of Rs. 10,000 was imposed upon the Michni Tarakzais, which they paid without demur. Though not active participators in the deed, they had failed to give warning of an act which they well knew was meditated.

At the end of the same year (1873) Captain Anderson, the officer commanding at Fort Shabkadar, was fired at, though happily without effect, by a member of the Hafizkor sub-section of the Tarakzai clan; but the insult was promptly avenged by confiscation of the lands held by members of the section, and their prohibition from entering British territory for a period of three years. From this time till the invasion of Afghanistan in 1878, our relations with the independent Mohmands continued undisturbed. In 1874, the arrest of Sirdar Yakub Khan by the Amir was the signal for rebellion at Lalpura, and Nauroz Khan, the chief at Lalpura, disobeyed the summons to go to Kabul, and retired to Gandab. The affairs of Lalpura continued in a very disturbed state, but these troubles did not extend to our border. In 1875, Muhammad Shah Khan, the son of Sultan Muhammad Khan, was installed as Khan of Lalpura. In 1877, Nauroz Khan died at Gandab, and his sons shortly after came in to Peshawar.

Operations against the Mohmands in 1879.

Affair at Kam Dakka.

When war was declared against the Amir of Afghanistan in 1878, Muhammad Shah Khan sent a Mohmand contingent to

[1] Then in Afghan territory.

co-operate with the Amir's troops at Ali Musjid, but they fled without firing a shot, and Muhammad Shah Khan came in shortly after to Lieutenant-General Sir S. Browne, at Dakka, and tendered his submission. He was recognized as Khan of Lalpura and did fairly good service. The sons of Nauroz Khan, Muhammad Sadik Khan and Akbar Khan, were at this time with the British Army. Moghal Khan, the Khan of Goshta, second in importance only to the chief of Lalpura, refused to come in, and held aloof. It is said that it was at his instigation that a raid was made by hill Mohmands on the village of Sarai, on the left bank of the Kabul river in the Kama district.

In consequence of this raid, and owing to the murder of two camel-drivers from the camp at Jalalabad while tending their camels grazing, a small column, as per margin, was sent into the Kama district on the 11th of January 1879, under the command of Brigadier-General F. H. Jenkins. No opposition was met with, and the village of Shergarh was surprised, the headman of the village and a ringleader of the marauding party being captured. A party of Mohmands was observed making for the hills, and the mountain guns opened on them with effect. On the following day the column returned to camp, having accomplished the object for which it had been detached.

Hazara M. B., 2 guns.
Guide Cavalry, 50 sabres.
" Infantry, 300 bayonets.

On the 6th of February 1879, a force of Mohmands, aided by Bajauris, and estimated at 12,000, made an attack on the village of a friendly chief in the Kama district. This chief, Azim Khan, the Khan of Chardeh, had previously tendered his submission to the British, and had been put in charge of the two districts of Goshta and Chardeh. This raid, like the previous one, was made at the instigation of Moghal Khan, the hostile Khan of Goshta.

On the 7th February, a small force, as shown in margin, numbering about 900 men, under Brigadier-General H. T. Macpherson, V.C., C.B., was sent from Jalalabad to attack the enemy. A simultaneous movement was ordered from Basawal by Chardeh towards Goshta, to intercept the Mohmands should they retire by the route by which they had advanced. This force, consisting of 2 mountain

10th Hussars, one troop.
Detachment, Rifle Brigade.
11th B. C., one squadron.
Det., 20th Punjab N. I.
" 4th Gurkha Regiment.

guns, 300 infantry and 1 squadron of Guides Cavalry, was under the command of Brigadier-General J. A. Tytler, V.C., C.B., and was accompanied by Azim Khan and a few followers. The two columns crossed the river, but the enemy, having received information of the intended movements, did not wait to be attacked, but retreated to the hills before the arrival of the troops. The columns therefore returned to their respective stations, and by the 11th all excitement in this district had passed over.

About this time an agitation was got up by the *mullas*, and much excitement was caused among the Mohmands by their fanatical preaching. This excitement found vent in an attack on Mr. G. B. Scott, Surveyor, at Zankai, above Michni, on the 28th of February 1879.

Arrangements had been previously made by the Deputy Commissioner of Peshawar, with the Tarakzai Mohmands, for the safe conduct of a party through their country for the purpose of surveying the Shanilo route from Peshawar to Dakka. Steps had also been taken to prevent any opposition on the part of the Halimzai Mohmands from Gandab. This was considered necessary owing to the preaching of a wandering mendicant *mulla*, known as the *fakir* of Mian Isa, from the Halimzai village of that name, in British territory, where he had long resided. On the outbreak of hostilities he had taken to the hills, and soon gained influence among the ignorant clansmen. On the 26th of February Mr. Scott arrived at Michni, and the following day went to Sahib Chin, and returned without any interruption or unfriendly demonstration whatever. An escort of seventy men of the 24th Punjab Native Infantry had been told off as a guard for him.

On the morning of the 28th of February, Mr. Scott, taking with him only two non-commissioned officers and twenty sepoys of his guard, accompanied by the *Tehsildar* and several *maliks*, proceeded to Zankhai. He was joined on the way by some men of the Tarakzai clan. On arriving at Zankhai he began to sketch, and had been at work some little time, when he observed a body of men approaching from Gandab. He at once determined to return, and gave the order to retire. The party had gone about two miles, when a body of the enemy began to open a brisk fire on them. At first no notice was taken of it, but soon the fire became too hot, and the sepoys were ordered to return it.

A skirmishing action then began, and the sepoys were ordered to retire in parties of at first ten each, and then five each, one covering the other. The country people who had remained with the party (about twenty or thirty in number), under the command of the *Tehsildar*, Shahpasand Khan, helped to keep off the enemy, but their ammunition soon failed. The retirement was continued until a mass of low hills was reached. Here Mr. Scott sent for reinforcements. Leaving the road, the party continued their retreat along an almost level spur for about half a mile, at the end of which was a steep descent to the bed of a small stream. Here the enemy charged, sword in hand, and succeeded in cutting down a naick and a sepoy, whose bodies had to be left on the ground. They were, however, eventually beaten off, and forced to seek cover.

After this the enemy seemed to have had enough, and the retreat was continued almost unmolested to Gidarnao. About a mile beyond this village the remainder of the guard, under Captain E. G. Newnham, was met, and the whole party returned to Michni. Our loss had been—one non-commissioned officer and one sepoy killed, one sepoy shot through the foot, and, in addition to this, Hidayat Khan, a *malik* of Sena, was shot through the face.

The sub-divisions of the Tarakzais and Halimzais implicated in this outrage were fined Rs. 2,000, which they eventually paid.

More serious than the Zankhai affair was the gathering headed by the well-known Mulla Khalil, in April 1879. This man was the grandson of a Swati from Pakli, in the Hazara district. A man of little education, but of great ambition, he had at this time risen to a position of much influence among the Mohmands. For some weeks before this, rumours had been rife of gathering of Mohmands of the Khwaezai and Halimzai clans, for the purpose of raiding on British territory, or making attacks on the British posts along the Khaibar route. On the night of the 20th April, a few Mohmands, numbering perhaps 200 or 300, began to cross over the Kabul river from Palosi to Shinpok. On the 20th April, the Khan of Lalpura sent to the officer commanding at Dakka (Major O. Barnes, 10th Bengal Lancers), to say that a large body of Mohmands were within three miles of that place, and had already exchanged shots with his outposts. The *Khan* asked for help, as he expected a night attack. Major Barnes made such arrangements as were practicable for the defence of Lalpura, but the anticipated attack did not take place.

C-3rd Royal Artillery, 2 guns.
10th B. L., 1 squadron.
Mhairwara Battn., 3 companies.[1]

As, however, reports from every quarter agreed in stating that the Mohmands were in large numbers, Major Barnes moved out the following morning with the troops as per margin, to ascertain the character and number of his neighbours. The road, as far as the foot of the Kam Dakka pass, was found clear of hostile tribes. Having halted the guns and main body of the cavalry at the foot of the pass, Major Barnes pushed forward the infantry and a few mounted orderlies to Kam Dakka, which is a village on the south side of the Kabul river, seven miles east of Dakka. No opposition of any consequence was offered to this reconnaissance, a few shots only being exchanged across the Kabul river. Kam Dakka was found unoccupied by the enemy, but all reports were unanimous as to the Mohmands being in great strength in Rena and Parchao, on the north side of the river. The Kam Dakka villagers were friendly, but expressed grave fear for their own property and lives, and begged that the reconnoitring party might not to be withdrawn.

The force returned to Dakka the same day without meeting any opposition, and, on a report of the intelligence gained by it being telegraphed to Lieutenant-General F. F. Maude, V.C., C.B., commanding the 2nd Division, Peshawar Valley Field Force, at Landi Kotal, instructions were issued to despatch two companies of the Mhairwara Battalion to Kam Dakka. This step was taken on the recommendation of the Political Officer, Major E. R. Conolly. That officer was in camp at Landi Kotal when the telegram from the Officer Commanding at Dakka arrived, and strongly advised that help should be sent to the people of Kam Dakka, as the inhabitants were, Major Conolly stated, friendly to the troops.

In consultation with the Political Officer, it was also decided to send a force from Landi Kotal to reconnoitre through the Shilman valley towards Kam Dakka. The object of this reconnaissance was to reassure the inhabitants, who were considered to be friendly, to open up and obtain topographical information of

[1] Now the 44th Merwara Infantry.

this part of the country, some of which was unknown, and to work round on Kam Dakka, so that should any of the Mohmands have crossed the Kabul river, they might possibly be caught between the troops from Dakka and this reconnoitring column.

11-9th Royal Artillery,	2 guns.	
1-12th Foot	2 cos.	
1-25th ,,	2 ,,	
24th Punjab N. I.	2 ,,	
Bhopal Battalion	2 ,,	

Lieut.-Colonel F. B. Norman, Commandant, 24th Punjab Native Infantry, accompanied by Major E. R. Conolly as Political Officer, marched from Landi Kotal in command of this column, consisting of the troops noted in the margin, at four o'clock on the afternoon of the 21st April. On the same day, in accordance with the orders received, a detachment of the Mhairwara Battalion, consisting of 130 men under the command of Captain O'Moore Creagh,[1] was despatched from Dakka at five o'clock in the evening to the friendly village of Kam Dakka, with instructions to protect that place against an enemy to be expected from across the Kabul river, and to hold the village for three days.

4 Native Officers.
11 Non-Commissioned Officers.
4 Drummers.
119 Sepoys.

This detachment, provided with entrenching tools, and carrying spare ammunition, and rations, did not reach Kam Dakka till a quarter past eleven o'clock that night, as great difficulty was experienced in getting the mules over the intervening hills.

As the orders to the detachment were to occupy the village of Kam Dakka, and to entrench it, Captain Creagh concluded its inhabitants would be expecting the troops, but he nevertheless sent forward a messenger to give notice of the arrival of the detachment.

On his arrival at Kam Dakka, Captain Creagh summoned the headmen of the village, and announced to them the object with which the troops had been sent. The villagers were, however, averse to the troops entering their village, and said they had neither asked for, nor did they require, any assistance, as they were quite able to protect themselves. They further expressed it as their opinion that the detachment would be defeated by the enemy, as it was unaccompanied by any mountain guns; they therefore had no wish to compromise themselves with their tribe

[1] Now Lieut.-General Sir O'Moore Creagh, V.C., K.C.B.

on account of the troops. Their demeanour was evidently anything but friendly.

That night the detachment bivouacked outside the village of Kam Dakka, throwing out the necessary picquets for its protection; and at four o'clock on the morning of the 22nd of April Captain Creagh again summoned the headmen, but they refused to have anything to do with the troops, and refused even to furnish a messenger to Dakka. They, however, said that in the attack which would take place they would remain neutral, and would not allow the enemy into the village of Kam Dakka.

Captain Creagh, in order to carry out his orders, took up a position covering the right and left front of Kam Dakka, with the understanding that the inhabitants of that place would themselves protect their own front, as they said they would do. He then reported all well to the officer commanding at Dakka, as the enemy did not appear too numerous, only a few of them being visible on the hill in front of his position.

About five o'clock in the morning, crowds of the enemy were seen crossing the river, and ascending the hill in front of where the troops were stationed, and threatening their flank. The impending attack was then reported to Dakka, and as the enemy opened fire upon the detachment at about half-past five o'clock, and the inhabitants of Kam Dakka became more sullen, the troops were withdrawn altogether from the latter place. A fresh position was then taken up, with the right of the detachment resting on the Dakka and Kam Dakka road, and the left towards the Kabul river, with a support and reserve in rear of the right, and the baggage in rear of the left; at the same time cavalry were applied for from Dakka, as the enemy were advancing into the open.

This position was held for about an hour, while continual reinforcements joined the enemy, who kept up a heavy fire on the troops; but the right flank being again threatened, the detachment fell back slowly through some cultivated ground. At about eight o'clock in the morning, a party of the Mhairwara Battalion, consisting of one jemadar, four non-commissioned officers, and thirty-one men, escorting ammunition from Dakka, came down through the pass to join the detachment. On seeing them the enemy withdrew to the hilltops, but continued to extend to the right.

From what this escort told Captain Creagh, he came to the conclusion that he could expect no reinforcements on that day, and therefore he resolved to take up the best available position, to enable him to maintain himself against the attack of the enemy as long as possible. Fixing upon a tomb in a graveyard to his left rear, Captain Creagh threw back the right of the detachment, and brought the skirmishers facing the hills, with the tomb in the rear.

Part of the supports, the reserve, and the *doolie*-bearers were set to work to build stone breastworks flanking each other, the baggage was placed under the river bank, where it was out of fire, while the skirmishers kept up a brisk fire, which prevented the enemy from attempting to come down the hills to close quarters, although they kept up a continuous fire. The hills commanded this position at a distance of about 500 yards, but no better was available, as it was necessary for the troops to keep near the river for the sake of the water-supply, and the ruined tomb and stones round it furnished materials for the rapid construction of breastworks.

Scarcely had this entrenchment been completed, about nine o'clock in the morning, and the baggage followers and animals been brought under cover, and a supply of water obtained in the *massaks*, when the enemy came down from the hills and completely surrounded the detachment. The attack and defence continued from nine o'clock in the morning till about three o'clock in the afternoon, the enemy several times making an assault on the entrenchment, and being repulsed only by bayonet charges. About two o'clock in the afternoon the enemy's circle had closed round the troops to a uniform distance of from 60 to 100 yards. About three o'clock in the afternoon the ammunition began to run low, and the position became most critical, when it was noticed that the enemy were moving from right to left, while for the first time they cleared away from the rear of the position. This movement on the part of the enemy was due to the approach of reinforcements, under the command of Captain D. M. Strong, 10th Bengal Lancers, accompanied by Captain L. H. E. Tucker, Political Officer.

On the situation of the Mhairwara detachment at Kam Dakka becoming known at divisional head-quarters, at ten o'clock on the morning of the 22nd of April, through the receipt of a telegram from the officer commanding at Dakka, Lieut.-General Maude immediately directed the Kam Dakka detachment to be reinforced from Dakka by one company of the 1-5th Fusiliers,[1] and by another from the Mhairwara Battalion, ordering at the same time three companies of the 1-12th Foot,[2] and two guns of 11-9th Royal Artillery (a mountain battery) from Landi Kotal to Dakka, and two companies of the 2nd Gurkhas, from Basawal to the same place. One company, 1-12th Foot, and the two mountain guns were subsequently diverted to Kam Dakka, direct across country from Haft Chah, midway between Landi Kotal and Dakka.

On the arrival of the reinforcements from Dakka at the pass overlooking the Kam Dakka plain, Captain Strong, who was in command of the party, seeing the Kam Dakka detachment in a low, irregular enclosure of broken walls, surrounded by groups of the enemy with red and white standards, advanced immediately with a company of the 1-5th Fusiliers, and one of the Mhairwara Battalion, at the same time ordering up a troop of the 10th Bengal Lancers, which was some distance in rear; while descending from the pass to the position of the Kam Dakka detachment, a small party of the enemy was attacked by the 1-5th Fusiliers, and driven with some loss into the hills. About half-way down a detachment of the Mhairwaras was posted on a ridge, where it greatly assisted in keeping the enemy off the flank of the troops, and in maintaining communications with the rear.

On reaching the position held by the Kam Dakka detachment, it was found that the enemy were under cover about 100 yards off, while a body with standards occupied a hill 500 yards distant, the only shelter for the troops being close under the walls of the enclosure, as the enemy's bullets were dropping inside it. The troops now received orders to cease firing, as the ammunition was running short, and awaited an assault with fixed bayonets, with instructions to fire only if the enemy showed at 150 yards distant. The British officers were told off to different posts to superintend the defence, and to carry out the gradual evacuation of the position. Still it was felt that this withdrawal would be with heavy loss so long as the enemy held their well-covered position

[1] Now 1st Battalion, Northumberland Fusiliers.
[2] Now 1st Battalion, Suffolk Regiment.

within 100 yards of the troops. The approach of Lieutenant C. E. Pollock, who had been sent to bring up the troop of the 10th Bengal Lancers, was therefore a welcome sight, as he rode across the plain to announce that the cavalry were under cover about 200 yards off.

From a point on the river bank, about 120 yards from the position of the enemy, Captain Strong, with Lieutenant Pollock, then led a charge of the cavalry to the cornfields, and dispersed the enemy, those who escaped the cavalry rushing down a steep bank into the river, their standards and turbans floating down the stream. The rest of the enemy fled to the hills on the right, from which a continuous fire poured down upon the cavalry during the charge. The Kam Dakka detachment, before retiring from the enclosure, charged the enemy, and then returned to carry off the dead and wounded, while the cavalry covered the further withdrawal of the infantry.

The mountain guns, with a company of the 1-12th Foot from Landi Kotal, had by this time arrived, and, coming immediately into action, shelled the enclosure, which, on its being evacuated by the Kam Dakka detachment, had been taken possession of by the enemy. The guns opened with common shell and percussion fuzes, and a shell from each gun having burst in the middle of the enclosure, the standards disappeared, and the enemy fled precipitately from this point, shrapnel being fired at them as they ran.

Major J. R. Dyce, 11-9th Royal Artillery, who had now assumed the command, considered it necessary to retire to Dakka. The retirement was consequently ordered, the cavalry leading, followed by the Mhairwara Battalion, baggage, wounded, etc., then the mountain guns, with the detachments 1-5th Fusiliers and 1-12th Foot, under Major H. L. W. Phillips, of the latter regiment, covering the rear. The withdrawal of the force was conducted regularly, but much time was lost by the number of *doolies* blocking up the road, and by the baggage mules, whose loads were constantly falling off.

Major O. Barnes, commanding at Dakka, had intended that the Kam Dakka detachment should be relieved from its critical position, but that the pass leading to that village should be held for the night, and the enemy attacked the following morning with all the available troops at his disposal, and for this purpose he had despatched rations and spare ammunition to the force; but Major Dyce determined not to hold the pass or to await the rations, as he considered it highly improbable that they could reach him after dark, and knew that they could not arrive till very late. The cavalry and battery mules would have necessarily been sent away, as there was no ground for them to stand on; water would not have been procurable, and none of the troops had tasted food since breakfast. The Kam Dakka detachment had been fighting since six o'clock that morning, the detachment 1-5th Fusiliers since midday, and that of the 1-12th Foot had been on the move since half-past eleven o'clock in the forenoon, while the cavalry were without forage or water.

Major Dyce, commanding the troops, followed in rear of the guns, watching if the enemy should attempt to descend from the opposite side to open fire upon them; but when quite up to the top of the pass, as the enemy had made no advance, the guns were ordered down to a position about 300 yards from the points where the path through the pass leads into the plain towards Dakka Kulan.

It was half-past six in the evening when the officer commanding the rear-guard reported all the baggage and *doolies* up to the top of the pass. The officer commanding the troops now instructed the rear-guard commander not to hold his ground longer than absolutely necessary, as, should the enemy get close up before he reached a spur which had to be crossed, the rear-guard would be taken in reverse.

As the position taken up by the guns was much cramped by the *doolies* and baggage animals, it was impossible to bring them into action; they were consequently retired to Dakka Kulan, where they were brought into action with the cavalry on the flank. Incessant firing was now taking place, but it was too dark to distinguish friend from foe. The guns remained in position till the main body of the rear-guard were well closed up, and then fell back to Dakka, where they arrived about eight o'clock in the evening, the rear-guard coming in about half an hour later. The enemy, though pressing the rear-guard closely and keeping up a heavy fire, occasioned very few casualties, as it was quite dark and the fire, though continuous, was misdirected.

On the following morning, the 23rd of April, a force under Lieut.-Colonel C. J. C. Sillery, 1-12th Foot, who had now assumed command at Dakka, marched at half-past six o'clock over the same ground to the pass. The column consisted of the troops noted in the margin. The field guns were halted in advance of Dakka Kulan, and two guns were sent to the extreme left, so as to fire down the river reaches in case of the enemy attempting to cross. The remainder crowned the pass, while the cavalry and the 2nd Gurkhas advanced.

C-3rd Royal Artillery.
11-9th " " 2 guns.
1-12th Foot, 2 companies.
1-5th Fusiliers, 1 company.
10th Bengal Lancers, 3 troops.
2nd Gurkhas, 2 companies.
Mhairwara Battn., 1 company.

Before reaching the pass, a raft was observed to cross the Kabul river, and men were assembling as if to embark in it. A mountain gun fired a shell at it at a range of 1,800 yards, which struck about 100 yards short, and appeared to *ricochet* into the raft. The enemy dispersed, and shortly afterwards the raft disappeared.

The 2nd Gurkhas and 1-5th Fusiliers being posted in the positions the enemy had occupied the previous day, the cavalry then advanced to Kam Dakka, and sent parties two miles ahead down the river.

The column under Lieut.-Colonel F. B. Norman here joined the Dakka detachment. This column, as already stated, had marched from Landi Kotal on the afternoon of the 21st; on that night it had halted about three miles from Kam Shilman, and reached Loi Shilman on the evening of the 22nd. During the day, Lieut.-Colonel Norman received news, by heliograph, of the threatened attack at Kam Dakka, and that the villagers of that place were unfriendly, and he, at the same time, received orders to press on as rapidly as he could, and, if possible, take the enemy in flank. On the morning of the 23rd, the force pushed on through the Shilman valley and reached Kam Dakka, as mentioned above, about 2 P.M.; but found that the fighting, of which reports had been received during the morning, was over, and that the Mohmands had dispersed.

On the arrival of Lieut.-Colonel Norman's force, the Dakka column was withdrawn to the fort. The troops under Lieut.-Colonel Norman remained at Kam Dakka during the 24th, and were quite undisturbed, and on the 25th they returned to Landi Kotal.

The casualties among the troops in the affair of the 22nd were 6 killed and 18 wounded; those of the enemy were very considerable, and were estimated at about 200 killed and wounded. It was computed that about 1,500 men were opposed to our troops.

The only cause for regret beyond the loss of so many gallant men was, the Commander-in-Chief considered, that the original intention of Major Barnes, to hold the pass during the night and to attack the enemy in the morning, had not been adhered to, as, had this been done, the enemy would have no doubt received a severer lesson than they got on the 23rd of April. The Commander-in-Chief also recorded his opinion that, "but for the coolness, determination, and gallantry of the highest order, and the admirable conduct which Captain Creagh displayed on this occasion, the detachment under his command would, in all probability, have been cut off and destroyed." For his gallant conduct this officer subsequently received the Victoria Cross.

Many of the Lalpura men came down armed to Kam Dakka, and, as they did not assist the detachment, it was naturally presumed that they joined the enemy. The Kam Dakka men also, after applying for the assistance of the troops, were many of them recognized in the ranks of the enemy. On this being brought to the notice of the Political Officer (Major Conolly) he stated that the Kam Dakka men had behaved throughout in the usual Pathan manner, doing their best to pull well with both sides. They were in a most difficult position, afraid of punishment from the troops if they were hostile to them, and afraid of the Mohmands if they gave help to the troops, lest they might cross over the Kabul river and burn Kam Dakka, to deter the inhabitants from again helping the troops, and also as an effectual way of annoying the British Government. It was to prevent any mischance of this sort, the effect of which would have been most injurious to the prestige of the Government, that he advised that Kam Dakka should be defended. The Political Officer, therefore, did not see how the inhabitants of Kam Dakka could have behaved otherwise than they did.

Lieut.-General Maude recorded his opinion that if such were the opinions of the Political Officer, and if he considered it probable even that the Kam Dakka inhabitants would act as they did, he should have informed the General Officer Commanding to that effect when he advised him to assist them with troops. Had he done so, the Lieut.-General would either not have sent any of Her Majesty's troops on such an errand, or would have taken care that their supports were nearer than Dakka, seven miles off, or Landi Kotal, about fifteen miles distant.

Operations against the Mohmands in 1880.

Action on the Gara heights in January.

In April 1879, the same month as the Kam Dakka affair above related, Muhammad Sadik Khan, the eldest son of Nauroz Khan, who was with Lieut.-General Sir S. J. Browne, at Gandamak, fled from the British camp and joined the Amir Yakub Khan [whose mother was a sister of Nauroz Khan], and, as soon as our troops left Dakka in June 1879, he was appointed Khan of Lalpura in the place of Muhammad Shah Khan.

When the second advance into Afghanistan took place, Muhammad Sadik Khan of Lalpura hesitated for some days, but at length appeared at Dakka, and for two months all went well at Lalpura, and also at Goshta, where Moghal Khan sat in an attitude of passive hostility.

The journey of the Amir Yakub Khan to India gave the first shock to the Mohmands, and further agitation was produced by the news of the fighting at Kabul. Moghal Khan was the first to go, in December 1879, but his gathering was speedily broken up by a cannonade across the river from Chardeh, the *Khan* of which place again remained loyal to the English, partly from inclination, and party from enmity to Moghal Khan. Mulla Khalil had for some time been rousing the impressionable tribesmen, and working on Muhammad Sadik Khan, who, at length, unable longer to bear the taunts and passionate messages of the *mullas*, retired from Lalpura to Rena, in January 1880, and put himself at the head of the men who had already collected there with Mulla Khalil. The movement, having gained the tribal chief as its leader, soon spread, and the Mohmands flocked down to

Palosi and Rena. Meanwhile, an important diversion was effected by detaching Akbar Khan, a younger son of Nauroz Khan, who was appointed by the British Government as Khan of Lalpura in the place of his brother. Under the circumstances, he was unable to render much active assistance; but one-half of the Nauroz Khan interest, the most powerful in the tribe, was thus secured to us. On the 11th of January the enemy began to cross the river; and on the 14th, about 5,400 men, under Muhammad Sadik Khan and Mulla Khalil, had crossed, and taken up a strong position on the Gara heights, about two miles from Fort Dakka, and between that place and Kam Dakka. This ground had been reconnoitred on the 7th by Colonel T. W. R. Boisragon, commanding at Fort Dakka, and almost every officer in the garrison had made himself familiar with its features, in anticipation of the enemy taking up this position. It was now determined that, while a column from Dakka attacked the enemy's position in front, another column should be sent from Landi Kotal to attack them in flank and rear, so that, surrounded on three sides, and the unfordable Kabul river in rear, escape would be impossible and destruction almost certain.

1-C R. H. A., 4 guns.
6th Dragoon Guards, 94 sabres.
1-25th K. O. B., 110 bayonets.
17th Bengal Cavalry, 50 sabres.
8th N. I., 100 bayonets.
30th P. N. I., 500 bayonets.

On the morning of the 15th, therefore, the Dakka column, as per margin, under the command of Colonel T. W. R. Boisragon, 30th Punjab Native Infantry, was drawn up in position facing the Gara heights by 11 A.M. The action had been purposely delayed to allow the Landi Kotal column time to arrive.

Brigadier-General J. Doran, C.B., had marched six hours previously from Landi Kotal, and, it was hoped, was now in a position to cut off the enemy's retreat. The Mohmands had, as usual, strengthened their position by constructing stone breastworks on all the commanding points, and had even thrown up during the night an entrenchment along the foot of the hills.

The action was begun by two guns of 1-C Royal Horse Artillery. These opened fire at a distance of 1,000 yards on the advanced *sangars*, and the first shot burst just over the crest of the most advanced work. In the meantime, Colonel Boisragon had drawn up the infantry in the plain in a position to threaten the enemy's left flank, which appeared the most vulnerable, and had been selected as the point of attack.

The attack consisted of 300 men in skirmishing line, 200 in support, and 200 in reserve, and in this formation the advance was made at 1-55 P.M. As they reached the foot of the hill, the right, finding itself overlapped by the enemy, involuntarily edged off to the right, thus leaving a gap in the centre, which was filled up from the supports. Captain E. H. Webb, 8th Native Infantry, commanded the whole of the fighting line. Much shaken by the well-directed fire of the guns, which had lasted for about an hour and-a-half, the enemy abandoned their foremost line of works, and also those which immediately commanded them, as the infantry came on. The hillsides were most rugged and precipitous, but the advance was covered by the fire of all the four guns, and the enemy evacuated one position after another, until, at 2-30 P.M., the Gara heights were gained, and the enemy, utterly routed, were flying down the reverse slopes towards Kam Dakka. The reserve having charge of the ammunition, etc., and not being required to take an active part in the attack, moved to the right, and eventually crossed over the Gara pass.

In the meanwhile, two guns, with a cavalry escort, were moved to the extreme right to shell the *kotal* upon the track from Haft Chah to Kam Dakka, in case the enemy should defend it. The remaining two guns were taken to the left, and, after clearing the heights near the river, opened fire upon such of the enemy as could be seen crossing, and upon those on the other side who had already crossed.

The main body of the infantry, after gaining possession of the heights, descended the spurs into the Kam Dakka plain, and formed up on the river bank at four o'clock in the afternoon. The Mohmands hardly attempted to hold the *kotal* on the Haft Chah and Kam Dakka road, and were easily dislodged by the infantry. As soon as the guns of the Landi Kotal column were heard, about 5 P.M., Colonel Boisragon's force pressed on and occupied the village of Kam Dakka, where they were joined by Brig.-General Doran about half-past six o'clock.

In the meantime, the enemy had made good their escape, either towards Rena or across the river.

The advance of the Landi Kotal column, which was composed of the marginally-named troops, had been delayed beyond all expectations by the unforeseen difficulties of the road. The troops assembled a little before half-past four in the morning at the fort in the Loargai valley. An advanced guard of 100 *Jazailchis*, under Lieutenant G. Gaisford, 5th Punjab Infantry, had gone on ahead an hour earlier to seize the Inzari Kandao, about eight miles from camp.

11—9th Royal Artillery, 2 guns.
5th Fusiliers, 200 bayonets.
25th K. O. Borderers, 200 bayonets.
17th Bengal Cavalry, 20 sabres.
"C" Co., M. S. & M., 30 bayonets.
1st M. N. I., 300 bayonets.[1]
4th M. N. I., 200 ,, [2]
31st P. N. I., 300 ,, [3]

Owing to the darkness of the night the progress of the troops was slow, and it was not till 7-40 that the head of the column reached the Inzari Kandao. Here a halt was made, to enable the rear to close up, and the Brig.-General received a report from Lieutenant Gaisford, who had ascended a peak near at hand, that no enemy was in sight.

At 8-45 A.M. the descent from the Inzari Kandao was begun. The track was so narrow and difficult that the troops could only move in single file. The battery mules could hardly be got along, and, although only the reserve ammunition, water mules, and a few *dandies* were with the troops, even these caused most serious delay. The path was, in fact, a mere goat track; some baggage animals fell over the precipices and were lost, and the rear-guard was sixty-seven hours in covering seventeen miles. At the foot of the Torsappar Hill, Brig.-General Doran received information that the enemy were occupying the Shilman Gakhe in force. Another halt was therefore ordered, to allow the mountain guns to come up, and a company of the 5th Fusiliers was detached to crown some commanding heights in advance.

At 10-30 A.M. the troops again moved forward. The road was still most difficult, some of it being over slippery rocks, on which the horses of the cavalry detachment, and even the unshod battery mules, could not keep their footing.

At about 11-30 A.M., during a third short halt, the guns of Colonel Boisragon's force were heard. After that the path was somewhat better, and the troops advanced more rapidly. It was

[1] Now the 61st (P. L. O.) Pioneers. [2] Now the 64th Pioneers.
[3] Now the 31st Punjabis.

nearly one o'clock before the gorge of the Shilman Gakhe came in sight. The pass was held by the enemy, who showed three standards, one of which was planted in a breastwork on a conical hill in front of the pass. A company of the 5th Fusiliers was extended to seize a rocky hill, about half a mile from the crest of the Shilman Gakhe, and a company of the 31st Punjab Native Infantry occupied some heights to the left, a company of the 25th Foot connecting the two. The mountain guns opened on the enemy from the hill held by the company of the 5th Fusiliers, and the first shell caused them to abandon their advanced breastwork. The leading companies then advanced and cleared the pass of the enemy, who retired to a high hill facing and completely commanding the descent towards Kam Dakka. As this hill had to be taken, and it rose a thousand feet above the pass, a further delay was inevitable. Fortunately, the enemy made but a feeble resistance, and the hill was quickly carried by two companies of the 5th Fusiliers, supported by two of the 31st Punjab Native Infantry. Another company of the 31st Punjab Native Infantry was sent down the pass to clear some lower hills in front, in which groups of the enemy were posted. The detachments of the 5th Fusiliers and 31st Punjab Native Infantry rapidly drove the enemy before them in the direction of Kam Dakka, and by half-past two the road was clear.

In the meantime, Brigadier-General Doran had established heliographic communication with Dakka, which could be seen from the crest of the Shilman Gakhe. By this means he learnt that Colonel Boisragon had crossed the Gara heights, and was between them and the Kabul river.

At 2-45 P.M. dense masses of the flying enemy could be seen moving down the right bank of the river and across the mouth of the *nala* running from the Shilman Gakhe to the Kabul.

Having stayed some time trying to ascertain the whereabouts of his baggage, regarding which no information could be obtained, Brig.-General Doran began the descent of the Shilman Gakhe at about 3-20 P.M. The path down to the Kabul river was nearly as bad as that between the Inzari Kandao and Torsappar, and it was not till five o'clock that the mouth of the *nala* was reached. Here, about six or seven hundred of the enemy were discovered on the opposite bank of the river, making their way across the sands from the ferry to the village of Rena. Another party was crossing on two rafts, and some on the right bank were making for the ferry. The mountain guns opened at a thousand yards, and a steady fire was kept up by the few British infantry at hand. Many of the enemy were seen to fall and be carried off, while a few bodies were found on the spot the next day. Brigadier-General Doran's troops reached Kam Dakka at 6-30 P.M., and there joined Colonel Boisragon's force, as already related. Both columns bivouacked without baggage, many without food, and some without even greatcoats.

The baggage of the Landi Kotal column was ordered to remain for the night near the Shilman Gakhe, but none of it got so far that night, or even the next. Very great difficulty was experienced by Lieut.-Colonel G. C. Hodding, commanding 4th Madras Native Infantry, who was in charge of the baggage with two hundred men of his regiment, in getting the animals over the extremely difficult road. The almost impassable nature of the path beyond the Inzari Kandao caused an immense block of animals at that place, and the confusion was increased by a false alarm, causing a panic among the mule-drivers and followers, in which some animals and loads were lost, and many drivers deserted. The baggage and guard bivouacked for the night on the Inzari Kandao, without water. Next day (16th of January) the march was resumed, and a detachment of sappers came out from Landi Kotal to improve the road; nevertheless, in spite of the exertions of Lieut.-Colonel Hodding and his officers, the baggage only advanced that day as far as the first water, four miles from the bivouac. On the 17th, the baggage struggled over the Shilman Gakhe, being met by a hundred men of the 31st Punjab Native Infantry, under Major Gordon Cumming, who came out to render assistance, and the bulk of it reached Kam Dakka about half-past ten that night; some, however, did not get in till the next morning.

On the 16th of January the troops halted at Kam Dakka, and the day was spent in collecting materials for rafts; and the following day, two rafts having been prepared, five hundred men, under Colonel Boisragon, were passed over, with orders to destroy Rena. The crossing commenced at 10-30 A.M., and was completed at 4-30 P.M. Rena was reached at six o'clock, and was found to be completely deserted, as was the neighbouring village of Parchao, and the whole country for three miles down the river. On the 18th, Rena was burnt, and its one tower blown up by a party of sappers, under Lieutenant A. R. F. Dorward, Royal Engineers. Pursuant to Brig.-General Doran's orders, the troops after this recrossed to the right bank, and, two additional rafts having been constructed, the operation was effected in less than three hours. The column then marched back to Dakka, which was reached at 4-30 P.M., without a shot having been fired during the day.

The defeat of the Mohmands on the Gara heights had caused a panic in the tribe, and the country was reported to be deserted for miles round. Brigadier-General Doran's column returned to Landi Kotal on the 18th January by the Gara Kandao and Haft Chah, and the baggage was sent by the Dakka pass.

Owing to the arrival of Brigadier-General Doran's column too late to intercept the enemy, the combined movement on the 15th had proved a failure. The Mohmands, however, suffered a severe defeat at the hands of Colonel Boisragon's greatly inferior force, and their loss was computed at 70 killed and 140 wounded. Out of the 70 killed, 21 bodies were seen by our officers lying in the ravines of the Gara heights; many were carried off, and others drowned, one shell bursting on a raft.

Our loss was slight. In the Dakka column there were only two killed and three wounded, and among the troops from Landi Kotal there were no casualties at all. 1-C Royal Horse Artillery expended, in the action of the 15th of January, 150 rounds, namely, 32 common shell and 118 shrapnel. The two guns, 11-9th Royal Artillery, with Brigadier-General Doran, expended on the same day twenty-one 7-pounder shells. The infantry of the whole force fired 13,286 rounds of small-arms ammunition.

The Mohmand force which was opposed to us consisted of men from nearly all the large clans. The Tarakzai proper do not, however, appear to have been present, although the Isa Khel and Burhan Khel branches were well represented. The Safis, and in particular the Kandahari section, supplied a strong contingent.

Major-General R. O. Bright, C.B., commanding the 2nd Division, Kabul Field Force, remarked, with regard to these operations, that a want of forethought was shown in not ascertaining with more care the nature of the route by which Brigadier-General

Doran's column was intended to advance. The baggage should certainly have been sent from Haft Chah by the Gara Kandao, which would have been cleared on the retirement of the enemy before Colonel Boisragon's troops.

The moral effect of the defeat of the 15th of January was very great, and for some months after this the Mohmands remained quiet. In June 1880, the united bands of Muhammad Sadik Khan and Moghal Khan of Goshta attempted to close the river at Basawal for the passage of our rafts, but were attacked by Akbar Khan and dispersed at night. About the time of Ayub Khan's success at Kandahar, preparations were made for a rising among the Mohmands, which collapsed as soon as the news arrived of his defeat. On the withdrawal of the British troops from Afghanistan, Akbar Khan was confirmed as Khan of Lalpura by the new Amir, and his relations with us continued to be satisfactory for some years.

In 1888 the Burhan Khel raided some sheep in British territory and came into collision with the villagers of Matta. Pir Dost Khan was held responsible for the misbehaviour of this section, and his annual allowance of Rs. 1,000, which had recently been granted in lieu of his *jagir*, was confiscated. This allowance was subsequently restored to the *Khan*, on condition that he distributed a portion among the Burhan Khel clan, and paid over their just shares to his brother Abdul Ghani Khan and another relative, who had claims upon him. The settlement now made put an end to the intrigues which had resulted from Pir Dost Khan's indolence, and his misappropriation of his allowance in former years.

Abdul Ghani was killed by Pir Dost Khan in 1895, and his allowance was continued to his nephew Abdul Rahman. In the following year the partisans of Abdul Ghani murdered Pir Dost Khan, who was succeeded by his son Ghulam Khan.

In 1890 the Mulla Khalil induced some Khwaezai tribesmen, who were joined by a few bad characters belonging to the Halimzai, to fire upon the Kabul river survey party. No damage was done however, and the Tarakzai *jirga*, who were with the surveyors, behaved well, and so did the Halimzai clan as a body.

In 1889 the Amir made an attempt to establish control over the Baezai clan " proposing a treaty of alliance and subordination on their part." He also demanded payment of tithes, and wished to build forts at Bedmanai and Mitai. These proposals, however, were not acceptable either to the Mohmands or to the Khan of Lalpura. The people of Mitai now became divided into two parties, one friendly to the Amir and the other anti-Afghan. The former was led by Malik Ghairat, who received a yearly subsidy of rupees 2,000 from Kabul; but in 1893 Ghairat was expelled from Mitai, in the course of a local quarrel, and was succeeded as leader of the pro-Afghan party by Malik Sultanai.

In February 1896 fighting broke out in the Mitai valley between the two factions of the Musa Khel Baezais. One side was led by Malik Ghairat, who now upheld the claims of Safdar Khan of Nawagai, while the opposing faction was commanded by Malik Sultanai, the protégé of the Afghan *Sipah Salar*, Ghulam Haidar. The first mentioned party had already met with some success, when on the 23rd April the *Sipah Salar* sent 400 *khassadars* (Militia) to seize Mitai village and take Malik Ghairat prisoner. Ghulam Haidar Khan claimed the whole of Mitai as the Amir's territory, and had previously warned the Khan of Nawagai to abstain from any interference within these limits. Accordingly he now peremptorily ordered the latter to withdraw from several villages in the valley to which he had laid claim. This action on the part of the Afghan commander-in-chief provoked a strong remonstrance from the Government, but Ghulam Haidar Khan declined to relinquish this portion of Mohmand territory or to withdraw his troops. Consequently a lengthy correspondence on the subject ensued between the Government of India and the Amir.

Settlement of the Assured clans, 1896.

Meanwhile the Government of India had decided to enter into relations with the Halimzai, Tarakzai, Utmanzai, Dawezai, and the Isa and Burhan Khel of Pandiali, with a view of bringing them under sole British control. The Baezai and Khwaezai, and the Safis, who inhabit scattered villages between the Mohmand country and Bajaur, were not included in this proposed settlement, as the policy to be adopted towards these sections had not yet been decided. In consequence of this decision the representatives of these six clans were summoned in October to assemble at Shabkadar in the following November, and Mr. W. R. H. Merk, I.C.S., then Commissioner and Superintendent of the Peshawar Divison, was entrusted with the task of effecting a settlement with them.

In answer to the summons over 1,000 representatives of the clans came into Shabkadar on the 7th November, and the next few days were employed in the business of the settlement. To begin with, the tribesmen were informed that they had now passed under the sole control of the British Government and they were, at the same time, assured that they would lose nothing by the change, inasmuch as our Government would continue the payments of the Kabul[1] and Lalpura allowances to those clans who had previously enjoyed them, and would grant similar new allowances to those who had not. In return the "assured" clans would be bound to render such services as the Government might demand, and the allowances would be conditional on their loyalty, fidelity, and good behaviour towards us. The assembled *jirgas* accepted the situation entirely, notwithstanding the efforts of certain partisans of the *Sipah Salar* who tried to raise doubts in their minds. After a discussion, lasting over some days, the details of the apportionment of the allowances amongst the clans were finally settled with the assistance of Muhammad Shah Khan and Muhammad Sadik Khan, ex-Khans of Lalpura, who were suitably rewarded by Government for their services on this occasion. Akbar Khan of Lalpura, who had been invited by Government to be present at the settlement, failed to appear, and, from the attitude of the tribesmen towards him, it was very evident that they had no wish whatever to have a *khan*, and no inclination to be dealt with through him. At a durbar held at Shabkadar on the 26th November by the Lieutenant-Governor of the Punjab, the settlement arrived at by Mr. Merk was finally confirmed, and the assembled *jirgas* then returned to their homes.

Before the assembly of the *jirgas* at Shabkadar in November, the *Sipah Salar* had vainly exerted himself to prevent the *maliks* from coming in. Malik Lalunai, the hereditary agent of the Khan of Lalpura, who was completely under the *Sipah Salar's* influence, entered Gandab in November with fourteen *khassadars* to attempt

1 The Kabul allowances were tribal subsidies given by the Afghan Government to the whole tribe or section, to secure their good conduct, loyalty and service; and every member of the clan received his share. The Lalpura allowances were personal grants made by the Chief to individual men of importance in the clan. The Halimzai and Tarakzai had been in receipt of these allowances under the former régime.

to gain over the tribes. Whilst the *jirgas* were assembled at Shabkadar these intrigues continued, and were then directed towards prevailing upon some of the elders to return to their homes and to renounce all relations with the British Government. It was also reported later that the houses of certain *maliks* of Yakhdand and Kamali, who went to Shabkadar were burnt by the Hadda Mulla and certain others.

Meanwhile the correspondence with the Amir, on the question of Afghan interference in Mitai, dragged on throughout the year 1896. The Amir ignored the request that he should withdraw his *khassadars*, and claimed that the Durand agreement had awarded the whole of Mohmand country to Afghanistan. Eventually he agreed to resume the demarcation of the Afghan boundary (which had been completed as far south as the Nawa Peak by Mr. Udny's Commission in 1895), and asked the names of the villages which were considered to be on the British side of the line. He was accordingly informed that the whole of the Halimzai, Tarakzai, Isa Khel, Burhan Khel, Dawezai and Utmanzai clans of the Mohmands, including the Safi villages, and the Mitai and Suran valleys, together with all Musa Khel villages east of the Kunar watershed must be held to be in British territory. But, in the hope of bringing about a speedy settlement, the Government of India offered to cede the Baezai, and Khwaczai villages in the Bohai Dag to Afghanistan. Mr. Udny and the *Sipah Salar* Ghulam Haidar Khan were appointed by their respective Governments to carry out the settlement, and met at Landi Khana on the 11th March 1897. But the difficulties raised by the Afghan representative made it impossible to proceed with the demarcation, and accordingly Mr. Udny's party was withdrawn.

In the following April the Afghan troops evacuated the Mitai valley, and, as Afghan interference with the Mohmand clans on the British side of the Durand line then ceased, the Government of India decided not to press the Amir to proceed with the delimitation. The boundary between independent Mohmand territory and Afghanistan consequently remained undemarcated, and though the question was revived in 1904-05, it has not yet been finally settled.

The Khan of Lalpura.

After 1884 the relations between the Khan of Lalpura and the Amir of Afghanistan became very strained. The former had declined to attack the Khan of Nawagai, with whom the Amir was much incensed on account of his action in expelling Dilaram Khan of Jhar for having paid a visit to Kabul. The Khan of Lalpura had pleaded want of money as his excuse for not obeying the Amir's commands, but the friendship and family ties which bound him to the Nawagai chief were probably the real reasons for his inactivity. As a punishment, the Amir deprived him of the *jagir* of Hissarak, which he presented to the *Khan's* brother Hassan Jan. During the next few years the *Khan's* grants and revenues were gradually reduced by the Amir; and his authority as titular chief of the Mohmands was disregarded by the Governor of Jalalabad and the *Sipah Salar*, who began to deal direct with the Halimzai and other sections.

In 1887 the *Khan* waged war, though with little success, against Moghal Khan of Goshta,[1] who had rebelled against the Amir and had fled to the hills. Later on he assisted the Afghan Commander-in-Chief in operations against the Sangu Khel Shinwaris. These services temporarily restored him to favour with the Amir, and in 1890 he was well received at the Kabul court.

In the following year, however, he again became discredited with the Afghan ruler, owing to his failure to crush Umra Khan of Jandol, against whom he had taken the field in support of the Khan of Nawagai.

A year later his revenues were still further reduced; and in 1894 certain allowances, hitherto paid to the Mohmands through him as their chief, were disbursed through the *Sipah Salar's* Agent, Lalunai. This individual soon became chief of Lalpura in all but name, and Akbar Khan was meanwhile detained in Asmar by Ghulam Haidar Khan.

In 1896 Akbar Khan was invited in his capacity of titular chief of the Mohmands to assist the British officials in the settlement of the "assured clans" which has been mentioned above. The *Khan*, however, failed to appear, and indeed he seems by this time to have lost all influence with the Mohmands, and the

[1] As the result of this rebellion the Khan-ship of Goshta was abolished by the Amir. Moghal Khan, the last chief, died in exile in 1893.

"assured" clans showed no desire to recognise him as their chief, or to have any dealings with him.

During the disturbances in 1897, which will presently be described, Akbar Khan's attitude towards the British was one of supineness, if not of open hostility. A year or two later he was virtually deprived of his position by the Amir and has since then lived with his son under surveillance at Kabul.

While Afghan influences were at work, as previously mentioned, to detach the Mohmands from their allegiance to the British Government, other intrigues were being prosecuted which had far more serious consequences.

The Hadda Mulla.

Early in the year 1897 it was reported that the Hadda Mulla was inciting the Mohmands to acts of hostility. He had even announced that the members of the *jirgas*, who had attended the Durbar at Shabkadar in November 1896, should not receive Muhammadan burial—a threat which, coming as it did from an acknowledged leader of their religion, must have been a terrible one in the eyes of his bigoted followers.

This *mulla*, Najm-ud-Din derived his title from the village of Adda or Hadda, in the Jalalabad district, where he was born about the year 1817. In 1883 he was expelled from Afghanistan by the order of the Amir, and took up his residence in the Jarobi glen, in the most rugged and inaccessible district of the Baezai Mohmand country. He acquired great power over the Mohmand clans, especially the Baezai tribesmen among whom he lived, and was able to exert very considerable influence over the Khan of Nawagai and the people of Bajaur. Although he was unable to bring about a general rising of the Mohmand clans in 1895, he is said to have led a contingent of his followers to oppose the advance of the Chitral Relief Force at the Malakand pass. He was also reputed to be a firm friend of the *Sipah Salar* Ghulam Haidar from whom he obtained assistance in the shape of money and arms. The *mulla's* efforts, however, to prevent the settlement with the "assured clans" signally failed; nor did he meet with any marked success when he endeavoured in the beginning of 1897 to intrigue with the Mian Guls of Swat and to foster an anti-British movement in Bajaur.

At the beginning of the fanatical rising of the Swat tribes in July, under the leadership of the Mad Fakir, there was no evidence of any disturbance among the Mohmand clans. In fact some thirty leading men of the Tarakzai and Halimzai sections visited the Commissioner of Peshawar and offered assistance.

At this date the Hadda Mulla was in Jarobi, and had so far shown no sign of activity, though he was doubtless only awaiting the development of the Mad Fakir's movement.

Raid on Shankargarh and attack of Shabkadar fort by Mohmands and others under the Hadda Mulla in August 1897.

On the 3rd August reports reached Peshawar that the Hadda Mulla had started for the Swat valley with a small following, and had summoned the Shinwaris, Ningraharis, and other clans to join him in a *jehad* against the British. The Mulla's call to arms was sounded in the following proclamation :

> Help from God awaits us and victory is at hand. Let it, after compliments, be understood by, and known to, the followers of the greatest of the prophets, *viz.*, all the people of Ningrahar, the Shinwaris and others, that the people of Swat, Bajaur and Buner have all united together and succeeded in annihilating the troops of the infidels stationed in Swat, and have plundered their property. All the Muslims are hereby informed that the Mohmands as a body have joined me in advancing upon Dheri (Shankargarh) *viâ* Gandab, for the purpose of carrying on a *jehad*. It is hoped that you on the receipt of this letter will rise up if sitting and start if standing. Taking the necessary supplies with you, come without fail as soon as possible. God be willing the time has come when the kafirs shall disappear. Be not idle, what more should I insist upon. Peace be upon you.

On the same day the Hindu inhabitants of Shankargarh, near Shabkadar fort, were greatly alarmed by rumours of an intended raid, and it was reported that the Baezai tribesmen, after meeting the *mulla* at Bedmanai, had declined to accompany him so far afield as Swat, but had volunteered to join in an attack on the above mentioned village. Sir Richard Udny, the Commissioner of Peshawar, regarded these rumours as extravagant and disbelieved that any real danger existed of a raid into British territory. He, however, despatched Subadar-Major

Abdur Rauf Khan, Commandant of the Border Military Police, to Shabkadar, with orders to take all necessary precautions. On the 5th, this officer reported that the *mulla*, with a small following of *talibs* and *murids*, was at Kung in the Bohai Dag, on his way to Gandab, and that he had demanded free passage through Halimzai territory with the avowed intention of making a raid across the British border. On the 7th August information was received that the *mulla*, with some 3,000 well armed tribesmen, chiefly Baezai Mohmands, and men from Lalpura and Ningrahar, had reached Gandab, and that an attack on Shankargarh was imminent.

Sir R. Udny relied upon the Halimzais, as members of an assured clan, and holders of land within our borders, to oppose the *mulla's* advance, and prevent any raiding party from moving through the Gandab valley. Consequently he declined Brigadier-General Elles' offer to reinforce the Shabkadar garrison with regular troops from Peshawar, and contented himself with instructing Subadar-Major Abdur Rauf to warn the villagers of Shabkadar, Matta-Moghal-Khel, and Kattozai, and the clansmen of Pandiali and the Gandab valley that they would be held responsible for repelling any raids within their limits. The Halimzais of Gandab were no doubt genuinely anxious to prevent the *mulla* and his following from passing through their country, and their leaders gave all possible information of his movements to the Police Commandant at Shabkadar. They, however, lacked the power to resist the great religious leader, supported as he was by a fanatical gathering from all the neighbouring clans; they were eventually compelled to yield, and some of their fighting men even joined the *mulla's* forces.

On the afternoon of the 7th August, the *mulla's* followers, numbering between 4,000 and 5,000 men, descended from the Sar Dheri hills on the north west and advanced across the plain towards Shankargarh. Then, dividing into two portions, half the force attacked Shabkadar fort, while the remainder swarmed into the village of Shankargarh, which they looted and burned.

Almost all the inhabitants had previously removed their families and property, and had either left the neighbourhood or had taken refuge in the fort. The attack on Shabkadar fort was easily repulsed by the garrison[1] under the command of Subadar-Major Abdur Rauf, who claimed to have inflicted a loss of forty killed and wounded on his assailants. One Hindu of Shankargarh who had remained in the village was killed and another wounded, but there were no other casualties on our side.

At about 5 A.M., on the 8th, the enemy drew off, and about a third of the *lashkar* recrossed the frontier, while the remainder retired out of range of the fort.

Action of Shabkadar, 9th August 1897.

At about 8 P.M., on the 7th, a message reached Peshawar from Subadar-Major Abdur Rauf stating that the *mulla's* force had crossed the border and was approaching Shabkadar. Sir Richard Udny at once requested Brigadier-General Elles to move out his troops in support of the Border Military Police, and shortly after midnight a column, strength as in margin, was despatched under command of Lieut.-Colonel Woon, 20th Punjab Infantry. All the transport at Peshawar had been taken for the troops operating in Swat, but 100 mules belonging to the Sapper Company were available and a number of two-wheeled carts (*tum-tums*) were obtained locally.

2 squadrons, 13th B. L.
4 guns, 51st Field Battery.
2 companies, Somerset. L. I.
20th Punjab Infantry.

On the arrival of the troops at Hajizai ferry at 2 P.M., a second message[2] was received from Shabkadar stating that the enemy had sacked and burned Shankargarh and were besieging the fort. Owing to the strength of the current and the paucity of boats, great difficulty was experienced in crossing the river, which was then in flood. At 6 A.M., one squadron was sent forward to reconnoitre, and Lieut.-Colonel Woon following with the advanced portion of his column, consisting of four and a half companies and two guns, reached Shabkadar at 10 A.M. After resting his troops for a couple of hours, Lieut.-Colonel Woon moved on to make a demonstration against the enemy, who were posted on the high ground to the west, commanding the entrance to the Gandab valley. The cavalry pushed forward to the foot of the hills, and tried to cut off some of the tribesmen who had descended on to open ground

1 The garrison of Shabkadar Fort on 7th August consisted of one native officer and forty-six men of the Border Military Police and thirteen men of the Peshawar District Police, all armed with Snider rifles.

2 This message had been sent off at midnight by the hand of a friendly Halimzai.

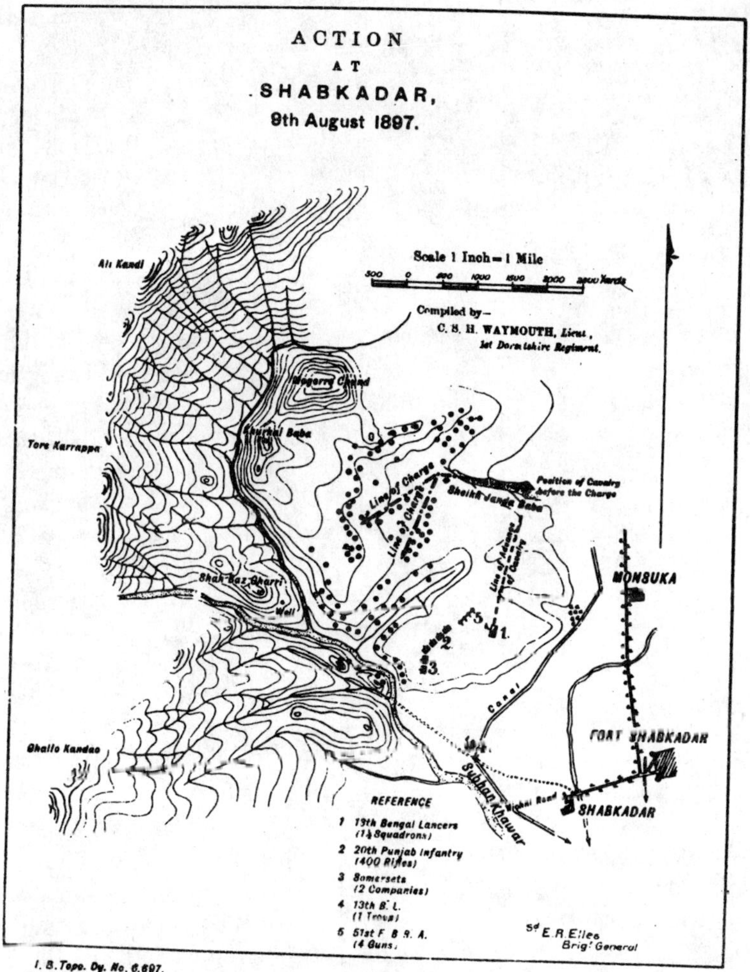

I. B. Topo. Dy. No. 6,897.
Exd. C. J. A., February 1907.

No. 4,057-I., 1907.

but finding the enemy in great strength they were obliged to retire. Meanwhile, as the troops were exhausted by their arduous march in the excessive heat, Lieut.-Colonel Woon decided to withdraw to the fort and await the arrival of the remainder of his force. The rest of the column, having been delayed at Hajizai ferry, did not reach Shabkadar till the evening. The casualties during the day were five men of the 13th Bengal Lancers wounded.

Early on the morning of the 9th August Lieut.-Colonel Woon again advanced, and found the enemy occupying a position on the undulating plateau at the foot of the hills. His intention was to make a frontal attack with the infantry, and to turn the enemy's left with the cavalry and artillery. The infantry began the action shortly before eight o'clock, but the field battery was delayed by bad ground and did not open fire till nearly an hour later. The enemy now made a determined attempt to turn our left flank, and Colonel Woon was compelled to order a retirement to avoid being cut off from the fort; at the same time he began to reinforce his left with a company of the 20th. At this moment Brigadier-General Elles arrived from Peshawar and assumed command. He found that the enemy's line extended for about two miles, and that the troops were outflanked and subjected to a cross fire; the guns had come into action close to the infantry, while the cavalry were posted a little distance in rear of the battery.

General Elles at once extended his infantry further to the left, and ordered the battery, which had begun to withdraw, to come into action again to support them. The cavalry were sent about a mile and a half to their right, and then moved up a dry *nala*-bed, which brought them on to the left of the hostile position near the village of Sheikh Janda Baba. As soon as the leading squadron had formed up, Major Atkinson, who was in command, gave the order to charge, and the troopers swept down upon the enemy's left rear; then moving in somewhat extended order, owing to the rough and broken ground, they rode along the whole front, which they completely cleared. As the cavalry approached under cover of the artillery fire which swept the ground in their front, the tribesmen, who were scattered about in small groups, promptly took to flight, and the greater number escaped along a large *nala* in rear of the position; others took cover behind the rocks which strewed the plateau, and fired at the horsemen as they passed. At the conclusion of this charge, the squadrons reformed on the left of the infantry, and a portion of the force afterwards advanced some distance to the front. The enemy had, however, now retreated to the hills, and General Elles, deeming it inadvisable to follow them up with the small force at his disposal, withdrew to Shabkadar.

The enemy numbered from 5,000 to 6,000 men, a considerable proportion of whom were armed with breech-loading rifles. Their losses amounted to more than 200 killed, including 30 or 40 head-men, besides a large number wounded; Malik Sultanai one of the leaders of the Musa Khel of Mitai received a mortal wound. The casualties on the British side amounted to four officers wounded, nine non-commissioned officers and men killed, and sixty-one wounded.

Great difficulty was experienced in obtaining reliable information as to the composition of the *mulla's* force. Subadar-Major Abdur Rauf who submitted a statement [1] showing the various clans who took part in the raid, estimated the total number present at 9,000 men, which is largely in excess of that given by General Elles. To quote, however, from the report of the Commissioner of Peshawar:—

It may be said that every tribe in the tract of country bounded on the east by the Panjkora and Swat rivers and the British frontier, on the south by the Kabul river, on the west by the Silala and Kunar watersheds, and on the north by Koh-i-Mohr range, was more or less implicated, including, besides Mohmands of all clans (except perhaps the Tarakzai), the Utman Khels of Ambahar and neighbouring valleys, and the Kandahari Safis who are under the jurisdiction of the Khan of Nawagai. The Mullagori Mians of Sapari on the left bank of the Swat river, just beyond the Abazai frontier, also joined, and lost several men killed and wounded; but what probably added most to the determination and impetuosity of the gathering was the arrival of large reinforcements from tribes who are subjects of the Amir, *viz.*, Shinwaris and Khugianis of the Ningrahar valley, Mohmands from the villages of Lalpura, Girdi Sarkani, Hazarnao, Basawal, Ambarkhana, and Chardeh, along the banks of the Kabul river, Utkhel Ghilzais, from the distant Lughman valley on the north side of the Kabul river beyond Jalalabad, and Safis from the still more distant valleys of Badel and Pech, which drain into the right bank of the Kunar river.

Of the Mohmands the Baezai clans, including the Musa Khel of Mitai, etc., seem to have furnished by far the most numerous contingent, and the Khwaezai were also largely represented, while of our own 'assured clans' the

[1] See Appendix.

Utmanzais, Dawezais, Isa Khel and Burhan Khel of Pandiali, and Halimzais of Kamali were all more or less conc-rned.

The question of the participation of Afghan subjects in the raid became the subject of correspondence between the Government of India and the Amir, who denied that his soldiers had ever joined the *mulla*, or that any of his people had done so with his cognizance. It was, however, reported that the Amir subsequently sent a *firman* to the Governor of Jalalabad, expressing his displeasure at men from that district having gone to join the Hadda Mulla, and directing that no more should be allowed to go.

On the 10th August the cavalry reconnoitred some three miles up the Gandab valley, but saw no sign of the enemy, who had retired further into the hills. The gathering, however, though discouraged by their defeat, did not disperse for several days, and the *mulla*, who had gone to Ghalanai, at once started to lay in stores of grain and ammunition with the intention of making another raid over the border at an early date. Meanwhile prompt measures were taken to reinforce the troops at Shabkadar; and by the 12th August the strength of the British force at that place was raised to 2,500 men. In order to improve the existing communications a bridge-of-boats was thrown over the branch of the Kabul river at Hajizai, and a field telegraph line connecting Shabkadar with Peshawar was completed by the 16th August.

In view, however, of the disturbed state of the frontier, and the possibility of the excitement spreading to the Afridis and other tribes, the Government decided that it would be a wiser policy to concentrate a strong force at Peshawar for immediate action wherever required than to undertake the immediate punishment of the Mohmands.

The question of an expedition against this tribe was therefore deferred, pending a full enquiry regarding the composition of the Hadda Mulla's gathering and the responsibility of the different sections, and until it should be more convenient to Government to send troops across the frontier.

Accordingly two moveable columns were formed, one at Peshawar and one at Shabkadar, and were held in readiness to move at an hour's notice. The fort at Michni was also garrisoned by 150 regular troops.

Meanwhile the Hadda Mulla's gathering had gradually dispersed, partly owing to their disappointment at the failure of the Mad Fakir's enterprise in Swat, and partly because of the difficulty of obtaining supplies in Gandab. Najam-ud-Din himself, after a fruitless attempt to obtain assistance from the Khan of Nawagai, retired to Jarobi.

As soon as the *mulla's* direct influence was removed, the Halimzai, Isa Khel, and Burhan Khel Mohmands attempted to justify their conduct in assisting him. The headmen of the first named section pleaded that they had been powerless to oppose his advance through their country and, admitting that they were now unable to resist the British Government, begged for mercy. Ghulam Khan of Pandiali, chief of the Isa and Burhan Khel, wrote to the Political Officer at Shabkadar saying that he was friendly to the Government, and warning him that the *mulla* was collecting a force in preparation for a second raid across the border. The Tarakzai *maliks*, who remained loyal to the British Government, also sent information regarding the movements of the other Mohmand clans, and stated that the Halimzai had urged the *mulla* to attack Michni in order to compromise their people.

Towards the end of August the Hadda Mulla was again on the move, but he failed in his attempt to collect the clansmen for another raid across our border in the direction of Shabkadar. About this time it was reported that he was in communication with the Afridis (who had attacked and destroyed the Khaibar posts on the 23rd and 24th August—*vide* Volume II) with a view to co-operating with them in simultaneous attacks on the British frontier. He had also written to the Mad Fakir in Swat urging the latter to attack the Khan of Dir, and shortly afterwards it transpired that he had again collected a force and was preparing for an invasion of Dir, as will be related in Chapter XIII.

The Mohmand Expedition, 1897.

This new move on the part of the Hadda Mulla materially altered the situation; and the Government, who had at first intended to

postpone the punishment of the Mohmands until the Afridis had been dealt with, now sanctioned the immediate despatch of an expedition against the former tribe.

The objects to be attained were the punishment of the Mohmands for their attacks on the British border, and the defeat and dispersal of the *mulla's* forces, so as to prevent any violation of Dir territory which might imperil the safety of the Chitral road.

The plan of operations was as follows; the Malakand Field Force under Sir Bindon Blood was to advance from the Swat valley through Bajaur, and co-operate with a force under Brig.-General Elles, which was to enter Mohmand country from Shabkadar.

The composition of the latter force is given in Appendix C.

Brigadier-General Elles was given the local rank of Major-General while in command of the Mohmand Field Force, and was given chief political control until such time as his troops should unite with the Malakand Force and come under the direct command of Major-General Sir B. Blood: Mr. Merk, I.C.S., accompanied the Force as Political Officer.

Major-General Elles assumed command on the 9th September. At this time the Hadda Mulla was said to be in Jarobi, and the Halimzai and Pandiali Mohmands, who were alarmed at our preparations, appealed to him to lead the Baezai and Khwaezai clans to their assistance. Small contingents from the various clans were reported to be holding the Kharappa pass and the Palewangai kotal, a little to the south of the Burjina pass, with the intention of opposing our advance by the Gandab and Alikandi routes. The friendly Tarakzai *jirga*, however, who came into Shabkadar, promised to prevent the hostile clansmen from entering their territory, and agreed to guard the Shanilo and Gatta-Gudar ferries over the Kabul river, and the Zankhai pass, thus securing the left flank of General Elles' force against raiding parties from the Khaibar side.

On the 15th September the Divisional Head-quarters with the 1st Brigade and No. 3 Mountain Battery marched to Ghalanai, eighteen miles from Shabkadar, and the 2nd Brigade moved to Dand. Though no opposition was met with, the long march and intense heat were a severe test of the endurance of the troops. The Kharappa pass proved exceedingly difficult, and the greater part of the transport was unable to cross until the following day. The track beyond Dand was quite impracticable for camel convoys, which were required to bring up supplies for Sir Bindon Blood's force at Nawagai as well as for General Elles' brigades; and consequently a halt was made at Ghalanai to allow time for improving the road. On the 16th General Elles, with a cavalry escort, reconnoitred the Gandab valley as far as Katsai; all the villages were found to be deserted and nothing was seen of the enemy. On the following day Brigadier-General Westmacott, with the marginally noted troops, marched to Katsai, two and a half miles south of the Nahaki pass. The pass was reconnoitred and found to be difficult and unfit for camel transport. An attempt to open up signalling communication with Nawagai was unsuccessful, but a letter was received from Sir Bindon Blood, stating that the Hadda Mulla was holding the Bedmanai pass with a force of about 1,000 men. The advance of the Malakand Field Force to attack this position was, however, to be postponed till the 18th, owing to the employment of Brigadier-General Jeffreys' brigade in the Mamund valley. By the 18th the camel road to Ghalanai was completed, and the field telegraph line was extended to that place from Shabkadar. The *jirga* of the Halimzai section in Gandab now came in and agreed to comply with the following terms, *viz.*, surrender of 300 *jizails*, 300 swords, and all rifles in their possession, payment of a fine of Rs. 5,000, and delivery of 2,400 maunds of grain. Supplies and forage were also taken without payment while the troops remained in the valley.

2 squadrons, 13th B. L.
No. 3 Mountain Battery.
2 Maxim guns Devon Regt.
20th Punjab Infantry.

The question of dealing with the principal supporters of the Hadda Mulla was reserved for future action,[1] and the *jirga* were informed that the slightest symptom of bad conduct would, notwithstanding full compliance with the terms, expose them to treatment as enemies. They were also required, as a guarantee of good faith, to bring back their families, which had been removed to the

[1] They were subsequently fined an additional 1,600 rupees, but their property was spared in consideration of good behaviour.

small Halimzai valleys draining into the Kabul river. In reply to their enquiry regarding their *jagir* in Panjpao and their allowances, they were simply informed that the orders of Government would be communicated to them hereafter.

The *jirgas* of the remainder of the "assured clans," who had also written for orders, were summoned to attend in Kamali on the 21st.

Meanwhile reconnaissances had been made in various directions, and the Khapakh pass and the route into Kamali over the Nahaki pass had been carefully examined. On the 19th the 1st Gurkhas, 28th Bombay Infantry, and half No. 5 Company, Bengal Sappers and Miners, joined Brigadier-General Westmacott's column, and marched with it to Nahaki village, at the northern end of the pass. Brigadier-General Macgregor also moved from Dand to Ghalanai with two battalions of the 2nd Brigade, escorting a large convoy of supplies.

During the day a message was received from Sir Bindon Blood stating that the Bedmanai pass was now held by a strong hostile force, and requesting General Elles to join him forthwith, as he did not consider it advisable to withdraw his troops to assist the brigade in the Mamund valley until the enemy in his front had been dispersed. Accordingly on the following day the Head-quarters, with two squadrons, 13th Bengal Lancers, and the Somersetshire Light Infantry, joined the 1st Brigade at Nahaki, while Brigadier-General Macgregor with a wing of the Oxfordshire Light Infantry and the Patiala Regiment marched to Wuchajawar, where an advanced depôt was formed. The remainder of the 2nd Brigade also moved up from Dand to Ghalanai. The cavalry reconnoitring in the Bohai Dag were fired on near the village of Kung, but no casualties occurred; another party examined the Danish Kol towards Mulla Kilai. On this date the Kamali-Halimzai *jirga* arrived at Nahaki, but General Elles was obliged to postone the settlement with this section and with the representatives of the other "assured clans" until a more convenient time.

On the 21st September Major-General Elles, with the 1st Brigade and the cavalry and artillery, marched to Lakarai, and one squadron reconnoitred as far as Khazina, meeting with no opposition. Nahaki was now occupied by three battalions of the 2nd Brigade and two guns of No. 5 Bombay Mountain Battery, while the 37th Dogras and the Nabha Regiment held the other posts on the line of communications.

At Lakarai village Major-General Elles was met by Sir Bindon Blood and received news of the two attacks by the Hadda Mulla's followers on the British camp at Nawagai, on the 19th and 20th September.[1] It was reported that the hostile force at Bedmanai now numbered over 4,000 men and had been augmented by a contingent of Ningraharis and Safis from Kunar under the Sufi Mulla. In order to enable Major-General Elles to deal with this gathering, and to clear the Mitai and Suran valleys, Sir Bindon Blood placed his 3rd Brigade and a mountain battery at the former's disposal, as he himself was obliged to join Brigadier-General Jeffreys in the Mamund valley.

On the 22nd General Elles moved his force on to Khazina, a small hamlet close to Kuz Chinarai, where he was joined by the 3rd Brigade of the Malakand Field Force from Nawagai.

Action of the Bedmanai pass, 23rd September 1897.

The Bedmanai pass lies about five miles west-south-west of Kuz Chinarai. The track leading from this village to the pass runs along the bed of a broad dry *nala*. About a mile and a half from Kuz Chinarai a narrow gap, between Gharibai hill and the northern end of a spur which juts out from the Yari Sar mountain, gives entrance to a broad valley. Crossing this, past the villages of Khalil Kor, Batan-Shah, Bar-Chinarai, and Sarakhwa, the path winds upwards along the *nala*, through a narrow gorge between the steep rocky spurs which branch out like the sticks of a fan from the Ilazai peak on the west, and the gentler slopes descending from the Yari Sar ridge on the east. The summit of the pass, 3,850 feet, is about 1,000 feet higher than Kuz Chinarai, and is commanded by the topmost peak of Yari Sar, which towers nearly 3,000 feet above it.

The plan of attack was as follows: the 1st Brigade with one battery was to make a turning movement along the Yari Sar ridge, while the 3rd Brigade, supported by the remainder of the artillery, advanced up the pass road.

[1] See Chapter XIII.

SKETCH PLAN OF ACTION AT BEDMANAI PASS

Scale 1 inch - 1 mile.

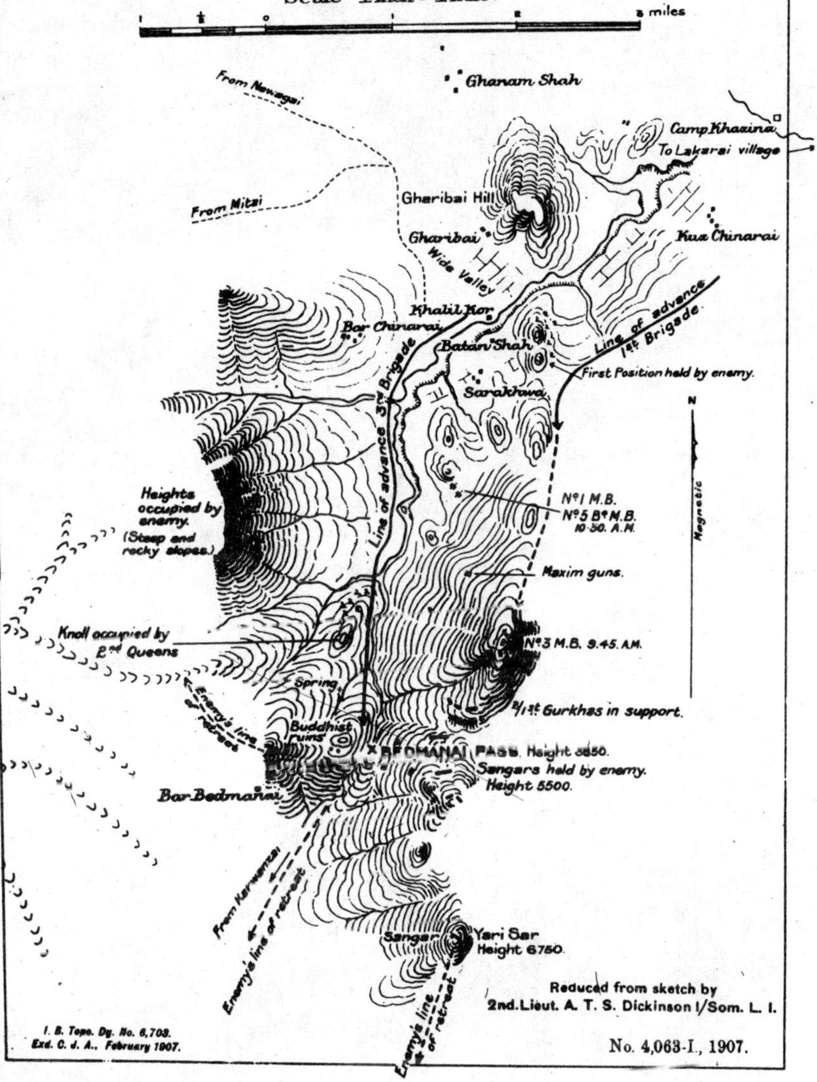

Reduced from sketch by 2nd. Lieut. A. T. S. Dickinson 1/Som. L. I.

I. B. Topo. Dy. No. 6,703.
Exd. C. J. A., February 1907.

No. 4,063-I., 1907.

At 7-15 A.M. the combined force under the command of Major-General Elles moved off from the camp between Khazina and Kuz Chinarai. The baggage and four squadrons of the cavalry remained in camp under command of Lieut.-Colonel G. W. Deane.

1st Brigade, Mohmand Field Force.

Commanding—Brigadier-General R. Westmacott, C.B., D.S.O.
1st Battalion, Somersetshire Light Infantry.
2nd " 1st Gurkha Rifles.
20th Punjab Infantry.
28th Bombay Pioneers.[1]
½ No. 5 Company, Bengal Sappers and Miners.

3rd Brigade, Malakand Field Force.

Commanding—Lieut.-Colonel B. C. Graves.
1st Battalion, The Queen's Regiment.
22nd Punjab Infantry.
39th Garhwal Rifles.
No. 3 Company, Bombay Sappers and Miners.

Royal Artillery.

Commanding—Lieut.-Colonel A. E. Duthy, R.A.

Batteries.

No. 1 Mountain Battery, Royal Artillery.
No. 3 " " " "
No. 5 (Bombay) Mountain Battery (4 guns).

The 39th Garhwal Rifles seized the Gharibai hill, which commanded the entrance to the defile from the Mitai valley and Nawagai. During their advance they met with slight opposition from a party of about 200 of the enemy who were posted in the village of Ghanam Shah. Four squadrons under Major Delamain, 11th Bengal Lancers, were sent on to watch the Mitai and Suran valleys. In the latter the enemy were seen in considerable numbers and kept up a continuous fire at long range. Accordingly Major Balfour, with one and a half squadrons, 13th Bengal Lancers, from the camp, was sent up this valley, but, coming under fire of the enemy in the hills, he was obliged to fall back after several horses had been hit. The cavalry then held the villages at the mouth of the valley and prevented the inhabitants from joining the tribesmen on the Bedmanai pass. Shortly after 8 A.M., the 20th Punjab Infantry with the maxims, supported by the 1st Gurkhas, 28th Bombay Pioneers, and No. 3 Mountain Battery, advanced up the wooded spur south of Khalil Kor, driving back the enemy's picquets, who were concealed among trees and rocks.

Meanwhile the Queen's and 22nd Punjab Infantry, with the other two mountain batteries, advanced through the gap at the foot of the southern slope of Gharibai hill. On the left of the British advance the enemy were driven back from ridge to ridge, and at 10-30 A.M., the 20th Punjab Infantry, well supported by the fire of No. 3 Mountain Battery, reached a *sangar*-crowned

[1] Now 128th Pioneers.

height (marked 5,500 on plan) which commanded the *kotal.* The enemy then retired in different directions, the majority moving further up the main ridge to the Yari Sar peak where they had built a large *sangar.* In the meantime the two batteries with the 3rd Brigade had come into action on a ridge 1½ miles south-east of Bar Chinarai, and shelled a party of the enemy posted in some Buddhist ruins on the *kotal.* After a short time these tribesmen retreated up the heights on the west of the pass, and the Queen's moving forward seized a wooded knoll in the centre of the gorge which commanded the summit of the pass. The ascent to the enemy's last position on the Yari Sar lay over a bare grassy slope, and was extremely steep. The supporting battalions were now ordered to close up, and the 20th Punjab Infantry again pushed on, covered by the fire of the Gurkhas and No. 3 Mountain Battery, which had advanced to the 5,500 spur. By 11 A.M. the Yari Sar was gained, and the maxims, which kept up with the firing line of the 20th throughout, were now turned on the retreating enemy. Save for a few parting shots from snipers on the western heights, all resistance now ceased, and the two advanced battalions of the 3rd Brigade occupied the pass, while the Sappers and Miners set to work to improve the road.

The casualties on the British side only amounted to one man killed and three wounded.

Had a determined defence been made by a strong body of the enemy, occpying the western cliffs in force as well as the heights to the east, the losses of the attacking force must necessarily have been great. The enemy, however, were never in very great strength, and subsequent information showed that there were not more than 700 or 800 men present, principally Baezais, with a contingent of some 120 men from Lalpura. Three or four dead bodies were found, but their losses, which must have been heavy, could not be correctly estimated, as most of the dead and wounded were carried off. That the resistance was so slight, was no doubt due to the heavy losses incurred by the enemy in their attack on the 3rd brigade camp at Nawagai on the 20th September, which caused a large part of the *mulla's* gathering to disperse; and also to the fact that the enemy were uncertain up to the last moment whether we meant to attack the Bedmanai pass or Mitai on the 23rd.

Moreover, as mentioned above, the contingent from the Mitai and Suran valleys were cut off by the cavalry, and were unable to assist in the defence of the pass.

At the conclusion of the action, the 1st Brigade, with No. 3 and No. 5 Mountain Batteries, moved down into the Bedmanai valley and occupied the villages of Kharwanzai and Bobak Kor, while the 3rd Brigade with the remaining battery and the cavalry, returned to Kuz Chinarai.

Operations in the Mitai and Suran valleys.

On the 24th September the 3rd Brigade entered the Mitai valley and destroyed all the Musa Khel villages and towers, with the exception of Dukhanuna. No serious opposition was offered by the enemy, but a few of their riflemen kept up a long range fire from the surrounding hills. The only casualties were two men of the Queen's wounded. On the completion of the operations the brigade returned to camp at Kuz Chinarai. On the following day a portion of this Brigade, under the command of Lieut.-Colonel Collins, moved up the Suran valley as far as the Shinwari village of Bahadur Kila. Some of the tribesmen fired occasional shots from the neighbouring hills, but otherwise made no attempt to interfere with the troops. The destruction of the whole of the Suran villages was completed shortly after midday and the column marched back to Kuz Chinarai.

The 3rd Brigade[1] now received orders to join the Tirah Expeditionary Force and accordingly on the 26th September the troops began their return march, and proceeding *viâ* Nahaki and the Gandah valley reached Peshawar on the 2nd October.

While the troops under Lieut.-Colonel Graves were engaged in the Mitai valley, the Divisional Head-quarters with the 1st Brigade moved down the Bedmanai valley to Sarfaraz Kila. No opposition was met with, but a few of the enemy were driven off from some water reservoirs which they had been trying to cut in order to render them useless for the troops. During the night several shots were fired into the camp and one sepoy was wounded.

[1] No. 1 Mountain Battery, Royal Artillery, and No. 3 Company, Bombay Sappers and Miners, accompanied this Brigade.

Engagement in the Jarobi glen, 25th September.

On the following morning the 1st Brigade continued its advance towards Jarobi, a wild mountain glen situated at the head of the Shindarra valley. A cavalry patrol, (half troop, 13th Bengal Lancers and half troop Patiala and Jodhpur Lancers) reconnoitred as far as Sarakhwa at the entrance to the Shindarra ravine. Finding the ground here impracticable for cavalry they were obliged to wait for the advanced guard, which consisted of the Somersetshire Light Infantry with two maxim guns and No. 3 Mountain Battery. Some small parties of the enemy on the hills on either side of the defile were quickly dispersed by a few rounds from the guns and long range volleys from the infantry. The Somersets, 28th Bombay Pioneers, and No. 5 Bombay Mountain Battery now took up a position at the mouth of the Shindarra gorge, while four companies of the 1st Gurkhas crowned the heights on the west. When these troops were in position, three companies of the 20th Punjab Infantry, with the Bengal Sappers and Miners and No. 3 Mountain Battery, advanced up the Shindarra ravine to the Fazal Kila tower, then, turning sharp to the right, they pushed on up the Jarobi glen to Tor Kila. Here the battery came into action and were joined shortly afterwards by the Gurkhas, while the 20th and the Sappers moved on to the Hadda Mulla's mosque, about half a mile further up the gorge, which here varies in width from 100 to 400 yards. As the troops neared the head of the glen a party of about 150 tribesmen armed with rifles opened fire from behind rocks and *sangars* on either side, and about a dozen *ghazis,* issuing from the mosque, charged down on the leading company. Six of the swordsmen were promptly shot down and the remainder fled.

By this time Tor Kila and other fortified villages in the gorge had been destroyed and as nothing was to be gained by remaining in Jarobi, where there was no ground suitable for a camp, General Elles gave the order to retire. The troops began to withdraw at 3-30 P.M., and were followed up by the enemy on either side of the ravine until they were checked by the fire of the Gurkhas on the heights above Fazal Kila. The force reached Tor Khel at 6 P.M. and bivoucked there for the night.

The casualties during the day were one man killed, and one Native officer and seventeen men wounded. The enemy were composed of Musa Khel from Mitai, Isa Khel of Jarobi, and other followers of the *mulla*. Their exact losses could not be ascertained, but they were known to have lost ten men killed. Three towers and five so-called forts in the Jarobi glen were also destroyed.

On the 26th the force moved from Tor Khel in two columns.

Punishment of the Baezai and Khwaezai clans.

The first column under Brigadier-General Westmacott, with the baggage and hospitals, marched down the broad valley which opens out eastward of Tor Khel, past Mamozai, to Khwarina, which was reached without opposition. All towers and forts met with on the way were demolished.

The second column under Lieut.-Colonel Sage, 1st Gurkha Rifles, after destroying the towers and fortifications of the large village of Manzari-China, moved down the Bohai Dag to Lashkar Kila. Here a group of four fortified villages, with strong towers, were destroyed. A portion of the defences of Koda Khel were next demolished, and a few of the enemy opened an ineffective fire on the rear guard as the column marched off to join the remainder of the Brigade at Khwarina.

On the 27th September Brigadier-General Westmacott with the marginally noted troops proceeded to complete the punishment of the Koda Khel Baezai.

No. 5 Bombay Mountain Battery.
2-1st Gurkha Rifles.
½ battalion, 28th Bombay Pioneers.
½ No. 5 Company, Bengal Sappers and Miners.
Oxfordshire Light Infantry.[1]
1 Squadron 1st Bengal Lancers.[1]

The villages belonging to this section lie on the right bank of the Bohai Dag watercourse, two miles south-west of Khwarina; and to the west and south of the group, within easy rifle range, are precipitous heights known as Kafaro Kotai and Rokai Manzai respectively. The villages, nine in number, were all fortified and possessed towers; they proved to be of a better and more substantial construction than most of those hitherto met with in the Mohmand country.

About a mile from the first village the Gurkhas formed for attack and moved forward, supported by the fire of the artillery. The Bombay Pioneers cleared the enemy out of a *sangar* on high ground to the north of the village, and occupied some low hills on the west. The Oxfords now arrived from Kung and opened long range fire on the enemy in the villages, while the cavalry moved

1 Joined the column from Kung.

off to watch the left flank. Driven from their villages by the hot fire, the enemy soon withdrew to the hills above, and, taking cover behind rocks and *sangars*, kept up a brisk fusillade on the troops, while the Sappers and Pioneers were engaged in demolishing the towers and forts. Accordingly the guns advanced to a second position in support of the Gurkhas, who then cleared the enemy from the Kafaro heights. Some *sangars* on the Bokai Manzai hill were next shelled, and after a few volleys from the infantry most of the enemy's riflemen dispersed. When nearly all the forts and towers had been destroyed, the troops were withdrawn under cover of the fire of the artillery and the Oxfords, which prevented the tribesmen from following up.

The casualties in this affair were five men wounded. A signaller of the Somersets who was reported missing rejoined his regiment unharmed on the 29th, having spent two nights in the hills.

As the column was proceeding to deal with the Khwaezai villages of Kutai, the *jirga* arrived and offered to submit. The troops accordingly marched on to join the remainder of the Brigade at Kung.

Meanwhile another column had proceeded to Torakhwa and Azimkilla (belonging to the Musa Khel Baezai), and after destroying the defences, had continued its march unopposed to Kung.

The Head-quarters and 1st Brigade halted at Kung on the 28th. The Oxfordshire Light Infantry now replaced the Somersetshires in the 1st Brigade and the latter battalion marched to Nahaki with a portion of the hospital and a convoy of sick.

The destruction of the Koda Khel forts and towers on the previous day had its due effect on the Khwaezai, whose *jirga* came in early in the afternoon of the 28th ; and by the evening all their villages, except Kung, had paid up their fine of arms and money, or had given hostages for payment. The Kung people, with characteristic Pathan wrongheadedness, stood out, owing to a domestic quarrel as to the appointment of their share. They were given until next morning to comply on penalty of having their forts and towers blown up. The remainder of the clan eventually paid up 220 guns and Rs. 1,600 in cash.

During the day the *jirgas* of the Halimzai of Kamali, Isa Khel, Burhan Khel, Utmanzai, and Dawezai, also came in, and terms were announced. They were required to supply free forage, grain and wood so long as the force should remain within their respective limits; to surrender all breech-loading and muzzle-loading rifles; to deliver up a specified number of *jezails* and swords; and to pay a fine varying from 1,000 to 2,000 rupees. These terms were to be complied with in full by the morning of the 4th October.

There was a good deal of sniping into camp during the night, although the heights were well picqueted: this was attributed to the inhabitants of Kung, who had refused our terms. Our casualties were two men wounded, and one or two animals hit.

The inhabitants of Kung remained obdurate, and on the morning of the 29th September their forts and towers were destroyed under a desultory fire from the hills. No casualties occurred, and the force marched to Nahaki down the Bohai Dag watercourse, the transport preceding the troops and moving for a great portion of the way on a broad front. No opposition was met with; the Khwaezai villages were for the most part deserted, but the Halimzais of Kamali had returned and were pursuing their ordinary avocations.

The 1st Brigade was now ordered to stand fast at Nahaki for the present, and Brigadier-General Westmacott assumed command of the line of communications.

2nd Brigade.
Commanding—Brig.-General Macgregor.
Troops.
No. 5 Bombay M. By.
3 sqds. 13th Bengal Lancers.
No. 5 Co., Bengal S. and M.
2nd Bn., Oxfordshire L. I.
9th Gurkha Rifles.
Patiala Regiment.

On the 30th September the 2nd Brigade, which had been reconstituted, marched from Nahaki, across the Kamali plain, to Bar Yakhdand. The country was bare and parched, and everywhere intersected by deep *nalas* impassable for transport, except at a few known crossings. The troops crossed the Palasang Nala, which runs into the Danish Kol, and camped just beyond Bar Yakhdand, a large Utmanzai village containing about 200 houses and several towers. No opposition was encountered and the villagers at Yakhdand were ostentatiously friendly. During the afternoon a reconnaissance was pushed on to the Shatai pass, and working-parties from the troops were employed in improving the track up to the *kotal* which proved to be very difficult.

Meanwhile the Utmanzai *jirga* brought in the arms due from the clan, but no rifles. The tribesmen stated that they had no weapons of this description in their possession : accordingly an additional fine of Rs. 500 was accepted instead.

On the 1st October Major-General Elles, with a portion of the 2nd Brigade, marched over the Shatai pass into the Pipal valley, and camped at Turu, near Ali-Sher in Dawezai territory. The Dawezai *jirga* came in during the day and complied with the terms which had been imposed upon them. On the following day the Turu column recrossed the Shatai pass and proceeded to Mulla Kili in Danish Kol, where they were joined by the remainder of the Brigade from Yakhdand. On this day a man of the 9th Gurkhas was reported missing, and it was subsequently ascertained that he had been murdered by some villagers from Dand who had stolen his rifle.

H.-Qs. and 1 sqd., 13th B. L.
4 guns, No. 5 Bombay M. By.
No. 5 Co., Bengal S. and M.
9th Gurkhas.
Patiala Regiment.

The Isa Khel of Pandiali and the Utmanzai were finally settled with at Mulla Kili, and on the 3rd a column under Lieut.-Colonel Wodehouse marched over the Garang pass to Lagham in Pandiali. The remainder of the 1st and 2nd brigades were now withdrawn from Mohmand country, by the Nahaki-Shalkadan route, and reached Peshawar on the 6th and 7th October, when the Field Force was broken up.

2 guns, No. 5 Bombay M. By.
No. 5 Co., Bengal S. and M.
9th Gurkhas.
Section No. 45 N. F. H.

Lieut.-Colonel Wodehouse's troops halted at Lagham on the 4th, while the Burhan Khel *jirga* proceeded to Ghalanai to pay up their fine to Major-General Elles. On the following day the column continued its march over the Alikandi hills. The track was difficult and required a considerable amount of road-making work to render it passable, so the troops did not reach Matta Moghal Khel until late in the afternoon.

The objects of the expedition had now been accomplished. The Mohmand tribe concerned in the raid on Shankargarh had been thoroughly well punished either by the destruction of the towers and forts of those who stood out against our terms, or by money fines in addition to partial disarmament. The Hadda Mulla's[1] gathering had been effectively dispersed; his stronghold at Jarobi destroyed, and he himself, discredited amongst the clans who had so lately flocked to his standard, had been obliged to flee before our

[1] Mulla Najam-ud-Din died at Jalalabad in 1903.

troops into Afghan territory. The payments of money fines and the delivery of arms had, in almost every case, been punctually carried out. The country of the hill Mohmands, never before visited by any troops, had been traversed from south to north and from east to west, and the *purdah* effectually lifted. Their fastnesses of Bedmanai and Jarobi had been entered by our troops with comparative ease, and the clans had had cause to regret bitterly their temerity in defying the authority of the *Sarkar* by joining in the raid of the 7th August 1897.

The Indian Medal, 1895, with clasp inscribed "Punjab Frontier, 1897-98" was granted to the troops employed in the action of Shabkadar and the subsequent operations in the Mohmand country.

The allowances of the five "assured clans" (Tarakzais excepted), who were implicated in hostilities against the British Government, were suspended after the outbreak in August 1897. In consequence, however, of the complete submission of the clans, their full compliance with the terms imposed, and their subsequent good behaviour, these allowances were renewed from the 1st April 1898.

By the terms of the Durand Convention the Musa Khel Baezais of Mitai had come under British control, and after the expedition of 1897 described in the preceding pages, they represented that the allowances which they had formerly received from the Afghan Government had ceased, and they therefore petitioned that they might share the privileges granted to the other "assured" clans. Accordingly in November 1902 the Musa Khel of Mitai became an "assured clan," and received allowances on conditions similar to those imposed on the other sections by the agreement of 1896, mentioned on page 467. The representatives of the clan further bound themselves to maintain friendly relations with their neighbour the Khan of Nawagai, whose claim, that the whole of the Mitai valley was the *daftar* or hereditary land of the Tarkanri tribe, and therefore formed part of his Khanate, had been a constant source of feud. Khan Muhammad Ali Jan, son of the Khan of Nawagai, was present when this settlement was made with the Musa Khel, and expressed himself satisfied with the arrangement.

It may be noted here that the Khan of Nawagai had temporarily gained the upper hand in Mitai in 1898, when fear of interference on the part of the Afghans no longer restrained him. But in the following year the Mohmands had combined against him and since then he had practically relinquished the Mitai and Suran valleys. The object of summoning the *Khan's* representative to witness the settlement with the Musa Khel, and the purport of the clause regarding friendly relations with Nawagai were to avoid giving offence to the Tarkanri chief, who might otherwise have resented the fact that the Government had subsidised a clan whom he claimed as tenants and subjects though they were in reality independent.

The Shinpokh-Smatsai affair, 1903.

About the end of April 1903 the crops and wells belonging to the villages of Shinpokh and Smatsai on the right bank of the Kabul river were destroyed by some Afghan *khassadars* and Morcha Khel tribesmen at the instigation of the *Sartip* of Dakka, who wished to punish the *maliks* for their dealings with British officials.

Shinpokh, which consists of three hamlets, each containing about twenty houses and a tower, is inhabited by Burhan Khel Mohmands who were formerly expelled from Dakka by the Morcha Khels. This village was admitted by the Amir, in 1896, to be within British territory. Smatsai, which is a Tarakzai village, inhabited by Shilman tenants from Loi Shilman, is also regarded by the Government as British. It is however situated in a part of Mohmand country which has not yet been delimited, and is claimed by the Amir as being on the Afghan side of the Durand line.

On the 29th April, Captain W. E. Venour occupied Smatsai with a small force of Khaibar Rifles, and on the next day a detachment was sent to protect Shinpokh. No opposition was met with and the marauders had withdrawn. On the 2nd May, however, some 300 Mohmands, several of whom were armed with Lee-Metford rifles, took up a position on the left bank of the Kabul river, opposite Smatsai, and opened fire on our levies. As the Khaibar Rifles were only armed with Sniders they were unable to reply to their assailants; the latter, however, contented themselves with sniping, and kept well out of range of the Smatsai garrison. Intermittent sniping continued for several days, and a small contingent of Khwaezais also joined in the demonstration—probably with a view to inducing Government to summon their *jirga* and grant them allowances on the lines of the "assured clans."

Correspondence ensued between the Government of India and the Amir regarding the action of the *Sartip* of Dakka. His Majesty eventually undertook to punish the Morcha Khel; and the Mohmands who were Afghan subjects were ordered to disperse. The Khaibar Rifles were then withdrawn from Smatsai and Shinpokh, and some thirty Shilman *khassadars* were specially engaged for the protection of these villages.

Raids on Jogin and Tangi in 1906.

On the 21st March 1906 a well-armed band of noted outlaws from Hazarnao in Afghan territory, accompanied by a number of Khwaezai and Tarakzai Mohmands, raided the village of Jogin, near Michni, and looted the houses of two well-to-do Hindus, carrying off property to the value of nearly 16,000 rupees. The action of the Afghan subjects, who participated in this raid, was brought to the notice of the Amir. The Tarakzais acknowledged their responsibility and surrendered twenty men suspected of complicity in the affair; seven of these, against whom sufficient evidence was obtainable, were brought to trial under the Frontier Crimes Act. It transpired later that the stolen property was publicly auctioned in Lalpura.

On the 9th April following, some Khoda Khel Mohmands, and a few Utman Khels, under the leadership of the Hazarnao outlaws made an attack on Tangi, a large village close to Abazai. Three Hindus and one Mussulman inhabitant were killed, the latter probably by accident, since the Muhammadans of Tangi were tacit abettors of the outrage, and made no attempt to repel the raiders, who confined their depredations to Hindu houses. A small party of Border Military Police, with some villagers of Abazai, pursued the invaders as they retired, and wounded a few of them, but were unable to make any captures. No Mohmands of the "assured clans" were implicated in this affair; and though the raiders passed through Safi Mohmand territory on their way to the border, the Safis were unaware of their intentions, and were not held responsible. The Tangi Mussulmans and Laman Utman Khels were heavily fined for their misbehaviour, and a protest against the conduct of the Khoda Khels was forwarded to Kabul.

A portion of the Hazarnao gang was ambushed at Tandi in July 1906 by a party of the Khaibar Rifles under Captain Bickford: two of the outlaws were killed and four captured.

The extension of the railway from Peshawar to the Afghan frontier through Shilman was commenced in 1906. The Mohmands have offered no serious objection to this undertaking and many of them have come forward to share in the work and profit by well-paid labour. The line now under construction runs only to a point, known as mile 300, on the Kabul river, about five miles below Gatta-Gudar ferry: beyond this the alignment has not been finally determined. The protection of the line is guaranteed by the Tarakzais, who receive a special additional allowance of Rs. 5,000 on this account. The allowance of the Mullagoris has also been raised from Rs. 2,000 to Rs. 5,000 in return for the right to open up communications through their country whenever Government may require to do so.

Although, with the exception of the Smatsai affair and the two raids at Jogin and Tangi on the Peshawar border described above, there has been no actual outbreak on the part of the Mohmands since 1897, our relations with the tribe are by no means satisfactory. The postponement of the delimitation of the frontier in Mohmand territory, and the uncertainty as to whether the final settlement will assign them to the Afghan or to the British Government have doubtless caused much of the unrest which now prevails among some of the clans. This has also been fostered, in no small degree, by the intrigues of Afghan subjects, who aim at seducing the "assured clans" from their allegiance to the British Government, and by the undisguised hostility of the *mullas*. Besides the Sufi Mulla, who brought a contingent of Ningraharis to assist in the defence of the Bedmanai pass in 1897, the most active of the religious leaders are the Kama Mulla, a priest called Abdul Baqi, and an individual known as the Gud Mulla—the last two being pupils and successors of the late Hadda Mulla. They are all bitterly opposed to the British and do their utmost to prevent the clansmen from having any dealings with our officials; indeed their threats have made some of the clans hesitate about accepting their allowances. The *mullas* have further threatened to interfere with the work of the Shilman railway line.

Trouble has also been caused in recent years by disputes with the Afghan frontier officials over the collection of dues on timber floated down the Kabul river below Dakka, and the seizure of drift wood. The Tarakzais have always had the privilege of collecting this toll, but the Amir's own property was specially exempted. Since 1898, however, the Amir has declared all timber exported to be a state monopoly, and therefore free of dues—a claim which, if substantiated, means a heavy loss to the Tarakzai clan. A quarrel over this business resulted in another collision at Smatsai in 1905 between some British levies and villagers and a party of Afghan *khassadars* who had been sent by the *Sarhang* of Dakka on the pretext of recovering drift wood. Protests to the Amir regarding illegal or unfriendly acts on the part of his officials in these regions have but little effect, since the latter are usually adepts in the art of misrepresenting facts and motives. It is hoped, however, that a speedy settlement of all debatable questions connected with this portion of the frontier will terminate the present condition of uncertainty among the Mohmand clans, and remove a source of disputes and quarrels between them and Afghan subjects. In 1904 when it was proposed to complete the demarcation of the frontier south of the Nawa peak, the Mohmands offered to be responsible for the safety of the British Mission while employed in their country. The question, however, was then deferred, and when it was revived a year later, it was held that the Mission could not depend upon tribal protection, nor was the time deemed opportune for the despatch of a military escort through Mohmand country.

In conclusion it may be said that, so long as present conditions prevail, the authority of the Government of India over the "assured clans" is none too firmly established, while little or no control is exercised over the remainder of the Mohmand tribe.

APPENDIX A.

Table showing principal divisions of the Mohmand tribe, and the affiliated and vassal clans.

MOHMAND.

- **Tarakzai.**
  - **Tarakzai (proper).**
    - Dadu Khel .. { Dalka Khel. / Shahmansur Khel.1 }
    - Kasim Khel .. { Khani Khel. / Khalil Khel. }
  - **Halimzai.**
    - Hamza Khel, Kadai Kor, Wali Beg Kor .. (in Gandab).
    - Ibrahim Khel, Hamza Khel, Busha Khel .. (in Kamali).
  - **Isa Khel.**
    - Kandai, Yusuf Khel .. (in Pandiali).
  - **Burhan Khel.**
    - Muhammad Khan Ror (Bar), Kharrappawal (Kuz) .. (in Pandiali).
- **Baezai.**
  - **Sepah.**
    - Musa Khel, Miro Khel, Bara Khel .. (Mitai).
  - **Usman Khel.**
    - Khuga Khel, Isa Khel, Attamar Khel, Koda Khel .. (Jarobi).
- **Khwaezai.**
  - Dawat Khel.
  - Maimana Khel.
  - Khadi Khel.
- **Dawezai.**
  - Kuchis or nomads .. { Hassan Khel, Mandozai, Hazar Buz, Za Khel } (in Ningrahar).
  - Wudredunkai or settled clans .. { Babazai Kor, Hassan Khel } (in Pipal).
- **Affiliated Clans.**
  - **Utmanzai.** — In Kuz and Bar Yakhdand.
  - **Kukkozai.** — Naraizai, Ahmedakzai, Baekzai .. (in Hazarnao and Basawal).
- **Vassal Clans.**
  - **Mullagoris. 2** — Ahmad Khel, Ismail, Daulat Khel .. (in Tartara and Kambela).
  - **Safis.** — Kandaharis, Gurbuz, Masand, Wader .. (in Surkamar).

1 The Morcha Khel, which is the Khan Khel of the Tarakzai to which family the Khan of Lalpura belongs, is a subdivision of the Shahmansur Khel.

2 The Mullagoris deny that they were ever vassals of the Mohmands.

APPENDIX B.

Estimate of the numbers of the Mohmand clans and others who took part in the action of Shabkadar on 9th August 1897, submitted by Subadar-Major Abdur Rauf, Native Commandant, Border Military Police.

Section.	*Men.*
Khwaezai	500
Baezai	3,000
Burhan Khel } of Pandiali Isa Khel } of Pandiali	400
Tarakzai[1]	300
Halimzai of Gandab	500
Halimzai of Kamali	200
Dawezai Utmanzai Kandahari Safis	1,000
Mullagoris Utman Khel Shaikhs (disciples of the Hadda Mullah)	1,000
Khugianis	200
Men of Badel glen	300
Shinwaris of Shigal in Kunar valley	400
Mohmands of Basawal, Hazarnao, etc., west of Dakka	300
Miscellaneous unclassed	1,000
TOTAL	9,100

NOTE.—This total exceeds General Elles' estimate which was about 6,000; but it may represent the numbers which took part in the raid on the 7th September, some of whom dispersed on the 8th.

[1] Tho Tarakzai clan did not join in hostilities against us and remained loyal throughout.

APPENDIX C.

Composition of the Mohmand Field Force, 1897.

1st Brigade.

Commanding—Brigadier-General Westmacott, C.B., D.S.O.

1st Battalion, Somersetshire Light Infantry.

20th Punjab Infantry.

2nd Battalion, 1st Gurkhas.

2 Sections, No. 5 British field hospital.

3 Sections, No. 31 Native field hospital.

1 Section, No. 45 Native field hospital.

2nd Brigade.

Commanding—Brigadier-General C. R. Macgregor, D.S.O.

2nd Battalion, Oxfordshire Light Infantry.

9th Gurkhas.

37th Dogras.

2 Sections, No. 5 British field hospital.

No. 44 Native field hospital.

Divisional Troops.

13th Bengal Lancers.

No. 3 Mountain Battery, R.A.

No. 5 (Bombay) Mountain Battery.

28th Bombay Infantry (Pioneers).

No. 5 Company, Bengal Sappers and Miners.

Patiala Regiment, Imperial Service Troops.[1]

Nabha Regiment, Imperial Service Troops.[2]

Maxim gun detachment (2 guns), Devonshire Regiment.

½ No. 63, Native field hospital.

1 Section, No. 45 Native field hospital.

[1] Attached to 2nd Brigade.
[2] Attached to Mohmand Field Force from 19th September.

APPENDIX D.

Commands and Staff of the Mohmand Field Force, 1897.

STAFF.

General Officer Commanding the Force (with the local rank of Major-General), Brigadier-General E. R. Elles, C.B.

Aide-de-Camp, Lieutenant M. R. Elles, R.E.

Orderly Officer, Captain K. MacLaren, 13th Hussars.

Assistant Adjutant General, Major C. L. Woollcombe, K. O. S. B.

Assistant Quarter Master General, Major G. H. W. O'Sullivan, R.E.

Deputy Assistant Quarter Master General (Intelligence), Captain F. A. Hoghton, 1st Bombay Grenadiers.

Commanding Royal Artillery, Lieut.-Colonel A. E. Duthy, R.A.

Field Engineer, Captain F. H. Kelly, R.E.

Principal Medical Officer, Surgeon-Colonel E. Townsend, A.M.S.

Chief Commissariat Officer, Captain G. Westropp.

Divisional Transport Officer, Captain F. A. Rideout.

Ordnance Officer, Major T. E. Rowan, R.A.

Survey Officer, Major W. J. Bythell, R.E.

1st BRIGADE.

Commanding, Brigadier-General R. Westmacott, C.B., D.S.O.

Orderly Officer, Lieutenant R. C. Wellesley, R.H.A.

D. A. A. G. Captain W. P. Blood, Royal Irish Fusiliers.

D. A. Q. M. G. Captain F. J. M. Edwards, 3rd Bombay Cavalry.

Brigade Commissariat Officer, Captain E. Y. Watson.

" Transport Officer, Captain W. H. Armstrong, East Yorkshire Regiment.

2ND BRIGADE.

Commanding, Colonel (with local rank of Brigadier-General) C. R. Macgregor, D.S.O.

Orderly Officer, 2nd-Lieutenant E. W. C. Ridgeway, 29th Punjab Infantry.

D. A. A. G. Captain G. M. Gloster, Devonshire Regiment.

D. A. Q. M. G. Captain H. Hudson, 19th Bengal Lancers.

Brigade Commissariat Officer, Lieutenant D. H. Drake-Brockman.

" Transport Officer, Lieutenant R. G. N. Tytler, Gordon Highlanders.

APPENDIX E.

***The disposition of the different corps and units of the Mohmand Field Force on the 28th September* 1897.**

At Kung.

Divisional Troops ..	No. 3 Mountain Battery, Royal Artillery. No. 5 Bombay Mountain Battery (4 guns). 13th Bengal Lancers ($3\frac{1}{2}$ squadrons). No. 5 Company, Bengal Sappers and Miners (2 sections). 28th Bombay Pioneers.
1st Brigade ..	2nd Battalion, Oxfordshire Light Infantry. 2 Maxim guns, Detachment Devonshire Regiment. 20th Punjab Infantry. 2nd Battalion, 1st Gurkha Rifles.
Medical units ..	3 Sections, No. 5 British Field Hospital. 2 ,, ,, 31 Native ,, ,,

At Nahaki.

Divisional Troops ..	Detachment, 13th Bengal Lancers (57 lances). 2 guns, No. 5 Bombay Mountain Battery.
En route to Peshawar ..	1st Battalion, Somersetshire Light Infantry.
2nd Brigade ..	9th Gurkha Rifles. Patiala Regiment—returned from 3rd Brigade, Malakand Field Force.
Medical units ..	1 Section, No. 5 British Field Hospital. 1 ,, ,, 31 Native ,, ,, 3 ,, ,, 44 ,, ,, ,, 1 ,, ,, 63 ,, ,, ,,

At Wuchajawar advanced Depôt.

Divisional Troops ..	No. 5 Company, Bengal Sappers and Miners (2 sections).
2nd Brigade ..	37th Dogras (6 companies).

At Ghalanai.

Divisional Troops ..	13th Bengal Lancers (1 field troop). Nabha Battalion, Imperial Service Troops. 1 Section, No. 44 Native Field Hospital. 1 ,, ,, 45 ,, ,, ,,

The 3rd Brigade, Malakand Field Force, was *en route* to Peshawar.

CHAPTER XII.

AKOZAI-YUSAFZAI AND TARKANRI TRIBES OF DIR AND BAJAUR.

As the limits of Dir and Bajaur do not coincide with the borders of any particular tribe or administrative area, it will be more convenient to deal with the two countries together. The people who inhabit these countries are the Akozai-Yusafzai, other clans of whom inhabit the Swat valley, and have already been described in Chapter VIII, and the cognate tribe of Tarkanri.

The country known as Dir roughly comprises the whole area drained by the Panjkora river and its affluents, as far south as its junction with the Bajaur or Rud river. The upper Panjkora valley, above Chutiatanr, is known as the Panjkora Kohistan, or Kohistan-i-Malizai, and is divided into two portions, of which the upper is called Bashkar and the lower Sheringal. The principal side valleys included in Dir are the Kashkar or Dir, the Baraul,[1] and the Maidan[1] on the right, and the Ushiri and Talash valleys on the left.

Bajaur may be described as the country watered by the river of that name, also known as the Rud river, together with its tributaries from the north and north-east, exclusive of the Jandol stream. This area includes the four valleys of Rud (or Bajaur), Babukarra, Watelai (or Mamund), and Chaharmung. South-west of the Chaharmung valley, but also included in Bajaur, lies a tract of country called Surkamar, belonging to the Khanate of Nawagai. It comprises the *nalas* of Kamangara, Chamarkand, and Guluna, whose waters flow into the Pipal or Ambahar stream, together with the Batai plain, which extends westward from the Shagai ridge to the mouths of the Mitai and Suran Nalas, near Kuz Chinerai and Karkano Shah, and southward to the Lakarai gorge.

The Jandol valley, which lies between the Maidan and Babukarra valleys, formerly belonged to Bajaur, but is now politically

[1] These two valleys were at one time included in Bajaur.

part of Dir; the people of the upper valley, however, at the present time do not own allegiance to the Khan, and are in reality independent of both Dir and Bajaur. For a description of this valley see page 512.

The northern limit of Dir is the crest of the mountain range which divides it from Chitral and Yasin. To the west the boundary is formed by the Durand line, which follows the crest of the Hindu Raj range, and separates Dir and Bajaur from Afghanistan. On the east and south, these two countries are bounded by Swat Kohistan and the Swat valley, and by the territories of the Utman Khels and Mohmands.

The whole country included in Dir and Bajaur is extremely mountainous. From the mass of mountains, which form an almost impassable barrier to the north of the Panjkora and Swat Kohistan, three principal ranges branch off in a southerly direction. The eastern chain, forming the watershed between the Swat and Indus rivers, runs south to the Dosiri peak, and thence in a westerly direction to the Malakand pass. The central range forms the watershed between the Panjkora and Swat rivers. This range, whose greatest altitude is 15,000 feet, sinks near the Laram pass to about 7,000 feet. Thence to its termination, at the junction of the Swat and Panjkora rivers, it is known as the Laram or Siar range. It is crossed by three main passes, the Laram, the Katgola, and the Badwai.

The western range is a continuation of the Hindu Raj which runs in a south-westerly direction, forming the watershed between the Panjkora and Bajaur rivers on the east, and the Kunar river on the west. From the Pushkari to the Shingara peak, this range forms the boundary between Dir and Chitral. Southwards from the Shingara peak, the Afghan boundary follows the crest and has been demarcated as far as the Nawa peak. The northern half of this portion of the Hindu Raj is also known as the Uchiri, while the southern half is called the Lakra range: further south again, it becomes the Kabul-Tsappar range. The Pushkari peak, the highest point of this portion of the Hindu Raj, is 16,500 feet. South of the Binshi peak (12,150 feet) the range sinks to an average height of 9,000 feet. A succession of almost parallel spurs, jutting out from this main range, divide the basin of the Bajaur river into several separate valleys.

The most important pass is the Lowari (10,200 feet) across which runs the main road from India to Chitral. It is considered fit for mule transport from April to November. Other passes are :— The Binshi, Trepaman, and Loegram, giving access from Bajaur to Asmar ; the Nawa pass, leading from Nawagai to Pashat in the Kunar valley ; the Kaga and Ghakhai (or Hindu Raj) passes, leading from the Watelai valley across the Lakra mountains in Mamund country.

The Panjkora river is fed from snows and glaciers and is, during summer, deep, rapid, and unfordable. In winter, its volume greatly decreases, and it can be forded in many places. The main valley of the Panjkora is considerably narrower and less rich in alluvial soil than that of Swat. The many subsidiary valleys, however, are extremely rich and fertile, and afford subsistence for the majority of the population. The principal tributaries of the Panjkora are the Dir (or Kunai), Baraul, and Maidan streams.

The Bajaur, or Rud river, and its affluents, rising in the lower mountains of the Hindu Raj, are not snow-fed ; and consequently are full in winter, and low during the summer months.

The climate of the Panjkora valley is generally temperate. In the upper valleys, it is cool in summer and intensely cold in winter. There is considerable rainfall in July and August. In Bajaur, the summer, though short, is extremely hot, while the rainfall is rather less than in Dir. Fever and ague are prevalent in the Panjkora and Bajaur valleys, but these localities have not such a bad reputation, in this respect, as the Swat valley. There are several suitable sites in the hills which could be used as sanitaria, should it ever be necessary to occupy this country with British troops during the summer.

In the Panjkora river basin, and the adjoining side valleys, the crops are similar to those of Swat with the exception of rice, which is cultivated in less quantities. Iron of good quality is smelted from sand obtained in the upper Baraul valley. The chief exports are *ghi*, hides, and a small quantity of wheat and barley ; imports are salt, crockery, and household goods.

There is also a considerable export of timber, which is obtained from the deodar forests in the Panjkora Kohistan, and floated down the Panjkora and Swat rivers. This trade, which was formerly in the hands of the Kaka-Khel Mians of Ziarat, near Nowshera, is now one of the main sources of the revenue of the Khan of Dir. In order to prevent the deforestation of the country, an arrangement was made in 1905, whereby the *Khan* agreed to the inspection of the forests by an official deputed by the Government of India, and to certain restrictions as to the amount of timber to be felled annually. In Bajaur, wheat, barley, and maize are grown. Fuel is scarce throughout this area.

It is difficult to estimate the exact amount of supplies available in Dir and Bajaur; but it is certain that from these countries and from Swat sufficient supplies could be obtained for a considerable force.

The most important route through the country here described is the road from the Swat valley to Chitral over the Lowarai pass.

Leaving the Swat at Chakdara it leads through Adinzai territory over the Katgola pass into the Talash valley, and thence by the Kamrani pass to Sado. Turning right-handed from Sado it runs up the Panjkora valley *viâ* Robat (or Shamardin), Warai, Darora (or Gandegar) to Dir, and thence up the Dir valley to the Lowari pass, which gives access to Chitral territory. An alternative route branching off from Sado runs westward to Ghosam, and then, turning northward, ascends the bed of the Jandol river to the Janbatai pass; after crossing this, the road leads along the Baraul valley to Chutiatanr and Dir, where it joins the first mentioned route. Both these roads have been greatly improved since 1895, and the first is used by the annual reliefs marching to and from Chitral. Further details regarding them and the arrangements which have been made for their protection will be found on page 551.

The people.

The four sections of the Malizai-Khwazazai branch of the Akozai-Yusafzai tribe who inhabit Dir and the Panjkora valley are the Painda Khel, the Sultan Khel, the Nasruddin Khel, and the Ausa Khel.

The Painda Khel.

The Painda Khel occupy the Ushiri, Niag, and Kharo valleys on the left bank of the Panjkora, and a sub-section, called the Akhund Khel, to which belongs the family of the Khan of Dir, have as their *daftar* the Dir or Kashkar valley, with its subsidiary *nalas*, as well as the district of Bibiaor on both banks of the Panjkora between Chutiatanr and Darora.

The Dir stream rises below the Lowari pass, and flows southwards through a narrow valley, with steep mountains on either side, till it reaches the Panjkora river just above Chutiatanr. Its tributaries are the small mountain streams draining the Jajurai, Dobandi, and Aleh Nalas on the right, and the Miana and lesser *nalas* on the left. Except for about two miles of more open country about Dir fort and village, cultivation is restricted to the river-bed and its immediate borders. Above Dir the valley is thickly wooded with fir and pine trees, and grass is plentiful. The upper portion of the valley, above the village of Kashkar, is inhabited by aliens—Katanis or Bashkaris, and there are also numerous Gujar settlements. The population of the lower valley is mixed, and includes a number of Swatis. The valley of the Dir, and the side *nalas* watered by its affluents (excepting the Dobandi Nala), together with the portion of the Panjkora valley, about a mile in length, between the mouth of the Dir and Chutiatanr fort, is also known as Kalandi district, and is all Akhund Khel *daftar*. The Dobandi Nala, which also belongs to the Akhund Khel, is a narrow valley watered by the stream which rises near the Zakhanna pass. It is thickly wooded and contains a fair amount of well cultivated land, but is chiefly notable on account of the iron smelting which is carried on there. The Dir river is generally unfordable, but is bridged in several places. The main route to Chitral runs up the valley.

The Bibiaor district contains some twenty villages. The Chitral road runs through this district and paths lead from it up the side valleys.

The Ushiri valley is about nineteen miles long and ten miles wide at its upper end, whence it contracts to a narrow gorge at its junction with the Panjkora valley. Its elevation falls from 11,000 feet at the head of the valley to 3,700 feet near Darora. Two branch streams, which rise near the Sidghai and Barkand passes, unite at Ushiri village to form the main stream which drains the valley. There is an ample water-supply, and plenty of cultivation, while the slopes of the surrounding hills are thickly wooded. The main route through the valley is a difficult track along the left bank of the stream. Three difficult passes, the Barkand, Shema-shami, and Sidghai lead into Upper Swat, the last two being only fit for men on foot. Paths run from Almas into the Niag valley, and from Jabbai to Upper Panjkora. The Ushiri stream is bridged in several places near the larger villages, but is seldom fordable. The villages of Darora and Jabbar, at the lower end of the valley, belong to the Sultan Khel.

The Niag valley, which lies between the Ushiri and Kharo valleys, has an area of some ninety-five square miles, and is fifteen miles in length by eight miles in width at its broadest part. Like the Ushiri, it is contracted at its lower end to a narrow gorge, through which its stream finds an exit to the Panjkora. The valley is extremely fertile, and its upper portion is well wooded. The Niag stream, except when it is swollen by melting snows or heavy rain, is insignificant. It is bridged at Mulla-gujar, Sundial, and just above its junction with the Panjkora river. There are roads along each bank; the southern road, which is fit for pack transport, leads over the Swatai pass into Upper Swat. The northern road, however, is impracticable for laden animals beyond Sundial. A side-path leads over the Shalga pass into Ushiri.

The Kharo valley is situated between the valleys of Niag and Tormung. It is ten miles long by six miles across, at its widest part, and has an area of about forty-eight square miles. The higher slopes of the mountains, which reach an altitude of 10,000 feet at the upper end of the valley, are well wooded and grassy. Fruit trees are very abundant, and there is a considerable export of fruit to Swat. The Kharo stream is unbridged, but is almost always fordable. The chief markets are Kotah and Kumbar.

There is a fairly good road up the valley as far as Dorial, whence paths lead over three difficult passes—the Sarlai, Landai and Tangu—into Upper Swat and the Deolai valley in Nikbi Khel country.

A number of men of the Painda Khel section, more particularly from the Kharo valley tribesmen, take service in India, chiefly in the Central India and Hyderabad States and in the Bombay Army.

The Sultan Khel.

The Sultan Khel inhabit the right bank of the Panjkora from the southern limit of Bibiaor to Khal and the whole of the Tormung valley on the left bank. They also possess the villages of Darora and Jabbar in the Ushiri valley. Their territory on the right bank thus comprises the Alakhun and Panjkora Nala, together with the Khal district, which includes the valleys of Rogano and Lukman-

Banda. This tract is bounded on the west by the ridge which divides it from the Aka Khel and Lajbok valleys, and on the south by Ausa Khel country.

The Panjkora Nala is watered by a stream which has its source near the Maidan peak (10,700 feet), and, after receiving numerous minor tributaries during its course, reaches the Panjkora river through a deep narrow gorge near Kotkai, midway between the mouths of the Niag and Ushiri streams. There is good grazing-ground throughout the valley, and the ravines and mountain sides in its upper portion are finely wooded with fir and pine. The chief villages are Sehrai, Patao, and Panjkora. Besides the Sultan Khel, a number of Gujars live in this valley.

The district of Khal comprises four villages collectively known as Khal, on the right bank of the Panjkora, two and a half miles above Robat, and the valleys of Lukman-Banda and Rogano. The Khal villages (Laorai Killa, Zarmundai, Bar Killa, and Kundai) are inhabited by Ibrahim Khel—Sultan Khel and Akhundzadas, and contain 160 houses, with about sixty acres of cultivated land. The Lukman-Banda Nala is a narrow treeless valley five miles in length, running north-west from the Panjkora about one mile above Khal. It contains thirteen hamlets inhabited by Rogani and Bakkar Khel, who are tenants of the Khans of Khal. The Rogano valley runs westward from the Panjkora from a point almost midway between the Niag and Kharo valleys. There is a good water-supply and fair grazing-ground. The chief village Jailar contains about eighty houses. Various paths lead to the adjoining valleys; that over the Danda pass to Lajbok being fit for pack transport. The inhabitants are all Rogani and hold the land as tenants of the Khans of Khal.

Umra Khan attacked Khal after he had expelled Muhammad Sharif Khan of Dir and forced the Khans to take refuge in Swat.

The Tormung is a small valley, with an area of about twenty-four square miles, situated on the left bank of the Panjkora, south of the Kharo Nala. Tormung, the chief village, has a loopholed tower, but other villages are unfortified. Roads lead up both banks of the Tormung stream: a path over the Manja pass into Nikbi Khel territory is fit for laden animals, and a more difficult route leads by the Batarai pass to Uch.

The Nasruddin Khel.

The territory of the Nasruddin Khel comprises the lower portion of the Maidan valley below the Ismailzai-Tarkanri boundary, together with the side *nalas* of Lajbok and Samalgai, the right bank of the Panjkora from Khal to its junction with the Maidan stream at Shazadgai, and the district of Robat on the left bank. This track is roughly bounded on the north-west by Upper Maidan, and on the south-east by the Laram range; while the lands of the Sultan Khel and Ausa Khel lie to the north-east and south-west, respectively.

Lajbok is a small valley running north-east from Lower Maidan at Shakartangai. It contains a population of a little over 500 people, who are mostly Akhund Khel Painda Khel, although the land belongs to the Nasruddin Khel.

The Robat district stretches in a north-westerly direction from the Laram pass to the Panjkora at Robat, where there is a large fort, the residence of the two Khans [1] who share the rulership of the district. The valley is rich and fertile, well cultivated and plentifully wooded. It contains a number of aliens—Rogani, Warkak, Mashwani, etc., who hold villages and lands as tenants. A road leads up the valley across the Laram pass to Uch.

The total poulation of the Nasruddin Khel amounts to about 5,000 people, distributed among seventy villages, of which the following are fortified, *viz.*, Shakartangai, Shazadgai, Bargulai, Barun, Ranai, and Robat. The tribe was continually opposed to Umra Khan during his wars of aggression. Their chief men are the *Khans* of Robat, and Fahm Jan of Bargulai and Barun.

The Ausa Khel.

The Ausa Khel occupy lands on both sides of the Panjkora. On the right bank their territory, which includes the valleys of Malakand, Makhai and Shatai, stretches from the Nasruddin Khel boundary at Shazadgai to the junction of the Bajaur river. Thence it ascends the left bank of that stream as far as Toratigga, a black rock between Ghosam and Ghobanai, which marks the Jandol boundary. On the left bank of the Panjkora, the Ausa Khel country extends from the Robat district of the Nasruddin Khel to the

[1] Abdullah Khan and Zarim Khan. The latter is a son of Khani Jan Khan who was the ruler of Robat in 1895.

junction of the Swat and Panjkora rivers at Sharbatai, thus including the Talash valley. To the east lies the Adinzai country, whose boundary runs from just west of the Laram pass along the Katgola ridge to Barchanrai peak and thence to a point about a mile below Chakdara.

The Malakand Nala is a small bare valley, with fair grazing-ground, through which a path runs *viâ* the Shalkandai pass into Jandol. It contains 1,400 inhabitants, who can muster about 280 armed men.

Makhai valley, on the left bank of the Rud, which it joins at Kotkai, is inhabited by Utman Khel tenants[1] of the Pai Khel sub-section of Ausa Khel. A road fit for pack mules leads over the Makhai pass at the head of the valley to Mundah.

The Talash valley, which has an average elevation of about 3,000 feet, extends some six miles from the left bank of the Panjkora eastward to the Topai Sar spur of the Laram range, which divides it from Adinzai territory. To the south, it is bounded by the Deolai peak and the Dusha Khel hills. It is watered by the Loi stream, into which several *nalas*—usually dry—run down from the slopes of the Siar range, which forms the northern boundary of the valley.

The main route to Bajaur enters by the Katgola pass and runs down the valley to the Panjkora river bank through a narrow defile about a mile and a half in length called the Shigu Kas on either side of which are rocky precipitous hills. The Chitral road leads over the Kamrani pass to Sado. Besides this, numerous mountain tracks, most of which are impracticable for laden animals, communicate with adjoining valleys.

The Ausa Khel, during a period of twelve years or more, prior to the extension of British influence over this trans-border country in 1895, were either under the authority of Umra Khan, or were subjected to his raids.

A sub-section of the Ausa Khel, deserving of mention is the Dush Khel (a branch of the Bahlol Khel division of the Sheikh Khel—Ausa Khel) who inhabit the mountainous district of that name lying along the left bank of the Panjkora, between the Talash valley and Sharbatai. They also share some land with the Khadakzai, in Swat.

[1] A few of these tenants also hold land in the Shahtai valley.

Owing to the inaccessibility of their territory, they were able to resist the encroachments of Umra Khan far longer than the Talash valley tribesmen, and only paid revenue to him for two or three years. They bear an ill reputation for raiding and robbery, and appear to be more independent than their neighbours, with whom, however, they keep on good terms. Their district now forms part of the Khan of Dir's territory.

A certain number of aliens live among the Dush Khel as servants or tenants, having received land in reward for past services. These are:— Dehgan, said to have come from Kunar in Afghanistan; Dalazak, a race of doubtful origin, who are also found in Sam Ranizai; Swati or descendants of original inhabitants; Gwari and Bajauri, supposed to have come from Utman Khel country and Bajaur, respectively.

The Tarkanri.

The Tarkanri, or Tarkanlanri, claim to be akin to the Yusafzai and Utman Khel, through their common descent from Kais or Abdur Rashid, who is said to have been the 37th in lineal descent from Talut, or Saul, King of Israel. They are supposed to have immigrated into Bajaur from Laghman, during the latter half of the fifteenth century. This tribe is divided into four sections, *viz.*, the Ismailzai, Isazai, Salarzai, and Mamund.

The Ismailzai.

The Ismailzai inhabit the upper Maidan valley, above the limit of Nasruddin Khel country at Aya Serai. They also own a number of villages in Lower Baraul and the Atan Nala. Two branches of the Atrapi stream, which take their rise from near the Tajka and Maidan peaks, unite south-west of the Mehrgram spur, and flow to Nagotal, where the combined stream is joined by the Kalut Khel, which rises near the Kalpanai pass. These two streams now form the Kunai or Maidan river, which waters the main Maidan valley, and flows into the Panjkora between Shazadgai and Udigram. The other affluents of the Kunai are the Aka Khel on the left bank and the Ananguri, and Katerzai on the right. Religious families of *saiyids* or *mullas* own no less than twenty-three villages in the Ismailzai district. These people are useless drones, cultivating very little land and paying no revenue, and are not liable to military service.

There are fortified villages at Gur, Maidan, Bandai, Kotkai, Dokrai, and Aya Serai.

The Maidan valley, which is some ten miles in length to the boundary of Nasruddin Khel territory (four miles above its junction with the Panjkora) is rich and fertile, and contains a large cultivated area. Paths, running up the various subsidiary *nalas* and over the passes and hills at their head, communicate with the adjoining districts. Only two are fit for pack animals, *viz.*, (i) up the Ananguri valley by the Inzar pass to Jandol, and (ii) up the Katorzai Nala over the Shalkandai pass to Barwa.

The Isazai.

The Isazai inhabit the Jandol and upper portion of the Baraul valley about Janbatai. They are divided into three chief sections, the Mast Khel, Musa Khel, and Ali Beg Khel, of which the Mast Khel is the Khan Khel, and claims hereditary rights over the whole of the Jandol valley. A large number of Mashwanis, occupy land as tenants of the Isazai. Other minor sections, who were either descendants of Kafirs or aboriginal tribes, though now considered to be Pathans and to belong to the Isazai clan, are Sheikh Khel or Shahi Khel, Khwazazai, Senzai, and Mandizai: the last three, however, are unimportant, and only own one or two villages each.

The Mast Khel occupy Barwa, and the surrounding hamlets, and the Tangai valley, together with a few outlying villages such as Anapia and Gol Bandai further south. The Musa Khel inhabit the Shalkandai valley, which runs north-north-east from Mundah.

The Ali Beg Khel have a few villages in the Shontalai valley, but their principal hamlets, Kanbat, Tyah, Tanglai, Baloda, Ghwa, and Rabanda are situated in a *nala* which runs from Kanbat north-west to the Shahi *kotal*.

The Sheikh Khel own some dozen villages in the Maskini valley above Gambir, on the west of the Jandol river. They have frequently been at enmity with the Mast Khel, and in their wars with them have several times lost and retaken the lands which they now occupy.

The Mashwani tenants of the Isazai hold lands in the upper slopes of the border hills on the northern limit of Jandol. They own between forty and fifty villages.

Besides the above-mentioned sub-sections and the Mashwani, there are numerous settlements of religious communities who have received villages and land in Jandol from the Isazai, as *seri* or freehold. In 1895 the number of these people in Jandol was estimated as follows, *viz.*, *Saiyids*, 1,790, owning five villages; *Akhundzadas*, 505, owning six villages; *Mians*, *Mullas* and *Sahibzadas*, 1,630, owning eighteen villages. Since that date their numbers and possessions have considerably increased. These people are exempt from taxation and are not called upon for military service.

There are also two important towns, Maiar and Mian Kilai, inhabited by a mixed population, and a number of small villages occupied by some 600 or 700 people of alien races and aboriginals. Maiar is a large town and trading centre situated just above the junction of the Maskini and Jandol streams. It belongs to *Akhundzadas* and contains about 1,500 houses with a large bazaar. It has a mixed population of Hindus, Muhammadan traders, Sheikh Khel, Utman Khel and others, estimated in 1895 at a total of 7,500 persons. Mian Kilai is owned by *Sahibzadas*, and is built on the right bank of the Jandol river just opposite Mundah. It is a trading centre for all the neighbouring countries and is considered to be the principal market between Peshawar and Badakhshan. The population, estimated at 5,000 people in 1895, includes Hindus, Muhammadan traders, and artificers.

The total population of the Jandol valley was estimated in 1895 to amount to close on 27,000 persons, but, as may be seen from the above description, a large proportion do not belong to the Tarkanri tribe.

Although the Mast Khel claim all the Janbatai district as *daftar* or hereditary land, the population there is very mixed. The Khan, however, belongs to the Mast Khel sub-section of the Isazai, and his followers may therefore be included in their fighting strength.

The boundaries of the Jandol valley inclusive of the Maskini Nala are:—On the north, the Janbatai range and the ridge between the Trepaman and Sargullo peaks. On the east the spur running south from the Suki peak to the Mohan peak dividing it from Maidan. On the south the Rud river. To the west the watershed between the Maskini and Babukarra valleys.

The valley is fourteen miles long and ten miles wide at its upper end narrowing towards the south to about six miles, its total area being about 144 square miles. It is extremely fertile and well cultivated but contains little forest except on the western side of the Maskini valley.

The Jandol stream, which provides an ample water-supply, rises in the Janbatai range, and has as tributaries the Maskini or Ram Gul and the Shontalai on the right, and the Tangai and Shalkandai on the left. The main route up the valley crosses the Janbatai pass, and several paths and tracks branch off in different directions from Mundah.

The Janbatai district or Upper Baraul is bounded on the north and north-west by the crest of the Uchiri range, and extends eastward to the watershed, between the Bin and Shingara Nala, which divides it from Lower Baraul. It thus includes the Janbatai, Binshi and Bin Nala. The district is part of the Mast Khel *daftar*, and revenue is paid to the chief of this clan, the Khan of Janbatai; the population, however, is mixed. Crops of wheat, barley, Indian corn, and rice are raised in the valley, and iron of excellent quality is exported, as also *ghi*, hides, and fruit. A local pattern of fire-arm manufactured at Jabo sells for Rs. 10 to 20. There are forts at Janbatai, Ido, Shai, and Shahkot.

The main road through the valley to Dir and Chitral crosses the Janbatai pass; it was improved in 1895 and is now fit for pack transport. Other routes lead by the Binshi pass to Asmar and by the Dolai and Jabo passes at the head of the Bin Nala to Narai or Narsat.

The Lower Baraul valley, which includes the subsidiary *nalas* of Maidan Khar, Shingara, and Atan, extends as far as the boundary of Dir proper at Ganurai, three miles above the Panjkora junction. It is well cultivated throughout, and the hills, especially on the south side, are thickly wooded. The whole of Lower Baraul, except the minor Khanates of Atan, Darikand, and Sandrawal, is known as the Baraul Bandai district, and belongs to the Bahadur Shah Khel sub-section of Ismailzai Tarkanri. The population, however, is very mixed and includes many Yusafzais as well as people of other tribes. The Atan Nala is inhabited mainly by Kohistanis, Swatis, and Gujars. Forts have been built at Darikand, Bandai, Dirkhan, Sandrawal, Sarbat, and Atan.

The Baraul river is formed by the junction at Janbatai Fort of the Janbatai, Binshi, and Bin streams; thence it flows for some seventeen miles north-east to the Panjkora at Chutiatanr. The river is periodically swollen to a rapid torrent by rains and melting snows. It is crossed at Darikand and Sarbat by bridges fit for laden animals, and there are fords at Ido, Darikand, and Dir Khan. The water is lowest in June, when it is used to irrigate the rice-fields.

The Salarzai.

The Salarzai inhabit the valleys of Babukarra and Chaharmung in Bajaur, and also possess lands in Shortan and Marawara, across the Afghan border.

In Babukarra, their territory is bounded on the north by the Hindu Raj, which divides it from Asmar, and on the east, the Takwara spur, running from the Trepaman Sar to the Shinkas peak above Mian Kilai, separates it from Jandol. On the west is the Mamund valley, and to the south lies the country of the Shamozai Utman Khel, on the right bank of the Bajaur river. The valley is about fifteen miles in length with an average width of five or six miles. At Ragha two forts, built by the Khan of Nawagai, on either side of a narrow gorge, guard the entrance from the south. About eight miles further north, near the chief village of Pashat, the valley divides into two branches. The eastern, or Batwar Nala runs up to the Trepaman pass, over which a difficult route leads into Asmar. The western branch, called the Loegram Darra, runs up to the Loegram pass, 7,750 feet. The easiest route from Jandol or the Babukarra valley is over this pass. Numerous paths lead into the Jandol valley, the best being over the Takwara or Rashakai Kotal to Mundah.

In this valley the Salarzai are divided into divisions called Madak and Sadin, which are again sub-divided into Upper and Lower, or Bar and Lar. In the lower valley, the Lar Madak are on the west, and the Lar Sadin on the east; in the upper portion the Bar Madak lands lie to the east and the Bar Sadin to the west. These divisions are distinct from the usual division into Khels.

The Chaharmung valley lies between the Mamund country on the north-east, and the Kamangara valley on the south-west, being divided from the latter by a spur which juts out in a south-easterly direction from the Nawa peak. From the southern end of this ridge, a line drawn across the valley through Kotkai and Tangai forms the boundary of the Khan of Nawagai's territory in this valley. The Salarzai in these two villages, and others to the south, own allegiance to the *Khan* and pay revenue to him, but the portion of the valley above this line is inhabited by the Saad-ud-din and Ahmad Din sub-sections of the Salarzai, who are independent.

The Khan Khel of the Salarzai is the Ibrahim Khel, to which belong the *Nawabs* or *Khans* of Nawagai, and the *Khans* of Khar, Jhar, Asmar, and Pashat (in Babukarra), who exercise a kind of feudal right over the rest of the Salarzai clans.

The Mamunds.

The Mamunds, the last and most important of the four sections of the Tarkanri tribe, inhabit the Mamund or Watelai valley, which lies between the two Salarzai valleys of Chaharmung and Babukarra. Like the Salarzai, the Mamunds also own lands in Shortan and Marawara, in the Kunar valley of Afghanistan. From the Lakra range, which forms its north-western boundary, a spur jutting out near Lakra Sar (9,370 feet) runs south-east, and divides the main Watelai Nala from a western branch called the Kakazai Nala. To the east of the Watelai, the valley is known as Wur Mamund, and to the west as Kakazai Mamund country.

The valley is about thirteen miles in length with a maximum breadth of ten miles, and is open and well cultivated, but much cut up by deep dry *nalas*. Considerable quantities of wheat, barley, and *bhusa* are obtainable, and small autumn crops of Indian corn and *jowar* are raised; firewood, however, is scarce.

The main *nala* is waterless above Inayat Kila, except when rains or melted snow send a freshet from the hills. The people in the open valley obtain water from tanks and wells. The principal villages are at the head of the valley close under the hills, where a good water-supply from springs is available.

Roads fit for pack transport lead up the valley, and branch off to all the villages. For about eight miles above Inayat Kila, the main route, though difficult, is practicable for field artillery. From Khalozai there are two routes along the Upper Watelai and the Kakazai Nala to the Kaga and Hindu Raj passes, which give access to Shortan and Marawara in the Kunar valley. The first of these passes is a mere foot-track, while the second is only practicable for lightly laden animals. Camping-grounds, suitable for a brigade of all arms, exist at Khalozai and Zagaderai, on either side of the Watelai Nala, five or six miles above Inayat Kila.

From the village of Tanai southward the valley is claimed by the *Khan* of Nawagai as part of his territory.

The Mamunds are said to muster 12,000 fighting men, all possessing fire-arms. They are perhaps the most warlike of the Tarkanri sections.

The position of the Khan or Nawab of Nawagai is somewhat peculiar. He is the head of the Ibrahim Khel Salarzai, but is also recognized as the hereditary chieftain of the whole Tarkanri tribe. In former days all sections of the tribe owned allegiance to the chief of the ruling family of Nawagai, but owing to internal dissensions the authority of the Khan as supreme ruler has greatly diminished. Although, however, the direct rule of the present Nawab is limited to a comparatively small area, and his authority over part of the territory claimed by him is only nominal, he still exercises considerable influence over the whole tribe, especially in matters of foreign policy. His influence also extends to other neighbouring tribes beyond the border of Bajaur, such as the Safis of the Kandahari plain, the Dawezai Mohmands of Pipal, and the Mandal, Alizai, and But Khel sections of the Utman Khel.

The Khan of Nawagai.

The actual territory of the Nawab of Nawagai is an irregular tract of country on the left bank of the Rud river, and the district of Surkamar. The boundary of the Rud river strip runs across the lower ends of the Chaharmung, Mamund, and Babukarra valleys, and has been a constant source of strife between the Nawagai Chief and the Salarzai and Mamund tribesmen who inhabit them.

In Surkamar the people are Mohmands, Safis and Shinwaris, the last of whom occupy the Chamarkand valley.

The Mitai and Suran valleys belonged in former days to the Tarkanri tribe, and were inhabited by Safi and Shinwari tenants, who paid tithe to the Tarkanri chief. Many years ago the Mohmands expelled these settlers and took possession of the two valleys, but they refused to own allegiance to the Khan of Nawagai, who claimed them as subjects, on the ground that they had immigrated into his territory. The Mohmands were supported by the Afghan Government in maintaining their independence of Nawagai, and after continuing the struggle for some years with varying fortune the Khan in 1899 finally abandoned the attempt to recover his possession in Mitai and Suran.[1] The Safis are all greatly under the influence of the Khan of Nawagai, and those who hold lands north of Lakarai may be considered as his subjects.

In addition to the two chief tribes of Dir and Bajaur described above, the following alien or non-Pathan races may be mentioned :—

Alien races.

The Bashkaris, who, like the Torwals and Garhis of Swat Kohistan, are probably descendants of races which peopled these countries before the Pathan invasion. These are found in the upper portion of the Panjkora Kohistan known as Bashkar.

The Mashwani, whose origin is doubtful, but who may possibly be akin to the Mashwani tribe of Afghanistan, are found in the Jandol and Maidan valleys, where they live as tenants of the Tarkanris.

The Sheikh Khel, Mandizai, Senzai, and Khwazazai in Jandol and the Haramzai and Shaibzai in the Maidan valley, are said to be of Kafir descent, but have now become Muhammadans, and are recognized as Pathans. The Rogani, Katni, and Guroh, who are of similar stock, are found in various parts of Dir. Gujars are also to be found in considerable numbers in all parts of the country.

The people of Dir and Bajaur are all Sunni Muhammadans. Though extremely bigoted they are probably far more superstitious than really religious ; and though not individually fanatical, like so many of the more southern Pathan tribes, they are extremely susceptible to the baneful influence of their *mullas*, who are able to excite among them a collective fanaticism to an extraordinary degree.

The country is infested by priests and religious communities, who make a handsome profit out of the ignorant and superstitious pilgrims to the numerous shrines. In addition to the *Saiyids*, or descendants of the Prophet, the other religious classes are *Sahibzadas*, descendants of well-known *mullas* ; *Mians*, descendants of saints and spiritual leaders ; and *Akhundzadas*, or *Pirzadas*, descendants of saints of merely local or tribal reputation.

In 1895 the most influential priest was the Hadda Mulla, Najm Ud Din who lived in Mohmand country, and whose career is described in Chapter XI. He was recalled to Afghanistan by the Amir in 1901 and died in 1903, when he was succeeded by Mir

[1] See Chapter XI, page 492.

Sahib Jan Badshah. A follower of the Hadda Mulla called Palam Baba has nowadays considerable influence in Dir, and is said to be bitterly opposed to the British.

The principal shrines are Sheo Baba at Hariankot near Dir, Khan Shahid, in Baraul, and Bibi Sahiba at Maiar in Jandol.

In character the people of Dir and Bajaur closely resemble the other Pathan tribes, though perhaps, in common with the Swatis, they excel them in treachery. A marked characteristic of the people of Dir, which is also shared by the Swat tribes, is a stern sense of discipline, which enables their leaders to exercise a control far more complete and effective than is usual among Pathan communities. This spirit of discipline also exists among the Bajauris, but to a much less degree than among the people above mentioned.

It is by the aid of this discipline that their leaders are enabled to incite these people to display that dangerous collective fanaticism which has already been mentioned as a notable trait in their character.

The Tarkanri, and more especially the Mamunds, have a rather higher reputation as a fighting tribe than the Akozai-Yusafzais of Swat and Dir, but these latter, as they have proved on the occasions when we have come into contact with them, are by no means to be despised.

The number of fighting men in Dir and Bajaur is estimated to be at the present time as under—

Dir—

Talash valley and Dush Khel	2,500
Malizai tribes (Akozai-Yusafzai) in Panjkora valley	26,500
Panjkora Kohistanis	5,200
Tarkanris	6,000
Khwazazai (*see* Upper Swat tribes)	11,150
Total ..	51,350

Bajaur —

Salarzai	8,000
Mamunds, Watelai valley	12,000
Other Tarkanris and tribesmen in Nawagai-Surkamar, including Mohmands, Safis, Shinwaris, etc.	10,000
Total ..	30,000

In the event of a general fanatical rising, the people of Dir and Bajaur would almost certainly be able to reckon on assistance from the Baizai and Ranizai of Upper and Lower Swat, who muster about 9,000 and 7,000 fighting men respectively, the Baizai clans of the Indus valley with 4,500 fighting men, and the Utman Khel to the number of 9,000. The Bunerwals also might have to be reckoned with. Although it is unlikely that the whole of these tribes and sections could simultaneously combine to fight as a single force, still it is not impossible that a religious war or a threatened invasion of their country might induce all to take up arms at one and the same time.

As will be seen in the account of the attack on the Malakand and Chakdara in July 1897 (*see* Chapter IX) nearly 20,000 men were able to collect with surprising secrecy and suddenness.

The system of land tenure in Dir and Bajaur is similar to that which holds good in Swat and Utman Khel country. When the Pathan tribes originally occupied these countries, all the land was divided up, and each section was allotted a portion, called *daftar* or *tappa*. Each *tappa* was then again portioned out among the sub-sections or *Khels*, whose individual members each received a share called *brakha*. All such shareholders are termed *daftari*.

Certain portions of the land have also been given as free grants (*seri*) to chiefs or tribal *jirgas*, but more usually to religious communities. These are often disputed lands which, if held by ordinary *daftaris*, would be a constant source of disturbance.

With the exception of *seri* grants, all land is subject to a peculiar system of periodical redistribution, called *khusanre* or *vesh*, which takes place at intervals of five, ten, fifteen or twenty years, according to local custom. This system, which applies to individual *daftaris* and to whole villages, is thoroughly bad in every way, since it naturally leads to interminable quarrels and disputes, and under it no man is willing to expend money or labour on the permanent improvement of his holding.

Both Dir and Bajaur are divided into numerous small *khanates* held by hereditary *khans*, or by nominees of the feudal chief, that is to say, at the present time the Khan of Dir in the case of Dir, and the Khan of Nawagai in Bajaur. In 1895, as has been already mentioned, Umra Khan of Jandol had established himself as paramount chief of all the country of Dir and a considerable part of Bajaur.

Revenue or *ushar* to the amount of one-tenth of the produce of the land is usually paid by *daftaris* to these minor *Khans* or to the ruling chief. The *khans*, who form a sort of aristocratic class, maintain two kinds of retainers, *viz.*, (1) *tiarkhor*, who are personal servants and receive food, clothing, and wife; (*ii*) *malatirs*, fighting men, partially trained, who are given houses and land near posts where they are stationed as guards or police.

The rule of the *khans* does not appear to interfere with the communal system of government by *jirga*, which is universal throughout these countries, and the system of which is as follows:—

The management of all matters relating to a village rests with the village council—*jirga*. Each village was originally represented in the *jirga* of its *khel*, each *khel* in that of its sub-division, and each sub-division in the *jirga* of the whole tribe. This system still holds good, except that it has been modified by one of party government, which has since come into existence. In each village there are two or more political parties (*dalla*) each represented by its own *jirga*. The party who by numbers or influence are the stronger are in power (*bande dalla*), and their *jirga* for the time being rule all matters concerning the village, administer justice, and control the village revenues. The party in opposition (*lande dalla*) have to bow to the will of the party in office, until such time as they can challenge the government. A few days' contest, generally accompanied by fighting, settles the matter one way or other, and the winners settle themselves in office. The same party system prevails throughout the whole tribe, and, according to the results of the village parliamentary contests, varies the power of the party *jirga* in the higher tribal councils. All these matters are regulated by an unwritten, but widely recognized, code of constitutional law.

This system of party government which is similar to that in Swat, Utman Khel, and Sam Ranizai, obtains throughout Dir and Bajaur, though it is somewhat modified in certain localities owing to the growth of an aristocracy belonging to the families of the numerous *khans* and petty chiefs.

An account of the rise of Umra Khan of Jandol (grandson of Faiz Talab Khan) and of his connection with Chitral affairs has been already given in Chapter II. By the end of the year 1893 this chief had established his authority over the whole of the districts of Jandol, Dir (including the Maidan and Baraul valleys), the Talash valley, and the territories of the Dush Khel and Adinzai. He had also invaded the disputed district of Narsat and occupied the villages of Nari and Sao. The tract of country which Umra Khan had brought under his control thus extended from the Dir-Chitral border in the north to the Swat river in the south, and included the whole of Dir, the greater part of Bajaur, and a portion of Swat. The Khan of Nawagai, for many years actively hostile to Umra Khan, had now made peace and entered into an alliance with his former enemy. Muhammad Sharif, the Khan of Dir, had been expelled from his former possessions and had sought refuge in Upper Swat.

The Chitral Relief Expedition under Lieutenant-General Sir Robert Low, K.C.B., in 1895.

It has already been mentioned in Chapter II that in consequence of the disturbed state of affairs in Chitral, and the dangers which threatened the British Agent and his escort interned in that place, the Government of India had, on the 14th March, ordered the mobilization of a division, in case it should be necessary to use force to compel Umra Khan's compliance with their demand that he should withdraw from that country.

On the 21st March news reached India of the attacks on the detachments under Captain Ross and Lieutenant Edwardes between Mastuj and Chitral. Thereupon the Government, recognizing that the Jandol Chief and the Chitralis had taken the initiative and entered on active hostilities, issued orders for the immediate despatch of the relieving force from India.

Peshawar had been selected as the base of operations, but, owing to the inconvenient nature of the communications between that place and Hoti Mardan, the base was moved to Nowshera. This alteration necessitated the construction of new railway sidings, and some amendment of the programme of concentration. The 1st division was selected for mobilization, as being the nearest to the theatre of operations; but some modifications were made, owing to the absence of certain units in Waziristan, and the fact that the full complement of cavalry and wheeled artillery was not required. The detail of troops composing the Chitral Relief Force was as follows :—

1ST INFANTRY BRIGADE.

Commanding—Brigadier-General A. A. Kinloch, C.B.

1st Battalion, Bedfordshire Regiment.
1st „ King's Royal Rifle Corps.
15th Sikhs.
37th Dogras.
No. 1 British Field Hospital.
„ 14 Native „ „

2ND INFANTRY BRIGADE.

Commanding—Brigadier-General H. C. Waterfield.

2nd Battalion, King's Own Scottish Borderers.
1st Battalion, Gordon Highlanders.
4th Sikh Infantry.
Guides Infantry.
No. 2 British Field Hospital.
„ 35 Native „ „

3RD INFANTRY BRIGADE.

Commanding—Brigadier-General W. F. Gatacre, D.S.O.

1st Battalion, East Kent Regiment.
2nd „ Seaforth Highlanders.
25th Punjab Infantry.
2nd Battalion, 4th Gurkha Rifles.
No. 8 British Field Hospital.
„ 19 Native „ „

DIVISIONAL TROOPS.[1]

11th Bengal Lancers.
Guides Cavalry.
13th Bengal Infantry.
23rd Punjab Pioneers.
15th Field Battery, Royal Artillery.
No. 3 Mountain Battery, Royal Artillery.
No. 8 Mountain Battery, Royal Artillery.
No. 2 (Derajat) Mountain Battery, 4 guns.
No. 1 Company Bengal Sappers and Miners.
„ 4 „ „ „ „ „
„ 6 „ „ „ „ „
Engineer Field Park, from Roorkee.
No. 4 British Field Hospital, A and B Sections.
Nos. 17 and 18, Native Field Hospitals.
No. 1 Veterinary Field Hospital.
1 Maxim gun and detachment, 1st Battalion, Devonshire Regiment.

LINES OF COMMUNICATION TROOPS.[2]

1st Battalion, East Lancashire Regt.
29th Punjab Infantry.
30th „ „
No. 4 (Hazara) Mountain Battery.
„ 4 British Field Hospital, C and D Sections.
No. 24 Native „ „
No. 2 Veterinary Field Hospital.
Field Medical Store Depôt.
British General Hospital, Peshawar.
Native „ „ „
½ General Veterinary Hospital, Umballa.
½ Base „ Store Depôt, Umballa.
Ordnance Field Park, Rawal Pindi.

1 The 34th Punjab Pioneers were mobilized towards the end of the month and joined the Divisional Troops in order to assist in the probable road-making requirements of the force.

2 About the 9th of April the General Officer Commanding the Force was empowered to draw upon the 9th Bengal Lancers, then at Hoti Mardan, for such additional cavalry as might be required on the lines of communication ; and No. 6 Company, Madras Sappers and Miners, were placed at the disposal of the Officer Commanding the lines of communication to assist in bridging the Swat river.

Nos. 5 and 6, British Field Hospitals „ 28 and 29 Native Field Hospitals	For sick and wounded returning from the front.

RESERVE BRIGADE.

Commanding—Major-Geneal G. N. Channer, V.C., C.B.

No. 7 (Bengal) Mountain Battery.	Sections C and D, No. 3 British Field Hospital.
3rd Battalion, Rifle Brigade.	
26th Punjab Infantry.	Sections A and B, No. 25 Native Field Hospital.
2nd Battalion, 1st Gurkha Rifles.	
„ „ 3rd „ „	No. 31 Native Field Hospital.

MOVEABLE COLUMN (ABBOTTABAD).

No. 8 (Bengal) Mountain Battery.	2nd Battalion, 5th Gurkha Rifles.
2nd Battalion, 2nd Gurkha Rifles.	A and B Sections, No. 26 Native Field Hospital.

The above details proceeded on the Field Service scale of strength, establishments, etc., as laid down in the Field Service Equipment Tables for the different branches, except that the number of British Officers with regiments of native cavalry and infantry were not increased above the peace establishment.

Railway concentration commenced on 26th March, and in seventeen days from the order to mobilize, 15,000 troops, rather more than half that number of followers, and 20,000 transport animals had been concentrated at Hoti Mardan and Nowshera, while, during the same period, about forty days' supplies for the whole force had been collected at and beyond the base.

The provision of suitable transport for the force was a matter of great difficulty, since, owing to the mountainous character of the country through which it was to advance, it was necessary to make use almost exclusively of pack animals. All available Government mules were collected, and a large number of animals were purchased and hired. Eventually 30,669 animals were procured for pack transport, representing a carrying power of 103,238 maunds.

The services of the Gwalior and Jeypore (Imperial Service) Transport Corps were also accepted.

Numerous other offers of Imperial Service troops were made, but the Government were unable to accept them, as they did not consider the occasion one of sufficient importance.

The following statement of the objects of the expedition was published in Government General Order No. 324, dated the 29th March 1895:—

Umra Khan, the Chief of Jandol, in spite of his oft-repeated assurances of friendship to the British Government, and regardless of frequent warnings to refrain from interfering with the affairs of Chitral, which is a protected State under the suzerainty of Kashmir, has forcibly entered the Chitral valley and attacked the Chitral people. He has failed to explain his attitude when asked to do so, or to withdraw when required, and, as he has disregarded all remonstrances, the Chitral Relief Force will be despatched against him.

The first object of the expedition is to relieve Chitral territory from invasion by Umra Khan, and assure it against such aggression in future. The force will advance into Swat, and thence proceed, as strategic and political considerations may show to be best, to the territory of Umra Khan, so as to coerce him into putting an end to the pressure placed by him upon the town and country of Chitral. If this object cannot be effected without passing through Bajaur and Dir, and attacking Umra Khan in Chitral territory, that course will be adopted, and should Umra Khan not make submission and reparation, he will be punished. If further measures for the relief and reinforcement of the British officers now in Chitral are necessary, the force will advance to Chitral to effect that object.

Every possible means will be taken to make known to the people of the countries on the Peshawar border that the reasons and objects of the expedition are as above set forth, and that the only cause of quarrel is with Umra Khan and with those who have supported him in committing aggression upon Chitral and defying the lawful authority of the Government of India. As little interference as possible will be permitted in the country through which the troops have to pass in order to reach the objective of the force, and neighbouring tracts will be untouched unless the people offer opposition or show active hostility. The length of time during which the force will remain across the border must depend on its having thoroughly assured the object to the expedition.

Our quarrel being, as stated above, only with Umra Khan of Jandol and the tribesmen who had joined him, every endeavour was made to secure the neutrality of the other independent tribes through whose territory the British force required to pass. On the 17th March a proclamation in the following terms had been sent to all the tribes concerned:—

To all the people of Swat and the people in Bajaur who do not side with Umra Khan.

Be it known to you, and any other persons concerned, that:—

Umra Khan, the Chief of Jandol, in spite of his often-repeated assurances of friendship to the British Government, and regardless of frequent warnings to refrain from interfering with the affairs of Chitral, which is a protected State under the suzerainty of Kashmir, has forcibly entered the Chitral valley and attacked the Chitrali people.

The Government of India have now given Umra Khan full warning that, unless he retires from Chitral by the 1st of April, corresponding with the 5th day of Shawal 1302 H., they will use force to compel him to do so. In order to carry out this purpose, they have arranged to assemble on the Peshawar border a force of sufficient strength to overcome all resistance, and to march this force through Umra Khan's territory towards Chitral.

The sole object of the Government of India is to put an end to the present, and prevent any future, unlawful aggression on Chitral territory, and, as soon as this object has been attained, the force will be withdrawn.

The Government of India have no intention of permanently occupying any territory through which Umra Khan's misconduct may now force them to pass, or of interfering with the independence of the tribes; and they will scrupulously avoid any acts of hostility towards the tribesmen so long as they on their part refrain from attacking or impeding in any way the march of the troops. Supplies and transport will be paid for, and all persons are at liberty to pursue their ordinary avocations in perfect security.

The Sam Ranizai consented to the passage of the British force through their country, and the *Khans* of the Khan Khel Baizai and of the Ranizai in Lower Swat endeavoured to restrain their people from any act of hostility. The attitude of the Manki Mulla, who had much influence in Swat and Utman Khel country, was doubtful, but a misunderstanding between him and the Mian Guls, grandsons of the Akhund, prevented the Upper Swatis from combining against us.

In return for a yearly subsidy of Rs. 12,000, and a present of 1,000 rifles, Safdar Khan, the Khan of Nawagai, agreed to use his influence over the Tarkanri tribesmen to induce them to keep the peace, and promised to furnish supplies and render assistance to the troops. He subsequently failed, however, to keep to the terms of his agreement, and contented himself with maintaining a neutral attitude, being probably fearful of the resentment of the Amir and the vengeance of Umra Khan, when the British should again withdraw from the country.

The *maliks* and leading men among the Bunerwals, Utman Khel and Mohmands also appeared anxious to restrain their people from joining in a quarrel which in no way concerned them.

On the 30th March, the Divisional Head-quarters, with the 2nd and 3rd Brigades, moved to Hoti Mardan from Nowshera, and were followed by the 1st Brigade on the 31st. Divisional troops were now allotted to brigades as under :—

1st Brigade.—11th Bengal Lancers ; No. 3 Mountain Battery, Royal Artillery ; No. 4 Company, Bengal Sappers and Miners.

2nd Brigade.—1 squadron, Guides Cavalry ; No. 8 Mountain Battery, Royal Artillery ; No. 1 Company, Bengal Sappers and Miners.

3rd Brigade.—1 squadron, Guides Cavalry ; No. 2 (Derajat) Mountain Battery ; No. 6 Company, Bengal Sappers and Miners.

One squadron of the Guides Cavalry was transferred to the lines of communication troops.

The 1st and 2nd Brigades had been ordered to take over twenty days' supplies for men and five days' grain for animals, and to maintain this supply intact as long as possible. The 1st Brigade was to be equipped with mule transport, the 2nd with mules and camels, and the 3rd with camels and carts; all corps, however, retained their obligatory mule transport.

No tents, except those for hospital use, were taken, and the allowance of personal baggage was 40lb for officers, 20lb for British soldiers, and 10lb for native soldiers.

On the 30th March, the following telegram from the Commander-in-Chief in India was communicated to the troops :—

I would like you to publish to the Chitral Field Force, before they march off, the following order addressed from me to you and them in wishing you and the force under your command the success upon which so much depends. I can best describe the importance and sanctity of the Mission on which the country now sends you forth by quoting the words in which His Excellency the Viceroy referred to it in Council on Thursday last. His Excellency said :— 'For the present we have before us a single issue, the claim of brave men, British and Indian, who have not flinched in the performance of their duty, to the support of their countrymen in their hour of need. It is a claim that I believe will go straight home to every British and Indian heart, and will inspire our councils with unanimity, and will quicken the steps of every man whose duty calls him forth on this expedition.'

On the 1st April Sir R. Low, with the 2nd and 3rd Brigades, marched to Jalala, while the 1st Brigade pushed on to Lundkwar. It was the intention of the General to advance into the Swat valley over the Malakand and Shakot passes, and to avoid the Morah pass, the use of which might arouse the susceptibilities of the Buner tribesmen on his right flank.

Late in the day, however, notwithstanding the supposed friendly attitude of the border tribes previously mentioned, it was reported that all three passes were held by tribesmen who intended to oppose our advance. The Morah and Shakot passes were said to be defended by 13,000 and 6,000 men, respectively, while only some 300 were believed to be holding the Malakand. In consequence of this information Sir Robert Low now decided to make a feint with his cavalry towards the Shakot, and to advance with the rest of his force by the Malakand, making a forced march that night to Dargai with the 2nd and 3rd Brigades. This plan had to be modified owing to heavy rain, which prevented the troops from moving before daybreak; all three brigades, however, concentrated at the foot of the Malakand pass by 8 A.M. on the 2nd April, and Lieutenant Cockerill, Intelligence Officer, with a company of the Guides, reconnoitred the enemy's position.

The road to the pass, after leaving Dargai, lay north-east for two miles up a gradually narrowing valley to the foot of the Malakand hills; then, turning north-west and leaving the bed of the valley, it ascended very steeply by zigzags to the crest, which was gained near a small village; from this, one track descended northwards into the Swat valley direct, and another, after running north-east for nearly three quarters of a mile along the east side of the ridge and just below the crest, crossed by a rocky cutting through a gap in the hills, and, descending, joined the other track. North-east of this gap, precipitous hills, which rise to a height of over 4,400 feet, formed the left of the enemy's position; while to the south-west of the village mentioned above, the crest of the range, sloping very steeply upwards, culminates in three peaks nearly 4,000 feet in height, on which the right of the enemy's position rested. The whole of the intervening ridge, including the village, was held in force, and thus the position to be attacked was over two miles in length.

It was the intention of the General Officer Commanding to force the pass with the 2nd Brigade, and then push forward the 1st Brigade, which was equipped entirely with mule transport, as far as the Swat river. Accordingly at 8 A.M. on the 3rd April the

2nd Brigade, under General Waterfield, advanced from Dargai in the order shewn in the margin. Each unit was accompanied by the 1st reserve ammunition, and the men carried their greatcoats and half a day's rations. The remainder of the baggage was left at Dargai, under small regimental guards, to follow later.

Order of March :—*2nd Brigade.*
Guides Cavalry, 1 squadron. } Advanced Guard.
" Infantry, 2 companies. }
Maxim gun detachment. }
Remainder of Guides Infantry.
3 Mountain Batteries.
Sappers and Miners, 3 companies.
King's Own Scottish Borderers.
Gordon Highlanders.
4th Sikhs ; rear-guard of 1 company.

The 1st Brigade marched off from Shakot village at 7 A.M. and followed the 2nd, while the 3rd Brigade was held in reserve at Dargai.

The plan of attack by the 2nd Brigade was as follows :—The 4th Sikhs and Guides Infantry were to scale the hills on the enemy's right and turn their position west of the pass, while the remaining battalions advanced up the valley supported by the fire of the three mountain batteries, which were to take up a preliminary position on a ridge marked A in plan.

On reaching a bend of the valley a little to the westward of the first artillery position, the 4th Sikhs began to ascend the spur on their left, while the Guides, after continuing up the *nala* for about half a mile, climbed a parallel spur on the right of the Sikhs, which rose steeply some 2,000 feet above the plain. Both these spurs were defended by the enemy's marksmen, who were posted in numerous *sangars* commanding the ascent, while numbers of the tribesmen, who were not in possession of fire-arms, were held in readiness to hurl down rocks and stones on the advancing troops.

The three mountain batteries, which were brigaded under command of Major J. Dacres-Cunningham, finding the range too great for effective fire, now advanced to a second position, marked B on plan. From here they shelled the *sangars* opposed to the flank attack of the Guides and 4th Sikhs, as well as the defences which stretched southwards in tiers below the pass itself. The ranges varied from 2,300 to 2,800 yards.

The remainder of the infantry now pushed on up the valley, passing ahead of the guns and cavalry. About noon Brigadier-General Waterfield, realizing that the turning movement was likely to be delayed by the difficulty of the ascent and by the stubborn

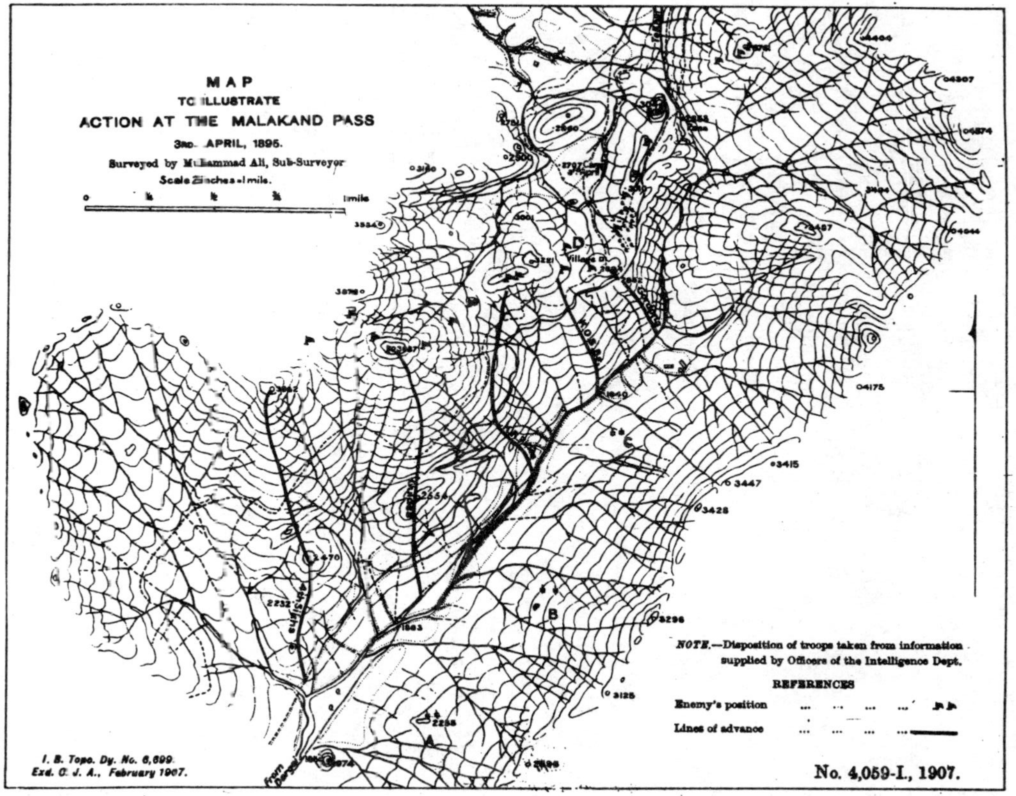
MAP
TO ILLUSTRATE
ACTION AT THE MALAKAND PASS
3RD APRIL, 1895.
Surveyed by Muhammad Ali, Sub-Surveyor
Scale 2 inches = 1 mile.
0
1mile
NOTE.—Disposition of troops taken from information supplied by Officers of the Intelligence Dept.
REFERENCES
Enemy's position
Lines of advance
A
B
C
D
Village D.
4th Sikhs
3415
3447
3428
3296
3125
2256
2232
2470
1863
1840
2554
3534
3876
4175
4307
4874
4644
4404
3487
2850
2500
3001
I. B. Topo. Dy. No. 6,699.
Exd. C. J. A., February 1907.
From Dargai
No. 4,059-I., 1907.

resistance of the defenders, decided to begin his frontal attack. Accordingly the King's Own Scottish Borderers, who had reached a point of the valley just north of C (*vide* plan), advanced up three separate spurs to attack the village marked D. The approach to the village, which appeared to be the key of this portion of the position, was over very steep, rugged ground, covered with low scrub jungle and commanded by several *sangars*. The Gordons moved some 600 or 700 yards further up the *nala*, and then sent four companies up a spur on the right of the Borderers, the remainder subsequently advancing still further to their right towards the crest east of the village. The maxim guns also accompanied the advance of these two battalions. Meanwhile, the artillery, having advanced to the close support of the infantry attack, came into action on the slope marked C, and opened fire at ranges of 1,000 to 1,400 yards.

The whole of the 2nd Brigade having been now launched to the attack, Sir Robert Low called up the 1st Brigade to support them. The 60th King's Royal Rifles were sent up the hill between the Guides and the King's Own Scottish Borderers, while the Bedfords and 37th Dogras, passing in rear of the Gordons, attacked the enemy's extreme left, which they overlapped considerably. The 15th Sikhs formed the reserve.

The Gordons and King's Own Scottish Borderers, well supported by the fire of the mountain batteries, which prevented the enemy from concentrating or reinforcing weak points, captured *sangar* after *sangar*, in spite of the dogged resistance of the defenders, and pushed their way steadily up the hillside. As they neared the summit a short halt was made, to collect the men; the advance was then sounded and the position was carried at the point of the bayonet by a simultaneous rush of the Gordons, King's Own Scottish Borderers, and 60th Rifles. The 4th Sikhs and the Guides having fought their way up the hill reached the crest on the enemy's right at the same time. The Sappers and Miners, following close on the fighting line, set to work to improve the rough track up the pass.

The action had lasted for about five hours, during which the enemy were under shell fire from sixteen guns. In holding on to their position to the very end, and standing up to the final bayonet charge, the tribesmen gave proof of the possession of fighting qualities of which the people of this part of the frontier had not hitherto been suspected.

The Bedfords and 37th Dogras pursued the enemy as far as Khar, where they bivouacked for the night, rejoining their Brigade on the pass the next morning. The 4th Sikhs passed the night on the ridge about a mile west of the pass, while the remainder of the 2nd Brigade returned to Dargai.

The enemy's strength was estimated at about 12,000 men; the number armed with fire-arms was at first supposed to have been 3,000, but was afterwards found to have been considerably greater. Their losses amounted to some 500 killed (the Swatis themselves admitting a loss of 300), but the number of wounded, among whom was an important leader called Sheikh Yamin, was not ascertained. It was noticed that the wounds inflicted by the Lee-Metford rifle, which was used by the British troops for the first time, were in many cases extremely slight; and the small bullet appeared to have insufficient stopping power when used against a semi-civilized or savage enemy.

On the British side eleven were killed and fifty-one wounded, including eight British and two native officers; 16,563 rounds of Lee-Metford and Martini-Henri ammunition were expended during the action, and the artillery fired 115 ring shell and 331 shrapnel.

During their advance, when about half-way up the hill, the 60th Rifles had come upon the remains of an old disused Buddhist road. This proved to be well aligned, and must originally have been most substantially built. After two days' work it was sufficiently repaired to allow of the passage of camel transport, and thus greatly facilitated the task of forwarding supplies.

At 1 P.M. on the 4th April the 1st Brigade moved down from the pass towards the Swat valley. The 2nd Brigade was ordered up to the top of the pass, and the 3rd Brigade remained at Dargai pending the passage over the Malakand of the baggage and supplies of the other two brigades.

As the advanced guard of the 1st Brigade, consisting of No. 4 Company, Bengal Sappers and Miners, and the Bedfordshire Regiment, under Lieut.-Colonel Patterson, approached the village of Piran, two miles south of Khar, the enemy was observed in considerable numbers on the hills north and north-east, on the right of the road. Lieut.-Colonel Patterson promptly occupied the heights on either side of the road commanding the passage of the defile. No. 3 Mountain Battery, Royal Artillery, coming up opened fire from the Piran spur just north of the village, and cleared the enemy from the low hills about 1,000 yards to the north, and checked their advance along the eastern ridge towards the pass.

The 37th Dogras, with one company, 15th Sikhs, were now moved forward, and drove the enemy off a low hill one mile south of Khar village, which formed the extreme right of their position and commanded the exit from the defile. After having followed the enemy for a short distance on to the open ground beyond, the Dogras were directed to fall back and hold this hill.

The guns had meanwhile advanced to a ridge on the west of the road and half a mile north-west of Piran, and the remainder of the infantry deployed below them. The enemy now made several attempts to retake the hill occupied by the Dogras, charging close up to the position, supported by the fire of their marksmen on the higher ridge to the south-east. The Dogras, however, with the company of the 15th Sikhs and No. 4 Company, Bengal Sappers and Miners, which had been sent to reinforce them, steadily repulsed each successive attack, inflicting considerable loss on their assailants.

The remainder of the Brigade, having again advanced about half a mile, once more deployed to cover the passage of the baggage. Towards evening a number of the enemy, leaving the ridge opposite the main body of the British Brigade, moved round the left flank of the Dogras' position. Here they were charged by two troops of the Guides Cavalry under Captain Adams which had just made their way across the pass, and had been sent forward to the attack by Brigadier-General Kinloch. Advancing over heavy cultivated ground intersected with *nalas*, the two troops resolutely attacked the enemy, who numbered some 1,200, cutting down thirty and driving the remainder in headlong flight to the hills.

The enemy numbered between 5,000 and 6,000 men, being mainly tribesmen who had come over from the Morah and Shakot passes in the hopes of being in time to assist the defenders of the Malakand. Their loss in killed alone was estimated at 600, of whom 350 belonged to the Swat valley. The casualties in the 1st Brigade were two killed and eighteen wounded.

The 1st Brigade bivouacked for the night close to Khar. On the morning of the 5th April nothing was seen of the enemy in the neighbourhood of the camp. The 1st Brigade halted at Khar, and was joined by the 2nd Brigade, less the Gordon Highlanders, who remained on the Malakand Kotal. Two squadrons of the Guides, accompanied by Brigadier-General Blood, Chief Staff Officer, moved up the Swat valley and reconnoitred the river opposite Chakdara. This village and the fort of Ramora, some two miles higher up, were seen to be undefended, but a body of men estimated at 3,000 strong was observed just beyond Thana, the chief village of Swat, situated at the foot of the hills on the left bank between two and three miles from the Chakdara fords. The people of Thana were warned that unless the gathering dispersed at once, troops would be sent against them.

Some of the leading men of the Adinzai valley, who had crossed the river to interview the British officers, were assured that their people would not be interfered with unless they opposed our advance. In the evening the *khans* and headmen of Thana and some men from Aladand came in and made professions of friendship. The tribesmen who had collected near Thana moved away from the village, but only to occupy a position commanding the approach to the river, whence they retired next day some four miles higher up the valley.

It may here be mentioned that Muhammad Sharif Khan, the ex-ruler of Dir, who since his expulsion by Umra Khan had sought a refuge at Mingaora in Upper Swat, had been interviewed by the Political Officer at Dargai, and had offered to assist the British force. Although the Government could not undertake any responsibility for the maintenance of his authority after the withdrawal of the troops from the country, he was promised aid in the shape of arms and money, and was encouraged by the prospect of recovering possession of his former territories. On the 5th April the Khan was permitted to cross the Swat river with the intention of raising the clans who still sided with him against Umra Khan.

Shortly after, it was reported that he had secured all the forts along the Panjkora and Maidan routes and had attacked the fort of Dir. This alliance with the Khan of Dir subsequently secured for our troops an unopposed passage through the Baraul and Dir valleys. It also prevented opposition from the powerful Malizai and Khwazazai clans of the Panjkora valley and the western portion of Upper Swat.

On the 6th, the 11th Bengal Lancers marched over the Malakand pass to Khar. The 2nd Brigade made a demonstration as far as Thana, and after marching through the village moved back to camp near Aladand.

No enemy was seen on the right bank of the river, but in the evening it was reported that a large force of Umra Khan's personal followers under the command of his brother, Muhammad Shah Khan, and occupied Chakdara and Ramora.

Early on the morning of the 7th April Major F. J. Aylmer, V.C., R.E., with No. 4 Company, Bengal Sappers and Miners, and one company from both the King's Own Scottish Borderers and the 4th Sikhs, was ordered to reconnoitre the river bank and select a site for a bridge. Captain Barton with one squadron of the Guides was sent at the same time to watch the enemy who had been seen above Thana on the previous day.

On approaching the river Major Aylmer's party was fired on from the hills on the opposite side. It was now seen that the enemy were holding the villages of Dalbar and Chakdara and a spur west of the latter village, thus commanding the low-lying open ground on the left bank. The fort of Ramora and surrounding villages were also occupied by armed parties of the enemy. Leaving two companies to guard the camp at Aladand, Brigadier-General Waterfield moved the 2nd Brigade down to the river, which was here about three feet deep and divided into several separate channels. About 9 A.M., Lieut.-Colonel Scott, with the 11th Bengal Lancers and one squadron of the Guides, arrived from Khar. He had been ordered to reconnoitre the Adinzai valley towards Uch, and brought instructions from Sir Robert Low to General Waterfield directing the latter to support the cavalry reconnaissance and to destroy Ramora fort across the river.

Meanwhile No. 8 Mountain Battery and a half battalion of the King's Own Scottish Borderers had opened fire on the enemy's position, and were shortly afterwards reinforced by the 4th Sikhs and maxim guns. Under cover of this fire the cavalry forded the river, but had only got part of the way across when the enemy, led by some 200 horsemen, broke into a hurried retreat up the Adinzai valley.

The 4th and 15th Sikhs, the latter having been sent on from the 1st Brigade, now crossed the river and occupied the villages of Dalbar and Chakdara, meeting with no further opposition. Some 300 of the enemy were taken prisoners, and a quantity of arms, cattle and grain was seized. The second half battalion of the Borderers, with the Bengal Sappers and Miners and No. 2 Derajat Mountain Battery, all under command of Lieut.-Colonel Dixon, moved up the river to a ford near Ramora, and a party was sent across to destroy the fort. The explosives carried were, however, insufficient to blow up the thick walls. On reaching the further bank the cavalry had at once taken up the pursuit and followed the fugitives as far as the Katgola pass, being joined on the way by Captain Barton's squadron of Guides, which had forded the river higher up. The cavalry succeeded in overtaking the enemy and killed at least 100 ; many of the mounted men abandoning their horses took refuge in the broken ground, and their leader, Muhammad Shah Khan, himself narrowly escaped capture. The force commanded by this chief amounted to some 4,500 men, amongst whom were other relatives of Umra Khan, and many fanatics from Upper Swat. Their losses were estimated at 250 killed, besides many wounded. Our casualties were three killed, one drowned, and nine wounded.

At about 4 P.M. the cavalry returned from the pursuit. The 4th and 15th Sikhs were left to hold the villages of Dalbar and Chakdara, and the hill to the south-west, while the remainder of the troops fell back to Aladand. The Gordon Highlanders and Guides Infantry rejoined the 2nd Brigade here the same evening.

The safety of the Swat valley being a matter of supreme importance, Sir Robert Low decided to leave his senior Brigadier, General Kinloch to guard it with the 1st Brigade, and the 2nd Brigade was thus ordered to lead the further advance. This brigade, reinforced by the 23rd Pioneers, crossed the Swat river on the 8th, and the 3rd Brigade moved up to Khar.

On this date the 11th Bengal Lancers reconnoitred the Talash valley as far as Shamshikhan, and bivouacked a mile south of Uch. Meanwhile the Guides Infantry with No. 2 Derajat Mountain Battery had occupied the Katgola pass, while a squadron of Guides Cavalry made a reconnaissance up the Adinzai valley to the Laram pass. The route through the Talash valley was reported fit for transport animals, and ample supply of water and fuel was said to be available ; the Laram pass, however, was found impracticable for the transport.

The delay in the Swat valley from the 4th to the 8th April was chiefly due to the difficulty encountered in conveying supplies over the Malakand pass. To feed the troops on the north side of the pass it was found necessary to use during the 4th, 5th, and 6th, all the mules of the force, as these were the only animals that could cross the pass by the zig-zag road then existing; and consequently it was not till the 8th, when camels had been crossing the pass for two days, that it was possible to re-equip the 2nd and 3rd Brigades with transport for their baggage and twenty days' supply.

The time thus lost in the actual advance was utilized in settling down the Upper Ranizais who had left their villages, and in impressing on them their responsibility for peace within their boundaries. After the final warning had been sent to the gathering near Thana, the conduct of Swat generally, notwithstanding repeated efforts to stir up fanaticism, remained excellent. The Mian Guls, who were anxious to pose as rulers, attempted to enter into correspondence regarding Government intentions in Swat, but a reply was sent informing them that, until they showed a *firman* appointing them rulers of Swat, no further correspondence would be held with them. No strong feeling against us existed among the true Pathan population in the valley, who openly cursed their religious leaders.

Reports were also received of unrest among the Bunerwals, Mohmands, and Utman Khel. Although it was considered unlikely that the former would give trouble so long as their own territory was not menaced, still, as a measure of précaution, the Reserve Brigade under Major-General Channer, V.C., C.B., was moved to Mardan. Orders were also issued for the mobilization of a second Reserve Brigade, but the troops of which it was composed did not leave their stations.

About the 5th April Sir Robert Low, having received information that Lieutenants Edwardes and Fowler were prisoners in the hands of Umra Khan, had asked for instructions with regard to possible negotiations with that chief for their release. The reply received on the 8th April was as follows:—

Your telegram of April 6th. The Government of India agree that you should not be the first to open negotiations with Umra Khan about the prisoners: it can only delay their release to let him see our anxiety about them. In case Umra Khan makes overtures, you are authorized to say that before we consider overtures, all Umra Khan's prisoners, both British and native officers and men, must be released; and if a hair of their heads is injured, the arm of England's just vengeance will pursue him to the end, leaving him neither land nor name; and her means will be spent in dealing out to him the just punishment for any ill-treatment of his prisoners, for whose safety he will be held personally responsible. Nothing will turn us from the enterprise on which we have entered, and Umra Khan now knows that the *Sirkar* never uses empty threats, and he will find every word now sent to him will be fulfilled.

On the 9th April the force noted in the margin made a reconnaissance as far as Sado on the Panjkora river. The stream though rapidly rising, was found to be still fordable for cavalry: the Shigu Kas defile at the end of the Talash valley was reported to be just passable for camels; but these animals could not be taken over the Kamrani pass, which otherwise was the best route, since it could be commanded by the enemy's fire. The cavalry bivouacked at Gumbat, while the remainder of the force spent the night at the junction of the Shigu Kas and Kamrani roads.

11th Bengal Lancers.
1 squadron, Guides Cavalry.
No. 2 Derajat M. B.
4th Sikh Infantry.
Guides Infantry.

On the following day these advanced troops pushed on to Sado, and the Guides Cavalry reconnoitred up the Rud-Jandol valley, being fired on by a small party of the enemy near Kotkai. The remainder of the 2nd Brigade, accompanied by Divisional Head-quarters and two companies of the 23rd Pioneers, marched to Gumbat, leaving a detachment to hold a post near Uch. A portion of the 3rd Brigade also advanced to a camp about three quarters of a mile from Uch.

It was now ascertained that Umra Khan was at Mundah. He had released six Muhammadan sepoys, who had been taken prisoners at Reshun, and they had arrived safely at Khar. In the hope of procuring the release of the two officers also, a further letter was sent to the Khan advising him to deliver up his remaining prisoners unhurt and to come in himself and submit to the terms imposed by the Government. The sequel to this attempt at negotiation is related below.

On the 11th April the whole of the 2nd Brigade was concentrated at Sado and Khungai. The baggage and rear-guard, which had been much delayed by the difficulties of the road through the Shigu

Kas, were fired upon by a small party of the enemy near Zulm Baba on the opposite side of the river. As the Panjkora had now become unfordable, Major Aylmer, V.C., with No. 4 Company, Bengal Sappers and Miners, and two companies, 23rd Pioneers, set to work to make a bridge. This was built on raft piers constructed from logs found on the river bank, and was made passable for men on foot by the evening of the 12th, when six companies of the Guides Infantry were sent across to guard the bridge-head.

The 3rd Brigade, which had completed the passage of the Swat river on the 11th, was ordered to concentrate at Gumbat, and to improve the road over the Kamrani pass.

On the evening of the 12th the distribution of the troops was as given in the margin.

Sado, Khungai and neighbourhood.	Divisional Head-quarters. 11th Bengal Lancers. 1 squadron, Guides Cavalry. No. 8 Mountain Battery, Royal Artillery. No. 2 (Derajat) Mountain Battery. 2nd Brigade. 2 companies, 23rd Punjab Pioneers. No. 4 Company, Bengal Sappers and Miners.
Gumbat and Kamrani pass.	3rd Brigade.
Uch	½ squadron, Guides Cavalry. 2 companies, 15th Sikhs.
Chakdara . . .	½ squadron, Guides Cavalry. 6 companies, 15th Sikhs. 6 companies, 23rd Punjab Pioneers. Nos. 1 and 6 Companies, Bengal Sappers and Miners.
Khar	1 squadron, Guides Cavalry. No. 3 Mountain Battery, Royal Artillery. 1st Brigade (except 1st Sikhs). 13th Bengal Infantry.
Malakand pass . .	1st Battalion, East Lancashire Regiment. 29th Punjab Infantry. Wing, 34th Punjab Pioneers. 2 companies, 30th Punjab Infantry.
Dargai . . .	1 squadron, 9th Bengal Lancers. No. 4 (Hazara) Mountain Battery. 2 companies, 30th Punjab Infantry.
Jalala . . .	1 squadron, 9th Bengal Lancers. 2 companies, 30th Punjab Infantry.

On the morning of the 13th Lieut.-Colonel Battye, in command of the Guides, acting on instructions received from Sir Robert Low, proceeded to punish certain villages from which the transport had been fired upon during its march through the Shigu Kas defile.

It was intended to send more troops across to support the Guides, but unfortunately the river had risen during the night, bringing down huge logs of timber, which carried away portions of the bridge, rendering it quite impassable by 9 A.M. The remaining company of the Guides, with a supply of ammunition, was, however, sent across in rafts.

Leaving two companies, under Lieutenant Johnson, to hold the entrenched position at the bridge-head, Lieut.-Colonel Battye moved off at 6 A.M. with five companies, and advanced up the left bank of the Jandol[1] stream towards Subhan Killa, which was reached at nine o'clock. On the way, parties were sent to burn the villages of Walai, Khazanai, and Dehrai. The Guides now forded the Jandol stream, and ascended the heights west of the Panjkora, destroying Garhai and some other small hamlets *en route.* By 10-30 A.M., Lieut.-Colonel Battye reached the crest of the ridge west of the bend of the river below the Jandol-Panjkora junction, and sent forward an advanced picquet to cover his front. Lieutenant Stewart with one company was now despatched to Harangai with instructions to burn the village, and Lieutenant Codrington with another company was ordered to move along the ridge in a south-easterly direction and support this party.

About noon the enemy was observed in considerable force near Kotkai, three miles further up the Jandol valley, and large parties were seen crossing to the right bank of the stream. It was not until 1 P.M. that Lieut.-Colonel Battye, in reply to his heliograph message reporting the state of affairs, received an order to retire to his entrenched position. He at once sent orders to Lieutenant Codrington to withdraw the burning party: meanwhile, Lieutenant Stewart, in compliance with that officer's instructions, had already collected his men near a village about a quarter of a mile south-east of Harangai. From here his line of retreat lay either up the spur to the position held by Lieutenant Codrington, or over a lower col and along a *nala* running north-east to the Panjkora, just above Zulm-Baba. Lieutenant Stewart chose the latter route, and, after reaching the river and ascending the right bank for about a mile, eventually joined Lieutenant Codrington's party.

Meanwhile Lieut.-Colonel Battye, being anxious for the safety of these detached companies on his left, whose movements he was unable to observe, held on to his position with the

[1] This portion of the stream is called indifferently the Rud (Bajaur) or the Jandol. The two unite just west of Ghosam and their combined waters flow into the Panjkora a little below Sado. The eastern limit of the Jandol valley proper is between Ghobani and Ghosam.

remainder of his force, in order to give the former time to complete their withdrawal. At length the order was given for the main body of the battalion to retire, but not before the enemy had begun to press onwards in formidable numbers. Lieut.-Colonel Battye with Captain Campbell and two companies moved down a spur running north-east, while Lieutenant Lockhart with a company and a half descended a parallel spur about midway between the first party and Lieutenant Codrington. When about a third of the descent had been accomplished, the enemy charged down one of the spurs, but were checked by steady volleys, though a few succeeded in getting within twenty paces of the defence.

Lieutenant Codrington's party had now reached a point opposite the upper end of the island just below the mouth of the Jandol stream, when he received a signal message from Brigadier-General Waterfield directing him to look out to the north and prevent surprise. He accordingly moved up the hill again, sending Lieutenant Stewart's company to reinforce the main body, while his own company took up a position on a lower spur some 500 yards in rear, to protect the flank.

As soon as the enemy were seen crossing the main ridge, the artillery on the left bank of the river opened fire; and, as the tribesmen came nearer, the supporting infantry were able to give valuable assistance and prevent them closing in upon the Guides.

Very deliberately the different companies retired, fiercely assailed on all sides, yet coolly firing by word of command and relinquishing quietly and almost imperceptibly one position only to take up another a few yards further back. As they came down on to the open ground at the foot of the hills, the enemy pressed forward with still greater boldness. At this moment Lieut.-Colonel Battye, who had been conspicuous among the last group at each successive retirement, fell mortally wounded, and the command of the battalion devolved on Captain Campbell.

When he saw his commander fall, Subadar Rajab, with a handful of men, rushed forward and shot down several of the tribesmen at close quarters, thus checking their advance at a critical moment. The Guides now retired across level ground through high crops along the river bank to the bridge-head, fording the Jandol stream on their way. During the latter part of this movement a body of the enemy moved along the left bank and tried to cut off their retreat.

They were, however, frustrated by the two companies which had been left at the bridge-head under Lieutenant Johnson, who had now moved out to support the main body from a position on the high ground north of Khazanai. Darkness had begun to close in when the last of the companies arrived at the bridge-head.

A company of the 4th Sikhs were sent across the river on *massak* rafts to reinforce the Guides, while the Gordon Highlanders and No. 2 Derajat Mountain Battery took up a position on the left bank to support them during the night. The remainder of the 2nd Brigade now withdrew to camp some 1½ miles from the river. The enemy kept up their fire till 11 P.M. It was subsequently ascertained that the enemy had planned a night attack, and intended to try and rush the entrenched post, but were deterred by the star shell fired by the Derajat Battery.

Firing was resumed after daybreak, and Captain Peebles, in charge of the maxim guns, was mortally wounded about 8 A.M.

Our losses on the 13th and 14th were two British officers and three men killed, twenty men wounded, including five followers. The enemy, among whom were a large number of Shamozai Utman Khel, subsequently admitted a loss of over 500 men, out of a total gathering of some 5,000 men.

In his report Sir Robert Low expressed the opinion that although the disinclination to retire was a fault on the right side, still, under the circumstances, it would have been better had the officer commanding began to retreat without waiting for orders: the retirement however, as it was carried out, was a splendid performance. For their gallant conduct in charging the enemy when Lieut.-Colonel Battye was wounded, Subadar Rajab and four men subsequently received the 3rd Class of the Order of Merit. The Commander-in-Chief also recorded his admiration of the manner in which the retreat was accomplished, and a special tribute was paid in Government orders to the memory of Lieut.-Colonel Battye.

From the 14th to the 16th April the two brigades halted at Sado, while a suspension bridge was constructed, the cables being formed with strands of telegraph wire.

On the 17th the 3rd Brigade and a portion of the 2nd Brigade crossed the Panjkora during the morning. But, the descent to the valley from the right bank being difficult, Sir Robert Low, in order to avoid undue delay, ordered Brigadier-General Waterfield to pass the 3rd Brigade baggage over the bridge and to follow with his own brigade on the next day.

The 3rd Brigade, preceded by the cavalry, now advanced up the Jandol valley. The cavalry scouts were fired on by a party of the enemy near Dagh, and when the leading squadron of the Guides reached Ghosam, a large body of tribesmen were seen advancing from Mian Kilai. The advanced cavalry fell back on Ghobani, and the enemy coming on down the right bank of the Jandol stream occupied the forts of Andak and Dherai and the spurs to the south. About midday the 3rd Brigade advanced to the attack from Ghobani, where the artillery came into action against the forts. First moving south towards Manugai, and then turning westward, the Seaforth Highlanders and the 4th Gurkhas drove the enemy from ridge to ridge, meeting with but little resistance. The cavalry meanwhile worked up the river-bed in the hopes of cutting off the enemy if they attempted to recross, but the tribesmen kept well out of reach of the sowars, and finally disappeared into the hilly country to the west.

Our casualties in this affair were eight men and nine horses wounded. The enemy, whose loss was not ascertained, numbered between 3,000 and 4,000 men, chiefly Mamunds and Salarzai Tarkanris, with a few Mohmands.

On the 18th April the 2nd and 3rd Brigades advanced to Mundah and Mian Kilai, which were both deserted, except for a few Hindu traders found in the latter place. A cavalry reconnaissance was made to the foot of the Janbatai pass and met with no opposition.

No. 2 Derajat M. B.
1st Battalion, The Buffs.
2nd Battn., 4th Gurkha Rifles.
Half No. 4 Co., B. S. and M
2 sections, Field Hospital.

Meanwhile, as no news had been received as to events in Chitral, Sir Robert Low decided to push forward the 3rd Brigade as rapidly as possible. Accordingly Brig.-General Gatacre continued his march to Barwa, with the troops noted in the margin. Seventeen days' supplies accompanied this force. On this day Sir Robert Low received information that Umra Khan, after spending the previous night at Maiar, had fled up the Maskini valley and crossed the Afghan frontier into Asmar, where he sought refuge with the *Sipah Salar*.

It will be convenient here to give a short account of the negotiations which had taken place between Sir Robert Low and Umra

Khan. On the 11th April two messengers from Umra Khan arrived at Sado and stated that their master desired to arrange terms of peace. The Native Political Assistant was sent to interview these men, but, failing to find them, went on to Mundah, where he was received by Umra Khan and permitted to see the captured officers, who were brought over from Barwa. Lieutenant Edwardes was now released and reached Sado on the 13th. He brought a verbal message from the Khan asking why he had incurred the hostility of Government, how long it would last, and what were the terms which would be offered to him. Sir Robert Low replied that the cause of quarrel had already been stated in former correspondence, but that if the Khan now released the remaining prisoners, and abstained from further hostilities, and assisted the troops in their advance on Chitral, he would not be dispossessed of his territories in Jandol. Umra Khan, however, asked for time to consider the matter, but was informed that no truce would be made. On the 15th Sir Robert Low, in accordance with instructions received from Government, informed the Khan that in consequence of the delay in accepting them, the terms offered in the previous letter must be cancelled. He added that until the other prisoners were released, no further intercourse would be held with him, and that the question of terms would be decided by the Government.

On the 16th Lieutenant Fowler and the remaining prisoners were sent to the British camp at Sado, bringing a letter from Umra Khan, of which the following is a translation :—

You wrote informing me that Government troops had arrived at my boundaries, and that if I wished to save my life and property from ruin, I should make over to you the two English officers, and should submit to whatever conditions the Government of India might impose. I have now acted according to this writing : one of the two officers has already been sent in and the other whom I had kept only to advise me, I now send in with the *Sahibzada*. The conditions you write in your second letter I have accepted, and I have recalled my forces from Chitral. I was not present in the fight of Ranikoji (that of 13th April). On the strength of former services rendered by me, I ask that the Government troops may go to Chitral by some other road, because Jandol is near to other tribes. If any one should show hostility, I shall get into trouble. I shall be obliged by your granting this. If Government come by Jandol, I shall withdraw from Jandol, and when the Government troops have returned to Peshawar, I will return to Jandol. You may trust whatever the *Sahibzada* may tell you. I ask to be informed of such as is agreed to.

To this Sir Robert Low replied :—

I am glad that you have sent to me Lieutenant Fowler and the remaining prisoners. I have also received your letter, in which you say that you have accepted the terms laid down for you; but you are aware that I informed you by letter yesterday that the conditions laid down by me were cancelled owing to your delay in accepting them, and I can now only inform you that I have sent your letter to the Government of India for their consideration and for such orders as they may see fit to give.

Sir Robert Low was now instructed to inform the Khan that the Government could only accept his unconditional surrender, but were willing to offer an honourable asylum in India for himself and family, together with a reasonable number of followers. Umra Khan, however, had fled to Afghanistan before these instructions were received, and it was therefore decided that no further communication should be held with him unless he first made overtures. Sir Robert Low was also directed to inform the Bajauris that, provided they ceased hostilities, their villages and property would be spared.

On the 19th April Brigadier-General Gatacre with the advanced portion of the 3rd Brigade marched to the Janbatai pass, and bivouacked for the night about two miles beyond the *kotal*.

On the following day the force moved to Bandai, where news was received that the Chitral garrison were being very hard pressed. Sir Robert Low accordingly authorized Brigadier-General Gatacre to push on at once with a small lightly equipped column of 500 men.

1st Column.
½ No. 4 Co., Ben. S. and M.
2nd Bn., 4th Gurkha Rifles.
2 guns, No. 2 (Derajat) M. B.
1 section, No. 10 N. F. H.

2nd Column.
1st Bn., The Buffs.
2 guns, No. 2 (Derajat) M. B.
1 section, No. 8 B. F. H.

On the 21st General Gatacre advanced his troops from Bandai in two columns, as shown in the margin concentrating them again at Dir on the 22nd. On the 21st information was received from the Khan of Dir that the siege of Chitral had been raised, and that Sher Afzal and his followers had fled. This news being confirmed on the following day, Sir Robert Low ordered General Gatacre to advance less hurriedly, and with due consideration for his troops.

Brigadier-General Gatacre now issued orders for the troops detailed above (with the exception of the Derajat Battery, which was replaced by two maxim guns of the Devonshire Regiment) to march from Dir to the Lowari pass, with ten days' supplies.

The route to Gujar, at the foot of the pass, lay for eleven miles up the Dir valley beside the tumbling snow-fed torrent that streams from the south side of the pass. The track was in general extremely difficult, frequently losing itself among the boulders that choked the bed of the stream, or rising steeply to traverse the face of a rocky b'uff, only to fall again with equal abruptness on the further side. This portion of the road had to be re-aligned and reconstructed throughout, the river had to be bridged in some four or five places, and stone staircase ramps had to be built in the water at more than one point, to enable laden animals to pass where the stream washed the foot of precipitous cliffs. From Gujar, 8,450 feet, to the summit of the pass, a distance of three miles, the track lay over frozen but often treacherous snow, at first at a fairly easy gradient, but growing steeper and more slippery as the pass was approached. Beyond the crest a great snow cornice, fifteen feet in height, overhung the head of the glen, down which the track descended for about 1,000 yards at a gradient of 1 in 3 or 4, over vast drifts of avalanche snow, in which great rocks and the uprooted trunks of gigantic trees lay deeply imbedded. From the foot of this descent the route lay down a steep and rocky gorge, now following the tangled bed of the torrent, now winding through fine forests of pine and cedar, or traversing open grassy slopes clogged with the drainage of melting snows. About three miles from the pass there is a camping-ground called Ziarat, situated high above the torrent at an elevation of 7,200 feet and surrounded by a forest of pine trees. Onwards from Ziarat to Ashreth, a distance of about six miles, the character of the valley remains the same. Throughout its entire length of twenty-three miles, f om Dir to Ashreth, the road was a mere goat-track, offering extraordinary difficulties to the passage of troops, and requiring extensive improvements before laden animals could follow it.

On the 23rd April an advanced party of Sappers and Miners with a half battalion of the Buffs, and one company, 4th Gurkhas, marched to Kolandi, improving the road and constructing a bridge on the way. Next day this party moved on three and a half miles to Mir a, making three bridges over the stream during the march. On the 25th the remainder of the Gurkhas marched from Dir to Kolandi, while the advanced party, reinforced by the other half battalion of the

Buffs, pushed on to Gujar. Here they set to work to clear the track leading up the pass. Wet weather now set in, which, added to the severe cold, was very trying to the troops, who were without tents.

At 3-30 A.M. on the 26th the first portion of the column resumed its march up the pass in the following order :—Advanced guard of Sappers ; two companies of the Buffs as a tramping party ; 200 coolies carrying light loads ; remainder of Sappers, followed by their mules carrying equipment and baggage ; one company, 4th Gurkhas, with baggage. Two more companies of the Buffs lined the route to the top of the pass to assist the column during the ascent, which, notwithstanding the extreme difficulty of the track, was completed by 7 A.M. A number of mules fell while descending the steep slope on the far side but none were injured, and there was but little damage done to the loads.

The Buffs, who supplied fatigue parties to assist the other troops across, were obliged to bivouack by detachments along the road. The remainder of the advanced party reached Ashreth at nightfall, and on the 27th the second half of the column crossed the pass. The next two days were spent in improving the road down the pass on the north side, and on the 30th the whole column, excepting two companies of the Gurkhas left at Ziarat, concentrated at Ashreth, where it was ordered to halt for the present.

It has already been stated on another page that Sher Afzal and a number of the leading men of Chitral, together with some of their followers, had been captured in Bashkar by the Khan of Dir's *lashkar*. The whole of these prisoners, numbering about 900 persons inclusive of women and children, were brought into the head-quarters camp at Dir on the 27th April. The majority were subsequently sent back to Chitral, and on the 1st May the following were despatched as prisoners to India :—Sher Afzal, Kokand Beg, Yadgar Beg, Danial Beg, Muhammad Afzal Beg and Inayat Shah ; and later Sher Afzal's daughter, the widow of Nizam-ul-Mulk, followed them.

The object of the expedition had now been successfully accomplished. The relieving forces had reached Chitral territory, and the British garrison had been rescued. Umra Khan, after releasing the prisoners who had fallen into his hands, had fled the country, while Sher Afzal and his principal confederates were in our custody.

The following gracious message from Her Majesty the Queen Empress was forwarded by the Viceroy to Sir Robert Low, congratulating him on the successful result of the operations :—

> Pray convey to my brave troops my admiration of their gallantry and endurance, my sorrow at the loss of valuable lives, and my anxiety for the recovery of the wounded and sick.

To return now to the troops south of the Lowarai pass.

The 2nd Brigade, with the exception of the 11th Bengal Lancers, who returned to the Swat valley, and certain other detachments, remained at Mundah. Reconnaissances were made in the Bajaur, Maskini, Maidan, and Panjkora valleys. While taking part in the last of these Captain W. R. Robertson was treacherously attacked and severely wounded by a tribesman from Dir, who formed one of his local escort. This fanatic was afterwards captured and executed. The 1st Brigade also made various reconnaissances in the Swat valley. No opposition was met with, and after the fighting at Chakdara on the 7th April the inhabitants of this valley refrained from any further exhibition of hostility.

Towards the end of April the line of communication was placed under the command of Major-General E. Stedman, C.B. The object of appointing an officer of this rank was to ensure his being senior to all the Brigadiers in the event of their commands being extended along the lines of communication, or in case it became necessary to form moveable columns. The line of communication was divided into four sections as under :—

No. 1, Base to the Panjkora.
No. 2, Panjkora to Dir.
No. 3, Dir to Ashreth,
No. 4, Ashreth to Chitral.

At Dargai	1,250	camels.
„ Khar	1,250	„
„ Chakdara[1]	1,200	„
„ Sarai	1,250	„
„ Panjkora bridge.	1,250	„
„ Mundah	1,250	„
„ Kanbat	3,000	mules and ponies.
„ Bandai	1,500	donkeys.
„ Dir	1,800	mules and donkeys.
„ Gujar	660	donkeys.
„ Ziarat	300	„
„ Ashreth	660	„
„ Drosh	500	mules.
„ Gairat	450	„
„ Broz	400	„
„ Chitral	200	„

Major-General Stedman's command extended from the base at Nowshera to Bandai, and later to Dir. A staging system of transport for the forwarding of supplies was established. During May the number of transport animals employed at the different stages was as given in the margin.

[1] Hired bullocks and 400 mules of the Reserve Brigade worked on this section. Maundage animals also worked up to Mundah.

Prior to this date, owing to the rapidity with which it had been necessary to push on the advance, no definite system of supply could be organized. Advanced depôts were now formed at Dargai, Chakdara, Mundah, Dir, and Kala Drosh. At each of these twenty days' supplies were maintained for troops in the section dependent on the depôt, and one day's supplies for all troops in front.

Twenty-five field post offices were established. Beyond Dargai the mails were carried by runners, disposed in stages, who were found to be more satisfactory than sowars, since they could use narrow mountain paths and were able to travel at night and without escort. In his report Major-General Stedman remarked—"considering that the mails are now carried from Nowshera to Chitral in less than 77 hours with satisfactory regularity, I think that high praise is due to the Postal Department for the care they have bestowed upon the training and supervision of the ignorant tribesmen from whom their postal runners were perforce recruited."

Telegraphic communication had been completed as far as Dir by the end of April, and was extended to Chitral in May. On mobilization 200 miles of field material and 20 offices had been sent to the base; but altogether 26 field offices were opened and 221 miles of posts and 403 miles of wire were erected. The erecting party at the front averaged five miles of line daily for thirty-seven days. In April constant interruptions were caused by transport animals breaking the light field posts, and during the next two months there was a good deal of trouble owing to wire-cutting and thefts of material by the tribesmen.

In addition to the trestle bridge thrown across the Swat river at Chakdara, a pontoon bridge with twelve pontoons, which had been brought up on elephants, was constructed in May; while a suspension bridge was completed by the end of June. A new suspension bridge of 200 feet span also replaced the temporary structure made on the Panjkora at Sado, and other bridges were constructed at Chutiatanr and Darora.

It has already been mentioned in Chapter II that the column from Gilgit under Lieut.-Colonel Kelly had remained halted at Chitral after the relief of the fort on the 20th April. As, however, the presence of this small force alone was not considered an adequate assertion of our military supremacy, and since it was also desirable to complete and maintain communication by the Dir route pending a decision as to future policy and action, Sir Robert Low was instructed to send a portion of his division on to Chitral.

1st Bn., The Buffs.
No. 2 Derajat Mn. Battery.
No. 4 Co., Ben. S. & Ms.
1 coy., 4th Gurkha Rifles.

Brigadier-General Gatacre, with the troops noted in the margin, was accordingly directed to push on to Chitral, which he reached on the 15th May.

The remainder of the 4th Gurkhas held the line of communication from Ziarat to Broz; the 25th Punjab Infantry remained at Dir and Gujar, while Bandai and Janbatai were garrisoned by the Seaforth Highlanders.

Sir Robert Low, escorted by one company of the Seaforths, arrived at Chitral on the 16th May, where he reviewed the troops composing the garrison which had held the fort during the siege, and the two relieving columns.

On the 10th May a 4th Brigade, as shown in the margin, was formed from troops employed on the lines of communications, and was placed under the command of Brigadier-General A. G. Hammond, V.C.

1st Bn., East Lancashire Regiment.
29th Punjab Infantry.
30th " "
1 squadron, 9th B. L.

During the next two months various movements of minor importance took place, and the troops were largely employed in improving the roads along the lines of communications.

After the relief of Chitral at the end of April, all organized opposition on the part of the tribesmen ceased. In the Jandol valley, however, shots were frequently fired into our camps, and attacks on individuals or small parties continually occurred. On the 15th May a British sentry was shot dead at Mundah, and at Kambat a party of the enemy attacked some Hazara coolies, killing four and wounding twenty-three. Altogether from about the middle of April to the date of the withdrawal of the forces the total number of killed and wounded in these numerous outrages amounted to two British soldiers and forty-nine followers killed, and one British, two native soldiers, and forty-seven followers wounded. Nineteen men, who had committed fanatical attacks, were arrested and executed, and six men were known to have been wounded by sentries.

Considerable annoyance was also caused by damage to telegraph material and thefts of wire, mostly in Jandol. These outrages were at first supposed to be nothing more than the natural outcome of the disorder which ensued after the flight of Umra Khan from Jandol, and were believed to have been committed by a few of his sympathisers who had not yet dispersed to their homes. Later on, however, parties of tribesmen numbering from 80 to 300 began to attempt attacks on our camps. These incidents, combined with the facts that the inhabitants of the valley made no move to cultivate their lands, and that a number of Peshawaris employed in collecting supplies on the lines of communication were desirous of returning to their homes, seemed to point to the possibility of further outbreak. Measures were promptly taken to put a stop to this unrest. The chief instigators—usually religious leaders—were arrested, and fines, payable in grain or cattle, were imposed on certain villages. Saiyid Ahmad and Sher Afzal of Shahi, relatives of Umra Khan, were employed to organize a system of tribal police, and the people were induced to set to work on the cultivation of their fields. In consequence of the arrest of leading men, *jirgas* came in from the Lower Salarzai and Shamozai Utman Khel; and it became evident that a serious endeavour had been made to raise the Jandolis and all the neighbouring clans.

The Hadda Mulla had assured the people of Nawagai and the Utman Khel and Tarkanri tribes that the British intended to annex their country and disarm them. The Manki Mulla, while abstaining from active help, consented to the proceedings of his brother priests. The people of Buner were also becoming suspicious, and occupied the Buner passes after sending their women and children into the hills. On receipt of a letter from Major Deane, however, explaining that no interference with their country was intended, they quieted down, and their fighting men dispersed.

On the 11th June the Upper Salarzai and Mamund *jirgas* also came to Mundah, accompanied by the Khan of Nawagai, who had been ordered to attend and explain the non-fulfilment of his promise to maintain order among his people. The *Khan* and the various *jirgas* were received by Sir Robert Low and appeared to be well satisfied by his assurance that the Government had no intention of taking over their country or of demanding revenue from them.

Henceforward the troubles in the Jandol valley sensibly diminished, but some disturbance was caused in the Baraul valley by people from Asmar. Some mule-drivers in a post near Bandai were cut up on the 19th June, and about this time several followers were killed and convoys were fired on. It was, however, not possible to deal with the perpetrators of these outrages without having recourse to action which would probably have caused undesirable complications, as they came from territory beyond the limits of British influence.

By the end of July the road to Chitral *viâ* the Panjkora valley had been extensively improved, and it was decided to abandon the Jandol–Baraul route and withdraw the troops stationed in those valleys. Accordingly by the middle of August the advanced troops were moved back to the left bank of the Panjkora, and the British units of the 2nd Division went into summer quarters on the Barchanrai hills south of the Talash valley.

About this time the Reserve Brigade at Mardan and the Abbott-abad moveable column were broken up.

During the withdrawal of the troops from Jandol no trouble was experienced from the tribes. After the completion of the movements, the Khans of Nawagai and Pashat came to Sado with the Shamozai and Salarzai *jirgas,* and stated that they had taken steps to prevent any disturbance. They also requested that the bridge at Sado might be left intact, and undertook to prevent any interference with it on the part of malcontents among the tribes-men.

About the middle of July a number of Umra Khan's relatives were sent to Peshawar by the Amir, who had refused their request for permission to proceed to Bajaur direct, lest their return to that country should be displeasing to the Government. These people were, however, sent back to Jandol, where lands were assigned to them by the order of the Political Officer, since they were unable to agree amongst themselves as to the division of the property of their late chief. Barwa was given to Saiyid Ahmad Khan; Satbar to Sher Afzal Khan; Shahi to the sons of Muhammad Zaman Khan; Chanda to Mir Hassan Khan; Damthal to Zanulla Khan; Tor to Mir Afzal Khan; Mundah to Abdul Majid Khan; Kaskothi to Abdul Ghani Khan and other cousins; and Maskini to the family of Muhammad Shah Khan, who did not himself return until September.

On the 4th September the troops composing the Chitral garrison ceased to form part of the Relief Force and on the following day the 3rd Brigade was broken up. On the 8th the Commander-in-Chief arrived at Malakand, and after inspecting the troops in the Swat valley, proceeded to the Laram pass and to Barchanrai. On the 16th the General Officer Commanding the lines of communications issued orders for the final withdrawal of the troops. The last convoy for Chitral left Gujar on the 18th, and on the next day the garrison of that post withdrew to Dir. The final evacuation began on the 20th and was completed by the 27th without any disturbance. The telegraph line from Drosh to Chakdara was dismantled, the stores necessary for its reconstruction being left at Drosh, Dir, and Chakdara.

On the 28th September the Divisional Head-quarters demobilised at Nowshera. In taking leave of the Chitral Relief Force Sir Robert Low, in his farewell order, placed on record his high appreciation of the fine services of the troops whom it had been his privilege to command in the field for the past six months.

The question of the future policy with regard to Chitral, and the means of communication with that country, had been under consideration since the beginning of the military operations. The Government of India had recommended the retention of a British force in Chitral and the maintenance of the road from Nowshera *viâ* Panjkora and Dir. In June the Secretary of State had informed the Government that, in view of the large number of troops which would be required to ensure the security of the road and the heavy burden which would consequently be thrown on Indian revenues, these proposals were not acceptable. Before, however, fresh arrangements could be completed for the settlement of Chitral and the evacuation of trans-frontier posts occupied by the troops, a change of government occurred, and the new Secretary of State informed the Indian Government that the matter would be reconsidered. In reply to a request for further information as to the proposed arrangements for keeping open the road to Chitral, the Government of India stated that, as the Khan of Dir and the Swat *khans*, were friendly, it was expected that the Panjkora-Dir route could be safeguarded by tribal levies and that it would only be necessary to employ troops at Chakdara and the Malakand pass. For Chitral the Government recommended a garrison of two battalions of Native infantry, one company Sappers and Miners, and one section of a Native mountain battery. It was added that the Native Infantry battalion in the Gilgit Agency could be withdrawn, and that the detachments at Mastuj and Ghizr would probably not be required.

This information removed the doubt which had hitherto been felt by the Home Government as to the feasibility of keeping open the road by peaceful means and without heavy expenditure. Accordingly on the 9th August formal assent was given to the proposals of the Government of India.

On the 10th August Sir Robert Low had been instructed to arrange for garrisoning the Malakand pass and Chakdara, and to settle terms with the Swatis and the Khan of Dir for the safeguarding of the road through their territories. The Khan of Dir in return for an annual allowance of Rs. 10,000, subsequently increased to Rs. 15,000, undertook to keep open the postal route, protect the telegraph line, maintain the road, levy-posts, and camping-grounds in good order, and to protect the route with levies, the cost of upkeep of the latter being defrayed by Government. An extra sum of Rs. 1,000 *per mensem* was also granted as postal subsidy, and Rs. 10,000 per annum was allowed in compensation for tolls and taxes, which the *Khan* agreed to forego in future. The *Khan* also received a present of Rs. 25,000 for his services during the relief operations. The Dir levies, numbering 310 men (subsequently increased to 350 infantry and 40 sowars), were to hold posts at Chakdara, Sarai, Sado, Robat, Warai, Darora, Dir, and Kolandi. They are recruited chiefly from the Malizai Yusafzai, the remainder being Tarkanri, Utman Khel, and other Pathans. They were at first provided with Sniders but have since been re-armed with Martini-Henry rifles.

The Khan of Nawagai was granted an allowance of Rs. 6,000 per annum. Arrangements were also made with the *khans* and *maliks* of Swat for the maintenance of the road through their valley—see Chapter VIII, and fortified posts were built at Chakdara and Malakand for the garrisons, noted in the margin, which were left to hold those places.

1 Squadron Cavalry.
1 Mountain Battery.
1 Company of Sappers and Miners.
4 Battalions of Infantry.

A Political Agency of Dir and Swat was established with headquarters at Malakand, and Major H. A. Deane was appointed as political officer in charge.

APPENDIX A´ (i).

Genealogy of the true YUSAFZAI descended from YUSAF, son of Mand or Mandai.

- YUSAF.
  - Uria or Badi, the insolent. —*Extinct.*
  - Isa.
    - 9 *others, all killed.*
    - Hassan . Hassanzai
    - Yakub . Mada Khel
    - Aka . Akazai
    - (Isazai, Black Mountain, Mahaban, and banks of Indus.)
  - Muss.
    - Ilias
      - Mami, married Ayesha . Ashazai
      - Taji . Gadai . Gadaizai
      - Salar . Salarzai
      - Naso . Nasozai
      - (Iliaszai. Buner.)
  - Mali.
    - Daulat . Daulatzai
    - Chagar . Chagarzai
    - Aba } Nurizai
    - Isorai } Nurizai
    - (Malizai, Buner and Chamla valley.)
  - Ako.
    - Halim } —Ranizai . Left bank of river in Lower Swat.
    - Utman } —Ranizai
    - Mukha } —Ranizai
    - Bazid
      - Suheil . Kuz Sulizai
      - Babu . Babuzai
      - Suleiman . Bar Sulizai
      - (Baziai; Left bank, Upper Swat valley.)
    - Khwajo
      - Allah din . Adinzai
      - Shammu . Shamozai
      - Nikbi . Nikbi Khel
      - (Right bank of Swat river.)
      - Mali .
        - Sheikh Khel
        - Nura Khel
        - Nasruddin Khel
        - Sultan Khel
        - Painda Khel
        - (Malizai. Dir and Panjkora valley.)
      - Sabit . } Sebujni
      - Chuna . } Sebujni
      - Shamai . Shamizai
      - (Right bank of river in Upper Swat.)
      - (Khwazazai.)
    - Khandak . Khadakzai
    - Aba . . Abazai
    - (Right bank of river in Lower Swat.)

APPENDIX A (ii).

Genealogy of the Malizai Khwazazai Akozai Yusafzai.

MALIZAI.

- *Ausa Khel by a wife named Ausa.*
  - Sheikh Khel.
    - Bahlol Khel
      - Dusha Khel (1).
      - The other 10 sub-sections of Bahlol Khel (2).
    - Pinze brakhe (3).
    - Pai Khel
      - War Pai Khel (4).
      - Adu Khel
        - Jaus Khel (5).
        - Janas Khel (6).
  - Nura Khel.
    - Umar Khel (7).
    - Jelal Khel (8).
    - Hassan Khel
      - Mirak Khel (9).
      - Wali Khel (10).
    - Ibrahim Khel (11).
- *By a wife called Sehsadda.*
  - Nasruddin Khel.
    - Mahi Khel (12).
    - Bakra Khel (13).
    - Fateh Khan Khel (14).
    - Kadar Khan Khel (15).
    - Yakub Khel (16).
    - Hamza Khel (17).
  - Painda Khel.
    - Zara Khel
      - Mubarak Khel (18).
      - Bamad Khel (19).
    - Karoi (20).
  - Sultan Khel.
    - Dalkha Khel
      - Ilias Khel (21).
      - Abbas Khel (22).
    - Babu Kar Khel
      - Ibrahim Khel, or Bar Toi (23).
      - Said Ahmad Khel, or Kuz Toi (24)

APPENDIX B.

Genealogy of the Tarkanri.

- TARAK (half-brother of Mand or Mandai, the father of Yusaf.)
  - Mamund.
    - (1) Wur } Watelai valley.
    - (2) Kakazai } Watelai valley.
    - Salarzai.
      - (3) Saaduldin } Babukarra and Charmung.
      - (4) Ahmad din. } Babukarra and Charmung.
  - Bezad.
    - Isozai. } Jandol valley.
      - (5) Mast Khel
      - (6) Ali Beg Khel (Shontalai valley)
      - (7) Musa Khel (Shalkandi valley)
      - (8) Mashwani (*not true Tarkanri*)
      - (9) Sheikh Khel (Miskini valley). } Not true Pathans. Are of aboriginal stock.
      - (10) Mandezai } Not true Pathans. Are of aboriginal stock.
      - (11) Senzai } Not true Pathans. Are of aboriginal stock.
      - (12) Khwazazai } Not true Pathans. Are of aboriginal stock.
    - Ismailzai. } Maidan valley.
      - Nura Khel.
        - (13) Jabbi Khel
        - (14) Bahadur Shah Khel
        - (15) Said Khel
        - (16) Tura Khel
        - Kalut Khel
          - (17) Fazal Khel
          - (18) Muradi Khel
        - (19) Abib Khan Khel
        - (20) Bucha Khel
        - (21 to 24) Atrapi Khel
        - (25) Haramzai } of aboriginal stock.
        - (26) Shaibzai } of aboriginal stock.
      - Aka Khel.
        - (27) Kata Khel
        - (28) Burhan Khel
        - (29) Ibrahim Khel
        - (30 to 32) Katurzai
        - (33) Sodi Khel

APPENDIX C.

Details of Commands and Staff of the Chitral Relief Force.

DIVISIONAL STAFF.

To Command the Division—	..	Major-General Sir R. C. Low, K.C.B.
Aide-de-Camp ..	..	Lieutenant R. B. Low, 9th Ben. Lancers.
Orderly Officer ..	..	„ A. A. Irvine, 3rd Bengal Infantry.
Chief Staff Officer	..	Colonel B. Blood, C.B., R.E. (with rank of Brigadier-General).
Assistant Adjutant General	..	Lieut.-Colonel J. H. S. Craigie, Highland Light Infantry.
Assistant Quarter Master General.	..	Lieut.-Colonel G. H. C. Dyce, 33rd Bengal Infantry.
Deputy Assistant Quarter Master General, Intelligence.	..	Captain J. E. Nixon, 18th Ben. Lancers.
Intelligence Officer	..	Lieutenant W. R. Robertson, 3rd Dragoon Guards.
Colonel on the Staff, Royal Artillery.	..	Colonel W. W. Murdoch, R.A.
Staff Captain, Royal Artillery	..	Captain M. F. Fegen, R.A.
Colonel on Staff, Royal Engrs.		Brevet-Colonel H. P. Leach, D.S.O., R.E.
Adjutant, Royal Engineers	..	Captain J. A. Tanner, D.S.O., R.E.
Field Engineer ..	..	Major C. C. Ellis, R.E.
Superintendent, Army Signalling.	..	Captain T. E. O'Leary, Royal Irish Fusiliers.
Principal Medical Officer	..	Surgeon-Colonel T. Maunsell, A.M.S.
Survey Officer ..	..	Captain W. J. Bythell, R.E.
Inspecting Veterinary Officer	..	Veterinary-Major R. Poyser, A.V.D.
Divisional Commissariat Officer		Lieut.-Colonel A. G. Yaldwin.
„ *Transport Officer*	..	Major C. M. FitzGerald.

1ST BRIGADE STAFF.

Commanding— ..	..	Brigadier-General A. A. A. Kinloch, C.B.
Orderly Officer ..	..	Captain J. G. Turner, 2nd Ben. Lancers.
Deputy Assistant Adjutant and Quarter Master General.		„ W. E. Bunbury, 25th Punjab Infantry.

Brigade-Major	Captain H. E. Stanton, D.S.O., R.A.
Brigade Commissariat Officer ..	„ R. P. Jackson, Commissariat-Transport Department.

2ND BRIGADE STAFF.

Commanding—	Colonel H. G. Waterfield (with rank of Brigadier-General).
Orderly Officer	Lieutenant P. E. Ricketts, 18th Bengal Lancers.
Deputy Assistant Adjutant and Quarter Master General.	Captain W. G. Hamilton, East Lanc. Regiment.
Brigade-Major	Captain A. C. Batten, 2nd Punjab Cavalry.
Brigade Commissariat Officer.	Captain C. G. R. Thackwell.

3RD BRIGADE STAFF.

Commanding—	Brigadier-General W. F. Gatacre, D.S.O.
Orderly Officer	Lieutenant R. G. Brooke, 7th Hussars.
Deputy Assistant Adjutant and Quarter Master General.	Captain L. Herbert, Central India Horse.
Brigade-Major	Captain G. C. I. Stockwell, Highland Light Infantry.
Brigade Commissariat Officer ..	Captain A. B. Williams.

STAFF OF DIVISIONAL TROOPS.

Brigade-Major	Captain G. J. Younghusband, Corps of Guides.
Commanding Royal Artillery ..	Lieut.-Colonel W. Aitken, R.A.
Adjutant, Royal Artillery ..	Captain G. C. Dowell, R.A.
Brigade Commissariat Officer ..	Captain R. W. Nicholson.

LINES OF COMMUNICATION STAFF.

Commanding—	Colonel A. G. Hammond, V.C., C.B., D.S.O. A.-D.-C. (with rank of Brigadier-General).
Orderly Officer	Lieutenant E. B. C. Boddam, 2nd Battalion, 5th Gurkha Rifles.
Deputy Assistant Adjutant and Quarter Master General.	Brevet-Major S. C. H. Monro Seaforth Highlanders.
Commanding Royal Engineer	Brevet-Lieut.-Colonel W. T. Shone, D.S.O., R.E.
Adjutant, Royal Engineers ..	Captain B. B. Russell, R.E.
Principal Medical Officer ..	Surgeon-Colonel G. Thomson, I.M.S.

Base Commandant, Nowshera	Major A. F. Barrow, C.M.G., 12th Bengal Infantry.
Road Commandant on the Lines of Communication.	Major F. S. Gwatkin, 13th Bengal Lancers.
Deputy Assistant Adjutant and Quarter Master General.	Captain C. W. Somerset, 12th Bengal Infantry.
Veterinary Officer at the Base ..	Veterinary-Captain F. W. Forsdyke,
Ordnance Officers ..	Major K. S. Dunsterville, R.A.
" "	Captain M. W. S. Pasley, R.A.
	" C. H. L. F. Wilson, R.A.

RESERVE BRIGADE STAFF.

Commanding—	Major-General G. N. Channer, V.C., C.B.
Orderly Officer	Captain B. H. Boucher, Hampshire Regiment.
Deputy Assistant Adjutant and Quarter Master General.	Major H. L. Smith-Dorrien, D.S.O., Derbyshire Regiment.
Brigade-Major	Captain H. H. Dobbie, 30th Punjab Infantry.
Brigade Commissariat Officer	Lieutenant W. T. Vincent.
Brigade Transport Officer ..	Captain A. B. H. Northcott, Royal Scots Fusiliers.
Brigade Signalling Officer ..	Captain W. E. M. Norie, Middlesex Regiment.
Field Engineer	Major J. W. Thurburn, R.E.

APPENDIX D.

Strength and distribution of the Chitral Relief Force on 1st May 1895.

Post.	Corps.	British Troops. Officers.	British Troops. Other ranks.	Native Troops. British Officers.	Native Troops. Native ranks.	Remarks.
Chitral	Details	..	..	1	2	
Ashreth	Staff, 3rd Brigade	8	1	..	..	
	Half No. 4 Company, Bengal Sappers and Miners.	2	1	..	80	
	1st Battalion, East Kent Regiment ..	24	805	..	..	
	Details	1	8	..	..	
Ziarat	2nd Battalion, 4th Gurkha Rifles ..	..	..	4	342	
Lowari pass ..	Half No. 4 Company, Bengal Sappers and Miners.	1	..	..	81	
	23rd Punjab Pioneers ..	..	..	4	347	
Gujar	2nd Battalion, 4th Gurkha Rifles ..	..	..	4	335	
Dir	Divisional Head-Quarters ..	27	3	..	30	
	Staff Divisional Troops	6	1	..	..	
	No. 2 (Derajat) Mountain Battery ..	..	..	3	176	
	2nd Battalion, Seaforth Highlanders ..	24	772	..	..	
	25th Punjab Infantry	..	..	8	556	
	2nd Battalion, 4th Gurkha Rifles ..	..	..	1	48	
Surbat	25th Punjab Infantry	..	..	1	181	
	23rd Punjab Pioneers	..	..	6	385	
Janbatai	4th Sikh Infantry	..	..	2	285	
Chashma (Kanbat) ..	Guides Cavalry	..	..	..	37	
	No. 3 Mountain Battery, Royal Artillery.	5	105	..	151	
	4th Sikh Infantry	..	..	8	330	
Mundah	Staff, 2nd Brigade	8	1	..	..	
	Guides Cavalry	..	..	3	106	
	No. 8 Mountain Battery, Royal Artillery.	5	110	..	156	
	2nd Battalion, King's Own Scottish Borderers.	29	798	..	..	
	1st Battalion, Gordon Highlanders ..	24	726	..	..	
	Guides Infantry	..	..	10	665	
Panjkora bridge ..	Guides Cavalry	..	..	1	135	
	No. 1 Company, Bengal Sappers and Miners.	8	8	..	171	
	13th Bengal Infantry	..	..	8	573	
Maidan valley ..	Guides Cavalry	..	..	4	65	On reconnaissance.

Post.	Corps.	British Troops. Officers.	British Troops. Other ranks.	Native Troops. British Officers.	Native Troops. Native ranks.	Remarks.
Serai	11th Bengal Lancers	..	..	1	61	
	15th Sikhs	..	..	2	176	
Chakdara	Staff, Lines of Communications	8	1	..	4	
	11th Bengal Lancers	..	..	..	56	
	No. 6 Company, Bengal Sappers and Miners.	2	2	..	164	
	No. 6 Company, Madras Sappers and Miners.	4	2	..	164	Arrived on the 21st April to assist in bridging the Swat river.
	15th Sikhs	..	..	7	552	
Khar	Staff, 1st Brigade	8	1	..	..	
	11th Bengal Lancers	..	..	9	378	
	No. 4 (Hazara) Mountain Battery	..	..	5	224	
	1st Battalion, Bedfordshire Regiment	26	764	..	..	
	1st Battalion, King's Royal Rifle Corps	26	745	..	..	
	2nd Battalion, Seaforth Highlanders	..	29	..	..	
	37th Dogras	..	..	11	734	
Malakand	1st Battalion, East Lancashire Regiment.	30	666	..	..	
	29th Punjab Infantry	..	..	11	731	
	34th Punjab Pioneers	..	..	10	611	
Foot of Malakand	30th Punjab Infantry	..	..	2	182	
Dargai	30th Punjab Infantry	..	..	6	369	
	Details	..	..	..	4	
Jalala	9th Bengal Lancers (2 squadrons)	..	..	1	95	
	30th Punjab Infantry	..	..	1	167	
Hoti Mardan	Staff	12	1	..	..	
	No. 7 (Bengal) Mountain Battery	..	..	4	232	Reserve Brigade less 3rd Bn. Rifle Brigade, which stood fast at Rawal Pindi.
	2nd Battalion, 1st Gurkha Rifles	..	..	10	727	
	2nd Battalion, 3rd Gurkha Rifles	..	..	9	755	
	26th Punjab Infantry	..	..	9	735	
	Details	2	26	..	..	

APPENDIX E.

Arrangements for the Lines of Communication, Chitral Relief Force, sanctioned in G. G. O. No. 478 of 10th May 1895.

Organization.—An officer of the rank of Major-General will command the Line of Communications from the base to the advanced depôt. The duties of the General Officer Commanding the Line of Communications will be as defined in the Field Service Manual, Part XI, paragraph 51.

The line will be divided into four sections, each in charge of a Road Commandant:—

1. Base to Khar, about 58 miles.
2. Khar to Mundia Khan, about 42 miles.
3. Mundia Khan to Dir, about 48 miles.
4. From Dir onwards.

The General Officer Commanding the Line of Communications will take orders only from the General Officer Commanding the Chitral Relief Force. His powers will be as defined in the Field Service Manual, Part XI, paragraph 52, with the following addendum:

> "Detached operations will be conducted entirely under the orders of the General Officer Commanding the Chitral Relief Force, but in the event of communication with the latter being, from any circumstances impracticable, the General Officer Commanding Line of Communications will assume the command and responsibility, but he must not himself leave the Line of Communications."

All requisitions that he may make on Brigadier-Generals, or other officers, for duties on the Line of Communications must at once be complied with.

The principal Commissariat Officer of the force and the principal Transport Officer will be under the orders of the General Officer Commanding the Line of Communications; as well as all Commissariat Officers and all Transport Officers, except Brigade Commissariat and Brigade Transport Officers who are under General Officers Commanding Brigades. The exception to this will be when Brigade Transport is used on the line apart from the brigades, and the Transport Officer accompanies it.

All Ordnance Officers and Depôts, as they stand, will be under the General Officer Commanding the Line of Communications.

The Inspecting Veterinary Officer and all other Veterinary Officers will be under the General Officer Commanding the Line of Communications.

STAFF OF THE LINE OF COMMUNICATIONS.

General Officer Commanding.	Major-General E. Stedman, C.B.
Aide-de-Camp ..	Lieutenant H. W. F. Cooke, 24th Punjab Infantry.
Assistant Adjutant and Quarter Master General.	Colonel I. S. M. Hamilton, D.S.O.
Deputy Assistant Adjutant and Quarter Master General.	Captain G. V. Kemball, Royal Artillery.
Principal Medical Officer.	Surgeon-Colonel G. Thomson, Indian Medical Service.
Chief Commissariat Officer.	Lieut.-Colonel A. G. Yaldwyn.
Chief Transport Officer	Major C. M. Fitzgerald.
Base Commandant ..	,, A. F. Barrow, C.M.G., 12th Bengal Infantry.
Deputy Assistant Adjutant and Quarter Master General at the Base.	Captain C. W. Somerset, 12th Bengal Infantry.
Road Commandants ..	Major F. S. Gwatkin, 13th Bengal Lancers. Brevet-Major S. C. H. Monro, Seaforth Highlanders. Major G. H. W. O'Sullivan, Royal Engineers. ,, A. J. Watson, Suffolk Regiment.
Commanding Royal Engineers.	Lieut.-Colonel W. T. Shone, D.S.O., R.E.
Adjutant, Royal Engineers.	Captain B. B. Russell, R.E.
Field Engineers ..	Major H. E. S. Abbott, R.E., Captain G. Williams, R.E., Captain W. G. R. Cordue, R.E., Captain H. C. Nanton, R.E.
Assistant Field Engineers	Lieutenant A. J. H. Swiney, R.E., Lieutenant A. Walpole, R.E., Lieutenant H. F. Thuillier, R.E., Lieutenant F. F. N. Rees, R.E., Lieutenant S. D'A. Crookshank, R.E., Lieutenant E. C. Ogilvie, R.E., Lieutenant H. A. L. Hepper, R.E.

APPENDIX F.

Agreement with the Khan of Dir.

Whereas the Government of India have no desire to annex the territory of the Khan of Dir, but require a road to be kept open from the Swat valley to Chitral territory, the Khan of Dir, on behalf of himself and of his successors, fully and freely undertakes :—

that he will keep open the road from Chakdara to Ashreth,
that he will make any postal arrangements required,
that he will protect the telegraph on any occasion when it is put up,
that he will maintain the road, levy posts and camping-ground enclosures in good repair, and
that he will protect the whole line with levies.

II.—In return for the above considerations the Government of India undertake to grant the *Khan* a payment of ten thousand rupees a year, and a present of four hundred Snider rifles with such a supply of ammunition as may be deemed advisable ; and they will defray the cost, as may be necessary, of the maintenance of the levies.

III.—The Government of India further undertake on their part, in consideration of the *Khan* accepting the conditions aforesaid and performing the services required by them, that they will not interfere with his administration of the country as fixed by its present boundaries.

IV.—In consideration of receiving from the Government of India an annual payment of 10,000 rupees the Khan of Dir, on behalf of himself and his successors, declares that trade passing along the road from Chakdara to Ashreth shall for ever be free from all toll or tax within his territories.

V.—The payments for the levies will be made at the end of every month ; the payment of the allowance to the *Khan* mentioned in clause II, and of the sum mentioned in clause IV in consideration of freedom of trade from taxes, shall be made in equal half-yearly instalments, one payment in the spring of the year, and one in the autumn. The first payments on these accounts will become due on the 1st of April 1896.

VI.—The Khan of Dir, on behalf of himself and of his successors, undertakes, at any time when the Government of India may wish to place troops temporarily on the Laram hill or on the Dusha Khel range, to give sufficient ground for their accommodation upon receiving a fair rent for the site or sites.

Laram :
The 12th September 1895.

(Sd.) MUHAMMAD SHARIF KHAN,
Khan of Dir.

CHAPTER XIII.

AKOZAI–YUSAFZAI AND TARKANRI TRIBES OF DIR AND BAJAUR—contd.

AFTER the withdrawal of the troops of the Chitral Relief Force at the end of 1895, the condition of affairs in Dir and Bajaur was on the whole satisfactory, although there was a certain amount of unrest among various local factions. The new political arrangements promised to be successful, and the levy system for keeping open the road through Dir worked well, mails and stores being passed through to Chitral without interference. Moreover, the abolition of tolls and taxes gave a welcome impetus to trade.

In January 1896 the Khan of Dir caused some trouble by invading the Jandol valley ; but when the British Political Officer, Major H. A. Deane, represented that such interference was likely to provoke the lasting enmity of the Jandolis, who were in a position to cause serious trouble on the flank of the Chitral road, he at once agreed to withdraw his followers. In May, troops proceeded from India by the Nowshera–Dir road to relieve the garrison in Chitral which returned by the same route. These movements were completed without any interference or disturbance on the part of the tribesmen.

During the autumn the Khan of Nawagai, wishing to extend his authority over the Salarzai people of the Babukarra valley, attacked the Khan of Pashat and seized two of his forts. The Khan of Dir, with Saiyid Khan of Barwa, also threatened to take part in the quarrel, but fortunately Major Deane was able to bring about a settlement which put a stop to further hostilities. During this year some anxiety was caused by rumours of the return of Umra Khan. He had been permitted by the Amir, with the consent of the Government of India, to proceed on a pilgrimage to Mecca. On his arrival in India on his homeward journey, the Government had proposed to grant him an allowance and a residence at Quetta. He, however, declined this offer and returned to Kabul.

At the beginning of 1897 it seemed not unreasonable to expect that the constant strife of former years was now about to be succeeded by a period of peace and prosperity. It was evident, however, that such a state of affairs would not be welcomed by the *mullas* and others of the priestly classes. These individuals, besides cherishing a fanatical hatred of all unbelievers, were bitterly opposed to any civilizing influence which might tend to destroy their supremacy among an ignorant and superstitious people. Consequently they were intensely suspicious of any advance on the part of the British, and did their utmost to discourage friendly relations between the tribesmen and the Government officials. The Hadda Mulla was known to be inciting the Mamunds and Nawagai clans to join with their neighbours, the Mohmands and Utman Khel, in a hostile demonstration against us. The Palam Mulla also endeavoured to stir up the fanaticism of the people of Dir, and urged them to attack the troops on their way to Chitral at the time of the annual reliefs. The Khan of Dir, however, seized and punished his messenger, and informed Major Deane that he would presently deal with the *mulla* himself, who, as he now discovered, had been tampering with the levies.

There was evidence, too, of Afghan intrigues amongst the Bajaur clans, and the Khan of Dir received a letter from Kabul enquiring what action he would take in the event of a general rising of the Muhammadan tribes. The *Sipah Salar*, Ghulam Haidar, who was still in Asmar on business connected with the demarcation of the Afghan boundary, also caused much mischief by spreading false reports as to the intentions of the Government with regard to Mohmand territory.

Notwithstanding these indications of unrest, and the undisguised hostility of the religious leaders, the Chitral reliefs were carried out in May without any disturbance.

In June the Khan of Dir established his authority over the tribes on the right bank of the Swat river, and early in the following month Major Deane received a number of Swati *jirgas* and effected a settlement between them and the Khan, [1] which appeared to satisfy all parties. The influence of the Mian Guls, who had been

[1] The title of Nawab of Dir was conferred by the Government upon Muhammad Sharif Khan in recognition of his friendly services.

a source of trouble in Upper Swat, was on the wane, and with the Khan of Dir paramount from the Lowari pass to Chakdara the safety of the Chitral road seemed to be assured. The attempts of the *mullas* and other intriguers had apparently failed, and the people appeared to be inclined to settle down to peace and quiet.

About the middle of July, however, a fresh complication was caused by the appearance of a religious fanatic called Mulla Mastan or Fakir Sartor,[1] who came to be known later as the Mad Fakir. This man arrived at Landakai in Swat from Buner, and in an incredibly short time spread a flame of fanaticism which culminated in an attack on the posts at Malakand and Chakdara by a large gathering of Swatis and tribesmen from many of the neighbouring clans.

This attack and the events in the Swat valley which immediately preceded it have already been described in Chapter VIII.

The fighting continued at the Malakand from the 26th July till the 1st August; and Chakdara, which was attacked at the same time, was not relieved until August 2nd, when the tribesmen were dispersed after suffering very heavy losses. The original gathering of about 1,000 followers of the Mad Fakir had been increased during this short period by numerous reinforcements to some 12,000 men at the Malakand and 8,000 at Chakdara. In addition to the Swat valley tribesmen, the following clans were included among the enemy, *viz.*, Adinzai, Dush Khel, Ausa Khel of the Talash valley, a small party of Painda Khel, and contingents from Bajaur, and the Maidan and Upper Jandol valleys. Sections of the Utman Khel and Bunerwals and some 2,000 British subjects from Yusafzai also took part in the rising.

The Khan of Dir was away in Kohistan when this fanatical outbreak occurred, and he had evidently been unwilling or unable to restrain his people. But though his attitude may have been uncertain at first, when he saw that the Mad Fakir's attempt was doomed to failure, he took prompt measures to prove his loyalty to Government. On the 5th August he reopened communication with Chitral and held the Panjkora bridge with his own retainers. He then visited Major Deane at Chakdara and promised to disarm and punish any of his subjects who had taken part in the rising.

[1] Bare headed.

The Khan of Nawagai, notwithstanding the efforts of the *mullas* and others to turn him from his allegiance, declined to encourage openly any hostility to Government.

It was soon evident that this was no mere local disturbance, but rather a preconcerted attempt of the combined tribes to drive the British from their country. Accordingly on the 30th July the Government of India issued orders for the despatch of a force to suppress the rising and to punish the tribes implicated in the attacks on our troops.

Operations of the Malakand Field Force in Dir and Bajaur.

The composition of this force, which was known as the Malakand Field Force, and was under the command of Major-General Sir Bindon Blood, K.C.B., has already been given in Appendix A., Chapter VIII.

The operations of the Malakand Field Force in the Swat valley, the Utman Khel and Mohmand countries have been fully dealt with in the chapters referring to these tribes. It is, however, proposed briefly to recapitulate these movements, before dealing in detail with the operations in Dir and Bajaur.

By the 8th August the concentration of the force was completed. The 1st Brigade was at Amandarra, the 2nd at Malakand and Khar, and the Reserve Brigade remained at Mardan to watch the Bunerwals. On this date news was received of an attack on Shabkadar by the Mohmands, led by the Hadda Mulla. This attack afforded still further proof of the general nature of the fanatical disturbance among the Pathan tribes.

Meanwhile the troops of the Malakand Brigade, which had been reinforced, had already started operations in the Swat valley for the punishment of the tribesmen. On the 9th August the Lower Swatis submitted unconditionally, and on the 17th the 1st Brigade advanced into Upper Swat, proceeding as far as Miangora, and returned to Thana on the 26th.

It was now decided to postpone the punishment of the Bunerwals to a later date and to proceed at once with the coercion of the Utman Khel on the left bank of the Swat river. Accordingly on the 30th August the 2nd Brigade marched down the valley with this object, and the Reserve Brigade was ordered up from Mardan and Rustam. At this time, however, events transpired in another portion of the frontier which necessitated the postponement of operations against the Cis-Swat Utman Khel, and the 2nd Brigade was recalled.

It will be remembered that the Hadda Mulla's gathering of Mohmand tribesmen, which attacked Shabkadar, was signally defeated on the 9th August by a force from Peshawar under Brigadier-General Elles, and dispersed to the hills. Towards the end of August, however, the *mulla* succeeded in collecting a fresh force, and on the 30th news was received that he was advancing into Dir in order to retaliate on the Nawab for his friendly attitude towards the British Government. On receipt of this information the 2nd Brigade was recalled from Cis-Utman Khel territory and the 3rd (or Reserve) Brigade under Brigadier-General Wodehouse was pushed forward to Uch in the Adinzai valley. This prompt move caused the Hadda Mulla to abandon his advance towards Dir, and his gathering dispersed. Nevertheless, on the 3rd September, the Government decided to undertake the punishment of the Mohmands forthwith; and a force of two brigades, under the command of Major-General Elles, was ordered to advance from the Shabkadar direction while two brigades of the Malakand Field Force were to co-operate from the east, moving through Bajaur, *viâ* Sado and Nawagai. The object of this expedition was to support the Chiefs of Dir and Nawagai and to safeguard our communication with Chitral, and then, in conjunction with the force under General Elles, to break the power of the Hadda Mulla and crush the hostile gathering in the Mohmand country.

Advance of Malakand Field Force through Bajaur to co-operate with Mohmand Field Force.

At this time the attitude of the Panjkora valley tribes caused considerable anxiety. The fighting in the Swat valley had naturally given rise to much unrest among them, and they were also stirred by the general spirit of fanaticism which had spread throughout the Pathan peoples on the border. Exaggerated reports had reached them of the Afridi successes in the Khaibar and on the Samana range; and the *mullas* diligently spread a report that a *jehad*, or religious war, had been ordered by the Amir, who himself intended to take part in it. The movements of the Hadda Mulla and the activity of the Mohmands also had a most disquieting effect on the Dir and Bajaur peoples.

2 squadrons, 11th Bengal Lancers.
10th Field Battery, Royal Artillery.
38th Dogras.
4 companies, 22nd Punjab Infantry.
½ No. 5 Company, Madras Sappers and Miners.
2 sections, Field Hospitals.

It has already been mentioned that the orders of the Government for an advance into Bajaur reached Sir Bindon Blood on the 3rd September. On the following day a column, as per margin, under Brigadier-General Wodehouse, marched from Uch to Sado with orders to secure the bridge over the Panjkora. This column was reinforced on the 5th September by No. 1 Mountain Battery, Royal Artillery, the 1st Battalion, West Surrey Regiment (The Queen's), and No. 3 Company, Bombay Sappers and Miners.

It transpired later that this move was only just in time to prevent the seizure of the bridge by the Bajauris and Shamozai Utman Khel. Information was received that these clans had met in *jirga* at Khar (in Bajaur) and had decided to oppose the Government. The minor *khans* of Bajaur and a representative of the Khan of Nawagai who were present had promised to lend arms and men, though, as they told the *jirgas,* they could not themselves join in active hostilities against the British troops.

The Khans of Nawagai, Jhar, and Khar, when called upon to explain their conduct, stated that they had been powerless to overcome the unanimous determination of the Bajaur clans to resist us.

The prompt advance of General Wodehouse's force to the Panjkora, however, had anticipated the action of the Bajaur tribesmen and for the moment frustrated their plans. Consequently they abandoned the idea of fighting for the present, pending a further meeting of the clans to reconsider their future policy.

On the 6th September the Shamozai Utman Khel expressed their willingness to submit to terms, and three days later, on the arrival of our troops at Ghosam, messages were received from the Khan of Nawagai and other Bajaur Chiefs offering to assist the Government.

On the 7th September Sir Bindon Blood, with divisional headquarters and the 2nd Brigade under General Jeffreys, marched from Chakdara to Sarai, and on the next day advanced across the Panjkora to Kotkai. This brigade was equipped entirely with mule transport ; five days' rations for men and one day's grain for animals were carried in regimental charge, while seven days' rations were carried by the Brigade Commissariat. Similar arrangements were made for the 3rd Brigade, except that its transport consisted chiefly of camels. Fourteen days' supplies were also carried by the Divisional Commissariat. The 1st Brigade was left to hold the Swat valley and the line of communications up to Sado : it was equipped with camels, carts, and a few mules.

On the 9th September the 2nd Brigade with Divisional Headquarters moved to Ghosam. The advance into Mohmand country was now postponed for three days in order that Sir Bindon Blood might deal with the Shamozai Utman Khel. A fine of 100 rifles was demanded from this section, but the time at the General's disposal was not sufficient to allow of punitive measures so as to enforce full compliance with the terms, and only fifteen breech-loading rifles and eighty-six guns were given up.

Meanwhile Major Deane, with a cavalry escort, proceeded to settle terms with the Jandolis, and went up the valley as far as Barwa. The Khans of Mundah, Tor Chandeh, and Shah were submissive and gave up over thirty rifles. But Umra Khan's brothers and his cousin Abdul Majid Khan, who had also participated in the rising in Swat, failed to comply with Major Deane's demand that they should surrender a certain number of rifles ; and as they had sent away their women and children, it was evident that they contemplated resistance. They were, however, promptly seized before they could put these plans into execution, and were sent under escort to Malakand, where they were detained until they had complied with the terms imposed.

On the 10th-11th September the 3rd Brigade concentrated at Shakrata, and a portion of the 1st Brigade, as shown in the margin, was moved up to Sado, to guard the Panjkora bridge and the advanced depôt which was formed there. Cavalry reconnaissances to the Batai and Shinai passes met with no opposition ; and on the 12th the 2nd Brigade encamped at Khar (in Bajaur), while the 3rd Brigade advanced to Shamshak at the southern end of the Watelai valley. At this place some Mamund and Salarzai *maliks* visited the camp, and enquired what were the intentions of Government with regard to their people, but no representative *jirga* appeared on behalf of either of these sections. The *maliks* were informed that, as a condition of peace, fifty rifles would be

3 squadrons, Guides Cavalry.
31st Punjab Infantry.
45th Sikhs.
½ No. 5 Company, Madras Sappers and Miners.

demanded from the Mamunds and forty from the Salarzai. Meanwhile the cavalry reconnoitred the Watelai and Chaharmung valleys, but except for a few harmless shots from the Mamund village of Zagai no opposition was encountered.

Sir Bindon Blood now intended to co-operate with the Mohmand Field Force, by sending Brigadier-General Jeffreys with a portion of the 2nd Brigade across the Rambat Pass to Butkor and Danish Kol, while he himself with the remainder of his force was to move into Mohmand territory by way of Nawagai. In accordance with this plan, the 2nd Brigade marched from Khar on the 14th September, and seized the Rambat Pass. Leaving the Buffs and the company of Sappers and Miners to hold the pass, the General moved the rest of his troops back to a camp on the right bank of the Chaharmung stream, about two miles from Markhanai. This village belonged to the Mandal Utman Khel who had taken part in the fighting in the Swat valley, and had hitherto made no sign of submission.

Attack on 2nd Brigade Camp at Markhanai by Mamunds.

The camp near Markhanai was a four-sided entrenchment, of the type usual in frontier warfare. The troops bivouacked on the perimeter, protected by a breastwork, while the hospitals, transport, stores, etc., were placed in the centre. The east face was on the edge of a wide *nala* about sixty feet deep, with precipitous banks, beyond which was a stony plain intersected by numerous small ravines. On the other three sides was open country, except that, in a fold of ground, about seventy yards from the west parapet, some terraced fields sloped down to a *nala* which ran northwards to the Chaharmung stream, about 1,200 yards distant.

Shortly after 8 P.M. three signal shots fired by the enemy were followed by a heavy fusilade from the east, west, and north, which caused considerable loss among the animals in the centre of the camp. The troops at once manned their trenches on the perimeter, and lights and fires were promptly extinguished. The attack, which was mainly directed on the east face, held by the Guides Infantry, was replied to by steady volleys, while the battery fired star shell to light up the enemy's position. The tribesmen made no attempt to rush the camp, but, utilizing the cover afforded by boulders and *nalas*, to approach to close range, kept up a galling fire till 10 P.M. Firing now ceased for a time and signal fires were seen to be lighted at several villages in the Mamund valley.

A little before 11 P.M. the attack was renewed with increased vigour and lasted for about three and a half hours. This time the main attack was made on the west face, held by the 38th Dogras. Brigadier-General Jeffreys ordered the Dogras to hold their fire in the hope that the enemy would attempt a charge; but the tribesmen could not be induced to leave the cover of the broken ground close to the parapet, and accordingly a counter-attack was ordered. While collecting their men for this purpose, Captain W. E. Tomkins and Lieutenant A. W. Bailey, 38th Dogras, were killed, and Lieutenant H. A. Harrington was dangerously wounded. The attempt was then abandoned, and shortly afterwards the enemy drew off. The casualties of the 2nd Brigade during this night attack were two British officers, two sepoys and two followers killed, one British and one native officer, and nine other ranks wounded; ninety-eight horses and transport animals were also killed or wounded. The enemy consisted of some 400 Mamund marksmen under the leadership of Muhammad Amin of Inayat Kila, with a few Salarzai, and some men of the Shamozai and But Khel Ismailzai sections of the Utman Khel. They lost twelve men killed besides many wounded.

Early next morning Captain E. H. Cole, with a squadron of the 11th Bengal Lancers, started in pursuit up the Mamund valley, and, overtaking a party of the enemy near Badan Kot, killed twenty-one of them, and drove the remainder into the hills surrounding Badan gorge. Being prevented by the difficult ground from following the fugitives any further, Captain Cole withdrew his troopers. On seeing this, the enemy as usual recovered their courage, and began to harass the retirement of the cavalry, but as soon as they observed the approach of supporting troops from Markhanai they dispersed.

Information of the affair at Markhanai had at once been sent to Nawagai, and as soon as Sir Bindon Blood had ascertained beyond doubt that the Mamunds were responsible for this attack on our camp, he instructed Brigadier-General Jeffreys to take prompt measures to punish them.

The previous orders for the advance of the 2nd Brigade over the Rambat pass were accordingly cancelled, and on the 15th September Brigadier-General Jeffreys concentrated his troops at Inayat Kila.

Meanwhile the 3rd Brigade remained in an entrenched position at Nawagai, where Sir Bindon Blood decided to await the advance of Major-General Elles' force from Peshawar. The reasons for this course were as follows :—(*i*) Sir Bindon Blood did not consider that his single brigade was strong enough to deal with the Hadda Mulla's following unsupported, or to force their position on the Bedmanai pass; (*ii*) it was inadvisable to join General Jeffreys, since the 2nd Brigade alone was strong enough to carry out the punishment of the Mamunds, and a retrograde movement in the face of the hostile Mohmand gathering would have been most unwise, especially as the country in rear was intricate and difficult; (*iii*) it was of the utmost importance that the Khan of Nawagai should be upheld by our present support; for, if left to himself, he would almost certainly have been powerless to resist the pressure brought to bear upon him to join in active hostilities against the Government.

Reconnaissances were made by the cavalry of the 3rd Brigade from Nawagai to the Kandara, Ata Khel, and Ambahar valleys. On the 15th and 16th September cavalry patrols reconnoitred the Bedmanai pass, which was found to be strongly held by the Hadda Mulla's forces.

On the 17th news of the fighting in the Mamund valley reached Nawagai, but the *Khan*, though strongly urged by his advisers, and by envoys from the *Sipah Salar*, to turn against us, remained true to his agreement to assist the Government. His retainers were employed in preventing any attack on the camp, and so far had been successful in their efforts. On the 18th communication was opened up with the Mohmand Field Force under Major-General Elles, which had reached the Nahaki pass.[1] On the 19th Sir Bindon Blood was directed from Army Head Quarters to proceed to Inayat Kila, but owing to the situation at Nawagai he was unable to comply with this order until the 22nd.

On the night of the 19th some 2,000 of the Hadda Mulla's followers from the Bedmanai pass made an attack on the camp, but were easily driven off. Our casualties were one man killed and one wounded. The camp was situated on stony terraced fields which sloped gently downwards towards the south. To the north the ground was open. On the east and west faces were deep *nalas*

[1] *Vide* Chapter XI.

about 150 to 200 yards from the camp, in which the enemy could collect, and on the west the terraces gave good cover even nearer. About a mile beyond on either side were steep rocky hills, and from the western ridge a low spur jutted out eastward to within 1,000 yards of the camp.

On the 20th a second night attack was made from the north and north-west by a body of tribesmen under the leadership of Sufi Mulla of Batikot who had joined the Hadda Mulla's force. Information had previously been given by the Khan of Nawagai that an attack was probable, and accordingly the troops were on the alert and well prepared.

The attack, which began about 9 P.M., was well carried out by rushes of swordsmen, covered by a smart fire of small arms; and the firing, with rushes at intervals, sometimes against three sides of the camp at the same time, went on till about 2 A.M., when the enemy drew off.

The steadiness of the troops during this somewhat trying action was quite perfect, and the safety of the camp was never in the slightest degree doubtful, although the enemy's swordsmen were so determined that many of them were shot down close to the entrenchment. The fire discipline of the infantry was shown to be excellent; the star shells fired by the mountain battery were most useful, and shrapnel and case were also fired at different times with great effect. Besides the 3,000 engaged in this attack the enemy had another body of some 2,000 in reserve. Their losses were heavy and amounted to at least 330 killed, besides a large number wounded, and several leading men were known to have been killed.

On our side the casualties were one man killed, thirty-one officers and men wounded, including Brigadier-General Wodehouse.

The cavalry were sent in pursuit at daybreak, but the enemy were not seen. On this date Sir Bindon Blood and Major-General Elles, Commanding the Mohmand Field Force, met at Lakarai. On the following day the former proceeded to the Mamund valley, while the 3rd Brigade, as shown in the margin, under command of Lieut.-Colonel B. C. Graves, 39th Garhwalis, marched to Kuz Chinarai, and was transferred to the Mohmand Field Force, vide Chapter XI. After taking part in the operations of this Force, the

1st Battalion, Royal West Surrey Regiment (The Queen's).
22nd Punjab Infantry.
39th Garwhal Rifles.
1 Squadron, 11th B. L.
No. 1 Mountain Battery, R.A.
No. 3 Co., Bo. S. and M.

3rd Brigade marched to Peshawar on the 2nd October, and was eventually employed with the Tirah Expeditionary Force.

We may now return to the operations of the 2nd Brigade. On the 16th September Brigadier-General Jeffreys advanced from Inayat Kila up the Watelai valley. His troops were divided into three columns as under :—

No. 1, Lieut.-Colonel Goldney, 35th Sikhs.	1 squadron, 11th Bengal Lancers. 4 guns, No. 8 Mountain Battery. 4 companies, The Buffs. 6 " 35th Sikhs. 2 sub-sections, No. 4 company, Bengal Sappers and Miners.
No. 2, Lieut.-Colonel Vivian, 38th Dogras.	6 companies, 38th Dogras. 4 sub-sections, No. 4 company, Bengal Sappers and Miners.
No. 3. Major Campbell, Guides Infantry.	2 companies, The Buffs. 5 " Guides Infantry. 2 sub-sections, No. 4 company, Bengal Sappers and Miners.

The plan of operations was as follows :—

No. 1 column was to advance along the Kaga pass road to Badalai, destroying the fortified villages of Tanrai, Munar, and Hazarnao *en route*. No. 2 column was to move along the eastern foothills against the villages of Shinkot, Lower Chingai, Damadolah, and Badan, while No. 3 column, moving more or less parallel with the centre force, was to direct its march towards Agrah, and deal with the villages met with on the west of the Watelai stream.

Lieut.-Colonel Vivian met with no opposition at Shinkot or Chingai, and having destroyed these villages, moved on to Damadolah. Here he found a considerable force of the enemy holding a strong position. Having decided that without guns his small force was insufficient to carry the position, he now withdrew, and was followed up for some distance by the enemy, who were driven off with loss. This column reached camp at Inayat Kila at 4 P.M., the only casualties being two men slightly wounded.

Meanwhile the other two columns moved up the valley. At about 7-30 A.M., the cavalry reported that the enemy were holding Badan, and Lieut.-Colonel Ommaney, with four companies of the Buffs and two guns was ordered to dislodge them. The enemy evacuated this position without showing fight, and the Buffs followed them up towards the hills as far as Dabar, leaving the village of Badan to be destroyed by No. 2 column, which was expected to come on later. Meanwhile the remainder of No. 1 column pushed on towards Badalai. When nearly opposite the village, Lieut.-Colonel Goldney received a report from the cavalry that the enemy were collecting in strength from the west. He accordingly halted and ordered the detachment of the Buffs at Dabar to rejoin the column. Shortly afterwards, however, the enemy were reported to be moving off towards the Kaga pass at the head of the valley. On receipt of this information Brigadier-General Jeffreys directed Lieut.-Colonel Goldney to push on without waiting for the remainder of the column; and at the same time he sent a message ordering Major Campbell to bring his detachment up on the left of the centre force. A few of the enemy who were holding Badalai were quickly driven off, and about 9-30 A.M., Captain Ryder, with 1½ companies 35th Sikhs, moved up the spur to the east of the village to protect the right flank. The guns, with 1½ companies as escort, also moved up the hill on the right of Badalai, while the remainder of the 35th Sikhs advanced against Upper Chingai. Having cleared this village two companies pushed on to Shahi Tangi, which was reached at 10-30 A.M. Here Lieut.-Colonel Goldney halted to await the arrival of the Buffs. As soon as they perceived that the advance of the troops was checked, the enemy began to press forward in considerable numbers. Lieut.-Colonel Goldney thereupon ordered the Sikhs to retire, and the two companies which had advanced rather far from their supports were hotly attacked as they fell back towards Chingai.

A body of the enemy advancing across some open ground on the west threatened to cut off their retreat, but were checked and dispersed by an opportune charge of the squadron under Captain Cole. This action relieved the pressure on the Sikhs, who now turned on their assailants and drove them off at the point of the bayonet.

At this moment the four companies of the Buffs arrived, and the two sections of the battery came into action on the ridge north of Chingai. Meanwhile No. 3 column under Major Campbell came up, and having occupied a position on the right bank of the Watelai stream, checked the advance of a large body of tribesmen who were crossing from the western side of the valley to reinforce the enemy at Shahi Tangi. During the retirement of the 35th Sikhs from that village, Lieutenant V. Hughes and one sepoy were killed and Lieutenant Cassels and sixteen men wounded.

Shortly after midday the Buffs, with the 35th Sikhs, again moved forward, covered by the fire of the artillery, to complete the destruction of the villages of Chingai and Shahi Tangi. This was successfully accomplished by 2-30 P.M., and appreciable loss was inflicted on the enemy, who had all the while maintained a stubborn resistance.

The Brigadier-General now began to withdraw his troops, with the intention of returning to camp at Inayat Kila.

The flanking party of the 35th Sikhs was still on the high ridge above Chingai ; orders to retire had been sent by signal to Captain Ryder earlier in the day, but had failed to reach him. About 3-30 P.M., however, Captain Ryder, observing the retirement of the main body, began to withdraw his men along the ridge, but in a direction which diverged from the general line of retreat. As this party fell back it was hotly assailed by the enemy on all sides ; but eventually, with the assistance of the Guides, who most gallantly came to their support, Captain Ryder's men succeeded in reaching the plain just as darkness set in. During their retirement the Sikhs had repulsed repeated charges of the enemy's swordsmen with heavy loss : but their own casualties were also severe, and amounted to fifteen killed, three missing, and twenty-four wounded, among the latter being both the British and two native officers. Twenty-two Martini-Henry rifles also fell into the hands of the enemy.

Brigadier-General Jeffreys had halted the covering troops in order to give Captain Ryder's party time to withdraw, but as soon as he was assured of the latter's safety, he continued the retirement. At about 7 P.M. the General reached Bilot, where he was met by four companies under Major Worlledge, who had marched to his assistance from Inayat Kila. This reinforcement was at once sent to support the Guides, since it was evident from the sound of firing that they were still engaged with the enemy. The Buffs, who were retiring in extended order, had now reached Munar, while the battery escorted by the Sappers and Miners and a company of the 35th Sikhs was moving to a position just north of Bilot.

Seeing that it would be difficult to reach Inayat Kila that night, and being anxious for the safety of the detachments on his right, Brigadier-General Jeffreys decided to occupy Munar and Bilot. Darkness had already set in, and in the confusion the order to hold Munar failed to reach the officer commanding the Buffs, who consequently continued to retire. A heavy thunderstorm breaking at this moment added to the difficulties of the troops, and they now became separated. The Buffs and the company of the 35th Sikhs, which had lost touch with the battery, made their way independently to the camp at Inayat Kila, where they arrived about 9 P.M. Meanwhile the guns with the Sappers and Miners had moved on to Bilot, where they were joined by about a dozen men of the Buffs. General Jeffreys now ordered this small force to take up a defensive position in the village, part of which was burning; but the enemy rushing up occupied some walls within close range, and poured in a destructive fire causing serious loss in men and animals. Lieutenant Watson, R.E., Lieutenant Wynter, R.A., and several men were wounded, and a number of the battery mules were hit. The guns fired a few rounds of case, and most persistent attempts were made by the Buffs and Sappers to clear the village; but their repeated charges, though most gallantly led by Lieutenants Colvin and Watson, failed to dislodge the enemy. Eventually about midnight, the four companies under Major Worlledge, who had been unable to gain touch with the Guides in the darkness, arrived at Bilot. With the assistance of this reinforcement the tribesmen were quickly driven off, and no further attack was made on the village during the rest of the night. For their gallant conduct in this affair Lieutenants Watson and Colvin, R.E., and Corporal Smith, East Kent Regiment, received the Victoria Cross.

The casualties during the day amounted in all to 2 officers (Lieutenant Hughes, 35th Sikhs, and Lieutenant Crawford, R.A.) and 36 men killed, 11 officers, 102 men, and 3 followers wounded.

On the 18th September the 2nd Brigade destroyed the village of Damadolah, where a large quantity of grain was obtained. During the operations the enemy kept up a desultory fire from the hills north-east of the village, and as usual followed up the subsequent retirement, but they were unable to get to close quarters. Their loss was not ascertained, but was probably severe: on our side two men were killed and five wounded.

On the following day Hazarnao and several other villages in that vicinity were destroyed without opposition, and a large supply of grain and *bhusa* was brought away. At Bilot it was found that the bodies of seven Muhammadan sepoys, who were buried there on the night of the 16th, had been exhumed and stripped, but not mutilated.

On the 20th the village of Zagai was attacked and destroyed without loss. This village belonged to some ex-retainers of Umra Khan, who were now led by one Ustaz Muhammad. During the withdrawal of the troops, the Buffs were closely pressed by the enemy while retiring over difficult ground from a spur on the north-east. The enemy, however, were driven back with heavy loss, and made no attempt to follow up the troops when they reached open country. Our casualties were four officers (Major Moody, Captain Hulke, Lieutenant Power and Lieutenant Keene, East Kent Regiment) and ten men wounded. During the return march a tower near Zagadherai, also belonging to Umra Khan's retainers, was demolished.

The next day was spent quietly in camp at Inayat Kila. A few shots were fired by the enemy during the night, but no serious attack was attempted. The village of Dag was next cleared and destroyed on the 22nd; the enemy offered little resistance beyond harassing the rear guard during the retirement, when one man was killed and two wounded. On this date Sir Bindon Blood arrived from Nawagai, escorted by two squadrons of the 11th Bengal Lancers.

On the 23rd the Brigade destroyed Tangai, about one and a half miles south-west of Dag. The enemy were seen in large numbers on the surrounding hills, but the excellent disposition of the Buffs and 35th Sikhs, aided by artillery fire, prevented them from seriously interfering with the Dogras and Sappers who were engaged in demolishing the defences of the village. On the completion of this work the force moved back to camp. Only two casualties occurred during the day.

On this date the Khan of Jhar visited the camp and reported that the Mamunds, disheartened by their heavy losses, were anxious to come to terms. Sir Bindon Blood accordingly agreed to suspend hostilities for forty-eight hours to allow the headmen to meet and arrange matters, and to send in a *jirga*.

Advantage was taken of this temporary truce to reorganize the 2nd Brigade, which had suffered considerably from casualties and sickness. No. 8 Bengal Mountain Battery, the Buffs, and 35th Sikhs were sent to the Panjkora, where they were employed on the line of communications. They were replaced by two squadrons Guides Cavalry, No. 7 Mountain Battery, R.A., the West Kent Regiment, and 31st Punjab Infantry. Supplies were also sent up from the Panjkora without interference, and a convoy escorted by three squadrons of the 11th Bengal Lancers was forwarded to the 3rd Brigade which had advanced from Nawagai to Kuz Chinarai to co-operate with the Mohmand Field Force.

To return now to the question of negotiations with the Mamunds. The tribesmen had been informed that a representative *jirga* must attend at Inayat Kila and that a fine of fifty rifles and Rs. 4,000 would have to be paid before terms could be discussed. On the 24th September the headmen of Dabar, Badan, and Upper Chingai brought in Rs. 400 and four fire-arms, and stated that they were trying to bring about the submission of the rest of the tribe. It was explained to these men that nothing less than the complete submission of the whole tribe would be accepted, and that terms of peace could only be arranged with a full and representative *jirga*.

At the request of the *khans* the armistice was extended for another twenty-four hours, and on the evening of the 26th a full *jirga* came in. They produced fifty worthless *jezails* and 3,575 Kabuli rupees, the Khan of Jhar standing security for the balance of the fine. During an interview with Mr. Davis, Assistant Political Officer, which took place on the next day, their attitude was unsatisfactory. They were told that fifty rifles must be surrendered as a penalty for their share in the attack on our posts in the Swat valley, and in addition they were ordered to return twenty-two rifles captured during the fighting on the 16th September. The *jirga* at first definitely declined to comply with these demands, on the ground that "all the world had turned out to take part in the *ghaza* at Chakdara," and that the rifles captured on the 16th had been carried off by men from Afghan territory who had joined in the fighting. They refused to give hostages as security for the return of the rifles, but promised to discuss matters further with their people and give an answer on the next day. The promised reply, however, was never received from the *jirga*, and it was afterwards ascertained that they had not even taken the trouble to make their fellow tribesmen acquainted with the terms imposed.

Though ostensibly friendly to the Government there is little doubt that the Khans of Nawagai, Khar, and Jhar secretly encouraged the Mamunds to resist compliance with the terms, and they evidently hoped that, owing to the disturbances which were taking place in other parts of the frontier, our troops would soon be compelled to evacuate their country.

Any expectations which might have been entertained as to the peaceful intentions of the Mamunds were dispelled by reports received on the 28th. It was even thought that an attack on the camp would be attempted during the night. The tribesmen, however, were fully employed in removing their property to the hills in preparation for further fighting. Their main object in securing these few days' respite had apparently been to gain an opportunity for sowing their land.

Operations were resumed on the 29th September, when the following villages were destroyed without opposition:—Zagaderai, Khalozai, Shagai, Amanatta, Jangzai, and Kamar. Fifteen large well-built towers, which formed part of the defences of these fortified villages, were demolished, and ample supplies of grain, *bhusa*, and fuel were taken back to camp.

On the following morning Brigadier-General Jeffreys, with the troops noted in the margin, marched up the valley to attack Agrah and Gat. These two villages are situated on the lower slopes of the spur which juts out from Lakra Sar and forms the watershed between the Kakazai and Upper Watelai Nalas.

Guides Cavalry 163 sabres.		
No. 7 Mountain Battery, R.A.		
Royal West Kent Regiment	380	Rifles.
31st Punjab Infantry ..	385	"
38th Dogras	342	"
Guides Infantry ..	364	"
TOTAL ..	1,391	"

As the column approached, a large hostile force was seen on the ridge to the west of the villages, and numbers of the tribesmen were collecting from other parts of the valley. The enemy's position was one of considerable strength. A rocky, precipitous ridge divided the space between the two villages, while on either flank were steep boulder-strewn spurs commanding the ground over which the troops had to advance. The action was begun by the cavalry, who, after advancing over very difficult ground for some distance up the Kakazai Nala, dismounted and opened fire on a number of tribesmen who were coming across from the west.

The plan of attack on the two villages was as follows:—The Guides Infantry were to advance up the spur on the west of Agrah, which was strongly held: the West Kent Regiment moving on the right of the Guides was to clear some wooded ground south of Agrah, and then advance to a certain point on the hill in rear of the village. The 31st Punjab Infantry were detailed to occupy the rocky ridge between the two villages, and the 38th Dogras were held in reserve.

The artillery, having taken up a position on the right bank of a small *nala* about a mile and a half south of Gat, opened fire on the ridge against which the 31st Punjab Infantry were to advance. Here the enemy, well protected by numerous *sangars* and huge boulders, stoutly opposed the attacking troops, and clung desperately to their position, until they were finally driven out at the point of the bayonet. While gallantly leading this attack Lieut.-Colonel O'Bryen fell mortally wounded, and Lieutenant Peacock, of the same regiment, also received a severe wound.

When Brigadier-General Jeffreys saw that the 31st Punjab Infantry were hotly engaged, he ordered two companies from the reserve to support them from a small knoll somewhat further to their right, while the battery advanced about half a mile to a second position whence they could shell the ground east of Gat.

The Guides Infantry, having occupied the spur on the west, were now fully employed in checking the advance of the enemy on their front and left flank. Meanwhile the West Kent Regiment had gained the slopes above Agrah, and the Sappers and Miners proceeded to demolish the village. A little later the West Kents moved across to support the left flank of the 31st, and in so doing they met with a desperate resistance from the tribesmen, who were well posted behind *sangars* and stone walls, which enclosed the terraced fields dotted about the hillside. In clearing one of these *sangars* Lieutenant Clayton Browne was killed and several men wounded. Following up this partial success, the enemy's swordsmen promptly charged the remainder of the party in the *sangar* and drove them back. Major Western, however, at once ordered a counter-attack, and the supports led by Captain Styles made a bayonet charge and dispersed the tribesmen.

Gat village was now partially destroyed, but as the enemy were observed advancing in large numbers from the direction of Zai, the officer commanding the West Kents withdrew his battalion.

As soon as the West Kent Regiment was clear of Gat, a general retirement was ordered. This was steadily and skilfully carried out, and the Brigade returned to Inayat Kila at 4 P.M.

The casualties in this action were two officers and ten men killed, seven officers and forty-two men wounded. The enemy's losses were severe; four leading *maliks* were killed, and many dead had been left in and near Gat village.

Sir Bindon Blood now determined to strengthen the force in the Mamund valley with a view to crushing all further resistance as speedily as possible. He accordingly left Panjkora for Inayat Kila on the 2nd October, accompanied by one squadron, Guides Cavalry, No. 8 Bengal Mountain Battery, and four companies, 24th Punjab Infantry. Brigadier-General Meiklejohn was also ordered to follow with a further reinforcement consisting of the 10th Field Battery, Royal Artillery,[1] No. 5 Company, Madras Sappers and Miners, and the Highland Light Infantry. This latter column reached Inayat Kila on the 4th.

On the 2nd October the troops of the 2nd Brigade were employed in foraging, and, after collecting some 1,100 mule loads of supplies, returned to camp without meeting with any opposition. On the following day Brigadier-General Jeffreys, with the troops noted in the margin, marched up the valley towards Agrah and Gat. The enemy, expecting that the latter village was to be attacked, collected in the hills above it: but on arriving opposite Badalai the troops turned off to the right and seized and destroyed that village, meeting with but little opposition. During the retirement, however, the enemy came boldly forward

Guides Cavalry, 2 squadrons.
No. 7 Mountain Battery.
No. 8 " " 4 guns.
Royal West Kent Regiment.
31st Punjab Infantry.
38th Dogras.
Guides Infantry.

[1] The advance of this field battery is noteworthy. Early in September it moved to the Panjkora over a very difficult road from Sarai to Sado. Four guns now marched to Inayat Kila over country entirely destitute of made roads and where no wheeled traffic had previously been seen.

from the direction of Chingai and the villages to the north-west, and made persistent efforts to surround the flanks, but were checked by the cavalry and the fire of the covering troops. The casualties in the 2nd Brigade on this date were two men killed and seventeen wounded.

AT INAYAT KILA.

1st Brigade (*Brigadier-General Meiklejohn*).
2nd Battalion, Highland Light Infantry.
24th Punjab Infantry (4 companies).
31st ,, ,,

2nd Brigade (*Brigadier-General Jeffreys*).
Royal West Kent Regiment.
38th Dogras.
Guides Infantry.

Divisional Troops.
10th Field Battery, Royal Artillery (4 guns).
No. 7 Mountain Battery, Royal Artillery.
No. 8 (Bengal) Mountain Battery (4 guns).
Guides Cavalry.
No. 4 Company, Bengal Sappers and Miners.
No. 5 ,, Madras ,, ,, ,,

On the line of communications—
1 squadron, 10th Bengal Lancers.
1st Battalion, East Kent Regiment.
16th Bengal Infantry.
20th Punjab ,,
21st ,, ,,
24th ,, ,, (4 companies).
35th Sikhs.

On the 4th October another redistribution, as shown in the margin, was made of the troops composing the Malakand Field Force.

The Mamunds being now aware of the arrival of fresh troops, and recognising that the Government was determined to bring about their submission at all costs, requested the Khan of Nawagai to intercede, and arrange terms of peace. Accordingly on the recommendation of Major Deane, who had arrived at Inayat Kila, hostilities were suspended in order to allow the *khans* to reopen negotiations with the tribesmen. Foraging parties were, however, still sent out daily, and on the 6th October the cavalry had a slight skirmish with the enemy in which a duffadar was wounded; but after this date no further shots were fired in the valley.

In consideration of the heavy losses which they had suffered in killed and wounded, and by the destruction of their villages, and the confiscation of grain and supplies, the terms originally imposed were somewhat reduced. The Mamunds were now required to make complete submission, but were only asked to return the twenty-two rifles taken from our troops. They were warned that if they failed to comply with these final terms, the Khan of Nawagai would be authorised to occupy the whole valley and seize their lands.

This time the Mamunds appeared to be in earnest in their desire for peace: they sent away their allies who had come from beyond the limits of the Watelai valley, and picquetted the approaches to our camp in order to prevent night firing by any possible malcontents. The restitution of the rifles and the final settlement were, however, delayed by intrigues from the Afghan side. Messengers from the *Sipah Salar* crossed the border and urged the tribesmen not to give up the arms; ammunition was also being forwarded from Kabul, and two mule loads were reported to have been received on the 8th October. Eventually, however, the tribesmen were persuaded to surrender the rifles which had been demanded, and on the 11th October the Mamund *jirga* came into Nawa Kila, about half a mile from the British camp.

The tribesmen were received in durbar by Sir Bindon Blood, and stated that they desired to make complete submission and secure a lasting peace; they also added that they had only fought against us in order to prevent the annexation of their country, which they greatly feared. A written statement was then given them to the effect that Government did not contemplate any such action, provided that the behaviour of the tribe was satisfactory and they continued to abide by the terms of their agreement. They were further assured that, although the question of the Afghan boundary line cutting through their land could not be discussed, no interference on the part of Afghan officials would be permitted in the portion of their territory which lay within the British sphere of influence.

The *jirga* appeared to be well satisfied with their reception and with the assurances given to them, and promised faithfully to observe the terms of settlement. They also agreed to expel Ustaz Muhammad and other adherents of Umra Khan from their valley.

The operations against the Mamunds were thus brought to a close, and on the following day the troops evacuated the Watelai valley and marched to Jhar.

From the 14th September to the 11th October the casualties in the 2nd Brigade were 6 officers killed, 24 wounded, 55 non-commissioned officers and men killed and 194 wounded: 135 horses and mules were killed and wounded or otherwise lost. The enemy's losses during the period were estimated at 300 killed and 250 wounded and they suffered severe punishment in the destruction of property and loss of grain and fodder.

In his report on the operations in the Watelai valley Sir Bindon Blood attributed the difficulties experienced in overcoming the resistance of the Mamunds to the following causes. The invasion of the valley was preceded by no decisive action which might have served as an object lesson to make the tribesmen realise our strength, while the physical features of their country gave the enemy many advantages which they utilised with no little tactical skill. Owing to the absence of water in the low-lying open country, many of the villages were situated near the rivulets in the lower slopes of the surrounding hills. Here the ground was invariably steep, broken, and very difficult. In retiring before the advance of our troops, and closely following them up during the inevitable retirement till they reached open country, the tribesmen chose the only tactics which could give them any measure of success. The fact that part of their lands lay in Afghan territory was a further advantage, in that they could easily remove much of their property beyond our reach.

The stubborn defence of their country in spite of continuous losses, gained for the Mamunds a well deserved reputation for bravery and good fighting qualities.

On the 13th October the troops under Sir Bindon Blood moved to Mattashah, three miles north of Jhar in the Babukarra valley in order to bring about a settlement with the Salarzai Tarkanri.

Settlement with the Salarzai Tarkanri, October 1897.

Although the Salarzai were implicated in the general rising, they had taken no very active part in the actual fighting and had not as a section combined with the Mamunds against us. Moreover, since the advance of the troops through Bajaur, they had abstained from any interference with the line of communication. It was therefore considered that a sufficient punishment would be inflicted by a fine of 20 rifles and 200 other fire-arms. The attitude of the Salarzai was at first uncertain; they were divided by internal feuds and the difficulty in arriving at a settlement was increased by the action of the Khan of Nawagai, who, in order to further his own designs upon their valley, was only too anxious to involve the inhabitants in hostilities with Government. After much discussion the Salarzai decided to submit; but a quarrel ensued between the Upper and Lower Salarzai as to the distribution of the fine, and, as they failed to agree, hostilities appeared to be imminent. Major Deane thereupon solved the difficulty by dealing with the Upper Salarzai separately, and on the 18th October they surrendered 100 guns which were accepted as full compliance with the terms, since it was known that they possessed no rifles. On the following day the Lower Salarzai also submitted ; they handed over 100 fire-arms and ten breech-loading rifles and gave security for the remainder.

During their stay at Mattashah the troops thoroughly reconnoitred the Babukarra valley. Snipers fired nightly into camp although it was protected by tribal picquets. Little damage was done, but on the 19th some twenty shots were fired and a sowar was wounded. As the *jirga* stated that this outrage was instigated by a recalcitrant *malik*, his villages and towers were destroyed by the troops and his lands were confiscated by the *jirga*.

On the 20th October the troops moved to Jhar ; and on the following day a Shamozai Utman Khel *jirga* came in and made submission. They surrendered twenty rifles and thirty-five other fire-arms ; as they had already given up a number of arms in September at Ghosam, and had since then assisted us by guarding the line of communication, this was now accepted as a full compliance with the terms imposed. On the 22nd October the Jandolis also brought into Ghosam the balance of rifles due from them.

Withdrawal of troops from Bajaur and Dir.

The last of the troops crossed the Panjkora river on the 23rd, and four days later the whole force returned to the Swat valley.

The following rewards were granted to the three *khans* who had assisted the troops during the operations in Bajaur ; *viz.*, to the Khan of Nawagai, Rs. 10,000 ; to the Khan of Khar, Rs. 3,500 ; and to the Khan of Jhar, Rs. 2,500.

After undertaking operations against certain other tribes, as described in previous chapters, the Malakand Field Force was broken up on the 19th January 1898. But in order to ensure the safety of our communication with Chitral a movable column was left in the Swat valley and the defences of the posts at Malakand and Chakdara were strengthened.

The Indian Medal, 1895, with clasp inscribed "Punjab Frontier, 1897-98," was granted to the troops employed in the operations in Bajaur and in the Mamund country.

The subsequent events in Dir and Bajaur, after the withdrawal of the Malakand Field Force, may now be briefly described.

The Chitral reliefs were successfully carried out during the month of May 1898. Later in the year the Chiefs of Dir and

Nawagai renewed their quarrel over the possession of the Jandol valley; but eventually a settlement was agreed upon. The Nawab of Dir retained possession of Jandol, in return for which he paid to the Khan of Nawagai a sum of Rs. 20,000 and abandoned all his claims in the Babukarra valley. For the next two years affairs in Dir and Bajaur remained quiet, though the Khan of Nawagai had some difficulty in maintaining his position in the face of constant internal quarrels among his people. To assist him in holding his own his subsidy was increased by Rs. 5,000 annually, and he received a present of 10,000 rounds of ammunition. During 1901 and 1902 the Khan of Nawagai became embroiled with the Salarzai of the Chaharmung valley and with the Mamunds, and the Nawab of Dir was only dissuaded from espousing the cause of the *Khan* against the latter section by the intervention of the Political Agent.

In the beginning of 1904 there was considerable friction between the Nawab of Dir and the subject tribes on the right bank of the Swat river, who complained of the oppressive rule of the Chief. The Adinzai were especially dissatisfied and were again anxious to secure the protection of Government, which they had previously requested in 1895. A settlement, however, was effected by the Political Agent, and the Nawab of Dir, being warned that any aggressive action against the Swat tribes would be displeasing to Government, abandoned his intention of coercing them. Later in the year a quarrel arose between the Nawab's two sons in Jandol. Mian Gul Jan, the younger son, who some time previously had been deprived of his governorship in the Adinzai valley, was now expelled from Mundah by his elder brother Auranzeb (better known as Badshah Khan) and fled to Nawagai. This Mian Gul Jan, son of the Muhammad Sharif Khan of Dir, must not be confused with the titular Mian Guls, who are descendants of the Akhund of Swat

On arriving at Nawagai, Mian Gul Jan persuaded the Khan to help him, and invade Jandol; but the attempt was foiled by Badshah Khan, who defeated the Nawagai *lashkar*. In December Muhammad Sharif Khan suddenly died, and was succeeded by his son Badshah Khan. Mian Gul Jan was then in Swat, where he was detained by the Khan Khel *jirga*; and subsequently he went to

Peshawar on the invitation of the Chief Commissioner. Badshah Khan's succession was recognized by the people of Dir and the tribes on the right bank of the Swat; but some trouble was caused by Saiyid Ahmad Khan of Barwa, who seized the fort of Tor and endeavoured to oust Badshah Khan from the Jandol valley. Failing in his first attempt Saiyid Ahmad withdrew to Bajaur, where he prevailed upon the Khans of Nawagai and Khar to assist him against the new ruler of Dir.

Late in December the combined forces of these three allied Chiefs invaded Jandol and occupied Barwa, Maiar, and Gambir. At the latter place 200 rifles which had been presented by Government to the late Nawab of Dir were seized. Matters were now further complicated by the action of the Salarzai and Mamunds, who attacked the Chief of Nawagai's nominee, Saminulla Khan of Pashat. They had been induced to create this diversion by Muhammad Ali, eldest son of the Khan of Nawagai, who had quarrelled with his father and had gone over to the side of the Khan of Dir. The attack on Pashat was repulsed by Saiyid Ahmad, who moved a force into Babukarra from the Upper Jandol valley, and at the end of January 1905 a truce was arranged between the Chiefs of Dir and Nawagai, and the forces dispersed. The Dir tribesmen were dissatisfied with the Chief for not having expelled the Bajaur *Khans* from Jandol, while the Ibrahim Khel Salarzai were equally discontented, since the only result of their enterprise was to establish Saiyid Ahmad in possession of Arif, Gambir, and Tor. It seemed probable therefore that a struggle would soon be renewed between this latter section and the Mast Khel for the possession of the Jandol valley.

On the 15th April a durbar was held by the Chief Commissioner of the North-West Frontier Province for the formal installation of Badshah Khan as Khan of Dir. The durbar was attended by all the notables of Dir and Upper Swat, including the Mian Guls. An agreement was made with the Khan, defining his obligations towards the Government, and granting him the same allowances as had been paid to his father. The Khan also consented to give an allowance of rupees 5,000 a year, and certain revenues, to his brother Mian Gul Jan, on condition that he did not return to Dir.

Little more than a month, however, had elapsed when Mian Gul Jan, breaking his engagements, escaped from Peshawar and appeared in Bajaur. Here he soon collected a following, and, having allied himself with Saiyid Ahmad, advanced against Badshah Khan with some 3,000 men. The Khan of Dir was outnumbered and the combined Bajaur forces succeeded in reaching the Maidan valley. As the defeat of the Khan of Dir, which now seemed probable, would have upset the arrangements for the security of the Chitral road, the Swat Valley Moveable Column was concentrated at Chakdara at the end of May with a view to supporting him. At this time Badshah Khan was reinforced by some Dir levies under Sardar Khan, ex-Khan of Bandai, and with the aid of the moral support afforded by the advance of the British troops he was enabled to hold his own. He now made terms with his brother and gave him the Khanship of Mundah. Mian Gul Jan had by this time discovered that Saiyid Ahmad was playing him false and had no intention of sharing the profits of his successes either in Maidan or Jandol. Saiyid Ahmad shortly afterwards withdrew his force from Maidan; and the Khans of Nawagai and Khar, who had again attacked Jandol, also evacuated that valley. On the 12th June Saiyid Ahmad and Mian Gul Jan, with the *jirgas* of the tribes concerned, came to Chakdara, and a settlement of the Dir-Bajaur dispute regarding the Jandol valley was arrived at.

The boundary between Jandol and Dir was defined: Mundah was assigned to Mian Gul Jan, and Saiyid Ahmad Khan retained possession of Barwa, Tor, and Gambir. The conditions, which are given in Appendix G, were to hold good for two years, during which time the chiefs promised to maintain a truce.

The settlement, however, is by no means entirely satisfactory, and it is not improbable that the struggle for the possession of the Jandol valley may be renewed at some future date. The Shahi Bibi, widow of the late Nawab of Dir, who espoused the cause of her favourite son Mian Gul Jan, and was the chief instigator in the previous quarrel, is said to be still busily intriguing against Badshah Khan. Although it matters little to the Government which chief eventually establishes his claim to the rulership of the Jandol valley, it is of the utmost importance to prevent any disturbance among the Dir and Bajaur tribes which might threaten the security of our communication with Chitral.

In December 1905 the Khans of Dir and Nawagai attended a durbar at Peshawar, and were presented to His Royal Highness the Prince of Wales.

Disagreements between the Nawab of Nawagai and his eldest son caused further disturbances in Bajaur during 1906, but the situation is now (1907) quiet for the moment.

END OF VOLUME I.